YALE HISTORICAL PUBLICATIONS

George Kubler, Editor

History of Art: 9

The publication of this work was aided by funds

provided by the Yale Department of the History of Art

deriving from a bequest of Isabel Paul.

Walton J. Lord

EARLY VICTORIAN

ARCHITECTURE

IN BRITAIN

by Henry-Russell Hitchcock

Volume 1: Text

New Haven: Yale University Press, 1954

FOR JOHN SUMMERSON DOROTHY STROUD FELLO ATKINSON

who have helped most

PREFACE

History, to be accurate, must be thick enough
to include the various levels of taste, to explain,
or at least to expound, survivals as well as
innovations, for frequently it is the conflict
between tradition and novelty which produces
the total culture of a time.

GEORGE BOAS

A satisfactory definition of Victorian architecture—Early, High, or Late—is not easily achieved. Neither "Victorian" nor "architecture," taken alone, is a word whose meaning need be obscure. Yet the complexity of their combined connotations gives a phrase that is ambiguous and even paradoxical to modern ears. Did any part of the Victorian Age produce *architecture* worthy of the name? Are Victorian ideas about architecture of any interest today? Or were they but confused heresies best ignored in a later age?

As some such questions arise in the critical mind around the phrase "Victorian architecture," so the historical mind may ask equally taxing ones: What, for instance, is properly meant by Victorian as applied to 19th-century culture? The Age of Victoria was a chronological entity defined by the sixty-four-year reign of the Queen; but can the same sixty-four years be considered also to frame a true cultural unit? If so, is that unit British only, more broadly Anglo-Saxon, or has it a wider significance in the general picture of 19th-century culture?

Above all, is the Victorian Age best considered as a single period? Or does it consist of a succession of subperiods, each more sharply characterized individually than continuous with the others? "Don't be Early Victorian," warned the Late Victorians; but our century abbreviated the warning to "Don't be Victorian." Now a change is well under way. By assuming that much of what is properly Early Victorian is but a happy aftermath of the respected Georgian—or at worst a playful excursus after the rigid rule of taste of the previous century—a great deal of the production of the 1830's and 1840's has in the last decade or two been removed from the artistic *Index Expurgatorius.*

The complete story of Victorian architecture rather resembles one of those endless novels typical of the period, over complicated in plot and subplot and crowded with quaintly named characters. The protagonists, moreover, are often so highly individualized that they seem like caricatures, or even

vii

fictional inventions, if their work and their opinions are merely sketched in outline. To attempt an over-all coverage of Victorian architecture in one volume is therefore as difficult—perhaps as futile—as to give an abridged version of *David Copperfield* or *Vanity Fair*.

This book is concerned with building production in Britain in the second quarter of the 19th century, or more precisely with that of the score of years from just before 1837 to just after 1852. Aspects of the history of construction are included that most Early Victorians did not consider relevant to the development of architecture as an art. Various characteristic manifestations of the period, moreover, which have generally been found unsympathetic in the past half-century will neither be excluded nor merely ridiculed. Willful omissions and blanket denigrations have hitherto tended to produce a picture of Early Victorian architecture that only Late Victorians, in their natural reaction against the ways of their fathers, would have recognized as plausible. An intentionally sympathetic study of Early Victorian architecture may hope to redress the critical balance without seeming to propose a "Victorian Revival."

Historians increasingly offer us an 18th century almost as full of movement and variety in the arts as the 19th was to be. The Georgians were never averse to new ideas in art, provided those who proposed them paid lip service to established cultural proprieties. As critics of art, moreover, and as technical aestheticians, the Georgians were more profound and subtler than the Victorians who later rang such curious changes on their most valid conclusions. Theory grew bolder, if also more confused, in the early 1850's just as the Early Victorian period was coming to an end.

Evidences of a lively eclecticism in Georgian taste are not difficult to discern in the byplay of surface fads patronized by a ruling elite. Among professional architects there was an unresolved mixture of real respect for the past, both Classical and medieval, untrammeled by excessive archaeological pedantry, and of serious enthusiasm for various new materials: some, such as iron, destined to be of major consequence later on; others merely shoddy substitutes like papier maché. Plenty of scandalous jerry-building went on in Georgian times; and in the handling of materials, old and new, there was both a continuing tradition of solid craftsmanship, even in machine work, and the most shameless gimcrackery. Time has distorted the balance, however, by wiping out most of what was *too* ill built or ill made in the 18th century.

In the present century those who are not specialists readily receive from the extant architectural remains of the Hanoverian period a single favorable image. If the 20th-century historian of Georgian architecture is to correct this popular image he must be coldly analytical, even cynical, in his approach. In presenting the architecture that succeeded the Georgian, on the other hand, one is perforce a sort of devil's advocate. To make out a plausible case for the serious study of Early Victorian building production, moreover, a more or less synthetic treatment is requisite. Broad categories, most of them already well recognized, must be utilized to subsume under a few headings the major new currents. Such a sorting out of the vast production of the period can help to make those currents comprehensible; they can then be recognized as valid expressions of continuing human aspirations, not mere manifestations of a perverse tastelessness. What seemed to contemporaries, even more perhaps than to posterity, a chaos of conflicting doctrine was by no means devoid of a few principles of positive taste that were widely accepted even by leaders in opposed critical camps. In controversy, naturally, the differences of position were loudly stated; the agreements were more usually tacit.

The Victorians were highly articulate and their self-critical writing is only too readily accepted today at face value. Some historians of the 19th century have been content to offer pictures of Early Victorian architecture that are, in effect, inherited from the period itself rather than freshly reconstituted. Lined up still with one or another Victorian critical faction, such writers have continued to present that faction's limited program as absolutely valid while dismissing the general run of Early Victorian building as laggard, preparatory, or outright vicious. Just as most political historians show their sympathies to be Whig or Tory, Conservative or Liberal, many writers on 19th-century architecture go all out for the "Greeks" or the "Goths." A few maintain that everything worth while derived from the continuance (or the revival) of some aspect of academic Classical tradition. Rather more historians and critics have continued to propagate the ideas of the medievalizing party. Many, for instance, accept its avowed functional principles and reject its practice; earlier in the century there were some architects who seemed to do exactly the reverse (alas, a few are around still). The learned and the professional world at least is unable to ignore Early Victorian architecture any longer, even if there is little current agreement as to its true value and meaning.

On the whole the ordinary cultivated person's grasp of what is Victorian, and even of why certain buildings are Victorian, is better than his assumed understanding of what is Georgian. It bears some resemblance at least to concepts that have historical and cultural reality, more perhaps than do some of the subtle and conflicting interpretations historians have been offering. But whether what is recognized as Victorian be rejected or embraced by the casual observer—and the public's reaction seems to grow more favorable all the time, at least to work of the Early Victorian decades—this general recognition remains highly uncritical. If we may judge from the faint manifestations of a Victorian "Revival" (fortunately almost entirely restricted to the realm of fashion, furniture, and decoration) what is most recognizably Victorian is the lowest vernacular of the age. Victorian leaders of taste, whether designers or critics, would have rejected as deplorably Philistine most of what now sells best in the antique shops.

Among those of more discrimination, a tentative distinction between Early Victorian and Late is often made today; the former, in principle, is considerably more widely appreciated than the latter, by laymen if not by specialists. (High Victorian is still pretty much a critic's and historian's term). But what is currently called "Early Victorian" may easily in fact be Late Georgian, not only in date but quite characteristically in style also—or, for that matter, it may be provincial work produced relatively late in the century. Blanket approval of the artistic production of an age is as stupid as is all-inclusive scorn. The wares of second-hand dealers turned merchants of the "antique" reveal how little the rising favor of Victoriana has yet developed any relevant artistic criteria. The shops still cater chiefly to that childish delight in the quaint with which the reassessment of the production of all periods of the past has begun.

Architecture is, properly speaking, not collectible. Certain preservation programs amount to collecting buildings, however, and some museums collect—perhaps unwisely—what are called "period rooms." In general the more closely the attitudes and the activities of enthusiasts for the architecture of any period approach those of the collector, the more harm they do. Yet the monuments of any period of the past require intelligent understanding and respect from posterity if they are not all to be destroyed outright or else quite denatured by unsympathetic renovation.

The present state of general interest in Early Victorian architecture is most unsatisfactory. The wrong things are too often selected for preservation merely because they conform to the public's naive idea of what is characteristic; the major monuments are either neglected or perhaps ruined by tactless remodeling. The possibility of arriving at a well-balanced picture of Victorian architecture is diminishing rapidly despite the tremendous volume of Victorian production which still remains intact. With the irony that plagues all preservation activities, the blanket refusal to consider any 19th-century structures worth saving has begun to lift, at least for much work of the 1830's and 1840's, before there is sufficient knowledge of what should be saved, and before proper techniques of maintenance and restoration without stylistic distortion have even been accepted as desirable.

The author aims to sort out the architectural remains of the Victorian Age into their principal categories in order that relative aesthetic quality and historical significance within those categories may become more recognizable. Such a sorting out must in the first place be chronological; therefore this book deals only with the late 1830's, the 1840's, and the early 1850's. But within that main chronological category there are typological and stylistic subcategories that require distinct recognition also.

Modern architectural theory often assumes that all types of edifice can (and even should), in any period, be designed in much the same way. The obvious readiness of the mid-19th century to utilize alternative stylistic forms in different fields, already deprecated by severe critics at the time, seems peculiarly reprehensible to us in a way it did not to the Late Victorians or even to most men of the early 20th century. But judgment should at least be suspended until Early Victorian production has been carefully examined. Even those mid-19th-century architects who were positive fanatics about "style" generally employed without shame a more or less extensive variety of modes when their practice included various different types of edifice. Other leaders of taste were quite frank in defense of a studied eclecticism, intentionally varied according to purpose and location. Different subcategories of type and of nominal "style," when broadly interpreted, therefore correspond to real subdivisions in Early Victorian production. They will also be found to be at least loosely interrelated; one type supposedly requiring one style and another, another, according to a tacitly accepted scheme of semi-functional symbolism.

Too strict a typological approach to Early Victorian building production tends to mask the relative unity of visual taste within the period. It also obscures the interchanges by which new architectural ideas, whether technical or visual, passed back and forth between groups of architects who specialized in different kinds of commissions. On the other hand, to take the supposed "battle of the styles," or even the actual confused free-for-all of stylistic factions, at face value is to ignore exactly the characteristics that are prime to the Early Victorian as a style-phase in its own right. Both the subcategories based on various building types and those based on what should be called "stylisms" or modes rather than "styles" must be kept elastic. The latter should be defined, as it were archaeologically, from the extant material rather than a priori, according to the pat terms of the period. Yet the contemporary terms, with their various favorable and unfavorable connotations, are themselves significant; for they provide a part of the data with which the historian must work in interpreting buildings of the period.

Certain individual Victorian architects, both Early and Late, have achieved fame out of proportion to their deserts, while others of as great significance have been totally forgotten. Accidents of contemporary publicity or even conscious campaigns, worthy of our own period of planned "public relations," explain some excessive reputations that now hardly need deflation. Then there are those men, often not conspicuously successful nor widely known at present, who have yet been widely accepted by later architects and critics as models of correct views and of conscientious devotion to their art—if not so often, in more absolute terms, as great masters of architectural design. It must be an important part of the historian's duty to seek out also the significant work of more obscure men with whom neither contemporaries nor posterity have been much concerned. And there are whole ranges of Early Victorian building production, ranges which the age largely ignored or consistently denigrated as architecture, which deserve total reassessment. The study of Victorian architecture need rarely be based on internal evidence only; most of what is of consequence can be linked by historical documentation with specific architects, engineers, or builders. Unfortunately, the examination of the total existing documentation must still proceed much further before all that ought to be known becomes readily accessible.

The disagreement, if one may so put it, between the scholars and the public on the subject of Early Victorian architecture is partly the fault of the former. Most writers have been excessively preoccupied with a few rather special edifices or with certain particular lines of development, ignoring too often the buildings with which the public is most familiar. Some of those special edifices were famous enough in their own day, like the Crystal Palace; others were hardly known outside a small inner circle of the aesthetic elite. Important as such things are, they cannot be considered to epitomize the whole Early Victorian period. No more can three or four of the more prominent urban edifices, such as the Houses of Parliament, the Reform Club, and St. George's Hall, when their images are projected on the screen in brief introductory lectures on the history of art, give any just idea of the general character of architectural production in the 30's, 40's, and early 50's.

Exceptional quality in Early Victorian building should be acclaimed wherever it may be found. The critical attitude that ignores all work without conscious artistic pretention and the opposing one which sees in architecture only more or less accomplished solutions of engineering problems are both forms of intellectual snobbery. It is therefore desirable to examine with equal care what the Early Victorians considered to be their most significant works and also those which our later age has accepted as worthy forerunners of its own architecture; they are often very different. The mass of ordinary buildings from which the public derives its understanding of Early Victorian architecture requires serious study too. That production was vast; nearly just is the estimate of those who have dismissed most of it as contemptible. Only a sampling technique, therefore, can hope to present its principal characteristics without tedious repetition and any analysis must perforce be almost more sociological than architectural.

Beyond the range of the better known architects who are mentioned in the existing histories, however, there are many modest individuals, men who never reached the metropolis or built a public monument, who are deserving of posterity's recognition for their personal achievement, or merely for their highly original ideas. Some anonymous buildings, moreover—anonymous at least thus far, in the absence of detailed local research—equal in quality the most conspicuous buildings by the most famous professional leaders. But even the work of those leaders who have already been the subject of individual biographies has rarely been illustrated thoroughly or with much discrimination. The lives and the opinions of such men are better documented than their buildings, with which this book is primarily concerned.

Northampton, Mass.
June 3, 1954

ACKNOWLEDGMENTS

During the ten years this book has been in active preparation there has accumulated a weight of obligation almost impossible to recall in full, much less to acknowledge in detail. Hazarding the accidental omission of some names, I must nevertheless attempt to set down here my thanks to all those who have been helpful and to express generic debts that are more precisely itemized in the separate entries of the List of Illustrations and, by implication at least, in various precise references to books and articles in the main text.

The three friends to whom this book is dedicated are those to whom my obligation is greatest. In 1945–46 John Summerson and Dorothy Stroud made me free of the Soane Museum, and in the comfort of their office serious work on this book began. Both of them, again and again, guided and accompanied me on expeditions through Victorian London and sustained me in all sorts of other ways. I am also using three photographs provided by Mr. Summerson; a plan from his *John Nash;* and much information, as well as short quotations, from his *Georgian London.* Over and above this, however, I know that a very large proportion of the 83 photographs in this book which come from the National Buildings Record were taken by him or for him during the war when he had the forethought to see that 19th-century as well as earlier architecture should be properly documented. Miss Stroud aided me in obtaining photographs from *Country Life,* of which ten are reproduced in this book with the permission of the proprietors. Fello Atkinson read most of my chapters and discussed them with me in detail. With him I have also visited many major monuments and never failed to see more through his eyes than I should have done with my own alone.

In the latest stages of the preparation of this book I owe a great deal to various friends at Yale: Lewis Perry Curtis, editor of the Yale Historical Publications, George Kubler, editor of the History of Art Publications, Sumner McKnight Crosby, professor of the history of art, and Carroll L. V. Meeks, associate professor of architecture. Mr. Curtis' meticulous reading of my text prepared the way for considerable stylistic improvement in the ultimate draft. Mr. Crosby played a most important part in arranging for publication by the Yale University Press. To Mr. Meeks I owe a special debt of gratitude. Some years ago we pooled all our graphic documentation on railway stations and a large part of the illustrations in chapters XV and XVI come from his files although it is the ultimate sources that are indicated in the List of Illustrations. I must also mention the continuous assistance of the staff of the Sterling Library at Yale; if this book was written from the resources of any other library than my own, it was that of Yale. In particular the willingness of the Sterling authorities to allow vast quantities of books and periodicals to be transported to Meriden, Connecticut, and kept there for weeks on end explains the high quality of the line illustrations which the Meriden Gravure Company could thus make directly from original wood engravings and other contemporary plates. Without this remarkable cooperation the high standard of the Yale Press in the matter of illustration copy could not have been maintained.

The expression of further obligations must be categorized: first, financial assistance; second, sources of information; third, access to buildings; fourth, illustrative material; fifth, reprinted material; sixth, technical assistance, etc.

Although much desultory research had been done before the war, work on this book really started with the opportunity to spend nine months in England in 1945–46 on a fellowship provided by the John Simon Guggenheim Memorial Foundation. While at Wesleyan University I was assisted by several generous research grants. A considerable contribution deriving from the estate of Isabel Paul of Newfields, N. H., helped to make publication possible.

With few exceptions, the writers whose books and articles are cited in the text have also notably assisted by providing information in conversation or in letters. Mr. Summerson's important aid has already been mentioned; that of H. S. Goodhart Rendel, perhaps the best informed person in England on Victorian architects in general, Nikolaus Pevsner, Carroll Meeks, Turpin C. Bannister, Graham C. Law, John Betjeman, J. M. Richards, Marcus Whiffen, and Phoebe Stanton should also be signalized. To the successive librarians of the Royal Institute of British Architects, Edward J. Carter, R. E. Enthoven, and James Palmes, who made available the resources of the world's finest architectural library, warm thanks are also due; and, in the United States, to the librarians of architecture and planning of the Massachusetts Institute of Technology and of Harvard University.

It is impossible even to list all the clergymen and institutional authorities who have facilitated access to buildings in their charge, frequently providing useful information as well. But I can take this opportunity to express my gratitude to the late Duke of Montrose, the Duke of Sutherland, Lord Carnarvon, and Lord Rosebery for the privilege of visiting their houses; and also to Lord Amulree for arranging for me to see in great detail, up to the very iron roofs, the Houses of Parliament. I would also like to thank those who, alas unavailingly, attempted to obtain entree to Balmoral Castle for me. How many terrace houses in London of the Victorian period I have at one time or another been inside is hard even to estimate; nor yet can I hope to enumerate all those friends and acquaintances whose dwellings have provided so much of the background of knowledge and experience on which certain aspects of the account of housing in Chapters XIV and XV are based.

A very large proportion of the illustrations come from 19th-century books and periodicals in the author's possession, above all from the files of the *Builder* and the *Illustrated London News* which between them provide so splendid a pictorial coverage of building history for all but the very earliest years of the Early Victorian period. As many more are from publications in the Sterling Library. Harvard supplied a copy of Baron Ernouf's *Art des jardins* as well as several periodicals not in Sterling Library, and Smith College furnished a copy of A. E. Richardson's *Monumental Classic Architecture*. To Professor Richardson and his publishers, B. T. Batsford, thanks are due for permission to use five illustrations from the latter work. A group of photographers, J. R. Johnson of Western Reserve University, Annan of Glasgow, Turl of Bristol, and Palmer of Manchester, took photographs especially for this work—in the case of Mr. Johnson in very considerable numbers. The photographs of the Coal Exchange were taken by Helmut Gernsheim for the author's article in the *Architectural Review,* and I am most grateful to the editors of the *Review* for allowing their use here, as also to Professor Rudolf Wittkower of the Warburg Institute for allowing the use of the photographs Mr. Gernsheim took for the Institute of Bridgewater House. I should also mention several photographs by R. H. de Burgh-Galwey and by Dell and Wainwright, covered by the *Architectural Review's* copyright, which are used here with the editors' permission. Mr. Gernsheim also generously supplied a copy of one of the early Crystal Palace photographs; the rest of these, as well as those of the Brompton Boilers in construction, I was allowed to have copied from originals at the Victoria and Albert Museum. To the Museum authorities, and particularly to Mr. C. H. Gibbs-Smith, I am most grateful.

Sixteen illustrations are from photographs especially made for this book from drawings, watercolors and lithographs in the library of the Royal Institute of British Architects, and these are used here with the kind consent of the Institute. Paxton's original sketch of the Crystal Palace is reproduced from a photograph supplied by the Royal Society of Arts, with whom it is deposited. A Pugin drawing at Scarisbrick is reproduced from Michael Trappes-Lomax's *Pugin, a Mediaeval Victorian,* with the author's generous permission and that of his publishers Sheed and Ward. Five illustrations were provided by the British Railways, or their predecessors the Great Western Railway and the London and North Eastern Railway, largely through the generous interest of Brian Lewis and Christian Barman. I am most grateful to the Town Clerk of Birkenhead for providing a photograph of an early plan. Mr. Whiffen has allowed me to use two of his photographs, and there is one of Mr. Law's, whose study of "Greek Thomson" has appeared in the *Architectural Review* (*115,* 307–16) since the main text of this book went to press. Messrs. Drake and Lasdun, the architects who are rebuilding so much of Paddington, provided a photograph of Westbourne Grove. To the Yale University Art Gallery I am especially grateful for permission to reproduce the Paxton watercolor formerly belonging to John Carter, who has all along taken a flattering interest in this book.

The continued assistance of Walter Godfrey and Cecil Farthing of the National Buildings Record has supplied me with almost innumerable photographs of Victorian architecture, of which 83, as has been noted, are reproduced. Additional photographs come from Messrs. Salmon of Winchester, Hammond of Leamington, the late F. C. Inglis of Edinburgh, McCann of Uttoxeter, Tuck and Valentine of London, Garratt of Bristol, Jay of Cheltenham, and Pickard of Leeds. Some half dozen or more photographs unfortunately provided no evidence of source whatsoever and for them it is impossible to make acknowledgment.

A very considerable portion of Chapters XV and XVI appeared in a pamphlet, *The Crystal Palace, The Structure, Its Antecedents and Its Immediate Progeny* (Northampton, 1951; 2d ed. 1952), issued in connection with an exhibition prepared in 1951 by the Smith College Museum of Art and the Massachusetts Institute of Technology and still, in 1954, being circulated by the Smithsonian Institution. The author wishes to express his gratitude to the *Architectural Review* for allowing him to incorporate the bulk of his articles published in that journal on the "Coal Exchange," on "Victorian Monuments of Commerce," and on "Brunel and Paddington," as also some material from that on "Early Cast Iron Façades." I am also grateful to Georges Wildenstein for permitting the inclusion of my article "Second Empire 'avant la lettre'" which appeared in the *Gazette des Beaux Arts.* The epigraph preceding the Preface comes from a review of André Malraux's *Voices of Silence* by George Boas in *Perspectives U.S.A.,* No. 7, and is used with the permission of Mr. Boas.

To my colleagues Ruth Wedgwood Kennedy, Phyllis Williams Lehmann, and Mary Bartlett Cowdrey, I am grateful for discussion of various technical points concerning the text; and most notably to Miss Cowdrey for advice and assistance in the preparation of the index. In the last six years Rita Halford has typed and retyped the manuscript so often she should know it by heart! Her devoted assistance in meeting a succession of deadlines has been supplemented by various members of the staff of the Smith College Museum of Art at times of particular stress. Alan Brooks, a graduate student at Yale, undertook the job of getting the books and periodicals out of the Sterling Library to be sent to Meriden.

No teacher can terminate a list of acknowledgments like this without mentioning his students. At Wesleyan University, at the Massachusetts Institute of Technology, at Smith College, at the Institute of Fine Arts of New York University, and at Yale large portions of the material in this book have been presented in seminars or lecture courses. The opportunity thus to put the results of research before intelligent and interested younger people is one no scholar should be without. More particularly I should like to mention, among my Yale students, Robert W. Duemling, Wilder Green, John Hoag, and James Evans, and among my New York University students, Ellen Kramer: Their researches have often paralleled or complemented my own, and discussion with them has always been of great value.

Finally, and not least, are certain friends, no specialists in 19th-century architecture, who have yet often accompanied me in London and through the British countryside in pursuit of buildings they sometimes thought totally unappetizing. I hope that Ivan Brodrick and Arthur O'Malley-Williams, in reading this book, will see how the various things we visited fit into place.

The length of this acknowledgment section—and, long as it is, I am only too sure it inadvertently omits many who have, in the last decade, signally aided me in one way or another—expresses the cooperative nature of historical research in the arts. Without financial assistance of various sorts, without libraries and photograph collections, without discussion with other scholars, without hospitable owners, without friends, colleagues, and students to aid and to comfort, no such work as this could well be completed.

CONTENTS OF VOLUME 1

CONTENTS OF VOLUME 2

CHAPTER I: THE STUDY OF

VICTORIAN ARCHITECTURE

"If the seed die not . . . ," it is written in the Bible; and sometimes, with buildings as with other artifacts of any particular period, only the loss of a large part of the finest work leads to recognition of the value and interest of what remains. For the student of Victorian architecture, as for the historian of any other aspect of the 19th century, the quantity and the availability of extant material are almost an embarrassment. Despite the blitz there is still much more building of the Victorian Age left in Britain than there is of any earlier period—perhaps even of all earlier periods together. In studying Victorian architecture seriously it is almost as important to decide what not to look at—or better what not to look for—as it is to consider the monuments of the age critically and historically at all.

The immediate Late Georgian background of the Early Victorian period will be discussed in the next chapter; here a different sort of preparation is needed: some discussion of the "how," if not so explicitly of the "why," of studying Victorian architecture. The Victorian Age well knew that its most conspicuous buildings were not always its best. In quality a surprising disparity exists between the large and obvious Victorian monuments of the 1870's—the Law Courts in London, say, or the town halls of the North—and earlier and generally more modest edifices which are little noticed today. Many of the former were built long after the several different kinds of Victorian design they exemplify were well past their prime, even though their architects had once been capable of really fine things. Too many critics base their judgment of Victorian architecture solely on these later monuments, so often worse than overripe, because the earlier work is inadequately known or less assertive in the urban scene.

Many of the finest examples of Victorian architecture have to be sought out in obscure places; even when found they require from the observer some effort of the historical imagination if they are to be properly appreciated. A book on Victorian architecture must therefore tell where the most significant edifices are to be found and also provide some explanation of their original cultural context. Even more important is the marshaling of a profusion of illustrative material; thus only can the generic image of what is

1

Victorian, which most people already recognize, be made more specific. Carefully selected monuments, thoroughly studied, should provide the basis for judgments of Victorian architecture, not blurred impressions of buildings glimpsed from a train or casually passed in the streets. Many excellent 19th-century edifices are never properly perceived today. Although Victorian work may be recurrently seen in its present shabby state, unless a conscious attempt is made by the observer to consider the builders' intentions, as well as to re-create in imagination the pristine condition and the original surroundings, much of it remains effectively as invisible as ruins still unexcavated.

Victorian buildings, it must be admitted, have not on the whole aged graciously. Perhaps this is merely because they are not yet quite old enough; more probably it is because their predominantly metropolitan sites expose them to excessive visual hazards in the way of surface grime and domineering later neighbors. The most admired productions of other ages, medieval castles and cathedrals, country mansions of the Tudor and Stuart ages, or residential squares and crescents of Georgian times have more often been spared such hazards or else have been completely destroyed. Victorian buildings are hard enough to see at first hand without a visual filter; somehow one's eyes must penetrate the grime that covers them and succeed also in shutting out the taller and brighter neighbors on either side. But 19th-century edifices are harder still to photograph satisfactorily; and most of us, alas, are conditioned to believe about architecture only what the camera records. Since the earlier Victorian monuments are less strident than the later ones, and more readily mistaken for Georgian, the lens often seems to miss their most characteristic virtues, and sometimes even to push them back a full generation in time. Too often the photographer himself has not recognized work of the 40's for what it is, but seen only quaintness and decay or an old-maidish sort of primness.

All Victorian buildings are in some sense on trial; their historian, however objective he might prefer to be, is therefore like a defense attorney before a diffident or hostile jury. The frequent use of contemporary pictures in this book may seem a little like producing childhood photographs of hardened criminals in the hope of swaying a jury in their favor; yet such pictures are most necessary if the subject of Early Victorian architecture is to be properly covered at all. Contemporary photographs of buildings of the late 30's, the 40's, and the early 50's are surprisingly hard to find; this despite the fact that calotypy and daguerreotypy were available from almost the beginning of the Victorian Age and more modern methods of photography from shortly after 1850. (Architecture, moreover, was a particularly good subject for the camera in days when exposures were unconscionably long.)

In the absence of early photographs other contemporary visual documents have very great value; the wood engravings of the 50's, moreover, were frequently based on photographs. The illustrations in the professional and general periodicals of the Victorian Age provided the means by which architectural ideas were spread as well as the images on which contemporary taste was formed. On them, furthermore, most contemporaries were forced to base their aesthetic judgments. Once one learns to interpret the documents a magic key is available to the architectural vision of the time such as line engravings of the 17th and 18th centuries provide for those earlier periods. If it is proper to appreciate Georgian architecture in the engraved plates of Colen Campbell and Robert Adam—and 18th-century design can hardly be understood without careful study of such plates—it is even more profitable to utilize the wealth of visual documentation which has come down from the Victorian Age.

An extremely rapidly flow of influence, not only within the British Isles but across the seas to the Dominions and the United States, characterized the whole Victorian Age and particularly its earlier decades. The speed with which submovements within the principal stylistic developments ran their course, from their first isolated introduction to their ultimate vulgarization, is both explained and chronicled by the contemporary visual documents. As in our own day, the effect of the design of a particular building on the general course of development did not have to await its completion, or sometimes even its initiation.

A present-day photograph of a Victorian building when labeled only with the original date of the architect's design or the date of its completion is likely to offer rather uncertain evidence as to the true place of that building in the history of 19th-century architecture. Pictures of the Houses of Parliament are often glibly dated "1837" (Fig. I 1), although Sir Charles Barry (1795–1860) * redesigned most of that enormous complex in the 40's and final completion, under the supervision of his son Edward Middleton Barry (1830–1880), came only well after his death in the mid-60's. The contemporary published view of Barry's Athenaeum in Manchester showed the original project (Fig. I 3), not the executed building (Fig. I 2) which is slightly different. In such situations contemporary graphic documents are obviously essential both to understand the architect's intention and to assess the possible effect of his original design as an influence on the work of others.

The available wealth of contemporary documentation in the form of plans,

* The points in the text where the principal biographical facts concerning important Early Victorian architects are given may be found by referring to the Index. Dates of birth and death will be supplied whenever possible where significant works by the various architects are first discussed.

3

sections, and technical details of construction offers advantages to the historian that are unobtainable for most earlier periods except through the preparation of modern measured drawings. It may not be so evident that wood engravings of details whose interest is visual rather than intellectual provide as good (or better) evidence as do photographs. The 20th century has come to accept photographs so naturally as substitutes for reality that much of our architecture is accused of being "photogenic": that is, designed to be appreciated more in photographs than in actuality. The parallel accusation that Victorian architecture was designed in considerable part to be appreciated in the reproductive media of the day is of course at least as true. For that reason, and because the judgment of all architecture, old or new, was necessarily based on familiarity with monuments studied through these media, contemporary illustrations have a special sort of psychological accuracy. They show what the architects intended—and also what the contemporary observer must have apprehended—far better than any photographs, even early photographs, can do.

The changing character of the visual documents may also be used to discriminate among the successive phases of Victorian style. Lithographs were used mostly in books rather than in periodicals (Fig. I 6); but in their delicacy of tonal contrast and their soft contours lithographs are perhaps truer to the architectural vision of the late 30's and early 40's than such simple outline drawings (Fig. I 4) and crudely vignetted perspectives (Fig. I 5) as could then be reproduced by the wood engravers working for the periodicals. By the 50's, however, with the rapid and climactic improvement in reproductive wood engraving, the qualities of the best illustrative craftsmanship came to parallel very closely the special qualities of the most characteristic new buildings. Bold black and white patterning and vigorous, rather than subtle, linear definition are successfully combined with strong illusions of three-dimensionality and coloristic rather than textural distinction of materials (Fig. XVII 5) to produce expressive images of the buildings of the day as contemporaries were seeing them.

Photography had by the 50's impinged considerably upon wood-engraving technique; for the camera had already set new standards of perspective presentation and of formalized value rendering. By then, moreover, the camera was often providing the intermediary documents from which wood engravers worked. But that development occurred, of course, only at the end of the Early Victorian period, and we are concerned here with its beginnings.

When *did* the Early Victorian period in architecture begin? "When" in cultural history, unless it be explained in terms of "how" and "why"—and also "where"—has little significance. The locus in the present instance presents no difficulty, since the scene has been set by definition in Great Britain. Few would deny that the United States had a Victorian Age in architecture quite as certainly as it had a Georgian one; and English Victorian influence was certainly not without importance elsewhere. But Victorian architecture had first to come into existence at home before it could be exported. The "why" and the "how" can be explained only with a broad preliminary examination of the British architectural scene in the 30's; more detail will be given in the next chapter.

Early in 1837 Sir John Soane (b. 1753), Architect of the Bank of England, died. His intransigent originality had perturbed the academic complacency of the profession for a full half-century. Yet in the 20th century he is often rated as the only Georgian architect later than Robert Adam (1728–1792) who belongs in the very first rank of achievement. Abroad only Karl Friedrich Schinkel (1781–1841), a generation younger, was his equal in distinction within his lifetime. Whether Soane's reputation ought to rival that of Sir Christopher Wren, as it does in many circles today, is a matter of taste; but that he was the greatest English architect of the High Romantic period can hardly be disputed, however much he may have owed to his first master, the younger George Dance (1744–1825). Soane, unlike Dance, was one of the few architects of the day whose production continued during the Napoleonic Wars almost unhampered by political and economic events. He could not, therefore, have many serious rivals in Europe between 1790 and 1815; and the New World was hardly yet ripe to produce architects of its own of so high a rank, even though the United States acquired in Latrobe its first professional, and one of great talent, at this very time.

Soane's death, therefore, rather than the accession of a 17-year-old female sovereign later in the same year, makes 1837 memorable in architectural history. But neither event need have signalized the termination of an architectural epoch in England, much less the opening of a new one. The final ending of individual careers, however distinguished, and the opening of new reigns, however prolonged, rarely mark except by coincidence major changes of historical phase in architecture.

Looking at early 19th-century cultural developments in Germany or France, a comparable change of phase—from High Romanticism to Late, from the world of David and Beethoven to that of Delacroix and Berlioz— seems to have come in 1830, a year of revolution in literature and the arts as well as in politics. In England also one might be led to select a date in the early 30's on political if not on musical or literary grounds, and various writers have done so. The crucial event would be not the death in 1830 of the last of the four Georges (which was so smoothly followed by his brother William's accession) but the stormy passage of the first Reform Act in 1832; for the passage of the act constituted a bloodless revolution from which the Victorian Age was to derive its special political character. But the reign of William IV lasted only a brief seven years, and the full results of the act's extension of the franchise were hardly felt before those years were over and William's niece established upon the throne. Events more directly related to building production must decide when the Victorian Age really began in architecture.

Soane built little in the 30's. As far as one can judge, now that almost none of his late work remains, that little was neither of the high quality nor of the assured originality of his earlier production of the period 1790–1830. The State Paper Office, in Duke Street, St. James's, for example, seems not to have continued any one of his established stylistic lines; rather it paralleled the new "Italian palace" mode that the young Charles Barry was introducing at the same time in the Travellers' Club house nearby in Pall Mall (Fig. I 7). The Law Courts at Westminster appear to have been virtuoso spacial compositions exploiting hanging vaults. But these represent, one must suppose, rather the willful diversions of an old master, delighting to shock the younger generation, than any advance beyond the superb interiors at the Bank of England.

Soane, for all his official appointments—or perhaps, such is professional jealousy, because of them—had long stood apart from most of his contemporaries, both younger and older, somewhat as does Frank Lloyd Wright in 20th-century America. Encomiums of a high order were finally granted him by the profession when he received a special gold medallion from the Royal Institute of British Architects in 1835, two years after retiring from a 45-year term as Architect of the Bank. But many of these tributes resembled, in their evident insincerity, those that Wright received from the American Institute of Architects in 1949 after 56 years of distinguished practice. The savor of this belated (and rather hypocritical) recognition from the middle generation, moreover, was soon soured by the biting satire of the youthful A. N. W. Pugin (1812–1852) in his *Contrasts,* which appeared the next year.

As if with some premonition of the short life which many of his principal buildings were destined to have, Soane devoted his last years to making a museum of his London house. No other architect has taken such care to insure that his ideas shall continue manifest to later generations. But it was to be almost a century before architects and critics began to appreciate his bequest; even today it is little more than a curiosity to the general public. To an amazing extent, despite the Soane Museum, Soane's fame died with him.

Of Soane's last two pupils one, George Bailey, became the first curator of the museum and effectively ceased practice. The other, Charles J. Richardson (1800–1872), was also drawn into the museum project, for it was he who provided the attractive lithographed plates in the monograph on the museum Soane published in 1835. But Richardson was already busy on his own with *A Popular Treatise on the Warming of Buildings* (1837, with two later editions) and, more significantly, with the preparation of a series of meticulously accurate lithographic plates of Elizabethan and Jacobean architecture which he began to publish in separate parts at about the same time. His *Observations on the Architecture of England during the Reigns of Queen Elizabeth and King James I* came out as a book in 1837 and was one of the first of a series of similar works by him and others.

It is of particular interest that Richardson included in his publications, besides modern views and measured drawings, facsimiles of original plans and sketches. Here was something Greek and Gothic archaeologists are practically never able to supply, and such plates introduced a new sophistication into the presentation of the architectural styles of the past. The group of plates Richardson copied from Wendel Dietterlin's *Architectura* (Nuremberg, 1598), one of the continental sources on which the Elizabethan and Jacobean designers of ornament leaned heavily, is less surprising to find than the reproductions of drawings by John Thorpe, then supposed to have been a leading architect under Elizabeth. How ironical it is that these drawings, among the choicest items in Soane's extensive collection, should thus have provided the inspiration for so much anti-Soanic architecture.

The Dance Cabinet, the central shrine of Soane's library, preserves the remarkable projects of his revered friend and master, the younger Dance. These are, moreover, the evident source of many of Soane's most brilliant conceptions of architectural form. But the Dance drawings were to remain unstudied, by Richardson or anyone else, practically until our own day. The great Adam portfolios, from which Richardson made a few unpublished tracings, had to wait only until the late 70's to be appreciated.

Richardson's career, long and busy enough as writer, teacher, and architect, was in no way distinguished after this moment in the late 30's. He is the first Victorian architect there is occasion to discuss; yet the illustrations in his late book *The Englishman's House,* first published in 1870 and reissued in several later editions both English and American, show how little his architecture was to be affected by the characteristic developments of three Victorian decades. Remote though Richardson's house designs are from what the world generally recognizes as Georgian, most can be matched in the plates of cottage books that other architects issued before George IV's death. To the end, therefore, Richardson's work may be considered characteristically proto-Victorian rather than truly Victorian.

Elizabethan and Jacobean architecture was to Late Georgians and Early Victorians neither Classic nor Gothic; but, being a local English amalgam of both, was deemed more "national" than either. Interest in old work of around 1600 was no novelty by the 1830's, moreover. Nikolaus Pevsner has lately shown (*Architectural Review, 107,* 117–120) that at one end of the 18th century Sir John Vanbrugh (1664–1726) drew inspiration from early 17th-century planning; and that at the other end Richard Payne Knight (1750–1824) used an unmistakably Elizabethan or Jacobean design to illustrate his Picturesque ideal of a country mansion in a naturalistically landscaped setting. But in the High Romantic period of the late 18th and early 19th centuries such design had not yet acquired the prestige or the popularity of the "Grecian" or the "Gothick"; nor had there been earlier attempts to document its monuments with any care. This new interest in the English architecture of the late 16th and early 17th centuries in the 30's was therefore especially significant of the approaching end of the Georgian rule of taste.

Among Soane's pupils of Richardson's generation only George Wightwick (1802–1872) in provincial Plymouth retained a place for the "Soanic" among the multiple stylisms he employed. Perhaps Soane's manner of design was too personal to be further developed by others and could only thus survive as an obsolescent variant of Late Georgian Classicism. However that may be, Soane's "modernism" was abjured even before his death as absolutely as the innovations of the Arts and Crafts group in England and of the Chicago School in America were rejected in the resurgent "traditionalism" that followed the first World War. Not until the 50's, when originality was once more vaunted, did critics find a good word to say for this "Boeotian"; for Boeotian was the name Soane's early enemies applied to him in a supposedly "Athenian" age. (He sued for libel but lost the case.)

The term "Victorian" is in some ways as meaningful—and should be as neutral—a stylistic designation in architecture as "Georgian"; certainly it ought not to be used as a libelous term. The accession of Victoria herself was, however, even less relevant to the change of phase in architecture than the death of Soane. Some at least of her Hanoverian forebears had been enthusiastic patrons of the arts; almost as a matter of principle she was not. Her personal tastes had in fact nothing at all to do with establishing the "Victorian" character of the architecture of her time.

Although in the course of two decades the actual settings in which the Queen lived became Victorian enough, her own tastes seem to have acted as a brake on those responsible for creating those settings. Yet she had neither the active interest nor the serious training to make her remain a convinced Georgian in the way of many leading aristocrats throughout the first part of her reign. The laggard manner in which she accepted new modes and the early death in 1862 of the Prince Consort, to whose judgment she had always turned in matters of art, insured that her surroundings remained Early Victorian, if in a rather commonplace way, to the very end of her life in 1901. But they had actually begun to be so only in the late 40's and early 50's when Early Victorian modes were already well established generally.

8

Even the more cultivated Albert's various connections with matters architectural are of real significance only in relation to the Crystal Palace. More than his wife he was led by personal inclination—and in conscious emulation of his Royal German contemporaries, of course—to take a rather direct interest, even to "dabble," in the arts. But duty seemed to require that he devote the greater part of his time to affairs of state. His own cautiousness, if not suggestions from the avuncular Baron Stockmar or from English associates, warned him of the unfavorable public reaction that could follow upon conspicuous expenditure by a mere consort of funds grudgingly voted by Parliament for Royal use.

The sort of Victorian taste the various Royal residences illustrate can be, without injustice, described as provincial or even suburban. Like the rather similar mansions which the rising provincial magnates were building in the suburbs of the Northern and Midland cities, the new portions of Buckingham Palace (Figs. IX 1–6) and the private retreats of the Sovereign on the Isle of Wight (Figs. VI 22–23) and in the Highlands (Figs. VIII 25–28) represent in their stylistic character a lag of a decade or more behind such architectural developments as were being patronized by the cultural elite. But for the exalted station of the clients, these houses would be almost beneath the notice of posterity. Only perhaps at the Home Farm near Windsor Castle, where Albert was eventually his own master, are there hints of an early response to "high" fashion in design.

In less private architectural matters into which the Prince was drawn, such as the campaign for the internal decoration of the Houses of Parliament (Chapter IX), the building for the Great Exhibition of 1851 (Chapter XVI), and the sponsorship of low-cost workers' housing (Chapter XIII), Albert's artistic tastes are less evident than his scientific and social enthusiasms. Choosing usually as his closest associates distinguished Victorians whose achievement was only incidentally related to architecture, he generally received advice that was more competent technically than aesthetically. Important though Albert's relation to Victorian building is, at least compared with his wife's, and particularly so in the early 50's, the architecture of the mid-century need not be called "Albertine." Neither his appearance on the English scene in the early 40's nor his death twenty years later can be correlated closely with architectural events.

It is convenient to divide the Victorian Age as a whole into successive periods, with one break in the early 50's and another around 1870. The architectural production of such short periods should not be considered to illustrate wholly distinct style-phases. But to confuse these style-phases or to merge them, as did those Victorians who wrote about the Victorian Age primarily in terms of a continuous "Gothic Revival," is to make more difficult rather than to simplify the problem of defining Victorian architecture as a whole. In certain fields of building—usually those fields in which self-consciousness about style was least cultivated by the Victorians—the continuity between the three subperiods is nearly unbroken. In such fields the stylistic breaks came so gradually and so belatedly that visual appearance often provides only ambiguous indexes for dating; yet the fact that most surface modulations did in the end reach all sorts of building production shows how unified the Victorian architectural world really was. A conscious snobbery may have set professional architects apart from mere builders as lawyers were set apart from their clerks; there were even within the profession itself diverse social categories as complex and mysterious as those stratifying the middle classes in county towns. But Victorian attitudes toward social status never seriously inhibited the flow of architectural ideas from one realm of building to another, although they undoubtedly made it rather slow and uneven.

To determine when the Victorian Age began one must have some idea as to when the Late Georgian period ended; for to recognize and attempt to characterize a seven-year "Williamite" phase of transition between is unprofitable (the term, in any event, is a barbarism). Precisely during those seven years, however, various cultural phenomena, mostly with roots deep in the 18th century but hitherto merely exceptions to more dominant patterns, developed a new sort of vigor. At last these forces were able to break through the general restraint imposed by the Georgian rule of taste that had so long held sway.

As in the case of the loose alliance of various contradictory political interests that passed the Reform Act, the supporters of new ideas in architecture, after gaining the upper hand in tacit concert, began to war lustily among themselves. Throughout the Early Victorian period what actually superseded the old rule of taste was no more, on the surface, than an uneasy eclecticism; yet under this variegated eclecticism certain visual criteria did hold general sway, even if no articulate body of doctrine concerning architecture was adumbrated. The writers of the day, so much less clear minded than those of the 18th century, had little ability or even desire to recognize and define these general criteria—in justice it must be admitted the task is not an easy one—since the nature of criticism was growing increasingly antivisual and absolutist at this very time.

The major new aesthetic categories recognized in the late 18th century represented the private attempts of a few highly cultivated connoisseurs to explain qualities which they thought desirable in the various arts even though those qualities were contrary to inherited concepts of "beauty." After nearly two generations these new categories were widely, if often implicitly, accepted. The visual concept of the Picturesque (though not so much that of the Sublime) had long been propagated by poets and novelists. Thus that concept was at least partially understood by all the articulate upper and middle classes (as I suppose the "nonrepresentational" or "abstract" is in the arts today). But in gaining wider currency, the idea of the Picturesque also lost precision. Almost anything might be considered picturesque, provided it was different from the standard productions of the previous age. The reaction against Georgian taste in the second quarter of the 19th century, once it had spread through the literate community, produced at first therefore a rather frivolous libertinism in the arts; yet within the frothy range of up-to-date architectural fashions hard centers of purpose were beginning to solidify by the mid-30's. These nodes of absolutist theory provided early evidence that the middle decades of the 19th century would not, in fact, be at all frivolous but rather deadly in their seriousness about the arts.

The rather sudden consolidation of the most earnest of these nuclei of purpose in the mature Gothic Revival around 1837 is often thought to epitomize the beginning of Victorian architecture. But to assign prime significance thus to one aspect only of the architectural scene, even to the Gothic Revival in its Puginian and Camdenian phases, cannot adequately explain the wide variety of types of design which actually characterizes building production in the late 30's and 40's. To do so, moreover, is to blame a few cranks and purists for a general confusion of taste they were in fact loudest in denouncing.

The third chapter of this book is devoted to "Pugin as a Church Architect," and the two that follow deal principally with the church builders who were his Anglican emulators. But that is so chiefly for reasons of dramatic organization. Such primacy of position must not be construed as a confirmation of the theory that assigns prime importance only to Gothic church building in the story of Early Victorian architecture. Following on those three chapters on church architects the next two are devoted to Barry's Italian palaces and their emulation by others in various fields of secular building.

Already introduced in the 20's, the *palazzo* manner (so to call it) had a considerably earlier start than did Pugin's Gothic, although it was not widely used, even by Barry himself, before the last years of the next decade. Once firmly rooted about the time of Victoria's accession, this 16th-century Italian mode remained as popular in England through the 40's and 50's as the 14th-century English mode of Pugin's churches. On the Continent a parallel manner was much more generally utilized. Thus some sort of revived Renaissance design, rather than the more exclusively English revived Gothic, must be considered the principal stylistic vehicle of Late Romantic architecture in general, of which the Early Victorian is merely the English variant.

The primarily stylistic preoccupations in these early chapters will be unsympathetic to many modern minds, but the terminology of the "revivals" can hardly be avoided if Early Victorian attitudes toward architecture are to be adequately presented. To balance these first five chapters, the next group deals largely with various building types rather than with surface stylisms. This section culminates in a discussion of those areas of building in which technical progress in construction rather than interstylistic strife was the chief preoccupation of the builders, whether they were engineers or architects or gardeners. To many Victorian leaders such a sequence, from the churches of Pugin to the Crystal Palace of the gardener Paxton, would have seemed a descent from the sublime to the all-but-ridiculous. To many modern readers, on the other hand, it is Pugin and his admirers who will seem ridiculous, not Paxton and his engineer associates Fox and Henderson. Let such, however, withhold their judgment awhile, for it is impossible to understand the Victorian Age unless the evangelistic purposes of the revivalists and the utilitarian motives of the technicians are fairly balanced and the entire work and thought of both honestly examined. Paxton, when building with conventional materials, was always an eclectic stylist; it was Pugin who was in theory a rigid "functionalist." (In practice, of course, he was inhibited by a lack of respect for functions and materials not closely similar to those familiar in medieval churches; but he did not hesitate to criticize the Crystal Palace on purely structural grounds.)

Pugin and Paxton are equally central figures in the picture of Victorian architecture, balanced like Plato and Aristotle in Raphael's "School of Athens." Knowledge of the two of them, both of what they really stood for and of what they in fact were able to accomplish, is as necessary to later architectural theorists as is knowledge of both Plato and Aristotle to philosophers. Pugin was much the more articulate of the two and his leadership began earlier and lasted longer. It is logical to present him first, even though Paxton's first great greenhouse (Fig. XV 29) was built as early as Pugin's first important church (Figs. III 6–9). Professionally speaking, Paxton was never either an architect or an engineer, much less an architectural critic. On the other hand the lively polemics of Pugin have confused rather than clarified later estimates of him as an architect and builder.

Both Pugin's theories and his mature achievement mark a turning point in the program of re-using medieval architectural forms which goes back to the mid-18th century. His mature emulation of 14th-century Gothic, with its ascetic rejection of all the later medieval fripperies which had delighted successive generations of Georgians, early established new standards for advanced church architects. His books of the late 30's and early 40's provided the basis for rigid new principles of "correct" Gothic building to which the new generation subscribed. But actually Thomas Rickman (1776–1841), a Quaker pharmacist turned medieval archaeologist, had preceded Pugin in several ways as a serious reformer of Georgian neo-Gothic. Even the accepted names for the successive phases of English Gothic architecture—Early English, Decorated, and Perpendicular—had first been introduced by him in his archaeological writing. After building fairly competent imitation-Gothic churches for nearly twenty years, Rickman was in the mid-30's a much more expert practitioner than the young Pugin when Pugin turned (at much the same time and in much the same spirit) toward Catholicism and a more careful revival of Gothic building methods. Occasional churches built a decade earlier by other men, such as Edward Lacey Garbett's church of Holy Trinity at Theale in Berkshire, had a medieval vigor and solidity that Pugin almost never equaled, except perhaps in his own church of St. Augustine's, Ramsgate. The vigor of Garbett's detailing derives from a study of Salisbury Cathedral, the asymmetrical composition from the principles of the Picturesque. Late Georgian Gothic, particularly as applied to churches, demands a more careful investigation than it has yet received. Such investigation will probably tend to minimize the revolution in actual building methods that Pugin initiated; but it will hardly modify the novelty of Pugin's controlling attitude toward Gothic design. For the "Revival of Christian Architecture" at which he aimed was not merely a matter of taste or even of archeological correctness.

Earlier the Gothick (to continue to give it a Georgian spelling) had been for the most part a whimsical or a pedantic or sometimes merely an economical alternative to the dominant classical modes, little more serious than the concurrent Chinese or Turkish fancies. Now the cause of "Christian or Pointed" architecture became for Pugin an essentially religious crusade deeply imbued with values both ethical and sacramental. This transfer to the architectural field of Evangelical earnestness was widely accepted by most Anglicans within a very few years—though *not* by those whose religious position was technically Evangelical. A comparable earnestness was henceforth the necessary moral garment of Victorian architectural leaders, however much they might, like the critic Ruskin, profess to scorn Pugin and his productions. Pugin's campaign thus provides a peculiarly topical subject with which to begin the Victorian story, even though only a relatively small part of Early Victorian architectural production was affected by his books and his way of building.

But an equally characteristic "Renaissance Revival," under Barry's unfanatical leadership, continued throughout the Early Victorian period to have a wider influence on general building production than Pugin's Gothic Revival. Barry and the other exponents of Renaissance design were less drastic than the Gothic men in their rejection of established Georgian ways of seeing and ways of building. Generally latitudinarian in all things and not at all nationalistic, these men tended to accept the modern world much as they found it. Although hardly utilitarians in a strictly Benthamite sense, they envisaged for 19th-century architecture a progressive sequence of modulations. Serving new functional needs with real sympathy and freely utilizing new materials and structural methods, the Renaissance practitioners were above all moderates: Whigs or Liberals in political terms, not Tories or Radicals. To acquire credit in their ranks no such patterns of repentance and and conversion were demanded as by Pugin and the Camdenians. The "traditional" architects of the early 20th century were the natural heirs of such Victorians in their cool professionalism, their worldliness, and their accommodating approach to their clients' needs—as also, for that matter, often enough in their actual designing.

Renaissance men had no less scorn than Gothic Revivalists for most of the production of the earlier Georgian Age and gladly renounced as well the Grecian rigidities of the preceding decades. Yet there was a real continuity in the way the main structural and visual problems of architecture were approached. The Renaissance men belonged, more or less consciously, to the academic line that went back in England two centuries and more to Inigo Jones quite as much as to the broader international current to whose 15th- and 16th-century fountainheads they were programmatically returning.

W. H. Leeds (1786–1866) was the first, in the introduction to his monograph on Barry's Travellers' Club house, to provide a full-dress defense of the Renaissance case (*The Travellers' Club House . . . Accompanied by an Essay on the Present State of Architectural Study, and the Revival of the Italian Style* [1839]). Characteristically, he was much less fanatical in his attacks on Late Georgian practice than Pugin had been in his *Contrasts* three years earlier; he was also much less coherent and forceful in proposing a new set of architectural principles based on Renaissance practice. This Renaissance movement, although characteristic of the Early Victorian style-phase from the very first, does not therefore, in the precise way of Pugin's so much more concentrated Gothic campaign, fix the opening of the Victorian Age at any particular moment in time. The 19th-century Renaissance Revival, moreover, was never so closed and consistent in its doctrine or so exclusive in its professional membership as was the Gothic Revival from Pugin's time down at least to the 70's. Yet as Barry's leadership became generally accepted in the 40's the palaces of early 16th-century Rome more and more replaced those of late 16th-century Vicenza as models for various sorts of secular edifices, and these models were widely emulated well down into the 50's and beyond.

The beginning of the Victorian Age in the late 30's brought the wide acceptance of new stylistic models, English or Italian, and a parallel rejection of stylistic originality as an acceptable architectural aim. A new attitude toward the whole problem of architectural style in "modern" times was also taking shape. This attitude is really more significant than are the new stylistic models themselves or the general distrust of innovation. Without citing the examples which later chapters of this book will present in considerable profusion the attitude is rather hard to define. On the one hand, the styles of the past were considered to be vehicles for various general ideas; the novelty here is merely the association of different styles with different ideas, and even that had deep Georgian roots. Concepts of pure architectural form, such as are almost always necessary to aesthetic innovators, were generally ignored as mere Platonic abstractions: The forms of architecture were considered incapable of dissociation from the specific styles which had originally brought them into being. Yet it was also allowed that the formal elements of the various styles of the past could, within certain limits, be manipulated when they were "borrowed" for modern use, always provided that this manipulation was not alien to such definitions of the several styles as contemporary architectural historians were establishing. (These definitions are, of course, highly conventional ones and by no means coincide with those of the 20th century.) Thus it is the particular ways in which the forms of the past were manipulated by the Early Victorians that give the architecture of the period such homogeneity as it possesses.

That this new attitude toward style which took shape in the 30's did not lead merely to a kaleidoscopic eclecticism—as to many observers it seemed, and still seems, to have done—is largely due to the programmatic "revivals" or attempts to canalize 19th-century architecture within certain stylistic ranges. There were as yet no widely accepted ways of manipulating borrowed formal elements abstractly such as would begin to crystallize in the 50's (Chapter XVII). Of these more or less rigid programs for 19th-century architecture, Pugin's Gothic one and Barry's Renaissance one were, of course, the most influential. Quite as typical, however, is a third, of which Soane's pupil Richardson has already been mentioned as an early protagonist.

To refer to this third program as a "Jacobethan" revival is certainly convenient; the coined word, which is already current, neatly telescopes the later decades of the 16th century with the first decades of the 17th. But the term Jacobethan is more than a justifiable verbal convenience since the development of architecture in England was relatively continuous during the latter part of Elizabeth's reign and much of James I's, despite the change of dynasty. The major break began with Inigo Jones' first royal commissions around 1617; and that break was hardly complete, as regards architectural production as a whole, until well after the Civil War. Later Stuart

architecture of the sort which Jones initiated was to find few Victorian admirers and almost no emulators before the mid-50's.

To refer to the 16th–17th-century stylistic aspects of Early Victorian building production as a "revival" is questionable, however, for the Jacobethan
did not really "revive," that is, come to live again with a new life of its own,
even to the extent that the Gothic did with Pugin or the Renaissance with
Barry. Moreover, the Jacobethan Revival (so to call it all the same) was never
a major cultural movement throughout the whole Western world such as the
earlier Greek Revival had been in the preceding High Romantic period.
Yet this Jacobethan Revival is perhaps more definitely symptomatic of the
architecture of the whole Victorian Age, High and Late as well as Early—
if for somewhat different reasons in each case—than either the rabid Gothicism of Pugin, on which attention is usually focused in studies of this period,
or the quite personal Italianism of Barry. In the general tradition of derivative
design in architecture, which lasted almost down to the present as an aftermath of the Victorian Age, the Jacobethan Revival likewise continued to have
a definite, if undistinguished, place. And on the Continent, above all in
France, parallel movements can readily be recognized in the 30's and 40's,
though they came rather later in Germany.

The obscure beginnings of the Jacobethan Revival in the 18th century are
only just being carefully studied by Pevsner and others. The Jacobethan was
certainly prominent, however, among the alternative stylisms offered in such
Late Georgian house-pattern books as P. F. Robinson brought out in the 20's
well before Richardson, Henry Shaw (1801–1873), and others had begun to
provide accurate documents for imitation. For Barry in the late 30's and 40's
a version he called "Anglo-Italian" once or twice provided a useful stylistic
vehicle. In 1836 Barry won the competition for the New Palace of Westminster with a Perpendicular project against competitors who interpreted
the "Gothic or Elizabethan" design demanded by the program in a Jacobethan
sense. At the same time he was confirming his personal predilection for the
Italian High Renaissance by winning the scarcely less important Reform
Club competition with a version of an early 16th-century Roman palace
(Figs. VI 4–6). But within a year he was also engaged on a project for rebuilding the Earl of Carnarvon's Georgian seat in Hampshire, Highclere
Castle, in an elaborate Jacobethan vein.

The building campaign at Highclere was slow to start and much prolonged, so that no illustration of it was published before that in the *Building
News* in 1858 (Fig. I 7), and Barry himself hardly ever utilized Jacobethan
forms again as such, except in restoring 17th-century mansions, any more
than he was to use the Perpendicular much outside his Westminster work.

16

On the other hand, many architects certainly seem to have emulated High-clere in the 40's and early 50's despite the fact that the design was not available in any book or periodical until so much later. The Jacobethan was so perfectly suited to the tastes of the Early Victorians and to the capacities of the building industry of the day that it would certainly have become popular even without the prestige of Highclere. However, there is a great difference between the general popularity of a given mode of design in any period and its real suitability to the creative capacities of the leading architects of the day. The neo-Jacobethan was very rarely as successful as at Highclere, and that fact was certainly widely recognized by architects if not by laymen in Victorian times. Paxton's Mentmore is the chief exception (Fig. VIII 24).

Men were naturally not aware in the late 30's that they would one day think of themselves as Victorians; hence no one then craved to establish a specifically "Victorian" style. Yet the more intelligent leaders of taste seem to have realized soon that they were no more cut out to be successful neo-Elizabethans than their fathers had been to be plausible neo-Grecians. Serious-minded men were naturally shocked by Elizabethan profligacy, which had nowhere been more evident than in the architecture of the time. The ease with which Jacobethan ornament could be produced in substitute materials like papier-mâché and cast stone roused justifiable suspicion; while the emphasis on ornament in the available books distracted attention from Jacobethan planning and fenestration, which might have been profitably emulated had as much been known about Hardwick as about Burleigh or Wollaton.

Among the less earnest Victorians, however, the Jacobethan had a vast success. It was much used for country houses, both new and remodeled, by landowners who suspected the fanaticism of the Gothicists as much as they did the cosmopolitanism of the Renaissance practitioners. The ornament also provided for schools, hospitals, and other institutional edifices a casual sort of surface embellishment that could be used in any quantity. This appealed as a contrast to the cold functional detailing of utilitarian buildings in the Late Georgian period, now hopelessly out of fashion even among the hard-headed members of charitable boards.

The hankering for this hybrid style of a great English age of the past was destined to continue well down into our own time. It is all the more significant, therefore, that even 20th-century architectural scholars have yet to arrive at a thorough and coherent explanation of the real character of Elizabethan and Jacobean design. Such an understanding the Victorians had achieved (or at least believed they had) for both Gothic and High Renaissance design well before they came to emulate either with much aesthetic subtlety or creative vigor. But the Jacobethan, as John Steegman has pointed out in *Consort of Taste* (1950), was for them just "Olden Time," not a fully recognized style with a clearly definable character.

In the Early Victorian period the Jacobethan mode encouraged much less than did Gothic or Renaissance modes the creation of one of those illogical amalgams of archaeology and originality that alone give cultural vitality to a revival. Architects of neo-Jacobethan edifices rarely succeeded in fusing into a new alloy what they borrowed and what they added; the bronze-like idiosyncrasy of character which the best—and the worst—Victorian buildings in other modes so definitely possess was almost always lacking. When, in later Victorian times, characteristic elements from early 17th-century sources were successfully incorporated in a modern mode of design, these elements were rarely identified as Jacobethan. In the 70's and 80's Anne, not Elizabeth or James I, was the nominal Royal patron of the last Victorian revival that really revived.

The revived Jacobethan is generally an unsatisfactory 19th-century manifestation. It is too typical of many of the Victorians' weaknesses and timidities, even if it is also highly symptomatic of certain of their strongest and most recurrent tastes in matters visual. Moreover the neo-Jacobethan is almost never novel in a creative way and hence could rarely be expressive of its time. Like the forgeries of earlier paintings or sculpture made in any period, the neo-Jacobethan helps to reveal what Victorians really liked; it certainly does not illustrate either the heights or the depths of which they were capable in architecture.

Harlaxton, a vast house near Grantham in Lincolnshire designed by Anthony Salvin (1799–1881), was begun before Highclere but even longer a-building. It is only too easy to mistake this pile, which out-Burleighs Burleigh House, for an authentic work of two centuries and more earlier—at least from a certain distance (Fig. I 9). That could never occur with the Italianate palaces or even with most of the English 14th-century Gothic churches that were built in the 40's and 50's. This remark is, of course, not intended as praise, for a work of art can express satisfactorily only its own age and no other. When means of expression are borrowed, as they frequently are in literature and music as well as in architecture, the justification for such loans does not lie in the artist's competence as a forger—which can rarely deceive for long—but in the new use the artist finds for what he has borrowed.

In the deepest sense the borrowed means of expression are not part of the form of the new work but rather part of what it expresses; that is, elements of its content or meaning. It is a convenience of speech to refer to "styles" in Victorian architecture, meaning the nominal vehicles of expression borrowed from the styles of the past; but Victorian "style," in the best sense of that abused word, is something quite different. Harlaxton and all the other Jacobethan works of the age that half persuade us of their plausibility are in that sense all but devoid of style. Decade after decade the architects of country houses and of various sorts of institutions continued to work the Jacobethan vein with little or no change. But true style in art has life, of which the changes resulting from growth and development are the evidence; and only living style makes significant history. Little account will therefore be given in this book of Jacobethan production, since it maintained only a sort of vegetable existence. Other aspects of Early Victorian architecture came fully to life and teemed with bold actions and dramatic conflicts.

The new functional demands of the second quarter of the 19th century might seem today to have required an approach to design unconfused by stylistic preconceptions derived from the past. Yet in practice the need to create or develop new building types more often seemed to inhibit than to encourage conscious innovation in design as such. The workaday Victorian architects to whom these problems were usually consigned were neither particularly sensitive nor creative; their clients were likely to be frank Philistines. Railway stations, produce exchanges, and even museums, for example, were effectively new architectural types at this time; and for them surprisingly successful (though quite illogical) stylistic expression was often found by run-of-the-mill architects using almost accidental combinations of new materials and old forms. Whether the forms were cinquecento Italian or trecento Gothic, the results generally have a peculiarly 19th-century vigor.

Many modern critics see a different central dilemma in 19th-century architecture from that produced by the continuous "wars of the styles" for which Victorian critics were always mobilized. Foreign versus native, Gothic versus Renaissance, eclectic versus revivalist, evolutionary versus revolutionary, "copyistic" versus "real," moral or "Christian" Pointed versus worldly and "Pagan" Italian—all such verbalisms these critics would throw out as irrelevant in order to concentrate our attention almost solely on functional changes and structural developments. The story of the successive technical advances in construction in England from the mid-18th century on, particularly as regards the prefabrication of building elements and the increasingly bold use of ferrous products, could be most profitably told; but it would be a division of the general history of science and its applications, not an account of *architecture* as that art has generally been understood.

The portion of the technical story devoted to the period 1835–55, for example, would deal directly with only a few aspects of many of the most characteristic (not to say the most famous) Early Victorian monuments and would altogether omit many other rather important buildings. One need not accept any of the rigid definitions of architecture favored by the Victorians in order to feel that such a reduction of the significant building production of the mid-19th century to a few lines of evident "progress" in technics would be to ignore many of the legitimate aspirations of the best architectural minds of the age. Such a critical position repeats an error of one of those minds, that of Eugène-Emmanuel Viollet-le-Duc (1814–1879), who is so well known for a "rational" (more accurately, mechanistic) interpretation of the development of medieval architecture by now quite outdated.

Gothic architects and engineers in the Middle Ages operated (or so there is some reason to believe) more like scholastic philosophers than like modern technologists, just as might have been expected of the clerical world in which they lived. Engineers in the 19th century were almost as different from their 20th-century successors as from their medieval predecessors. On occasion 19th-century architects could produce better engineering-architecture than did their engineer rivals, work more comparable to the finest productions of the first real engineers, the men who were active just before the Victorian Age began.

Thomas Telford (1757–1834) and John Rennie (1761–1821) designed their stone bridges—and I mean "designed" in both the engineering and the architectural senses of the word—just as the ablest architects of their own Late Georgian day would have done. Engineering in masonry was still a part of architecture, and these men had been trained in architecture either by older architects or by self-instruction and experience. Scientific engineering theory was barely in its infancy, not an independent intellectual discipline.

The later 19th-century engineers were often poor architects. Isambard Kingdom Brunel (1806–1859), for example, in his Egyptian suspension bridge above the Clifton Gorge and in his castellated station at Temple Mead, two of the chief Early Victorian monuments of Bristol, echoed with enthusiasm the sillier stylisms of the day (Figs. XV 17, 20–21). The architect Francis Thompson's collaboration with Robert Stephenson (1803–1859) on the Britannia Tubular Bridge (Figs. XV 34–36, 38) and that of M. D. Wyatt with Brunel on Paddington Station (Figs. XVI 34–39), on the other hand, made of these far finer monuments than any that the Victorian engineers, who were generally without the sound architectural training of their Georgian predecessors, were capable of achieving on their own. Early Victorian engineering is partly separate from architecture, partly inextricably involved with it. To hypothesize a sequence of technical or engineering works uncorrupted by contemporary architectural ideals is only to dream—if indeed it is not consciously to falsify history in aid of a particular critical position of the present day.

20

If one wishes to give any serious consideration to Victorian architecture at all—an activity which appears now to occupy many critics and historians besides myself—it must be considered as a whole. The peculiar interest of the production of the period is not restricted to a few rather peripheral monuments of iron and glass like the Crystal Palace and the great railway sheds (Chapters XII and XIII). On the other hand to restrict one's study to the high-minded work of the Gothic Revivalists is equally wrong (Chapters III–V, XVII). The church builders enjoy the prestige of having been less loudly damned than most of their confreres by that great, if confused, Victorian architectural critic John Ruskin; but one must not take the Victorian scene at the Revivalists' own valuation any more than at Ruskin's.

Too much special pleading of various sorts, some of it inverted and ironic, has obscured the richness and vitality of the total Victorian story by concentrating attention on only one or another of its subplots. Early Victorian architecture, or all that matters of it, was not just the Gothic Revival, already the subject of several excellent books; nor was it merely some idealized "academic tradition" which even its admirers admit was much enfeebled after the 30's. Nor yet can Early Victorian architecture be restricted to the pure line of technical development, a line in any event not of uninterrupted progress but of bright hopes alternating with dismal slumps. Early Victorian architecture included all these things (and many others almost equally significant); it was in fact the sum of them, almost the result of their multiplication.

The many-voiced architectural music of the Victorian Age is complex in its orchestration after the harpsichord-like effects of the previous century. But it is the more intense dynamics of Victorian architecture even at its beginnings, characterized by crescendos and fortissimi rather than by soft passages, that remind us that this was the age of Berlioz in music as well as of the "Gothic Revival" of plainsong by the Benedictines. To understand Early Victorian architecture, and even perhaps to obtain from its special harmonies a pleasure no other age can provide, one must be ready to accept the piling up of large visual orchestras and choruses. A healthy suspicion of what both the 19th and the early 20th centuries have thought to be the "absolutes" of taste in the arts is also necessary.

An approach that is as charitable and uncensorious as that of the critics who have revived interest in later Roman architecture or in the divagations of style that followed the High Renaissance in Italy is required. The queasy attitude of those early 20th-century writers on the Victorian Age who tried to protect their own reputations for taste either by extreme selectivity or by excess of humorous reference should be avoided. I shall not eschew humor and occasionally must exhibit a touch of queasiness. But cold objectivity never did any humanistic subject good, however pathological its character; let us therefore laugh and be sick if we must, but as far as possible in concert with the Victorians. The 20th century certainly has no right to patronize the 19th.

CHAPTER II: THE 1830'S

The best preparation for the study of Victorian architecture, as for that of any other age, is some familiarity with the building of the preceding period. Fortunately in the last twenty-five years critics and historians have explored with particular sympathy and subtlety that Late Hanoverian period which extends down through the Regency and the reigns of George IV and William IV to the accession of their niece in 1837. In the typically Victorian view this, the age par excellence of taste, was a dark one when taste had sunk to abysmal depths. Much later, when scorn for things Georgian eventually gave way to renewed admiration, the Classicism and academic restraint of the more monumental productions of the early 19th century were too much stressed by historians. Yet in architecture the Late Georgians were, like George IV and his brothers, those wicked uncles of the virtuous Victoria, the wicked uncles of her Victorian subjects. One must be more concerned with the artistic vices of the Late Georgians, as the early 20th century saw them at least, than with their virtues in approaching the new architecture of the Victorian Age.

Because the Late Georgian period was an age of taste, it was also an age of amateurs. The building production of amateurs was of course rather restricted; yet altogether a great many laymen were intermittently active, from that enthusiastic builder the Regent (who did no designing himself in actual fact), through the old aristocracy and the new nabobs, down almost to the lower clerkly levels of the middle class. The architectural profession, on the other hand, was expanding rather slowly, for new personnel came in only through the inadequate channel of articled training in private offices or by self-recruitment from the ranks of the builders.

Is it healthy that crowds of amateurs, as opposed to a well-trained profession with a high esprit de corps, should influence architecture as markedly as they did in the Late Georgian period? It ill becomes one whose own status in architecture is that of an amateur to decide the question. However superior, in that particular period, the top production of a really great professional genius like Soane may have been, a great amateur like William Beckford obtained from James Wyatt (1746–1813), and a generation later from H. E. Goodridge (1797–1865), rather finer things at Fonthill and at Lansdowne than those professionals were always able to build without his backing.

The highly literate critical writings of amateur theorists like Richard Payne Knight and Uvedale Price (1747–1829), while sometimes only incidentally concerned with architecture, compare more than favorably with those of contemporary French architect-academicians such as A. C. Quatremère de Quincy (1755–1849). One may also well prefer the furniture and interior design of the English connoisseur Thomas Hope (1770–1831) to those of the contemporary French professionals Charles Percier and P. F. L. Fontaine (1764–1838; 1762–1853). Among the leading British architects Soane was not only a professional but technically at least, being Professor of Architecture at the Royal Academy, an academician. John Nash (1752–1835), however, the other leading architect of the time, was almost an amateur, if not merely a speculative entrepreneur with excellent connections at Court.

Building production was repeatedly shut down almost to nothing by wars and their aftermath in a way that the Victorian Age would never know. The significant proto-Victorianism of the period is nowhere better realized, therefore, than in the cottage and villa books that were brought out in such profusion in the 50 years between 1785 and 1835. For these books catered to the aspirations of a public of amateurs who could not even build their castles in Spain on account of the Peninsular War.

The Picturesque became in this period an aesthetic category as important as the Beautiful; it also quite overshadowed, at least in practical significance for architecture, the almost unachievable Sublime. Twenty-five years ago Christopher Hussey devoted to *The Picturesque* (London & New York, G. P. Putnam's Sons, 1927) a thick and compendious volume. Subtitled *Studies in a Point of View,* his book was a serious historical treatise on the origins of a new aesthetic concept and the effect of that concept on literature, gardening, painting, and architecture. In the compass of a single volume the treatment of no one of these arts could be complete; yet Hussey's chapter on architecture summarized admirably the theoretical background. It also sketched in outline, with relevant illustrations, the most characteristic manifestations. The influential cottage and villa books of the Late Georgian period begin, he noted, with John Plaw's *Rural Architecture* in 1785; he further stated that "this phase of architecture culminated, so far as books are concerned, in the prodigious *Encyclopedia of Cottage, Farm and Villa Architecture and Furniture* compiled by Loudon [John Claudius (1783–1843)], published in 1833 . . . [new ed. 1842]" Since then the late Donald Pilcher in *The Regency Style 1800–1830* (1948) has dealt in even more detail with the Picturesque in architecture as it was made manifest in the first quarter of the 19th century.

The Victorians, when high on their critical battle horses, almost consistently abjured the Picturesque as such, yet it might be still more accurate to say that they were rather seeking extra-aesthetic sanctions for what had become ingrained visual preferences. "The true picturesque follows [only] from the sternest utility," wrote one of the Camdenians in the 50's, thus reducing to a sort of epigram Pugin's ethical and antivisual attitude. "Reality," as the word was used by Victorian architectural critics in the 50's, became more or less equivalent to what would be called "functional expression" today. It was the favorite keyword among the high-minded of the mid-century in England, as also with the painter Courbet in France. Looser thinkers accepted the clumsy term "architecturesque." That word was proposed by Robert Kerr to denote the concept of the Picturesque as it had been revised by the critical writers of the mid-century. Later, under Eden Nesfield's and Norman Shaw's leadership, the Picturesque flowed back in the 60's almost unchastened and continued to color the architectural scene well through the frivolous 80's.

In examining here the illustrations in Late Georgian cottage and villa books those which display aspects of the Picturesque that are specifically proto-Victorian must naturally be emphasized; unfortunately this means ignoring more attractive illustrations which were at least as characteristic of the production of the period. In so doing I may seem to parallel the error of those 20th-century historians who have sought in the Victorian Age only such ammunition as might fit their own guns. But Hussey and Pilcher, as well as the cottage and villa books themselves, will readily provide a broader view.

If told that the "Pleasure Cottage" (Fig. II 1) from *An Essay on British Cottage Architecture* (1798) by James Malton (d. 1803) was dated somewhere between 1835 and 1855, no one would be surprised or, for that matter, very much interested. The irregular asymmetrical massing, the variety of materials of different textures and tones, and the crudity of execution were, however, a striking novelty when the book first appeared. And that novel quality resulted, we are told, from a conscious "attempt to perpetuate on principle, that peculiar mode of building, which was originally the result of chance, in dwellings for the Peasant and Farmer, and Retreats for the Gentlemen." A "rude Saxon Hutt" had made an early appearance among the garden pavilions built by William Kent at Stowe at least half a century earlier. Later Robert Adam had designed rustic structures for Horace Walpole and other distinguished clients, even as Hubert Robert had prepared a whole artificial village for Marie Antoinette at the Petit Trianon. But these were "fabricks," mere casual embellishments of the landscape, representing no attempt to perpetuate anything on principle. Generally, though not always, the earlier

25

ornamental cottages were symmetrical in design and often highly artificial in the choice and treatment of the materials by which their "rude" surfaces were obtained.

A double cottage (Fig. II 2) shown in Sir John Soane's *Sketches in Architecture* (also published in 1798 but, according to Hussey, prepared as early as 1793) helps to suggest how significant were Malton's designs. In this the same or similar rustic materials are used; but the façade is symmetrical, even basically academic, in composition. The patining, so admirably suggested by the aquatint process, is nevertheless even richer than in Malton's plate. That patining alone should reveal that both these designs are Georgian, not Victorian; for in general the Victorians liked their surfaces hard, and their vision, at least before the 60's and 70's, was less tonally pictorial than that of the 18th century.

There is a rather appealing sentimentality in Malton's description of one of his cottages as "a small house in the country; of odd, irregular form, with various harmonious coloring, the effect of weather, time and accident, the whole surrounded with smiling verdure, having a contented, cheerful, inviting aspect, and the door on the latch ready to receive the gossipy neighbor, or weary, exhausted traveller." It belongs to a simpler and friendlier world than that of the mid-19th century. Studied casualness was to be expressed by "a porch at the entrance; irregular breaks in the direction of the walls, one part higher than another; various roofing of different materials, thatch particularly, boldly projecting; fronts partly built of walls of brick, partly weather-boarded, and partly brick-noggin dashed; [and] casement window lights." Such things, Malton assures us, are all "conducive, and constitute [the ideal cottage's] features." All of them were to return, with greater sophistication, in Nesfield's and Shaw's work in the 60's, reaching a new peak of popularity in the 70's. They had remained popular with the less sophisticated right through the Early Victorian period.

The best nearly contemporary examples of cottages in the Malton spirit are to be seen at Blaise Castle near Bath, where in 1809 Nash built a whole hamlet. Such things are not Victorian; as executed they are not even proto-Victorian. But the increasing appreciation of them was peculiarly corrosive of inherited Palladian standards of design and execution.

The Late Georgian "Rustic Cottage" is only one of several vehicles of the Picturesque. The asymmetrically towered "Italian Villa" is equally important. This model traced its origins to the fabrics in the 17th-century Italian landscapes of Claude and the Poussins, just as the Rustic Cottage did—at least in part—to those in the 17th-century Dutch scenes of Ruysdael and Hobbema. The first Italian Villa fabrics, in this special sense, were probably realized in French gardens just before or just after the Revolution. Later at

26

Clisson near Nantes, in the heart of an area devastated by the bitter military operations in the Vendée, the brothers Caccault built in the years before 1810 a whole village in the spirit of the landscapes of Claude and Poussin. The wild terrain reminded these enthusiastic amateurs of the Campagna they had known so well in their long stays in Rome. But this village was as rustic in its Mediterranean way as was Nash's thatched hamlet, and more literally picturesque in the sense of being directly suggested by paintings. The aquatints after drawings by C. Thiénon and the anonymous text of *Voyage pittoresque dans le Bocage de la Vendée, ou vues de Clisson et de ses environs* (Paris, 1817) give the best idea of the work of the Caccaults.

But the first Italian Villa in England was Cronkhill, near Shrewsbury (Fig. II 3). It was probably also the first anywhere to serve as a modest "retreat" for a gentleman and hence was a type of house to which the suburban middle class might snobbishly aspire. It was built, according to John Summerson, about 1802 by Nash (*John Nash, Architect to King George IV* [1935], pp. 71–73). What was to be perhaps the most significant of the Picturesque modes of house design, born of the fabricks in 17th-century painting, appeared here almost full blown. The heterogeneity of its ultimate origins is rather clearer than in later examples, some of which are as late as the 80's. Like the fabricks in paintings, Cronkhill presupposes a vague but complex legend: Part of the walls would have been the ruins of a Roman villa; these the Middle Ages repaired, adding a round and a square tower for defense; the Renaissance introduced large oblong windows for light and air, and also surrounded the main square block with an elegant arched loggia. This last was of course equivalent, in its modest convenience, not to a classical portico but to the low verandahs like permanent awnings that had been borrowed originally from the bungalows of the East. By this time, indeed, verandahs popularized by returning Anglo-Indians were coming to be generally accepted as a desirable facility for outdoor living, even in the doubtful summer climate of Britain. Later, after Waterloo, Nash would use them extensively in more Oriental guise on the Royal Pavilion at Brighton.

Nash, or whoever in his office prepared the design for Cronkhill, had primarily in mind the pleasant three-dimensional pattern which the simple and irregularly piled masses and voids would make as a largish fabrick in the landscape. The composition was no abstract exercise in form; it was rather intended to seem "the effect of chance," in Malton's words, and the proportional relationships were not very carefully studied. Some advantage was taken, however, of the opportunities for a new and more elastic sort of domestic planning. But the principal immediate importance of the Italian Villa, on its first introduction, was the evidence it provided that Italianate design could readily be made Picturesque. Such design need only be eclectic in its choice of forms and loose in composition—something John Vanbrugh had known a century earlier and frequently exploited—in order to throw off the stigma of old-fashioned Augustan formality.

Italian Villas, as such, are not of much consequence after 1837. They continued to be built well down into the 80's but, as the Victorian Age advanced, the later examples display a steadily declining ease and grace. The new type of asymmetrical composition, on the other hand, carelessly or carefully organized about a major vertical accent, such as the earliest villas particularly prefigure, is of the greatest importance in the Victorian Age. No matter what the widely varying surface stylisms, from Early Christian through various kinds of Gothic to Late Stuart or even French Second Empire, the results are unmistakably 19th century in character. There are, for example, two grand and bold Victorian monuments—designed in the late 50's and neither of them an Italian Villa in the Regency sense at all—which well illustrate the latent capacities of this sort of composition. These are Barry's Halifax Town Hall (Fig. VI 3) and the St. Vincent Street Church in Glasgow by Alexander Thomson (1817–1875). In them the underlying concept was finally apotheosized, even though Barry's nominal style at Halifax was the Late Renaissance of France and Thomson's at Glasgow Grecian enough to justify his nickname "Greek" Thomson. Actually, however, the neo-Gothic architects were to be the most consistent masters of towered asymmetrical composition in the next generation.

Among the qualities which indicate that neither Malton's cottage nor Nash's villa can be Early Victorian in date are their real simplicity of design and their delicacy of scale. Much more proto-Victorian is the rustic double cottage that Robert Lugar offered in his *Architectural Sketches for Cottages, Rural Dwellings, and Villas in the Grecian, Gothic, and Fancy Styles* (1805) (Fig. II 6). The chamfered corners here, the hipped gables, and the general gawkiness of the exteriors produce a coarse-grained and inelegant effect, despite the tonal refinement of the aquatint process.

Lugar's cottage contrasts also, both in character and in quality, with the grouped cottages illustrated in another book of the same year, *The Rural Architect* by Joseph Gandy (1771–1843) (Fig. II 4). This boldest of all Soane's pupils scarcely practiced at all, and his modest cottage projects must not be considered an accurate index of what was actually being built—even occasionally—in these war-torn years. Rather they are among the most distinguished examples of what never *could* have been built in that period, as are the abstract and surrealist projects designed by the brilliant French architect Claude Nicholas Ledoux (1736–1806) for his *Ville idéale* (1808), so pathetically dedicated to the Emperor Alexander of Russia. The Late Georgian functionalism of Gandy's projects can be matched in Early Vic-

28

torian times only in certain fine works of engineering-architecture. His cottage designs exaggerate all that Early Victorians most detested in the executed work of the Regency period and were hardly admired again before the present century.

Another of Lugar's house projects in *Architectural Sketches,* an Italian Villa, is also proto-Victorian in its heavy though simple detailing (Fig. II 5); but the sharp dichotomy between the dull, symmetrical front elevation and the off-center accent provided by a tall octagonal tower is more significant. The possibilities of exotic or eclectic elaboration of the towered villa formula, which led eventually to Barry's and Thomson's fine late works, are still better suggested by Lugar's "Garden Pavilion in the Egyptian and Turkish Taste." Here the tall tower has become a slender minaret set well back on one side; a more or less Egyptian entrance doorway on the front is flanked by a shorter onion-domed tower; while behind this a verandah of scalloped segmental arches extends to the rear.

A design of Lugar's in what he calls the Castle Style proposes a considerable mansion (not a cottage, villa, or modest retreat) in which the large rounded masses are elaborately casual in their grouping, although the planning, which is in the Adam tradition, seems merely dislocated from its axes and not related to the asymmetrical organization of the exterior. This is quite unlike most of the large "castles" which prominent professional architects were actually building in Regency days. These usually have plans of almost academic formality; only some of Nash's more modest castellated work shows the characteristic loosening of the domestic plan in this period.

Gwrych Castle at Abergele is more comparable to Lugar's project and was possibly built in part from the designs of its amateur owner Lloyd Bamford Hesketh. Charles Augustus Busby (1788–1838), later the architect of Kemp Town in Brighton, had exhibited at the Royal Academy in 1814 a drawing for "A castellated mansion to be erected in Denbighshire for L. B. Hesketh, Esq.," but Hesketh must at least have been playing Beckford to Busby's Wyatt. Gwrych is, however, a far finer example than Lugar's project of a pictorially organized composition made up of bold cubic blocks and cylinders (Fig. II 7). Set against a hanging wood, it seems almost like a piece of large-scale abstract sculpture; in such things the High Victorian architecturesque was already happily prefigured.

Beside Gwrych, Lowther and Eastnor Castles by Sir Robert Smirke (1780–1867) seem no advance on Adam's Culzean; and James Wyatt's Belvoir, as well as Windsor after it was remodeled and enlarged by Sir Jeffrey Wyatville (1776–1840), are saved from dullness only by their sites and, at Windsor, by the incorporation of genuine medieval elements. Nash's castles, designed presumably by the elder Pugin, are generally preferable not only because of their less schematized planning but also for their not unskilled architecturesque massing. Yet these were soon to be as much anathema to the Victorians as the others because of their almost total lack of archaeological plausibility.

The beautiful book by John (Buonarroti) Papworth (1775–1847), *Rural Residences* (1818; 2d ed. 1832), was illustrated throughout with delicately hand-colored aquatints. In this no designs for castles were offered; but there are the usual thatch-covered Rustic Cottages, here quite symmetrically composed, and also a fine towered Italian Villa, "designed as the residence of an artist" (Fig. II 8). The forms of this villa were "selected from works of pictorial beauty" by great Italian painters and it belonged, Papworth states, to what "may be termed the painter's style of building." In addition to these charming designs there is a remarkable Cottage Orné (i.e., a gentleman's retreat, not a mere dwelling for an agricultural laborer) prefiguring the mid-20th century in the extreme simplicity of its detailing (Fig. II 10). The positive compositional use of the voids of the verandahs, which are arranged on two levels around the solid core of the house, is most interesting but was not developed further in England in Victorian times.

More proto-Victorian is the recurrent emphasis in Papworth's book on small, detached, freely planned houses ornamented with modest Tudor trim (Fig. II 9). These are said by their designer to be peculiarly suited for parsonages since they would harmonize with the old Gothic village churches. The "Tudor Parsonage" was an amazingly popular formula, quite outclassing the Rustic Cottage and the Italian Villa through the rest of the Late Georgian period and well on into the next. Its unpretentious and commodious planning eventually provided the basis from which Philip Webb was to begin developing the modern house plan in the late 50's. By that time the surface style of such houses had already become "earlier" and the handling of detail more "real." This can be seen in the vicarages erected for the High Church clergy by Butterfield and other neo-Gothic architects in the 40's and 50's (Fig. V 13).

The principal purveyors of Tudor Parsonage models in the 20's were Peter Frederick Robinson (1776–1858) and Thomas Frederick Hunt (1791–1831); but almost all the cottage books offer them in profusion. Robinson's Swiss designs, first shown in his *Rural Architecture* in 1822 (later eds. to 1836) and again in a wider range of examples in *Designs for Ornamental Villas* (1827; later eds. to 1836), are presently still more significant.* To the

* Robinson's and Hunt's bibliographies are very complex. I shall not try to list later editions or all their titles. Hunt's *Designs for Parsonage Houses, Almshouses . . .* (1827) and his *Exemplars of Tudor Architecture Adapted to Modern Habitations* (1830) both provide prime "exemplars" of the Tudor Parsonage, needless to say.

Romantics and their successors Switzerland was very paradise. In the mid-century Ruskin maintained the Alpine cult among aesthetes after it had already been taken up by a heartier group. Hence anything Swiss long continued to have a special prestige.

Swiss folk architecture is, of course, generally rustic like that of English late medieval cottages; but it had certain bold and positive features, in the way of projecting wooden galleries and wide eaves supported on tremendous brackets, that the modest native edifices, admired since Malton's time, could not match (Fig. I 6). As characteristic as the assertive silhouette and the coarse timber-scaled articulation of the walls of the Swiss Chalet was the rough-and-ready peasant-Baroque detail, usually touched up with color. The latter provided a new repertory of "gingerbread" ornament, the word deriving from continental ginger-cakes stamped in chalet shape. This Swiss mode was considerably more influential in Germany and France in the mid-century than it ever was in England; but Alpine gingerbread, executed with the jigsaw, provided a most characteristic sort of Early Victorian ornament in England. In America the Swiss influence coming from England was much reinforced from German and even French sources.

Robinson's designs for large Jacobethan houses may be passed by here. Several of them were actually executed in the late 20's and one usually passes these by also, readily assuming that they are unimportant examples of Early Victorian country houses built as late as the 40's or early 50's. Yet for all their ambiguity of character they are not—at least in any positive or interesting way—proto-Victorian.

The verandahs so regularly incorporated in Robinson's and Hunt's house designs, whatever their nominal mode, were more generally adopted in America than in England. So also were the Grecian temple houses offered in another particularly attractive book published in 1827, *Retreats* (2d ed. 1840) by James Thomson (1800–1883). One of these, however, should be memorable for its Firbankian name "Irregular House." Thomson had been the architect this same year, under Nash's general supervision, of Cumberland Terrace in Regent's Park, a superb example of Picturesque Classicism. His later work of the 40's is less appealing (Fig. VIII 35).

In *Landscape Architecture,* also of 1827, Thomas Laing Meason presented a whole bookful of Italian Villa compositions all extracted directly, the author assures us, from the works of Italian painters from Giotto to Solimena. But more characteristic of the archaeological-minded 30's were the first two "books" of Charles Parker's *Villa rustica* (1832 and 1833; a later "book" came along in the 40's as well as a complete edition of the whole work). In this, actual rustic buildings which the author had examined in Italy are represented by what may almost be called measured drawings (Fig. II 11). But

31

Parker, like Thomson, continued to work well into the Early Victorian period, maturing with it. His executed work belongs in later chapters, as also some notice of his considerable influence in the early 40's on Lewis Cubitt and others (Fig. III 47).

A more interesting architect, already active in the 30's, who grew up to be a real Victorian was Edward Buckton Lamb (1805–1869). He made his debut in Loudon's *Encyclopedia of Cottage, Farm and Villa Architecture and Furniture* (1833; 2d ed., with supplement, 1842) and then purveyed almost unbelievably proto-Victorian designs to Loudon's *Architectural Magazine* throughout the rest of William IV's reign. His "Country Tavern," shown in the *Encyclopedia,* is in the Italian Villa mode—but with what a difference from Parker's plausible documents of the previous year (Fig. II 16). A curving stair rises around the loggia tower, quite destroying the elegance of its form; while the verandah roof on the other side is supported on crooked tree trunks of the most uncolumn-like Y-shaped form.

Here is an architect who already seems to hate "beauty" of the older Georgian sort as much as William Butterfield was ever to do. Lamb, however, earned in the 40's only the bitter enmity of the pious Camdenian critics who were—and only a very few years later—to defend Butterfield's "realism" with vigor. Lamb's Gothic was usually Perpendicular—but again with a difference. Both his "late" nominal style and that "difference," which modernized and personalized his detail, partly explain the antipathy of the ecclesiologists to his work. But it was his frank scorn for the ritualistic planning of churches that roused their malicious enmity. The crankiness of Lamb's Gothic is already very apparent in the coarse detail and nervous irregularity of silhouette of a large project shown in the *Encyclopedia* (Fig. II 12). Like his later client Disraeli, also an extreme individualist among Victorians, the architect who was to remodel Hughenden in the 60's was already making his characteristic mark in the 30's.

Two of Lamb's suburban villa projects, published in the third volume of the *Architectural Magazine* in 1836, are precisely contemporary with the appearance of Pugin's *Contrasts* and may well terminate the present discussion. One is Gothic of an order rarely seen in the work of others before the 60's; the Italianism of the other is so corrupt that it looks even later in date. The Gothic villa is said to be "of the second class," that is, in Pugin's language "Middle Pointed" or 14th-century Decorated (Fig. II 13); but it could hardly differ more sharply from the norms that Pugin and the Camdenians were to establish for the "revival" of this sort of Gothic in the next five years.

The materials are extraordinarily varied and boldly scaled, not crisp and delicate as in the Gothick villas of the opening of the century. A curious L-shaped group of chimneys plays almost the part of an Italian Villa tower

32

in the composition. Instead of an open gallery in front of the overhanging upper storey, such as appears on most of the Swiss chalets shown by Robinson (Fig. I 6), the braced wooden truss of the roof is brought well forward of the wall plane—a treatment for which Lamb (as usually with his wildest ideas) professed to have archaeological precedent. Let us not, like the Camdenians, succumb to nausea at the sight of this design; in it one catches an amazingly revealing glimpse of what was coming in architecture, not so much in a few years as in another two or three decades. In America, where the character of such a design can in fact best be matched, its progeny appeared in numbers only in the 60's and 70's.

Curiously enough the finest houses Lamb himself was eventually to build in the 50's and 60's do not resemble this early conceit, nor were they much like the strange Italian Villa which he also published in the 1836 volume of the *Magazine* (Fig. II 14). In that, however, he played quite as boldly with a different repertory of forms. The details throughout are few and heavy, but they are also almost "real" (in the sense of the critics of the 50's) because of the perversely structural way they are treated. One must assume, as regards the youthful Lamb, that he knew precisely what he meant to achieve; certainly he always did later when he matured into the eldest of the really wild Victorians. But either architectural illiteracy or imitation of Lamb's easily accessible designs made his early solecisms commonplaces of mid-Victorian villa building. He had less influence in the 40's, however, than in the 50's and 60's.

With Lamb in the mid-30's the post-Georgian period seems almost to have begun. Lest his early designs be refused credence or supposed to owe their appearance of extreme corruption to the crude woodcuts in Loudon's publications, comparable designs by an older man such as Francis Goodwin (1784–1835), who built the respectably Grecian Town Hall in Manchester and the Gibbsian spire of St. Paul's, Birmingham, should be consulted. In the aquatints of his *Domestic Architecture* (2 vols. 1833–34; supplement, 1835; 2d ed. 1843) appear most of the generic qualities of Lamb's house projects of the 30's. Goodwin handles his designs with considerably less personal gusto, but they are most elegantly presented in aquatint (Fig. II 15), not in crude wood engravings, so that we must assume we see them as he intended they should look.

Many more important Victorian architects than James Thomson and Parker and Lamb began their careers in the 30's and even earlier. For the most part it will suffice to suggest their Georgian background in a few words when introducing their earliest Victorian work. But in one instance, that of Sir Charles Barry, the pattern of his architecture was so firmly set in the 30's and his accomplishment already so great that he would certainly be con-

33

sidered a Late Georgian architect of distinction had his career terminated in 1837. Since Barry was also to be one of the two or three chief architects of the 40's, it seems well to sketch here at some length his training and his work in the years before 1836. It was then that his success in the competition for the design of Westminster New Palace made him suddenly the recognized head of the profession.

A compendious *Life and Works of Sir Charles Barry* (1867) was written by his son the Reverend Alfred Barry; the present account is largely based on that. The late Arthur T. Bolton had begun a study of Barry before his death. At present Marcus Whiffen has in hand a full-length book on Barry, something which is very much needed, as the gaps and uncertainties in the several sections of this book devoted to Barry's work will make evident. Whiffen's *Architecture of Sir Charles Barry in Manchester and Neighbourhood* (Manchester, Royal Manchester Institution, 1950) is very useful as far as it goes.

Born in 1795, Barry began to practice in the early 20's and first made a personal reputation with his Travellers' Club house at the conventional age of 35. Like many of his Georgian predecessors, he was essentially self-educated. He had, however, been an articled pupil with Middleton and Bailey, an obscure London firm of architects and surveyors to whom he was sent at the age of 15 and with whom he remained until he came of age. Then he started out on an unusually extensive grand tour of Europe and the Near East lasting for several years. During his time with Middleton and Bailey, Barry at least learned the business side of architecture, at which he rapidly became expert. And during those adolescent years he was also submitting projects to Royal Academy exhibitions and amusing himself by redecorating his own room as a garden grotto with landscapes seen through gaps in ruinous rockwork walls. He was a romantic young man, but still in a rather 18th-century way, not at all either a bigot or a Bohemian, as Pugin was so strangely to be at one and the same time.

Barry's father had been a Westminster stationer who supplied the government Stationery Office. The father had evidently accumulated considerable wealth, and the legacy of £200 he left his son encouraged him to embark on his tour in 1817. Down to 1815 the Continent had been largely closed to English travelers by the Napoleonic Wars; now in these postwar years they were flocking there again. For a young man of the English middle class, just entering the architectural profession, travel had social (and ultimately economic) advantages as well as its more obvious value as "postgraduate" training. A stay in Rome, for example, brought desirable contacts outside one's own class, as well as offering opportunities to study the monuments of antiquity at first hand.

On the first part of his travels in France and Italy Barry proceeded alone. With a catholic enthusiasm he devoted almost as much attention to collections of painting and sculpture as to buildings. Despite the fact that he had become engaged before leaving home, he decided in Rome to go on to the Near East to study Greek monuments. With the approval of his future father-in-law (and one may hope of his fiancée) he joined a party headed for Greece. Traveling alone in Greece would then have been dangerous, if not impossible, and Barry was not a particularly adventurous young man. Barry's party included Charles Eastlake (1793–1865, later President of the Royal Academy from 1850 and Director of the National Gallery from 1855); William Kinnard (d. 1839), who edited the supplementary volume which finally completed James Stuart and Nicholas Revett's *Antiquities of Athens* (4 vols. 1762–1816) in 1830; and a Mr. Johnson. Together they undertook an extensive tour of Greece and eventually of Turkey. Just as Barry prepared once more to return to England from Athens, a Mr. David Baillie offered him a salary of £200 a year to accompany him to Egypt and record the principal monuments there in sketches such as Baillie had admired of the Athenian buildings.

This visit to Egypt seems to have been the climax of Barry's travels. For the first time he passed outside the range of the conventional modern and classical world which students of architecture had been visiting intermittently for generations. Despite his vast enthusiasm for the monuments of ancient Egypt, however, he was not tempted to imitate Egyptian forms in his own later work. Even generic influences from this source are lacking, for it is a matter of biographical rather than internal evidence that the hieroglyph-covered walls of Egypt encouraged Barry to a freer use of ornament—freer, that is, than the severe taste of English Grecians allowed in the 20's.

After Egypt, Baillie and Barry visited Jerash and Baalbek in Syria but failed to reach Palmyra because of a clash with the Bedouins. That the scale and magnificence of the Roman ruins in these cities definitely impressed him (although not so much as those of Egyptian monuments) is at least obliquely interesting, for to modern eyes Imperial architecture in the Asiatic provinces certainly does suggest some of the peculiar qualities of Victorian monumental work. Yet Barry's own later buildings show rather less similarity to the edifices of Baalbek and Jerash than do those of his less traveled contemporaries.

Returning to Italy through Sicily, Barry examined with his usual catholicity the Norman monuments as well as the Greek ruins. Then, on his arrival in Rome, he found himself lionized as an expert on Egyptology. His final studies before returning home were made on a tour of various Italian towns with another young English architect, J. L. Wolfe, a pupil of Joseph Gwilt. It is these latest studies which seem most to have influenced his practice. The palaces of Rome and Florence evidently struck him as more suitable models for 19th-century architecture than the temples of the Greeks, now that his bright memories of Athens had been dimmed by his more intense Egyptian and Syrian experiences. Barry's son and biographer notes that his interest in the Gothic of Milan cathedral was greater on his second visit in 1820. In general medieval Italy had no appeal for him; nor for that matter the earlier Georgians' favorite city Vicenza.

It would not be worth while to sketch the itinerary of Barry's travels were it not symptomatic of the general modulation of taste in these years. The shift away from preoccupation with ancient Roman architecture and its traditional reinterpretation by such late 16th-century academic architects and theorists as Vignola and Palladio was by no means peculiar to Barry or even to English students. The principal interest of cognoscenti was now the temples of Greece; but increased admiration for Egyptian architecture, although never very influential on actual production, provided a sort of solvent for the absolutism of the Grecian faith. Increasingly, however, most architects visiting Italy turned their attention to the palaces of the High Renaissance with immediate effect on their own designing. In the work of Percier and Fontaine in France, even as early as their first project of 1802 for the Rue de Rivoli, and in the work of Leo von Klenze (1784–1864) in Munich from the mid-20's a sort of international Renaissance Revival was following rapidly on the heels of the Greek Revival. This Renaissance Revival had been initiated considerably earlier but was delayed in most of its manifestations by the endless Napoleonic Wars and the resultant interruption of building on the Continent.

In England the authors of cottage books were popularizing an informal Italian Villa mode, as we have seen; on the Continent there came a flood of more serious archaeological publications. Beginning with Charles Percier and P. F. L. Fontaine's *Palais, maisons et autres édifices modernes dessinés à Rome* (1798), a considerable French literature had already been devoted to the architecture of the Renaissance. To this A. H. V. Grandjean de Montigny (1776–1850) and A. Famin, Pierre Clochar (1774–*post* 1830), M. P. Gautier (1790–1855) and J. I. Hittorff (1793–1855) had contributed before Paul Marie Letarouilly (1795–1855) began the issue of his monumental *Edifices de Rome moderne* in 1840. No comparable flood of Renaissance documents appeared in Britain; architects like Barry, Cockerell, and Walters who had themselves traveled abroad (and there were of course many others) depended chiefly for Renaissance precedent on their memories and on their own sketches. These men will also have utilized the French treatises since their cultural background was cosmopolitan. Other architects soon imitated the leaders or copied details which they found in the pages of the architectural magazines of the day.

The natural thing for Barry to do on his return to England would have been to publish a book on Egyptian architecture; but a project for bringing out such a work, in collaboration with the wealthy amateur William Bankes of Kingston Hall in Dorset, fell through. Perhaps the failure of the project was just as well for Victorian architecture. Barry's career might otherwise have become trammeled with "Egyptian Revival" ideas in much the way Owen Jones (1809–1874), although rather an original designer, never quite escaped the "Moorish Revival" implications of his handsome treatise, *Plans . . . of the Alhambra* (prepared with J. Goury, 2 vols. 1842–45).

The best professional opportunity for a young architect in 1820 lay in obtaining commissions for new churches to be built in pursuance of the Act of Parliament of 1818. Unfortunately for Barry, the commissioners under the act took no interest in either Egyptian or Italian Renaissance design; indeed they actually tended to prefer Gothic to Grecian as being less expensive to execute. So Barry hastily turned his attention to the study of English Gothic (as it was understood at the time) and soon became a conspicuously successful practitioner of "Commissioners' Gothic." A decade later the young George Gilbert Scott (1811–1878), cannily taking advantage likewise of a new act of Parliament that required much inexpensive new construction, was to become (together with his partner William B. Moffatt [1812–1887]) a busy specialist at building workhouses—"Poor Law Bastilles" later reformers dubbed them.

The cornerstone of Barry's first Commissioners' church, that of All Saints', Stand, at Prestwich in Lancashire—a mere box, spireless, and with internal galleries—was laid in 1822 by the Earl of Wilton. Whiffen makes out a good case that Barry owed this job to Soane, to whom William Weston of Mandesleys, Prestwich, had applied for a design for the church in 1821. St. Matthew's, Campfield, whose cornerstone was laid in August 1822, is almost a twin of All Saints', Stand. The latter was consecrated in 1825, the former in 1826. St. Matthew's has the spire that economy forced Barry to omit at Stand.

In the next five years Barry built some ten Gothic churches and chapels, as well as altering or enlarging several others. For the parish church of St. Peter at Brighton he won the commission in a competition held in 1823. This edifice, built in the years 1824–28, is the most considerable of all his churches (Fig. II 18); to it George Somers Clarke (1825–1882) added a deep chancel in the 80's, more or less in the original style but denaturing its simple Commissioners' Gothic plan. Barry began no less than three churches for the rector of Islington in London in 1826. These were adequate examples of Georgian Perpendicular, while the richer Brighton church was more or less Decorated according to the very loose stylistic standards of the day.

The Royal Institution (today the City Art Gallery) in Manchester, which

Barry designed in 1824, is more significant (Fig. II 17), for that is one of the best examples of the Grecian museums that are so characteristic a product of the first decades of the 19th century in all countries. It illustrates better than do any of the churches the young architect's capability as an academic designer. Barry won the commission in a limited competition against the local architect Francis Goodwin, J. B. Papworth, John Foster (probably the younger [1786–1846] since the elder died in 1824) of Liverpool, and Lewis Wyatt. Their designs are not known, but it is likely that we would agree with the contemporary decision in favor of Barry. Buile Hill, now the Salford Natural History Museum, designed in 1825 by Barry, is a highly original Grecian house which has been damaged by the addition of a third storey.

More relevant to Barry's later career than his Manchester work was his intimacy in these years with the Holland House circle to which he was introduced by Lord Lansdowne, an acquaintance of his Roman days. There he met the great Whig aristocrats who were soon to be his chief patrons. It must have been in part as a result of Barry's own reputation as a traveler, and even more because of his new aristocratic friends, that he was invited to compete for the design of the new Travellers' Club house in 1829; it was certainly due to the predominantly Italian travels of its members that his Renaissance design was chosen. This was Barry's first important opportunity to build according to his more individual stylistic preoccupations; moreover, the clubhouse occupied a prominent West End site. But his earlier Brunswick Chapel (now St. Andrew's, Waterloo Street), built at Hove in 1827–28 for the Reverend Edward Everard (whom Barry knew in connection with his work on the Brighton parish church), was already a modest exercise in Italian Renaissance vein, interesting chiefly because it is not Gothic. Barry was also designing at this time a multiple-villa project in Brighton to which we will be returning shortly.

Large and elaborate clubhouses were really a post-Waterloo development in architecture, the handsomest being the new Athenaeum by Decimus Burton then rising in Waterloo Place. The new Travellers' Club house was to stand beside the Athenaeum in Pall Mall. The Travellers' is not a Victorian monument since it was completed in 1831; but it was as basic to Victorian stylistic development in many fields of secular building as Pugin's churches erected a decade later were to be in the ecclesiastical and related fields. As has been said, it also received in 1839 the honor of being presented by W. H. Leeds in a special monograph. This publication, with its fine engraved plates, made the design generally available for study and emulation. The Travellers' Club house must therefore be discussed in some detail here. Although Barry's much larger Reform Club house next door in Pall Mall, built at the opening of the new reign, later provided a still more perfect paradigm of the Italian palace mode, the Travellers' had already established Barry's reputation as the English leader of the international Renaissance Revival. Throughout the 40's it was the Travellers' as often as the Reform which was the immediate prototype of innumerable new edifices. Some of these were completely designed in the Italian palace mode; others merely utilized certain characteristic features of it such as the heavy terminal cornice or the windows framed with small orders.

Because of the restricted site of the clubhouse, a symmetrical disposition of the plan on four sides of a central court was not feasible; but of course the courts of many palaces in Renaissance Italy had been equally small and off-center (Fig. II 19). The main entrance lobby was forced to one side by this open court, becoming merely a corridor instead of a large central hall like those in Burton's Athenaeum and other earlier clubhouses. So also the staircase, instead of being a monumental axial feature, runs up modestly in returning flights behind the court. The chief rooms—coffee room below and library above—occupied the full width of the Carlton Gardens façade at the rear. (The present uses of the rooms differ somewhat.) Because of the entrance lobby on the right the morning room on the ground storey and the drawing room above were neither so monumental nor so symmetrical. Barry's planning here is undoubtedly more dexterous and less pretentious than in earlier clubhouses, illustrating his practical modern mind quite as much as any canonical formula.

The two-storey front and rear façades of the clubhouse are both astylar; that is, they have no giant order of columns or pilasters—as few other clubhouses of the 20's do for that matter (Figs. I 8, II 19). There is not even a projecting one-storey portico at the entrance such as there is on the neighboring Athenaeum. The Pall Mall front is necessarily asymmetrical (which Barry regretted) because of the unbalance of the plan. Hence the actual entrance doorway received little emphasis. It barely breaks the even line of the ground-storey openings despite its greater width and the scrolled brackets which support its somewhat heavier cornice. The upper-storey window range is absolutely regular; but the relief of the individual window frames is very emphatic because they are all edicular: That is, each is like a little flattened porch made up of a pair of Corinthian pilasters supporting a full entablature and a pediment. Unlike those framing the windows of Raphael's Pandolfini Palace (which Barry was accused of imitating too closely) the edicules here are not linked together either by a continuous entablature or by panels in the intervening wall spaces. Each stands out from the wall plane independent and equal in interest. The edicules are solidly supported and linked by plinths resting on the richly ornamented stringcourse which crowns the ground storey; and they are also echoed,

39

with less elaboration and less relief, by the simpler window frames in the lower wall. In other words, the openings are articulated, not the wall surface itself as is the case when classical orders are used to subdivide a façade.

Although this façade was intended to take its place in a row of buildings, it was not conceived merely as a two-dimensional composition. The bold cornice at the top is of the sort—henceforth usually given the Italian name *cornicione*—that is scaled to the full height of the building. In Palladian buildings of several storeys the terminal cornice had been scaled to the order, visible or implied, of the upper storey only, except where a giant order was used. The cornicione here is also returned around the corners, defining the base line of the visible hip roof. This treatment emphasizes the façade as the front surface of a cubic mass, not just a portion of a continuous street elevation. The rusticated quoins enhance this effect more subtly by providing a plastic binding at the corners. Also important in individualizing the clubhouse is the balustrade at street level; this masks the areas and basement windows and also sets the solid block of the building free from the pavement plane.

Thanks to the careful distribution of the ornamental features, this façade appears considerably less bald and severe than most contemporary Grecian work even though there is little ornamentation other than that provided by the moldings of the cornicione and the window frames. A simple guilloche pattern decorates the stringcourse between the two storeys; a close-set line of flat rosettes provides a sort of frieze below the dentils and modillions of the cornice: That is all.

The rear façade was much less influential on Victorian design and less attention need therefore be devoted to it here (Fig. II 19). Instead of the absolutely regular spacing on the Pall Mall front, the three central openings are close set here with single windows at either end. The ground storey is entirely rusticated; the corner quoins, as well as the quoins and voussoirs of the flat-arched windows, are delicately vermiculated to distinguish them from the rest of the wall surface. The pilasters flanking the first-storey windows support reeded archivolts instead of entablatures; thus the effect is more quattrocento than cinquecento. The tympana of the upper window arches, moreover, are filled with conventionalized shells, a motif much used later to enrich edicular window tops. The balconies at the base of these windows project on consoles rising across the paneled stringcourse below; the balcony railings are of pierced work instead of balusters. Even the cornicione is more delicate and fussy on this side; for it is supported on scrolled brackets above a decorative frieze of which the strapwork-like ornament resembles closely that on the balconies below. (The central superstructure, added later, was part of Barry's original design for the clubhouse;

40

but as this did not appear in the plates of the Leeds monograph it was not part of the Travellers' façades as Victorians knew and studied them.)

The interiors, which were on the whole quite simple in treatment and pale in their original coloring, have been too much pulled about to be worth describing. In any event they had no such long history of influence on Victorian architecture as did the exterior façades; their still very Georgian character can be studied in Leeds' plates.

In addition to his two churches in Brighton and Hove, St. Peter's and the Brunswick Chapel (St. Andrew's), Barry obtained the commission for the Sussex County Hospital there in a competition held in 1825–26 and began the structure in 1828. This brought him in contact with Thomas Attree. Jointly with the Reverend Edward Everard, Barry's client for the Brunswick Chapel, Attree was the honorary secretary of the hospital and a very prominent Brighton figure. He had already bought the tract to the northeast of the town called Brighton Park. (Subsequently this was named Queen's Park by Attree in honor of Queen Adelaide.) Desiring to move out of the house in which his office was located, Attree employed Barry to build him a villa there. This is now occupied by the Xaverian College.

In *Fashionable Brighton 1820–1860* [1947] Anthony Dale gives Thomas Attree as the builder of the villa; in *The History and Architecture of Brighton* [1950] he says it was his father William, so-called "King of Brighton" in these years and in fact Lord of the Manor of Atlingworth. But the link through Everard to the Sussex Hospital, St. Andrew's, and St. Peter's suggests Dale was right the first time.

The house for Attree was erected during exactly the same year as the Travellers' Club House. It differs from the more original Italian Villas of the Late Georgian period such as Cronkhill (Fig. II 3) in being completely symmetrical. Equally regular balustraded terraces provide what Barry called an "architectural garden"; for his concept of a proper villa setting represented a sharp break with the landscape gardening of the English 18th-century tradition; but that of course had been going out of fashion for some score or more years already. Near the house, however, stood a circular Italian tower now called the Pepper Box which masked a windmill. Although this picturesque feature was not attached to the main block of the house, as in the case of Nash's Cronkhill or of Goodridge's Lansdowne Tower just built above Bath for William Beckford, it was a conspicuous asymmetrically placed accessory in the general design of Attree's small estate. The score or more of additional villas, some Italian, some Tudor, with which Barry planned to surround the open and naturalistic central area of Queen's Park were never built.

For Barry the most important thing about the Attree project, so soon to prove abortive, was the favorable attention it attracted from the first from potential patrons. In particular the Duke and Duchess of Sutherland, whom Barry had already met at Holland House, came to see the new villa and its gardens and were much impressed. The duke and his younger brother Lord Francis Egerton, both members of the Travellers' Club, were in the next twenty years to pour out their enormous fortunes, largely derived from the Bridgewater Canal, on architectural projects, usually employing Barry as their architect. Extending well through the Early Victorian period, the major works done for these two clients find their proper place in Chapters VI and VII.

Barry, a Gothic church architect in the 20's, had become with the Travellers' Club house and Attree's villa better known in the early 30's as an architect of Italian palaces and villas. The clubhouse was certainly a palazzo in its design and also more or less of a palace in purpose, being intended for the group use of certain male members of the ruling class. While more modest in size, the Brighton house was a country mansion in the old Italian sense of the word "villa" rather than a small suburban residence in the Regency sense.

Barry was also acquiring considerable reputation as a skillful enlarger and modernizer. In 1833 he remodeled and enlarged the College of Surgeons in Lincoln's Inn Fields. There he preserved the original Greek Ionic portico but extended the main block upward with an attic and also widened the front. By capping this more extensive façade with a heavy cornicione he so subordinated the portico that it seemed but an honorific adjunct to a rather large and severe palazzo.

Barry had entered a Grecian design in the Birmingham Town Hall competition in 1831; but his projects for a London club to be built in the City (of 1832) and one in Manchester (of 1833) were presumably both Italianate. The project for the National Gallery of 1833, Bramantesque with pilaster orders, was so like von Klenze's Königsbau in Munich of the late 20's that some influence from that source may well be assumed. In 1834 Barry prepared designs for enlarging Holland House, presumably in the original Jacobean style, for his friend Lord Holland. These schemes suggest both the extent of his professional ambitions and the stylistic range of his designing activity during the early years of William IV's reign.

Barry's most important work in progress at this time, however, was Gothic: the King Edward VI Grammar School in New Street, Birmingham. And it was with the much more ambitious Gothic project which won the competition for the Houses of Parliament, held in 1835–36, that his national reputation was shortly established. Thenceforth Barry's career became a major thread in the Victorian architectural story; indeed that story has often been supposed to begin at just this point.

Did the Victorian period in architecture open with the acceptance of Barry's Gothic design for the seat of the national legislature in Westminster? Many would answer with an unequivocal "Yes"; some historians, who should know better, have even credited Queen Victoria herself with the selection of the winning design. And that design has by many been considered to mark some kind of a turning point in the history of the Gothic Revival, regardless of whether it is considered already to be Victorian. To complicate the situation further, Barry's credit for the design has often been disputed in favor of Pugin who was in fact merely an obscure collaborator of Barry's at this time.

The problem of the historical position of the Houses of Parliament, more properly known as Westminster New * Palace, including that of their disputed authorship, requires rather detailed discussion. As regards the structure above the embankment level, the Palace was actually begun only in 1840, four years after the competition was decided in Barry's favor and three years after Pugin had severed his connection with Barry. This was not to be renewed until 1844, by which time considerable portions of the vast complex were well advanced toward completion. The Palace was by no means entirely finished, however, when Pugin died six years later in 1852—although the House of Commons was opened in that year—or even by the time of Barry's death in 1860. These two architects must share credit between them for the design in its entirety, however, even though Barry's son Edward Middleton Barry supervised the final completion of the building in the 60's and is personally responsible for certain terminal touches of no great intrinsic importance. Just how the credit should be divided between the elder Barry and Pugin remains a very delicate question.

There was little to see at Westminster, except for the gradual construction of the embankment along the river, in the early years of the new reign; and the edifice remained far from complete at the end of the Early Victorian period. Even by the time of the opening of the House of Commons in 1852 the stylistic character of the unfinished Palace had already become distinctly unfashionable. The New Palace cannot be considered to open the Early Victorian phase of architecture in the late 30's when none of it was yet visible above ground level; nor does it represent Pugin's personal style in his early prime which, as we shall see in Chapter III, came precisely in the seven years while he was *not* associated with Barry on the Palace. To date the Palace in the early 50's, when it first became available to serve its principal function, is equally incorrect; for of that period it is as completely uncharacteristic as

---

* "New," incidentally, as of the time of William Rufus, not William IV, in relation to the "Old Palace" of Edward the Confessor. For the full story of the Palace see Maurice Hastings, *Parliament House* [1951].

it is of Pugin. The problem must therefore be approached in another way.

The original design for the Palace was prepared by Barry in 1835 for the competition held in that year, with considerable assistance from the then 23-year-old Pugin. This competition had followed on the burning of the earlier palace, a congery of edifices of various periods, the previous year. Although the scheme was considerably modified before construction above ground really began in 1840, and although it was to be still further elaborated during the long years of execution, the general design of the New Palace belongs to the original date of its preparation under William IV. Barry's major architectural decisions were all made two years before Victoria came to the throne and at a time when Pugin was still practically unknown as an architect and almost without practical experience at building.

Pugin undoubtedly redesigned most of the details of such exteriors and interiors as were executed between his recall by Barry in 1844 and his death in 1852; but he had already accepted Barry's commitment to a Perpendicular or Tudor Gothic style for the detail when he first assisted Barry on the competition drawings in 1835. That was long before he arrived, around 1840, at his own mature conviction that English Middle Pointed or Decorated Gothic was the only medieval style worthy of modern revival. For these reasons this important monument is necessarily something of a stylistic and historical anomaly; nor can it possibly be of Pugin's design if it is considered as a complete structure.

It would confuse rather than clarify this account of the general course of Early Victorian architectural development if the whole story of the New Palace were told here. A brief résumé of the prehistory of the edifice may better conclude this chapter on the 30's. The execution of the Palace will be discussed later in a chapter following those in which the principal stylistic and typological developments of the 40's are described and analyzed. Only with some such arbitrarily split treatment can the place of the Palace in the general sequence of Early Victorian development be understood and the ambiguity of its joint authorship somewhat clarified. Current investigations by Marcus Whiffen from the Barry side and by Phoebe Stanton from the Pugin side should ultimately resolve the latter problem much more completely.

The New Palace is the subject of important chapters in the two histories of the Gothic Revival, Charles Lock Eastlake's *History of the Gothic Revival* of 1872 and Sir Kenneth Clark's *Gothic Revival* of 1928 (2d ed. 1950). In Alfred Barry's life of his father, already mentioned, the chapter on the New Palace almost outweighs the rest of the book. Benjamin Ferrey's earlier account of the Palace, in his *Recollections of A. N. Welby Pugin and His Father, Augustus Pugin* (1861), is less considerable. But the two chapters on the

Palace in Michael Trappes-Lomax' *Pugin, A Medieval Victorian* (1933) amply make up for Ferrey's lack of detail. Running reports of the controversies about the Palace were published in the periodicals of the time and various documents issued by committees of Parliament, not to speak of the relevant debates in the two Houses, round out a very extensive bibliography which need not be listed in detail here. Finally, there are the pamphlets in which Pugin's and Barry's sons exchanged vicious blows in the 60's, well after both protagonists were dead, and thereby produced more heat than light. Two modern monographs may also be mentioned. *The Houses of Parliament* [1945] is chiefly a collection of photographs by Hans Wild, with a brief introduction by James Pope-Hennessy. Hastings' book has already been cited and is excellent, particularly for the history of the Palace before 1834. With all this literature already in existence it will be sufficient in this account merely to summarize the facts, adding as little comment as possible on controversial points where the facts are still in dispute.

A great many drawings of the Palace are now to be found in the Library of the Royal Institute of British Architects, some deposited by C. A. B. Barry in 1938 and others by Pugin's descendants since World War II. Even though these are only now being studied in detail, they already make possible at least a summary differentiation between the competition designs of 1835 and the building as executed after 1840. Such a differentiation has hitherto not been seriously attempted, I believe, by those writing about the Palace.

Because of the faulty firing of the heating apparatus under the old House of Lords, the complex of buildings that constituted Westminster Palace burned on 12 October 1834. The fire made a spectacular sight, as may be seen in the handsome painting by Turner now in the Cleveland Museum of Art. Barry observed it from the stagecoach as he returned to London that evening. According to his son, he at once realized the tremendous architectural opportunity the fire was creating—an opportunity he at once resolved to grasp.

The finest element in the earlier Palace was Westminster Hall. This had been remodeled from its Norman original by Henry Yevele in the 14th century and roofed by Hugh Herland with what is the ranking masterpiece of medieval carpentry. Fortunately the hall survived the fire as it was later to survive the blitz. The decision to preserve the hall, together with other historical considerations, led the Select Committee of Parliament, which was appointed by William IV early in 1835, to require that the designs for a new palace to be built on the old site should be "either Gothic or Elizabethan."

The archaeologist John Britton (1771–1857) at once rose before the newly established Institute of British Architects to protest against the vagueness of the latter term. As he pointed out, it might then mean anything from Tudor Gothic to full Renaissance; perhaps, however, the ambiguity was intentional. In any event none of those architects such as David Rhind and Anthony Salvin who sent in plausibly Jacobethan—as we might say—designs were any more successful in the competition than were the sophists, led by the great C. R. Cockerell, who offered compositions of academic late 16th-century Italian character. Cockerell's justification for his choice of style was that Englishmen of the Elizabethan period *ought* to have designed that way but unfortunately lacked the proper training.

From a total of 97 entries the committee selected four (according to some authorities five), and these were submitted to William IV. The King (presumably with ministerial advice) picked Barry's, leaving John Chessel Buckler (who had succeeded to his father John Buckler's practice in 1826), David Hamilton (1768–1843) of Glasgow, and E. Kempthorne with consolation prizes of £500. When the decision was announced on 29 February 1836 a major "battle of the styles" broke loose. (This might more appropriately have occurred, it would seem, when the original stylistic prescription was first announced.) It is unnecessary to quote again, as Eastlake and Clark have done at some length, the curious arguments with which another Scottish Hamilton, W. R., attacked the Gothic and defended the Greek as an imitation of "Nature," since the government stood firm against the onslaughts of Classicists both from south and from north of the Border. The government's decision could well have been made on practical grounds alone, without reference to the "style" of Barry's project. But Barry's designs were well within the prescribed area of "Gothic or Elizabethan" and even split the difference between by being Early Tudor.

Barry's plan was most comprehensive and logical (Fig. II 21). It incorporated in a vast grid, between the river (whose marshy edge was to be embanked) and Westminster Hall, most of the facilities for which the old buildings had provided, although it is not quite clear to what extent the Law Courts were included in the actual competition scheme. The masterly general layout of the executed Palace, which differs very little from what Barry originally worked out, is only really intelligible today from the air. The location of Westminster Hall, preserved nearly intact yet skillfully utilized as a magnificent entrance lobby, mars the regularity and symmetry of the scheme if one approaches from the west; while the long river front provides a continuous screen on the other side that quite masks the articulation of the grid as a whole. This river front was intended from the first to be occupied by libraries, refreshment rooms, and various accommodations for committees, with taller end blocks to house the Speaker on the right and the Usher of the Black Rod on the left (Figs. II 25). (Since the main elements of the plan remain as originally determined in 1835–36 the rest of the description is best put in the present tense.) The presence of the octagonal hall occupying the central point in the grid is suggested by a lacy lantern of which the top is just visible above the river façade. To this Octagon the main line of access leads from Westminster Hall through St. Stephen's Hall. This is built over the old Lower Chapel precisely where the Commons had sat in St. Stephen's Chapel for so many centuries.

North and south of the Octagon the principal apartments are lined up (Fig. II 20). To the south lie the Peers' Lobby, the House of Lords, the Royal Gallery, and the Sovereign's Robing Room. A separate Royal approach leads into this last, coming up a grand stairway from the southwest porch at the base of the tall tower which was soon named for Queen Victoria. A southwest wing joins the tower to the east end of St. Stephen's Hall. To the north of the Octagon are the Commons' Lobby, the House of Commons, and beyond that, in the range facing New Palace Yard, the Ministers' Rooms. At the end of this range and thus not in line with the Victoria Tower—which stands farther to the west—is the Clock Tower in which Big Ben hangs.

No less than a dozen interior courts, of various shapes and sizes, lie between the cross arms of the grid. They separate the principal suites of apartments, for which they provide light, from the external ranges of the complex. North of St. Stephen's Hall and on the inner side of Westminster Hall is the old cloister of the medieval St. Stephen's College of which little else now remains. This Barry restored as the Cloister Court. His son Edward Middleton Barry restored the old Lower Chapel below St. Stephen's Hall in the 60's. Even farther to the west Barry planned, but never built, additional wings to incorporate the Law Courts and to mask the open west flank of Westminster Hall (Figs. II 21, 24). Throughout the rest of the century various architects prepared designs for similar wings in this position; perhaps fortunately none of them was ever carried out.

Westminster Hall lies at a slight angle to Barry's north and south axis as well as entirely to the north of his east and west axis (Fig. II 21). Because of this awkward relationship of Westminster Hall to the western side of his grid, Barry's principal and most highly organized façade had necessarily to be that on the east toward the river. Originally this faced the marshy Lambeth shore; much later the tall and endlessly repeated pavilions of St. Thomas's Hospital (built in 1868–71 by Henry Currey [1820–1900]) rose above another embankment there. Both before and after the hospital was built the river façade of the Palace had to be seen in sharp perspective from one of the bridges at the two ends. The tremendous extension and formal balance of the composition as it is seen in elevational drawings is therefore quite unreal and has always been so.

Although Barry in time did make plans for an appropriate development of the Lambeth shore across the Thames, he had doubtless originally designed the river front, in part at least, with the conscious thought that the diagonal foreshortening of the views from the bridges at either end would produce those picturesque effects now so familiar to everyone. He provided no tall central feature such as might have marked the cross axis of the Palace and terminated a grand approach from south of the river. This would almost certainly have been planned by any continental architect of the day.

Barry's aversion to axial emphasis is well known, however, and is equally well illustrated in other major works. Always preferring to build up the ends of his compositions rather than the center, he introduced pavilions with coupled towers at the extreme ends of the façade. Rather taller towers rise at the ends of the central block also; but the axial bay is nowise distinguished from its immediate neighbors, nor is the central lantern to the rear of it particularly noticeable.

The general composition of the façade in the competition drawings of 1835–36 followed closely that of King Edward's Grammar School in Birmingham which Barry was building at this time (Fig. II 26). In each of the three main divisions of this long river façade there are eleven arched bays instead of the seven on the so much smaller Birmingham building (Fig. II 25). The projecting oriels of the terminal pavilions of the school were repeated at Westminster almost without change on all six towers of the river front. The embankment wall was to rise straight from the river edge broken only by two water gates on the axes of the end pavilions; no such subbasement had been necessary in Birmingham, of course. Above this unmembered wall the ground storey of the superstructure was originally intended to have two small windows in each bay coupled under rectangular drip-molds. Stepped buttresses would have risen between the bays, each one terminating (as at Birmingham) in a tall thin finial above the parapet masking the low roof.

The windows of the two principal storeys were to be linked vertically in continuous sunken panels; thus they would have much the same effect as the tall two-storey windows of the large schoolroom that ran along the front of the school in Birmingham. (They were even more like the side windows of St. Peter's, Brighton, which likewise have paneled transoms at gallery level.) But because of their greater size these windows were to be divided by grids of mullions into a much larger number of oblong panels, each headed by Perpendicular tracery.

Above the arches of the second storey a taller and richer parapet than that used on the school was proposed; on the central block another paneled stage was to intervene between the arches and the crowning parapet. But Barry

48

reserved the richest treatment for the towers flanking the central block. On these, octagonal corner buttresses, elaborately paneled, were to confine the oriels; while above the oriels in the topmost stage each tower was to contain a pair of huge windows like those in the belfries of Perpendicular church towers.

Barry was already employing young Pugin to work out the Perpendicular detailing of the Birmingham school. It was not unnatural, therefore, that Barry should also employ that youthful expert at medieval ornament on this much more elaborate but very similar design; especially since Barry, in spite of the considerable number of churches he had been building since the 20's, was well aware of his own deficiencies at Gothic design. He paid Pugin £300 more or less for his assistance (the actual sum varies in different accounts). This seems generous, since Pugin was receiving at the same time considerably less—some say only £200—from James Gillespie Graham for whom he is supposed to have provided a complete set of drawings submitted in the New Palace competition under Gillespie Graham's name. But the latter was a personal friend, who had taken him in after a shipwreck off the Scottish coast, and probably also a coreligionist.

It is sufficiently evident, I think, that not only the plans but the major compositional decisions must, in the circumstances, have been Barry's, even though there is an unlikely theory of Edward Welby Pugin's that Barry obscured from his own office force the full extent of Pugin's assistance. Looking at the early drawings as reproduced here at small scale, one may even go so far as to say that Pugin's contributions are all but invisible (Figs. II 22-24). In execution the quality of the detailing would, of course, make a great deal of difference, particularly as regards the richer passages; but what gives individual character to the elevations, the distribution of the principal structural elements and ornamented areas, must have been decided by Barry.

So also the idea of setting a tremendous keep-like tower at the southwest corner of the otherwise regular complex of the grid, with nothing to balance it except the smaller and more lacily profiled Clock Tower in a noncorrespondent position at the other end, should also be Barry's. Such an asymmetrical arrangement of vertical accents is certainly suggested in some of Barry's early Italian Villa projects for Attree at Queen's Park, Brighton, if not in the one villa he executed there. The arrangement parallels more closely still the two unmatched towers Barry added to the Duke of Sutherland's symmetrical mansion at Trentham Park, although one of these is certainly later and both may be. The informal placing of the towers did not at all affect the symmetry and regularity of the river front since they were set so far back of the eastern edge of the grid. But the towers enhanced the picturesque asymmetry of the north and south elevations, which had to be irregular in any case unless Westminster Hall were to be completely blocked off at both ends by additional wings (Figs. II 22, 23).

The elevations of the two towers were both very richly detailed in the early drawings. That at the southwest had six storeys of windows which were to be ranged in four bays and framed at the corners by octagonal stair turrets. The treatment at the top was an elaboration of that proposed for the towers at the ends of the central block on the river front, the crowns of the corner turrets being developed into openwork spires. At the base the great arches of the Royal Porch rose to a height equaling that of the top of the first storey in the other sections of the Palace. These arches were to be set in a solid paneled wall and crowned with a gallery of kings' statues in niches. The motif is very like the Perpendicular west fronts of several English cathedrals and seems rather too ecclesiastical for a secular structure. Lines of niches set between the bays of the six storeys would have completed the reticulation of the skyscraper-like shaft of the tower. A similar treatment was later employed for all the exterior walls of the Palace.

The slimmer Clock Tower was originally to have had, below the clock stage, stepped corner buttresses set at right angles like those on the end pavilions of the river front. Above the parapet of the main Palace wall the tower would have had two open stages of tall triple lights, richly traceried at their tops and linked vertically by traceried panels. The clock stage above was to have been much ornamented around the clock faces and crowned by a sort of spire. The tall, concave roof of the tower was to rise in two diminishing stages between corner finials to an open lantern at the top; this would be set diagonally in relation to the square plan of the tower below, a rather fussy idea later given up.

The somewhat churchy elaboration of the two towers seems particularly to reflect the taste of Pugin. Since the much improved treatment of the Clock Tower as actually executed in the late 40's (Figs. I 1, IX 23) was evidently based on Pugin's small clock tower at Scarisbrick Hall (Fig. VIII 3) which he began to remodel in 1837, it seems very likely that Barry again gave his associate, after 1844, a relatively free hand in the final design of this conspicuous feature. On the other hand, it must have been Barry himself who redesigned the lower stage of the larger tower, since this was carried up during the years while Pugin was not working on the Palace drawings at all.

The two-towered corner pavilions of the river front were to have had, on their north and south ends, plain unbuttressed areas of ashlar flanking two storeys of oblong mullioned windows linked by paneling (Figs. II 22, 23). The proposed treatment of the rest of the north and south walls was even plainer; no buttresses rose between the coupled bays, and at the top of the wall there was only a plain battlemented parapet like that on the ends of the Birmingham school (Fig. II 26). Thus these north and south walls represented a considerable simplification of the elaborate vocabulary of the river front, and only the vertical rows of niches between the paired windows echoed the more ecclesiastical elaboration of the two towers.

Even the original design of the shaft of the Victoria Tower, though the over-all paneling may well have been Pugin's contribution, depended intimately upon the number of storeys and the spacing of the windows, both of which matters only Barry, presumably, could have determined. Elsewhere Barry's control must have been even more complete.

Pugin left Barry's employ at the end of 1836, just before preparatory work for the foundations of the Palace began; between then and 1844 he had no part in preparing any of the working drawings. Up to this point it is evident that his contributions to the design, while certainly considerable, could not have been major ones. The fact that all the detail was Perpendicular and even Tudor rather than the 14th-century Decorated associated with Pugin's maturity, however, is not one of the reasons why his responsibility must be considered to have been subordinate in elevations that were essentially Barry's. The use of "15th century" in the subtitle of his book *Contrasts* (prepared in 1835 and issued at this very time) shows that Pugin had not yet come to believe that the Decorated or Middle Pointed was the only acceptable form of Gothic. It was in emulating the ornament of the 15th and even the 16th century, which he later considered "Debased," that Pugin was then proudest to be recognized as a virtuoso as his other publications of 1835–36 clearly display.

The principal reason why Pugin's contributions to the original designs for Westminster New Palace must be considered unimportant—particularly in the absence of visual documentation on the competition project which he was preparing at the same time for Gillespie Graham—is that in 1835–36, as indeed to the end of his life, Pugin would scarcely have been capable of developing an architectural scheme of this size and this degree of complexity. Moreover, he knew his limitations; he was quite well aware that he lacked the conventional architectural training of the Late Georgian period and he was proud rather than ashamed of that lack. He had confined his own studies, moreover, chiefly to the churches, the castles, and the manor houses of the Middle Ages. Pugin would have been the first to admit that the ancient work he knew best offered few suggestions for organizing the elevations of so vast a complex, particularly when the designer of the elevations could have no control over the essentially academic planning. He even once overtly disowned all responsibility for the river front, calling it (rather inaccurately) "All Greek" when he passed by with a friend on the river.

Newly converted to Catholicism, Pugin might have suspected that he would not be commissioned to carry out so important a government building even if he won the first prize. More probably Pugin did not even care to enter, less from modesty than from lack of interest in so secular a program. Pugin, it has been suggested, felt that he could not alone prepare all the multitude of drawings required even then for so enormous a structure, but that suggestion accords ill with his known speed and assiduity as a draftsman. These were, moreover, put at the service of two other architects in this competition. If his friend Gillespie Graham, although probably a Catholic too, cared to gamble on the chance of acceptance and wished to pay Pugin for drawings, Pugin was ready to oblige. Gillespie Graham was much more experienced than Pugin, having been practicing at least since Waterloo; he was therefore probably quite competent to supervise the execution of the Palace had "his" design won. If Barry wished to hire Pugin's assistance, Pugin was equally ready to help him, but in so doing he was consciously avoiding all real architectural responsibility. Only the 19th century, with its tendency to believe that "architecture" was merely (or at least chiefly) ornamental detail—"the embellishment of structure," as Gilbert Scott later put it, and Ruskin at times went further in that direction—could have considered Pugin to have been, to use his son's ridiculous phrase, the "art-architect" of the New Palace.

Because of the essentially Late Georgian character of the 1835 design the New Palace as a whole is less novel than Barry's High Renaissance Reform Club house or his Jacobethan Highclere Castle, both designed in the next year or two. The character of the Gothic detail, whether or not it is all due to Pugin, can certainly add no further proto-Victorian significance to the original decision of the Select Committee to require a "Gothic or Elizabethan" design. But, one may properly ask, how bold or premonitory had that decision actually been? It was bold, I should say, not qualitatively but merely in a sense quantitatively; for the New Palace would be big, conspicuous, and of focal importance as a national symbol. Yet a similar decision could certainly have been made as easily under George IV as under William IV if the taste of the Sovereign were at all involved—and in 1835 it probably was not. Moreover, in the reign not of George IV but of George II, William Kent, that crown prince of neo-Palladianism, had already prepared Gothic designs for the extension of the Old Palace, thus deferring stylistically to the prestige of its medieval antiquity.

On the strength of the resemblances between Barry's project and the work of Sir Jeffrey Wyatville at Windsor Castle one may surely go further: If George IV could have seen the results of the New Palace competition he might well have been delighted by Barry's general handling of the composition. Wyatville's east front at Windsor may even have suggested to Barry the five-part division of his river front by means of towers. The asymmetrical placing of the taller towers, set well behind the eastern range, is also not dissimilar to the location of the old medieval towers, which Wyatville heightened at Windsor, in relation to his rather regular new garden front.

The more ecclesiastical elaboration of the ornament on the New Palace could be matched, still earlier, at the Regent's Carlton House in the delicate scale and the richness of the iron and glass conservatory designed by William Porden (1755–1822). (The use of new materials in the New Palace was for the most part to be inconspicuous rather than thus brashly exuberant however.) Pugin, whom Barry selected as his ornamental expert on the New Palace, had already been employed by Wyatville nine years before, when he was only 14, to design Gothic furniture for Windsor. He was also the son of a man who had been head of the "Gothic Department" (so to put it) in the architectural factory of the King's old friend Nash. That Barry should employ the younger Pugin after his father's death would have seemed only natural to George IV.

William IV was no connoisseur in these matters, whereas George had as Regent been a famous leader of taste. The Sailor King might well have followed here what he thought would have been the lead of his late brother, the First Gentleman of Europe. But what these suppositions really imply is that neither the Select Committee's original stylistic prescription nor the ultimate selection of Barry's design of 1835 need be considered proto-Victorian at all.

The tale just told has therefore dealt with a terminal episode of Late Georgian architecture. Of the executed Palace, whose cornerstone was not even laid until 1840, there will be much more to say in Chapter IX; but the Victorian Age was already well under way before the Palace began to rise above its new embankment. The ultimate appearance of the Palace, outside as well as in, owes a great deal to the contributions Pugin made after 1844 when he returned to assist and even, one may perhaps say without prejudice, to collaborate with Barry. In those eight years between 1836 and 1844, however, Pugin had become the first and the most famous of Victorian church architects. Barry's private work in those years, moreover, had maintained and increased his already very considerable reputation along lines that bore little relation to the particular character of the design of the New Palace. The time has now come, therefore, to turn to Pugin's and to Barry's other work of the late 30's and 40's as well as to the work of those architects who followed their lead.

This chapter, almost as much as the first, has been an introduction; and introductions, like overtures, can announce only a few principal themes of

53

extensive works. Now the house lights may begin to dim before the curtain rises on a curious dramatic episode: the prolific production of a sincerely pious church architecture in an age more and more riddled with doubt and shortly to be self-accused of the most brassy materialism.

By 1837 the great technical strides in building construction made in the late 18th and early 19th centuries already lay in the past. The series of early iron bridges, first arched and then suspended by chains, starting in the later 1770's, and the early development of iron-skeleton construction, begun by William Strutt in a calico mill he built in 1792 at Derby, belong to the Late Georgian architectural story. But when the simple and highly original design of the masonry towers from which the great Georgian engineer Thomas Telford hung his Menai Suspension Bridge of 1819–24 is remembered with admiration, the castellated design of the towers of his other coeval bridge at Conway should not be forgotten. Suggesting a fantastic architectural metaphor, it makes this suspension bridge into a sort of giant *pont-levis* leading to the ruins of the real Edwardian castle behind. If an early 19th-century engineer in designing a suspension bridge could thus pay stylistic tribute to the military architecture of the 14th century, how much more understandable it is that churchmen and church architects, stirred to new piety by the Assize Sermon John Keble preached in 1833 at Oxford on "National Apostasy," should have sought in that same age of the far past appropriate settings for a religious revival. Churches in the Late Georgian period had become pagan temples without and galleried lecture halls within; now Taste would take its orders from Religion and the warm glow of Faith (somewhat dimmed by feeble stained glass) would challenge again the cooler light of Reason, as in the days before the Renaissance and the Reformation.

The Victorian Age in architecture should have opened—or so many writers seem to think—with a vast public structure of national significance such as the New Palace; too often, alas, historians have cut their cloth to fit the coat they wished to make. Others would evidently prefer to enter across Brunel's Clifton Suspension Bridge, begun in 1837 but designed as early as 1831, into Paxton's Conservatory at Chatsworth (Figs. XV 17, 29). Actually it was a religious episode that signalized the opening of the new age more definitely than any other set of events in the realm of building. The first great protagonist in the drama was a fanatical convert to Roman Catholicism in a country whose established religion had long been Protestant. This was possible in part because of the Catholic Emancipation Act of 1829 which permitted the building of new Catholic churches; but that this Catholic should so signally have influenced Anglicans, and eventually even Nonconformists, may at first seem surprising.

54

One of the principal effects of the passage of the Reform Act of 1832 had been to release the forces of political Nonconformism. Partly by reaction a large faction within the Established Church soon wished to be Catholic in a more or less medieval but non-Roman way. The Dissenters' rising threat to the supremacy of the Establishment led to a revival of Anglican church building in which the more consciously Catholic Anglicans naturally took the lead. The Nonconformists, growing richer all the time, were not slow to rival the architectural fervor of Catholics and Anglo-Catholics and even, surprisingly enough, to imitate their edifices.

The general character of the Victorian Age is in many ways the result of the Reform Act of 1832. Yet the most vigorous architectural development at the beginning of the new age owes less to the positive influence of the act than to the curious sequence of reactions that its repercussions in the field of religion were already inducing. Such an apparent paradox, not unfamiliar to historians concerned with the architecture of other epochs, explains why the next three chapters deal with Early Victorian church architecture, Catholic, Anglican, and Nonconformist.

CHAPTER III: PUGIN AS A
CHURCH ARCHITECT

On the whole, the church architecture of the beginning of the Victorian Age is hardly pleasanter to look at than that of the preceding Late Georgian period; to 20th-century taste it has thus far been considerably less acceptable. Yet many reasons, several of which have already been mentioned, give special historical importance to the churches that were built in the late 30's and early 40's. Soon, moreover, Victorian England was more than rivaling medieval England in the extent, if not in the quality, of its church-building program. Despite the ravages of neo-Georgian taste and 20th-century bombing, an immense number of Early Victorian churches still remain intact. The rise in the curve of ecclesiastical construction, which had first turned upward around 1820, was paralleled within two decades by a marked change in architectural style; quite coincidentally that change came in the early years of Victoria's reign.

In the early 20's a Gothic guise for churches, such as had hitherto been little favored by trained architects, became the accepted alternative to a Grecian one. Other alternatives, Norman, "Lombardic," or basilican, were but little exploited until the Georgian rule of taste finally collapsed in the late 30's. The Gothic of the new churches, frequently called "Commissioners' Gothic" in derogation (from the Parliamentary Commission for Building New Churches set up in 1818), is one of the feebler manifestations of the Late Georgian period and generally inferior in visual interest to the Gothick of the 18th century. Yet this early 19th-century Gothic could provide the foundation at least for a significant stylistic development, once new religious convictions gave energizing force to the re-use of ancient ecclesiastical forms in building new churches. The accepted function of a church had long been merely that of a hall holding a preacher and his congregation; now churches were once more to be holy edifices designed for sacramental worship under a dedicated priesthood, as they had supposedly been in the Middle Ages.

When fear of revolution stirred Parliament in 1818 to pass the Church Building Act, under which the Commissioners for Building New Churches operated, the controlling reasons for new church building had been evangelical and precautionary. But the 30's saw the rise of a new fervor within the Anglican Church fired by the tracts of Pusey and Newman which poured forth from Oxford. One effect of the Oxford Movement on church building was to stimulate rich and pious laymen to vie with the state as patrons of ecclesiastical achitecture. But it also provided the background for a new attitude toward medieval archaeology: Ancient monuments came to be admired, studied, and accepted as models for emulation not because they pleased the eye but because of their "ecclesiological" virtues.

"Ecclesiology" was a new word and it defined a new intellectual activity. This activity was partly archaeological, a matter of research and theory concerning medieval practice; but it soon became even more a sort of pseudo-science of "correct" church building, dogmatic and bigoted in the way that only a pseudo-science can be. The usual program of church design was completely changed after 1840 by the activities of "ecclesiologists" banded together into societies and equipped with periodicals to spread their propaganda. The simple solution of providing a large unified auditorium, from all parts of which the congregation could see and hear the preacher, was soon outdated. Ecclesiology prescribed a new method of assembling characteristic elements borrowed from medieval English churches into a complex shell within which various sacramental rites could be "rubrickally" performed.

The rubrics, or regulations for worship of the Anglican Church, were open to various interpretations; but more and more a High Church party found sanction in them for a ritual of considerable elaboration that seemed distinctly un-Protestant to their Evangelical opponents. Thus the new attitude was not consciously aesthetic but rather, in a special if rather metaphorical sense, functional. Even to talk in purely visual terms of proportion and of other objective qualities in church architecture was in certain circles soon castigated as pagan; just as today some "Functionalists" condemn consideration of purely aesthetic values as antisocial.

Ecclesiological functionalism was of course more symbolic than practical. Particularly characteristic was the concern with structural methods and building materials as matters of ethical rather than mechanical or visual import. The satisfaction of the builder's conscience as a Christian and a craftsman soon came to be considered more desirable than the provision of pleasure for the observer's eye. This ethical approach, with its emphasis not merely on what was most "honest" but (by extension) on what looked most "honest," has proved to be the chief continuing value later generations have found in the prolific theoretical writing of the 40's. But in practice the avoidance of architectural "shams" by the Victorians also implied the avoidance of materials and methods not known in the Middle Ages. Hence advanced church architecture was for a long period divorced from contact with significant new structural developments. The interest of Early Victorian church architecture is almost purely stylistic even though it is also (rather paradoxically) more intellectual than visual.

As everyone knows, Newman and others under his influence overshot the original goal of the Oxford Tractarians as reformers of the Anglican Church. Almost against their will they found themselves converted to Romanism. It is perhaps not altogether fanciful to believe that the tremendous energy expended on ecclesiology in the 40's by so many of the Anglican clergy and the more pious and enthusiastic laymen was often sublimation induced by social inhibitions against Roman conversion. The logic of the doctrinal position which the Tractarians came to occupy must seem, to an outside observer, to lead all but inevitably to Rome. However that may be, the focus of the new attitude toward church building certainly lay in the "Higher" areas of the Establishment. And it was powerful enough, before the 40's were over, to affect all sorts of Anglicans and even a large number of Christians outside the Establishment. Yet the adoption of ecclesiological doctrine by English Nonconformists was for the most part quite superficial, barely more than a retarded acceptance of an upper-class fashion. This was true also as regards the various independent Presbyterian sects in Scotland; the Presbyterian Establishment built no churches at all for many years after the Disruption of 1843.

The Roman Catholic hierarchy because of its close continental connections was generally unsympathetic to the Gothic. Yet at the beginning it was a Roman convert who led the way in architecture, supported by a few rich and influential Catholic laymen. These men sought to emphasize the continuity of English Catholic tradition with the period before Henry VIII's defection, now that Catholics had been re-enfranchised by the Whigs. *Lord Shrewsbury, Pugin and the Catholic Revival* [1946], by Denis Gwynn, although modest in length, gives an excellent picture of the interests of the lay leaders of English Catholicism in the 30's and 40's and their differences with the hierarchy.

The remaining glories of ancient Gothic architecture, the old cathedrals and parish churches, belonged legally to the Establishment; but the revived use of English Gothic in the new church edifices Catholics were now free to build, without even the nominal protection of a foreign embassy as hitherto required, might underline a conveniently obscured fact: Gothic architecture had certainly once been Catholic architecture except, of course, for the most decadent Late Perpendicular of the end of the 16th century and the beginning of the 17th.

When Augustus Northmore Welby Pugin became a Roman convert in the mid-30's he had hardly begun to be an architect. Yet he could already be considered, even at the age of 22, a mature archaeologist, for he had been assisting his father Augustus (Auguste) Charles Pugin (1762–1832) from childhood in his ambitious publishing ventures. To list the elder Pugin's multifarious works on medieval architecture is unnecessary; suffice it to say that they long continued, down even into the present century, to be used as crib-books by later architects. The last of his publications, *Examples of Gothic Architecture,* had been left unfinished at his death in 1832, with only the first volume in print. His son at once undertook to complete the work and not only added two more volumes in 1836 to that published in 1831 but also brought out a second edition of the whole in 1838.

The young Pugin was known already, at least to a small circle, as a versatile decorative designer. He had been only 15 when Wyatville employed him to design Gothic furniture for Windsor Castle; four years later, in 1831, his scenery for the ballet *Kenilworth* at Covent Garden had been a resounding success because of the splendor and accuracy of its medieval details. But, when Pugin started a business of his own for supplying carved Gothic ornaments to builders, he rapidly failed for lack of commercial ability. Up to this time he had had no proper architectural experience at all—which is not surprising considering his extreme, if very precocious, youth.

The years 1833 and 1834 Pugin spent traveling about the country making drawings of ancient monuments for use in the *Examples.* Perpetually shocked at the lack of respect with which Anglican incumbents treated their churches, he wrote plaintively to a friend in January 1834 and concluded his letter with a surprising non sequitur: "I can assure you that, after a most close and impartial investigation, I feel perfectly convinced the Roman Catholic Church is the only true one, and the only one in which the grand and sublime style of church architecture can ever be restored. A very good chapel is now building in the North, and when it is complete I certainly think I shall recant." This new Catholic edifice must have been either St. Peter's, Stonyhurst, begun in 1832 at the well-known Jesuit school, or St. Ignatius's, Preston, built 1834–35. In any event it is ironic that the architect of both these churches should have been John Joseph Scoles (1798–1863); for Scoles, a born Catholic with close Jesuit connections, soon seemed to Pugin a quite shameless latitudinarian in the way he handled Gothic forms.

Pugin's upbringing was Protestant. Whatever his father may have been, his mother was a devoted follower of the evangelist Edward Irving, whose interminable sermons may well have predisposed the youthful Augustus against all Protestant services, whether Anglican or Nonconformist. Catholic writers have discussed at some length whether Pugin's conversion was induced by his belief that the Roman Church was "the only true one" or because he judged it "the only one in which the grand sublime style" could be restored. Yet according to the ideology of which Pugin was the forerunner, the restoration of the "true" faith—whether Roman or Anglo-Catholic—and its housing in grand and sublime style were soon to appear almost a single problem. Upon his conversion Pugin's relations grew closer with the rich Catholic magnate John Talbot, 16th Earl of Shrewsbury (1791–1852), and with the scholarly convert Ambrose Lisle March-Phillipps (1809–1878), later known as de Lisle. For Lord Shrewsbury Pugin had already begun to do some decorative work at Alton Towers; now, spurred on by March-Phillipps, the earl became a generous contributor toward several of the churches Pugin built but not, as Trappes-Lomax implies, by any means the only important source of funds then available for such work.

Somewhat irrelevant to the concerns of this chapter are Pugin's volumes of designs for *Gothic Furniture in the Style of the 15th Century* (1835); his *Designs for Iron & Brass Work in the Style of the XV and XVI Centuries* (1836); and his *Designs for Gold and Silversmiths* (1836). More architectural in subject matter but also without relevance to Pugin's churches was his *Details of Antient Timber Houses of the 15th and 16th Centuries* (1836); this is remarkable, however, in that the material offered is entirely French. These publications indicate how little Pugin was inclined at this time to restrict Gothic orthodoxy to the English 14th century and to that phase of medieval architecture Rickman had called Decorated. They show him rather as a precocious virtuoso at medieval ornament of later periods, just as we would expect from the Tudor detail he had been providing for Barry's school in Birmingham (Fig. II 26). The Pugin of these volumes of plates was obviously the perfect collaborator for Barry and for Gillespie Graham in the preparation of their competition projects for the New Palace in 1835; indeed there can rarely have been such an ideal "ghost."

In the last year of William IV's reign Pugin was only 24 and still generally unknown. What reputation he had, outside a limited circle, he owed in considerable part to the confusion of his name with his father's. (Curiously enough a similar confusion has continued ever since, although today it operates in reverse.) But in this year, 1836, Pugin issued in addition to his three volumes of plates an architectural manifesto at his own expense, having in the previous year sought vainly to find a publisher. This book, called *Contrasts*, at once brought him notoriety if not fame; as much as any other single event its publication marked the end of the Georgian Age in architecture.

In *Contrasts, or a Parallel between the Architecture of the Fourteenth and Fifteenth Centuries, and Similar Buildings of the Present Day* (to give the complete title) Pugin attacked the characteristic methods of Late Georgian design with every polemic weapon at his command. The work of the leading architects of the beginning of the century—Nash, Soane, Smirke, Wilkins, and the Inwoods—received the roughest sort of graphic and verbal treatment at his hands. Because of his father's employment by Nash, Pugin must have known the methods of that office best; probably his excoriations are least unjust to that Late Georgian "plan-factory."

Various characteristic modern types of building appeared in the plates of *Contrasts*, etched in all their baldness and barrenness and with no mercy for their designers' superficial use of Grecian or Gothic forms (Figs. III 2, 21–22). Beside each caricature (for they were that) he offered a rich 15th-century monument, elaborated with the laciest detail of which his needle was capable and presented wherever possible with the most tendentious connotations. In the 20th century even Frank Lloyd Wright, inveighing against the "white boxes" of Functionalism or the eclectic parade of "traditional" stylisms, has rarely been so violent; and Osbert Lancaster's architectural cartoons are positively generous in intention compared to Pugin's caricatures of Late Georgian work.

At the same time the violence of the attack often seems doubly to misfire—at least nowadays. On the one hand the polemic, while always intellectually diverting, is hopelessly unhistorical if not consciously unfair; on the other hand 20th-century eyes are quite likely to prefer, because of their cleanness and simplicity, the buildings that are pilloried to most of the medieval alternatives Pugin offered. It must also be stressed that Pugin was still not an architect even *in posse* (except for his own house, Fig. VIII 1); the medieval buildings in his plates were all actual old buildings, however prettified, not alternative new projects of his own. *Contrasts* prepared the way for Pugin's career as an architect but it did not initiate it. He was still almost entirely a critic and a decorator, hardly at all a real builder. In later years, moreover, he felt that practically none of his executed work except St. Augustine's, Ramsgate (Figs. III 34–36) achieved the standards of pseudomedieval design he set from the first as a critic.

Before turning to Pugin's earliest churches it is worth while to examine a Roman Catholic edifice just erected at the outer end of the Lisson Grove in London near Lord's Cricket Ground by the same Scoles whose Lancashire churches played some part in Pugin's conversion. To cultivated Early Victorians this building of 1833–34, generously paid for by the Misses Gallini (granddaughters of the remarkable Georgian dancer and entrepreneur "Sir" John Gallini), was soon to seem quite demonstrably a mere compilation of ecclesiological solecisms.

That Our Lady's, St. John's Wood, was Early English or First Pointed in style (to use the quaint terms that Rickman and others of the preceding generation had established for the Gothic of 1190–1250) would perhaps have been the first thing to strike a later Victorian critic's eye (Fig. III 1). But that was not a serious objection in the mid-30's; even a decade later, when the primacy of the later 14th-century Decorated or Second Pointed had been generally established, the earlier Gothic style-phase continued to be frequently emulated. St. John's Wood had once belonged to the Templars; through one of those complicated exercises in historical connotation that appeal to the antiquarian mind, this historical accident justified to contemporaries the choice of Temple Church in London as a model for the detail—if not so much of Salisbury and Southwark Cathedrals, which Scoles also declared to be his inspiration.

The plan and the construction of the church were (and to some extent still are) really shocking. The external transepts are "shams" in that they incorporate a clergy house and are in no way expressed internally; the vaulting was executed in plaster and the vaulting shafts are of cast iron—to mention but a few of the more egregious ecclesiological faults. It was still bad form at least for a Roman Catholic "chapel" to be built with a tower, even though the law no longer forbade the use of this prime symbol of a "church"; to contemporaries the lack of a tower was therefore justified.

To modern eyes the chief vices of the building are rather different from those the Victorians noted. The silhouette, with its three gables of nearly equal height, lacks unity and builds up to no such climax as a tower might have provided. The thin buttresses are merely nominal, not actual, features of either the construction or the design. This complaint doubtless blends some atavistic ethical objection to shams (in the Victorian sense) with a feeling that what is really a Late Georgian composition in planes is merely corrupted by these projecting buttresses which quite fail to become positive elements in a composition of more three-dimensional character. All the detail, whatever its august prototypes, is clumsy in scale and execution; the materials, moreover, are sensuously horrid both in themselves and in the way they are used. Scoles seems to be apologizing for the yellow stock brick that economy required him to use; he does not glory in its matter-of-fact quality in the way of Telford and the other builders of contemporary warehouses at the docks in the East End. Inside, the plaster vaults do not round out the amorphous spacial volumes of the interior but rather confuse them the more. As a result the interior is neither unified, as in the best Georgian preaching halls, nor yet clearly articulated, as it was soon to be within Pugin's linked naves, aisles, and chancels.

The emancipation of the Catholics in 1829 had led to a great increase in both the number and the size of the churches they undertook to build in the 30's. The most ambitious—still incomplete today—was the vast pseudo-peripteral temple of the Holy Apostles (now the Procathedral) which H. E.

Goodridge of Bath, William Beckford's architect for Lansdowne Tower, began in 1834 at Clifton, above Bristol. More typical in scale, if doubtless exceptionally high in quality for this time, is St. Augustine's, Tunbridge Wells (Fig. III 4). Begun at the opening of the new reign, this was completed in 1838 by the veteran Catholic architect Joseph Ireland, to whom Scoles had gone as an articled pupil in 1812. With advice from the archaeologist John Carter (1748–1817), Ireland had erected two Gothic chapels as early as 1818, just before Scoles left him to begin independent practice; but he seems never to have been an enthusiastic Gothicist and is at best an extremely obscure figure.

The Tunbridge Wells church must have been much closer to what the Catholic clergy in general expected in the 30's than were the Gothic churches by Ireland's pupil in Lancashire and London. As much a mere preaching-box as any Dissenting conventicle, St. Augustine's is nevertheless solidly built of coursed ashlar. It has many modest virtues, but it was already markedly out of date stylistically. Except for the absence of a tower—the existing tower was added some fifty years later—it reminds one of the modest Early Georgian churches of the English countryside and the American Colonies built a century or more earlier. It is in comparison with such Roman Catholic churches as this and Scoles' Our Lady's, St. John's Wood, that Pugin's first actual productions as a church architect, following immediately after the appearance of *Contrasts*, must be measured.

The first edition of *Contrasts* was not a financial success although a few years later the enlarged 1841 edition prospered phenomenally; but few books written by architects in their youth can have caused so much excitement. In a sense the whole architectural profession had been pilloried and several architects and writers issued counterblasts. Pugin had therefore to return to the battle in 1838 with two vigorous pamphlets. English Catholic intellectuals and aesthetes, on the other hand, had now found both a cause and a hero. Led by Shrewsbury and March-Phillipps, they rushed to employ Pugin on ecclesiastical commissions. With a cause so holy and a designer so devout, Pugin's services were often given free and he never became very rich; nevertheless, his professional success before he was thirty has rarely been equaled by young architects of other periods: Within five years after the appearance of *Contrasts* he had built or was building more than twenty-five chapels, churches, and cathedrals, not to speak of the various restorations and the commissions for stained-glass windows and other individual features in churches, old and new, that were soon coming his way—from Anglicans on occasion as well as from Catholics.

The first things—after his own house outside Salisbury (Fig. VIII 1)— that Pugin built were small chapels. Holy Cross Chapel, holding about 200 worshipers, at Whitwick in Leicestershire, was consecrated 12 October 1837 and demolished in 1905; Holy Sepulchre Chapel at High Cademan nearby, already in use in 1837, was hardly more than a wayside shrine. Both chapels were presumably commissioned by March-Phillipps, who lived at Garendon in the vicinity. Late in 1837 (and providing one of the architectural events that give that year special historical significance) Pugin began a more considerable work, St. James's at Reading, using rubble taken from the nearby ruins of Reading Abbey. This church was not carried very rapidly to completion; the foundation stone was laid 14 December 1837 but it was not opened until 5 August 1840, a long campaign considering its modest size.

Perhaps out of pious deference to the style of the ancient Abbey— though Pugin was ready enough to plunder its substance—St. James's was Norman, not Gothic of any epoch. With a simple rectangular nave and a modest apse—the ambulatory, west porch, and other extensions are modern (1925)—the plan of St. James's was quite unremarkable. The later accretions so disguise Pugin's work here that it cannot well be illustrated in its present form; at the church itself it is possible to puzzle out what is original.

Neither in the detail nor in the general composition does the edifice pass beyond the range of contemporary Norman work by other men. Indeed, one of the projects published by G. E. Hamilton in 1836 in his *Designs for Rural Churches* is considerably more elaborate, being provided with aisles, a clerestory, and a square west tower, as well as a projecting chancel (Fig. III 3). This project and the very similar though unchanceled church of St. Clement's, Oxford (Fig. III 5), are both more "correct" exercises in the Norman mode. I do not know who designed St. Clement's or the precise date: P. F. Robinson, at least, had built similar churches in the 20's, and Soane had already offered the Commissioners a Norman design in 1819. This is perhaps of 1835–40 and might be by John Buckler (1770–1851) or more probably by his son J. C. Buckler who won one of the prizes in the New Palace competition.

The interior proportions of Pugin's St. James's are pleasant enough; the simple detail is well scaled; the construction of re-used rubble is quite solid. Though extremely modest and unpretentious, this church provides a more convincing beginning for Pugin's career as an ecclesiastical architect than might have been expected from the controversialist and decorator he had previously been.

What is usually considered Pugin's first church (because it was entirely completed by 1839 and dedicated on 9 October of that year, even though it was not begun until early 1838 some months after St. James's) is St. Marie's— the spelling was a favorite archaism of Pugin's—in Bridgegate, Derby. A large edifice of the local Derbyshire gritstone, the Derby church is definitely

Perpendicular. St. Marie's at Uttoxeter in Staffordshire, begun at just the same time, is Early English. Much enlarged in 1913–14, the Uttoxeter church is barely recognizable as Pugin's work today even though the main features of his design were preserved. This edifice, which is not far from Alton, was entirely paid for by Lord Shrewsbury, the coeval Derby church only in part.

Because of the "late" style of St. Marie's, Derby, and the general slickness of the interior finish (perhaps exaggerated by the latest scheme of redecoration carried out in 1930) this "first" church by Pugin is in many ways merely an improved version of various revived Gothic edifices built in the previous fifteen years or so by Late Georgian architects (Figs. III 6–9). Indeed, St. Luke's, Chelsea, built in London in 1819–25 by James Savage (1779–1854), can be considered more ambitious since it is vaulted in stone throughout; the Derby church has a vault only over the polygonal sanctuary. St. Luke's is a very large edifice, designed for an Anglican congregation of 2,500; and it cost some £40,000, much more than Pugin could expect to spend on a Catholic parish church.

If St. Marie's is compared with an almost exactly contemporary work by the leading Gothic architect of the previous generation, however, Bishop Ryder's Church in Birmingham (Fig. III 15), built by Rickman with the aid of his partner R. C. Hussey in 1837–38, one can see that Pugin already had a distinctly better command of medieval detail. Rickman's St. George's, Birmingham, erected in 1820–23, more than fifteen years earlier, would actually provide a fairer comparison since it is in the same nominal style.

Pugin already knew how to give real distinction to the vertical proportions of his tower and his aisle-flanked nave in a way Rickman rarely approached. This distinction would have been even more notable if the fine spire he projected had been built and the chancel with its flanking chapels had been extended to the east as he planned to do. In a later building campaign, begun after Pugin's death and terminating in 1855, E. W. Pugin (1834–1876) added a northeast chapel in his father's manner and introduced a rather fragile iron chancel screen as well as other embellishments; but the sanctuary itself was never deepened.

Both in his detail and in his proportions Pugin owed a great deal to having made a more intimate and better correlated study of ancient monuments than Rickman; but he also had a greater aptitude for design in the abstract. This aptitude had undoubtedly been sharpened by his study of old work; yet it is also definable in other terms than those of relative "correctness." There is, however, little that is markedly post-Georgian here: no asymmetry, no major elaboration of the masses, nor any increased complexity of the interior volumes. The buttresses are rather thin—as indeed real Perpendicular buttresses often were; the walls themselves are thin; while the moldings, if not wiry, are more metallic than stony—again as real Perpendicular moldings were likely to be. But the shapes of the wall surfaces, both inside and out, seem to have been carefully predetermined; the openings are precisely cut in the walls; and the whole has, without the fussiness, something of the delicacy of Pugin's etchings.

There is, therefore, a recognizably personal stylization of the borrowed Gothic forms at St. Marie's, although no very piquant new qualities appear. It is exactly the things that are *not* present here which were principally to characterize, within a few years, the mature Early Victorian ecclesiastical style, not alone that of Pugin but of "advanced" Anglican architects as well. It might pain Pugin to have it said, but this church still belongs pretty much with the secular Gothic work of Barry for which Pugin had, after all, been providing the details for several years past. The "neatness" (to use a favorite contemporary critical word) and the sense of serious professional study certainly recall Barry.

The Derby church has, of course, little beyond its nominal style in common with Barry's tedious churches of the 20's; but it does resemble his grammar school in Birmingham of 1835 (Fig. II 26) and also the early designs for the New Palace (Figs. II 22–25). It has not, I think, been suggested previously, but is it really unlikely that the young Pugin, in his first considerable work, should show some influence from the only established and experienced architect with whom he had been closely associated?

In the same year that St. Marie's, Derby, was begun, Pugin produced an ambitious project for a London parish church in Southwark, south of the Thames. This vast cruciform scheme was planned with the presumption that the edifice would soon be ranked as a cathedral. The length and height of the clerestoreyed nave, the elaboration of the arcaded front and transept façades, and the great central tower not surprisingly terrified the Catholic authorities (Fig. III 12). They saw no hope then of obtaining money for an edifice on such a scale; and they had no intention, unlike their medieval forebears, of embarking on a building venture that might take several generations to complete.

The interior, as we see it in Pugin's sketch dated 1838, is certainly impressive (Fig. III 14). But it is impressive in the earlier Romantic way, reminding one of Wyatt's immensely tall stairhall at Fonthill Abbey or of the overwhelmingly vertical cathedral projects of Schinkel for Berlin and of Latrobe for Baltimore of a generation earlier, known likewise only from drawings and prints. The height and slimness of the nave arcade seem much more exaggerated than at Derby. The linked clerestorey and triforium repeat at smaller scale the dominating verticals of the vaulting shafts. Above them the polygonal ceiled roof encloses the volumes of nave and choir more cleanly than do the rather flimsy open trusses of the Derby roof. Surely Sir Kenneth Clark chose an unfortunate ground for complaint when he wrote that Pugin had no feeling for volume. St. Marie's, Derby, and this project rather indicate that he was too concerned with the expression of spacial volume at the expense of providing an adequate sense of support in his freestanding piers and surrounding walls.

Pugin always inveighed against the use of cast iron in church building either structurally or ornamentally. It is ironic, therefore, that he should so often—and perhaps at his most characteristic, if not at his best—have turned out projects and even executed buildings that look as if they ought to be poured in metal rather than erected with stone and wood. That sort of architectural expression was inherent in his nature and in that of most of his contemporaries; but he and they fought against it from this point on with only too great success. It is not in church architecture that one finds effective Early Victorian use of metal. When iron columns returned to ecclesiological respectability in the late 50's and 60's, they were to be used in a very different way under what was called "Early" French influence (i.e., that of the 12th-century Gothic of the Ile-de-France).

The Southwark authorities turned down Pugin's project of 1838 the next year and did not commission him to build what proved to be a considerably less ambitious edifice until a year later (Figs. III 11, 13). His first church of cathedral scale was therefore St. Chad's in Bath Street, Birmingham, of which the foundation stone was laid on 29 October 1839. This was opened less than two years later on 21 June 1841. St. Chad's was built with the intention of providing a local cathedral for the Catholics, but it did not receive the designation until the Roman sees were established, with so much political uproar, a decade later.

By 1834 the Birmingham Catholics, having already determined to have a Gothic design, obtained drawings from Rickman, who had settled there after his Liverpool beginnings. Rickman, although a Quaker, was quite as willing to oblige the Catholics as he was the Anglicans for whom he generally worked; but this scheme of 1834 soon fell through for lack of adequate funds. When it was revived several years later Pugin was first called in merely to advise on the design. With no regard for professional ethics, he soon took over the commission—need one behave ethically toward a Quaker who had the presumption to design a Catholic church?

The result is very curious: For one thing, although St. Chad's is neither First nor Third but Second Pointed, i.e., Decorated, it is (surprisingly enough) scarcely English at all, but rather Germanic, in character. The two west towers, so rare in medieval England, with their spindly spires; the local Warwickshire red brick (little used for churches in England before the Perpendicular period but ubiquitous in 14th-century Germany); and especially the continuous roof slope covering both nave and aisles: All these things are very poor English Gothic archaeology (Fig. III 16). The three narrow windows of the apse—itself even shorter proportionately than that at Derby—look almost Italian in their meager tracery. Although five rather similar apse windows were used in the Southwark project, they appear less un-English. Hardly before the late 50's was so "continental" a Gothic church to be built in England again even for Catholics.

Thus this church is strangely out of the main stream of Early Victorian development. Yet, because St. Chad's is well built and in good physical condition (despite the thinness of its walls and the skimpiness of its roof timbers), and also because its decorations have been refreshed in modern times with taste and tact, the Birmingham Cathedral may well be, for many observers as for the critic John Summerson, the most impressive of all Pugin's works. Externally the grouped volumes of apse, Lady chapel, and sacristies at the rear rise against the tall transept with an effectiveness only partly due to the way the hill slope falls away behind. This composition in terms of associated volumes is no accident; the finely textured surfaces of common red brick and the delicate stone edging of the great windows were consciously selected to produce the visual result. It represents a most skillful exploitation of particular economic and topographic circumstances for which Pugin should receive full architectural credit.

Not much good can be said of the west front of St. Chad's. The openings are awkwardly related in size and shape; the towers above are not integrated with—nor are they clearly articulated from—the tall gable of the nave (Fig. III 18). The figure sculpture, despite all the attention Pugin gave to it, might as well be the most conventional plaster saints such as were then produced in series in the Place St. Sulpice in Paris. Above all, the balance of stone and brick is awkward: Too much stone detail breaks up the fine, if grimy, brick surfaces; yet there is not enough to produce any effect of plastic or bichromatic richness and variety.

The interior of St. Chad's, for all its continental character, is a triumph of personal expression, less coherent doubtless than St. Marie's, Derby, less "sublime" than that proposed in the Southwark project, but considerably more original (Fig. III 17). The nave and aisles constitute a single volume barely subdivided by the tall slim lines of the clustered shafts that help carry the roof. The slightness of these structural members actually becomes a major virtue, for they appear merely as a transparent screen rather than as ranges of major supports.

The same cannot be said for the trusses of the roof. The queenpost construction is gauche and irrelevant in design; the matchstick slightness of the scantlings seems quite inadequate to span so wide a nave. There is, furthermore, considerable confusion in the organization of the associated spaces at the east end in contrast to the effectiveness of the exterior. The precise relationship of the transept to the nave, for example, cannot readily be apprehended in the interior. A heavy choir screen, moreover, projects awkwardly into the crossing in order to increase the area of the exigous sanctuary. This rather masks the terminal volume of the apse in a way the rood arches of Derby and Southwark do not; it also breaks the continuous cross volume of the transept.

Pugin, here, had bitten off more than he could chew, not merely financially (which doubtless partly explains the pinchpenny trusses) but also conceptually. A church of cathedral pretensions required in his estimation both transepts and west towers; but he was as yet little more capable than his contemporaries of coping with the resultant elaboration of internal volume and external mass. The intended central tower would have helped to compose the exterior but it could hardly have improved the interior. Although Pugin was destined to build several more cathedrals and at least one abbey of cathedral proportions, he was not properly a cathedral builder; nor, for that matter, was the Early Victorian period a cathedral-building epoch. Pugin was himself most successful with edifices of parish church scale; and parish churches were to be the characteristic ecclesiastical products of the whole Victorian Age.

In addition to the Birmingham cathedral-to-be and the first Roman Catholic abbey built in England since the Reformation (about which the less said architecturally the better), Pugin began at least five parish churches in 1839. The abbey project was sponsored by March-Phillipps; it is in Leicestershire near, or possibly on, his estates. The advocation is to St. Bernard, the name is Grâce Dieu, but the address is—Coalville! Lord Shrewsbury gave £3,000 toward its construction—a mere drop in the bucket for so enormous a building scheme—and coal revenues never provided enough to carry out the work except in the simplest and crudest way (Fig. III 10).

Of the five new parish churches, that of St. Michael Archangel, at Gorey (Co. Wexford) in Ireland, has some interest. It is Norman in style—his last church that was not Gothic—and provided with the central tower which Pugin usually reserved for his cathedrals and abbeys. Because of the complexity of the plan, with aisles, transept, and rounded apse as well as a great tower (possibly never completed), the Gorey project was one of his most ambitious (Fig. III 10).

But St. Michael's, Gorey, lacks the significance of St. Wilfrid's, Hulme, near Manchester, built in 1839–42. This is a small church, accommodating 800, which cost only some £5,000 even with the attached priests' house included. St. Wilfrid's was intended to demonstrate that a "correct" Gothic church need not be expensive. To save money Pugin avoided the Perpendicular and used 13th-century Early English as at St. Mary's, Uttoxeter. But he was using 14th-century English Decorated, probably for the first time, for the tiny chapel of St. Ann at Keighley in Yorkshire, opened 21 November 1840, and St. Ann's must have been building at precisely the same time as St. Wilfrid's. Pugin was evidently only just coming to believe in 1839 that the Decorated was the most suitable style for emulation; it would be several years before he abjured completely the earlier and later phases of medieval style.

St. Wilfrid's tower is quite modest and capped with a plain pyramidal spire above a solid parapet (Fig. III 19). This tower is placed not in the center of the front but at the northwest corner. The plan is very nearly an unbroken rectangle except for the slight projection of the sacristy to the southeast and the modest south porch. This last feature was henceforth to become almost an essential of English 19th-century church design, having always provided in the Middle Ages a most characteristic insular note.

The perspective view which Pugin chose for the wood engraving in the *Dublin Review*, No. 20 (1841), where examples of executed work by Pugin were first illustrated, and which he used again in his book called *The Present State of Ecclesiastical Architecture in England* in 1843 is taken from the northeast in order to show the complexity of the articulated masses (Fig. III 19). Only where the Lady chapel on the northeast is incorporated under a continuation of the aisle roof does any section of the plan fail to receive autonomous expression in the external massing. The buttresses, doubtless because of the red Lancashire brick of which the church is built, are slight of projection though broad and sturdy in proportion. Yet St. Wilfrid's is in general less "advanced" stylistically than a project that was shortly to appear in the second edition of *Contrasts*.

To the original text and plates of *Contrasts* Pugin added in the new edition of 1841 a 28-page article in French by the French Catholic leader Montalembert as well as controversial notes of his own. But more interesting in the present context is the additional illustrative material: four etched plates, a plate filled with small wood engravings, and other new wood engravings on the text pages. (The plate showing Soane's house contrasted with an Early French Renaissance half-timber front was rather significantly dropped—it had been Pugin's only example of even vaguely Italianate design.)

The most important new material is in the etched plates, particularly one illustrating a radially planned modern workhouse together with an "Antient Poor House" as "Contrasted Residences of the Poor," and another showing a

"Catholic Town in 1440" in opposition to "The Same Town in 1840." The churches in these compositions, although merely sketched in perspective at very small scale, indicate the sort of edifice that Pugin craved to erect rather better than anything he was actually building at this time.

Attached to the "Antient Poor House" is a largish cruciform church with square crossing tower, aisles, clerestorey, and traceried west window (Fig. III 21). It looks very solid compared with most of Pugin's executed work of 1840–41, but it also looks very big and expensive. Lately Gothic had come to be considered more satisfactory than Grecian for churches partly because it was cheaper, no tall porticoes of stone being needed. The Catholics who were Pugin's clients had little money for church building, as the emphasis on the cheapness of St. Wilfrid's indicates: The hierarchy might well, as at Southwark, fear that Pugin's ideas were too ambitious if this was what he considered proper in the way of a mere poorhouse chapel!

When Pugin contrasted his English towns of 1440 and 1840 he showed, in the modern view, a river lined with what appear to 20th-century eyes as very dignified and functional warehouses, but disfigured on all sides by kilns, gas holders, and innumerable smoke-belching factory chimneys and with the medieval churches standing ruined or desecrated (Fig. III 22). On the other hand, in the view of the "Catholic Town in 1440" 14 complete churches and chapels are shown. Of these, two appear completely enough to suggest they are quite as much actual "projects" by Pugin as reflections of ancient monuments. In the left distance is a great cruciform abbey with a square central tower and a tall slender spire; this is even more ambitious in scale and richness than the church attached to the "Antient Poor House." In the right foreground is a more modest parochial church. This is aisleless, but it has two bays in the chancel to three in the nave and carries a tower on the right side of the west front. This sketch, which calls for close comparison with St. Wilfrid's, Hulme (Fig. III 19), is the prototype of a very large proportion of the most characteristic Victorian churches.

A sharp break in the mass is produced by the differentiation in height between the nave and the chancel. This break and the asymmetrical position of the tower are not entirely unknown in Late Georgian churches but they are both distinctly rare. The strong emphasis on the projecting chancel and the corner tower introduces a new approach to external composition that is most significant. In perspective the considerable horizontal extension of the chancel balances the equally considerable but vertical mass of the tower; therefore the church must be seen from an angle, not elevationally, to be properly appreciated as a composition in the round. The side walls themselves have a plastic effect because of the heavy stepped buttresses that flank them. The prominence of the high roof with its broken skyline is further accented by the little belfry set over the east gable of the nave. Far more than the Manchester church, this "project" adumbrates a new visual ideal of asymmetrically articulated massing. The new ideal had been explored playfully for a generation in villas and other modestly ornamental structures, but it had hardly been proposed hitherto as suitable for monumental or public edifices even though there is a hint of it in the unmatched towers of the New Palace.

Pugin and the Anglican ecclesiologists who soon echoed his principles verbally abjured the Picturesque; they emphasized rather the symbolical functionalism of such complex church compositions and contrasted their "natural" irregularity with the "mock" regularity of contemporary monumental design in Classical modes. Thus the little belfry on the east gable here was intended to hold the Sanctus bell whose ringing marked the presence of the Host on the altar, not just to provide a piquant visual accent. The tower was at the corner because otherwise, on an aisleless church, it would hide the nave from the front; the deep chancel was required for a revived medieval ritual; and so on. The purely aesthetic arguments for irregularity, long put forth by the critical champions of the Picturesque, were scorned as hedonistic; but the Picturesque lesson had nonetheless been thoroughly learned. As often before in architectural history, a non-aesthetic theory apparently had to be developed in order to defend—and even finally to crystallize—a change in visual taste.

Which, one may ask, is the truer Pugin—the still somewhat Late Georgian master of volumes, by whom many more excellent edifices were to be built, or this experimenter with articulated massing who was the inventor of the "realistic" or functional version of the Picturesque? I do not know, but there is no question which was to be the more influential. St. Wilfrid's, Hulme, together with the church in the foreground of the 1440 town, rather than any of his earlier parish churches, provided one of the few basic models for the Early Victorian church. From this time on almost all Pugin's churches were generically Decorated, moreover, and virtually devoid of non-English elements. St. Alban's, Macclesfield, his last Perpendicular church, was built in 1839–40; but several of his important and influential churches of the early 40's were Early English. None of the later churches has anything of the continental look of St. Chad's.

In 1840 Early Victorian Gothic became an article of cultural export when Pugin began the chapel and the refectory of the Collège de Saint-Edmond at Douai in France, an edifice that has not been used since 1903 and may no longer exist. In America, moreover, Richard Upjohn (1802–1878) was already persuading the vestry of Trinity Church in New York to allow him to rebuild their 18th-century Gothick meetinghouse in conformity with new standards, although those standards were only what Pugin had introduced at St. Marie's, Derby. Hence Trinity, like the Westminster New Palace, was to be out of date in the eyes of its architect (who was soon a leading American ecclesiologist) even before it was completed in 1846.

This was because of the instant success on both sides of the Atlantic of the new models provided by St. Wilfrid's, Hulme, and by two other churches begun by Pugin in 1840. One of these was St. Oswald's, Old Swan, Liverpool, opened 7 August 1842; the other was St. George's, Lambeth Road, later the Southwark Cathedral, which was carried out in the 40's on a much less ambitious scale than Pugin's earlier Southwark project of 1838.

The foundations for St. George's were begun 8 September 1840, the cornerstone was laid 28 May 1841, and the church was opened 4 July 1848. *The Builder*, 3, 13–14, gives a description of the construction through 1843, and G. and C. White published an official *Description of St. George's Cathedral* in 1851. The official organ of Anglican ecclesiology, *The Ecclesiologist*, 9, 151–161, upon the opening of the church, discussed it at length, calling it "of not small importance in the ecclesiological movement," and mentioned the confessionals which had been added between the buttresses (not given in the plan of 1841 in Fig. III 13). The west front was shown by Pugin at the Royal Academy Exhibition of 1840. Houses for the clergy and for Sisters of Mercy adjoined the church and were built by Pugin at the same time. Only ruins remain since the blitz.

Of these two new church models, that provided at St. Oswald's is much the more important however: Here for the first time the "ideal" 14th-century English parish church, as Pugin understood it, was recreated. The very deep chancel, the low side aisles, the south porch, and the centrally placed western tower are all characteristic (Fig. III 20). This sort of tower with broached stone spire, more or less elaborately gabled and pinnacled, became the accepted 19th-century symbol of a real church—"non est hic aliud," its form seems to proclaim, "nisi domus dei"—and at its base opened the accepted "porta coeli" of the Victorians. The tracery on the ideal church is richly Geometrical or (preferably) Curvilinear Decorated. The body of the church inside and out is usually low and pyramidal in massing. It is heavily buttressed externally and even more heavily trussed within. The interior is rather dark on account of the labyrinth of dark-stained wooden beams overhead and because clerestorey windows are either lacking altogether or very small and widely spaced.

The accessories are many and elaborate: a baptismal font (at the west end), a stone pulpit and a brass lectern at the chancel entrance, and preferably a screen of wood or metal to isolate still further the deep inner cavern of the sanctuary; in that the altar is laden with Pugin-designed brummagem

73

brasswork—actually made in Birmingham by his fellow Catholic John Hardman. In the nave stained wooden benches replace the comfortable pews demanded by Georgian congregations; while, for the clergy, elaborate stone
sedilia provide equally comfortless niched seats at the side of the chancel.
If the bishop did not object, even Anglican churches have a piscina, or sacramental drain, in the side wall of the chancel, but that was a peculiarly Romish
abomination in the eyes of sound Protestants.

Much literary talent has been expended, worthy of a better cause, in
describing such interiors whose very odors inspire the poetic muse of John
Betjeman. What is architecturally important is that here in this tiny suburban
Roman Catholic church of St. Oswald's, Old Swan, costing only £5,000,
Pugin first established a new model, almost a new building type, quite discontinuous with Georgian church architecture. The obscurity of the interiors
of such churches was increased over the generations by the darkening of
the walls and even more by the filling up of all the windows with memorial
stained glass. But the desire for this warm gloom and the acceptance of this
ascetic lack of physical comfort, accompanied by a profusion of elaborate
accessories only occasionally used, have survived among churchmen of most
faiths well into our own day. The sort of architectural hair shirt the model
provided evidently solaced the Victorians' sense of sin by offering all the
physical discomforts Georgians had so successfully avoided in their churches.
Such interiors also offer a sense of escape from the wicked modern world,
something that has continued to appeal to successive generations of the
devout of all churches. It is still a legitimate aim for church architects today,
although Gothic forms are surely not necessary to provide it.

St. Oswald's is better than many of its progeny, for it is handsomely executed in reddish Cheshire sandstone laid in rather large ashlar blocks. Because of the need for economy, carved ornament was kept to a minimum. The
roof timbering is neither so low nor so clumsy as it was often to be in the late
40's; the interior is therefore neither excessively dark nor heavy despite the
lack of a clerestorey. No excessive accumulation of paraphernalia clutters
the interior—even Pugin's screen, once standing at the chancel entrance,
has now been moved to the west end.

As regards the external composition, Pugin achieved in the massing of St.
Oswald's a maximum of variety despite the frontal position of the western
tower and the nearly continuous slope of the nave and aisle roofs (Fig.
III 20). A corner stair turret unbalances the symmetry of the tower and a
boldly projecting south porch, unmatched on the north, provides the chief
entrance. The aisle roofs, moreover, do not (as at St. Chad's, Birmingham)
precisely continue the pitch of the roof of the nave; while the main roof line
breaks sharply at the chancel as at St. Wilfrid's, Hulme. The chancel is flanked

by accessory masses which do not balance—here only a small sacristy on the south as the church was originally designed; usually there are one or more side chapels at the rear. But the convention of complex articulation and unbalance of mass has not yet become a bore as it would so soon. The essence of Pugin's mature capacities as a designer is already concentrated in this modest edifice.

The site at Old Swan was originally village-like although it lay on the fringes of a great city, and the district remains fairly open even today. Pugin was perfectly capable of distinguishing between such a more or less rural site, in which a complex composition could be assimilated into the natural landscape, and the restricted urban sites for which most of his larger churches had to be designed. Urban surroundings clearly demanded taller and less ramified compositions—not to speak of clerestoreys—if the interior were to have any light at all, and these he regularly provided. The Camdenians who accepted and promoted the new models were not, at least for another decade, much aware of this important distinction between the requirements of open and of shut-in sites.

The Anglican leaders of the ecclesiological reform were generally country born—some in vicarages, some in country houses—if not, they wished they had been. A rather snobbish nostalgia for a medieval world in which the "pure" countryside and its life were more important than the wicked towns —and also, undoubtedly, certain aesthetic prejudices deriving from Picturesque landscape painting—made village church types, paradoxically enough, the established convention of an increasingly urban age. As late as 1848 the *Ecclesiologist, 9, 163,* for example, referred to St. Oswald's very favorably as a "good reproduction of a country church." Very shortly advanced ecclesiologists were to change their tune and criticize sharply, if for some years ineffectively, the building of low sprawling churches in built-up areas.

Early Victorian churches, in fact, generally stand in what are now suburban areas. It should be noted in justice that when they were built, as was the case at Old Swan, massive estate development had in most cases hardly yet begun around them. Patrons and architects may often have had reason to hope that later building in the vicinity would follow a rather open, village-like pattern, the recurrent ideal of the 19th century which J. M. Richards has hymned again in *The Castles on the Ground* [1946]. It rarely worked out that way, however, around the larger towns before the 70's by which time most Early Victorian churches had been engulfed by solid terrace building.

Pugin's third basic church model, that best represented by St. George's, Southwark, as built, is better suited to really urban sites. There aisles as tall as the nave admit considerable light, while the higher walls and the less broken silhouette fit better into a built-up street. On the other hand, the frequent use (as here) of three gables of nearly equal height, like those on Scoles' Our Lady's, St. John's Wood, the resultant lack of any sort of pyramidal composition, and the frequent omission of a crowning tower—St. George's west tower was taken over from the earlier project with little change but never carried up very far—generally produce an exterior composition that is distinctly dull. Indeed such churches are often duller than the preceding Late Georgian ones whose "insipidity" Early Victorians so loudly protested.

As has been said, St. George's was badly blitzed in World War II (Fig. III 11); but it had barely survived Ruskin's far more damaging critical blitz in Volume 1 of *The Stones of Venice* (1851). There is no need to discuss here Ruskin's harsh dictum that Pugin was "one of the least possible or conceivable architects" in relation to this particular church on whose deficiencies the judgment was admittedly based; not even Ruskin can have considered St. George's typical of Pugin at his best. The High Victorians, even when most influenced by Ruskin, wrestled valiantly with the problem of designing urban churches of brick; but they found it almost as difficult as did Scoles or Pugin to handle the London stock brick, which Pugin was forced by economy to use here, in a visually satisfying way. Pugin said his *mea culpa* often enough concerning St. George's. Though one need not accept the sincerity of all the protestations he made about his executed work, the existence of the 1838 project (however impossible it might have been both practically and artistically to bring it to fruition) indicates Pugin's real ambitions for the Southwark Cathedral. St. George's compares well, moreover, with the architectural projects with which Ruskin was himself most directly concerned; it is at least architecture, not mere exterior decoration.

In 1840 Pugin received from his fellow Catholics the academic recognition that architectural rebels always seem to crave. He was appointed Professor of Ecclesiastical Antiquities at St. Marie's College, Oscott, the designation of the chair implying a retrospective rather than a prospective view of church building. Now he martialed his doctrine, as adumbrated in two lectures given earlier at the college, in a book on *The True Principles of Pointed or Christian Architecture* which came out in 1841. This time his new book was sponsored by John Weale, the leading London architectural publisher. Pugin's didactic and proselyting talents were very considerable; the many historical and theological digressions in these published lectures are always lively if frequently almost unintelligible today. He also included plenty of those witty verbal and graphic attacks on ordinary contemporary work which had made *Contrasts* so effective as propaganda—a new edition of that book, indeed, was required this very year. But the time had come when

Pugin really expected others to begin to build in his way; therefore he set out in his new work to clarify his doctrine and present it in a systematic way.

The publisher's announcement promised six "true principles" which may be succinctly paraphrased here: (1) All ornaments of "pure pointed" edifices were merely "decorations to the essential construction." (2) The construction of old "pointed" architecture was always varied to accord with the properties of the different materials employed, i.e., stone, timber, or metal. (3) No features were introduced which were not essential either to convenience or to propriety (propriety as used by Pugin covered a multitude of sins or, more accurately, a multitude of holy practices). (4) A variant of 1: Pointed architecture "decorates" the useful portions of buildings instead of concealing or disguising them. (5) The "true principles" of architectural proportion are found only in "pointed" edifices (such is Pugin's claim to exclusive beauty, the claim made by every logical revivalist of any style of the past whatsoever, Roman, Grecian, Gothic—or, for that matter, Renaissance and even Georgian). (6) The defects of modern, i.e., post-medieval, architecture lie principally in departures from ancient principles (which amounts to saying departure from Pugin's own "true principles").

Much of 20th-century Functionalism, not to speak of intervening architectural doctrine, is to be found in principles 2, 3 and 4 once they are divorced from principle 6; in them, therefore, lies the core of Pugin's long-term significance as a theorist. But at the opening of the 40's his doctrines seemed more restricted in meaning, as Pugin certainly intended that they should. The only "proper" ornaments were those used on ancient buildings. All materials, and particularly metal, should be used only as they were in the Middle Ages, thus effectively inhibiting major structural developments in the architectural use of iron. The useful portions of buildings must not merely be unconcealed and undisguised, they must be decorated and indeed preferably Decorated. Only an interpretation of medieval conventions can decide what is useful or proper. Departure from ancient principles will produce nothing but defects—as by implication it had then done for almost three hundred years.

To the architect or client desirous of conforming to these principles the most useful things in the book were the illustrations showing good and bad practice. By means of these Pugin could explain in detail the practical purpose of various Gothic features such as drip molds and buttresses that had hitherto been imitated for their picturesque effect (Fig. III 25). Pugin was undoubtedly a good teacher. Just what the budding priests of Oscott made of his instruction one cannot know; but the serious young Anglican ecclesiologists, the amateur students of medieval architecture banded together in societies at Cambridge and Oxford, and many an aspiring young architect learned Pugin's lessons from *True Principles* only too well. Repentance for ignorance and, among architects, for sins already committed (chiefly with plaster, henceforth forbidden for vaults and moldings, and soon even for interior walls) was now the order of the day.

In line with principle 6 little 19th-century work, executed or unexecuted, was illustrated except for satirical purposes. But one half-plate showed a very magnificent project for a 14th-century parish church with a high clerestorey and a tall spire heavily buttressed and airily pinnacled. The very large and deep chancel was flanked on the northeast by a Lady chapel of almost equal size and elaboration. The Decorated detail throughout was very rich and very "late"; indeed the chancel windows had tracery that was definitely Perpendicular (Fig. III 24). The silhouette was less characteristic than that of St. Oswald's; but it was enriched by two asymetrically placed stair turrets at the east end of the nave, as well as by the large chapel, and it was accented by a small Sanctus belfry placed over the east gable of the nave. As an adjunct to an "Old English Mansion," a smaller rural church was also shown; but this was only a variant of the small church in the view of the 1440 town included in the second edition of *Contrasts* (Fig. III 22).

The two years 1841 and 1842 represent the apogee of Pugin's career. Once the Oscott lectures had appeared in book form his new Gothic gospel could no longer be considered unrevealed. As a result of the concurrent activities of the Camden Society rejection of the new architectural gospel had become, in a certain Anglican milieu, suspiciously close to rejection of the tenets of the Anglo-Catholic faith (see Chapter IV). Most architects wishing to work for the Tractarians, who were now sponsoring a campaign of church restoration as well as of church building and church decoration, hastened to "correct" their use of Gothic forms and to avoid all ecclesiological solecisms. Even though the older professional spokesmen who wrote for the press still generally rejected—and with some vehemence—the authority of Pugin and those Anglicans who echoed his gospel, few of the younger architects refused to give at least lip service to the new ideals. As in the case of later conservatives who have tried to fight off stylistic changes in architecture, one may justly suspect that the older men wished to protect a vested interest—the accumulated professional capital of their Classical training and their Georgian experience.

The effect of this successful revolution, initiated so short a time before, did not reach its peak for another decade. By that time the original doctrine had already begun to be modified almost beyond recognition by an architect more talented and more original, if also less articulate, than Pugin. But discussion of the "New Law," so to say, of William Butterfield belongs in a much later chapter (XVII). The tale of Pugin's own career must now be completed by describing in some detail what are probably his best works, those begun in 1841 and 1842. After those years his public success tapered off gradually in the decade that preceded his madness and death. The significant work of the Anglicans who took up his doctrines so avidly was just beginning when his own best days were coming to an end (see Chapters IV and V).

Paradoxically, the seeds of Pugin's declining reputation were probably already sown as a concomitant to the very events that signalized his triumph. When his works began to be better known, Pugin's failure in practice to maintain his own exalted standards became as evident to others as it had always been to himself. His many honest statements concerning the inadequacy of his executed buildings could readily be turned against him. Thus his early work was damned by quotations from his own books as soon as maturing post-Georgian tastes made manifest its weaknesses; and the first to criticize were naturally those he had best trained to judge architecture in the new way.

That Pugin chose to illustrate his article on "The Present State of Ecclesiastical Architecture in England" in the *Dublin Review*, No. 20 (May 1841), with very modest wood engravings of his own work, both completed and still in production, was unfortunate for his later reputation. Hitherto connoisseurs had really known little about Pugin's buildings. Many who were primarily literary or religious minded had doubtless presumed their excellence from reading his tracts—an architect with such pious principles could not but produce buildings of distinction. Pugin's frank humility about his work seemed to indicate a truly Christian character; for the pious it perhaps counterbalanced that un-Christian lack of charity toward others so evident in his attitude toward erring contemporaries. Those who were more impressed by ocular evidence judged Pugin's work by the delicate etchings in his early books or, if they chanced to see them, by his even more exquisite drawings.

The delicacy and freshness of Pugin's sketches can still appeal. If they fail today to evoke medieval work as they once did, we must remember that Pugin's own generation still knew Gothic buildings mostly through Late Georgian illustrations of which the elegant engraved plates in his father's books were among the most plausible. Even when students examined ancient edifices for themselves, they undoubtedly saw chiefly what their study of existing visual documents led them to expect; just as we often make judgments from photographs today long before we actually see famous medieval or later buildings.

Only a few ecclesiologists or specialist-architects would by 1841 have studied Pugin's own buildings in construction or when completed; for they were located (as the first manifestations of an architectural revolution tend to be) in what contemporaries considered unlikely, even unget-at-able, places. Victorians did not as yet expect much in the way of art from Derby or Birmingham or Manchester. There is, moreover, about a building of a new type when it is seen in construction or newly completed something very disarming: If it still lacks, for want of funds, the full decorative treatment which the architect has planned, one can easily make generous allowances. Pugin's own early response to Scoles' Lancashire churches well illustrates this reaction; and everyone who visited the early works of the leading modern architects when they were new twenty years or so ago will recall over-enthusiastic judgments which had later to be drastically revised.

Particularly with regard to the work of men whose own writings provide a new critical canon, a Pugin or a Frank Lloyd Wright or a LeCorbusier, optimism colors the response of the youthful student (if not always that of his cynical elders). The young feel that the persuasive revelation of the written text is quite certain to be confirmed as the executed work proceeds toward its completion; everything that is evidently missing can be explained by the cruel exigencies of the particular situation. Lack of real sympathy on the part of the client is readily assumed and deficient training of the workmen is taken for granted. Above all, lack of funds—so much more is always needed above the estimates to realize the architect's intent—is usually no mere assumption but cold fact.

The little wood engravings in the *Dublin Review* article of 1841 reappeared when *The Present State* was published in book form in 1843. Though doubtless made from Pugin's drawings, they are bald and cold (Fig. III 19); the mysterious haze of rich detail in the etchings (Fig. III 24) gives way to a few coarse lines that merely sketch the forms. In most of the interiors shown, if not always perhaps in the exteriors, the earlier magic seems almost wholly absent; the buildings look for the most part as dead and dull as they too often are in reality. If Pugin had refused to allow his own work to be illustrated at all, his position would have been more consistent; for he considered it better that students, whether ecclesiologists or architects, should not waste the time they might spend studying ancient work by examining any new buildings, even his own. Moreover, the models which he was providing were certainly not, in his estimation, yet worthy of imitation—not even the relatively well-executed churches on which he was now at work in the early 40's.

The initial stage of mere study of the past according to new and more "Catholick" ideas and of violent partisan protest against the defects of conventional contemporary practice was now nearly over. Churchmen and architects alike were anxious to try producing actual edifices in a new and presumably better way. Bullying the incumbents of ancient churches into "restoring" their medieval treasures was no longer enough to assuage the ecclesiologists' passion for "correct" church architecture. The architects were gladly accepting—as they would throughout the Victorian era—commissions for restoration; they even extended these commissions on many occasions— usually with full ecclesiological sanction—into what amounted to a complete rebuilding of ancient fabrics. In the process they learned a lot "the hard way"—hard on the churches, at least, if not on the architects. But no books could have given the knowledge the restorers were rediscovering through this plastic surgery carried out on the living architectural flesh of the medieval past. In the process, alas, the integrity of almost every Gothic building in England was destroyed. Nevertheless, architects naturally found still more of a challenge in calls to design and build completely new structures and, if they were to build such new structures, what more convenient models could there be than those the modern Gothic masterbuilder Pugin was setting before them in these wood engravings of his own work?

"Do as I say and not as I do," teachers always cry even though pupils rarely listen. Pugin's architect disciples certainly looked long, as he instructed, at ancient models; but when they were called on to prepare a design for a particular church on a particular site they generally fell back on imitating what he had already built in the previous five years. Church architects, like so many lawyers, were ready to quote every "antient" precedent they could think of for the various elements introduced in their new work. Yet all but the few who denied entirely the new Gothic light usually followed one or another of the church models that had first been clearly, if unappetizingly, presented in the plans, elevations, and perspectives of Pugin's *Dublin Review* article. At the same time, moreover, young architects began to feel that their own imitative results were not unworthy of comparison, if not with Pugin's medieval originals, at least with these crudely presented structures.

Thus, as so often happens in the careers of revolutionary leaders, Pugin's work within a very few years began to seem unsatisfactory to many who owed their whole professional stock of ideas and of forms to him. But in 1841 and 1842 Pugin was still well ahead of the crowd; these are, indeed, the years when he began his finest parish church and what ought to have been his finest cathedral. Some dozen other churches started in these two years also testify that his popularity with the Catholics was still rising and his capacity for work quite incredible. If he was beginning to burn out, as is often the fate of neurotics with a narrow creative streak, he was not yet aware of the fact; the downturn in his production began only in 1843.

St. Giles's, Cheadle, as originally designed for Lord Shrewsbury in 1841, was to have been a relatively inexpensive church, costing some £5,000 like St. Oswald's, Old Swan. Indeed, as one sees the design presented in the *Dublin Review* article in 1841 it appears very similar to St. Oswald's. For one reason or another Lord Shrewsbury later decided to lavish much larger sums of money on St. Giles's and the finished church (consecrated 21 September 1846) is much finer than St. Oswald's or any other of Pugin's early parish churches.

Although the plan and the basic concept of the church were little changed (Fig. III 26), Pugin was enabled with the extra funds to carry up his spire to a much greater height than he had at first intended and also to elaborate it with many spirelets and gables. If an essentially derivative work may ever be really fine, this spire is; for the silhouette has real elegance and the scale true grandeur as the tower soars up from the valley high above the small Staffordshire town of Cheadle. Neither too bare, as are many of the best High Victorian spires, nor too fussy, like most ambitious spires of the 30's and 40's (including those of Pugin's own earlier projects), the tower displays a really "monumental" quality (in the best sense of that ambiguous word). Two hundred feet tall, it quite dwarfs the relatively low church; but a spired tower should belong more to the whole town picture than to the individual structure of which it is a part.

The church profits enormously from the rich orange-brown sandstone of which it is built. The surfaces of the ashlar are pleasantly tooled so that the stone has weathered most plausibly. The moldings and other details, although extremely refined, have a certain sturdiness lacking in the earlier churches of Pugin, so often either papery or metallic in effect. The windfall of additional funds, which provided for heightening the spire, doubtless made possible more and better carved work on the exterior; chiefly it was expended on the decoration of the interior, however.

The other churches of Pugin, particularly as one sees them today with most of their original painted decoration obliterated, are likely to be rather bare, cold, and even overlighted. In the interior of St. Giles's, on the other hand—and the difference will surprise the more, the better one knows the general run of Pugin's churches—the warm darkness of the interior is the most notable first impression. This effect is only partly due to the rather feeble colored glass of the aisle windows through which the daylight seeps into the unlighted nave; for here is a magnificently colored darkness not unlike that of St. Mark's in Venice or other Byzantine churches lined with rich mosaics. Every square inch of the interior is painted either with gold or with color chiefly in repeating patterns—diapers, chevrons, and brocaded effects —which are infinitely various in design and yet consistently harmonious in scale (Figs. III 27–28). Least happy is the figural painting over the chancel arch; but so perfect is the evenness of tone in all the decorations that the mural does not offend as do the garish windows, certainly among the poorest Pugin ever designed.

The over-all tonality is brownish gray highlighted with gold; and time, in this cleanly Staffordshire town, has only slightly darkened the general effect. The combination of colors in the various areas of pattern is bolder and richer than this general effect would at first suggest: The floors, for example, are of red and cream tiles, and a dado of yellow and deep gray-blue figured tiles lines the aisle walls. The special significance of this sort of "permanent polychromy" in tile will become evident in Chapter XVII. The chancel screen is brown, red, and gold, while around the font in the southwest corner is a screen of bright polished brass. The roof trusses, of the rather awkward X type, are richly colored and patterned, as are also the rafters, the curved braces, and the flat areas between them. Thus the whole roof structure acquires a special sort of solidity and expressive meaning—just as one of Pugin's principles implied that structure should—merely from the handling of the decoration on the useful elements.

There are many, undoubtedly far too many, accessories. But the darkness tends to merge them in the total effect of subdued richness. One is reminded forcibly by the sumptuous quality of patterned tone on patterned tone, of form dissolved in drenched color, of a Baxter print—or even of the orchestration of the great Romantic composers. Doubtless this interior was once not so unique as it seems today; yet the decoration and the tall spire as seen from a distance must always have set this Cheadle church apart from the rest of Pugin's work and even more from the work of his imitators. Not before the next decade was a more satisfying church completed within the main stream of the Gothic Revival. It is, moreover, a major monument of Late Romanticism; for it recalls, among contemporary works in other arts, not the music of Queen Victoria's favorite Mendelssohn but rather that of Berlioz; it may even be compared not unjustly with the coloristic painting of Turner and Delacroix.

The other parish church of the early 40's that should be specifically mentioned is St. Mary's, Stockton-on-Tees (Durham), completed in 1842. Though without aisles, this is a more conspicuous and better example of the corner-towered model than St. Wilfrid's, Hulme (Fig. III 19). The tall tower with its broached spire balances more effectively the rather broad front gable of the nave. The detail is Early English, not Decorated, and the characteristic lancet arcades are an excellent device for making evident through their clusters of tall colonnettes the real thickness of the masonry walls (Fig. III 23). This church has a rather more masculine quality than St. Giles's, preparing the way for that special vitality which certain later Victorian architects were to achieve by an even more plastic and articulated use of early Gothic detail.

Another St. Mary's, later the Roman Catholic cathedral of Newcastle-on-

Tyne, was begun in 1842 and opened 21 August 1844. It has three aisles of nearly equal height, each with an independent gable roof, like St. George's, Southwark. The low and dark interior has a special interest in its arrangement. The chancel is not separated structurally from the nave but only set off by a screen; thus the interior volume of space becomes quite continuous from west to east. On the exterior the tower (with a tall spire added later by another hand) was set not at the front but against the side of the south aisle some distance back from the west façade of the church. The undifferentiated chancel and the tower at the side are both premonitory of important aspects of later Victorian church architecture even if neither is especially effective as handled here.

The near-equality of the three aisles conflicts in the interior with the effect of horizontal flow of space toward the altar. On the exterior the three high-gabled roofs distract from that concentration of vertical accent which Pugin must have hoped to achieve by placing his tower in the position usually occupied merely by a low south porch. Yet both the placing of the tower and the treatment of the chancel indicate that Pugin was far from through with making experiments in mass and space composition even if he always followed readily citable medieval precedents. Before the beginning of Butterfield's mature work, which came at the very end of the decade, no other neo-Gothic architect was at once so "correct" and so original in his use of borrowed medieval elements as was Pugin (see Chapter XVII).

St. Barnabas's, Nottingham, dating from the same years as St. Mary's, Newcastle, and also later a cathedral, did not please Pugin very much. Despite a contribution of £10,000 from Lord Shrewsbury, economy dictated here simple Early English detailing with plain lancet windows; yet the way the vast black * stone masses pile up like a mountain range from the east to the great central tower bespeaks a serious interest in abstract three-dimensional composition (Fig. III 32). Pugin might easily have studied this effect in a preliminary model; it is certainly far removed from papery "façade architecture." The nave is plain and dull internally as well as externally (Figs. III 31, 33); but the very tall and narrow transept windows have something of the "sublimity" that Beckford and Wyatt had sought at Fonthill Abbey—how Pugin would have loathed such a comparison!

The east end, not the nave, was the most important part of a church to the sacramentally minded Pugin. Here the east end is almost as large as the nave and the transepts combined (Fig. III 30). Around the sanctuary he created

* Actually the material is a creamy gray gritstone, but grime has made it a rich and even black all over. The irregular diagonal pointing of the ashlar blocks, with smoother cut edges and dressings, provides an excellent texture. Bold imbrications are cut into the stonework of the spire.

84

a fascinating agglomeration of related volumes of differing height opening into one another through arcades. Even in its present denuded state this eastern arm of St. Barnabas's retains something of the mystery, something of the sense of holy places behind holy places, of multiplied ritual areas and graduated degrees of sanctity at which Pugin always aimed. Decorated as he intended it to be, with a richness comparable to that of St. Giles's, Cheadle, the effect should have been extremely fine (Fig. III 29); even as it stands the east end displays the most complex planning Pugin ever attempted. Yet, despite all the sense of mystery, the associated spacial volumes remain as clearly defined as the masonry forms that clothe them on the exterior. Above all, the vertical dimension is fully exploited at St. Barnabas's, both inside and out, as it rarely could be in Pugin's small parish churches.

In a project for St. Gregory's Abbey at Downside in Devonshire, prepared in 1842 also, Pugin proposed a much larger Early English church with a central tower and a similarly complex grouping of subsidiary masses at the east end. But the vastly longer nave and considerably longer transepts, together with the paired western towers, compromise the compactness and concentration of form that distinguish St. Barnabas's. Despite their abbatial propriety these expensive features must have played a considerable part in discouraging the English Benedictines from initiating the revival of their building activities with so ambitious a scheme.

In the next year, 1843, Pugin began few new building projects; but it was for him a year of strenuous publishing activity. The article in No. 20 (May 1841) of the *Dublin Review*, already discussed, and a second article in No. 23 (February 1842) reappeared together in a book entitled *The Present State of Ecclesiastical Architecture in England*. The second article was fortunately illustrated not with wood engravings but once more with Pugin's own etchings. These plates include three of St. Barnabas's, one of the Downside project, and another of the monastery then being so penuriously executed at Coalville in Leicestershire. A very attractive etching is of Jesus Chapel at Ackworth Grange, Yorkshire (opened 12 October 1842); this is very small but comparable in the completeness of the original decorative treatment to St. Giles's, Cheadle. The rich screen in St. Chad's, Birmingham, is also illustrated, as well as such semisecular buildings as the Birmingham Bishop's House, the Birmingham and Liverpool Convents of Our Lady of Mercy, and St. John's Hospital, Alton. The illustrations in this book offer without question the most appealing graphic documentation of Pugin's work, with only a single plate devoted to the visual casuistry of *Contrasts* and *True Principles*. The comparison Pugin provided in that plate between the section of an aisleless Classical preaching-box and that of an aisled "Catholic church" is probably specious in suggesting how much less masonry the latter required; yet

85

the argument could appeal to the practical minded. Two additional plates are devoted to the work of other Catholic architects.

Poor Scoles, twenty years older than Pugin and with a firm hold on Jesuit commissions, was sternly taken to task for his new St. John's, Islington. But he was chastised more in a spirit of friendliness than of anger: "We are unwilling to attribute all the defects . . . to the architect, who has on former occasions shown himself capable of doing very much better, and who would be a valuable ally in the good cause, if he would seek to do what is positively right and correct, rather than what may please for the moment . . . These are not times for compromise." Thus speak leaders in every period after their causes have become all but victorious to the older rivals and forerunners who have not swallowed the new doctrines whole.

What, one naturally wants to know, were Scoles' sins in Pugin's eyes? Poor St. John's may be considered an architectural sin by almost anyone; even if less heinous than the earlier church in Lisson Grove, it is still pathetically unreal as architecture. But what was to Pugin its chief fault was venial for an architect working for Jesuits: The plan was not that of a 14th-century English parish church—nave, side aisles, and deep chancel—but rather (at much reduced scale) that of the Gesù in Rome, with a very wide nave, two ranges of side chapels, and a semicircular apse (although, of course, no dome over the crossing). The Romanesque detail, although somewhat continental in character, could hardly be castigated by Pugin; for his own St. Michael's, Gorey, just then being completed, was Norman, it will be recalled.

The use of two towers at St. John's—and very skimpy ones at that—on a church that was in Pugin's words "neither collegiate, conventual, nor cathedral," he considered a serious ecclesiological solecism. And the character of the façade illustrates the "all-front principle of the Dissenters"; indeed "it is by no means equal to the Puritan edition of York Minster at the Scotch kirk, Regent Square." That was the final insult! for this rather ridiculous edifice, built in the 20's by Sir William Tite (1798–1873), was one that Pugin had known well ever since he had been dragged there by his mother to sit through the sermons of Edward Irving. Moreover, the modest Irvingite auditorium is in very truth but a "preaching-box" or "conventicle" internally and the façade a manifest "sham."

Instead of Scoles' church Pugin suggested (with plan and perspective generously provided) that the demolished St. Mary's, Islington, originally dating from the 14th century, ought to have been rebuilt on the Catholics' new site complete with aisled nave and northwest tower. At St. Mary's, as in many late medieval town churches, there had been no other chancel than that created by screening off the two easternmost bays of the nave; this may well have provided the particular source of Pugin's Newcastle plan.

But if the older Catholic architect Scoles was thus so effectively admonished—he actually began soon to mend his ways—another Catholic architect, Matthew E. Hadfield (1812–1885), Pugin's precise contemporary but in experience considerably his junior, received very warm, even too lavish, praise. In Pugin's flattering etching Hadfield's St. Bede's, Masborough, at Rotherham (built 1841–42), looks almost exactly like one of Pugin's aisleless and towerless Decorated chapels. With its larger windows, it is in fact considerably more attractive than St. Ann's, Keighley, or St. Mary's, Southport, completed by Pugin in 1840 and 1841, respectively, at least as one sees them in the wood engravings of the *Dublin Review* article of 1841 which were republished in the *Present State.* Hadfield had learned Pugin's simpler lessons well; when he embarked on more ambitious commissions, however, his lack of a personal style became only too evident (Fig. III 38). With very few exceptions the distinguished followers of Pugin were all Anglicans.

In Pugin's other book issued in 1843, *An Apology for the Revival of Christian Architecture in England,* he was less exclusively concerned than usual with churches. Attacking contemporary eclecticism, he urged the use of Gothic for all modern structures and discussed various building problems with which he had little or no actual experience. Graphic parodies of contemporary works are balanced not, as in *Contrasts,* with real medieval work —since there were no ancient railway bridges or grocer's shops—but with projects of his own; to these further reference will be made in Chapters XII and XV (Figs. XII 23, XV 9).

Pugin also devoted several plates and much of his text in *An Apology* to various kinds of church accessories such as sepulchral brasses, sculpture, and painting; and also to the various furnishings for the sanctuary now being produced to his designs by his friend and associate John Hardman of Birmingham. None of this was architecture, but no architectural revolution can be complete until almost all related furnishings have been redesigned. Very often, indeed, general enthusiasm for the new sort of furnishings proceeds more rapidly, if also more confusedly, than the acceptance of the new architecture itself. That was certainly true in the churches of the 1840's, just as it was to be in the houses of the 1930's with their light wooden furniture and general "industrial-art" gadgetry.

The most remarkable thing about *An Apology* is its frontispiece (Fig. III 10). Here, gathered together in a single perspective as in the famous composite view Cockerell prepared of Wren's City churches, are *two dozen* cathedrals, churches, and chapels, a large proportion (but by no means all) of those Pugin had built or was building since St. Marie's, Derby, had been begun only five years earlier. This plate certainly provides most impressive evidence of Pugin's energy and his phenomenally rapid success. Indeed Pugin has been accused of displaying here a shameless vainglory; for such cathedrals as St. George's, Southwark, and St. Mary's, Newcastle, are shown with their tall towers and spires complete, while St. Chad's, Birmingham, has a central tower, never even begun, to crown it.

Such an accusation is unjust since Pugin had actually built considerably more churches, particularly small ones, than the plate indicated. St. Giles's, Cheadle, moreover, was destined to receive at his hands in the next few years a spire much taller and richer than that shown here, one equal in height to any of the unbuilt spires and finer in design (Fig. III 26). Then, except for a gatehouse at Oscott College in Warwickshire and St. John's Hospital at Alton in Staffordshire, none of his non-church work is included. Pugin was punished, if not by the fates at least by the judgment of many contemporaries, for his presumed boastfulness. There was too much disparity between the suggestion of richness and finish in this etching and the barrenness of many of the executed edifices; moreover, Pugin's churches were now widely distributed in fairly accessible places and hence were becoming well known at first hand to interested students.

Pugin began only some half-dozen new churches in 1843 and 1844; after 1845 the curve of his church production went sharply downward. Fewer than half a dozen of his churches can be dated, apparently, from the last seven years of his life. The researches of Phoebe Stanton are adding many unknown works to the Pugin canon; but the proportional relationship of his early and his late production will presumably not be significantly changed. Of the late works, moreover, only one demands detailed discussion, that which he began to build for himself beside his house at Ramsgate in 1846. This church was completed, except for the top stage of the central tower and the intended spire, in 1851, just before his madness and death. Yet St. Mary's, Liverpool—built 1844–45; moved and rebuilt in the mid-80's by Pugin's youngest son Peter Paul Pugin (1851–1904); then destroyed in the blitz—had certain features which the younger men were to admire and emulate at the end of the decade. The Liverpool church was definitely a town church with a tall clerestorey; as at St. Mary's, Newcastle, there was no break in plan at the chancel, but the chancel received a paneled arched ceiling although the roof of the nave rested as usual on spare polygonal trusses. The effect was perhaps not altogether happy but it was rather more suggestive of a new approach than Newcastle. Much later, High Victorian church architects saw how to develop Pugin's idea: Such unified spacial volumes are indeed quite characteristic of the best church interiors of the 60's.

St. Augustine's, Ramsgate, is not suggestive of any new approach as regards the treatment of spacial volume; on the contrary the several parts—

the nave, the south aisle, the crossing, the transept, and the southeast chapel
—are so separated from one another by heavy arches that the interior has
almost as little unity as a Late Byzantine church (Fig. III 34). Externally the
local material, napped flint, produces a delicate, etching-like continuity of
surface reminding one of Pugin's best earlier work (Fig. III 35). Narrow bands
of freestone set in the flint walls offer on the other hand a premonition of the
flat polychromy of the 50's (see Chapter XVII). But the stone trim in general,
if very plausibly scaled, seems by its plastic vigor to contradict the general
continuity of surface in a way the rather pinched trim around the openings
in Pugin's earlier churches had not. The equally heavy members of the nave
arcades conduce to the effect of congestion inside the church; while overhead the close-set polygonal timbering of the nave and aisle roofs and the
sturdy paneling of the chancel, transept, and chapel roofs are almost too
heavy and solid. No "roof-tree has been starved to gild the altar" here, to
reverse a characteristic negative judgment on Pugin's churches.

The walls are all of cream-colored Caen stone, not of painted plaster; the
beams and ceilings are of dark oak, not stained and varnished pitchpine.
Everything is "real" in a most medieval way and Pugin's delight in these
honest materials can still be contagious. It is not difficult, therefore, to understand why Pugin derived from this church a satisfaction no other had given
him: This was certainly the way a neo-medieval church ought to be built.
The archaeologically minded for several generations were ready to give
him credit here for exceptional authenticity of detail also, a matter of little
interest today. The floor tiles, however, well illustrate his best manner in
flat pattern work (Fig. III 36).

As often occurs when architects build for themselves—perhaps because
there is no set time limit for the completion of the work—there is no over-all
controlling conception here but rather too great a profusion of separate
trouvailles. Thus St. Augustine's can remind one of Frank Lloyd Wright's
two Taliesins. But it is well to conclude the discussion of Pugin's work as a
church architect with St. Augustine's. Many younger men had come to feel
by the late 40's that they had learned all Pugin's lessons and could build
better neo-medieval churches than he had done at the opening of the decade. This church demonstrated that Pugin also—at least as a craftsman—
had continued to learn. If Pugin could have built over again in the late
40's some of the churches he ran up so cheaply and hastily in the early 40's
he might have answered most of the complaints of his Victorian critics;
considering the characteristic modern response to this "model" church, however, one may wonder whether much might not thereby have been lost
which today gives attraction to his earlier work.

The initiatory monuments of any series always have a special charm, even perhaps special virtues. Not least is this true of those overly ambitious Roman Catholic edifices of the late 30's and early 40's with which Pugin opened the series of Early Victorian churches. How often one speaks of a picture as a "fine early work" of some master; St. Augustine's at best is only a fine late work even though Pugin was still under 35 when he began it.

Before turning to the churches built in the Early Victorian period by and for Anglicans, which constitute the great bulk of ecclesiastical production in the 40's, a few of the edifices that were built by Pugin's Roman Catholic rivals in the mid- and late 40's ought to be mentioned. In 1844 Scoles began two important churches for his usual clients the Jesuits, one in Liverpool and another in London. Both are Decorated in style and, so far as modern eyes can discriminate in such a dead issue, they are in the main as "correct" in plan as Pugin's. St. Francis Xavier's, in Salisbury Street, Liverpool, was opened in 1848. A large church holding some 1,600, this has a nave and side aisles, a polygonal apse (less correct than a deep oblong chancel but, as we have seen, used by Pugin in several of his large early churches), and a tall square corner tower placed to the right of the façade, with the main portal at its base. A peculiar and unmedieval feature is the row of confessionals, forming a sort of subsidiary aisle, that opens off the north side of the church —peculiar, but certainly useful for modern Roman Catholic practice. Such confessionals were also introduced by Pugin at St. George's, Southwark, sometime before it was opened in 1848, and those may just possibly be the earlier.

St. Francis Xavier's is perhaps overrich internally and the Geometrical details are less authentic than Pugin's. But the nave compares favorably in its proportions with many of his, certainly a more important consideration. A polygonal paneled roof, such as Pugin had used only in chancels and chapels, covers the whole nave. This sort of roof is certainly cleaner and more volume defining than the rather feeble open trusses usual in Pugin's interiors. The shafts of the nave colonnade are of polished gray-green Drogheda marble from Ireland. They could thus be of so slight a section (because of the relative strength of the material) that they have often been deprecated—or sometimes admired—for being of cast iron. The *Ecclesiologist's* reviewers did not agree about this church. In 1847 (8, 217) it was said to be "exceedingly satisfactory in many respects"; the next year (9, 163) it was called a "decided failure" with a "sprawling apse" and nave shafts like "iron pipes."

This structural use of a stronger material such as marble, with conscious emphasis on the decorative value of its permanent coloring, is a significant premonition of the "structural" or "permanent" polychromy so popular from the early 50's on (see Chapter XVII). The relative naturalism and boldness of the foliage carving is appealing also in comparison with the dryness and daintiness of Pugin's foliage; it is also rather premonitory of High Victorian ornament. The random ashlar, once of mixed beige and orange limestones, is now of course all weathered to the same dark gray; the interior is of beige stone with but little painted polychromy.

Scoles had come a long way from Our Lady's, Lisson Grove, in ten years; and much of his improvement was undoubtedly the result of a sincere desire to reach the new standard of neo-Gothic design set by Pugin in the interim. But the taste of St. Francis Xavier's is not Pugin's, nor was it that of his Anglican admirers. The general effect is at once coarser and more lush; it is also more related to continental Gothicism of this same Late Romantic period. Even though this church has more vitality than many designed by Pugin's ablest Anglican disciples in these years, it lies outside the main line of development—as do most Roman Catholic churches, for that matter, at least down to the 70's.

The Catholic patrons of the mid-century were less aesthetically sophisticated than Lord Shrewsbury and March-Phillipps, while the prejudices of the Catholic clergy, most of whom had spent their years of training abroad, were now consciously continental and often definitely anti-Gothic. As Gwynn has pointed out in *Lord Shrewsbury, Pugin and the Catholic Revival* (1946), the activity of the Oratorians in Early Victorian England, members of an order founded by St. Philip Neri in 16th-century Italy, had much to do with the preference for Renaissance models such as they used for their own churches and houses in London and Birmingham.

Just as the more Protestant-minded Anglicans feared that the revival of Gothic forms might imply the revival of Popery—as indeed, to Pugin, it did—the Roman hierarchy feared the intensely English bent of the revival and, even more, its close association with the new militancy of the High Anglicans. Enthusiasm for medieval art might lead Anglicans to conversion but, as I have suggested, ecclesiology seems quite as often to have provided a respectable way of sublimating extreme Catholic tendencies. Some aesthetic converts to Catholicism, such as the Reverend Richard Waldo Sibthorp (a client of Pugin's in Lincoln, for whom he built St. Ann's Bede Houses there in 1842), actually returned from Rome to their original allegiance. (Sibthorp went over in 1841, returned in 1843, and ended as a Catholic again in 1865.) In his later life even Pugin began to show some sympathy for the Anglican Church, chiefly because it was "sounder" on the subject of chancel screens than were his co-religionists in England. To the Roman clergy the Gothic Revival and the Catholic Revival in England were quite different things; they could not, therefore, give Pugin as wholehearted support as did the High Anglicans.

All this background one senses in Scoles' other important Jesuit church, that of the Immaculate Conception, Farm Street, Grosvenor Square. This was completed in 1849, the year after the Liverpool example. Located in the heart of Mayfair, the church is nevertheless quite inconspicuous, being without a tower (Fig. III 39). Rich and almost French Flambuoyant in its Late Decorated way, the Farm Street shrine contains many elaborate accessories by other designers such as the high altar by Pugin, of the original date of the church, and a sumptuous Chapel of the Sacred Heart by Henry Clutton (1819–1893), added in 1858–59 to the right of the chancel. The interior has been so much embellished over the years with all sorts of colored decoration that it is hard to tell just what the inside was like originally. It certainly does not look today particularly English or even as characteristically Early Victorian as St. Francis Xavier's.

When the design was shown at the Royal Academy Exhibition in 1847, the *Ecclesiologist, 8,* 206, found it "decidedly too foreign and flambuoyant in character" and with too short a chancel; nevertheless it was considered a "laudable attempt to design a town church" and even the tall clerestorey was approved. To the *Builder,* 1847, 213, it was "a clever design." Charles Lock Eastlake in *A History of the Gothic Revival* (1872) called it one of Scoles' best productions, noting favorably the glass by Wailes and the polychromy and gilding by Bulmer added after the church was completed. A curious feature of the church was the handling of the aisles which could not extend all the way to the "west" (actually south) front because of the exiguity of the site.

In 1844 Hadfield, whose Masborough chapel Pugin had praised, began the large church of St. John's, Salford, in association with his partner John Gray Weightman (1801–1872), a pupil of C. R. Cockerell. Finished in 1848, this later became the Roman Catholic cathedral (Fig. III 38). St. John's is a cruciform church clumsily pieced together out of disparate features borrowed from various 14th-century English models. The tower and spire of Newark, the nave of Howden, and the choir of Selby were all supposedly copied here, "not absolutely in proportion but in detail," as Eastlake remarked. The *Ecclesiologist, 9,* 161–163, dismissed the architects as mere "copyists"; yet Eastlake assures us that St. John's had "elicited the admiration of Pugin" (which is hard to believe). The Salford Cathedral may be closer superficially to Pugin's standards; but in every serious architectural way it is below the quality of Scoles' churches; nor did the work of Hadfield and Weightman improve much during their long and successful career as Roman Catholic church builders—not at least until after the Early Victorian period when their pupil George Goldie (1828–1887) took over as designer.

At St. Chad's, Manchester, begun later but completed in 1848 at the same time as St. John's, Salford, Hadfield and Weightman continued to use Romanesque forms. This church was disapproved by the *Ecclesiologist* in the review cited above as "italianizing." In part this was because of the very rich internal polychromy for which ironically the *Ecclesiologist* was within a year or two to be so actively campaigning (see Chapter XVII). Gillespie Graham, who had earlier had the advantage of Pugin's friendship and collaboration, provided equally sumptuous polychromy in the Chapel of St. Anthony the Eremite, at Murthly in Perthshire. This Norman edifice provided the subject of a handsome monograph (Edinburgh, 1850) whose chromolithographed plates of elephant-folio size give an excellent idea of what the polychromy of the 40's was like when fresh.

As we shall see in Chapter V, Anglicans likewise continued in the late 40's to use pre-Gothic models on occasion despite the frowns of ecclesiological purists. The Roman Catholics, for their part, were still drawing inspiration from even more dubious sources, at least from a Puginian or advanced ec-clesiological point of view. When the vast carcass (begun in 1834) of Good-ridge's church of the Holy Apostles, later the procathedral at Clifton, Bristol, was at last fitted up for use in 1847–49, the broad nave was filled with a re-markable framework of timber with round wooden arches dividing it into three aisles (Fig. III 40). The spirit is that of the best contemporary metal construction as we shall see later (Chapters XV–XVI); the "style"—if a reminiscent name must be applied, and the age always demanded it—is more or less Romanesque. This interior, in its strength, grace, and suitability to the needs of 19th-century Roman Catholic services, put all but the finest work of Pugin to shame; it must also have been very inexpensive to carry out. But it could only make Pugin and his disciples writhe in anguish; for it was "utilitarian," not "Catholic," in spirit. Perhaps it was fear of ecclesiological lynching that has kept the architect's name a secret—there is no reason why it should not be Goodridge whose Bath work of this time was Romanesquoid.

There was other less original but equally non-Gothic work being done for Roman Catholics. Charles Parker, because of his influential publications, might almost be called the "Pugin of the Italian Villa mode" had he done more actual building of consequence. In 1846 he added an Italian campanile to the Classical Spanish Embassy Chapel in London (1797, by Joseph Bonomi [1743–1824]) now long since destroyed. At the same time he was building two churches near London whose basilican elements he grouped in a sort of parody of such a Puginian model as St. Oswald's, Old Swan. One is at St. Albans; the other at Kingston-on-Thames. The campanile in both cases is in the middle of the west front; the oblong chancel is lower than the nave; and the aisle and clerestorey windows are coupled in an approximation of simple tracery (Fig. III 41). The chancel screen at Kingston-on-Thames was of cast iron, the roof tiles copied from samples imported from Florence.

93

On the Continent, both in France and in Germany, basilican and Italian Romanesque exemplars provided the characteristic plans and conventional decorations of most Catholic churches in the 40's. The grandest and most important Italian church of the age, San Paolo fuori-le-mura outside Rome, was also basilican, being a reconstruction of the 5th-century original which had burned. In England, however, such Catholic churches as Parker's were as much exceptions to the general rule as were the few Italian Romanesque churches built by Anglicans in this period. The most considerable basilican structure, St. Peter's, Hatton Garden, intended primarily for the foreign Catholics of London, was begun in 1853 from the designs of Francesco Gualandi, a Bolognese architect. As far as the story of Early Victorian churches goes, this is completely irrelevant, although not to later developments in the 60's and 70's.

The ablest of the Roman Catholic architects working in the tradition of Pugin appeared only in the late 40's. William Wilkins Wardell (1823–1900) built his first church when he was only 23; between 1846 and his emigration to Australia in 1858 he had completed half a hundred. His work, therefore, falls chiefly in a later period; but his most consequential London church, that of Our Lady of Victories in Clapham Park Road, was built in 1849–52. It is an edifice that Pugin ought to have approved much more highly than anything by Hadfield. Solidly built of squared Kentish ragstone, this has a rather fine corner tower with a spire of considerable height. Rich but crisp 14th-century detail is effectively concentrated at the portal under the tower. Inside, the nave is tall and well lighted with a heavy polygonal-trussed roof like that in St. Augustine's, Ramsgate, although rather flattened in section (Fig. III 37). There is also a deep, rib-vaulted chancel. The church received many sumptuous additional features from the hand of J. F. Bentley (1839–1902) who came to live in the parish in 1874; but the general effect of the original portions is not unworthy of comparison with all but the best Anglican work of the date.

Wardell's other London churches of the late 40's are St. John Baptist's, Hackney, opened in 1848, and St. Alexis's, Fitzroy Place, Kentish Town, begun in 1849. Other Roman Catholic architects, such as Joseph Aloysius Hansom (1803–1882), got their start as builders of Gothic churches in the late 40's and early 50's; but their mature work belongs, as regards both its vices and its virtues, to the High Victorian 50's and 60's.

It is possible to deal with Pugin's work as a church architect before touching at all on Anglican and Nonconformist churches because he was at first so completely an isolated revolutionary. In his early years he was, moreover, remarkably productive. Very few Anglican churches showing his influence were even begun before 1843 by which time most of his were already at least under way. Even as a writer Pugin was less prolific on strictly architectural matters after the publication of *The Present State* and *An Apology* in 1843.

His *Glossary of Ecclesiastical Ornament and Costume* (1844) was a remarkably complete compilation, in the tradition of his father's books and his own early treatises on metalwork, which at once became a standard work. It has, of course, little to do directly with architecture. *Floriated Ornament* (1849) is a very charming book entirely illustrated with color plates. This helps one to realize the sort of bright and delicate painted decoration with which Pugin's interiors, ecclesiastical and secular, were meant to be covered. The rather somber tonality of St. Giles's, Cheadle, was perhaps not altogether typical of Pugin's usual intentions in color and design, or so these plates would suggest. Moreover, the specific identification of the plants from which the patterns were conventionalized illustrates an important Victorian conviction soon to be much publicized by Ruskin: Victorians generally were coming to believe that pseudomedieval ornament ought to be stylized on the basis of real botanical knowledge of particular plant forms, not copied directly from old work nor yet arbitrarily invented.

Sir Kenneth Clark has suggested that the chromolithography of the plates in this book is none too accurate. Yet I feel sure that these plates really do give us something of the bright, sharply contrasted, and intricate polychrome effects which the Early Victorians were seeking in their interiors of the 40's as the relatively monochrome—or bichrome—Late Georgian tradition broke down along with other aspects of the preceding rule of taste. The general tone is pretty, not heavy; delicate and various, not broad and even—surely this is characteristic of many works of minor art of the period, such as china painting and chintzes, long recognized as having charm if not beauty. It would not be a bad idea to enliven the now dreary interiors of so many of Pugin's churches and the still more drab churches of his Anglican contemporaries by stenciling such patterns on light grounds across the walls and the roofs.

The stained glass of the epoch, still surviving in considerable quantity, only occasionally has a comparable freshness and gaiety. But the study of stained glass, a most important accessory in Victorian churches, is too large a subject to embark on here. The early glass, good or bad, can rarely even be commented on; only with the work of William Morris (1834–1896) and his associates in the 60's and 70's do Victorian windows become of much independent merit. Pugin was rather active at window design himself; working with Hardman of Birmingham he contributed stained glass to many Anglican churches, old and new, as well as to most of the Catholic churches he built himself. One of his largest and best is the west window in St. Mary's, Beverley, designed at the very end of his life as part of a general campaign to restore that magnificent 14th-century parish church.

Pugin's last publication to be concerned, at least nominally, with architecture—a spate of writing on other controversial matters can be ignored here—was a *Treatise on Chancel Screens and Rood Lofts,* published in 1851. It was chiefly illustrated with medieval examples most of which were continental, not English. Pugin's feelings about screens were even more intense than they had been earlier and so nearly pathological that it is not surprising madness followed a year later. Had he not gone mad, some have conjectured that he might have returned to the Anglican fold; his reconversion would certainly have been an appropriate response to the success of his architectural reforms among Anglicans.

This chapter has been concerned with Pugin as a church architect. Much of his other architectural work, intrinsically less important, is dealt with in Chapter VIII; but it is by his churches that he must stand or fall. Was he "one of the least possible or conceivable architects" in Ruskin's words? No, that is clearly a wicked libel. But it would be presumptuous to assert that the intrinsic architectural value of his production compares with its historical significance. Before his death few Victorian churches were built by others however—and none perhaps completed in Gothic—that have stood up as well in the considered estimate of posterity.

Pugin's biographers and the historians of the Gothic Revival have in general done him a disservice. They have accepted his stated aims as a reviver of old forms too literally; they have even paid him the unwise compliment of comparing his work—as he himself perpetually did—with the incomparable real work of the Middle Ages. The condemnations which he uttered at one time or another on all of his work except St. Augustine's, Ramsgate, have therefore been too much echoed by his most sincere admirers. I have tried to show that he was truly an architect, if not perhaps of the first rank *sub specie historiae.* Further consideration of Early Victorian churches will only serve to show that for his day, at least, he was a remarkably good designer and builder.

CHAPTER IV: ANGLICAN AND NONCONFORMIST CHURCHES OF THE LATE 30'S AND EARLY 40'S

To indicate how various was the accomplishment of the Early Victorians in church architecture it will be well to depart for a while from what men of the 50's and 60's believed to be the main line of development. To Gilbert Scott, to Beresford-Hope, or to C. L. Eastlake the dramatic revival of English church architecture—which certainly began around 1840—was so completely associated with the progress of "The Revival" (i.e., the Gothic Revival) that their views were somewhat biased, particularly as both Scott and Beresford-Hope had been from almost the first important actors in the play. About the main plot of the initial episode there can be little dispute although there may be differences of emphasis; with that main plot the previous chapter concerning Pugin, its principal protagonist, has dealt. As regards the relative interest of the various subplots, the perspective of the 1950's must differ considerably from that of the 1850's when the drama was reaching its climax. Yet many 20th-century writers, following a tradition of historiography that has its roots in the mid-19th century, tend to omit what seem to them irrelevant, or even comic, interludes in the story of church building of the 40's somewhat as the French do in their productions of Shakespeare.

Pugin in the late 30's was able to initiate singlehanded a revolution in English church architecture because he was the spearhead of a new generation; but that generation was hardly destined to come into its own generally for another decade. Pugin and his contemporaries were born within the new century. To them the old mid-Georgian sanctions of the period before the Napoleonic Wars had early lost their strength, as did the old Victorian sanctions to those of us who were born after 1900. Gothic, which had been to their fathers' generation hardly more than a diverting whim or hobby, was like a revelation to them. Born serious, the younger men could not but despise the latitudinarianism of their elders in every field. In architecture Pugin was the first to make a mark; from earliest youth, indeed, he had been a prodigy. In a profession where a mature career is normally not under way before the age of 30 or more, Pugin's most active period of production began when he was 25; by 40 he was dead. All his contemporaries in architecture—except for Richard Cromwell Carpenter (1812–1855) who died at 43—had much more time ahead of them.

The architects who were building Anglican churches at the opening of Victoria's reign—and not many Nonconformist chapels were as yet being designed by architects—divide into two groups. On the one hand are the older men, of whom several must be considered pioneers of the mature Gothic Revival if hardly of mature Victorian architecture: Thomas Rickman, Anthony Salvin (1799–1881), Ambrose Poynter (1796–1866), and Edward Blore (1789–1879), for example, were all Pugin's elders by a decade or more. Of these Salvin alone developed into a Victorian architect of any consequence; but even he is really important only for his secular work (see Chapter VIII). On the other hand are various younger men within two or three years of being Pugin's precise contemporaries.

So rapid was the modulation of style in church architecture after 1840 that the older men who had been building Gothic churches of a sort since the 20's were rarely able to keep up to date after the early years of the decade. Their considerable (and apparently very relevant) experience and their Classical training had accustomed them to accept the obvious needs of the Anglican Church as they were understood in the first third of the century. They never really learned the new ecclesiological tricks; therefore they soon lost prestige to younger and more fanatical men when the new forces of Tractarianism had successfully reformed the doctrines and the rites of the Anglican Church.

Rickman was the only older man who was primarily a church architect and also untrammeled by the usual Classical training. He died in 1841 before his competence came to be seriously questioned. In a world grown intensely conscious of doctrinal differences this Quaker would have stood little chance of obtaining important Anglican commissions much after that date. Fortunately for the other men of Rickman's generation, they were by no means so restricted to ecclesiastical work by their interests and their experience. Among them, Salvin at least had a very successful Victorian career as a castle builder; Blore inherited the Royal patronage—such as it was—from the previous reign (see Chapter IX).

The new day of the dedicated specialist in church architecture began with Pugin, but the intense younger men who were his followers did not achieve their near-monopoly of the field much before the later 40's. In the opening years of Victoria's reign such opportunities as were Pugin's rarely came the way of Anglican architects. The Anglican opposite numbers of his Catholic patrons, so numerous later on, were still undergraduates at Cambridge or Oxford. However enthusiastic the patronage of these youths, it was likely to be rather limited in financial scope at this time. The earliest Victorian churches built for the Establishment which have architectural distinction comparable to Pugin's were mostly the work of architects who were specialists neither in church work nor at Gothic design.

The later chapters of Whiffen's *Stuart and Georgian Churches* [1947–48] give the most detailed and accurate picture of English church architecture in the 20's and 30's. The account in Basil F. L. Clarke's *Church Builders of the 19th Century* [1938] is somewhat more conventional. Clarke, however, continues the story forward, and his appendixes, giving brief biographies of church architects and lists of churches, are full of information. His book is a useful supplement to the histories of the Gothic Revival by Sir Kenneth Clark and C. L. Eastlake that have already been mentioned.

The great majority of "Gothic" churches built around 1840, as in the mid-30's, were the work of hack architects; and they were of course Gothic only in a rather limited sense. But a crude sort of Pointed detail of vaguely Early English character was being widely used to denature or to disguise the inherited Late Georgian meetinghouse, and by far the greater number of new churches were now avowedly non-Classical in their nominal "style." Of the six completed churches listed in the Report of the Parliamentary Commissioners for 1837, only two were Classical. Four years later, when 15 churches were reported by the Commissioners as built and 19 more as under construction, all but one were either Gothic or Norman.

Of course many churches, and usually the more ambitious ones, were built without assistance from the Commissioners; these were somewhat more likely to be Classical. St. Paul's, Valetta, on the island of Malta, founded by the Queen Mother Adelaide in 1839 and costing £15,000, is important if remote in location. Externally St. Paul's still follows closely the century-old formula of Gibbs' St. Martin's-in-the-Fields except for the omission of a tower and spire. Internally it is even more academically Classical (Fig. IV 2), for a flat paneled ceiling covers the wide nave, while the side colonnades are continued as a pilaster order around the semicircular apse. Considerably less ambitious but no more original are two Classical churches in London: That of Holy Trinity, built in 1837 in Gray's Inn Road by Sir James Pennethorne, has a stock brick façade and a stubby belfry; Trinity Chapel, Poplar, in the East India Dock Road, designed by the engineer William Hosking (1800–1861), is glibly described by contemporaries as "Grecian Corinthian."

The most popular alternative to Gothic in these years was some sort of Norman. Pugin's St. James's, Reading, begun in 1837, and his St. Michael's Gorey, begun in 1839, illustrate the Norman of the 30's as do also several of the plates in Hamilton's *Rural Churches* (1836). Late Georgian Gothic had grown very conventional in its dry Early English guise. Those who wished to build edifices of individual distinction—whether they were rich private sponsors or ecclesiastical authorities—tended therefore to follow Roman-esque models, English or continental, or else to use some sort of near-Perpendicular. For Perpendicular a new level of elaboration was being set in Barry's and Pugin's original designs for the New Palace; and the profession, of course, was well aware of this long before the walls rose high enough to attract the eyes of the general public. The Decorated of the 14th century, soon destined to be the acknowledged queen of all church modes, was hardly yet distinguishable as such in revived work; even Pugin's principal Decorated paradigms for churches, as we have seen, were hardly adumbrated before the early 40's.

Such analysis of production in terms of past styles nominally imitated can be tedious and in most periods is rather meaningless; but the development of Early Victorian architecture was so canalized by concepts of style revival that it is absolutely necessary to provide it here. The widely held assumption that Decorated models for church design, so firmly established by the end of this period, had proliferated already at its start needs to be corrected. The best new churches of individual distinction built around 1840 were admittedly exceptions to the general run in many ways; but they were not exceptions from any new stylistic norm that had yet come into being, even in the work of Pugin himself.

At the opening of his career, moreover, the Roman Catholic Pugin had no real rival among Anglican church builders. Not unjustly, Rickman had the highest prestige, for he had a considerable knowledge of real Gothic work and a sincere desire to imitate it plausibly. But he was at the end of his career, already turned 60. A late church of his, Bishop Ryder's in Birmingham of 1837–38 (Fig. III 15), is hardly the equal, much less the superior, of his St. George's, also in Birmingham, built as early as 1820–23. The most sumptuous new Anglican church of the late 30's in the Gothic mode, among the many built by architects of the older generation, is St. Peter's, the parish church of Leeds. R. D. Chantrell, who designed St. Peter's, had been building Gothic churches in Leeds almost as long as had Rickman in Liverpool and Birmingham. Chantrell's life dates are elusive but he was probably nearly 60 by the time he built St. Peter's—he had exhibited a design for a church at the Royal Academy as early as 1813. Less archaeological than Rickman's, his churches of the 20's are often rather more attractive examples of Late Georgian Gothic.

The other most remarkable churches of this moment were by much younger men, notably James William Wild (1814–1892) and Thomas Henry Wyatt (1807–1880), the latter working in partnership with David Brandon (1813–1897). Though Wild was Pugin's junior by two years his early reputation as a church architect did not survive the rapid success of Pugin's revolution; he soon left the English scene, reappearing only at the end of the 40's.

100

In Wyatt's prolific professional career church building was to be only a secondary interest even though he continued to design churches in some quantity throughout his long life. The churches these men—Chantrell, Wild, and Wyatt and Brandon—built around 1840 are no longer Georgian; but they are, like most of Pugin's contemporary work, still quite regular if not absolutely symmetrical in design. In their proportions, however, and in their general feeling they are by no means merely Classical compositions disguised with medieval detail any more than are Pugin's.

In the placing and the prominence of his towers, particularly at St. Wilfrid's, Manchester (Fig. III 19) and St. Oswald's, Liverpool (Fig. III 20), Pugin struck one of his strongest new notes; with them he set the guide lines of his vertically massed compositions. In their towers these other architects also broke most sharply with Georgian traditions of church design. Yet the general complexity of the exteriors of their churches is still in the older Picturesque tradition, so long exploited in cottage and villa architecture, not a positive expression of changed internal functions as it was with Pugin. Yet churches by these men could readily be utilized for the new High Church ritual: Wyatt's at Wilton was; and Dean Hook of Leeds, the client for the Chantrell church there, was considered relatively "High" in the early 40's. The new architectural symbolism of multiple religious functions expressed by articulation of interior volume and exterior mass was still largely lacking in all but Pugin's own churches however.

By their richness of ornament and complexity of form these churches of around 1840 appealed to new, post-Georgian, visual tastes. And when their architects' supposed deference to medieval authority—not as yet open to doubt—came to be questioned within a few years that distrust was factional rather than objective. If these earliest Early Victorian churches had been called upon to serve religious functions less subject to rapid modification they might well have continued longer to please connoisseurs. Incredibly tedious, at least to modern eyes, are the first Anglican churches that aimed to provide for the new functional needs of Tractarian "sacramentality." Chantrell's and Wild's and Wyatt's edifices, on the other hand, all remain quite interesting visually. Although these churches were soon left behind by the rapid crystallization of new ritualistic patterns and rigid stylistic inhibitions, they deserve attention as significant Early Victorian structures—something they have thus far rarely received.

St. Lawrence's, Southampton, was begun in August 1839 by Wild. It occupied an area 30 feet by 80 feet with more than a third of the length given over to a vaulted chancel; thus the plan was actually more "advanced" ritually than many of Pugin's. But the church was not freestanding and the façade in the High Street was flanked by regular four-storey houses; thus the articulated plan could not be the determinant of the only possible exterior view. The greater part of the width of the front was to be given up to a great tower and spire rising three times as high as the neighboring houses (Fig. IV 3). Because of the deep-sunk portal at its base and the piled-up buttresses at the corners, not to speak of the broached and gabled spire above, this would have contrasted markedly with the flat domestic fronts on either side. But the tower was not built until much later and then by another hand, while the church in any event is now entirely destroyed. (The front with its tower was, however, exhibited in a drawing at the Royal Academy in 1839 and hence well known as a design to interested contemporaries.)

The Academy drawing not being available, the effectiveness of this church front can only be guessed today from the modest wood engraving in the Companion to the *British Almanac* for 1839. The porch was of Caen stone as were some of the moldings; but the rest was chiefly of white local brick, a material that does not age gracefully. The Early English detail, while apparently well scaled, can hardly have given much body to so ghostly a paleness. It was in his sense of the "nature of materials" that Pugin, already in the late 30's, most excelled men like Wild at Gothic work. A design such as this for the front of St. Lawrence's demanded stone or at least red brick; but of course even Pugin was reduced to using yellow stocks at Southwark and for his own house at Ramsgate.

Despite dreary materials, Wild's other Gothic church of the late 30's, that of Holy Trinity, Blackheath, is more effective. Slightly larger than St. Lawrence's this had the further advantage of an open, rising site. There are side aisles and a polygonal apse, such as Pugin often used in these years, to elaborate the massing. The cost, some £5,000, was a third of that of a pretentiously porticoed Classical church like St. Paul's, Valetta.

Since the street lies to the southeast of the church, the polygonal apse forms the principal feature of the main façade (Fig. IV 1). This is flanked by two towers patterned after some memory of a Rhineland cathedral. The over-all modeling of the external mass is made still more complex by the addition of a gabled southeast porch. The frontispiece, showing the abbey church of Maria Laach, in *Architectural Notes on German Churches* (Cambridge, 1835; 3 eds. to 1842) by Sir William Whewell, then Master of Trinity College, Cambridge, could well have provided Wild with a suggestion—or perhaps it was some traveled architect's sketch which he saw. In its turn Wild's design was available to influence others since it was shown at the Royal Academy in 1838 as well as later in the Companion to the *British Almanac* for 1840 after the church was finished.

Because of the yellow stock brick of the walls, relieved only by a few stone moldings, even the contemporary who wrote the account there commented that Holy Trinity was "not only unpleasing in colour, but has also a certain heaviness not apparent in a mere drawing of it." The design is poorly scaled— as indeed many of Pugin's churches had been up to this date—and the actual building is considerably smaller than might be expected from the sketch. Yet the general plastic effect is of a richness Pugin hardly essayed before St. Barnabas's, Nottingham. Much can surely be forgiven so ambitious an edifice designed by a young man of 25 or 26.

Wild's early promise as a church architect was soon forgotten when the new, avowedly anti-aesthetic, doctrines of Pugin took hold. He was not an archaeologist nor was he a nationalist—even St. Lawrence's tower had a "foreign," presumably French, look to contemporaries. Worse, he was not a ritualist, despite the relative depth of his chancel at Southampton and the chancel screen he introduced at Blackheath. The new visual values for which he sought so frankly in his first Gothic churches did not become widely acceptable until they had received support from ancient national precedent and become the vehicles of a revived medieval symbolism. Fortunately the Tractarian tide did not rise so rapidly but that Wild was able to build one more Early Victorian church in England: His Christ Church, Streatham, to which we will return shortly, is perhaps the most original of all Early Victorian churches.

The other important Gothic church of the late 30's is less original than Wild's but much larger: Chantrell's St. Peter's, Leeds, begun in 1839 and consecrated in 1841, is especially remarkable for the complexity of its plan and for the elaboration of the detail. Above all, the position of the tower, not at the west end but in the middle of the north side, gives it distinction. Even Pugin praised this tower; yet Chantrell's probable reason for placing the tower where he did was not one Pugin could have approved. The church stands sidewise to the road and the tower was presumably set in the center of the side front in order to mark the transeptal entrance in an axial way, not for either picturesque or functional reasons (Fig. IV 4).

This tower is handsome in its own right; for it is all of stone, richly paneled in the Late Decorated or Early Perpendicular manner, and carried out with sturdier membering than most contemporary work in a 14th–15th-century vein. It is, for example, much more solidly buttressed than Pugin's tower on St. Marie's, Derby. But the body of the church behind the tall tower seems too low and too broad. A shallow clerestorey barely rises above the low-pitched roofs of the aisles; a low subsidiary aisle on the north flanks the base of the tower. The tall three-sided apse appears rather like a great bay window attached to the east end of the main block; at the west there is no plastic elaboration of the flat front at all to balance it.

Inside, the church is also low and broad with the low-pitched ceiling supported on heavy wooden trusses decorated with paneling (Fig. IV 5). The extremely ornate gallery front of dark varnished wood does not break the vertical lines of the piers except at the west end; but the galleries themselves have the effect of cutting off the subsidiary areas in the aisles from the main spacial volume of the nave. The ribbed plaster vaults over the crossing, the transepts, and the apse also break the unity of the interior, but they do not produce that effect of meaningful articulation of which Pugin was sometimes master.

For its time there was some serious archaeology in Chantrell's work and a due respect for national tradition. In 1847 a writer in the *Ecclesiologist, 8,* 132, commented, however, that "six years are a long time these days," so that (he claimed) St. Peter's could already be studied only as "an historical monument"! He paired it nevertheless with Newman's Littlemore church as an early instance of the "Catholic feeling of the church energizing" Gothic design. But there was only rudimentary "sacramentality" here even though the whole eastern arm might almost be considered to provide a deep chancel —indeed it is now thus arranged. Rich and elaborate, as befitting the £26,000 Dean Hook spent on it, St. Peter's still belongs to the world, as more or less to the mode, of Westminster New Palace. Such a church could satisfy many of the actual visual tastes of the Early Victorians, but it was not sufficiently serious in its ecclesiological program to impress them for long. St. Peter's continued to be admired and even imitated by Nonconformists, however, as the Mill Hill Chapel of the Unitarians here in Leeds, built nearly a decade later by Bowman and Crowther, illustrates so well (Fig. IV 9).

The most considerable Anglican edifice begun at the opening of the 40's was Wyatt and Brandon's church of SS. Mary and Nicholas, Wilton (Figs. IV 6–8). Begun in 1840 and many years a-building, it cost some £20,000. This was provided by Florence Nightingale's friend the Hon. Sydney Herbert (later Lord Herbert of Lea) and his mother the Dowager Countess of Pembroke who was a daughter of Count Worontzow-Dashkow, the lord of Alupka (Fig. VIII 5). A marble and Cosmati-work altar, brought from South Italy by the countess for incorporation in the church, undoubtedly served to suggest the Italian Romanesque treatment of the whole structure; but the Bishop of Salisbury forbade the use of a stone altar as being contrary to the rubrics, and real Romanesque fragments were incorporated only in the pulpit.

Even C. L. Eastlake, the Victorian historian of the Gothic Revival, called St. Mary's, Wilton, the most important Anglican church of its time, remarking that "the liberal munificence of the benefactor[s] . . . and the sumptuous nature of its decoration exercised in course of time a great and valuable influence on private patronage and public taste in architecture." The Wilton church provided precedent for a good many edifices of the 40's in what was then called the "Lombardic style" (to distinguish it from the national Norman Romanesque) even though the reviewer in the *Ecclesiologist*, 6, 169–174, reporting on its completion in 1846, was quite scornful of its foreign flavor. (But see Chapter XVII, for the ecclesiological "party line" was destined to change sharply a few years later.)

Although the general effect was evidently too continental to please the cognoscenti when it was new and most in the public eye—it was shown at the Royal Academy in 1840 and again in 1842—a model of the church was still considered worth displaying at the Great Exhibition of 1851. St. Mary's was, moreover, one of the few English churches of the 40's to be published abroad—in the Vienna *Allgemeine Bauzeitung*—since it was in a mode that was fashionable for churches all over Europe, and particularly in Germany, as the Camdenian Gothic was not. It may be recalled that at this time Frederick William IV of Prussia brought an apse mosaic home from Murano for incorporation in Persius' basilican Friedenskirche at Potsdam.

The exquisite quality of the cream-colored ashlar masonry, now subtly lichened, enhances the consistent character and scale of the rather eclectic Italian Romanesque detail used on the exterior (Fig. IV 6). The mosaic in the semidome of the apse, the patterned marble floors (reputedly from Sta. Maria Maggiore in Rome!), and other polychrome features are still the most noticeable things inside the church. But the simple basilican plan, with wide nave arches, and the cross-vaulted choir bay before the semicircular apse provided quite satisfactorily for the needs of an advanced Anglican ritual (Fig. IV 7). Because of the unusually tall proportions and, above all, the clear articulation of the nave, aisles, choir, and apse as related but distinguishable spacial volumes, the Wilton church is not unworthy of comparison internally with Pugin's best work (Fig. IV 8). The heavy trusses of the roof are particularly sturdy and structural as compared to Pugin's matchstick roofs of the time. Externally the masses are likewise clearly articulated except for the lack of any break in the roof at the west end of the choir. The freestanding tower in the Italian tradition is rather too remote from the main body of the church to compose well from most angles of approach; but the raised stone parvis before the west front is extremely effective and really Italian in character.

Wild's Christ Church, Christchurch Road, in Streatham, a southern London suburb, likewise begun in 1840, was much less expensive, costing only some £6,000 without the internal decorations; it is also larger, providing no less than 1,200 sittings. Although nominally Lombardic too in the usual terminology of the day, Christ Church is more original in every way than the Wilton church (Fig. IV 10). The material, as at Holy Trinity, Blackheath, is yellow brick; but the bricks were carefully selected for their intense color and superbly laid with an almost Regency emphasis on thin joints and smooth unbroken surfaces. (The walls actually recall those of the Duke of York's Headquarters in Chelsea, built by John Sanders in 1801.) At the arches and in the frieze below the bold and original cornice white and red bricks were introduced to form simple bands and diapers—the earliest "structural polychromy" of the Victorian Age (see Chapter XVII). Inside the church, side galleries are fully incorporated into the essential structural scheme of the clerestorey supports. The arrangement resembles what Soane had proposed in a Romanesque project prepared for the Commissioners twenty years before; he had also utilized it in a more personal way at St. Peter's, Walworth, in 1822.

Such galleries or tribunes, giving a three-storey elevation to the interior nave walls, had of course the precedent of the later Roman basilicas and also of the great continental Romanesque and Gothic churches of the 12th century; for that matter, they were often present in the earlier English cathedrals. The younger John Shaw (1803–1870) recommended them at this time (together with the Lombardic style) for churches to be built in the East End of London in a letter he wrote to Bishop Blomfield. Shaw also used them himself between two ranges of brick arcades carried on slim iron columns, at Christ Church, Watney Street, in London, completed in 1841. Internally this is almost identical with Wild's church and of considerable intrinsic interest.

If galleries were still to be put in churches—and they were, as a sort of horrid concession to economy, in many churches of the early 40's—this was obviously the most effective way of incorporating them instead of pushing them as much out of sight as possible behind a tall nave arcade as Chantrell did. But galleries were already by 1840 beginning to be red rag to English medievalists; even more reprehensible in the eyes of the fanatical new critics of church architecture was the restriction of the sanctuary to a mere semicircular apse here at Streatham. Wild's masterpiece therefore had a very poor reception for nearly a decade until Ruskin warmly commended its polychromy; it then became, by adoption, the first example of Ruskinian Italian Gothic.

The interior of Christ Church, Streatham, was (in the summer of 1952) being radically restored and may or may not, when the restoration is complete, reveal Wild's original intentions. But the exterior still stands clean and sharp, its planes defining accurately the relationship of the principal interior volumes. The whole composition is made singularly piquant, moreover, by the height and the marked vertical emphasis of the southeast tower. This tower has a steep pyramidal roof diapered with polychrome tiles. That roof and the slot-like belfry openings, so simply grilled and set between pilaster strips that rise unbroken from the plain solid base, offer a curious premonition of the finest towers of the High Victorian period; certainly Wild's design quite lacks the fussy elaboration which Early Victorians most admired. The tower is a fragment of Victorian architecture with strong positive quality; with this campanile of Wild's, as much as with any of Pugin's early spires, a new architectural age opened.

Wild's next important commission took him in 1842 to Egypt before the intended interior decoration of the Streatham church was even begun. There he was supposed to build an Anglican church at Alexandria. This edifice was to rise inside a high paneled wall with a semicircular apse at one end and a narthex flanked by low masses at the other. Dominated by a tower standing free in the southeast corner of the compound, the whole promised to form an effective and highly original three-dimensional composition. At the suggestion of the Turkish viceroy, who donated the site, the decorations were to be of Islamic character; to Victorian eyes the design had more the air of a mosque or a synagogue, therefore, than of an Anglican church. But then Christ Church, Streatham, was usually accused by contemporary critics of looking Saracenic also. This non-Christian look, together with the small number of permanent British residents in Alexandria, may explain why the construction of St. Mark's had to be suspended in 1848 for lack of funds; only then did Wild return to England.

While these handsome and interesting Lombardic churches of Wyatt and Wild were being designed a major twist in the architectural plot was occurring. This twist was destined to give considerable historical significance to various small churches then a-building—if hardly, even so, to make them much worth looking at. The new "science" of ecclesiology had been born and the gospel of Pugin was rapidly being recast in Anglo-Catholic form. In 1839 a group of young men at Cambridge founded the Cambridge Camden Society and issued their first pamphlet. This was called, modestly enough, *Hints for the Practical Study of Ecclesiastical Antiquities* (1839, 2d ed. 1840, 3d ed. 1842, 4th ed. 1843). The banding together of a few university undergraduates under their tutor to study medieval churches appeared singularly unlikely to affect the current practice of architecture. But the new ecclesiology, which the Society at once began to formulate into a system of rigid doctrines, soon made church design no matter of taste but practically one of Anglo-Catholic dogma. The Camdenians' study of medieval churches early led them to note that most of those extant had, over the centuries, been much altered from their original condition. The fact that these shrines were then being used in a very Protestant and not at all a "Catholick" way, moreover, seemed still graver to young men who were even more inflamed by the theological tracts of the Oxford Movement than by the architectural writings of Pugin.

The membership in the Society—which rose from 8 to 180 within the first year—was in fact more preoccupied with religious controversy than with architecture. Whether or not the members were planning to take orders, it seemed to them a matter of religious and not merely (as we would say today) of cultural and humanistic importance that the old Gothic churches should be physically restored. Even more important was the Camdenians' insistence that churches should again be used exactly in the way Camdenians supposed them to have been used in Archbishop Laud's time before the Civil War— or, better (though more dubious polemically), before Henry VIII's Reformation. From this essentially antiquarian position it was but a step to interfering —at first usually where family connections made it easy—with the arrangement of various churches newly built or still in construction.

The Oxford Tractarians had not taken much interest in architecture. The tiny church of SS. Mary and Nicholas that John Henry Newman built at Littlemore near Oxford in 1834–36 had neither aisles nor chancel. Costing only £1,011, it was 60 feet by 25 feet and was based on the chancel only of the church at Moreton Pinckney, Northamptonshire, of which Newman's brother-in-law the Reverend Thomas Mozley was the incumbent. Mozley himself made drawings of his chancel and these were handed to an unnamed Oxford architect (to whom £46 was paid) for execution. H. J. Underwood's *Church of St. Mary the Virgin, Littlemore, Oxfordshire* (1840) illustrates the modest and quite unecclesiological edifice Newman built. (Joseph Clarke [1798–1861] in 1848 added a chancel and a southwest tower and made alterations in the nave, so that the original design is now completely denatured; he even added Purbeck marble shafts in the arcading, a relatively early instance of this sort of "structural polychromy.") It was not at Oxford but at Cambridge that 19th-century religious fervor first sought an architectural outlet.

In 1839 Viscount Beresford together with other subscribers had begun, as landowners were continually doing, the construction of a small district church at Kilndown in the parish of Gouldhurst in Kent, employing no architect at all but using detail that was vaguely Gothic. The original edifice might have been modeled on one of the simpler designs in Hamilton's *Designs for Rural Churches* (1836), but more probably something even more rudimentary served—perhaps, indeed, there was no proper model at all. In many instances in the 18th century the patron's specifications and the builder's own decayed village traditions had been responsible for quite attractive Gothick work. Whatever the source of the design, there were no chancel and no aisles any more than at Newman's Littlemore; the roof, moreover, was of a sensible low pitch like that of most Georgian meetinghouses.

Anthony J. Beresford Hope (1820–1887), later known as A. J. B. Beres-ford-Hope, one of the original members of the Camden Society, was a younger son of Thomas Hope. That *richissime* Regency connoisseur, descendant of a Dutch banking family, was the author of several popular treatises on furniture and costume design. He also wrote a general history of architecture, published posthumously in 1835, in which the illustrations, surprisingly enough, were mostly Gothic—and Italian Gothic at that. Beres-ford-Hope was also a relative through his mother (a daughter of Lord Decies, Archbishop of Tuam) of Lord Beresford, who somewhat later married the mother, a widow after Thomas Hope's death in 1831. In 1840 young Hope induced Lord Beresford to allow some modification of his new church. (As Hope was already very rich after the death of his father and later extremely generous in paying for churches, one may hope that he footed the bills even though he was not yet of age.)

Anthony Salvin was an architect of the older generation who came of a good family in County Durham. Already in the late 20's he had achieved something of a reputation as a builder of Tudor country houses and he was, of course, already at work on Harlaxton (Fig. I 9). So it was to Salvin, not to the Roman Pugin, that Hope turned to obtain a design for a solid stone altar raised on three steps, the first "Catholick" feature introduced at Christ Church, Kilndown. (The Archbishop of Canterbury was perhaps less on the lookout for Popery than the Bishop of Salisbury.) On the advice of Whewell, who was considered an authority on Gothic because of his book, stained glass was also ordered from Munich for the east windows which were installed in 1841. This glass was later published in a monograph, *Abbildungen der Glasgemälde in der Salvator-kirche zu Kilndown in der Grafschaft Kent* (Munich, 1852).

Most significantly, to make up for the lack of a structural chancel, a space some 15 feet deep at the east end of the church was set off as a sanctuary by means of a screen. This was based on that of Beaulieu Abbey and had been designed by an architect considerably younger than Salvin but destined to be more famous. He was R. C. Carpenter, who came as close as anyone to being the Anglican Pugin in the late 40's. Another still younger man, William Butterfield (1814–1900), who would play a sort of super-Pugin role in a later act of the Victorian Gothic drama, designed a brass lectern and two coronas, probably a year or so later than the initiation of the reforms in 1840. Among the lot of them the little church was in time completely reorganized ritually although without any actual structural changes. Stone sedilia and oak stalls were installed in the chancel space east of Carpenter's screen; a stone pulpit (by Carpenter and copied, like the screen, from the one at Beaulieu) was

109

corbeled out from the south wall of the nave; finally the low-pitched roof was masked externally by a stone parapet pierced with trefoils, and a stone lychgate was built to lead into the churchyard.

This work was not all completed in a few years; throughout his life Beresford-Hope continued to take an active interest in his stepfather's church. The interior walls, however, were all covered with painted decorations by Roos and Willement by 1845. In this little Kentish scene there first appeared several of the new characters who were to dominate the church-building drama for the next two decades—not Roos and Willement, of course, who were decorators only, but Hope himself and Butterfield and Carpenter (although the last died in 1855).

While all this activity was going on at Kilndown, other landowners were taking thought to the new "church-principles," for thus they were now called in Charles Anderson's *Ancient Models; or, Hints on Church-building*. In the edition of this modest work which was issued in 1841—there had apparently been an earlier edition in 1840—the author was able to discuss some ten churches which he could approve, at least at this early state of ecclesiology; few would have passed muster even a year or two later. Most of them were nominally Early English in style; three were Norman and one Tudor. (None, however, was Decorated, it is worth noting.) Most of these churches had been designed by architects of the older generation of whom only Ambrose Poynter had previously had much experience or success with medieval design.

Poynter's church at Scofton, near Worksop, in Nottinghamshire, built entirely of stone "at the sole expense of George Savile Foljambe, Esq.," the local landowner, seems to be the most elaborate if neither the largest nor the most correct of the group. It is Norman and provided with aisles, chancel, and west tower. Internally the sanctuary is deeper than the slight eastward projection beyond the aisles indicates externally (Fig. IV 12). There is a gallery only at the west end, and in the nave are open seats, with stalls in the aisles. The cost, including the stained glass for the windows (probably from Munich) and the architect's commission, was £3,808; but the result was hardly the equal of some of Hamilton's Norman designs of 1836 (Fig. III 3). The other churches cost much the same, except for Newman's at Littlemore which, it will be recalled, cost only a little over £1,000.

Several of the churches praised by Anderson seem to have been the work of amateurs. For example, St. Matthew's, Otterbourne, in Hampshire, and the Anfield church nearby were from the designs of W. C. Yonge, who was a local squire not an architect. St. Matthew's, presumably just completed in 1841, has no aisles and a very short eastern arm. Very simply built of dark blue brick with trim of Caen stone, some third of the total cost of £3,850 went for the elaborate interior fittings. The funds were put up by Yonge himself, by Sir William Heathcote (who also paid the entire cost of the Anfield church, smaller but similar in style and construction), and by a Mr. Chamberlain. The principal interest of St. Matthew's, Otterbourne, is that the detail is Decorated though the church as a whole is not otherwise very Puginian (Fig. IV 13). Amateurs, however, were already becoming aware of their deficiencies and soon ceded the practice of "correct" church building to architects specializing in such work.

Among the professionals Poynter and most of his generation (as has been said) very soon fell behind the procession. George Wightwick, indeed, the Soane pupil who built the Tudor chapel at Bude in Devon for Sir Thomas Dyke Acland described by Anderson, was very shortly to appear as a very acid critic of the Camdenians and their architect friends. But one new name of significance is introduced in *Ancient Models*, that of Benjamin Ferrey (1810–1880). He was a pupil of the elder Pugin, two years older than his famous son, and destined later to be that son's first biographer. Ferrey's church at Compton Valence in Dorset, much praised by Anderson, was an old one, now merely "enriched and repaired"; that was a process, however, that only too often entailed a nearly complete rebuilding at the hands of ambitious Camdenian architects.

Ferrey had already begun to do country house and institutional work— most of it Tudor—and had laid out the new seaside resort of Bournemouth, building groups of Italian Villas and Tudor Cottages there also in the late 30's. In his long life Ferrey built more than fifty churches and restored at least as many old ones. His St. Mary's, Southwark, built in 1840–41, was praised at this time for its "discreet" design: It was said Ferrey had endeavored there "to produce effect rather by form than by decoration." Actually this is almost as dull an exercise in Early English as those being produced by the older church builders at this time; lacking a tower, it may be considered even duller (Fig. I 4). But it has aisles, a clerestorey, and transepts; while the chancel, if not very deep, is yet marked off by a break in the roof line and by flying buttresses at the chancel arch. St. Mary's is merely the tentative essay of an apt pupil. For all its complexity of mass the church shows little more grasp of the new possibilities of articulated composition than does Hadfield's Salford Cathedral (Fig. III 38). Ferrey's churches soon became more correct and more archaeologically plausible but they generally remained rather uninteresting and impersonal in character.

Ferrey's name is all but forgotten now; another Anglican church architect who came on the scene in these years was soon to be so successful that his name eventually became almost synonymous with Victorian Gothic. Sir George Gilbert Scott, although born in 1811, a year before Pugin, was des-

111

tined to outlive Pugin by more than a quarter century; and it was in the 50's and 60's after Pugin's death that he rose to nearly unchallenged professional primacy. His *Personal and Professional Recollections* were edited by his son, the second G. G. Scott, and published in 1879 the year after his death. They provide a fascinating account of a phenomenally busy life in architecture; but for all Scott's intelligence they do not persuade the reader, any more than do most of his buildings, that he had more than a middling talent. A modern account of his life and work would be a most worthwhile undertaking, for his career would provide a significant case study of what makes for worldly success in architecture. Scott's name will recur in these chapters; but no consecutive recounting of his achievements, such as was devoted to Pugin in the last chapter, would be relevant since he was not really so dominant a leader in the Early Victorian period as he and most of his later contemporaries believed. His major works belong to a period well beyond that covered in this book; in the 30's and 40's he was just making his reputation, and doing so in competition with other architects such as Carpenter and Butterfield who were better at Camdenian Gothic than he.

Scott's background was clerical; his father was a rector and his grandfather Thomas Scott the Biblical commentator. He was articled early to a minor architect, the elder James Edmeston, in London, and in Edmeston's office he met William B. Moffatt who was to be his partner through the first rather undistinguished decade of his building career. After leaving Edmeston, Scott worked briefly for the building firm of Grissell and Peto, later the contractors for the Westminster New Palace in its early stages, and then spent two years 1832–34 in the office of Sir Robert Smirke's pupil Henry Roberts, who was at that time building Fishmonger's Hall in London, his only monumental work.

Scott's opportunity came in 1834 with the Poor Law Act of that year requiring the construction of workhouses for the new Poor Law Unions into which the country was divided. At first he helped Sampson Kempthorne—an architect concerning whom little is known since he emigrated to New Zealand in 1841—in designing workhouses. Then, upon his father's death, he set up his own practice, shortly bringing in Moffatt as his partner. In the next ten years they designed altogether more than fifty workhouses; but we are concerned here with the beginnings of his career as a church architect. His first church, St. Nicholas's, Bailgate, in Lincoln, was built in the same year as Pugin's "first" church, St. Marie's, Derby, but with no such pretensions to medieval correctness as the latter. Scott was to disown St. Nicholas's in later years along with such other early churches of his as St. Mark's, King Edward's Road, Birmingham, which followed immediately after.

It would be kinder to draw a veil over these clumsy, fumbling edifices; not because of their plaster moldings, shallow chancels, and other purely ecclesiological sins for which Scott was so penitent later, but just on account of their abysmal dullness which more than rivals that of his workhouses. Yet St. Nicholas's—and following it several others—has its bald tower placed in that same northwest corner position which seemed a significant innovation of Pugin's at St. Wilfrid's, Hulme, actually begun a year later. As was to be so often true in his later career, Scott already knew in his twenties how to pick up a novelty early—if he didn't actually introduce it himself as he may well have done in this instance—and then to plug it hard if rarely with any real distinction. His first corner towers are not well related to the massing of his churches; they have no characteristic outline and provide no really effective accent. Yet when they were new the piquancy of their asymmetrical placing naturally attracted a great deal of attention.

Scott had not as yet studied, much less accepted, the gospel of Pugin; indeed it was only gradually being revealed in Pugin's successive books. Although Scott found grace for a few brief years in the sight of the Camdenians after he absorbed Pugin's ideas, he was by nature not an extremist but an opportunist. His earliest successes in what was (ironically) the very lucrative poorhouse field indicated this quality as clearly as did the way he bowed to Lord Palmerston in the long row about the "style" of the Foreign Office, a famous episode just outside the period covered by this book. But no revolution would succeed if its leading figures all had to be fanatics; the surest indication of the immanent success of a new movement is the hurried attempt of opportunists like Scott to land early on the bandwagon. Discussion of Scott's well-heralded "arrival" as a church architect may better be postponed for a few pages, however.

The year 1841 was an important one in Pugin's life as we have seen. It was important for the young Anglican architects also, not so much for new churches begun as for the crystallization of doctrine that then occurred. Pugin's *True Principles* and his *Dublin Review* articles made both his theories and his executed work more accessible to interested students. The initiation of the Camden Society's journal *The Ecclesiologist* provided a lively forum for the discussion of the virtues and vices of the new churches as the young fanatics saw them. The Society's next two pamphlets, which appeared this year also, *A Few Words to Church Builders* (with two more editions by 1844) and *A Few Words to Churchwardens on Churches and Church Ornaments*, were intended to indicate how architects, clergymen, and others responsible for the care of churches might avoid the acid strictures of these energetic young reformers. There were two versions of the latter pamphlet: "No. 1 Suited for Country Parishes," of which no less than 14 editions were needed by 1846, and "No. 2 Suited to Towns and Manufacturing Parishes," of which there were (significantly) only half as many editions, six over the years 1841–43 and a seventh in 1871. The new 1841 edition of Anderson's *Ancient Models,* to which reference has already been made, listed in an added chapter some of the things already accomplished in the previous year or two by the Society and their friends, an unimpressive record as we have seen.

There was still much confusion about "style." In the first number of the *Ecclesiologist* Norman was recommended to the Bishop of New Zealand for new parish churches; yet Wild's Christ Church, Streatham, was strongly condemned for its Italian Romanesque character. A principle of stylistic nationalism was rapidly being established in the neomedieval field. As the practice of Ferrey and others throughout the 40's indicates, there was by no means so rigid a principle of chronological limitation of style, even if from this time on the Decorated was definitely preferred to earlier, and above all to later, styles for emulation.

Perhaps the handsomest church begun in this year 1841 by any other architect than Pugin was not Gothic at all; it was also neither Anglican nor Roman Catholic. The Great Thornton Street Chapel in Hull by F. H. Lockwood (1811–1878) and Thomas Allom (1804–1872) is an octostyle Corinthian temple of fine Harehill freestone with subsidiary side pavilions linked by colonnaded screens (Fig. IV 11). The *Illustrated London News,* 27 May, 1843, illustrating the edifice before its opening in August, remarked that "the design presents a striking improvement upon the general style and character of places of worship not belonging to the Established Church [showing] the great advance of refinement and taste in the Fine Arts observable among Dissenters." Although executed at an estimated cost of only £7,000, the Hull Independent Chapel with its 160-foot front and its auditorium holding 1,800 put all Anglican churches of the period, except such an example of private beneficence as St. Mary's, Wilton, to shame.

But is it Victorian? Perhaps not; yet a very similar temple model, increasingly large in scale, coarse in detail, and without the side pavilions, continued well into the 60's to be a favorite with Dissenters. The most comparable Nonconformist church, an equally distinguished example of a Classical temple executed in fine masonry, was built for the Irvingites on St. Augustine's Bank in Bristol in 1839–40 by Richard Shackleton Pope (1781–1884). (This was later acquired by the Roman Catholics and is now known as St. Mary's-on-the-Quay.) Is it also non-Victorian because it is Classical? In Chapter X, which is devoted to Early Victorian corporate architecture, it will become evident that Classical design can definitely be Victorian in secular work. And, to the mind of the Camdenians, Nonconformist churches were hardly religious edifices at all but merely lecture halls.

114

English Dissenters had by no means entirely eschewed medieval forms in Late Georgian times any more than they had in America. Edward Irving's own church by Tite in Tavistock Place near Regent Square in London, built as early as the 20's with a façade "reduced" from that of York Cathedral, has already been mentioned. The Cavendish Chapel, completed in 1840 at Ramsgate by James Wilson of Bath, was Norman; and there are other examples dating from the years between. But the association of the new excitement about revived Gothic with the Roman Catholic Pugin and the markedly Anglo-Catholic character of the Camdenians' doctrinal position could not but discourage Nonconformists from participating very actively in the new movement. Thus they tended to turn back after 1840 toward Classical models, if for a few years only.

Ritualistic sacramentality must obviously be either so meaningless or so obnoxious to Nonconformists that it is surprising their antipathy to Gothic did not last. It is a remarkable testimony to the strength of the ecclesiological movement (and perhaps to a certain snobbery among the wealthier Dissenters) that Gothic was so frequently accepted as an appropriate style for important chapels after the mid-40's. The less tendentious Norman was, however, generally preferred; so it was likewise through much of the 40's by Anglican parishes and individual patrons who wished to dissociate themselves from the Tractarian party. Thus variations of neomedieval style served to symbolize variations in the theological position of different churches as determined by their incumbents, their patrons, or their parishioners. But it is wrong to suppose that it was always the "Highest" Anglicans in the early 40's who got the highest quality of design as is admittedly true after about 1845.

To compare the Camdenian Carpenter's St. Stephen's, Selly Park Road, Birmingham, perhaps the most "correct" example of the 14th-century English parish church model being built in 1841 by any architect other than Pugin himself (or so we are told), with Walker Rawstone's very Low Church St. Jude's, Manningham, at Bradford of 1841–43 is perhaps unfair. St. Stephen's was built of so soft a red sandstone that Carpenter's work has largely melted away and must therefore be taken on faith as the earliest example of his considerable talent. (The church was also much modified later by W. H. Bidlake [1862–1938]; for even the most correct of Early Victorian churches rarely satisfied the ritual needs or the visual tastes of the next generation.) But it is at least probable that St. Jude's was always as good a building. Its short transeptal aisles and its shallow apse, the well-lighted nave, the construction of good Yorkshire freestone throughout, and the rich and quite plausible Norman ornament about the east end provide a considerably more attractive and not less worthy or typical example of the earliest Victorian church architecture (Fig. IV 14). The actual purposes of a contemporary church were well served here; the structure was solid and not ill proportioned. If it seems today somewhat barren internally, so for that matter do Carpenter's churches, even those that have remained in better physical condition than the one in Birmingham.

There was no long-term future for churches like Rawstone's although many more of them were to be built throughout the 40's. They deserve, just the same, a critical attention hitherto denied them. Their plans are no more open than those to which the High Anglicans were to return in the 60's; and the galleried transeptal aisles flanking the east end provide a convenient enlargement of the area within range of both service and sermon that is available for the congregation. (This the American H. H. Richardson [1838–1886] realized when planning his epoch-making churches, also Romanesque in their detailing, at Boston, Massachusetts, in the early 70's.) The carved ornamentation on these Norman churches often has a vigor and a justness of scale that is lacking in most contemporary Gothic work. Their interiors, however, would profit even more than the standard Gothic models of the day from sympathetic redecoration.

In 1842 and 1843 many prominent new churches were Norman or Lombardic including one or two of the best. These were designed not only by older men, such as Henry Edward Kendall (1776–1875) and the elder John Foster of Bristol, but by Ferrey, Henry Clutton, and others who were just beginning their careers. Kendall's St. John Evangelist's, Harrow Road, in Kensal Green or J. D. Hopkins' church in Argyle Square, Gray's Inn Road, both in London, un-aisled but with two-towered west façades, were pathetically pretentious and tawdry like Tite's Irvingite church; Ferrey's are no more interesting than his contemporary Gothic work. But the tall, round-arched nave arcades of John Foster and Son's St. Mary's, Bute Street, in Cardiff (consecrated 1843), with their big round columns and Byzantinesque capitals, already suggest the bold scale and vigorous detail of the younger John Foster's fine secular work of the 60's in Bristol.

Even the reviewer in the *Ecclesiologist*, 8, 254–255, found this "Romanesque-Byzantine" edifice superior to John Shaw's Christ Church, Watney Street, which has been mentioned earlier, and the many other Norman churches in the East End of London, perhaps because the apse is rib vaulted and has a quite inappropriate blind arcade of Early English character. The obnoxious galleries in the aisles are now gone from St. Mary's, but the roof is still as "miserably flat" as when the writer in the *Ecclesiologist* first so described it. The presence of an elaborate but blind west portal in the two-towered eastern street front immediately behind the hidden apse is as disconcerting to 20th- as to 19th-century Functionalists. The interior would

116

profit from tactful redecoration—presently the polychromy in the apse is too heavy and rich while the nave walls and ceiling are badly faded and stained. The exterior is of a pleasant gray-green random ashlar with cream-colored Bath stone trim. It is the unsympathetic exteriors of grimy stock brick which make most Norman churches of the 40's in London so inferior to this Cardiff example. But there are exceptions.

Clutton's St. Jude's, Old Bethnal Green Road, in London (opened in 1846), is a blasted ruin today yet there is still a remarkable grandeur in its vast cruciform mass. This mass is also effectively elaborated by a great semi-decagonal apse and by two towers placed at the western transept angles. The simple, rather German, sort of Lombardic detail is also very suitable for execution in stock brick. The interior with its ribbed vaults (executed doubt-less in plaster) has an amazing breadth and dignity of scale and a minimum of nonstructural detail (Fig. IV 15). Clutton himself, and perhaps others as well, may have recalled the effect of this fine interior when the reaction against excessive articulation of interior spacial volumes came in the 50's and 60's. Clutton, in fact, was to be more prominent in that later period and his best work of the early 50's has already ceased to be typically Early Victorian. Eventually he even won the plaudits of the *Ecclesiologist* although he was never a Camdenian himself and worked more for Catholics than for Anglicans.

When the designs for St. Jude's were shown at this time at the Royal Academy Exhibition of 1845 the *Ecclesiologist's* reviewer noted it only as "deserving of severe condemnation." Two years later (8, 317–318) the Society's view was already more generous: "with all its faults and irregularities, this church looks better than many a badly attempted Pointed Church." But their critic went on to say that this did not "excuse Mr. Clutton for his adoption of German Romanesque." Within another year, however, the *Ecclesiologist* was to be recommending the brick churches of Germany for emulation, although of course only the Gothic ones (see Chapter XVII). From the early 50's on Clutton's cosmopolitanism paralleled the later Camdenian modes. His name and his work, beginning with St. Jude's, deserve a much higher reputation than they have been granted by historians of the Gothic Revival.

A tiny church at Llanymynech, near Oswestry in Shropshire, by R. Kyrke Penson (1816–1886) cost only £1,450 and held but 480 (Fig. I 5). Although St. Agatha's was praised at the time for being "pure Norman" and also for the then rather novel use of terra-cotta trim, its interest today is chiefly the asymmetrical location of the tower part-way back on the north side; for most Early Victorian churches of Norman design still preserved a Georgian symmetry. But it was not with such churches that young Anglican architects in the years 1842–44 during which St. Agatha's Llanymynech was building first began to vie directly with Pugin. The better known new work was now all Gothic.

At St. Giles's, Camberwell, Scott and Moffatt at last had a major opportunity to show what Anglicans could do with a big freestanding Gothic parish church in a London suburb if given adequate financial support (Figs. IV 19–20). Ferrey's Christ Church, Endell Street, in London itself, indicated what could be done with less ample funds and the more restricted opportunities of a confined urban site (Fig. IV 18). In the provinces St. Saviour's, Leeds, built by John Macduff Derick (d. 1861) for Dr. Pusey was as ambitious (at least in intention) as St. Giles's, Camberwell (Fig. IV 17). And in the country Edmund Sharpe (1809–1877) at Lever Bridge, near Bolton-le-Moors in Lancashire, was able to exceed in the richness of his Decorated detail anything Pugin had yet built, and without excessive expenditure, by using terra cotta for the entire edifice (Fig. IV 22).

Other London churches, Gothic in design and of considerable pretention, were begun in these years, such as Christ Church, Westminster (in Caxton Street), by Poynter and St. Michael's, Pimlico, by the second Thomas Cundy (1790–1867), the Grosvenor Estate surveyor. But in their confused massing and ill-proportioned detail these serve chiefly to show how hard it was for the older men to learn Pugin's lessons. In the provinces and in the country Gothic churches more or less up to Camdenian standards were now being built in profusion, however. They illustrate how sharp a change of style had already taken place in the five years since the beginning of Victoria's reign, yet they rarely indicate that it had been altogether a change for the better. Many modest country churches by Carpenter and Scott and Ferrey are, of course, unexceptionable despite their extreme dullness. In Basil Clarke's words, "from a quarter of a mile away [they are] pleasing to the eye and almost indistinguishable from old buildings. But the difference is obvious when one approaches very closely." Even that is perhaps too generous an appraisal for most; usually they are less interesting to visit than those of the first third of the century.

Yet even excepting the principal churches of the day by Scott and Ferrey and Derick in London and in Leeds (to which we shall be returning shortly and which certainly merit the considerable attention they have always received from writers on the Gothic Revival) by no means all Gothic churches built in the early 40's are retardataire, or boringly dull, or shrinkingly modest. In Leamington, for example, the Reverend John Craig began in 1843 the reconstruction of All Saints' parish church at cathedral scale and with considerable elaboration of plan and detail.

The nave as planned was to be 130 feet long, 32 feet wide (with 10-foot aisles), and 75 feet high. Craig also intended to have a central tower 120 feet high with a spire above rising to 250 feet. Only 50 feet of the nave were opened in 1844 but the chancel was complete by the next year. The north transept, with a gallery, was opened in 1849; the tower at its corner was finished by 1852. After that little more was added, however, for a long time. Craig broke with his professional aide, a draftsman from Coventry named Mitchell, and became so deeply involved financially in his ambitious project that the bishop had to intervene. The south transept was not built until the later 60's nor was the nave completed, with the tall southwest tower and the very dry west front by Sir Arthur Blomfield (1829–1899), before the beginning of the present century.

The breadth and the height of the nave and the great expanse of the windows in the polygonal apse, reputedly copied by Craig from Cologne Cathedral, are most impressive (Fig. IV 16). The detail of all Craig's work is surprisingly literate, while the very dislocation of the various parts produces something of the variety of form characteristic of a real medieval church. Thus the effect, while somewhat incoherent, is anything but dull. But the day of the amateur church designer was coming to a close; and of all the various methods of financing Victorian church building the one least likely to produce a satisfactory result was Craig's, in effect a private speculation in the sale of sittings.

All Saints' has received little attention from historians, perhaps because its confused story is so difficult to disentangle. But the interior, at least, offers a major specimen of Early Victorian church architecture beside which many of the churches most praised by contemporaries seem very inconsequential. In its great size and in some of its features—the German apse windows and the transept window borrowed from Rouen—it is more continental than English. That helps to explain why it was received with so little favor in the 40's when it was being built. To the casual observer Blomfield's west front so completely masks Craig's work that few visitors to Leamington are aware of what lies behind.

The original design for St. Giles's, Camberwell Church Street, was submitted by Scott and Moffatt in a competition held immediately after the old parish church burned down early in the year 1842. This was nearly as ambitious as Dr. Craig's intentions or those of Pugin for his various cathedrals and abbeys. As Scott was well aware, an appropriation of £20,000 from the parish rate had been voted for erecting the new edifice. Since the insurance money received for the loss of the old church was also available the building fund would amount to considerably more than the Herberts were spending on St. Mary's, Wilton. The church as first projected in the architects' winning design was to have been much larger than St. Mary's, holding 2,000, and was

119

furthermore to be crowned with a central tower rising more than 225 feet; a successful protest against the high parish rate, however, made necessary a reduction in the appropriation. Scott, always obliging, then prepared a more modest design with an interior intended to hold 1,500. This was eventually built for only £ 14,500, the precise figure he had estimated. Such a feat is so remarkable in any period that this fact alone goes far to explain Scott's great popularity with his Victorian clients. Nevertheless, unlike most of Pugin's churches, St. Giles's does not show the effects of parochial parsimony (Fig. IV 19). It is very solidly built of Kentish rubble, faced inside with Streaton stone from Yorkshire, and trimmed with Caen stone; moreover, the work was not delayed but went forward rapidly to a consecration late in 1844.

The interior disposition at St. Giles's met at the time with the full approval of the Camdenians (Fig. IV 20). In the main it might well have been approved by Pugin as well, whose most fervent admirer Scott now professed himself to be. The chancel was deep, deeper indeed than in many of Pugin's churches—Eastlake calls it "one of the first chancels of proper length." The altar was of stone, but it was still a "table" (i.e., not solid) in order to meet Protestant objections although raised on several steps to provide visibility and liturgical honor. The reredos (altar screen in the terminology of the time) was a richly cusped and crocketed arcade; its side panels were filled with the Commandments and the center arch with a cross—therefore not too Catholic, yet not too Protestant. The galleries in the aisles (since removed by later ecclesiologists) destroyed any resemblance to Scott's presumptive medieval models but they likewise indicated his canny ability to come to terms with his clients. Fortunately for Scott the full anathema of the Camdenians had not yet been unleashed against galleries; the reviewer in the *Ecclesiologist,* while rather disturbed by an "incorrectly placed" baptismal font, found the galleries "the least offensive . . . we have seen." Moreover, even the sort of Gothic detail used seems to indicate Scott's genius for compromise, being late 13th century of the time of transition between the Early English and the Decorated. Henceforth this period was always to provide Scott's preferred models when these were English and not continental.

The nave columns are alternately round and octagonal with boldly, though not very sensitively, carved capitals. The arched trusses of the wooden roof are simple and sturdy. There is a rib vault (we may assume of masonry) under the crossing tower and a polygonal ceiled wooden roof over the chancel. Although the church is 153 feet long and 87 feet wide at the transepts it has little sense of spaciousness. With all its real size, and despite Scott's solidly professional command of his worthy materials, the interior has in fact little positive quality of any sort. It is not squat or even particularly barren; but there seems to be none of that conscious mastery in relating various spacial volumes that gives distinction to Pugin's best work.

The exterior is considerably happier; for the chancel, aisles, and transepts build up very effectively to the solid central tower with its octagonal stone spire only some 20 feet lower than the original design proposed (Fig. IV 19). Perhaps it would not seem excessively ornamented (as the *Ecclesiologist* complained) were it not for the strong tonal contrast between the grimy walling stone and the cleaner Caen stone trim. The walls and buttresses are solid, the tracery is well scaled, and the grouping of the masses is much better handled than is that of the voids within. Yet even the exterior does not have any serious archaeological plausibility nor does it have much individual flavor. It actually seems rather commonplace today; but that is in part a measure of its contemporary success. The model of St. Giles's was so much followed by Scott and by many other architects when building large parish churches in this decade and the next that St. Giles's, although the real original, seems today but another instance of a ubiquitous type.

Ferrey's Christ Church, St. Giles, in Endell Street near High Holborn, was completed about a year later than the Camberwell church, but it exists no more. Financed by the various church-building societies of the time, with additional assistance from several individual benefactors, it was intended primarily to serve the poor of this notoriously congested district. Ferrey was able to provide a church two-thirds the size of St. Giles's, Camberwell, for a small part of the cost. (To do so, of course, he also had to include galleries.) To judge from contemporary wood engravings (Fig. IV 18) it was externally very like Pugin's St. Mary's at Stockton-on-Tees (Fig. III 23) but with the addition of aisles; in the vigor of its vertical proportions it was even superior, although presumably not in the quality of the detail. The "style" was outright Early English, as that of Ferrey's St. Mary's, Southwark had been, and for economy's sake there was little carved work. However inappropriate the markedly asymmetrical design may have been to the solid rows of contiguous houses, it must certainly have been quite striking. For some time it was the most monumental structure in the new street which Pennethorne, as Architect to the Commissioners of Woods and Forests, had just cut through the horrid slums of St. Giles. Interestingly enough, the reviewer in the *Ecclesiologist*, 6, 61, was rather lukewarm about the church. He even thought "the architect might have derived some useful notions from foreign town churches," although he hastened to add that he was "not of course intending to recommend such novelties." The significance of this suggestion, of course, is its deviation from the nationalistic bigotry then at its peak in Camdenian circles.

St. Saviour's, Cavalier Hill, Leeds, was an ambitious church begun by that same Dr. Edward B. Pusey who had been one of the earliest Tractarian leaders in the 30's (Puseyite, indeed, is frequently used as a synonym for Tractarian). On a high site to the east of the city, in an outlying region perhaps not yet as run down as it is today, Pusey and Derick projected a great cruciform edifice of Decorated design for which the cornerstone was laid 14 September 1842. Slow in building because of financial stringency, it was opened, incomplete, in October 1845. (The Pusey Chapel was added in 1890 while the tall crossing tower was not completed before the present century.) In part because there is so little carved ornament, St. Saviour's does not have the complacent professionalism of Scott's St. Giles's, Camberwell; it also lacks the strong, if obvious, silhouette of Ferrey's Christ Church. But the high narrow nave and the very deep chancel of equal height, together with the great windows at the east and west ends—the latter designed by Pugin, as is also one of the transept windows—seem to express a deeper religious sentiment (Fig. IV 17). St. Saviour's is in some ways a primitive of the High Victorian—not in obvious ways, but in its more intense emotional conviction. Even Pugin had hardly achieved so churchly a church, and it is therefore not quite typical of the period in which it was begun.

Derick never again repeated the promise of this church at Leeds. Later he seems to have settled in Ireland and thence he is supposed to have emigrated to the United States where no trace of his activities has been found.

Yet one other Derick church, in building at the same time as St. Saviour's, may well be illustrated. His Memorial Church in Colabah in Afghanistan (Fig. IV 21) will serve to emphasize that long before Victoria became Empress of India the sun had ceased to set on the Victorian Gothic; for its dominion already extended by 1850 from San Francisco eastward to Hong Kong. Even the Pacific Islands, for that matter, are not without characteristic monuments of 19th-century Anglican ecclesiology. This church, built "in memory of those who fell in the wars of Scinde and Afghanistan" the *Illustrated London News*, 6, 68, informed its readers, "will form no mean specimen of the architectural arts of the home country . . . The design is a modification, on a plain and cheap principle, of the florid Gothic; a style admirably adapted to the climate, and calculated to have a good effect in the midst of the *florid* scenery of India." The writer found the entrance "too small" and the substructure "much too slight and mean." "The purpose of the church, however, disarms criticism," he said—and disarmed let it remain at this distance in time and space.

Edmund Sharpe's Lever Bridge church, about a mile from Bolton-le-Moors, is also in florid Gothic (Fig. IV 22). St. Stephen's, built in 1842–45, is not very correct ecclesiologically, having no aisles and only a shallow chancel. But the technical innovations in the construction attracted a great deal of attention; a model of it was even shown at the Great Exhibition in 1851. Various synthetic materials for ornament had been used in architecture since the late 18th century. Penson was already using terra cotta for the Norman detail on his inexpensive stone church at Llanymynech. Here the whole church, including the pulpit, the organ screen, and even the benches, was built of baked clay and in a style more properly called florid than Derick's "plain and cheap" church in India. The west front culminates in an openwork octagonal spire rather like that at Freiburg-in-Breisgau. The so-called Ladyshore terra cotta used at Lever Bridge was made from a special fire clay found in the nearby colliery of John Fletcher; he was the chief promoter as well as the largest subscriber to the venture and had proposed that this novel material be tried.

St. Stephen's held 350 and cost £2,600 which was about half or even less of what such an edifice would have cost if built with equivalent elaboration in stone. But it was immediately dubbed the "Pot Church" and being thus derided was little emulated. The tendency of the Early Victorian period, at least in church building, was to reject all materials not hallowed by ancient usage, largely on irrelevant ethical grounds. Early Victorian carving, particularly that of a florid order, is rarely very appetizing; but to cast similar ornament in iron or mold it in clay for ecclesiastical use was felt to be somehow immoral, even by men who were hardly aware of Pugin's doctrines.

In its floridity the Lever Bridge church is exceeded only by the Scott Monument in Edinburgh (Fig. IV 29). This is built entirely of stone and cost £15,650 (more than five times what the terra-cotta church cost), exclusive of the statue of Sir Walter himself but including the sculptured figures of his heroes and heroines. In the competition for this structure, which was held in 1836, Rickman received the first prize, Charles Fowler (1791–1867) the second, and an Edinburgh carpenter turned architect, E. Meikle Kemp (1795–1844), the third. In 1838 the local competitor received the commission; work did not begin until 1840 however. Structurally complete by Kemp's death in 1844, the monument with all its statues in place was not dedicated until the summer of 1846. The stained glass was introduced into the windows considerably later still.

Debatably Early Victorian, because of the pre-Victorian date of the original design, the Scott Monument is a very exceptional edifice even less characteristic of the period than Sharpe's church. The prototypical monument of these years was Gilbert Scott's Martyrs' Memorial in Oxford (Fig. IV 24), a "neat" and "chaste" copy of a 14th-century Eleanor cross. This was completed in 1841 after an unseemly quarrel between the "Protestant" and "Catholic" parties of the Established Church in which Pugin actively participated, although not an Anglican at all.

Sharpe built one more terra-cotta church in the mid-40's, Holy Trinity, Platt Lane, at Rusholme outside Manchester, which was erected in 1844. The founder and donor was a member of the Worsley family, Lords of the Manor of Platt, who became an Anglican at that time (his family having been Independents since the 17th century) because the local Independent chapel had turned Unitarian. Despite the extremely Low Church services for which it was intended and which have been maintained ever since, Holy Trinity is much more correct in plan than Lever Bridge, with a relatively deep chancel and broad side aisles (Fig. IV 25). The tall spire, moreover, shows no continental influence. Sharpe used rather less detail this time throughout—in part for technical reasons—and the style here is the regular Late or Curvilinear Decorated rather than the fancier "florid" of St. Stephen's. The church is in excellent condition, having been restored in 1891 and 1906 and the spire rebuilt in 1911, always with intelligent respect for the original design. What seem today like very Low Church accessories, including a 17th-century secular table of oak used for Communion, are all as they originally were; strangely enough they were actually approved by the *Ecclesiologist*, 9, 137–138, as late as 1848. The only complaint then, and a sound one, was that terra cotta should not be made to imitate stone.

The favored style of the mid-40's, if architects had plenty of money to spend, was one or another sort of Late Decorated—so late sometimes that it approached the Perpendicular as closely as did the style of Chantrell's Leeds parish church although the total effect is usually rather different. An interesting example in the London area of the less ecclesiological sort of church of the day is Holy Trinity, Bishop's Road, Paddington, by Thomas Cundy II, which was opened in 1846 (Fig. IV 23). The rich, sharply pointed, western spire of this church, which rises to a height of 210 feet, forms a striking accent to the north seen between the rows of small Italianate houses in Gloucester Terrace which were built in these same years.

The *Ecclesiologist* found this church "very dangerous" and saw in it "nothing but a combination of discordant and impossible elements." That judgment reflects both the Camdenians' ascetic rejection of the visual appeal of tall slim proportions and their well-founded suspicion that "such monsters" (to use the *Ecclesiologist's* strong language) crossed the forbidden boundary line between the latest of Decorated and the Perpendicular. Holy Trinity was "too late" in a double sense: too late in style by a century and too late in its actual construction by about five years for that late style to be appreciated in advanced circles.

124

In the provinces, St. Alkmund's, Derby, by Isaac Henry Stevens (1810–1876), which was built opposite Pugin's St. Marie's in 1844–46, is dull but plausible archaeologically (Fig. IV 26). Since it lacked the uncanonically vertical proportions which give so lithe a shape to both the exterior and the interior of the Paddington church as well as its "late" detailing this was approved by the *Ecclesiologist;* it certainly has rather less appeal today than Cundy's church.

Both these edifices have their towers symmetrically placed at the west end as perhaps the greater number of churches still did. But the more piquant possibilities of other locations for the tower and spire were being increasingly tried out even, as we have seen at Llanymynech, on churches of Norman style. (Many modest country churches, of course, still had no more than a belfry carried on the western gable like Yonge's St. Matthew's, Otterbourne.) In the handling of towers the lead provided by Pugin at St. Wilfrid's, Hulme, and by Scott at St. Nicholas's, Lincoln, was followed by all sorts of architects. In 1843, for example, Alexander Dick Gough (1804–1871) and his partner in architectural crime Robert Lewis Roumieu (1824–1877) were called on to "modernize" Barry's St. Peter's, Islington, even though it was still not even a score of years old. Such men operated with no thought of Camdenian approval; yet beside their new Early English front, of most uncanonical proportions and very gawkily detailed, they placed a thin tower at one of the front corners with a tall toothpick of a spire.

St. Mark's, Swindon, was built in 1843–45 by Scott and Moffatt to serve the new railway town there. Costing some £5,500, this was intended to be something of a model church but not necessarily a Camdenian model church. Here the 140-foot tower was set outside the line of the north aisle and slightly back from the west front more or less in the position of Garbett's tower at Theale in the 20's. The reviewer in the *Ecclesiologist,* who otherwise approved the plan and the "Flowing" Decorated detail of St. Mark's, thought this placing was "affected and unnecessary" (Fig. IV 28). Down to the middle of the decade, at least, the position considered correct for the tower, if it were neither over the crossing nor in the middle of the west front, was in the plane of the west front at the end of the north or the south aisle. Again one finds Scott at Swindon being more original than is generally recognized since this placing within a few years became all too common. Still more exceptional—and most piquant in effect—is the small square bell turret rising at the right side of the west nave gable on Scott's St. Andrew's, Leeds (Fig. IV 27).

St. Andrew's, built in 1844–45, is in general one of Scott's best early churches, simple and solid, with a generous clerestorey and a very deep chancel. It was ornamented externally with continuous Early English ar-

125

cades, and the sturdily detailed interior was of pleasant, if not very individual, proportions. Because of the eclectic confusion of Scott's more conspicuous later works of the 50's and 60's it has too generally been forgotten that in the early 40's, when he was first making his reputation, he was undoubtedly one of the most carefully archaeological of neo-Gothic practitioners at the same time that he was one of the readiest to try out new ideas in composition. He was always quite competent professionally, even if uninspired, but in his early work this competence is easier to appreciate. Churches such as St. Giles's, Camberwell, St. Mark's, Swindon, or St. Andrew's, Leeds, may lack any strong personal flavor to modern eyes, but they are rarely as dull as are all but the very best by Ferrey or Carpenter. Scott also had the courage to maintain his independence of the Camdenians. Though he met their increasingly precise ritualistic demands when they actually employed him he was always ready to bend "Low" or "High" in his churches according to the doctrinal altitude of particular clients.

In 1844 Scott's partnership with Moffatt came to an end. He entered alone in that year the important foreign competition which first brought him international fame (see Chapter V). Henceforth, although he attracted to his office the ablest young men as his assistants, he worked nominally by himself. The figure of Moffatt is so dim, and his own later work so little known (Fig. VII 18) that it is difficult to judge how much of a contribution he made to the partnership with Scott even while it lasted. At best it would seem that Moffatt had been an executive assistant, particularly in their poorhouse practice, not a co-designer. It is probably not unjust, therefore, to discuss Scott, the youthful church designer of the early 40's, as an individual and not as a member of a partnership (as has in fact always been done hitherto). A few years later, when his practice began to be really large, there is more reason to give credit to other designers in his office, particularly as they were often young men of marked individuality whose personal tastes and abilities are known from their writings and their own later buildings.

The semiofficial list of Scott's nearly 750 works, prepared by his secretary and published in the *Builder*, 36, 343, begins only with 1847; but Basil Clarke has correctly stated that "1844 was the year of the beginning of a new era in Scott's professional life." Nevertheless there is no over-all break in the story of Early Victorian church architecture at this point to justify bringing this chapter to a close: So involved are the various threads of the plot that they cannot all be clearly cut off in 1844.

As we shall see, there were major alarums at the end of that year but they would not be intelligible without some backtracking to the previous year. The tale told so far corresponds in time with the period of Pugin's greatest activity at church building up to his return to assist Barry on the New Palace;

126

the new churches discussed in this chapter are those most strictly contemporary with his finest ecclesiastical work (St. Augustine's, Ramsgate, begun in 1846, being alone excepted). The next chapter takes up the story at the point where Pugin's leadership, now generally accepted in High Church circles, gradually passed into the hands of Anglican architects.

CHAPTER V: ANGLICAN AND

NONCONFORMIST CHURCHES

OF THE LATE 40'S

The years 1843 through 1845 were full of ecclesiological excitement which is rather more diverting to read about than the churches then being built are to visit. Pugin's publications of 1843 crystallized the image of his work for his own generation and rounded out his message. Yet these pronouncements seem likewise to have signalized the culmination of his direct influence and to have presaged already a decline in his reputation. Anglicans could not employ Pugin, in any case, because of his faith (or at least they did not, except for restorations and accessories; presumably he would not have accepted commissions to build them complete new churches). But Anglicans could now console themselves with the belief that designs could be obtained from such young men as Benjamin Ferrey or Gilbert Scott that would equal in correctness those of their revered but Romish master; very soon sophisticated Camdenians began to feel that from Carpenter and Butterfield they were getting an even better brand of revived Gothic.

Curiously enough the young Butterfield's first work, Highbury Chapel built in Bristol in 1842, had been erected for Dissenters and was also, at least nominally, Perpendicular. This is a difficult edifice to characterize, particularly as the tower and various other elements were added or modified by Edward William Godwin (1833–1886) in 1862. It is solid, it is simple, and its Perpendicular detail is quite stony, not crisp and metallic like Pugin's at St. Marie's, Derby, completed only three years earlier. Doubtless the later emendations affect the general impression, but this first church of Butterfield's is quite manifestly post-Georgian and, despite the Congregationalists for whom it was built, it has less flavor of the Dissenting conventicle about it than many Anglican churches of its period. Butterfield could receive no credit from Camdenians for designing a Nonconformist chapel and his reputation with them must have begun with his work—probably of about the same date —at Kilndown. By that time Carpenter's credit was well established, not to speak of Scott's and Ferrey's, even though the latter were never to be in the inner circle of the ecclesiologists in the way Butterfield, quite as much as Carpenter, was from this time on.

William Butterfield was born in 1814, two years after Pugin and Carpenter. From 1831 to 1834 he had been apprenticed to a London builder, Thomas Archer, after which he seems to have worked for some time in a Worcester office. His beginnings remain extremely obscure and it would be most desirable to know more of his activities before he designed Highbury Chapel. Richard Cromwell Carpenter's start is somewhat better documented but there are many gaps in the story of his early years also. Son of a Deputy Lord Lieutenant of Middlesex, he went to Charterhouse School and was then articled to John Blyth, an architect practicing in the City of London. At the age of 19, presumably while he was with Blyth, Carpenter made designs for a Gothic church which was, of course, never executed. He became a friend of Pugin very early and was probably the first of the younger architects to join forces with the Cambridge students in the Camden Society.

As with Butterfield, Carpenter's earliest known work seems singularly inappropriate to his later reputation; this is a whole square of terrace houses in Islington competently executed in a rather Georgian sort of Tudor (Fig. XIII 3). The work in Lonsdale Square is dated 1838; what, if anything, preceded it and what followed in the year or two before he joined the group Beresford-Hope marshaled to work at Kilndown is not clear. Considering his presumptive financial resources and his early reputation as an ecclesiologist much of his time in the late 30's may well have been devoted to the detailed study of ancient churches. Certainly he must have participated actively in the preparation of the propagandistic publications of the Camden Society before as well as after he began to remodel and restore churches himself. One at least imagines that Carpenter would have disavowed his terraces in Lonsdale Square almost immediately after they were built. St. Marie's, Derby, had been opened and the Camden Society founded the next year; these events might well have decided him to devote all his energies henceforth to ecclesiological study and the holy vocation of building "correct," not to say "sacramental," churches.

The Camdenians went on issuing and reissuing their pamphlets in the early 40's, as has been noted. Their *Few Words,* now become a great many, increasingly reached church builders to whom Pugin's frankly Roman doctrines would have been anathema. In 1843 came (in two successive editions) *A Few Words to the Parish Clerks and Sextons of Country Churches.* More important, however—and doubtless read by few parish clerks and sextons— was the translation published in this year by J. M. Neale and Benjamin Webb (1819–1885), the two founders of the Camden Society, of a 13th-century treatise on *The Symbolism of Churches and Church Ornaments* by Durandus,

Bishop of Mende. Medieval symbolism or "sacramentality" (to use the translators' own term) was expounded in a long introduction. Neale's and Webb's interpretation of sacramentality retains a certain perverse fascination as a complete Victorian system of architectural iconography, and builders of Catholic and Anglican churches must still consider some at least of its tenets.

The introduction included many other things besides a recondite theory of symbolism. Down to his death in 1841 the Quaker Rickman had been an active builder of Gothic churches for the Establishment; now it was revealed —and one almost means "revealed" in the doctrinal sense—to Neale and Webb that only architects who were good churchmen should build Anglican churches at all. "Church architects," moreover, should not soil their hands with secular commissions as Carpenter had done at Lonsdale Square; above all they must never work for Dissenters as Butterfield had done even more lately. But the production of new Anglican churches and the restoration of old ones were by this time so well supported that Anglican architects could now afford to accept these restrictions on their professional range of activity. Henceforth some of the ablest Victorian architects were content to build little but churches and associated edifices, of which a good many were required, of course, as Anglican religious life revived—vicarages, parish houses, schools, and even occasionally nunneries. Country houses, moreover, seem in practice not to have fallen under the Camdenian ban.

In America Richard Upjohn (1802–1878), an early convert to ecclesiology, solved the problem of working for Dissenters, who were there the immense majority, by refusing to design for them in Gothic; frequently, however, he housed their heterodox services in Lombardic edifices. He even made a project for a basilican chapel with a tall campanile for that headquarters of Socinian heresy Harvard College. There Professor Andrews Norton (the father of Charles Eliot Norton, Ruskin's friend), who was generally known as the "Unitarian Pope," would doubtless have occupied the episcopal throne at the rear of Upjohn's apse, had the chapel been built.

The additional restriction which Neale and Webb wished to impose on churchmen architects—that they should work *only* in the English Decorated Gothic of the 14th century—Upjohn did not accept even for Anglican churches. One of his best, St. Paul's, Baltimore, is basilican, doubtless because the incumbent and his services were too "Low" to rate Gothic in Upjohn's estimation. To such an exclusive stylistic position Pugin himself had only gradually come; but it was henceforth established ecclesiological law in the Higher Anglican circles. Actually, from 1845 on, probably the majority of new churches were Decorated in style, even though a good few were always Early English for economy's sake.

Few of the architects who received the support of the ecclesiologists continued any longer to design Norman or Perpendicular churches; yet Ferrey's Norman church at Enshanger, near Peterborough, was built in the early 50's, as was also his Perpendicular St. John's, Brixton, one of his best works. Architects less subservient to the Camdenians—which meant in practice those who worked chiefly for Low Church clients or were not specialists in church architecture—continued to build Norman and even Lombardic churches on occasion well after 1845; very few, however, still tried to use Perpendicular except E. B. Lamb. Thus by the end of the Early Victorian period in the early 50's the triumph of the English styles of the 13th and 14th centuries was all but complete. Other medieval modes were definitely obsolescent, though never entirely obsolete, quite as Classical forms had been among Anglicans since the 20's.

The Camdenians, like Pugin, were riding high in 1843. The proscriptions in the new editions of their pamphlets had grown stiffer and their authority was widely accepted. Protests there were from both architects and laymen, but the protestant (and Protestant) party was fighting a losing battle. Their utilitarian arguments were admittedly mundane; moreover, the compromise solutions they continued to propose did not offer such satisfying visual effects as the churches approved by the ecclesiologists. That fact was probably more important than anyone cared to admit at the time.

Earlier, when Georgian taste was being battered down, almost any novelties of style and composition which differed from the Grecian and Gothick church models of the first decades of the century seemed exciting and temporarily acceptable. Now a new Victorian taste had definitely been formed at least as regards ecclesiastical architecture; like any taste in process of crystallization this required its crude rules of thumb. Rather wide agreement now existed that churches should have something, at least, of that articulation of plan and mass Pugin and the Camdenians were providing, chiefly (they claimed) for nonvisual reasons. It was therefore convenient in practice to require that the particular models provided by English 14th-century parish churches (as they were then understood) should generally be followed.

The avowed members of the Camdenian "party," the 700 or so in the Camden Society itself with perhaps as many in the less fanatical Oxford Architectural Society and in various other diocesan archaeological societies, were supported by an immense body of "fellow travelers" among the clergy, the more pious churchmen, and the younger members of the architectural profession. But the strength of the Society's position as arbiter of taste—the fact that its architectural conclusions derived from its sacramental postulates—could also be its weakness.

A crisis was now at hand. In architecture the least trace of foreign influence was decried by most Camdenians; but with their perpetual insistence on the use of pre-Reformation churches as models and their insistent talk of the necessity of "Catholick" worship—not to speak of their active propaganda for the elaborate symbolism of a 13th-century French bishop—how could they avoid being accused of forming a "common front" with the Roman Catholic Pugin? Might not the restoration of ancient English churches to their 14th-century condition—an activity considerably more widespread than the building of "correct" new churches—be merely a subtle preparation for changing back the allegiance of the national church to Rome?

Newman did not become a Roman Catholic until 1845. But several of his associates had preceded him as converts a year or two earlier. The departure of these men from the Established Church seemed at last to expose what many had long suspected: The Oxford Movement and all the developments associated with it, including what might be called the "Cambridge Movement" in church architecture, had a goal as well as a direction, and that goal was Rome. Late in 1844 the storm broke. A sermon with the resounding title "The 'Restoration of Churches' Is the Restoration of Popery" was preached by the Evangelical Dr. Francis Close, a leader of Cheltenham society and later Dean of Carlisle, in Christ Church, Cheltenham, an edifice of markedly un-Camdenian character which had been built for him by the local architects W. C. and R. Jearrad in the late 30's. Close's sermon was soon widely distributed as a pamphlet in which his charge was "proved and illustrated from the authentic publications of the Cambridge Camden Society," or so he asserted. First the fellow travelers and then the Camdenians (after violent personal attacks on Close as a Nestorian heretic) broke and ran. The Oxford Society, in order to insist on its still Protestant position, dissociated itself from the more extreme views so frequently voiced in the *Ecclesiologist*; in 1845 the Camden Society itself cut all ties—at least nominally—with its own powerful and official organ of opinion.

By the next year, however, the crisis was suddenly over. The Camden Society changed its name to the Ecclesiological Society (including, in all frankness, the phrase "late Cambridge Camden" in its formal title) and began again to sponsor the *Ecclesiologist*. What I have called the "Cambridge Movement" went forward once more, as indeed did the Oxford Movement; but both were now clearly established as programs of reform within the Established Church, not underground routes to Rome.

The real triumph within the Anglican Church of the doctrines both of the Tractarians and of the ecclesiologists actually dates from this moment. Despite occasional conversions and local controversies over particular points of ritual or articles of church furniture the High Church party could no longer be pictured as a fanatical conspiracy whose members might at any moment

132

reveal their true Roman colors. Its members now constituted a weighty body in the religious life of the land; their ideals—particularly in architecture—were very broadly influential; and not alone in England but wherever there were Anglicans or even any other Protestants of British origin.

While all this was taking place among the Anglicans, the Nonconformists were beginning to follow the lead of the Establishment, surprising though that must seem. Perhaps snobbery influenced them, as has already been unkindly suggested; but the increasingly complete breakdown of 18th-century standards of taste (in the formation of which, as members of the still submerged middle classes, they had never very actively shared) can be represented as a cultural protest on the part of the new Liberal democracy against a Whiggish classicism. That is certainly partially true even if it has sometimes been too heavily stressed. Since the Camdenian Gothic was a creation of the new post-Georgian age, advanced Liberals could have a positive sympathy for the movement despite its "Catholic" connotations, just as the Liberals were those who put through Catholic enfranchisement in 1829.

Although there was an upheaval within the Church of Scotland at this time—in 1843—which broke up the homogeneity of Scottish religious life, the Presbyterians in Scotland were still the ruling class there. As it was the new Free Church, however, breaking away from the Establishment, that needed accommodation in the 40's (the existing church edifices remaining in the possession of the Presbyterian Establishment) the Free Church alone built new churches. Relatively more Protestant than the parent body the Free Church was, nevertheless, not afraid of the Gothic in the way of the more bigoted Baptists in Wales and in America. Although the old Gothic cathedrals belonged to the Church of Scotland, it is not really surprising that John T. Rochead (1814–1878) should have begun, immediately after the Dissolution of 1843, the large and prominent Regent Street Free Church in Glasgow in the 13th–14th-century style of Glasgow Cathedral. Admittedly, however, none of the finest Victorian churches of Glasgow are Gothic.

In Edinburgh the Victoria Hall, intended for the annual assemblies of the Free Church but serving between times as a church under the name of Tolbooth St. John's, was also built at the time of the Dissolution. This was designed in the form of a richly decorated Perpendicular meetinghouse by Pugin's friend Gillespie Graham, himself probably a Catholic. Although it is hard to believe, Pugin is reputed to have assisted Graham in the design of this super-conventicle. But the tower, so worthy of Pugin and such a feature of the silhouette of the Old Town from Prince's Street, is said to be neither by Graham nor by Pugin (Fig. X 40). At Aberdeen the local architect Archibald Simpson (1790–1847) built no less than three Free Churches that are Gothic although they are all very retardataire in style and ex-

133

tremely Protestant in plan. In London, however, where Presbyterians were Dissenters, the National Scotch Church was rebuilt in a very picturesque and unecclesiastical Norman.

In Birmingham the Wycliffe Chapel of the Independents was rebuilt early in 1843 by Philip Hardwick (1792–1870) in Perpendicular. But there was no general re-use of medieval forms by English Nonconformists before the end of the decade when their own specialist church architects first began to be active. The more pretentious conventicles of the earliest Victorian years were generally neither Gothic nor designed by Nonconformists.

For the Belvoir Street Particular Baptist Chapel in Leicester, which was completed in 1845, the architect chosen was the Catholic Hansom. That the authorities of the Free Church in Edinburgh employed Catholic architects is surprising enough; it is certainly more surprising that the Leicester Particular Baptists should have done so. But it may indicate to what an extent Anglican architects had already become subservient to the Camdenian party and hence more or less unavailable for Dissenting commissions. When Gilbert Scott in 1844 received the compliment of being selected as the one architect to represent England in the international competition for the Nikolaikirche in Hamburg and accepted the invitation with enthusiasm, he was castigated by the *Ecclesiologist* for his willingness to work for heretics. Although he attempted, with elaborate doctrinal polemics, to justify purveying to Lutherans the peculiarly Anglican blessings of 14th-century Gothic, his excuses were considered in sound Camdenian circles to be the special pleading of a theological amateur and he was never again trusted as an ecclesiologist. To work for Baptists, and Particular ones at that, would surely have been even more reprehensible.

Hansom's Belvoir Street Chapel is Classical in style but most original in plan and disposition (Fig. V 3). The circular auditorium, surrounded by galleries, is lighted by a monitor above and was provided with "other fittings peculiar to the Particular Baptists," according to the *Illustrated London News*, 8, 268—I suppose a font for total immersion. The entrances are in two round bays set at either side of that segment of the circumference which faces the street. This is no mere repetition of a Late Georgian Grecian temple, therefore, like the Irvingites' church in Bristol or the great Thornton Street Chapel in Hull (Fig. IV 11) of a few years earlier.

The ingenuity of Hansom's planning for the special needs of the Particular Baptists—so very remote from the ritual requirements of the Tractarians—and the rich articulation of the mass composition with two major cylindrical forms, one above the other, flanked by subordinate cylinders is characteristically Early Victorian. So also is the broad and plastic—not to say coarse—treatment of the Classical detail, such as the use of heavy rusticated bands on the engaged Doric columns. But the chapel is essentially secular in character and quite unrelated to the main developments of the day in ecclesiastical architecture; it might almost as well be an exchange or an institute of some sort.

Baptists, among all Dissenters, remained even down to the 70's or 80's the most allergic to neomedieval styling, although their Buckingham Chapel at Clifton, begun in 1847, was already in a rather Batty Langley sort of Early English. In 1845 John Gibson (1819–1892), a former assistant of Barry who had just started his own practice, designed for the London Baptists a large and conspicuous edifice which was at least Romanesquoid. In Bloomsbury Street, just north of Pennethorne's new Endell Street in St. Giles in London, the Central Baptist Chapel began to rise near Ferrey's Early English Christ Church and beside a towerless and aisleless Decorated church that had just been built by Poynter for the French Protestants in 1844–45 (both of which are now demolished). It was opened late in 1848. The chapel is a square, galleried meetinghouse; but the broad front façade, of stock brick with limestone trim, is flanked by two towers and pierced by three deep-sunk arched doorways set under a large rose window in a not unmedieval way (Fig. V 4). The detail, consisting chiefly of pilaster strips linked by corbel table stringcourses and cornices, is literally Lombardic; even the curiously square proportions of the façade can be matched in many 12th-century Italian churches, although the paired towers would have been rather exceptional.

There is not much relation here between the façade and the interior. The corner towers, which disguise the extreme breadth of the auditorium, contain the stairs leading up to the galleries but their principal raison d'être is visual. The interior is singularly dismal and uninteresting as if the money had run out before it was completely finished. The contract cost was £8,700, largely given by S. Morton Peto (1809–1889), one of the contractors for the New Palace and a rich railway entrepreneur. Peto was not stinting John Thomas on his own Norfolk house (Fig. VI 18) but perhaps he grew tired of the young and inexperienced Gibson's "extras," or a puritanical reaction may have set in against the relatively elaborate treatment of the façade. It is also to be noted that Peto employed Barry's associates to design for him, never Barry himself—at least we may suppose that he called the architect here since he paid for his Italian tune.

Considered merely as a piece of urban street architecture, a monumental façade and nothing more, this Bloomsbury chapel is clearly the work of a serious designer; it well deserves to have survived the hazards of taste and of bombs. By means of stone colonnettes and stringcourses Gibson successfully reduced the dreary stock brickwork to a mere infilling for the panels between in a way that would have been quite impossible with Puginian 14th-century

135

Gothic. Unfortunately the arcaded storey at the top, added later to replace the original low gable seen in the illustration, has now reduced the apparent height of the towers and thus excessively exaggerated the horizontality of the composition. But on the whole this chapel still deserves its prominence as the most conspicuous extant Early Victorian edifice built by Dissenters in central London. The *Ecclesiologist*, 8, 373, itself was forced to admit that the towers were really good even if the walls were thin and the moldings poor; but the reviewer also remarked sourly, "Dissent is not what it was that it perches itself in would-be churches."

Wightwick's modest Norman chapel in Courtenay Street, Plymouth, was also completed in 1848. Being for Congregationalists, this hardly deserves mention; for by then that denomination had two church architects of its own, John Thomas Emmett and John Tarring (1806–1875), consistently building Gothic edifices, the former at least with considerable real ability. Just after 1845 the Wesleyans, who did not consider themselves remote from the Establishment, and the Independents and Unitarians, who in many provincial cities included among their restricted numbers the local commercial aristocracy, also turned to Gothic with an almost Anglican enthusiasm.

The Wesleyan Chapel in the East India Road in London, completed in 1848 from the design of James Wilson of Bath, is large and ornate. Although not at all orthodox from the Camdenian point of view it was intended to be a "model" Methodist church. No aisles flank the nave and the roof is low pitched; at the east end no chancel projects and a large organ rises immediately behind the communion table. The ribbed arched ceiling was certainly of plaster; but the windows were filled with stained glass, "dight with appropriate symbols," as a contemporary account in the *Illustrated London News*, 13, 176, remarks (appropriate, one may query, to whose ideas— Wesley's or those of Durandus?). This colored glass in the windows imparted to the interior, so the account goes on, "an unusual degree of richness and solemnity, akin to the 'dim religious light' of our cathedrals." The detail is Decorated and nearly as "florid" as that of Sharpe's Lever Bridge church. There is no tower, for towers were still considered the proper appurtenances of real Anglican "churches" only while this was but a humble Nonconformist "chapel." Two prominent polygonal buttresses flank the great west window like turrets, however, breaking into frothy pinnacles above the traceried parapet of the front gable.

Nor was Methodist acceptance of Gothic restricted to London by this time. A modest chapel in a more restrained sort of Decorated was rising in 1847 at Wantage in Berkshire from the design of R. W. Ordish. Small though this is, the form and the details (if not the plan) are much more correct than those of Wilson's East End chapel. If the favored Decorated mode of the

Camdenians was henceforth increasingly popular with Dissenters their larger and more prominent churches were still quite as likely to be Perpendicular. The Free Kirk in Manchester, begun in 1846 by the local firm of Travis and Mangnell, is; so also the Kentish Town Congregational Church of 1847–48 in London by Hodge and Butler. This has aisles and a clerestorey but still no tower and closely resembles Wilson's contemporary Methodist chapel.

The conspicuous Mill Hill Chapel (Fig. IV 9), built for the Unitarians of Leeds by Bowman and Crowther in 1847–48, is a large and apparently cruciform edifice. But it is not very advanced in Anglican terms, for there is actually only one transept, providing a principal side entrance as at the local parish church, and the "eastern" arm was by no means all devoted to a chancel. These architects, Henry Bowman (1814–1883) and Joseph Stretch Crowther (d. 1893), knew medieval work intimately. In 1845 the first volume of their work on the *Churches of the Middle Ages, Plans, Sections, and Details* (2 vols. 1845–53) had been published; and their detail here, if not much more correct, is almost as rich and quite as suave as Chantrell's on the Leeds parish church. The roofs of nave and transept were now carried quite high, for example, although the lower aisle roofs are completely masked by pierced parapets. Elaborately pinnacled octagonal buttresses flanking the transept as well as the two ends of the nave take the place of a tower; for Unitarians still remained somewhat dubious about the propriety of towers on their "chapels" in Britain, if not on their prominent churches in America. The actual chancel, of course, was very shallow; the present altar-like communion table and other very churchly fittings are much later.

The very large Cavendish Street Independent Chapel in Manchester, intended to hold up to 1,500, was begun in 1847 by Edward Walters (1808–1872), soon to be favorably known for his palatial warehouses (see Chapter XII). This is perhaps the first Dissenting church to appear, at least superficially, quite like a contemporary Anglican church (Fig. V 2). Early Decorated in general character and in detailing, there are aisles, transepts, and a prominent southwest tower. Unlike the Mill Hill Chapel, however, this has no chancel at all. Except for its flat east end, the Hope Street Chapel, built in Liverpool for Dr. James Martineau's Unitarian congregation by T. Denville Barry (d. 1905) and his partner Brown at the same time, is also a complete and elaborate (if dreadfully ugly) example of the regular Decorated parish church model of the day complete with tall northwest tower and spire. More original in composition and quite pleasant to look upon is the same architects' Haverstock Hill Congregational Church of 1848–49 in Maitland Park Villas on the northern edge of London.

In Grafton Square, Clapham, to the south of London John Tarring, already

137

the principal specialist at building Gothic churches for Dissenters, began in 1850 a pretentious Congregational chapel with a western tower and spire 178 feet tall. This is all built of Kentish ragstone with Bath stone trim. The Clapham edifice was well in advance of Tarring's Horbury Independent Chapel in Kensington Park Road, Notting Hill, of 1848–49, which is little more than a "Pointed preaching-box" as Pugin would undoubtedly have dubbed it. The interior arrangements at Clapham remained unorthodox, however, with no separate aisles, galleries carried all around the auditory, and no chancel at all. Costing some £8,000 by the time it was completed in 1852, the chapel could hold 1,000 although the dimensions were only 113 feet by 48 feet.

Such compromises between style and convenience had by now become anathema to Anglicans but they were still acceptable to the rich and intellectual Congregationalists of Clapham. By resorting to them the architects who specialized in Dissenting commissions were readily adapting Camdenian models for Nonconformist use. Soon they made the results acceptable even to the less sophisticated Dissenters, but to the continued disgust of ecclesiological purists who saw in them only parodies of "Catholick" architecture. Posterity on the whole tends to agree (if for nonpartisan reasons) with the purists, although it finds something humorous rather than revolting in the mildly stylized heads of Luther, Calvin, Bunyan, and other Dissenting heroes that replace the saints around the Clapham church's Decorated portal.

Even as late as the beginning of the 50's most Dissenting churches, however ornate their Decorated detail, continued to look retardataire and even makeshift; and the use of Gothic forms by Nonconformists was never to be so nearly universal as among Anglicans. Classical forms continued in favor, particularly with the Baptists. Many chapels of around 1850 remain of a rather appealing, if unsophisticated, post-Georgian simplicity to which John Betjeman, with the help of John Piper's illustrations, has called almost too much attention of late years. Norman and Early English, but in both cases of a fantastic character recalling Anglican work of the 20's and 30's, continued in rather extensive use with Dissenters both in Britain and in America.

The most accomplished Gothic architect among the Nonconformists was J. T. Emmett. He had already shown a design for a Holloway Congregational church in London at the Royal Academy in 1846 but his best work came a few years later. The Independents' church in Glasgow of 1852, with a tower and spire 220 feet tall at the northwest corner of the front and a well-proportioned nave with clerestorey and aisles, is probably the nearest approach to Camdenian standards Scotland saw in this period (Fig. V 8). His Independent College, in the Finchley Road near Swiss Cottage in London, the commission for which he won in competition in 1849, was on the whole a finer specimen of Collegiate Tudor than was built at Oxford or Cambridge in the Early Victorian period. It has now been demolished.

More original are such Congregational churches by Emmett as that in the Upper Clapton Road, begun in 1850, or the similar one in Avenue Road, Hampstead. Both have boldly scaled Early Decorated detail and show skillful adjustment of Gothic themes to Dissenting practice. Transepts and a rich south porch give plastic interest to the exterior of the Hampstead church; there is also a tremendous traceried west window above a modest but deeply sunk portal. In the Clapton church, which cost £7,316, the galleries are carried on delicate iron columns set back of the masonry nave arcade. Overhead is a fine open timber roof. Emmett's early death, even before his Independent College was finished, cut off a rather promising career.

In general the most interesting Early Victorian Dissenting churches of Gothic design are the earlier ones. In them the architects, although generally less able than Emmett, were still struggling to work out types which would incorporate the principal inherited features of the meetinghouse in articulated compositions appealing to the new Victorian taste for elaboration of ornament, complexity of mass, and irregularity of silhouette. Once they and their clients accepted the superiority of the mature Camdenian church models, which had been developed in accordance with a totally different conception of the functions of ecclesiastical edifices, no real integrity of design was possible, but only a superficial masquerade. This was rarely even intended to fool the observer, though it might well do so at first in the case of Emmett's Glasgow church.

An Early Victorian Dissenting architecture of distinction might have been possible. Other functions as definitely carried over from the Georgian Age without real change as those of the Protestant meetinghouse received positively new expression. Everyone rightly recognizes, however, that the representative churches of the late 40's and early 50's are those built by Anglican specialists for churchmen, High, Broad, or Low. Most churchmen now took for granted, without excessive partisan fervor, the new functional needs of sacred edifices since Anglicans in general had come to find them satisfying to their revived spiritual cravings.

This does not mean that no good Anglican churches were built in the Norman and Lombardic modes in the second half of the decade. Wyatt and Brandon's St. Matthias's, in Chilton Street, Bethnal Green, in the East End, completed in 1848, is a cheaper version of St. Mary's, Wilton, but in some ways more satisfactory. The basilican nave with its half-round apse, though of much more modest dimensions and materials, is better proportioned (Fig. V 12). The *Ecclesiologist*, 8, 392–393, surprisingly enough, did not damn it, perhaps because of the "timid symptoms of polychromy" the reviewer discerned (for the Camdenian leaders were all in favor of internal polychromy by 1848). The final verdict was that "the interior really looks church-like, although built in a style which is exotic to England."

The tower attached to the south aisle, set one bay back from the west front, is better related to the main mass than that at Wilton. The transition from square to octagon in the tower is somewhat clumsy; but the tall octagonal roof, consciously assimilated to the shape of the conventional Decorated spire, forms a sharper accent than does the plain hip of the earlier campanile even if it lacks the assurance of Wild's simple Streatham pyramid. The materials, stock brick with a minimum of stone trim, are horridly begrimed; but they are intrinsically no more disagreeable than the Kentish ragstone rubble which was generally used for the more pretentious churches of the period in the London area. Moreover, St. Matthias's could, in a pinch, be rehabilitated easily with a coat of paint inside and out if anyone were still interested in its appearance. (The contiguous schools with their flush window trim of stone are surprisingly attractive just as they are.)

The East End is particularly full of Early Victorian churches of Romanesquoid design: Clutton's nearby St. Jude's, Bethnal Green (Fig. IV 15), and John Shaw's Christ Church, Watney Street, have already been mentioned. Still earlier had been Blore's Christ Church in the New North Road in Hoxton; opened only in 1839, this was by 1846–47 already receiving a Camdenian "restoration" (*sic*) at Butterfield's hands. In other parts of London there are several more, generally of less interest. All Saints', York Street, in Southwark, is a cheaply built church with a tall detached tower to the rear: "Very unworthy," pontificated the *Ecclesiologist*, 8, 205, "a step backward rather than forward; as a specimen of Romanesque it is contemptible." But those interested in structural developments should note that not only the columns supporting the gallery but the gallery rafters and also those of the main roof were of iron. The architect was William Rogers (d. 1857), and the date of building 1844–46.

St. John Evangelist's, Charlotte Street, in Soho, by Hugh Smith was also consecrated in 1846. This has two rather tall towers which give a Rhenish look to the narrow west front—"a most unsatisfactory composition," the *Ecclesiologist*, 7, 123–124, pronounced. The Kentish Town Parish Church in the Highgate Road, of 1845, is more interesting and even less correct. This also has two towers, but on the eastern façade toward the road like the Fosters' St. Mary's, Bute Street, in Cardiff, and short aisles behind them in the transeptal position as at Rawstone's St. Jude's, Manningham, in Bradford. This edifice had apparently been preceded by one of Peter Thompson's tem-

140

porary, not to say prefabricated, churches of wood built for only £5,000 two or three years earlier.

The rather archaeologically basilican church of All Saints, in Ennismore Gardens off Knightsbridge in London, is by Lewis Vulliamy (1791–1871), an architect best known for his Renaissance work (see Chapter VII). This had been planned for erection on another site as early as 1837 but it was not carried out on this site until 1846–49. The polychrome decorations in the apse by Owen Jones persuaded the critic in the *Ecclesiologist* to be lenient when he discussed All Saints' upon its completion. Christ Church, Bermondsey, in the East End, built by W. B. Hays in 1847, with a clerestorey, side galleries behind the nave arcade, and a tall southwest tower, might be mentioned also. But few of these churches show any individual distinction of design.

Since almost all of them are provided only with basilican apses, or else with very shallow rectangular eastern projections, in evident avoidance of the deep chancels insisted on by the Camdenians, one may assume that their sponsors were all Low Churchmen intentionally eschewing Decorated Gothic as well as ritualistic planning. Except in the case of Vulliamy little is known of their architects' stylistic preferences; the considerable influence of John Shaw's report to the Bishop of London doubtless explains their generic Romanesquoid character.

Outside London one of the best churches of the late 40's is St. Peter's in Tewksbury Road, Cheltenham. This edifice, built in 1847–49, is by Samuel Whitfield Dawkes (1811–1880), generally known as the architect of the Middlesex County Lunatic Asylum at Colney Hatch, an enormous Italian Villa sort of institutional complex of precisely the same date. Dawkes had just completed St. Andrew's, Wells Street, in London (reerected in Church Lane, Kingsbury, Middlesex, in 1933–34). Begun in 1845, that church was recognized as a model of ecclesiology in its arrangements despite its Perpendicular detail (Fig. V 6)—"Considered from a ritual point of view, it is the most satisfactory church yet built in London," the *Ecclesiologist*, 8, 79, stated approvingly. But the incumbent at Wells Street was the Camdenian leader Benjamin Webb; at Cheltenham the redoubtably Protestant rector Francis Close called the tune. (For Close, Dawkes also built the Church of England Training College in Cheltenham in a simple but early sort of Collegiate Gothic; this was begun in 1849 and the design was shown that year in the Royal Academy Exhibition.) St. Peter's is an aisleless, cruciform edifice with transeptal galleries terminating at the east in a rib-vaulted apse (Fig. V 10). The most unusual feature is the circular stone lantern supported on stone pendentives which gives space and light to a church otherwise low and dark. The open wooden roof is plain and straightforward, as roofs based on 14th-century models rarely were at this time, and the rich but simple

Norman zigzag moldings were more within the capacity of contemporary masons than Decorated detail. The massing of the east end, although gauche, has considerable vigor of the sort critics would soon be calling "architecturesque" (Fig. V 9).

Here at Cheltenham the choice of style had a special sort of topical interest. The nave and crossing were intended to imitate those of the old Norman church of St. Sepulchre in Cambridge concerning whose restoration Close had successfully battled with the Camden Society on their home grounds. In the account of St. Peter's given in the *Ecclesiologist* in 1849 the arrangements were allowed to be "nearly correct." Afraid of arousing again a dangerous enemy, the writer was evidently being coy and avoiding such denunciation as was freely bestowed on East End churches of Romanesque style backed by less combative sponsors.

A good many small village churches of Norman design were still being built. Admittedly exceptions, and appealing today in part for that reason, these non-Gothic churches of the mid- and late 40's are certainly not negligible in the production of the Early Victorian period. But the larger and more elaborate Anglican churches, after 1845, were generally Decorated and these attracted the greatest contemporary attention. That may explain why the others have thus far been so largely ignored by English historians, although Carroll Meeks has lately shown in the *Art Bulletin*, 35, 17–33, how well they fit into the international picture.

It was in 1844 that Scott, separating now from his partner Moffatt, was selected as the lone English representative in the competition for the Nikolaikirche in Hamburg. On the strength of his St. Giles's, Camberwell (Figs. IV 19, 20), by this time nearly completed, not to speak of such other excellent churches then in construction as St. Mark's, Swindon (Fig. IV 28), and St. Andrew's, Leeds (Fig. IV 27), this was an understandable choice. Poynter was perhaps the most prominent church architect of the older generation; but he had not been able to meet the new standards as his large and prominent Christ Church, Westminster, just finished and opened, sufficiently indicated. Ferrey did not begin his chief London church (Figs. V, 25, 26) nearby in Westminster for several years. The young architects most closely associated with the Camden Society were unlikely yet to receive very general support; in any case their doctrinaire command of the new "church principles" had thus far been illustrated only in very modest churches located in obscure places. Carpenter's first real opportunity did not come until he began St. Paul's, Brighton, in 1846 (Figs. V, 21–23); what is usually considered Butterfield's "first church"—rather than his Highbury Chapel—that at Coalpitheath outside Bristol, was begun only in 1844.

Scott won the Hamburg competition in 1845 with a most ambitious project

(Fig. V 5) for a large vaulted church of cathedral scale in the English Decorated style tactfully modulated toward "German Middle Pointed." The Nikolaikirche was expected to cost no less than £85,000; even though the design was considerably simplified during the long years it took to build— 1846–63—it must in the end have cost considerably more than that. When drawings of the exterior and the interior were shown at the Royal Academy Exhibition in 1847—Scott's first appearance there curiously enough—they could not help attracting a great deal of attention. Scott's general reputation as a church architect was now made even though he lost the approval of the Camdenians by thus dallying with Lutherans.

To that large middle body of the Established Church which accepted the greater part of the Camdenian program without fanaticism Scott was henceforth the new architectural leader par excellence, the obvious man to employ for important commissions, and so he remained for the rest of his life. Many preferred to deal with an architect who was a businessman rather than an aesthete; and this businessman, who could tell you what a church would cost and stick to his estimate, also appeared to be competent at archaeology, knowledgeable about ritual, and even skillful in doctrinal casuistry, as was evidenced by his lively and usually intelligent intervention in all the church controversies of the day.

Yet Scott was never a true church specialist in the way of his High Church rivals, nor was he even a particularly conscientious or personal church designer. In his well-organized office he knew how to employ his draftsmen effectively on a great range of different commissions, leaving to the more talented and experienced among them considerable individual responsibility in design. Beginning at least with St. Matthew's, City Road, in London, which was designed in 1847, rumor often attributed his best churches to this or that young man in the office. Many of his assistants were later to earn a higher personal reputation than Scott among connoisseurs of church architecture; the fine Early English tower of St. Matthew's (Fig. V 7) is supposed to be from the hand of the young George Edmund Street (1824–1881) whose own great career as a Victorian architect only began when he started independent practice the next year.

Through most of the 40's, however, Scott deserves a large part of the credit for what came out of his office. Although the complaints of more highbrow architects against his work have echoed down through the generations, inspection of a characteristic group of his churches will readily persuade that Scott was, in the context of the period, probably the most important Early Victorian practitioner in the Gothic mode after Pugin. But the qualification "Early" must be made, for a far greater Victorian Gothic designer was just getting his career under way in these years.

143

The first architect of considerable personal talent to appear after Pugin in the Gothic field, William Butterfield, did not reveal his cranky individuality for several more years. His St. Saviour's, Coalpitheath, consecrated in 1845, is an admirable essay in imitative 14th-century parish church design but little more than that. It is splendidly built of fine materials, well proportioned, skillfully composed, and correctly detailed; yet it is more the "thesis" of a superior student than a mature work of architecture. Only the stone lychgate (Fig. V 14), with its simple forms and curious juxtaposition of angles, suggests the pungent sort of originality Butterfield's finest work was to display later.

What the *Ecclesiologist, 4*, 189, rightly called the "very unaffected" vicarage of St. Saviour's, simple in detail and compactly massed, is also more significant for important later developments in its restrainedly picturesque way than is the church. The interior of the vicarage has been much pulled about but the original disposition can still be recognized. Deriving from the Tudor Parsonage models of the 20's and 30's, the plan looks forward to the innovations of Philip S. Webb (1831–1915), W. Eden Nesfield (1835–1888), and R. Norman Shaw (1831–1912) in the 60's. Around an entrance hall that was a real room, not a mere lobby, and out of which the main staircase rises, are loosely grouped the principal living rooms, with the modest service quarters conveniently contiguous to the dining room. This is an early instance of that "agglutinative" domestic planning (so to call it) which was transmitted from England to America in the 70's and which has there a real place in the genealogy of the modern house.

Here at the Coalpitheath vicarage "realism"—almost Functionalism of the modern sort—makes its appearance in house design (Fig. V 13). The elaborate frippery of the revived Tudor of Late Georgian times, lacy bargeboards, complex chimneystacks, and multitudinous piquancies of detail, gives way to plain walls of local rubble, simply gabled, set off by a minimum of cut-stone trim at the ample windows. The effect is rather barren, however, since the irregularities of massing and window placement are only those which the convenient disposition of the rooms make necessary. Yet as an expression of the asceticism of the early Tractarian parsons it could hardly be bettered.

It was from this sort of semi-secular work by Butterfield, rather than from that of Pugin or his own employer Scott, that Street took off in the parsonages and schools he began to build at the end of the decade. And it was in Street's office in the 50's that Webb and Shaw learned a comparable approach to domestic building. Thus, by a sort of paradox, it was in the by-products of Camdenian church building that the most important contributions to the general advance of house architecture were made in the Early Victorian period. High Church parsonages carried forward the advances of the Picturesque period at a time when architects specializing in small residential work were, with a few exceptions, content to stagnate. In many ways the Coalpitheath vicarage is more important historically than the castles of Salvin, the palaces of Barry, or the manor houses of Pugin. Yet it is evident that only a few cranky young men ever realized at the time that this was so. By most contemporaries this small house would barely have been noticed when they came to study and admire the church to which it was but an accessory.

Carpenter died too young to reach full maturity. As in the case of Ferrey it is doubtful if he ever felt the need for that sort of highly personal expression in church design which would soon make Butterfield the first of the High Victorians (see Chapter XVII). His St. John Baptist's, Cookham Dean, in Berkshire, a small church intended to hold 300 and costing some £1,300, was built in 1844–45. This drew warmer praise from his fellow Camdenians than did Butterfield's Coalpitheath; "a most satisfactory design, very simple yet not mean or starved" was the *Ecclesiologist's* verdict. Modern commentators with a real sympathy for the period—John Betjeman and John Piper writing in *Murray's Berkshire Architectural Guide* (1949)—are less enthusiastic. They find it "untidily planned" although they call attention to "the plain but rather successful interior" with its interesting early Pre-Raphaelite stained glass (of about 1850 they claim, which seems unlikely).

At Coalpitheath or Cookham Dean one may well feel that by the mid-40's Scott's archaeology was correct enough for anybody. His opportunities for building were certainly much more varied and considerable than Butterfield's or Carpenter's. Scott was not hidebound about style—indeed in the 50's he became an early champion of eclectic Gothicism—but in the mid- and late 40's he followed 13th-century models more consistently than 14th-century ones. His best churches of the period, St. Andrew's, Leeds (Fig. IV 27), and St. Matthew's, City Road (Fig. V 7), in London, were frequently straight Early English, not "Transitional" like St. Giles's, Camberwell (Fig. IV 19, 20). He utilized freely various asymmetrical positions for his towers; but several of his best churches have massive central lanters, sometimes simple and modest as on little St. Ann's, Alderney (Fig. V 11), sometimes as rich as at St. Giles's, Camberwell. Above all his churches were solidly put together and they do not usually appear so barren as the more correct Camdenian churches when devoid of their intended decoration and accessories. Inside and outside they have carefully considered scale and a judicious amount of respectable, if impersonal, detail.

In the Newfoundland Cathedral at St. John's, begun in 1846, the cruciform mass piles up splendidly against the sloping hill (Fig. V 15). The buttresses, by their vigorous spread around the east end, suggest the ribbed masonry vaults within; while the plate tracery, so rarely used in the 40's, suggests that the young Street may have had a hand here as well as at St. Matthew's, City

Road. Before Scott took over the Newfoundland commission an Irish stone-mason had provided a plan, and more elaborate designs had also been obtained from Derick. The building looked very large and impressive in the drawings shown by Scott at the Royal Academy Exhibitions in 1848 and 1849; but construction, largely with stone imported from Scotland, proceeded very slowly. As the cathedral was finished only in the mid-80's by Scott's son George Gilbert Scott II (1839–1897) it cannot be credited as a whole to the Early Victorian period.

Butterfield and Carpenter had a more subtly Puginian approach than Scott to medieval structure of one particular period and kind—that exemplified in the wooden-roofed English parish churches of the 14th century. With their more restricted practice they could supervise their work more closely, and their feeling for materials was undoubtedly sounder. Yet Scott's St. Philip's, Leeds, which seems to have been the first church since Savage's St. Luke's, Chelsea, that was actually vaulted in stone throughout, is for that reason more convincingly medieval today. Rightly or wrongly, stone vaulting seems to the 20th century so much the essence of Gothic that a church vaulted throughout, and even one with merely a vaulted east end like the Newfoundland Cathedral, satisfies our present archaeological ideas better than anything Butterfield or Carpenter ever built.

Despite all that may justly be said in Scott's favor, it remains true that his churches are almost always too representative to be either very interesting or very memorable. To round out the picture of the Early Victorian church some typical Gothic churches by architects less able than he must be described as well as a few exceptional ones by men more dedicated to their art. Out of the enormous production of the decade between Pugin's apogee in 1842 and his death in 1852 only a relatively small number can be mentioned at all. It is always important, and ought to be interesting, to trace the steps by which a revolution is made or an election won; but reporting the results tends to be monotonous. Excitement enters church architecture again only when the High Victorian period begins in the early 50's (Chapter XVII).

St. Thomas's in Southgate Street, Winchester, is by E. W. Elmslie, a provincial architect of little reputation; but this church, built in 1845–46, is considerably more effective externally than that of Holy Trinity, North Wall, which was erected in Winchester in 1852 for £6,000 by the highly esteemed Henry Woodyer, the only early pupil of Butterfield. (It is chiefly the rich internal polychromy—including figure subjects on the walls, dated 1902, and much red and white pattern work on the roof, as well as what seems to be Morris stained glass in the windows—which gives interest to Holy Trinity today.)

As St. Thomas's stands to the west of the street the architect made the most of the complex massing of the east end (Fig. V 19). Since the gables of the eastern aisles are lower than the chancel gable they build up handsomely, together with the north transeptal gable, toward the high roof of the nave. The chancel projects eastward of the side aisles and is flanked by two rather heavy octagonal pinnacles so that the total effect is very plastic indeed. The tower was not completed until 1857 and the spire is more angular and nervous in detail than the earlier work carried out in the mid-40's. Originally the tower was to have been central; but when the *Ecclesiologist, 6,* 155, 190, reported (moderately favorably) in 1846 on what was called the "semi-Catholic" interior arrangements the reviewer also expressed disappointment at the decision, then already made, to move the tower to its present position.

Churches designed with such pyramidal effects of mass as this and tied to the ground by spreading buttresses are ill adapted to urban settings; but they can be extremely rich and interesting on an open site like that St. Thomas's occupies on the edge of Winchester. The interiors of such churches, as has already been remarked of St. Oswald's, Old Swan, are likely to be low and dark. But here at St. Thomas's the additional height and light provided by the modest clerestorey serves to reveal the clumsiness of the interior detailing not to create an effect of greater spaciousness.

A considerably larger church, also designed by architects whose headquarters were not in London, is St. Paul's, Manningham, in Bradford, built in 1847–48 by the local firm of Mallinson and Healey (Fig. V 18). Set on a slope rising from east to west this clearly articulated cruciform edifice still forms a conspicuous pile. The central tower, capped with a plain spire, is even on axis with St. Paul Street which leads up to it from Manningham Lane. There are long transepts and the aisle windows have cross gables, a German feature first used by Scott on the Nikolaikirche which was now becoming popular as a device for elaborating the otherwise simple relationship between a conventional English nave and side aisles. As usual the interior is dull, the clerestorey being very small, while the expensive marble columns in the nave arcade no longer seem a particularly desirable luxury. Far better is the external random ashlar masonry of local Yorkshire stone left quarry faced; for this ashlar forms a pleasant irregular surface pattern, modestly scaled, to set off the cut-stone trim of the lancets and the plate tracery of the larger windows.

Neither Elmslie nor the Bradford architects represent pure Camdenian doctrine; but by this time the Camden Society's particular favorite Carpenter had had his first real opportunity when he was called on to build a large church for that generous patron Dr. Wagner, the rector of Brighton. St. Paul's in West Street was begun in 1846 and opened in 1848. The curious spire of wood covered with lead is a much later work by Carpenter's son. By 1854 R. C. Carpenter had carried the tower up to the height of the middle of the belfry windows, capping it with a bold wooden saddleback roof. At the same time the present wooden passageway, leading in from the street to the western narthex, was built. In 1873, when the parish was formally inaugurated, Richard Herbert Carpenter (1841–1893) added his dubious spire, which cost over £3,000. Today this spire and the later 19th- and 20th-century commercial buildings on either side make the original east end look unduly modest.

Actually the scale of the very deep chancel of St. Paul's, projecting eastward toward the street, is quite bold as one of the rare plates published by the *Ecclesiologist* helps us to realize by providing Carpenter's complete original design (Fig. V 21). But the local napped flint, of which the walls are made, and the contrasting whiteness and crispness of the Caen stone trim produce a Pugin-like effect of smooth surface and precise proportion. A similar almost metallic sharpness gives distinction to the eastern portal which is set between the deep buttresses at the base of the tower (Fig. V 23).

St. Paul's has no clerestorey and the nave is rather dark. But the immense east window and the south windows in the chancel provide, at least relatively, a flood of light in the sanctuary (Fig. V 22). There the rather delicately paneled polygonal ceiling is enlivened by bright ornamental stenciling doubtless renewed since Carpenter's time. The proportions of the nave are generous and the open timber construction of the roof over it is sturdy without being clumsy. The delicate chancel screen and the enormous rood, together with the painting above the chancel arch, concentrate the decoration (like the illumination) around the sanctuary. The mural on the east wall of the nave may be by Dyce who was expected, according to the *Ecclesiologist*, *10*, 204–207, to execute a mural on the north wall of the chancel. If so, it is rather superior to his better known work for Butterfield at All Saints', Margaret Street, in London.

A special interest of this Brighton church is the array of excellent glass, much of it dating slightly later than the fabric of the church but almost all consistent with it in style. The earlier windows, designed partly by Carpenter and partly by Pugin, were executed by John Hardman, Pugin's Birmingham associate. A large three-light window of the Annunciation, the Resurrection, and the Pentecost, designed by Alfred Bell and executed by Lavers and Barraud, was installed in 1855.

All Saints', Hove, begun in 1848 by Carpenter but not consecrated until 1852, is rather similar to St. Paul's, with separate gables over the aisles and an unfinished northwest tower. It is a good though dull Early Victorian church of the most doctrinaire sort. Carpenter's "restoration" of the old Brighton parish church (begun in 1852 as a memorial to the Duke of Wellington and completed in 1854) turned it also into a strictly Camdenian edifice, with very little of the original fabric left visible. The *Ecclesiologist* (*7*, 155–156, 203; *8*, 188–189; *9*, 55–56; and *10*, 204–207) was recurrently enthusiastic about Carpenter's Brighton churches but also noted, rather sourly, that "the very high opinion we have of [his] talents makes any praise of his work suspicious in some quarters."

Carpenter's most important church is probably St. Mary Magdalene's in Munster Square, London, which was started in the summer of 1849 and consecrated in 1852. Built at the entire cost of the incumbent, the Reverend E. Stewart, it was intended from the first to be a model of ecclesiological correctness. The fact that the tower was never built—Carpenter had unusually bad luck with his towers—is unfortunate; but once more a plate in the *Ecclesiologist* reveals the complete original design (Fig. V 16). The north aisle, omitted in the original campaign of construction, was eventually completed according to Carpenter's original plan.

The concentration of almost all the external, as well as all the internal, decoration on the sanctuary leaves the west front rather bare and humble. But it is the difficulty of obtaining adequate lighting in a city church with no clerestorey and the extreme dinginess, to which the stained-glass windows by Pugin and by Clayton and the painted decorations by J. G. Crace have alike succumbed, which make St. Mary Magdalene so unimpressive to 20th-century eyes and all but impossible to photograph (Fig. V 17). The east window is by Pugin and was ordered by Carpenter. The west window, erected as a memorial to Carpenter after his early death in 1855, was designed by J. R. Clayton (later the partner of Bell) who had designed windows for Carpenter at St. Paul's, Brighton; this was executed by Hardman.

In the very years during which this church was being built Butterfield, with the full blessing of the Camdenians, was initiating the High Victorian Gothic in another London church which was very, very different (see Chapter XVII). The *Ecclesiologist*, *13*, 167, nevertheless pronounced St. Mary Magdalene's in 1852 to be "the most artistically correct new church in London." Later generations of ecclesiologists have continued to praise its correctness, if not its artistic qualities, down to our own day.

If Carpenter had lived longer there might perhaps be more to say about him, but I doubt it. He was one of those single-track perfectionists who took the doctrine of an architectural revolution quite literally. By the conscientiousness with which such men follow their artistic creeds they often freeze into sterility whatever innate creative capacity they may have originally had. The architectural vigor of Pugin and the individuality of his work are the better appreciated by comparing his churches with Carpenter's;

for Carpenter was in many ways more what Pugin, in his writings, insisted a church architect ought to be than Pugin ever was himself, except perhaps in his own Ramsgate church. One can readily sympathize with contemporaries who preferred to employ men of less total artistic integrity such as the facile and competent Scott from whom something showy could always be expected.

In justice to Carpenter, whose opportunities were so much more limited by his early death than were those of the long-lived Scott and Butterfield, two major projects of his should at least be mentioned. His design for an Anglican cathedral at Colombo in Ceylon was very ambitious compared with any of his executed churches. Although including many elements the scheme was surprisingly compact in plan for the period and also in mass composition; all those features which might have provided external accents to the large cruciform shape were either omitted or minimized (Fig. V 20). There was neither a crossing lantern nor west towers, and the west front itself was to be quite hidden behind a rather blunt Burgundian forechurch. Open loggias, intended like the forechurch to provide protection against the intense heat and light of the tropics, masked the projection of the transepts at ground level and continued around the polygonal apse, thus producing a plan that recalls that of Notre Dame in Paris. Although the church was to be vaulted throughout, the design is otherwise typically English and 13th century in character, not the usual 14th-century Decorated. Clerestorey passages in the thick walls were expected to reduce the tropical light entering the small plate-traceried windows. The proportions were somewhat squarish, for Carpenter seems to have rejected vertical emphasis as consciously as he did any unnecessary complexity of massing. There could hardly have been a more curious Victorian export to the East.

Carpenter was not only too correct for his age—for all its lip service to correctness—but he actually seems to have been out of sympathy with many of its prime aesthetic demands. At its best his work is somewhat premonitory of the tastes of the Late Victorians in the 70's and 80's, not of those of the intervening period. His other cathedral project, for a west front on the Episcopal cathedral of Inverness in Scotland with deep-sunk portals and two flanking towers, is remarkable for its French character; this suggests, even more than does the Colombo design, that irregularity was not much to his taste.

Carpenter's principal secular works—if Early Victorian schools can be called secular when started under Tractarian auspices—were St. John's College, Hurstpierpoint, and the College of SS. Mary and Nicholas at Lancing, both in Sussex. The former was built in 1851–53, at a cost of £20,000, for the education of some two hundred sons of farmers and tradesmen (Fig. V 24); the latter, a still larger establishment, was designed in 1854 and begun just

150

at the time of Carpenter's death in 1855. The Lancing college was gradually completed, with many additions and emendations, by William Slater (1818–1872), Carpenter's partner and successor (with whom Carpenter's son was associated as a partner after 1863). The Hurstpierpoint school has a business-like simplicity about it but on the whole is rather dull; the Lancing college as executed must be considered largely Slater's work, too late to be properly called Early Victorian.

The alterations to Beresford-Hope's country house Bedsgebury Park, begun by Carpenter and completed by Slater, were not Gothic but Italianate, supposedly in keeping with the original design, and need not concern us here. His most extraordinary venture, which also fell to Slater to complete, was a scheme for an all-iron church commissioned by the Ecclesiological Society in 1853. This will be referred to again in Chapter XVI. Despite his early death Carpenter's production was considerably more extensive than might have been expected, though not up to that of Pugin who died at an even earlier age. The very few examples discussed and illustrated here do justice to his production, I believe, although they hardly explain his tremendous contemporary reputation of which echoes have lasted right down to the present.

Ferrey was more ready than Carpenter to meet the actual—as distinguished from the avowed—tastes of the Early Victorians. Toward the construction of his chief London church Miss Angela Georgina Burdett-Coutts (later Baroness Burdett-Coutts) who was the principal heiress, through her fantastic step-grandmother the Duchess of St. Albans, to the fortune of her grandfather the banker Thomas Coutts, provided very large sums. St. Stephen's, Rochester Row, Westminster, which was begun in 1847 and consecrated in 1850, is a large Curvilinear Decorated church—one may assume that Ferrey's continued devotion to earlier styles in his small country churches was mostly due to lack of adequate funds to pay for the richly carved detail the Decorated seemed to require. The interior of St. Stephen's is quite conventional (Fig. V 26). Because of the adequate lighting provided by the clerestorey windows (which the *Ecclesiologist*, 9, 331, thought should be "reconsidered") and the tactful renewal of the painted wall decorations it looks today more like contemporary views, such as were shown at the Royal Academy Exhibition in 1849, than do most Early Victorian churches. There are windows by Wailes and by Powell and in the reredos the diapering of St. Dunstan's Shrine at Canterbury was copied in Minton tile—something of which the *Ecclesiologist*, *11*, 114, usually so enthusiastic over polychromy by 1851, "queried the legitimacy" because it was an "application of mechanical art."

The exterior of the church is dominated by an elaborate tower and spire rising in the south transeptal position (Fig. V 25). The usual south porch and a modest group of related school buildings further enriched the picturesque massing. For the horrid Kentish ragstone rubble that was used for most contemporary London churches Ferrey substituted a harder stone laid in random ashlar; this is quite delicately scaled and very dark gray now in color. The rich tracery of the windows and the crocketing of the pinnacles at the corners of the tower and the chancel are graceful and refined.

Lacking in any real originality—even of the rather negative sort that Carpenter's work displays—St. Stephen's represents a sort of post-Puginian norm. Ferrey and many others were to continue building such churches long after Butterfield set a new pace for the High Victorian period. They provide the prototypes also for the more literate Episcopal churches of the mid-century in America. Frank Wills (1827–   ) (who was English trained and did much work in Canada) in a considerable group of churches and John Notman (who came from Edinburgh) at St. Mark's, Philadelphia, came closest to this norm in quality. The Ecclesiological Society supplied a set of plans by Carpenter for St. Mark's. These were not used but may have assisted Notman in preparing his design which is certainly not far below Carpenter's standards. The more famous church work of Richard Upjohn is at once cruder and somewhat more original, yet it represents on the whole the same norm.

Before the decade was over a younger architect, John Loughborough Pearson (1817–1897), easily went beyond this norm, but in the same direction of increased suavity and elegance, in his church of Holy Trinity, Bessborough Gardens, also in Westminster (Fig. V 30). But this cruciform church, with its tall central tower and spire, is very little premonitory of the fine works which would later make Pearson's great reputation. Only the great height (200 feet) and the vigorous but refined silhouette of the central tower prepare one for his churches of the 60's, 70's, and 80's, for at this time Pearson's command of medieval detail was still almost as impersonal as Ferrey's.

Holy Trinity is dated 1849–52 and was built with £12,000 entirely provided by Archbishop Bentinck. The materials were Bargate stone with Bath stone for the trim. The chancel was 42 feet long compared with the nave's 125 feet. Perhaps for that reason the *Ecclesiologist, 12,* 231–232, approved it in general even though their reviewer "could detect many traces of Perpendicular feeling in the mouldings" of what was supposed, of course, to be a Decorated church. But then the Society's agents could pick up an occasional—and to them nauseous—whiff of Perpendicular even in Butterfield's, if not perhaps in Carpenter's, work!

Most other London churches of the late 40's and early 50's are quite without individual interest regardless of whether they were built by church architects or by architects in general practice who accepted the new conventions for Anglican churches. Curiously enough one of the best is—at least nominally—by Thomas Cundy II, the Grosvenor Estate surveyor, most of whose other churches, except that of Holy Trinity, Paddington, are worse than routine. The site for Saint Barnabas's, Pimlico, was donated by the ground landlord, the Marquess of Westminster, which explains the choice of Cundy. However, it was "understood that Mr. A. J. B. Hope, M. P., had been one of the principal contributors" toward the total of £19,000 which the whole complex eventually cost. It would be he who brought in Butterfield to assist on the final designs. Butterfield was then engaged with Benjamin Webb in preparing the first part of *Instrumenta ecclesiastica* which was published in 1847. This was a compendium of old and new designs for correct church fittings which Butterfield had undertaken at the specific request of the Ecclesiological Society and presumably with financial support provided by Beresford-Hope.

St. Barnabas's itself was begun in 1846 and consecrated in 1850. Very similar externally to Ferrey's Christ Church, St. Giles, it is unfortunately built of Kentish ragstone rubble like Cundy's other Pimlico churches (Fig. V 27). With the attendant schools and clergy house, the whole ecclesiastical group occupies considerable ground and has sufficient open space around it so that the boldly articulated composition can be seen in the round from various angles. The subsidiary buildings were the first schools and such to be designed in 13th-century style; they are supposed to have terrified the young ladies of Pimlico by their conventual appearance (Fig. V 28). However that may be, they certainly form a very simple and harmonious foil for the tall proportions and vigorous lancet openings of the northwest tower and the west gable of the church.

The interior once impressed by the richness and variety of its decorations (Fig. V 29). Glass by Wailes filled all the windows; the brass gates in the chancel screen and the hanging corona were by Hardman, the eagle lectern by Potter, and the painted diaper on the chancel walls by Bulmer. There was even a "warning apparatus" generously paid for by Sir J. Swinburne.

The relatively tall proportions and the sturdiness of the nave columns and the roof trusses are still notable. There are certain details of the roofing, especially the notching on the nave principals and the scalloped beams that divide the panels of the chancel ceiling, that specifically suggest the bolder hand of Butterfield. Internal evidence therefore tends to confirm the rumor that he supplemented the low-level competence of the regular Cundy office force at some point in the designing of the church. St. Barnabas's was completed just as Butterfield was initiating a new phase of the Victorian Gothic at All Saints', Margaret Street, for the same patron, Beresford-Hope. The

Pimlico church may be considered, therefore, in some of its aspects a sort of primitive of the High Victorian almost as much as Butterfield's contemporary work (partly restoration, partly new construction) for Beresford-Hope at St. Augustine's College, Canterbury. The college was also carried out in the years 1846–48 although initiated in 1845, and similar notchings and scallopings are to be found in its principal interiors.

There is literally no end to the roster of Early Victorian churches. One could go on indefinitely singling out early works by men such as G. E. Street, Ewan Christian (1814–1895), or Samuel Sanders Teulon (1812–1873) who were, like Butterfield and Pearson, to make their real mark in Victorian church architecture rather later. Or one could note with some amusement the conscientiousness with which men previously unwilling to accept the new gospel, various successful London architects with general practices like Wyatt and Brandon, Philip Hardwick and his son, or John Gibson, now turned out designs of the standard type whenever their offices were called on to produce churches. So, a century later in America, famous "traditional" firms like McKim, Mead, and White would set up their "modern" departments and the restorers of Colonial Williamsburg learn to design laboratories and gymnasiums of relatively advanced design.

One church by the serious medievalists Edward Sharpe of the "pot churches" and his partner Edward Graham Paley (1813–1895) must serve to illustrate the integrity of the better churches being built all over England at the end of the Early Victorian period. Such churches could certainly not have been designed so plausibly or constructed so solidly, even by Pugin himself, around 1840. They provide the well-cultivated stock onto which the more exotic blooms of the High Victorian Gothic were soon to be grafted (Chapter XVII).

Sharpe and Paley's St. Thomas's, Coventry, was begun in 1848 and consecrated in 1849. Costing £3,350 and holding 576 people, this is sturdy and structural throughout, not fussy and trivial in detail or barren here and over-rich there like so many others in the same nominal Decorated mode. The local red sandstone gives a particularly warm and varied tone to the walls; the interior volumes are clearly and straightforwardly articulated; and the well-proportioned exterior massing expresses directly the interior articulation without further elaboration (Fig. V 33). For example, there is no tower, although one was originally intended; but a bell turret placed to one side of the west gable, as on Scott's St. Andrew's, Leeds, provides a modest asymmetrical accent in a quite unforced way. The buttresses are simple but solid, not too spreading, not too thin; and all the stonework of the walls is sound and normal looking, neither excessively varied in pattern and texture nor yet laid up in overscaled blocks of smoothly regular ashlar.

154

Inside St. Thomas's the molded capitals and the intrados profiles of the nave arcades are notably clean and firm (Fig. V 34). The carved angels on the brackets beneath the roof principals are undistinguished but not excessively sentimental or silly. Touches of strong color still remain on the shields the angels hold although the general effect is monochrome. The plaster walls are not so unbroken as to appear bare nor are they stenciled all over with wallpaper-like patterns. The fine interior has real architectonic interest and can therefore do without the various ecclesiological frills and fitments which often pre-empted in these years attention and funds better spent on more essential things.

St. Thomas's is certainly a far sounder church than most of those being built in the years just before the new reign began. There is more devotional feeling than in the large Classical churches of the Late Georgian period; while the execution and finish is professional throughout not amateurish or experimental as in the pre-Puginian Gothic ones—or, for that matter, in Sharpe's own "pot church" at Lever Bridge which had been begun only a half dozen years earlier. It was not necessary, however, that this sort of church design should remain supreme indefinitely despite its solid virtues. Already architects of strong personal talent, as we shall see in Chapter XVII, were feeling their way toward drastic modulations—in formal composition, in the use of color, and in the scale of detail—that would provide a livelier visual interest. But this church well illustrates an Early Victorian formula of design and construction which was perhaps the most positive result of the long decay of Georgian taste. Inapplicable though it was to most types of building other than churches, it represented a real cultural achievement of its period like the Georgian terrace house or the mid-20th-century factory. In too many other fields of architecture the virtues of Early Victorian production are more the result of good habits inherited from the immediate Georgian past than to absorption-by-emulation of the qualities of medieval or Renaissance work.

Yet the correct Early Victorian church represents a rather narrow canalization of the new post-Georgian visual tastes. The growing desire for richer effects, for more articulated organization of the interior spacial volumes and the external masses, and for greater plasticity of surface treatment, could obviously have found equally effective expression elsewise than by conscientious emulation of 13th- and 14th-century English parish church models. This, the subconscious "will-to-style" of the age (if I may be pardoned a Germanism) had already achieved in the early 40's in such churches as Wyatt's and Wild's at Wilton and Streatham; it continued to do so, moreover, if with diminishing success, in milieus where High Church influence was not strong. Because of the nature and background of the Camdenian doctrines it is sur-

155

prising, not that Low Church Anglicans and Dissenters were slow to reach viable compromises with those doctrines, but that conscientious Protestants were ready to accept them at all.

The Low Church acceptance of standard Early Victorian Gothic was all but complete by the early 50's, although the Protestants were somewhat slow once more to follow the next bold architectural adventures proposed by the "Higher" leaders of taste. Because Dissenters were mostly content to follow the Anglicans rather than to strike out on a line of their own, almost all their Early Victorian churches, whether Grecian, Romanesque, Early English, Perpendicular, or Decorated in nominal style, remained somewhat retard-ataire. Worse, their architects always seemed to be apologizing, as has been said, for such elements of the Georgian meetinghouse as they had to retain for functional reasons. These elements should rather have given a special symbolic character to their architectural expression comparable to that character the architects serving High Anglicans achieved in their settings for elaborate ritual. The vigor of 19th-century Protestantism did express itself in much secular architecture, as we shall see in later chapters, but hardly at all in ecclesiastical edifices in Britain. For obvious reasons American church architecture of the 40's and 50's outside Anglican circles is more original and idiosyncratic.

An exception of a sort to these statements is the Independent Chapel and its schools built in 1849 at Boston in Lincolnshire by Stephen Lewin. Schools of their own were particularly vital to the Dissenters' scheme of things since the older foundations were not usually accessible to their children; and the schools here are not a mere adjunct but occupy the entire ground storey below the auditory. The moderately wide nave of the latter is high roofed and ends in a semicircular apse. A tall tower rises all but free of the west front as proudly as Wild's at Streatham and topped, like Wild's, by a steep pyramid of decorative tiling (Fig. V 31).

The fairly elaborate ornamental features are all executed in pale, stone-colored molded brick. They must be described merely as "round-arched medieval" since they conform to no particular Norman or continental Romanesque models. (Lewin had issued the first part of a book of *Designs for Churches in the Norman and Gothic Styles* at Oxford in 1844 but had no very considerable knowledge or understanding of old work.) Inside, the pulpit is placed within the apse, with seats around the rear in the true basilican tradition. The roof trusses are laminated semicircular arches of wood, ingenious technically and effective visually, like those shortly to be used at much larger scale in the transept of the Crystal Palace and the sheds of King's Cross Station.

The whole cost was only £1,300 and the tower is but 110 feet high, with the other dimensions in proportion; but the architect at least attempted to make a brave showing. With the sums at his disposal nothing resembling the conventional Anglican models of the time could have been plausibly built— above all not with school accommodations included—for no architect had yet realized how to simplify 14th-century Gothic forms successfully for execution in brick. Doubtless, moreover, in this old Puritan district the inhibitions against Anglican models were especially strong. Lewin was almost forced to be original but he did not know how to be original enough—to move further, say, in the direction that Wild had already started almost a decade earlier in designing his brick church at Streatham.

In the Georgian Age good architecture did not necessarily require much expenditure, as many modest dwellings and meetinghouses make evident both in England and in America. But to appeal to the new Victorian visual tastes an architect needed to have either real genius—which was in these years almost wholly lacking in all camps—or the considerable funds required for good stone masonry and carefully carved ornament. Lewin's was a cheap church and it looks it, in every sense of the word.

In contrast to the Boston chapel, one of the most expensive non-Anglican churches, the Catholic Apostolic church in Gordon Square in London, stands up with all but the best Anglican work of its day even though it is quite without originality. For one thing, the architect John Raphael Brandon (1817–1877) was one of the most serious Victorian students of old medieval work. With his brother Joshua Arthur Brandon, by this time dead, J. R. Brandon had issued a manual called *An Analysis of Gothick Architecture* (2 vols. 1847; new eds. 1849, 1860; reprint 1903); following that came an excellent book with examples of medieval *Parish Churches* in 1848, and in 1849 an even better treatise on *Open Timber Roofs of the Middle Ages* (new ed. 1860). These Brandons apparently were not related to Wyatt's partner David Brandon.

The Catholic Apostolic Church body, which had grown up out of Edward Irving's preaching, later worked out for itself a ritual as elaborate (and, for that matter, doubtless quite as authentically medieval) as that of the Camdenians. (A writer in the *Ecclesiologist, 15,* 83–88, denounced that ritual violently as a horrid parody of the Anglo-Catholic and could barely discuss the architecture of the Gordon Square church for fury at the Irvingite heresy when reporting on the design as shown at the Royal Academy Exhibition in 1853.) By this time the Catholic Apostolics could accept without any Puritan inhibitions an elaborate 14th-century cathedral project for their principal London edifice. And, with a contract price of £27,157, Brandon could afford to use good Bath stone ashlar throughout and to propose, at least, a profusion of elaborate figural carving even though much of it, in fact, still remains in the block (Fig. V 36). This is also the only Early Victorian church with a real triforium as well as a clerestorey.

Despite its archaeological completeness, really grand scale, and excellent materials, the Gordon Square church is singularly dull. Even the Victorians themselves, by the time it was building—the foundations were laid in 1850 and it was begun in 1851; although opened in 1854 it has never really been completed—seem to have realized that archaeology without some use of the imagination or at least unconscious originality of treatment could be as uninteresting when medieval as when Classical. The *Ecclesiologist* went so far as to say that "more artistic feeling" in the design would have led to grudging approval despite the dubious rites the edifice was to house. But since most Early Victorian churches are small and dark the interior of the Catholic Apostolic church, like that of the Leamington parish church, has a certain impressiveness deriving from its great size and its ample illumination. The church is 210 feet long and the nave is 90 feet high; had the west front been built the nave would be 60 feet longer. How tall the central tower was intended to be and whether western towers were planned I do not know; without them the exterior seems much more incomplete than the interior (Fig. V 35).

Not all churches of this period are correct and dull; plenty of them are just dull. On the other hand, some churches by architects outside ecclesiological circles were Gothic with a significant difference. To a certain extent this difference merely meant a continuation of Late Georgian ways of handling Pointed forms. In America, where ecclesiologists were few and knowledge of medieval works second- or thirdhand, most churches of the 40's and early 50's not built for Anglicans are negatively post-Georgian rather than positively Early Victorian in character. In England, on the other hand, the "rogue-architects," as H. S. Goodhart Rendel has called them (meaning in this period those who did not join the Camdenian camp), must have been quite conscious of their independence.

The wild fantasies of men like Gough and Roumieu are hardly worth considering although it should be recognized that there were many clients who admired their work. But the aberrations of E. B. Lamb, whose proto-Victorian projects of the 30's were discussed in Chapter II, have greater interest. The way Lamb contrasts coarseness and delicacy in his handling of form continues to offer more than a suggestion, like his earliest designs published by Loudon, of the direction Victorian Gothic was going to take after 1850. Lamb's almost obsessive passion for broken lines and for the articulation of structural elements, his ubiquitous segmental-pointed arches, and his curious notchings and chamferings are even more premonitory of the High Victorian.

Feeling no compulsion to use the ritually correct plans of the Camdenians, he often developed the eastern end of his churches in a rather complicated way in order to provide near the pulpit and the communion table (which he characteristically placed in the very shallowest of chancels) a large amount of usable space for the congregation. At times his churches seem almost to be centrally planned although there is always at least a short nave.

Lamb's church of All Saints, Thirkleby, in Yorkshire, illustrates most of these points (Fig. V 32). This was built in the late 40's (consecrated 1850) by the widow of the local landowner Sir Robert Frankland Russell to replace an Early Georgian church; for Lamb's clientèle, although necessarily Low Church, was by no means predominantly middle class. It cannot be said that All Saints' is any more successful than it is typical.

Lamb's peculiar methods of personal expression, exemplified in most of his work of all periods, were consistently rejected as tasteless if not outright illiterate by Camdenians. But his churches of the 40's such as All Saints' have already something of the perverse vigor and the haunting formal dissonances which were to be so typical of the next period of church architecture; and in the 50's and 60's such qualities were to be highly approved by ecclesiological purists—at least when other architects than Lamb purveyed them. It is well to remember that these qualities were already possible, although rare, before the 40's were over.

Sometimes, as in his not very interesting chapel for the Consumption Hospital in Brompton, built in 1849–50, Lamb's styling was recognizably Perpendicular—not to say "Debased" as his enemies always did—but it was nevertheless unmistakably Lamb-like, to make a tempting pun. His addiction to the unfashionable Perpendicular explains neither the individuality of his works nor their contemporary condemnation. To continue to use the Perpendicular in the mid- and late 40's was for most architects merely to be behind the current mode; Lamb's fault to his contemporaries lay rather in moving ahead of that mode too rapidly. Yet there is apparently some curious law of stylistic growth according to which only those can fully succeed in a particular phase of art who have mastered in their youth the preceding phase. Lamb refused to master the Camdenian phase and so he could never become a real leader even when his aberrations were being consistently paralleled in the work of many young architects in the later 50's and 60's. It was then that his own best work was done, however, culminating in St. Martin's, Gospel Oak, in Kentish Town, London, and its fine parsonage which were built in 1864–65.

Lamb tried to exploit his undoubted originality too early and he was therefore caught in a sort of cul-de-sac during the whole Early Victorian period. Remarkable though his most mature work of the 50's and 60's was to be, even that represents on the whole a private, not a public and generally acceptable, sort of achievement. It is more interesting to posterity than it ever was to most contemporaries. But it was Lamb's proud refusal to conform to the formulas of ritualistic planning in the 40's which caused his ostracism by the ecclesiologists far more than their distaste for the strange forms he was then adumbrating. This independent attitude continued quite unabated to the end of his career and warned off the young from following too frankly in his roguish footsteps.

What might be considered by many the finest Early Victorian church in Britain was built in 1856–57 in Glasgow at a cost of £8,000 by Alexander Thomson. Thomson was quite as original as Lamb if not, being a Scot and a Presbyterian, so isolated from his own milieu. But this church, so very late in date, is even less related to the dominant currents of the Early Victorian period than were Lamb's in the 40's (Fig. V 37). The Caledonia Road Free Church, though completely without influence on other British architects, may serve nevertheless to wind up this chapter just because it is so extraordinarily handsome. Too many of the buildings illustrated in this chapter and the preceding are unappealing visually.

Insofar as Thomson's work can be related to general stylistic developments in Britain at all it belongs at least as much to the High Victorian as to the Early Victorian phase. But more truly it seems to realize certain of the possibilities implicit in the Romantic Classicism of the beginning of the century which Soane, almost alone in England, approached at the time. Specifically, of course, Thomson owed a great deal in this church to Schinkel, not only to Schinkel's Berlin churches but also to his secular buildings, all of which were accessible for study in the great monograph on his work. It would be inappropriate to analyze the Caledonia Road Church here in detail although the plan and section merit the most careful study—almost more than do the superbly crisp elevations. (Measured drawings of it were published in the *Architectural Review, 15,* 189–190.) There will be more to say about Thomson, however, in Chapter XIV.

In 1852 Pugin died. His death no more affected current production than Soane's had done in 1837; but like Soane's death it provides a convenient landmark to close off a period, at least in church architecture. Actually it was architects of Pugin's own age or but little younger who now took the lead. But Pugin's success had come very early while most of the new men began to make their mark only when they were about thirty-five; that was in the 19th century as in most other periods the usual age for the opening of a mature career. How Pugin might have reacted to the turn which Anglican church architecture was to take in the 50's it is hard to say (see Chapter XVII). But at the end of his life, as has been noted, he was so impressed by the acceptance of his architectural doctrines by Anglicans generally, as compared with the very uneven response of his fellow Roman Catholics, and so flattered by the number of Anglican architects currently building churches according to his highest standards that he almost recanted.

No one was likely to become again a Roman convert for architectural reasons as Pugin had done in the mid-30's. It was now clear enough that the Anglican church was "the only [one] in which a revival of the grand and sublime style of church building was to be expected," to quote his own words of twenty years earlier. For this reason the Gothic Revival in its later phases must be considered an essentially English manifestation, characteristic only of Britain and the Anglo-Saxon lands beyond the seas. Even if one were to disregard the contrast between the ultimate extension of the use of Gothic forms to almost every field of architectural design in England and its relatively rare use for anything but churches on the Continent, still the neo-Gothic churches built abroad in the mid-century rarely illustrate such a high norm of current practice as do most Anglican churches by 1850.

If it is ever justifiable to use the metaphor of "revival"—and I have avoided using even the *word* as far as possible in this chapter—the Gothic was "revived" in the 40's in English church architecture; some simulacrum of the medieval corpse was pieced together again and made, however perilously, to stand up. Then, in the next decade, the corpse was actually reanimated and for a time an architectural miracle seemed to have occurred as Gothic design once more moved forward into new channels. Most of this new life ran out by 1870, nevertheless, despite all the acres of fake Gothic that have been built since then. When "Gothic" buildings are designed and erected in Anglo-Saxon countries today—and amazingly enough they still are—they do not possess even the relative vitality of the dullest Camdenian parish churches of the 40's.

Yet Pugin's neo-Gothic church architecture had a full century of some sort of life. The campaigns of few architectural reformers in modern times have had such long-continued effect. Hence the episodes with which this chapter and the two preceding ones have dealt remain exceptional in the history of the 19th century; only the Victorian innovations in building technique have shown a similarly enduring life, and that of a wholly different order (Chapters XV–XVI); for the history of scientific development is cumulative however much it may be interrupted. The more humanistic story of architecture consists of successive and of parallel episodes which have independent value. Of these the Early Victorian Gothic church development is an example, but only one among the many in the total Victorian story.

CHAPTER VI: BARRY AS AN

ARCHITECT OF "PALACES"

Pugin as a personality is one of the most colorful Early Victorians. Because of the remarkably complete acceptance of the reforms he initiated in church architecture and the repercussions of those reforms in other fields he must be considered one of the most influential men of the mid-19th century. Yet as an architect Pugin can hardly be considered quite characteristic of his time despite the many Camdenian church architects who modeled themselves after him. His fanaticism, his single-minded emulation of a very limited period of the past, and even more the integrity of his concern with structure and its expression set him apart from the great majority of his professional contemporaries. Among church architects Scott, in most respects Pugin's inferior, is much more typical. But the really representative Early Victorian architect, the true head of the opposition to the Puginian party, and also Pugin's equal in influence if not in talent was Sir Charles Barry.

By a curious and ironic twist these men whose positions in the architectural scene were so nearly polar not only maintained friendly relations but cooperated professionally throughout most of the Early Victorian period. A deadly feud broke out after Pugin's death between his family and Barry's; difficult though the sons found it to understand their fathers' relationship, however, so long as Pugin lived it seems to have troubled the fathers themselves very little. Nor has it been difficult for later posterity to accept that they operated comfortably enough as a two-man team even though the scope of their individual architectural responsibilities at Westminster differed so notably. The story of the New Palace on which they worked together cannot properly be treated as a mere part of the career either of Barry or of Pugin, for the Palace was characteristic of neither. Not because Barry was the architect of the Palace of Westminster therefore—which in any case no one thinks of as a palace—is he called here an architect of "palaces."

In many periods of the past the two chief divisions of monumental architecture are best exemplified by the church and the palace. In 19th-century England, with all the varied fields of architectural activity inherited from the preceding period and all the new fields commercial and industrial development were opening up, neither church nor palace building provided more than a small segment of the range of architectural production. In the technical sense of a representative Royal residence the Early Victorian period saw only two minor pieces of palace construction; those are both mere additions to an existing structure even though they may have appeared as independent edifices when seen from the Green Park or from Buckingham Gate. Neither the new front of Buckingham Palace nor the ballroom wing were designed by Barry, nor are they in one of his characteristic modes (see Chapter IX). Barry was also not concerned, except in a very incidental way, with the most considerable and famous building of the period which was miscalled a palace, Paxton's Crystal Palace which housed the Great Exhibition of 1851.

But considering the conventional use of the Italian word *palazzo* for the large formal residences of feudal and commercial magnates in Renaissance Italy and the functional similarity of Barry's great private and semiprivate edifices to these, one may not improperly balance against Pugin, par excellence the church architect, Barry as the leading contemporary palace architect. His palatial clubhouses and mansions were also widely imitated in institutional and commercial work, and they influenced much domestic and other secular building to a lesser degree. The term "palace architect" is all the more appropriate because Barry's favorite exemplars—and certainly those most influential on his contemporaries—were in fact Italian palazzos of the early 16th century.

In the same way that the extent of Pugin's influence can be broadly measured by the profusion of Victorian structures that emulate English 14th-century Gothic models, the importance of Barry's professional leadership can be read in the much greater variety of Victorian edifices whose design was based—even if at times rather sketchily—on Italian 16th-century originals. In neither instance were the proposed and accepted standards as restricted as this statement must seem to imply. Barry's influence can be sensed in various strains of academic design which range in their prototypes all the way from ancient Greece to 17th-century England; while Pugin's influence, although most significant and clearly definable in the field of church architecture, affected secular work in various medievalizing modes from the Norman to the early Elizabethan. In recounting the story of Barry's career in some detail in this chapter and the next—or at least of that portion of it which falls between 1837 and the mid-50's—examples of parallel and comparable work by other men may appropriately be discussed also.

In 1836, when Pugin's *Contrasts* appeared, Barry was already one of the most successful English architects of his generation as the account of his early career in Chapter II will have made plain. His early Sutherland commissions must have been rather unsatisfying to Barry for reasons that will soon appear. But it was the Sutherland patronage which started him on his way as an architect of private palaces in the city and in the country. His Westminster commission and his Pall Mall clubhouses, which provided the first complete examples of his characteristic palazzo mode of design, were much more important for his general reputation.

York House in London had been built by Benjamin Dean Wyatt (1775–1850) for George IV's brother the Duke of York in 1825 with money borrowed from the Marquess of Stafford, the father of the Duke of Sutherland. (Later it was rechristened Stafford House by the Sutherlands and today it is known less appropriately as Lancaster House.) According to Alfred Barry, the redecoration of the interiors here was discussed as early as 1835 although the project was presumably not pursued very far until the duke actually acquired the property—on which he already had at least a moral mortgage —in 1841. But this may well have been, as a tentative scheme at least, the first of that series of remodelings of Georgian mansions which was to occupy so much of Barry's later professional life.

Such jobs undoubtedly brought him a handsome income, but they also limited his original production and restricted his creative opportunities. The continual experience of Italianizing in an early 16th-century mode mansions which Georgians had originally built according to Palladian ideals tended to soften the distinction between the Georgian and the Victorian in Barry's mind. As a result these remodelings provide architectural historians, whether of the 18th century or of the 19th, with confused pastiches which almost defy analysis without the aid of contemporary documentation. The Stafford House interiors are particularly hard to sort out because they are all of one century; fortunately the problem is not very relevant here. Most of them are not cinquecento at all but rather a sort of Louis XIV or even Rococo, whenever and by whomever they may have been designed.

Barry's work for the Sutherlands at Trentham Park, their principal English seat in Staffordshire, is not involved with that of other 19th-century architects nor is it confined to interiors. Operations definitely began several years before 1837 even if no sharp line can be drawn between the original scheme of the mid-30's and what was decided on only as several building campaigns succeeded one another through the next decade and later. Trentham must therefore be discussed more fully than Stafford House. Among other things the project entailed the creation of an enormous "architectural garden" on the flat terrain near Stoke-on-Trent where stood the rather bald late 17th-century brick mansion of the Marquesses of Stafford. In laying out the gardens at Trentham Barry had the collaboration of the landscape gardener William Andrews Nesfield (1793–1881) who was henceforth to be his usual associate in country house work.

The site must have appeared almost as hopeless in its lack of "capabilities" as the surroundings of the old Louis XIII hunting box at Versailles when Louis XIV set Le Nôtre to work. Even the Leveson-Gowers, moreover, with all their Bridgewater Canal and Sutherlandshire incomes, were not ready to spend as much as the Sun King. The results are certainly not impressive today in the way of many great 18th-century gardens, grand and gracious as ever though now untended. The empty parterres run flatly out to the edge of a considerable lake providing a rather ill-kept suburban plaisance for the inhabitants of the nearby pottery towns. Wood engravings of the period show what the gardens were originally like and early 20th-century photographs reveal that Trentham long remained a worthy memorial of Barry and Nesfield's strenuous efforts (Fig. VI 1).

In 1837, when the new reign opened, the Trentham Park operations were already being described in the Companion to the *British Almanac* as surpassing "for their variety and extent . . . everything else of the kind." The colonnaded hemicycle, providing a grandiose new entrance at the left of the old 17th-century block, as well as the one-storey private wing to the right had certainly been designed by then if not yet completely executed (Fig. VI 2). Next, the old block itself was refaced in cement, with giant pilasters (such as Barry in principle scorned) set at the corners and at intervals along the façades. A balustrade over the main entablature masked the old hip roof behind but the general effect remained rather makeshift. This part of the work was taken in hand in 1838. The great loggia-topped tower which once rose on the rear corner of the main block toward the stable court must be somewhat later (but before 1847). Although possibly planned earlier the less massive and more ornate tower across the stable court, which is fortunately still extant, is posterior to 1847. (The date derives from published views which show one tower but not the other.)

Today the main block and the private wing are entirely gone. But the arcades of the hemicycle on the left, with their engaged columns, and the longer straight arcade of the orangery on the right still remain on either side of a blank space on the low terrace where once stood the core of the complex. These fragments look like nothing so much as the remains of some exposition of the early 20th century. The tawdry cement, the endless repetition of conventional academic features, and the impossibility of reading any meaning into their disposition in the absence of the main block between make what remains unsatisfactory even as garden ruins. Another more ornate pavilion still stands to the far right; this is at the intersection of the orangery arcade with the sculpture gallery which runs along the far side of the stable court. This pavilion has a certain pathetic and frivolous fantasy about it that is rather appealing in the way of a Victorian ball gown found in an attic.

The stable court, which is almost completely extant, has more positive architectural quality. Not only are the various elements freely and organically disposed but the decaying ochre-painted stucco and the simple detail do suggest real Italian work, if not necessarily of any particular period. The remaining tower, set against the long high wall of the sculpture gallery on the right, is a rather brilliant piece of virtuosity in what the 20th century calls a Mannerist vein. Because of the considerable height and the skillfully verticalized arrangement of the decorative features this is premonitory of Barry's fine late tower on the Halifax Town Hall designed in 1859–60 at the very end of his life (Fig. VI 3). The special character of this tower at Trentham makes a late date (perhaps after 1850) probable; the comparable stable tower at Cliveden is not by Barry but by Clutton and still later in date.

There is a certain perverse fascination about Trentham even today; but it can never have represented very coherently Barry's concept of what a palatial modern mansion with its adjuncts should be and so it set no integrated model for imitation. Only the idea of using asymmetrically placed towers, such as had hitherto been used only on small villas, to provide massive vertical accents for large plain mansions was much copied. These towers were not merely striking and novel in their visual effect but were useful for storing water now that country houses began to have some interior plumbing. Other examples of the Italian Villa genre by Barry—for despite its size this is really as much a villa as a palazzo, if a quite gargantuan one—will be mentioned further on in this chapter and the next. But the progeny of Trentham are really exceptions to the main line of development in Early Victorian country house architecture; that took a rather different direction which will be discussed at some length in Chapter VIII.

Just as the work at Trentham got under way a new stage in Barry's career began in 1836 with his success in the Westminster competition. But this commission for the New Palace, although it provided his chief occupation for the rest of his life, did not pre-empt his entire time and energy; nor was it influential, in the way the Travellers' Club commission had been, in setting a major trend of style with Barry as its leader. Between the appearance of *Contrasts* in this year and 1845 Pugin built, or at least began, some forty cathedrals, churches, and chapels. In this same range of eight years, the first half of the Early Victorian period, the roster of Barry's individual works was naturally much less. Only about a dozen were of any consequence besides the New Palace and that modest number includes several remodelings. But even so the variety of Barry's work was much greater than that of Pugin's, and its influence was therefore wider if not so deep.

Throughout this period Pugin was not assisting Barry on the Palace. Only in 1844 did Barry commission him to take charge of all the ornamental part of the work, particularly that in the principal interiors. If Pugin apparently accomplished so much more building, many of his commissions were very small and very few were really carried through to completion. The range of his practice was also extremely limited. He did a little country house work for Catholics (see Chapter VIII) and various convents and schools; but essentially he was a specialist in church building for a minority sect.

Barry's practice in these years had a much more considerable scope and his worldly success—as also of course his income—was much greater too. There was other important government work for him to do besides the New Palace, one major urbanistic "improvement" in London, two churches, an institute, a major clubhouse, part of an Oxford college, and a good deal of country house work including the continuing operations at Trentham Park. In addition there was a British Embassy abroad on which he at least "advised," one or more suburban mansions (possibly), and even an important London prison. In each of these fields, except the ecclesiastical and the collegiate, Barry's contributions were distinguished and usually much imitated by others. He therefore richly deserved the honor when he was made a Royal Academician in 1844—he had been an Associate of the Academy since 1838.

Of all this varied production, it is the institute, the clubhouse, several of the country houses, the government building, and the prison that deserve the most attention; the projects for urban improvement and many other commissions, both executed and unexecuted, need only be touched on. It is his palaces, in the city and in the country, that establish Barry's very high rank, if not his absolute primacy, among Early Victorian architects.

The Manchester Athenaeum was planned in 1836 (Figs. I 2–3). In his pamphlet on Barry's work in Manchester Whiffen describes this institute as a "venture in adult education" which had been initiated in 1835. He also says that the building cost £18,000, of which two-thirds were raised by subscription, the other third on a mortgage. Construction began in 1837 and the institute was opened for use two years later in 1839. Unlike the Manchester Unitarian chapel, nominally Early English, which Barry was building in Upper Brook Street, Chorlton, in the same years, the Athenaeum is very typical of Barry. The character of its design stimulated a strong interest in Italian palace formulas among Manchester warehouse architects and thus had very important results locally in the late 40's (see Chapter XII).

The Athenaeum is larger and much more severe than the Travellers' Club

167

house; all but freestanding, it has a fine cube-like unity even if it lacks the grace of the earlier palazzo. The attempt to mask the lecture theater in the upper storey behind the cornicione made the proportions somewhat top-heavy. (The present balustrade and the ungainly mansard above it are later emendations; originally there was a low-pitched hip roof covered with Italian pantiles.) The trim of the windows, with little cornices over those of the ground storey and pediments over those above, is too modest to hold its own against the broad expanses of plain wall at the top and between the storeys.

An earlier version of the elevation, published in the *Surveyor, Engineer and Architect* in 1843, shows a range of attic windows linked in a sort of frieze and is distinctly superior to that executed (Fig. I 3). (This illustration must have done as much as the plates in Leed's monograph on the Travellers' Club house [Fig. I 7] and the elevation of the Reform Club house which provided the frontispiece of the first volume of the *Surveyor*, etc., in 1840 [Fig. VI 4], to familiarize contemporaries with Barry's palazzo mode.) The present solid frieze, however, ornamented only with a well-cut inscription, does provide a handsome frame to the plain upper wall surface. This frieze is a very refined version of a type, usually with sansserif letters in relief, that was to give distinction to many commercial buildings in the 40's.

The axial entrance to the Athenaeum is more emphasized than is usual with Barry and very correctly Roman of the High Renaissance. Engaged pilasters flanking the doorway carry an entablature of which the cornice corresponds to the stringcourse at the sill level of the first-storey windows. Broad steps bridge the front area which is masked by a balustrade as at the Travellers'.

If the atmosphere of Manchester had not coated the fine ashlar with so continuous a bloom of soot the refinement of the moldings and the precision of the detail in general would perhaps be more readily appreciated. The actual effect is somewhat flat and dull though enormously dignified in a frock-coated way. By the mid-40's, when the Negroid fate of all stonework in Manchester became evident, the local architects learned to increase the scale of their relief and the boldness of their detail. Thus the later Italianate façades nearby "read" more clearly despite their equally sooty patina.

The Manchester Athenaeum is chiefly interesting today as a fore-study of the Reform Club house, a commission Barry won in a limited competition just after the Athenaeum was begun. According to Whiffen, the design was produced by Barry between June and November 1837. The other invited competitors were Blore, Decimus Burton (1800–1881), Sir Robert Smirke, George Basevi (1794–1845), and C. R. Cockerell (1788–1863), all except Smirke more or less of Barry's generation. Of this lot of prominent architects of the 30's only Cockerell—and perhaps one may add Basevi—besides Barry himself were displaying in these years any leadership in post-Georgian design (see Chapters X and XI). The almost unanimous vote of the Club's building committee on 15 December 1837 to award Barry's design the first prize of £500 and to commission him is evidence of the members' desire to be up-to-date in matters of taste.

Like the Manchester Athenaeum, and unlike its neighbor the Travellers', the Reform is effectively freestanding. To protect the Travellers' from being overshadowed by its larger and taller neighbor Barry introduced a low recessed link in which the entrance and stairs to the bedroom floors of the new clubhouse were placed (Fig. VI 4). Thus the cornicione could continue unbroken around all four sides of the main block. The lack of a more important entrance was criticized from the first but Barry held out firmly against such a feature. His Manchester façade had led him to disapprove of strong central accents; they seemed to him to detract from the unity and regularity of a palazzo block despite the weight of actual Italian 16th-century precedent for their use.

The court, originally intended to be uncovered, received in the end a roof with plentiful glass areas. This was probably the first of the central halls soon to be a favorite feature of Victorian monumental planning. Although possibly suggested here by the treatment of the similar hall in Cockerell's competition project, this roof (in which iron beams played an important part) represented no more than a common-sense adaptation of the Italian *cortile* to the English climate by utilizing the new possibilities of glass and iron. This is quite characteristic of Barry's usual attitude toward modern or local functional needs and toward new materials and new methods of construction, all so very different from Pugin's.

The greater width of the site permitted a regularization of the Travellers' plan at the Reform (Fig. VI 5). But the staircase here is even less prominent than in the neighboring clubhouse, rising and turning between solid walls at one end of the central hall. The treatment of the open colonnades surrounding the hall is rich and indeed rather gorgeous now the gilt has been renewed with real gold leaf in a postwar refurbishment. Although (in deference to Pugin's violent attacks on shams) Barry is said to have "regretted the imposture," he used scagliola, gilding, and paintwork freely here, the cost of real marbles and real metal ornament being considered prohibitive. (The original tenders for the building ranged up from Grissell and Peto's £38,400 to Jackson's £42,586). The color treatment of the dining room as lately renewed is supposed to be original although it seems rather pale and Georgian. The rich brown and gold of several of the other rooms is certainly more satisfactory, although not Barry's. Nor is this the scheme for redecoration, with ceilings in white and gold, shown by E. M. Barry at the Royal Academy Exhibition in 1855, of which the *Builder, 13*, 220, remarked, "It is scarcely a step in advance"; most probably it belongs to the campaign of redecoration by Crossley of Newark in 1869. Less than with Pugin, however, is decoration in color important in Barry's architectural interiors.

In their praise of this major new clubhouse on its completion in 1840 contemporaries stressed the modernity and the technical elaboration of the kitchens. The equipment in them had been worked out by Barry in detail with the distinguished French chef of the club Alexis Soyer (d. 1858). T. L. Walker published the complete specifications of the steam-kitchen apparatus and other fittings in the seventh part of his *Architectural Precedents* (3d ed. 1841) together with a detailed plan of the basement. Soyer himself devoted much of the text of *The Gastronomic Regenerator* (1852) (said to be a "simplified and entirely new system of cookery"), as well as many illustrations, to this practical wonder of the age. It is well to remember that Barry, who was apparently so preoccupied with matters of visual taste, could thus cater on the highest international standard to the demands of taste in another sense. It was not for nothing that Barry had received in early youth an essentially practical training while he was articled to Middleton and Bailey. The mind boggles at the thought of Pugin coping with the culinary department of architecture—the abbot's kitchen at Glastonbury Abbey, later to provide the model for Deane and Woodward's Clarendon Laboratory at Oxford, would doubtless have been his ideal.

The exterior of the Reform has splendid dignity and scale. Grander in its proportions than the Travellers', it is also bolder in the treatment of the architectural features (Figs. VI 4, 6). Yet these are, as regards the first two storeys, so similar as to be nearly identical. The order of the first-storey edicules consists of half-columns instead of pilasters, while the cornices of the windows below are supported on scrolled brackets like those used only over the entrance door at the Travellers'. The central portal is nearly the same in design but it breaks the even line of the windows by its greater height as well as by its greater width. The balconettes at the first-storey windows are supported by consoles which interrupt the stringcourse below somewhat as on the rear of the Travellers'.

It is said that Barry regretted not using a third range of tall windows in the second storey like those on the Farnese Palace in Rome. He has, of course, often been accused of copying that façade too closely as it is; but his attic is actually more San Gallesque in feeling than the top storey which Michelangelo designed for the Roman palace. The line of nearly square windows, linked together by the strongly molded stringcourse below, provides a sort of frieze below the cornicione like the treatment originally proposed for the

Manchester Athenaeum. The tremendous modillioned cornice is absolutely, and also relatively, heavier than that crowning its lower and earlier neighbor.

On the front and the rear the evenly spaced ranges of windows are all but identical; the only difference is that the pediments of the edicules on the rear are segmental rather than pointed as on the front. The façade toward Carlton Gardens, facing south, also offers a more vigorous pattern of light and shade. On the west end the openings are grouped: two, four, and two. The center ones, corresponding to the middle section of the large room at this end on the first storey, have segmental pediments while the terminal pairs have pointed ones. These breaks in the regular rhythm of the western wall are accented by four chimneys that rise above the roof, two at the corners and two above the wider wall spaces. The corner chimneys provide rather mild examples of Barry's favorite end accents that were so characteristic of his design for the river front of the New Palace from the first. He would handle the same motif much more boldly at Bridgewater House ten years later (Figs. VII 7, 10).

The continuity of the balustrade around the basement areas provides a visual platform for all three façades. Suggesting a slightly projecting terrace below the great solid block of the building, this feature has much to do with creating that sense of aloof dignity Barry always sought and here so successfully achieved. Above this balustrade, along the Pall Mall front, a range of cast-iron lamp standards, rising in front of the plain wall spaces between the windows, suggests an imaginary frontal plane behind which the building seems to rise.

The effect of severe dignity in the façades—which actually makes most of Pugin's churches look rather frivolous—is doubtless in large part produced by the broad unbroken wall planes above the two lower ranges of windows, fortunately not so excessive here as on the Manchester Athenaeum. But the superb adjustment of scale and relief in the various conventional features—note, for example, the plain chamfering of the corner quoins—is almost equally important. Often as the essential scheme of this façade was to be imitated in the Victorian period, few architects were ever able to approach the sureness of Barry's hand. One may even prefer it to the Farnese itself where the relation between San Gallo's lower storeys and Michelangelo's top storey and cornicione always seems rather awkward. The even more confused relation of the elaborate central features there, in the two lower storeys, to the unbroken rhythm of the other openings helps to explain Barry's refusal to elaborate the central portal.

The Reform Club, of course, was founded to record the passage of the Reform Act of 1832. The mode of its new clubhouse was readily accepted as a symbol of the rising political power of the middle classes. In 1844 Henry

Flower used the astylar mode of Barry's two Pall Mall clubhouses for the Gresham Club in the City. Earlier still, at Liverpool, the Williams brothers in their Brunswick Buildings, built in 1841, first emulated the Italian palace in an office building, even to including a central court (Fig. XII 1). George Alexander had already borrowed the model for a bank at Bath designed in 1840, just as the Reform Club house itself was being completed (Fig. XI 6). But the next large West End clubhouse, the Conservative, was quite naturally somewhat conservative in its architecture.

Begun in 1843 and completed at least externally by 1844, this was the joint work of Sydney Smirke (1798–1877), who had earlier assisted his brother Robert on the Oxford and Cambridge Club house of 1835–37, and of George Basevi. This was Basevi's last commission of importance before his untimely death in 1845. The *parti,* or plan scheme, is much less clearly organized than that of the Reform or even of the Travellers'. The main entrance at one end is only approximately balanced by a bay window at the other; and from the entrance vestibule the main line of circulation has to turn at right angles into the central hall. This hall does not itself rise to two-storey height as at the Reform but a large circular hole in the ceiling allows light from the glass dome over the first-storey hall to reach the ground storey. The elaborate staircase at the rear, with a landing and double return flights, occupies rather more space than does the central hall, somewhat as at Burton's Athenaeum. The principal rooms are irregularly disposed along the St. James's Street front and down the right side, quite belying the pseudosymmetry of the main façade.

Externally the ground storey is entirely rusticated between the entrance porch and the bay window, both of which terminal features are flanked by Doric columns (Fig. VI 8). On the first storey engaged Corinthian columns are used all along the wall between the projecting end bays. In those, triple windows are introduced with complex pilaster clusters between them. (The motif rather resembles the central window group on the Farnese Palace which Barry had so carefully avoided copying.) The roof is masked with a conventional balustrade above a modest cornice. Despite the size and elaboration of the composition almost nothing is really novel here. The interior decorations are also very rich but they are just that—mere "interior decoration." The delicate painted arabesques in the central hall are the work of the German Sang, who was to do so much secular decorative work throughout the Early Victorian period. But post-Georgian seems to define both the inside and the outside of this clubhouse better than Early Victorian.

Before the Conservative Club house was finished the other Tory political club, the Carlton, determined upon an extensive remodeling of its Pall Mall quarters. The existing clubhouse had been built by Sir Robert Smirke in the

172

20's and was now most embarrassingly overshadowed and outshone by the new Reform next door. Sydney Smirke and Basevi, Barry, Cockerell, and Burton—all the established club architects except the elder Smirke—were among those invited to compete for the commission. The elderly Thomas Hopper (1776–1856) and the youthful Matthew Digby Wyatt (1820–1877), a brother of Thomas Henry Wyatt, were also invited, as well as several men of varying ages best known for their Gothic work, Poynter, Salvin, and even Pugin himself. The relatively obscure William Railton (1803–1877), architect in 1839 of the Nelson Column and of some rather feeble Gothic churches, not to speak of Lee and Duesbury, who had just completed the Town Hall at Derby, were on the list too. Sydney Smirke easily won the competition, having followed the line of outbidding Barry's severely Roman "Farnese Palace" with an ornately Venetian "St. Mark's Library." The alterations began in 1847 but were held up after only a small portion of the refacing had been completed; only in 1854 did the remodeling go forward again.

The new façade followed Sansovino's model very closely (Fig. VI 7). The completely plastic and articulated wall arcade of the first storey was elaborated as in the Venetian original with bold figure carving in the spandrels and garlands held by putti in the frieze; this arcading was destined in the mid-50's to have a considerable influence on commercial architecture. The ground storey could not, of course, have the open-arched loggia of its original in the Piazzetta; Smirke therefore repeated the arcade of the storey above except that the arches here were rusticated and the only carved work the boldly projecting heads on the keystones. The three central bays projected slightly and were flanked by coupled pilasters instead of engaged columns. This doubling of the order in the center was also repeated above modifying Sansovino's original even rhythm. The corners were strengthened by pairing a pilaster with a column in both storeys; this same combination of pilaster and column emphasized the entrance also which was in a single bay breaking still farther forward from the three-bay central projection.

On the garden side the central three bays also came forward and even rose into a tall attic that cut most awkwardly through the terminal balustrade. Compared to the Reform, the Carlton was much less correct in its use of a High Renaissance formula; but the more boldly modeled surfaces and the profusion of carving well illustrate the modulation of Early Victorian taste in the late 40's away from the severity of Barry's early prime. Unfortunately the Carlton was again refaced in this century and then badly blitzed; the extant ruins show no trace of Sydney Smirke's work.

The Army and Navy Club house across Pall Mall early rivaled the Carlton in its Venetian splendor and is still in pristine condition externally. A first open competition for this was held in 1846–47; 68 architects entered and

George Tattersall won. After a larger site had been obtained, a second competition was held for six invited architects; this time C. Octavius Parnell (d. 1865) with his partner Alfred Smith won. Begun in 1848, the building was opened in February 1851 while Sydney Smirke's new front on the clubhouse across Pall Mall still remained but a fragment.

Here the model was Sansovino's Palazzo Cornaro, and most of Sydney Smirke's archaeological solecisms were avoided (Fig. VI 9). Three tall arches at the entrance, ornamented with vermiculated rustication, provide an emphatic central feature without requiring any break in the plane of the façade. The range of rusticated piers joining the ground storey with a mezzanine above was to prove as suggestive as the rich arcades of the upper storeys to later commercial architects. (Actually, Cockerell had already approached this treatment in the Westminster Bank, as we shall see in Chapter XIII, but with a more Georgian restraint.)

Although the Venetian façades of these later Pall Mall clubhouses of the 40's were to have an influence on commercial architecture a few years later, the Roman design formula of the Reform, rapidly decreasing in severity as window frames became richer and bolder, remained the favorite model for most clubs well into the 60's and even beyond. In the second (1848) competition for the Army and Navy Club house young George Truefitt (1824–1902) submitted a richly pinnacled and gabled Gothic project with broad square-topped windows set between buttresses and a projecting tower above the entrance porch. Not until the mid-60's, however, did any major club in London or the provinces relinquish in favor of Gothic the Roman or Venetian palace models of Barry and Sydney Smirke. In America the clubhouse formula of the Early Victorian period, first introduced by the Scottish-born John Notman at the Philadelphia Athenaeum in the 40's, was to continue down into the 20th century with very little change and no improvement. The best late exterior would be that of McKim, Mead, and White's University Club house in New York which has been admired even by Le Corbusier; the best interiors perhaps Willis Polk's in the Pacific Union Club in San Francisco.

The social and political club was a 19th-century British institution that was as characteristic of the new age, for all its long Georgian ancestry, as the "de-reformed" Anglicanism of the Tractarians. For it Barry had established at a very early date a clubhouse model as enduring as that provided by the churches of Pugin and the Camdenians. The relevance of the palazzo connotation for urban clubhouses may have been rather more remote and arbitrary than it was for commercial edifices (see Chapter XI); but because the new clubs were major centers of mundane influence Barry's type of

174

Italian design early came to be accepted as expressive of urban wealth and power, and so it long remained. Characteristic of the confused approach of the Early Victorians toward expression in architecture, an approach destined to last well into the present century, is the fact that the "club style" (so to call it) was also used for buildings whose purpose was very different indeed from those of the Travellers' and the Reform.

Perhaps because of the prominence of Barry's Manchester Athenaeum the palazzo mode was soon widely used for housing cultural agencies which had the worthy intention of extending to the middle classes, and even to "industrious mechanics," opportunities for self-improvement little known in earlier Georgian times. The first Victorian examples of such institutions were still completely Grecian. The Leicester General News Room and Library, opened in 1837 and designed by a local architect, W. Flint, had Greek Ionic engaged columns set between more solid corner bays. The still more conservatively designed Royal Institution of South Wales in Swansea by Long of Liverpool, begun in 1838, had an Ionic portico projecting in the middle of a plain oblong block just like a Palladian mansion of the 18th century.

Moxhay's Hall of Commerce in Threadneedle Street in the City, built in 1842, was one of the first comparable structures to be astylar more or less in the way of Barry's clubhouses (Fig. VI 10). The heavy frames of the ground-storey openings carried cornices supported on very bold scrolled brackets, only that of the central doorway being capped with a pediment. There were no openings in the upper wall; instead an allegorical relief extended nearly the full length of the façade. The whole composition was then crowned with a cornicione above a rich scrolled frieze. The new monumental scale introduced here must have been as striking as that of Cockerell's Westminster Bank and his Sun Assurance buildings nearby (Figs. XI 2, 4), for the tremendous cornice was on a line with the parapet tops of the neighboring four-storey houses. Moxhay's venture was a personal speculation without public support and not a success; it is sad to report that it soon degenerated to more profit-reaping use as a bank.

In the Nottingham Mechanics Institute, completed in 1844 by Robert Jalland, in the Physicians' Hall in Edinburgh of 1844–45 by Thomas Hamilton (1784–1858), and in the Museum at Ipswich, completed in 1847 by the local architect Fleury, various modifications of the Grecian as used for institutional edifices appear, all aimed at producing richer and more plastic effects. Of these Hamilton's hall, in Queen Street on the North side of the New Town, is the most successful (Fig. VI 11). This carries only a moderate cornice; but a columned central edicule, with a special sort of Corinthian detail, projects boldly at the first-storey level above a wider entrance porch. Of course Hamilton's forms are Greek—if like Cockerell's rather subtle and scholarly in character—but the total effect here is Victorian in the rather transitional way of the later Greek Revival in America.

The Ipswich Museum is neither subtle nor scholarly. Giant Doric columns are set in the hollowed-out corners of the façade, surely an extraordinary device for achieving bold plasticity since it is at once clumsy, arbitrary, and expensive. The precise purposes and backing of this institution are not entirely clear but it was generically educational in intention. The Nottingham Institute, of the three the most characteristic of the genre functionally, has the least visual interest.

The Southampton Yacht Club—not exactly a cultural institution, but similar in scale and pretensions—was built by Thomas Sander Hack in 1845. His name is almost too good to be true for a provincial architect of this period, but his Italian palazzino was considerably better than hack work. Although symmetrical in design and compounded of conventional elements this was as unashamedly picturesque as the Italian Villa compositions in Charles Parker's books (Fig. VI 12). The first storey rose over a Tuscan portico to display a range of shell-arched windows like those on the rear of the Travellers' Club house (Fig. II 19). Above this was a wide expanse of plain wall and then tiny attic windows set between the unusually bold scrolled consoles supporting the cornicione. From the corners of the hip roof, which was covered with special Italian pantiles, there rose paneled and corniced chimneys. In the center of the main roof was a low arcaded observation loggia with its own little tile-covered shelter; this was doubtless suggested, like the shell-filled arches below, by Barry's intended crowning feature on the Travellers' Club house. Yet Hack's was a very different Italianism from the severe dignity of the Manchester Athenaeum and the Reform. Piquant and original, it catered more happily to Early Victorian tastes, however, than did the corrupt Classicism hitherto usual for provincial institutes and clubhouses.

George Alexander's Sheffield Athenaeum and Mechanics' Institution, begun in 1847 at a contract cost of some £4,500, was almost literally a "little Reform Club house" like his earlier bank in Bath (Figs. VI 15, XI 6). Occupying a site in Surrey Street at the corner of Tudor Street among low and vulgar houses, this rose foursquare with its three tall storeys crowned by a relatively modest cornicione. Of course in this much smaller building (60 feet by 56½ feet and but 26½ feet high), with only five openings across the front and six on the side, the Reform model was slightly modified as well as reduced in scale. The entrance had Doric pilasters and an entablature above the door arch; the pediments over the first-storey windows were alternately pointed and segmental, while the attic window frames had their own little cornices.

In Manchester the Mechanics' Institute in Princess Street was built by John Edgar Gregan (1813–1855) as late as 1854–55, just before his early death. This rivals Barry's Athenaeum of nearly twenty years earlier in dignity if not in the correctness of the proportions. The windows on the front are larger here and more closely spaced in three even ranges; the parapet is solid and rises rather too high above the severe cornice. Muted though it is by Manchester grime, the color contrast of the superbly laid red brick of the walls with the crisply cut gray stone trim is also very handsome and provides an interest not found in Barry's comparable work. The arched entrance is set under a bracket-supported cornice that rises into the line of the first-storey stringcourse. This is excellently proportioned and rather less conventional than Alexander's entrance at Sheffield.

The Institute has altogether a *tenue* comparable to Barry's Athenaeum and yet rather more character withal; for the external expression of the irregularities of the plan, which includes lecture theaters as well as ordinary rooms, is made at once clear and visually effective by the asymmetrical but carefully ordered design of the exposed left flank of the building. A mere repetition on this side of the three ranges of windows of the front façade, while closer to Barry's original formula, would have been much less satisfactory than are the varied window sizes Gregan used; for these clearly suggest the sequence of rooms of different shapes within, yet are nicely related by their harmonious proportions.

Alexander had been partly trained on the Continent by the French architect A. N. Caristie (1783–1862) and his travels had been as extensive as Barry's. Gregan had no such early advantages. But the work of both men illustrates that a new discipline of rather restrained academic design had become established in the 40's which was generally capable of producing edifices of at least modest distinction; this lasted well through the middle years of the next decade. Such design did not lead forward but it is often very satisfactory in itself, like the design of many modest Georgian structures.

To consider examples from the work of one architect only, the academic sobriety of Sydney Smirke's Athenaeum at Bury (Fig. VI 20), begun in 1850 in New Market Street next to the municipal building he had just completed there, may well be preferred to the Sansovinesque elaboration of his Carlton Club house (Fig. VI 7). At Bury a dignified range of pedimented windows occupies the upper storey with plain panels sunk in the wall spaces between. These panels illustrate the tendency to move away from the isolated window trim characteristic of early examples of the palazzo mode toward a richer surface treatment; but the effect is still very restrained and severe here. At the Carlton, where there was no more plain wall or flat surface left, Smirke had already led the way toward a complete articulation of masonry structure such as would later produce the finest commercial façades of the succeeding High Victorian period.

Before leaving the subject of Early Victorian cultural buildings in small cities a word should be said about the Plymouth and Cottonian Library erected by George Wightwick in Cornwall Street, Plymouth, in 1851–52. Here the interior was lighted by a central monitor with only the simplest and most delicate divisions (almost certainly of iron) between the large clerestorey windows. But the cove over the cast of the Panathenaic frieze from the Parthenon that crowned the wall, as well as the ceilings above and below the monitor, was ornamented in a fashion at once lush and flat, recalling the exotic decorations on his master Soane's very latest works at Westminster. But this post-Soanic richness is more or less peculiar to Wightwick in its lack of the new Victorian boldness of relief.

On the exterior of the library similar ornament, used in moderation, is successfully associated with a very personal version of the palazzo mode (Fig. VI 16). In the ground storey triple windows of almost Grecian severity flank a flat entrance edicule. A quite Soanic panel rises above the façade in the middle of the crowning balustrade over a cornice that is definitely no cornicione. The balconettes below and the pediments over the three first-storey windows, supported as they are on heavy scrolled brackets, provide bolder relief. The band of rosettes on the architrave of the main entablature recalls the friezes on Barry's clubhouses even though the fret on either side of the fine raised inscription in the frieze is still Grecian and geometrical.

This library and various other Plymouth buildings by Wightwick of the 40's and 50's should remind us that retardataire architecture may sometimes have positive virtues even though it is almost always inferior in assurance and integrity to earlier work in its particular tradition. Wightwick sought to retain the urbane virtues of the old Georgian modes long after they had become obsolescent while also catering to some aspects of the new Victorian taste. He had real talent, moreover, and his work is generally preferable to that of many bolder Early Victorian architects in the provinces such as poor Fleury in Ipswich.

It was not in the British provinces or even in London, curiously enough, that the palazzo mode of the Reform Club house was first consistently applied to the design of a mansion. The British Embassy in Istanbul, built in 1845–47 by W. J. Smith, seems to have provided the earliest example of a really palatial Early Victorian residence in the Italian manner. It was known at home only through the publication of a rather crude perspective (Fig. VI 17). Apparently Smith had based his design on sketches made by Barry as early

178

as 1842; later, when the building was nearly complete, Barry "modified [Smith's] design . . . to an extent that greatly determined the general effect," according to his son and biographer. This Constantinopolitan variant of the Reform had little immediate influence on house building in Britain. The depressed economic climate of the mid-40's was not particularly conducive to the building of large urban mansions in Britain.

Two five-storey houses flanking Albert Gate in Knightsbridge, erected in 1843–45 by the builder Thomas Cubitt (1788–1855), are something of an exception to these statements and remain conspicuous even today. They are not, however, really convincing examples of palazzo design (Fig. VI 14). Not surprisingly, the larger of the two (that to the west) was taken on completion by one of the most prosperous of the nouveaux riches, George Hudson, the railroad "king" from York, then at the peak of his career. This is now the French Embassy and has been considerably enlarged. The two houses were designed by someone in Cubitt's office but probably not by his architect-brother Lewis. Characteristic features of the Reform were utilized to introduce a new and fashionable note into what are really oversized terminal terrace houses, semi-isolated though they stand between Knightsbridge and the edge of the Park. The edicules of the first-storey windows, the balconettes at this level and below the second-storey windows, not to speak of the tall bracketed cornice, give unusual boldness of relief to the cliff-like stucco walls. But there is no particular individuality or refinement in the designing of the façades as a whole or in the cinquecento detailing. The planning includes a glass-domed central stairhall in each house, and throughout the size and the disposition of the rooms is more generous than in ordinary terrace houses of the period.

A more ambitious London project was undertaken by a man named Blashfield in 1844. Leasing land which the Office of Works had just made available on the site of the kitchen gardens of Kensington Palace, he arranged for the building of 21 large freestanding houses. These were mostly supposed to be "Italian" and were erected from designs provided by Wyatt and Brandon, Owen Jones, and H. E. Kendall. According to the account given in the *Builder* in 1852, "for a time the speculation languished and some who built there early must have suffered." Other architects besides those just mentioned certainly began houses in Kensington Palace Gardens in the mid-40's although several may have remained in carcass down into the 50's as Decimus Burton's Harrington House certainly did.

One of the finest houses in Kensington Palace Gardens (No. 15) is frequently attributed to Barry although his biographer does not list it among his works and other evidence assigns it to James T. Knowles. Certainly this mansion, now also an embassy, is much handsomer than the Cubitt houses at Albert Gate and most carefully designed (Fig. VI 13). The façade has Corinthian edicules at the first-storey windows and there are small attic windows above which cut through the frieze below the rich cornicione. The ground storey is rusticated and flanked by two small wings at either end. The entrance is emphasized, in the way Barry deprecated, by a pair of engaged columns and an entablature. The execution in stucco is excellent but naturally lacks the firmness and weight of Barry's work in stone—though no more than do his own additions to Trentham Park.

Another slightly smaller mansion in Kensington Palace Gardens—five windows wide instead of seven—was designed by Robert Richardson Banks (1813–1872). Like Gibson, Banks started as an assistant of Barry's, in his case from 1838 to 1847. He later practiced in partnership with the younger Charles Barry until his death. This earlier house was rather the superior of the two, being less crowded in design and having its square attic windows set below and not across the frieze, here very richly ornamented. The pediments were over the ground-storey windows but the entrance motif was practically identical (Fig. VI 21). From the date of construction, 1845, it is evident Banks was still working in Barry's office at the time he designed this house. Knowles' house was built in 1847 and presumably derives from Banks'.

These two very Barryesque houses seem to have set a pace for the rest of the mansions in this select development; but most of them have been so rebuilt or altered at various periods from the 60's on down to our own day that it is hard to know what they were like originally. The houses Owen Jones built here in the 40's were not Italian; instead they carry the sort of Moorish ornamentation which might be expected of the famous author of the *Alhambra*. They seem more like oversized Georgian garden fabrics than serious Early Victorian mansions. When Alderman Moor's house, supposedly founded on the Alhambra, was shown by Jones at the Architectural Exhibition in 1849, the *Builder*, 7, 109, found it "clever but unsuitable." The house at No. 3 was shown by Jones at the Architectural Exhibition as late as 1863 (*Builder*, 21, 255) and may well be of that date.

The Earl of Harrington's mansion, originally designed and begun by Decimus Burton in the 40's, was finally finished by C. J. Richardson only in 1852 (presumably with the profits from the sale of his South Kensington estate to the Commissioners of the Exhibition of 1851). It is of a pinched and dry Tudor rather casually applied to a symmetrical body in the Late Georgian way. Like Jones' oriental super-villas, this mansion seems decades out of date beside the more characteristic Italian houses. Another even more prominent, as well as far finer, Gothic house of the late 40's in London will find a place in the next chapter.

180

A decade before Barry's indirect connection with the design of the finest houses in Kensington Palace Gardens his country house work had got under way at Trentham Park, and there operations continued through these years at a rather slow pace. Because of the tremendous scale and the piecemeal nature of the alterations Trentham provided no viable model for imitation by others. It was in Barry's considerably more complete remodeling of the ancestral seat of the Earl of Tankerville at Walton-on-Thames, quite near London, which began in 1837, that a complete Italian exemplar was first offered for Early Victorian country houses.

The relatively modest main block of the earlier Georgian house at Walton was not much modified. The evenly spaced windows were given strong but simple academic enframements and the roof was covered, above a bold cornicione, with pantiles of Italian pattern (these were, in fact, especially made for this job and used here for the first time in England). A new vaulted and arcaded entrance gallery masked the extensive service quarters which were grouped around a court at one end of the main block; but the gallery's principal purpose was to provide a grand approach to the saloon.

At the outer end of the gallery a tall, loggia-topped tower, rising over the carriage porch, dominated more effectively than that at Trentham the mass of the house. Unlike the designers of small villas in the 20's and 30's, Barry made no attempt to break up the main block and group it asymmetrically around the tower; but the strong accent of a tall tower, usually placed as at Walton toward one end of the house, became a favorite feature henceforth in various kinds of country house design, as has already been noted. Not many large new houses followed this enlarged and half-regularized Italian Villa mode at all strictly; but what Barry had accomplished with a minimum of alteration to the Georgian block of Walton House did suggest a useful formula for modernizing 18th- and early 19th-century houses that remained more or less popular down through the 70's.

Of course Wyatville had already attempted something of the sort at Chatsworth for the 6th Duke of Devonshire, beginning in the 20's. But the new service wing there and its very large loggia tower were not really integrated with the composition of the 17th-century house. Chatsworth, in any event, had always been too large and too grand to be much imitated by landowners of less than ducal pretensions. When the Queen bought Osborne House to use as her private summer residence in 1845 it was certainly her friend the Duchess of Sutherland's private apartments at Trentham Park rather than the Duke of Devonshire's service wing at Chatsworth that suggested attaching a new Royal block of Italian design by means of an arcaded gallery to one corner of the simple old house on the estate. She and Albert had visited

Chatsworth in 1843, but it seems to have been Paxton's conservatory rather than Wyatville's work that made an impression on them (see Chapter XV)—that and the illumination of the gardens at night, also Paxton's doing.

At Osborne the new block, which went up rapidly in 1845–46, was built by Thomas Cubitt without benefit of any architect at all. Cubitt doubtless carried out fairly specific instructions from Prince Albert; but the result rather resembles the Albert Gate mansions which were then just being completed (Fig. VI 14) and the designs are presumably from the same anonymous hand in the Cubitt office. Thus this rather amorphous stucco-covered lump, although detached, has quite the air of an enlarged terrace house and is curiously inappropriate to a country site or to Albert's pretensions to cultivated taste (Figs. VI 22–23). Osborne was bought and enlarged with the Royal family's private funds, now rapidly increasing thanks to Albert's excellent management; thus the consort was almost as much one of the new-rich as "King" Hudson who took the larger of the two Albert Gate mansions.

If the design of Osborne was commonplace, the construction throughout was nevertheless remarkably solid despite the rather tawdry use of cement for the exterior. All the floors are carried on iron girders, with brick jack-arches between, so that the edifice was more nearly fireproof than most urban buildings of the day. The roof is flat and raised on two ranges of brick arches with an air space between for insulation. Leveled up with asphalt, it provided a usable terrace reached by a solid teak staircase in the tower. As we will note in other connections, Albert's technical standards were well ahead of those of most of his contemporaries. But his architectural standards, as evidenced here, seem to indicate that he had little real understanding of the new Victorian work of Barry and other professional leaders of the day.

The loggia-topped tower rises from one of the rear corners of the 1845–46 block at Osborne in total disregard of the absolute symmetry of all the façades (Fig. VI 22). But for its heavy Italianate trim, the curving bay window in the center of the garden front, with its metal awning shading the first-storey balcony, might perhaps have had some Regency grace of a quite domestic order; instead it is clumsy and makeshift in appearance quite as if it were an afterthought. The polygonal bay in the center of the terrace front is still more domestic and unpalatial in character. Additional awkward breaks on the other sides of the block fritter away any unity of effect this rather bumptious cube of cement might have had.

The detail is much heavier and cruder than on the Barryesque houses in Kensington Palace Gardens, lacking even the relative virtue of that on the Albert Gate mansions. A few edicular windows are used in the first storey but not consistently enough to provide, as on the London houses, a coherent rhythm. Even the heavily—too heavily—bracketed cornice at the top cannot unify the design because of the many breaks in the plan. The effectiveness of the tower—the only feature that really recalls Barry—is spoiled by the way this cornice cuts across it, reducing its apparent height and breaking the vertical outline.

When, in the immediately succeeding years 1847–49, the old house was torn down and a large new main block built on its site, the virtue of the original tower as a dominant vertical accent was further weakened by the addition of another slighter tower at the far end of the new work. The terrace façade of this lengthy new block, also designed in the Cubitt office, is markedly symmetrical; an elaborate triplet motif marks the center in all three storeys and two-storey wings project at the ends to connect with the earlier square pavilion and the new tower (Fig. VI 23). The prominent use of Palladian motifs on these low wings and along the long side façade makes evident, even more than the clumsiness of the original block, how little either Albert or Cubitt grasped the true character of Barry's Italianism either in the outright palatial version of the Reform Club house or the more villa-like one of Walton House.

Undoubtedly the arcading of the subsidiary features at Trentham Park suggested—together with some of the later and poorer Italianate work at Potsdam such as the Orangerieschloss—the fussy elaboration of the features here at Osborne. But the stupid result confirms the suspicion, based on the employment of a builder rather than an architect, that the Royal family had no real respect for the profession. Doubtless they would actually have preferred to live in one of the new stucco terraces of Bayswater—or at best in Mr. Hudson's mansion—rather than in a country house designed by any of the leading architects of the day. According to an old-established English tradition the aristocracy continued to outbuild Royalty in the Victorian Age. As in the 17th century the Herberts got the finest work of the day.

According to his son and biographer, Barry was first consulted by the Earl of Carnarvon in 1837 about remodeling Highclere Castle near Burghclere in Hampshire. The earliest drawings preserved, those at the Royal Institute of British Architects, carry the date 1840, however; and an account published along with a perspective view in the *Building News* in 1858 stated that construction was not even begun until 1842. Although the *Builder* reported in 1844 that the refacing of the exterior was then "quite completed," as well as the erection of the lofty tower, the modernization of the rather plain old Georgian block here certainly dragged on for many years, probably at least into the 50's as at Trentham Park.

Barry's son remarks that although "the whole constructional framework of the house was retained . . . yet the building became in the strictest sense new and original." Original in any strict sense it certainly is not, since the basis of the design is Jacobethan, but new it was (Figs. I 7, VI 19). The picturesqueness and irregularity of the pre-academic styles of English architecture, hitherto so much emphasized in most 19th-century country houses not Classical in design, is very much under control here. The result can be considered a triumph for Barry's skill at adaptation and his real architectonic talents.

Although he himself described the mode of Highclere as "Anglo-Italian," not Elizabethan or Jacobean, the character of the detail is definitely early 17th-century English. It has, moreover, a delicacy and richness of effect quite different from the severity of his cinquecento Italian work. Probably it was the close spacing of the window openings in the original house that determined the choice of Anglo-Italian rather than Palatial-Italian. Barry considered that the windows should be much more widely spaced in his preferred mode; but it was his desire to achieve breadth of effect rather than a respect for academically correct proportions that controlled his thinking. Here at Highclere breadth was to be obtained through over-all reticulation of the surface, as on the New Palace. The vertical linking of the many openings and the elaboration of the skyline with an open strapwork balustrade and finial-like obelisks, as well as the tall slim towers Barry added on the corners of the original block, produced at Highclere a composition remarkably similar to that of the river front at Westminster.

Particularly characteristic of Barry is the strong end-emphasis these towers provide. Contrary to his usual practice he emphasized the center also, at least on the entrance front. Not only is there a projecting porch on the ground storey; ranges of strapwork-ornamented pilasters frame the three central bays in each of the upper storeys and an attic rises over those bays nearly as high as the corner towers. Even more characteristic of Barry is the great keep-like main tower. This is actually in the middle of one of the sides of the block, but it forms a strong asymmetrical accent as seen from most directions. In the original design for this main tower, as seen in a water color preserved in the Royal Institute of British Architects Library, the range of openings in the top storey would have recalled the loggias atop his other country house towers; the corner turrets, on the other hand, suggested those on the Victoria Tower as it was finally to be completed two decades later. The executed tower is a more independent and unified invention.

Barry's Anglo-Italian depended so much on the use of a profusion of rather small-scale motifs that it cannot be analyzed with the precision appropriate to the more cut-and-dried Italian palace mode. The over-all reticulation at Highclere is produced by continuous horizontal and vertical members of generically Renaissance order. The window frames are linked from storey to storey by carved panels above and below, while ornate pilasters on the corners of the towers and between the bays in the center of the front provide richer vertical accents. The horizontal lines of the entablatures above each storey and the stringcourses at the window-sill levels cross all these verticals thus paneling, in a sense, the entire wall surface. The verticals, moreover, are carried up past the cornice at the top of the main block onto the attic walls of the corner towers and the parapets between. In the subordinate turrets at the corners of the main tower and in the little obelisks above the "stiles" of the parapets the ascending lines finally terminate in ranges of sharp points against the sky almost as profuse as those on Milan Cathedral. Highclere is thus quite as much—and as little—Gothic in spirit as the New Palace. Inside, moreover, the entrance lobby and the great central hall are also Gothic, the former in a surprisingly advanced Victorian way with colonnettes of brilliantly colored marble, a note of polychromy that suggests a date in the 50's.

The significant thing about the great hall is not the Tudor character of the detailing but its position in the plan. Possibly the old Georgian Highclere may have been quadrangular, although that is rather unlikely. However that may be, the plan of the present house represents an adaptation of that of the Reform Club house to country house purposes. The Renaissance colonnades surrounding the hall of the clubhouse in both storeys are here reinterpreted as Tudor arcades, while the open timber roof overhead has sufficient skylights in it to provide light for what is the principal apartment of the house, not a mere center of circulation. Although the staircase on the right, which rises in the lower portion of the great tower, is screened from the hall by the arcading, it is not of the enclosed type between walls which Barry used at the Reform but rises around a square open well and is brilliantly lighted by windows in the outer wall of the tower.

The other main rooms at Highclere, the dining room occupying the right half of the entrance front and the library extending back from the other side of the entrance front along most of one of the garden fronts—the other garden front is occupied by smaller apartments—are of no great interest since Barry's work is much confused by various elements that are both earlier and later in date. Even the hall, whose original dark varnished oak has been pickled by the present Lord Carnarvon to provide a more cheerful 20th-century air, is not distinguished in detail. Barry evidently had no assistance here from Pugin, whose more authentically medieval great hall at Scarisbrick, also designed in the late 30's and many, many years a-building, he was perhaps consciously attempting to rival.

It is the planning of Highclere that gives it considerable historical significance. On a quite different scale from that of Butterfield's tiny Coalpitheath vicarage Highclere provides another early essay in agglutinative planning.

185

Two rooms could hardly be more different in effect today than what remains of the small stairhall at Coalpitheath and this tall toplighted central space with its contiguous monumental staircase at Highclere. But in their essential conception as real living areas, not mere passages, and in the irregular grouping around them of the more specialized living rooms of different sizes and shapes, both are premonitory of the advanced house planning of the 60's.

Evidently contemporaries saw some connection not evident today between the planning of Highclere and its Jacobethan exteriors, for at least two other important country houses, both considerably later, follow Barry's model in the two respects. Paxton's Mentmore, at least, more than rivals Highclere in size and in the profusion of the Jacobethan ornament, as also in the amplitude of the glass-roofed central hall (Fig. VIII 24). Externally it is less original, following Wollaton much more closely than does Highclere; inside, the real 18th-century French *boiseries* and the magnificent old furniture and pictures somewhat obscure the Early Victorian character of the total effect. Banks and Barry's Bylaugh Hall, empty if not demolished today, was never a real rival to Highclere (Fig. VIII 34).

Both at Highclere and at Mentmore the superb surrounding parks enhance the total effect. Indeed, as one sees these crisp and intricate stone piles, at once monumental in scale and varied in silhouette, one cannot but recall that Richard Payne Knight, a generation earlier at the height of the Picturesque period, had shown a large Jacobethan house in a naturalistic park as his *beau idèal* of an English gentleman's mansion. The ideal was originally, therefore, a Late Georgian one but Barry's realization of it at Highclere was an Early Victorian triumph. As much as at the Reform and less ambiguously than at Westminster he displayed here his very real architectural talent. Fello Atkinson has said of Highclere—and he was thinking of Vanbrugh's Blenheim as well—"English architects achieve their greatest architectonic effects when they design pictorially." By its very existence Highclere somewhat negatives the general criticisms of the Victorian use of the Jacobethan set down in the first two chapters. Yet it is an exception: typical of Barry but not typical of the Barryesque, which was to contemporaries the palazzo mode of his clubhouses.

Highclere is in fact Barry's only important work in the Anglo-Italian vein. This is curious since it seems to have been a favorite work of his—perhaps because of the completeness, so unusual in his remodelings, with which the character of the original house had been transmuted. Only Gawthorpe Hall in Lancashire is at all similar. That is an old Elizabethan house which Barry modified slightly by raising the towers and the chimneys and by adding a pierced parapet to mask the roofs. But the model he provided at Highclere was generally influential well into the 50's on various other architects doing country house work, even if few of them except Paxton and his own son Charles understood the value of his innovations in planning or approached his skill in architectonic organization of the exterior.

Haphazard imitation of Jacobethan architecture had become fairly frequent by the mid-30's but it was usually greeted then with disapproval as being "debased" or "corrupt" in detail. A new visual documentation rapidly brought a change of attitude. To the series of carefully prepared books by C. J. Richardson and Henry Shaw of the late 30's to which reference was made in Chapter I, Joseph Nash added his monumental *Mansions of England of the Olden Time* (4 series, 1839–49) which began to appear in parts in 1837. The many extremely pictorial lithographs of exteriors and interiors in this, animated with figures in early 17th-century costume, fed the growing delight in the period and the style at the opening of the new reign. The contemporary interest in Italian Renaissance palace architecture produced no serious archaeological documents in England, as has been said, nor even any popular imagery of the Nash order. A scholarly Renaissance Revival in Britain was therefore restricted to architects like Barry—there were actually a good many of them—who had themselves been in Italy and made their own drawings; the most intelligent clients were those who had themselves made the grand tour. It required little travel or cultivation to relish the Jacobethan.

Yet the Jacobethan Revival was soon almost as well provided with accurate published plates of old work as was the Gothic Revival. One may assert, indeed, that illustrations of 16th–17th-century work were better than those available of 13th–14th-century work; even if the available visual documentation on the Jacobethan was much less profuse the monuments had generally been more sympathetically seen and more accurately drawn. In any event the old detail often had those particular qualities of hardness combined with fussiness which seem to have been natural to Early Victorian carvers. Barry probably had made little personal study of real Jacobethan work and depended on published material for the details of Highclere as he would not have done to the same extent for Italian Renaissance details. Yet because of his sure sense of scale and the crisp workmanship he obtained from his carvers the detailing of Highclere may well be preferred to that of much original work of Elizabeth's or James I's time. Certainly one would never mistake its peculiar hard elegance for the production of any century but the 19th. Innumerable less sensitive designers, leaning on the same plates in Shaw's and Richardson's books, turned out Jacobethan buildings in the 40's and 50's that were considerably more plausible than Barry's—as also more plausible than even the best Gothic of the Camdenians.

This is notably true of Harlaxton, near Grantham in Lincolnshire, by Anthony Salvin which has already been mentioned in this particular connection. Considerably larger than Highclere and not a remodeling, this house was begun before 1837 and built gradually through the 40's and 50's for Gregory Gregory whose mother was a de Ligne heiress. In 1853 the *Builder*, *11*, 569, reported that construction had been going on "during the last fourteen years" and that more than £ 100,000 had already been spent. Ten years before, however, the *Illustrated London News*, 7 May 1843, p. 357, had provided a wood engraving of the new mansion which was described as "now approaching completion," the construction according to the writer having then "occupied nearly twenty years at a cost, it is said, to the proprietor of from £ 8,000 to £ 10,000 a year." Fortunately for the Gregory family the old house at Harlaxton, which was on a different site, remained more or less habitable while the endless campaign of building what the writer referred to as the "'proper house' of the English gentleman" went forward.

Harlaxton is an enormously complex pile and entirely executed in good freestone like Highclere, the stone here having been brought from Ancaster. It does not look much like Highclere because of its extremely broken outline with many high, scalloped gables and bay windows (Figs. I 9, VI 24). The plan is predominantly symmetrical, but it follows the authentically Elizabethan combined E and H scheme rather than the block-with-central-court model of Highclere. The inspiration evidently came from Burleigh House for the exterior though not for the plan.

Harlaxton is surprisingly correct archaeologically not only in its planning but even more in the profusion, the large size, and the variety of the mullioned windows. The particular character of the detail, which is coarser and less crisp than at Highclere, is also more authentic. An English magnate of the late 16th century might have been better pleased with Harlaxton than a Roman noble of the Renaissance with the Reform Club house—or a medieval prelate with a Pugin church, for that matter. But the endless elaboration of the skyline, with its clustered chimneys, its intersecting gables, and its domelike turret tops, however correct, produces a disordered picturesqueness that contrasts unhappily with the clear silhouette of Highclere topped by its regular hedge of obelisks and dominated by its massive tower (Fig. VI 33). The lack of a principal vertical accent, such as Barry's great towers provided, denies Harlaxton the real novelty of Walton House or even Trentham. In its total effect, as presumably in the date of its original design, it is pre-Victorian in a way Highclere is not.

The Jacobethan mansions of Edward Blore, because of the somewhat earlier version of the mode he favored and his predilection for asymmetry, belong rather with the manorial type of country house to which Chapter VIII will be devoted. But one of the very few really large and almost completely rebuilt houses of the mid-40's, Somerleyton Hall in Norfolk, is clearly modeled on Highclere rather than on Blore's or Salvin's characteristic work. Samuel Morton Peto—he was knighted only in the 50's—was, like Hudson, one of the new railway millionaires; but the foundation of his vast fortune had come from the early contract for building the Westminster New Palace for Barry which he took with his partner Thomas Grissell. Curiously enough, Peto did not employ Barry for Somerleyton but had his house designed (in 1844) by John Thomas (1813–1862) who was not an architect but the chief sculptor on the Palace. Thomas had first been discovered by Barry when he was working as a stonemason on the Birmingham grammar school and by now was much in demand everywhere for architectural sculpture. Presumably Peto had found him more accommodating to work with than Barry.

An earlier house—in this case really of Elizabethan date—was not merely refaced but completely buried. The very extensive new work went on for nearly a decade and the village nearby was not reconstructed, with a large Baptist chapel of Gothic design now demolished, until 1854. Somerleyton has only two storeys, but high roofs of moderate pitch and strange arched dormers provide an ample attic storey (Fig. VI 18). The windows are linked together vertically, as at Highclere, and broad tower-like pavilions flank the garden front. The two-storey bay windows set against these corner towers and the central pavilion, with its round oriel above an open porch, are more like Salvin's characteristic features at Harlaxton. Such things, of course, are far from being incorrect archaeologically but they break up that continuous reticulated pattern which gives the best sort of 19th-century order and scale to Highclere. The feature most obviously borrowed from Barry here is the tall tower rising at one of the rear corners of the main block. With its rather plain shank and its open-arched loggia, this resembles more closely Barry's Italian Villa towers at Trentham (Fig. VI 2) and Walton than it does the broader Highclere "keep" (Fig. VI 19); it certainly bears no resemblance at all to the Victoria Tower at Westminster (Fig. I 1).

Unlike Highclere and Harlaxton but like much other Jacobethan work of the 40's, the material used for Somerleyton is a local red brick with the profuse trim executed in imported Caen stone. The plan of the house is, as might have been expected of a sculptor-turned-architect, somewhat amateurish in organization, with many unlighted interior corridors. That section of the principal suite of rooms which runs across the garden front on the west is large and well lighted; but the rooms on the north received no light except through the conservatory (now demolished). This feature once covered almost as large an area as the whole main block of the house, but it was completely unrelated to it in scale and design as were most other such metal-and-glass adjuncts to masonry buildings. Behind the site of the conservatory

189

is a large stable complex masked from the entrance court by a screen with a central gateway. The service wing rambles off behind the great tower, with the kitchens as remote from the dining hall as it was possible to put them. Thomas was no rival of Barry either as a designer or as a planner.

As has been said, most of Barry's country house work consisted of alterations. Only a few more such jobs initiated in the early 40's need be mentioned here. The work at Harewood House was planned as early as 1842 and ran on through the rest of the decade; the additions to Duncombe Park were begun in 1843. At both places Barry apparently had too much respect for the original 18th-century architects (reputedly Vanbrugh at Duncombe; Carr of York, and later Adam, at Harewood) to undertake such drastic remodeling as at Highclere or the complete submergence of the existing houses in new accessories as at Trentham Park. At Harewood, with his usual interest in producing a striking skyline, Barry raised the height of the wings and added a balustrade and high chimney stacks to the main block. But his chief work there was the extensive terraced garden carried out in collaboration with Major Nesfield.

At Duncombe he added an entrance portico, despite his avowed disapproval of such features, and flanked the entrance court with blocks of buildings in which he tried to maintain the Vanbrughian scale. Here also he laid out the Italian gardens, again in collaboration with Nesfield. The gardens represent the finest aspect of Barry's country house activities, for his remodelings too often recall the "tasteful" changes and additions with which early 20th-century architects have denatured so many 17th- and 18th-century houses in England and America, all the while professing a pious respect for their original character.

Barry's career offers no obvious stopping point in the mid-40's, partly because all his jobs tended to run on for so many years. Moreover, there are important projects and executed works initiated before 1845 which have so far only been listed. The succeeding chapter therefore continues the Barry story with no real break.

CHAPTER VII: THE BARRY

STORY CONTINUED

It is time to turn to some of the more public aspects of Barry's multifarious professional activity. His rearrangement of Trafalgar Square (originally laid out in 1829) was his only urbanistic project to be carried out, and even that gave him little satisfaction. Disapproving, like most Victorians, of the National Gallery which William Wilkins (1778–1839) built in 1832–38 along the north side of the square, Barry hoped to lend its rather episodic front more dignity by providing a handsome base. His embanked terrace, which continues Pall Mall East across the top of the square, was to some extent dictated by the terrain; but it also served admirably to give breadth and some sort of unity to the long façade behind and above it.

Barry disapproved not only of Wilkins' building but also of Railton's Nelson Column in the center of the square. He would have preferred to place balancing masses of statuary on either side of an open north-south axis in order to maintain a clear view of the National Gallery portico. But since Railton's giant column, just being erected in 1840 when Barry was called in, could no more be removed than Wilkins' façade, Barry flanked it by large fountains to left and right. Instead of providing a central flight of stairs leading up to the terrace and the Gallery portico, he doubled his staircases and set them at the two outer corners of the terrace. Considered as what might be called "ameliorative urbanism," the result is not unsuccessful if hardly a fair example of Barry's real ideas for monumental public squares.

Of a very different order was another public commission of Barry's dating from the opening of the decade. The Pentonville Prison, built in 1841–42 off the Caledonian Road in London, followed closely the plan—at once radical and radial—of the Eastern Penitentiary in Philadelphia (Fig. VII 2). That American model prison, the first transatlantic edifice to have real influence abroad, was built in the years 1823–35 by John Haviland (1792–1852), an English-born architect who had settled in Philadelphia in 1816. From the tall central hall at Pentonville the doors of all the ranges of cells were visible, as in Haviland's scheme, along the sides of the radiating wings. The central corridors of the four wings rose the full three storeys without any visual obstructions and were covered at the top with plain barrel vaults. The upper ranges of cells were reached by narrow iron balconies bracketed out from the stone walls and linked by bridges and circular stairs of iron in the central hall. These delicate metal elements contrasted with the massive simplicity of the surrounding masonry in a most striking way.

A perverse ingenuity provided complete isolation for each prisoner even when in the chapel, while the exercising yards were divided into tiny segmental pens. Yet each cell had its own toilet facilities, as well as a fair-sized window, so that the accommodations were far superior physically to anything most prisoners would have known before their incarceration. The plans had been submitted by the Inspectors of Prisons to Lord John Russell, the Home Secretary, and the government of the day on his advice spent altogether some £85,000 on the structure, most of it for the comfort of the prisoners. Unfortunately various changes and additions make it difficult today to appreciate the real monumentality which Barry achieved here; the prison, considered as a work of architecture, must be discussed in the past tense.

From the central hall a short wing projected forward to house various offices. Outside the surrounding walls, which are 20 feet high and provided with corner guard towers, was the entrance block. This had only two storeys but a tremendous projecting porch, arched on three sides, provided the chief architectural feature of the whole complex (Fig. VII 3). The prison was not castellated in design like the Eastern Penitentiary. Rather, the bare handling of the tall outer walls with their flat structural buttresses and the domestic simplicity of the corner bastions were as much in the tradition of Late Georgian engineering-architecture as the great warehouse-like cell blocks within. But the administrative wing, the modest front block outside the walls, and the entrance porch received a massively plastic treatment.

Doric pilasters, banded with roughly rusticated blocks, defined the bays of the front wing and supported a heavily bracketed cornice; above that a solid parapet with strips of rusticated blocks over the pilasters masked the roof. Under the cornice, giant keystones in a similarly Piranesian vein accented the segmental arches of the upper windows. At the corners of the entrance porch, which rose well above the two-storey front block, banded Doric pilasters appeared again; these were set in pairs between the great arches and the bracketed cornice broken forward above them. The corners of the front block itself were defined by bold rusticated quoins and similar rusticated trim surrounded the two ranges of rectangular windows in the side walls. Near the center of the whole prison complex rose a rather slim square tower, rusticated all the way up, with a projecting metal balcony near its top for the use of the watch.

Representing the most advanced ideas of the day in penal planning, this

192

prison of Barry's soon had a high reputation. But it did not have so great an influence as his clubs and his remodeled country houses. Moseley's Middlesex House of Detention, begun in 1846, was somewhat similar in external treatment as well as in plan. The even larger Surrey County Prison by D. Hill, in construction in 1850, had a separate three-winged section for women as well as the main five-winged complex. At this prison rusticated stone trim provided the only decoration on the front gateway and the ward houses. The entrance arch was flanked by low towers topped with curious obelisk-like features somewhat in the Vanbrugh tradition. But the flanking ward houses were domestic rather than monumental in scale, each of them being in effect a small Italian Villa with tiny round-arched windows and a corner tower. Thus the whole composition was rather suburban in tone with little of the solemn grandeur of Barry's Pentonville.

A more characteristic Early Victorian prison is Reading Gaol by Scott and Moffatt. This was begun immediately after the completion of Pentonville and completed two years later, in 1844, at a cost of £40,000. The chosen style was avowedly that of a 15th-century castle, and Reading Gaol still makes quite a show (Fig. VII 4). The bright red brick walls are diapered with the handsome local "blue" brick and extensively trimmed with cream-colored Bath stone. Although the detail is rather feeble the functional elements of a prison lent themselves rather better to castellated treatment than those of most Victorian structures.

The long walls, with their corner watchtowers, are pleasanter to look at—at least from the outside—than those of Pentonville, and not less practical. The Governor's House and the matching unit flanking the gateway in the front wall, so clearly seen from the railway as one enters Reading from London, are naively composed in the fashion of a child's castle of sand or wooden building blocks. But these features lead up effectively to the larger and plainer masses of the administrative wing and the tall cell blocks behind; while the petty octagonal stair turrets are nobly echoed above by the great ventilating tower that rises from the central hall. (It is doubtful, however, if these once-fashionable architectural amenities comforted that premature post-Victorian Oscar Wilde when he became the most famous inmate of Reading Gaol a half-century later.)

Holloway Prison in London was built in 1851–52 by the City Architect John Bunstone Bunning (1802–1863). This is rather similar to Reading Gaol but more strikingly articulated. The usual ward houses, standing well forward at the front, are of red brick and rather clumsily composed and detailed. But the tall central block, rising behind the low entrance gate, has a more plausibly medieval character than that at Reading Gaol partly because it is based on 14th- rather than 15th-century models. Machicolations, crenella-

193

tions, and turrets, half seen through the trees along the Camden Road, pile up as on some Late Georgian fake castle toward the tall ventilating tower which is placed off-center at the rear (Fig. VII 1).

It is hard now to associate this picturesque and romantic mode with the grim functions of 19th-century penitentiaries. But the Early Victorians were influenced in designing their new gaols by the continued utilization of real Royal castles of the Middle Ages as prisons; there were also certain obvious identities of function such as the need for unbroken walls and frequent watchtowers. Since Bunning in his other official work was usually Italianate his use of the castellated mode at Holloway is the more significant. Other architects also, although ready to accept the practical innovations of Barry's model prison, preferred castellated to Italianate design for gaols. Thus Barry cannot be said to have initiated an Early Victorian mode in this field even though Pentonville was once perhaps the best single example of a major prison of the period.

As exceptional as Pentonville is Barry's other principal public commission of the early 40's. Soane's range of offices for the Board of Trade, in Whitehall at the corner of Downing Street, had been only partly executed in the 20's. By 1844 the tremendous increase in the Board of Trade's business—particularly as a result of Gladstone's railway act of that year—had come to require additional accommodation. At first the intention was merely to complete the original composition by repeating at the eastern end the porticoed block on the Downing Street corner. It soon became evident that such a new portico would impinge on the Whitehall roadway, and in 1845 Barry determined to refront the whole range omitting both porticoes and increasing the height to three storeys. This decision seemed to justify a façade treatment wholly different from Soane's although the engaged Corinthian columns of the original two-storey edifice were to be re-used above a new ground floor.

By raising these giant columns on individual rusticated piers and breaking the entablature forward over each of them Barry introduced strong vertical accents. Thus he substituted a dynamically plastic rhythm of almost Baroque character for the Classic serenity of Soane's near-colonnade (Fig. VII 6). The ground-storey piers and the engaged columns above them are set against rusticated wall segments. In between these the window casings in the three storeys are linked vertically by balconettes under the first-storey windows and by carved panels over their console-supported cornices. A rich scroll ornaments the frieze of the main entablature and a balustrade with urns enlivens the skyline. The continuity of the range of engaged columns is barely broken by the very slight projection of the corner pavilions; but above them Barry obtained the end emphasis he always sought by adding attics. The short pilasters in these attics project as far from the wall surfaces between as do the columns below and the rather heavy attic cornice is also broken forward over each of them. The front surface of each pilaster is enriched with a carved swag while a frieze-like band of bold foliage links them above the square attic windows. Out of the corner urns rise finial-like balusters recalling the obelisks at Highclere. The offices inside are provided with extremely bold cornices carried on heavy scrolled modillions; their paneled ceilings are also ornamented with plaster wreaths and garlands of almost Jonesian boldness.

Completed in 1847, the Board of Trade had little immediate influence but it was a portent of great changes to come after the Early Victorian period was over. Ten years later, when designs were being solicited for new government offices, this most ornately plastic of Barry's London buildings set a pace for all competitors who were not convinced Gothicists. Yet the competition projects of 1856–57 actually owed more to Second Empire influence and are all rather typically High Victorian. Even Barry, in his own project of 1857 which was not entered in the official competition, proposed capping all the government buildings along Parliament Street and Whitehall, including his Board of Trade block, with the mansard roofs which were so characteristic a feature of Visconti and Lefuel's New Louvre.

In the 40's Barry's work owed little to France however parallel it may have been to French work of the day. The design he made in 1844 for remodeling and enlarging Dunrobin Castle, the Scottish seat of the Sutherlands, was exceptional, for there he apparently intended to produce something resembling a high-roofed French chateau of the later Renaissance. The castle, as carried out by a man from Aberdeen named Leslie between 1845 and 1848, shows important changes from Barry's scheme which made it rather typically British in the end. The duke had evidently demanded a more feudal effect—and naturally he got what he wanted from his Aberdonian architect (Fig. VII 5). Barry never entirely lost touch with the work at Dunrobin; in 1848 the great tower was altered at his suggestion and one of his elaborate Italian terrace gardens was laid out below the castle. But as a whole Dunrobin can hardly be considered his; of its actual character there will be more to say in the next chapter in discussing that characteristic Early Victorian mode called "Scottish Baronial" of which it was an aberrant but influential example.

Barry's major work of the late 40's, and one of the major monuments of the entire Victorian age, is Bridgewater House in London. This was begun in 1847 for the brother of the Duke of Sutherland, Lord Francis Egerton, who had just been created Earl of Ellesmere. (It was tactfully named for the earl's grandfather, the canal-building Duke of Bridgewater, whose family name he had assumed and whose principal heir he was.) Already in 1840, when he was working at Trafalgar Square on the eastward extension of Pall

Mall, Barry had also proposed continuing Pall Mall westward from St. James's Street to the Green Park. He wanted to re-erect Nash's Marble Arch, then standing before Buckingham Palace, as the central feature in a screen running across the entrance to the park rather like Decimus Burton's screen at Hyde Park corner. As early as this, then, Barry had probably envisaged balancing Stafford House on the south side of his new street with another palatial block on the north. Whether Lord Francis Egerton was already the destined client is not clear—he was at that time employing Blore, not Barry, to build Worsley Hall for him near Manchester (Figs. VIII 8–9).

When Bridgewater House was actually planned in 1847 the grand scale of the mansion was more than comparable to that of Stafford House. As the space between the two houses was never cleared the main south front is best seen diagonally from Cleveland Square (Fig. VII 7). The west or garden front is as completely visible from the Green Park as if this were a country house, for Bridgewater House is set farther back from the park than Stafford House and almost in line with Vardy's Palladian Spencer House to the north. Thus there is room for a considerable formal garden and, as is usual with Barry, a balustraded terrace along the base of the house plays an important part in the general architectural effect (Fig. VII 10).

The basic *parti* or plan scheme of Bridgewater House as executed is quite similar to that of the Reform Club house: a central hall, here of vast size, surrounded by arcaded corridors, with the main stairway rising between walls to the east (Fig. VII 8). In the earliest extant plan the hall was to have been an open court, as also originally at the Reform, but with a monumental enclosed staircase rising T-wise through the center. The principal rooms are all on the first storey facing the park. A long skylighted gallery, also on the first storey, runs along the north side to hold the magnificent Bridgewater Collection of paintings. In order that the public might have direct access to this art gallery—visitors began to be admitted by ticket in 1851—a separate staircase was provided in a tower at the northeast corner. Beyond this tower a wing projecting farther to the east contains stables below and servants' rooms above. A one-storey block, attached to the east end of the south front and originally providing additional equine accommodation, masks the small stable court from Cleveland Square. Thus the massing on the north and east is quite irregular; but those are the unimportant aspects of the house and the irregularities were not exploited by Barry in a picturesque way.

The entrance façade facing south is longer and lower proportionately than that of the Reform Club house, the general treatment very much richer. An early project, shown at the Royal Academy Exhibition in 1847, included engaged columns rising over a rusticated ground storey like those on the Board of Trade but with an unbroken entablature above. This was rejected as too expensive and a scheme of all-over paneling, with much carving in relief, was next proposed by Barry. His experience with Perpendicular at the New Palace—and doubtless also the success of his Anglo-Italian treatment at Highclere—will have encouraged this drastic modification of the severe San Gallesque scheme used at the Reform. Probably for reasons of economy he determined in the end on the present handling of the façade which represents merely an enrichment of his basic High Renaissance formula.

The whole ground storey is rusticated and broad raised bands, which are not only rusticated but vermiculated, replace plain quoins at the corners (Fig. VII 7). The segmental pediments of the first-storey windows are filled with intricate carving designed by John Thomas. Between the attic windows raised panels suggest a continuous broad frieze (of which Alfred Barry says, rather curiously, that Barry did not really approve). The cornice above has rather tall scrolled brackets, more elaborate versions of those at Pentonville, with a balustrade above to mask the low hip roofs.

At the corners there are ornamental chimneys of the full width of the vermiculated bands below; these are ornamented with pilaster-like members, also banded with vermiculation, and provide considerably stronger end accents than do the modest stacks on the Reform. But there is also a strong central accent on this façade in the form of a projecting porch. This is flanked by coupled Doric columns banded with vermiculation. Like the pilasters on the Pentonville porch these enframe a central arch, here provided with a richly carved keystone and vermiculated voussoirs cutting across a molded archivolt. Carving on the stringcourses, the window cases, and in between the cornice brackets, although rather restrained in character, increases the generally ornate effect of this front; as a result it is richer, if considerably less bold, than that of the Board of Trade.

The elements of the garden front are mostly identical with those of the entrance front but the general rhythm is quite different (Fig. VII 10). Wide bays, corresponding to the terminal rooms of the principal suite, project slightly at each end of the façade. The corner bands of vermiculation are repeated at the inner edges of these bays, and chimneys rise over these inner bands as well as over the actual corners. In these end bays the standard window units are flanked by half-windows in a semi-Palladian way. At the first-floor level balconettes also project below the window groups; elsewhere, as on the south front, the balustrades of the first-storey windows are set inside the casing. The tripartite organization of the garden façade is more expressive than that of the entrance front, definitely suggesting the range of three great reception rooms on the principal storey that lie behind (Fig. VII 8). The strong end emphasis provided by the broader bays flanking the façade and the pairs of finial-like chimneys above the crowning balustrade recall the corner towers at Highclere and the terminal attics of the Board of Trade. Like the gabled pavilions flanking the Birmingham grammar school façade and the towers on the river front of the New Palace, these end bays illustrate how Barry imposed his own taste in composition regardless of the nominal mode in which he was working.

The decorations of the great hall of Bridgewater House were carried out only in the mid-50's by a German named Götzenberg: fussily figural, they were not approved by Barry when he saw them in 1858. But the ceilings, doorcases, and mantels in the principal rooms are of Barry's own design and extremely handsome (Figs. VII 9, 11). The mode is perhaps intended to be "Louis XIV" but there is, as always with Barry's ornamental work, much restraint and strong emphasis on the geometrical framework of the features. The detail has a distinctly personal flavor with very little Rococo feeling and the execution is uniformly of very high quality. Unfortunately such rich ornament was soon much imitated in tawdry machine-made papier-mâché. But Barry need not be blamed too much for providing decorative models that could readily be vulgarized; so also—and even more directly—did the unworldly Pugin through his connections with brummagem firms of ecclesiastical furnishers.

Here at Bridgewater House Barry was not so much leading as following the general taste of the mid-century for greater and greater richness. His authority merely sanctioned a movement, already well started, away from the original severity of the Italian palace mode. This movement had progressed considerably further at the hands of others by the time the exterior of Bridgewater House was completed in the fall of 1848 than it ever did in Barry's own work before the late 50's.

A few words should be said about the materials. The south and west fronts are all of Portland stone; the other sides are cement coated, with some stone trim. The ground-storey ceilings were arched in brick and the domical vaults of the galleries around the great hall were likewise of brick. The elliptical-arched principals of the gallery roof were of wrought iron tied above the suspended subceiling. Behind the inner skylights, gas burners were placed so that the artificial illumination might come from the same source as the daylight (Fig. VII 12). (Actually the *Builder, 10,* 358, complained in 1851 that the "lighting of the gallery is very unsatisfactory," a complaint only too familiar to art gallery directors of every period.)

As with the Reform Club's kitchens, Barry's technical modernity here was considerable; but it was, as always, subordinated to his fixed conception of the proprieties of palatial design. No visual expression of new materials or structural elements seemed to him necessary. The Gothicists under Pugin's leadership insisted upon direct expression of construction; yet they abjured all materials and methods which could not be reconciled with a somewhat bigoted and parochial conception of medieval practice. The many architects who followed Barry's lead, on the other hand, were quite willing to utilize fireproof construction and to exploit all sorts of new materials so long as they could be disguised with applied Renaissance decoration.

Designed in 1848, the year Bridgewater House was completed externally, but executed only very slowly through the 50's, one other Early Victorian mansion in London rivaled Bridgewater House both in size and in splendor. Dorchester House in Park Lane, indeed, was in the end even more magnificent. Erected by the shipping magnate Robert Stayner Holford, it was the principal architectural production of Lewis Vulliamy, whose earlier work hardly prepares one for this highly competent exercise in palace design.

Four years older than Barry, Vulliamy had worked for Robert Smirke and studied at the Royal Academy where he won the Gold Medal in 1815. Then he had traveled in Italy and Greece in practically the same years as Barry (1818–21) on a Travelling Studentship from the Academy. He doubtless took little more interest than Barry in the cheap Gothic churches he was called on to build in the early years of his practice; but at All Saints', Ennismore Gardens, designed in 1837 though not built till a decade later, he essayed with more success a basilican church, as has already been noted. His most prominent work before Dorchester House is the façade of the Royal Institution in Albemarle Street. Built in 1838 to refront an earlier structure, this is a long pseudoportico of engaged columns. Rather like Soane's Board of Trade before Barry altered it, the façade is more Late Georgian than Early Victorian in character. The Royal Institution was the most exalted of all the Early Victorian cultural centers; there the upper classes in full evening dress acquired some of the new scientific knowledge at lectures and demonstrations quite as "industrious mechanics" were doing in humbler provincial institutes.

At Dorchester House both client and architect were determined to outsplurge Lord Ellesmere and Barry; and this they were actually able to do, partly because the client had acquired a site that was more open and partly because the architect adopted a bolder and more plastic treatment for the two main façades. Vulliamy not only carried up the greater part of his palace to full three-storey height but also articulated the two upper storeys with pilaster orders above a rusticated ground floor (Fig. VII 13). Much more important than the extra height and the applied orders, however, was the strong end emphasis Vulliamy created on the park front by omitting the second storey in the five middle bays and the massive central emphasis that a projecting entrance porch three full bays wide gave to the other

199

front (Fig. VII 15). Arches carried on a subordinate order in the three first-storey bays above this porch recalled the Sansovinesque treatment of the Carlton Club house and provided that richness of form and complexity of rhythm the late 40's were beginning to seek in Renaissance design. The open entrance court, with screen to the west, allowed the public a more generous view from Park Lane than one gets of Bridgewater House from Cleveland Square.

Unfortunately, in the working out of his compositions Vulliamy was somewhat clumsy, committing solecisms that the better trained Barry would have avoided. The paired bays of the corner pavilions, for example, flanked by coupled pilasters but with only a single pilaster in the center, were not very happy even if they did have the precedent of Peruzzi's Farnesina. The small arched windows in the top storey, with their continuous archivolts and low segmental pediments, derive from an earlier stage of the Renaissance than the bold, console-supported pediments of the windows in the principal storeys. Bramante may have used such window detail but its delicacy and flatness contradicted the controlling scale of Vulliamy's whole composition. The very flat pilasters of the attic, with their tiny fluted capitals, were well related to these windows; but the window frames and pilasters alike were overpowered by the heavy scrolled brackets and carved swags in the frieze above.

On the other hand, the entrance porch with the architrave of its entablature omitted over the central bay in order to allow a taller central arch had a somewhat Vignolan air, as did also the detailing of the arcaded screen closing in the forecourt on the east (Fig. VII 15). These earlier and later notes seem inharmonious with the Roman High Renaissance character of the façades as a whole. Such detailed stylistic analysis emphasizes by contrast the greater consistency and even the relative originality of Barry's treatment of the Bridgewater House façades.

The planning of Dorchester House did not differ much from that of Bridgewater House except that it was somewhat less clearly and axially organized (Fig. VII 14). As at Bridgewater House the east and the north façades were irregular, particularly the latter, since many of the service facilities were arranged on mezzanines between the main storey levels. The reception rooms in the first storey occupied the other three sides around the relatively small central court. The court itself was glass roofed and contained a great open marble staircase. This and several of the other principal rooms eventually incorporated the major decorative achievements of that distinguished Victorian sculptor Alfred Stevens (1817–1875); but Stevens did not begin to work for Holford here until 1858. High Victorian in date, if not so clearly High Victorian in style, the interiors need only be touched on here.

All in all, Holford had some £6,000 worth of Stevens' work at Dorchester House of which a certain amount has been salvaged by museums and hotel owners. The fireplace caryatids now in the Tate Gallery are, despite their obvious derivation from Michelangelo, among the recognized masterpieces of 19th-century English sculpture. The dining room fittings, sideboards and so forth, are apparently no longer extant. With their carved mahogany frames, cut and engraved mirrors, and edicular construction they could well have been the inspiration for the lush decoration characteristic of later Victorian "gin-palace" interiors.

The sad story of Stevens' employment, or more accurately lack of employment, by architects in the mid-century is covered in detail by K. R. Towndrow in his life of *Alfred Stevens* (1939). That a sculptor working with such sympathetic aptitude in the cinquecento tradition should have been called on so rarely by Victorian architects employing the idioms of that period is something of a tragedy. John Thomas, whose work seems of little intrinsic interest today, must have been more accommodating to work with since it was he who executed most of the sculptural commissions connected with large and prominent buidings of Renaissance design in the 40's and 50's. Distinguished sculptural accessories cannot redeem thoroughly bad architecture but they can add subsidiary interest to such merely competent work as Vulliamy and most Early Victorian architects other than Barry generally achieved when they worked in the Renaissance mode.

This period produced in London almost no other great individual mansions, competent or otherwise, to compare with Bridgewater and Dorchester houses. In refronting Hertford House in Piccadilly in 1849–51 the builders' firm of William Cubitt (1785–1861), Plunkett and Company introduced few innovations beyond a bracketed cornice and an ornately carved frieze above a conventional pilaster order. If this bow-fronted house appears still to be Georgian—as of course it is essentially—the Hope mansion (later occupied by the Junior Athenaeum Club) farther along Piccadilly, designed a year earlier by a French architect, seemed already almost High Victorian (Fig. VII 17). But the character of this house is so exceptional for the late 40's that its full significance can hardly yet be made evident. It will be necessary first to consider more carefully than hitherto in this book the general relation of English architecture to that of the Continent in the Victorian Age, a matter better left for discussion toward the end of this chapter.

Just one Gothic mansion of any consequence seems to have been built in London in the 40's. Charles Russell's house at No. 19 (now No. 23) Park Lane was very modest compared to Holford's Dorchester House farther north but, unlike that, it survived the early 20th-century rebuilding of Park

Lane and has been restored since World War II. The house was completed in 1848 from the designs of W. B. Moffatt, the former partner of Gilbert Scott. It is in width no more than a regular terrace house; but it stood out from its Georgian neighbors as much by its greater height and its all-stone façade as by its Late Gothic features (Fig. VII 18).

A broad rectangular oriel filled with mullioned lights occupies almost the whole width of the first and second storeys. In the low ground storey the Tudor-arched entrance door to the right of the central buttress below the oriel is balanced by a traceried window on the left. In the third storey two mullioned windows occupy the same proportion of the wall as does the oriel in the storeys below. Twin dormers of stone with crocketed gables project from the high curb roof.

Except for the reticulated pattern provided by the molded window mullions, Moffatt used little detail. There is a band of carving on the molding below the oriel and a range of shields in the panels between the first- and second-storey windows; parapets of pierced and paneled crenellations also rise above the oriel and at the eave in front of the dormers. The walls are of random ashlar with molded trim and irregular quoining of a lighter freestone. The interior included a great dining hall for which a monitor with a clerestorey above the open wooden roof provided the only natural light.

It may seem surprising that the façade of the Russell house, so well suited to simplified repetition in matching house fronts, should have had almost no influence on Victorian builders. But Gothic, even the regularized Late Gothic of Tudor times, was not yet acceptable for urban domestic use however much it might already be the dominant mode for churches and, almost as much, for schools and other institutions controlled by churchy patrons. The reasons for this avoidance of Gothic by builders will be better understood when the general conditions of Early Victorian house production in London are considered in Chapters XII and XIII. But the paucity of individual Early Victorian mansions of medieval design in London is nevertheless an anomaly since the Tudor manor was undoubtedly the favorite country house model of the 40's. Barry's Italian Villa and Anglo-Italian modes were but exceptions to established norms which will be discussed in the next chapter.

The tale of Barry's executed buildings should now be continued through the late 40's and into the early 50's; after the opening of the House of Commons in 1852 his production practically ceased coincidentally with the end of the Early Victorian period. The Halifax Town Hall, designed in 1859–60 just before Barry's death and executed in the next two years with some changes by his son E. M. Barry, is really his only late work of consequence.

In 1847 Barry was called in to "style," as 20th-century slang would put it, the Keyham Factory of the Royal Navy at Devonport outside Plymouth. The foundries, smithies, turning shops and so forth of this establishment had already been planned and their structure determined by naval engineers. For the exterior of these very extensive one-storey buildings Barry provided a simple Italianate trim somewhat like that on the Pentonville Prison. Chains of rustication, plain heavy stringcourses, and simplified entablatures give weight and dignity to the long walls even though they have no relationship whatsoever to the internal ironwork of the engineers.

Dominating the group rises a tall clock tower quite similar to those Barry added to several of the country houses he altered. This tower is in many stages with boldly rusticated walls. Like the later tower at Trentham it has heavy, rather Mannerist, detail toward the top, and there is a small balcony carried on a boldly bracketed cornice just above the clock stage, somewhat as at Pentonville. In the tapered outlines of these later towers of his, so different from the simpler loggia-topped towers of the earlier Italian Villa mode, Barry was clearly attempting to vie with the silhouette of Gothic church spires. Finally, in his last work, Barry provided the Halifax Town Hall with a remarkably satisfactory Italianate equivalent to a Gothic church tower, even to setting it on the corner of a public edifice in the center of a city (Fig. VI 3). But that is not only High Victorian, it is one of the real High Victorian masterpieces and hence outside the proper scope of this book.

Shrubland Park, near Ipswich in Norfolk, has the latest and most successful of Barry's loggia-topped towers of the standard sort (Fig. VII 20). Called in 1848 by Sir William Fowle Middleton to modernize the existing house, Barry added this tower to provide the main accent in an elaborate scheme of alteration. But at Shrubland, as elsewhere, Barry's energies went chiefly toward the laying out of the expensive terraced gardens. (For the upkeep of these Middleton, on his death, set up a trust fund with an income of £2,000 a year.) The original building had already been modified by John Peter Gandy-Deering (1787–1850) in 1830 and his pilastered fronts were retained by Barry. But the crowning pediments were removed and the roof was hidden by balustrades to harmonize with the square balustraded top of the new tower. As at Duncombe a new entrance was added, flanked in this case by low galleries for sculpture.

The principal feature of Shrubland, superbly coordinated pictorially with the new tower, is the tremendous staircase leading down a steep slope to the lower parterres. This is approached from the upper terrace in front of the house through a pavilion loaded with amazingly Mannerist detail rather recalling that on Pirro Ligorio's Casino in the Vatican gardens. At the far end of the balustrade-surrounded lower parterre terminating the axis of the staircase an open-arched gazebo stands out against the rich and extensive view of the distant landscape.

At Canford Manor near Wimborne in Dorset, whither Barry was also called in 1848 by the Welsh ironmaster Sir John Guest, his opportunities were less. The house had been built by Blore over the years 1826–36 in the hard dry Tudor of the Late Georgian period. The material was buff brick with wiry stone trim, and the surrounding grounds were perfectly flat. Behind the garden front Barry added a tremendous great hall, its steep roof rising in the center of the complex above the lower roofs of Blore's main block. New service quarters were also built around a court to the west of the hall, and an elaborate main staircase was introduced, somewhat as at Highclere, between the hall and the court.

The principal external feature added by Barry was a great keep-like tower at the southwest corner. This dominates and accents the whole confused group of gables and turrets by its height and its broken outline. Of the four corner turrets of this tower, which rather recall the corner finials on the Highclere "keep," one is octagonal and carried higher than the rest. This excessively piquant touch is quite uncharacteristic of Barry although not out of keeping with the irregularity of Blore's original composition. Neither the keep nor Barry's cloister-like conservatory that extends to the north of the main block (masking, perversely enough, the only really medieval feature at Canford, which is the old kitchen) satisfies the highest standards of manorial design at the end of the Early Victorian period. Barry's special talents and wide experience as a modernizer of country houses could not cope effectively with a situation that required Gothic design which was even less to his taste now than it had been earlier.

At Cliveden in Buckinghamshire, where the Duke of Sutherland wished to rebuild completely the old central block after it burned in 1849, the final result of the extensive operations was not much happier; nor is it quite characteristic of Barry even though there is nothing medieval about it. The necessity of utilizing the old foundations cannot have been particularly onerous; but the first scheme of design, which Barry preferred, for an astylar palace block with corner towers was rejected by the difficult duke as too costly. The next scheme, introducing engaged columns with the entablature breaking out over them as on the Board of Trade, was itself later modified to the present range of Ionic pilasters under an unbroken entablature, presumably for economy's sake. As a result the upper storeys of the garden front appear almost more like an imitation of the original late 17th-century mansion than of anything Italian of the 16th century (Fig. VII 21).

The long balustraded terrace, with the elaborate doubled and quadrupled flights of stairs in the center leading down to the extensive gardens along the river, is very typical of Barry's architectural gardening at its best. An extensive range of rusticated arches gives an almost loggia-like character to the ground storey along the terrace. Beyond the ends of the main block are similar one-storey wings ornamented with engaged columns between arches. This long arcaded base is most effectively related to the terrace, if not to the heavier main block above it. On the left the terminal wing contains the dining room which connects directly with the main suite of breakfast room, drawing room, and library running across the garden front. On the right the balancing wing provided a private suite for the duke and duchess as at Trentham. The center of the entrance front was occupied by a large hall running through to the drawing room in the 17th-century Anglo-Palladian way. In the front corners of the house an additional drawing room was balanced by a very large staircase hall, itself more Anglo-Palladian than Barry-like; behind these rooms longitudinal corridors led to the private suite and the dining room in the end wings. It is at least possible that Barry's planning of the front half of the main block was controlled by existing foundation walls.

The small two-storey blocks flanking the entrance court are connected to the main block by curved corridors; these had survived the fire and were not much modified by Barry. Farther forward, on the right as one approaches the house, is a considerable complex of Italianate stable buildings arranged around a court, somewhat like those at Trentham and dominated again by an extremely ornate tower. But this picturesque feature was added only in 1861 by Henry Clutton and is no part of Barry's main composition: That is as formal and symmetrical as the 17th-century Cliveden that had burned. The new work here is all of brick covered with Portland cement and hence has not weathered very gracefully. The interiors were completely done over by the 1st Lord Astor in the Newport or Fifth Avenue manner of the turn of the century. Therefore, although Cliveden is Barry's most extensive remaining country house, it is by no means to be considered among his most satisfactory or characteristic works. Trentham rather than Cliveden should have gone to the National Trust.

The corner towers of the first Cliveden project turned up again on a megalomaniac scheme of 1857 for burying Clumber House, the Duke of Newcastle's seat in the Dukeries, behind extensive ranges of new construction. Once more a remodeling, this project represented Barry's ultimate ideal for the country palace of an English peer. As we have seen, however, even the Earl of Ellesmere at Bridgewater House and the Duke of Sutherland at Cliveden had to restrain Barry's ambitions on the score of expense. The Duke of Newcastle can have had no serious intention of proceeding with this fantastic venture; it is much too late in any event to be considered Early Victorian and also much too boldly plastic.

In the early 50's Barry was at least indirectly concerned with the design of both the first and the second Crystal Palace the story of which will be told in Chapter XVI. His other work of the 50's lies as definitely outside the chronological and stylistic limits of the Early Victorian period as do the Clumber project and the Halifax Town Hall. Mention has been made already, however, of his Government Offices scheme of 1857 in which the influence of the New Louvre was evident; and from this project, marking the effective beginning of the High Victorian in Renaissance guise, it will now be well to turn back to consider certain buildings of the late 40's and early 50's which first suggest a closer relationship to France than was characteristic of British architecture in the earlier decades of the century.

At the opening of the century wars discouraged close cultural contacts with the Continent and the postwar generation seems to have remained standoffish, traveling abroad as tourists with little interest in contemporary production. In painting and literature currents of influence flowed outward from England and, if English architects were dependent on French books for Italian Renaissance material, the international Greek Revival had depended from the first on the volumes of Stuart and Revett. The Jacobethan was, of course, wholly nationalistic; and, after the very first, Pugin and his Anglican followers rejected foreign models with chauvinistic bigotry. But there were more respectable reasons why the English found little to interest them in the new work done abroad in the 30's and 40's, however much they sought there the architectural treasures of the Gothic and the Renaissance past. Romantic Classicism, passé in England from approximately the time of Victoria's accession, lived on in Germany and France; in the newer Romantic modes England, partly for economic reasons, had long had a considerable headstart, as also in various technical developments. In the estimation of those interested in propagating these new modes on the Continent that headstart still continued throughout the whole Early Victorian period. From churches to business buildings and railway stations England was either stylistically or technologically ahead. Her own architectural achievements of the late 30's and 40's might seem feeble enough to that stern young critic Ruskin when he appeared on the scene, but he had even less good to say in *The Seven Lamps of Architecture* (1849) of modern work abroad—on the rare occasions when he deigned to consider it at all.

In the international realm of the Gothic Revival England was patently leading the Continent in the 40's and early 50's. From the winning of the Nikolaikirche competition by Scott in 1845 to the winning of the Lille Cathedral competition by Henry Clutton and William Burges (1827–1881) ten years later—a major architectural event which lies beyond the compass of this book—the outside world was ready to recognize English leadership in neo-Gothic work. It was only with the general circulation, beginning in the mid-50's, of Viollet-le-Duc's *Dictionnaire raisonné de l'architecture française du XIe au XVIe siècle* (10 vols. 1854–68) that a counterinfluence from France upon England began in this field. Within the international Renaissance Revival of the second quarter of the century Barry, in retrospect at least, seems to stand second to none of his rivals abroad even if his position was confused for foreign contemporaries by his responsibility for the conspicuously Gothic New Palace. Englishmen around 1850 could well ask: Why imitate what you are already doing better at home?

One aspect of French art, however, was not without influence in the England of the 30's and 40's: Rococo ornament. This had been the great French innovation of the early 18th century and was now associated (not incorrectly) with the prestige of Louis XIV. The skilled craftsmanship of French decorating firms continued—and would still continue almost down to the present day—to purvey not alone Rococo furniture but whole interiors to all the world. England had never had a real Rococo period of its own, doubtless because the Rococo was considered only as an alternative mode of interior design for use in a few reception rooms. But like Chinoiserie, Rococo never passed entirely out of fashion even at the height of Grecian enthusiasm. In the Early Victorian period it continued to find considerable favor with English commercial decorators as also with furniture designers.

Many of the interiors at Harlaxton were described in the 50's as "Louis XIV," which to the 19th century meant Rococo. Their design probably dates from the 40's but may go back to the late 30's whether or not the ingredients were locally produced from Salvin's drawings or imported from Paris. Other rooms there were Jacobethan, of course, like the exterior. The problem of dating the various aspects of the decoration of Stafford House has been mentioned in the previous chapter. A successful disentanglement of its epochs (and doubtless a study of similar work in other great houses) would almost certainly reveal Louis XIV elements of a relatively authentic sort added in the late 30's or 40's.

Victorian interior design, whether of Rococo or other inspiration, is too complex a subject to be more than touched on in this book. It is French influence on architecture which concerns us at this point.* What has been said of the use of Rococo in decoration merely gives evidence of a certain cosmopolitanism on the part of clients to which architects catered rather grudgingly throughout most of the Early Victorian period (if, indeed, the imported French interior work was not introduced without their approval).

* My article "Second Empire 'avant la lettre'" in the *Gazette des Beaux Arts*, Sept. 1953, pp. 115–130, corresponding to pp. 206–215 of this chapter, illustrates this subject considerably more fully.

Just before the Victorian Age began and again near the end of the Early Victorian phase, one country house, Wrest Park in Bedfordshire, and the Hope mansion in London which has already been mentioned, stand apart as unique examples of consistent and dignified French design. At the time the 2d Earl de Grey (1781–1859) became first president of the newly founded Institute of British Architects in 1834 he was engaged in rebuilding Wrest Park, which he had inherited along with his earldom the previous year. Of earlier work there he retained only the splendid early 18th-century domed pavilion by Thomas Archer (1668–1743), most nearly Baroque of all English architects. The special, quite continental character of this feature may have suggested the mode chosen for the new house, which is generically late Baroque as well as specifically French. This great mansion of the 30's, with its tall segmental-arched windows, its low mansards, and its central and terminal pavilions, is a far better scaled and more soberly detailed imitation of the French architecture of the early 18th century than was ever achieved by later architects, French and American, who set out in the late 19th and early 20th centuries to "realize" with cold exactitude the measured drawings of old chateaux. It is also not unworthy of comparison with Petworth and, like that great Late Stuart mansion in Sussex, very much of a fluke and a mystery. It would be outside the scope of this book to attempt to elucidate Wrest Park, since it is in no sense an Early Victorian monument even though it is a most untypical Late Georgian one. Despite the prominent position of its owner and (at least nominal) designer as a patron of architecture, the location of Earl de Grey's mansion deep in the country and its complete lack of those qualities either conservative or advanced taste admired in the 30's and 40's must explain why it was so completely without contemporary influence.

Some other country houses of the 40's besides Dunrobin designed in the Scottish Baronial mode have a French flavor; but for the most part that flavor arises naturally from the stylistic ambiguity of the native 16th- and 17th-century models. The extreme formality of certain Jacobethan elevations by William Burn (1789–1870) seems Gallic; yet that is in fact more due to his naturally tight planning than to any inspiration from abroad. His much later Montagu House, built in London beside the Thames for the Duke of Buccleuch in the 60's, alone illustrated a programmatically French design. But by that time the mansarded mode was in general use in England and had been for almost a decade.

The Hope mansion at 116 Piccadilly on the corner of Down Street was the first edifice that illustrated a serious French influence on Victorian architecture, just as Pentonville Prison was the first to owe anything of consequence to America. The client was Henry Thomas Hope (1808–1862), eldest son of Thomas Hope, the early 19th-century historian of architecture and connoisseur of interior design. This Hope was also the elder brother of Beresford-Hope who was signally assisting in the very same years, as the effective client for Butterfield's new church of All Saints', Margaret Street, in launching the High Victorian Gothic.

After Henry Thomas Hope inherited Deepdene in Surrey on his father's death in 1831 he added to that extensive Regency villa a new southeastern front; this is a tame and conventional Italianate exercise, advanced for its day but with little positive character. The church he sponsored at Dorking likewise shows none of the serious, if amateur, preoccupation with architectural matters of his father and brother. Inheriting the magnificent family collection of paintings, chiefly Dutch, formed by his ancestors in Amsterdam, Henry Thomas Hope like his father early became a vice-president of the Society of Arts; he was also one of the founders of the Art Union. The mansion in Piccadilly was built primarily to house the Hope Collection on the demolition of his father's famous galleries in Duchess Street and not, like All Saints', as an architectural manifesto. One can only guess at Hope's reasons for employing Pierre-Charles Dusillon to design his London mansion; for this obscure French architect, although trained at the Ecole des Beaux Arts under Vaudoyer and Lebas, practiced chiefly in Switzerland and never very extensively even there.

Hope's brother's aristocratic tone, ecclesiological preoccupations, and strictly Anglican aestheticism must have derived from the mother's family. She was a daughter, it will be recalled, of Lord Decies, Archbishop of Tuam; long after Thomas Hope's death she married Lord Beresford, a cousin. A. J. B. Hope's eventual assumption of her maiden name, which was also Beresford, as part of his own surname—it was already one of his given names—reinforces this suggestion, as does the fact that his earliest exercise in ecclesiology was the remodeling of Lord Beresford's little church at Kilndown into the first Camdenian shrine. Beresford-Hope's marriage to a daughter of Lord Salisbury will only have increased his well-established leanings. Henry Thomas Hope, on the other hand, is best known as the chairman of the Eastern Steam Navigation Company while Brunel's *Leviathan* was being built, and was generally a man of the modern financial world. As a connoisseur he was chiefly active in adding to his father's Classical collections. He was thus in every way in the cosmopolitan tradition of the Amsterdam founders of the family banking fortune and little likely to employ his brother's favorites Carpenter and Butterfield.

Henry Cole (1808–1882), one of the principal begetters of the Great Exhibition of 1851 and long a most influential member of the Society of Arts, had been impressed by the superior quality of French "art-manufactures" at least since 1845 when he first coined the term. The greater part of the decorative adjuncts of Hope's new house, the original contract for which was signed in 1848, were to be ordered in Paris, very probably on Cole's recommendation.

The construction of the Hope house, which began in 1849 and lasted well into the Great Exhibition year 1851, was supervised by Thomas Leverton Donaldson (1795–1885), also a member of the group associated with Cole and the Exhibition, but there is no reason to suppose that he modified Dusillon's original design. That was late 16th-century French in character—in one of the "Henri" rather than one of the "Louis" styles, so to say—but hardly either strikingly or archaeologically so. Even though the Hope house was not at all a typical London dwelling but a *hotel particulier* or large Parisian sort of mansion in three storeys with a low dormered mansard, it was the solid ashlar construction and the breadth of its front along Piccadilly that made it conspicuous in the Victorian West End. The general composition was curiously unimaginative (Fig. VII 17). Five identical double bays faced Piccadilly and an almost Belgravian porch at pavement level cut awkwardly into the central bay in Down Street. (Perhaps this was an afterthought of Hope's and designed by Donaldson rather than by Dusillon.) Inset panels of colored marbles in the "pilasters" between the bays and in the friezes over the windows seemed to echo the novel "constructional" or "permanent" polychromy of Butterfield's All Saints' and Ruskin's *Seven Lamps* which will be discussed at considerable length in Chapter XVII.

This was probably fortuitous; certainly these polychrome touches were handled in a most discreet and un-Butterfieldian way. Of the various motifs of decoration, these bits of external color would nevertheless have struck contemporaries as most novel, even though the scrolled ornament in the curved pediments over the main-floor windows and the narrow vertical brackets descending below the principal cornice must also have been rather unfamiliar. The effectiveness of the crowning mansard owed more to the boldly plastic effect of the chamfered corner and the recurrent dormers that broke its lower slope than to its height or shape, for there was no extravagance of concave or convex profiling such as would become so popular about ten years later. But this roof treatment did offer a real premonition of the vigorous modeling of the building mass which High Victorians would soon be achieving with borrowed French elements.

No mature "Second Empire" mode as yet existed in France for Dusillon to follow—nor for that matter any Second Empire. Under the Second Republic the Constituent Assembly had voted in 1848 to undertake the repair and restoration of the old Louvre and this work was now proceeding at the hands of Felix Duban (1797–1870); but it was not until the Prince-President

210

had made himself Emperor as Napoleon III in 1852 that the erection of the New Louvre to join the old palace with the Sovereign's actual residence in the Tuileries was decided on. The lavish character of the New Louvre as executed was not really determined until two years later still after Hector Martin Lefuel (1810–1880) took over the commission on the death of Louis J. T. Visconti (1791–1853) who had prepared the original 1852 project. Thus the Hope mansion preceded by several years the most characteristic Parisian monument of the Second Empire.

There is one other London monument of what may well be called "proto-Second Empire" character since its design also antedates that of the New Louvre by a year or two. This is still a familiar landmark, while the Hope house was destroyed in 1936. For a dozen years the Great Western Railway had no adequate station at Paddington. With the approach of the Great Exhibition of 1851 the inferiority of the principal London terminal facilities to those then reaching completion at Liverpool and Newcastle, and even at smaller places like Chester, had become shamefully evident (see Chapters XV–XVI). Shaken by the Hudson collapse of 1849 and by the London and North-Western stockholders' attacks on the expensive splendor of Hardwick's Great Hall at Euston, the Great Western directors nevertheless found courage to embark at long last on the construction of their permanent London terminus. That they should have begun their ambitious station-building project with a great hotel in Conduit Street East was surprising; that they employed Hardwick to design it, with a pretentiousness new for English hotels, was perhaps unfortunate. Because of the "Arch" of Euston I and the Great Hall of Euston II behind it, Hardwick (which name must stand for both Philip, to whom most of the commissions had been nominally assigned, and his son Philip Charles Hardwick [1822–1892], who had long done most of the work of the office) was certainly the most prominent London station architect. But Sancton Wood or Lewis Cubitt or even William Tite built better stations and might well have designed a better railway hotel.

The Great Western Hotel was described at the time merely as "one of the largest in London"; but with some 150 rooms it must have exceeded the combined accommodations of the twin hotels the Hardwicks had just completed in front of Euston. Despite the stone-built dignity of the station hotels at York and Hull by T. G. Andrews and the great size of the structure William Livock was rearing at this time (to contain both railway offices and hotel facilities) at Grand Central, Birmingham, the Great Western was really the first grandiose and monumental hotel in Britain. It consciously vied with the handsome hotels that had been built by Isaiah Rogers (1800–1869) in America in the 30's and 40's, as well as with the chief urban hotels of the

211

Continent, in elaboration of design if not in variety of services. "Motives of economy," the *Illustrated London News, 21*, 538, stated, "much reduced the scope of Mr. Hardwick's exertions [yet] the whole object of the proprietors [was] to provide the public with every comfort and luxury at moderate charges, and to produce a substantial building as comfortably arranged as possible with due regard to a handsome exterior, without exceeding the limits of strict economy."

The *Civil Engineer and Architect's Journal, 14*, 355, opens the account of the hotel it published in 1851 with a statement characteristic of the more modern-minded milieus of the day: "It was with our fathers a subject of regret that they had dwindled to the days of little buildings and little men. They looked back with envy on times when the piety of the middle ages erected gigantic cathedrals and cloisters and to a later time when the profusion of princes raised up widespread palaces; and they grieved that great works were not in their days. A different state of society has altered these things, and the aggregation of the public in masses has restored the desire for colossal buildings. Such are the Crystal Palace, the railway stations, the concert halls, hippodromes, winter gardens and railway hotels." This quotation reflects the attitude of clients proud of the obvious achievements of their own age with its new comforts and luxuries and frankly out to make a profit by appealing to the up-to-date tastes of the prosperous middle classes. And they did; in the first half-year after the hotel opened it paid at the rate of 10 per cent per annum, with an additional bonus to the proprietors.

The new monster hotel was naturally not to be Gothic, nor yet Grecian like those of Boston and New York built a decade or more earlier. One would have expected the mode to be "plain Italian," like those of Andrews and Livock; but no, "the selected style was," so the *Illustrated London News, 21*, 538, informed its readers in 1852, "French of Louis XIV or later" (Fig. VII 16). To 20th-century eyes the high mansard lined with pedimented stone dormers and the central pavilion crowned with a convex curb roof appear very much later, too late in fact to be possible. For this plastic massing definitely suggests the Second Empire. Rare this sort of design was to remain in France even in the late 50's and 60's; when Hardwick began the Great Western Hotel it was all but nonexistent. The design has therefore a peculiar priority as being even more notably Second Empire *avant la lettre* than the less pompous Hope house.

For this epoch-making, but not ingratiating, monument the models from which Hardwick worked are not easy to spot. It is very unlike anything built in Paris in the 40's in its general effect and even more unlike anything French that really dates from the late 17th or early 18th century. But the puzzle is perhaps not worth solution; for the prototype of most later Victorian work in the Second Empire mode was to be the New Louvre once that was seen by English visitors and published in English magazines in the mid-50's.

The design of the Great Western Hotel was heavily publicized. It was shown complete at the Royal Academy Exhibition in 1851, and various details again in 1852. It was illustrated in 1851 in the *Civil Engineer and Architect's Journal;* in the *Illustrated London News* the next year; and in the Companion to the *British Almanac* for 1853. It was always recognized as the precursor of the London hotel-building boom which began late in the decade with the Westminster Palace and the Grosvenor at the two ends of Victoria Street. Their architects, the Moseleys and J. T. Knowles respectively, followed Hardwick's model in using prominent mansard roofs and more or less Parisian detailing. The climax of English Second Empire was eventually reached in the Grand Hotel at Scarborough built in 1863–67 by Cuthbert Brodrick (1825–1905). The more one examines 19th-century mansarded hotels outside France, from the Great Western on through those built in Rocky Mountain mining towns like Virginia City or Leadville almost a generation later, the more one realizes how very nominal is their French character. This Second Empire mode is almost as characteristically Victorian and Anglo-Saxon as is Victorian Gothic but it is characteristic of the High, not the Early, Victorian phase.

Before leaving the Great Western it should be noted how completely British this dreary Paddington pile is: Above all the cement coating of the exterior ties it in with the Early Victorian stuccoed terraces of the surrounding district (see Chapter XIV). If the exterior be somewhat tawdry the internal construction was nevertheless solid. For example, the staircases and passages, though not the rooms, were built fireproof in the manner of the best contemporary country houses. The ubiquitous John Thomas modeled the giant caryatids on the front. Such facts link the hotel with other pretentious urban structures then building in Britain; but it is the nominally "French" styling of the exterior and the strong, if clumsy, plasticity of the masses, of an order not yet essayed in Paris, that for a few years set it apart until a whole series of later London hotels, beginning with those by the Moseleys and by Knowles that have been mentioned, outbid it in every way.

A much more attractive and original building, designed in 1852 in a somewhat similar mode, is the Bristol General Hospital. The competition for this edifice was won by a local architect, William Bruce Gingell, after the building committee had received advice both from George Wightwick, by then retired to Clifton, and from T. H. Wyatt. Whether or not French influence should be recognized here remains a question (Fig. VII 19). The dormered roofs are high though hardly true mansards. The double-S-curved capping of the principal tower provides a dominant motif more Central European

213

than French. Above all, the corner position of the tower and the general Italian Villa character of the asymmetrical massing differentiates the building sharply from the severe and regular hospitals which official architects were building in France in the mid-century.

The excellent quality of the Bristol General Hospital derives rather more from the fine local materials of which it was built than from its novel design. Random ashlar of blue Pennant stone was used for the walls, as in so many of the great Victorian warehouses of Bristol, and cream-colored Bath stone was freely introduced in the rusticated voussoirs and pilaster strips. The projecting and slightly battered basement storey on which the building is so firmly supported provided 8,000 square feet of warehouse space. The bold scale of the rusticated entrances, as also the simpler treatment of the arched window groups between, suggests the attribution to Gingell of the excellent warehouse at No. 12 Temple Street (Fig. XII 28). If this warehouse, as seems possible, dates from some time in the years 1852–57 when the hospital was being designed and built, its completely arcaded façade must vie for priority with that of Deane and Woodward's Ruskin-inspired Royal Insurance office in London. It is certainly a more advanced and coherent example of commerical architecture whatever its date. Both the hospital and the warehouse in Temple Street contrast markedly with the sumptuously Sansovinesque West of England Bank in Corn Street, designed in 1855, for which this architect is best known.

Functional efficiency in planning is hard to evaluate in a hundred-year-old hospital like that in Bristol. But Gingell's use of fireproof ceilings throughout on the Fox and Barrett system, with a hard cement finish on all floors and dadoes to facilitate cleaning, as well as the elaborate heating and ventilating equipment, evidence technical standards higher than Hardwick was allowed for his luxury hotel in London. The contract price was £14,959.

The three buildings just discussed are generally premonitory of things to come; they are even more premonitory, as has been noted, of certain aspects of Barry's final phase as illustrated in the Government Offices project of 1857 and the Halifax Town Hall. (The mansard roof with which that is capped was not in his original project, however, but was added by E. M. Barry when the building was executed.) Because they are thus ahead of their time they have not so much concluded the present chapter as carried it beyond its natural terminus. The hints they offer of the new direction in neo-Renaissance design that Victorian architecture would follow after the mid-50's can easily be paralleled in Gothic work of the years 1848–52 during which the Hope house, the Great Western Hotel, and the Bristol General Hospital were all designed. The concluding chapter of this book is devoted to the metamorphosis of English neo-Gothic in those years. No such elaborate explanation of the steps that led from the Early Victorian to the High Victorian on the Renaissance side is needed here, if only because the British in their own estimation were following in the 50's the international lead of Paris and produced after Barry no recognized master of neo-Renaissance design of their own.

The High Victorian Gothic was destined to be a specifically English manifestation, influential though it was throughout the world; but many (though not all) High Victorian buildings of generically Renaissance character can be termed Second Empire with some propriety because of the Parisian ideals and standards of their designers. Early manifestations of this international mode are paradoxically hard to find in France; the Hope house can best be paralleled not in Paris but in the mansarded Shiff house, built in New York in 1849–50 by a German-born but French-trained architect Detlef Lienau (1818–1887), and in some Berlin work of the mid-century by Friedrich Hitzig (1811–1881). The Second Empire mode of the 50's and 60's was certainly not deeply rooted in the England of the 40's.

This chapter and the preceding one have centered around the work of Barry and, particularly, what can be called his private architecture as represented in country houses and city mansions. It will be well therefore to bring the account of Barry as a major Early Victorian architect to an end by attempting to sum up his achievement and the achievement of those who followed his leadership in the 40's. To do so at this point, before the account of the building of his Palace at Westminster has been completed, may seem at first sight perverse; but in fact that major edifice occupies so special a position in his career, as in the total production of the time, that one may fairly say the general story of Early Victorian architecture—and above all of Barry's major position in it—would be the same whether or not he built the New Palace. More serious is the fact that material which will be presented in later chapters on commercial architecture and urban housing is really needed to round out the picture of his very extensive influence upon his contemporaries. A trial balance, none the less, may not be out of place here.

The occasional comparisons, implicit and explicit, that have been made throughout this chapter and the preceding one of the work of Barry with similar productions by his contemporaries should already have indicated how significant his leadership was even when measured by that of Pugin. The full extent of his influence cannot be established yet, but the range of his own accomplishment at least should already be evident. This accomplishment is curiously time bound nevertheless. It is not really surprising that Barry should have built very little after the early 50's, even though he was only 57 at the time of Pugin's death in 1852. Barry's achievement is further restricted by the fact that he worked chiefly for rich private clients. Despite the various fields in which he was active at one time or another, private architecture was his true realm; that is why he has been characterized in this book as a "palace architect."

Private architecture had been through much of the 17th and 18th centuries the chief field of English professional activity. It was of considerably less importance in the Early Victorian period. Success at church architecture won a higher reputation; the architecture of business provided richer opportunities; and civic architecture was now more conspicuous in an England grown increasingly pious, commercial, and urban. Some aristocrats still built on a very large scale, usually with income from new industrial interests rather than from agricultural land; a few bankers, railway contractors, shipping magnates, and ironmasters were beginning to rival patrons with inherited wealth in the size of their building commissions. But there was no such continuous demand for great new mansions in London and in the country as in the Georgian Age when patronage was more confined to the aristocracy; nor yet as in the later Victorian decades when throngs of industrial magnates, at a certain stage in their careers, set themselves up as landowners in the country.

The clubs and the institutes, expressing new group activities of the upper and lower middle classes, are more typical of the Early Victorian period than are private palaces whether in the city or the country. In the cities commercial architecture, as we shall see in Chapters XI and XII, was already vying with private architecture in scale and magnificence. The characteristic urban housing of all classes, as in the Georgian Age, was not the custom-designed mansion but the ready-made terrace house (see Chapters XIII–XIV). Yet private architecture still had considerable inherited prestige.

It was on account of Barry's clubs, mansions, and country houses, not because of his public commissions, that he had so great an influence over various fields of architecture in which he himself never practiced. Together with the 14th-century parish church model which Pugin standardized for Victorian use and the neo-Tudor manor house mode which had already come into wide use in the Late Georgian period, Barry's Italian palazzos—and to a less considerable extent his large-scale towered villas—provided basic stylistic paradigms for the Victorian Age.

The Early Victorian period was essentially eclectic as Barry was eclectic—that is, in a rather limited way. Few of its leaders really aimed at the exclusive revival of one particular style of the past in the way of the Grecian enthusiasts earlier in the century. Even Pugin, as we shall see in the next chapter, followed later models for his country houses than he did for his churches. Characteristically, the Early Victorians were seeking not one but rather a group of viable modes for use in various different fields of architecture, and for several of these modes Barry provided exemplars that long remained satisfying. Each mode was to have more or less exclusive dominion within its own field as

216

also in what might be called functionally contiguous areas; but none was considered universally valid. Despite his Brunswick Chapel at Hove, built back in the 20's, Barry would not have expected (or perhaps even have wished) to build a church of Renaissance design in the late 30's or the 40's. Whatever mode Pugin may have followed in the design he entered in the Reform Club competition in 1837 it is most unlikely to have been the 14th-century Decorated of his mature churches.

The available documentation on the admired styles of the past in the 40's was uneven in accuracy and completeness. Only a few architects had Pugin's or Barry's direct knowledge of the models they tried to follow. The practical requirements of the various functional programs differed a great deal in their effect on design, as will be more evident in later chapters. Yet the introduction of new materials, either for internal fireproofing or for novel features such as glass-roofed courts and conservatories, necessarily affected even the most conscientiously derivative architects. Therefore all Early Victorian paradigms differ, although in varying degree, from their ancient prototypes. In reaction from the latitudinarian attitude of the Late Georgians toward every past style but the Greek, however, the rigor with which the chosen models were *supposed* to be copied in the late 30's and early 40's generally increased. Architects of serious professional pretension vaunted their stylistic erudition and prated of their devotion to "correctness" in the use of borrowed forms.

Yet after the mid-40's a definite, though uneven, tendency toward a broader interpretation of chosen models made its appearance. This is sufficiently evident in the contrast between Barry's two chief London buildings, the Reform Club house of the late 30's and Bridgewater House of a decade later. On the one hand, new historical studies provided justification for richer variants of the basic paradigms (as had already been true for Grecian work in the 30's); on the other hand, severity and delicacy in the handling of detail gave way to an avid pursuit of more ornate, and also of coarser, effects in all the current modes. In the work of the more conscientious architects like Barry—and also Salvin, as we shall see in the next chapter—the choice of more complex or bolder ancient models for emulation in the late 40's seems to explain a good part of the changed character of the detail. Less learned architects merely elaborated or coarsened their handling of established paradigms in order to meet the cruder tastes of mid-century clients; this is especially evident in commercial architecture and in urban terrace design.

In larger matters of composition the basic visual differences between the various Early Victorian modes makes it hard to state in a few words the direction of the general modulation. The essential similarity between a Barry clubhouse and a Pugin church is intellectual rather than a matter of appearance. It may be fairly said, however, that the interpretation of all modes tended increasingly to emphasize surface plasticity as the 40's moved on. The early tendency (which might well be called centrifugal) toward the use of peripheral accents, such as a tower set at one corner of the main mass or raised pavilions at the ends of a long façade, was beginning to be balanced in the late 40's by a contrary centripetal tendency. More centralized, but not necessarily more symmetrical, massing was returning to favor. Shrubland or, a fortiori, Cliveden are more tightly composed than Trentham. The earlier, purely pictorial asymmetry—literally "picturesque"—which was primarily concerned with the silhouette, began to be replaced by a more restrained use of occult balance. Often this is at least pseudofunctional in character as Pugin demanded; in any event it is likely to be more a matter of over-all plastic massing than of consideration for the outline against the sky. (This is, of course, most evident in the proto-Second Empire buildings just discussed which lead forward to the High Victorian.)

Such conclusions, based as they must be now almost entirely on churches and on the work of Barry and some of his followers, will seem premature, and so they are. But it was in the fields which Pugin and Barry dominated that Early Victorian architects operated with the greatest aesthetic freedom, or at least with the most hope of sympathy from cultivated clients for their own aesthetic ideals. Unfortunately the cultivation of private clients was chiefly historical and lay for the most part in that range of so-called "general education," based on a little conventional knowledge, which is as little conducive to imaginative patronage of architecture as to sound judgment about any subject.

The creative possibilities of the Early Victorian period can barely be sensed in the types of buildings that have chiefly been covered thus far in this book. The ignorance of the rising middle classes has frequently been considered responsible for the deterioration of architecture after the Georgian Age; it might as justly be asserted that the restrictions of snobbery and the connotational superstitions of the educated upper classes which provided most of Pugin's and Barry's clients were more to blame. Barry, however, was able in the field of private architecture to cater rather successfully to whatever remained of an innate tradition of post-Renaissance taste among the upper classes. In other fields it was the rising elements in the community that provided the most challenging opportunities for Early Victorian architects. Yet the actual architectural capacity of the men who attempted to grasp these new opportunities was rarely so great as Pugin's or his Anglican rivals', not to speak of Barry's. It is one of the basic cultural tragedies of the 19th century in this Early Victorian period that architectural literacy and architectural invention were so often at odds.

Insofar as the second quarter of the 19th century was the beginning of a new age, so different quantitatively from preceding ages that it differed from them qualitatively also, neither church architects nor private architects really had much occasion to meet its most difficult problems head on. Barry could probably have done so most effectively, or so such commissions as the Pentonville Prison and the Keyham Factory may suggest. But within the late Whig world where he chiefly operated he had little more direct contact with the commercial and industrial 19th century than Pugin and his clients preoccupied with their Catholic Revival.

Barry utilized new materials quite as did the Georgians of the previous generation if perhaps with slightly less enthusiasm. His attitude toward completely new methods of construction, however, if we may judge by his suggestions for the first and second Crystal Palaces, was skeptical; what he might have done with such new problems as railway stations offered is not at all clear. In his planning he was in fact rarely called on to provide for wholly new needs. Intelligent adaptation rather than innovation was his forte. He was primarily a well-trained academic architect who could have been a success in England at almost any period after the High Middle Ages from Yevele's time to Holland's; but he would never have achieved originality in design. Thus he was the prototype par excellence of the so-called "traditional" architects of the early 20th century. In a period like our own, more aware of the creative inadequacy of its immediate predecessors than of their uninspiring virtues, it is hard to do an architect of Barry's sort full justice. His best work is too much like that of the most conventionally "tasteful" architects of the early 20th century and, indeed, provided the only real "tradition" they ever followed, whether they knew it or not.

Barry did not renew English architecture by the establishment of revolutionary new standards in the way that Pugin, however peculiarly, was actually doing. He merely maintained long-established European standards, modulating them knowledgeably to meet new conditions and providing sufficient superficial novelty to hold contemporary attention. In other hands and in newer fields of building, however, his Italian paradigms proved to be as basic to Victorian architecture as were Pugin's Gothic ones. He was less typically English than the half-foreign Pugin, more adaptable and less self-righteous, more cosmopolitan and less cranky. Barry's equals are his opposite numbers on the Continent, men like Henri Labrouste and Louis Joseph Duc (1802–1879) and Duban in France, or Gottfried Semper (1803–1879) and the other Renaissance Revivalists who succeeded Schinkel in Germany. Beside their work his own stands up well, far better than that of most of the architects, including even Pugin, whose country houses are discussed in the next chapter.

CHAPTER VIII: MANORIAL AND

CASTELLATED COUNTRY HOUSES

The stream of country house architecture was not much diverted from the general direction it had taken in Late Georgian days by Barry's Italian palace and villa models. The most characteristic mansions built in the country in the 40's continued the line of those earlier 19th-century houses that were neither Palladian nor Grecian but vaguely Tudor. Moreover the standards of the architects who designed them were only slowly raised by the high-flown ideals of Pugin and the Camdenians. But once a new Victorian program for country house design had become stabilized it tended to continue with little modification long after the end of the Early Victorian period in the 50's. Because the patronage was so similar much the same can be said of a great deal of other construction in the country: schools and other village institutions, almshouses, and the other necessary facilities in the rural scheme of living which were still mostly provided by feudal condescension or private charity rather than by some arm of the State.

Unlike the situation with urban housing there is little strictly anonymous country work which is of much visual consequence. Even the tiniest "National" schools were usually architect designed or at least derived from models provided by books. So also rows of cottages put up by landowners were no longer works of traditional craftsmanship but followed published models, many of them dating back to the Picturesque period of the 20's. The most modest new dwellings built for their own occupancy by the landed classes and such of their country houses of earlier periods as were altered and redecorated in Victorian times had architects, even if these architects were in fact only builders from the nearest county town who had assumed the higher professional title.

In the towns the house production of builders without professional pretensions is so enormous and so massive that the general picture of the Early Victorian city, with its characteristic patterns of urbanism, is for the greater part of their creation, and even more so than in Georgian times. However low their quality, the serried ranks of terrace houses cannot be altogether ignored even though the names of the responsible designers are lost on the forgotten payrolls of speculative entrepreneurs; for these houses provided the

220

basic cellular elements of which the urban organism as a whole was compounded (see Chapter XI). But new work of the Victorian Age in the country often lies quite unseen within its own park; or else it is half hidden in the village street among earlier edifices of indeterminate date whose materials and modest scale it happily echoes. Nonecclesiastical edifices of this period arouse no such curiosity as do Victorian village churches even though they may be by the same excellent (or execrable) architects. Only complete "model" villages, always the exception, attract much attention to themselves. Early Victorian work, therefore, is usually no such blemish on the general village picture as are the chain stores and council houses of the present century. Age has been kinder also to modest work of the 40's and 50's in the country than to that in cities and suburbs—age and, of course, veiling mantles of green vegetation.

It is just as well to let most simple country building lie unnoticed in its near anonymity and relative datelessness. If it survives, it presumably continues still to be useful, and a century's patina makes it less alien in the country scene than anything built today could hope to be for a long, long time. And, when demolished, the loss is only statistical, not absolute as with more individualized structures. However great the chances may be of vast programs of replacement of Victorian construction in cities and towns, a widespread destruction of minor Victorian accretions in the countryside is unlikely for a generation or more. Victorian country houses, on the other hand, are unprotected by the conventional respect and legislative piety that succor earlier monuments unless the Victorian mansions were the homes of famous men (who did not always employ the best architects, alas). For them there is real danger of all but complete demolition such as has already overtaken Trentham Park. Belated appreciation may help save a few, but probably not more than a few. It is worth while, therefore, to signal here certain examples as being especially fine and typical or of major significance in the development of domestic architecture. Schools, asylums, sanatoriums, country clubs, hostelries, even museums have come to occupy a good many; but accidents of location more than relative merit have thus far determined which should receive a new lease of life through adaptation to public or semi-public use. Adaptation, moreover, as in the gutting of Alton Towers to make a picnic resort for the Midlands, with only the gardens properly maintained as a profit-making show, may so distort the character of country houses that they might better be completely destroyed (a fate which has, in fact, now befallen this seat of Lord Shrewsbury). In any event a Victorian date is generally considered to justify the most drastic sort of remodeling if such big houses are taken for some new use, and thus their original character becomes completely denatured.

221

In considering the country architecture of the Early Victorian period one may properly be highly selective, following closely only the work of those architects who were specialists, like Salvin or Burn, or else leaders in some other field. A Jacobethan mansion by Paxton, or a castellated one by Clutton, is not necessarily better than similar big houses done by provincial architects whose careers never carried them outside their own county towns; but knowledge of such houses is relevant to our understanding of the ideals and capacities of men who are justly famous for work of quite a different order. Therefore the range of Victorian achievement in this field can be adequately presented with rather a small cast of characters, all named.

The previous chapter dealt with Barry's country house work and with some, at least, of the work of other men that paralleled his. Among these Anthony Salvin can be considered a more important leader than Barry himself in this field; moreover, he entered it a decade earlier. Salvin also was as much Pugin's rival at country house building as he was Barry's. Other men, such as Blore and Burn, though their production was less distinguished than Salvin's, provide even more than he a meaningful link with the Late Georgian period. Clutton and Teulon, on the other hand, carry the story forward, for their best and most characteristic work was to be done later in the High Victorian 50's and 60's. Although country house work is much-of-a-muchness, with few high peaks of accomplishment, the professional personnel was quite varied. There were not only men like Salvin and Blore and Burn who concentrated on country house work and men like Pugin and Clutton and Teulon who were primarily church architects; there were also many whose normal practice was urban—either commercial or else concerned with monumental public and semipublic edifices—who turned their hand to a few country houses, usually of a rather conventional order. The castles of academic bank architects or the manors of men who built railway stations are not, needless to say, likely to be the best of their kind.

Pugin himself was not very active at building castles and manors; certainly he had fewer opportunities for erecting or remodeling country houses than Barry did. As much because of his own Catholic prejudices, which were fanatically bigoted through most of the 40's, as because of the Protestant prejudices of most of the landed gentry, he was hardly employed at all on country house work except by fellow religionists. Rich Catholics coming up from the middle or lower classes did not appear much as clients for architects until later in the century; the aristocratic converts of the 30's and 40's mostly confined their patronage to church and convent building. Few old Catholic landowners needed new country seats nor could they often afford to remodel their ancestral houses. Any considerable money they might have available for building ventures was supposed to go for the erection of churches. Since the Catholic religion was still almost on a missionary basis in England, those Catholics who spent money on their own houses could be considered disloyal to the cause of reconverting Britain.

Pugin's own first house, and the first thing he ever built, was St. Marie's Grange, near Salisbury, which he began in 1835 just after his conversion and his second marriage. This tiny edifice is probably the crankiest honeymoon cottage an architect ever provided for his bride (Fig. VIII 1). Three storeys tall, the kitchen and scullery occupied most of the basement, although there are living rooms there today. Of the first storey almost one-third was originally given up to a vaulted chapel; that floor, moreover, was entered by a drawbridge under which was placed the stable. (Drawbridge and stable have both gone today.) The three bedrooms on the floor above were reached only by a circular stair; all of them opened into one another, with the water closet off the middle room! This convenience was in a small square turret which also provided space for water closets off the library and off the kitchen on the two floors below in the original arrangement of the house. The walls are incredibly thick in relation to the size of the house; but this permits ranges of what would today be called "storage-walls" in the principal rooms.

Built of red brick, with stone-mullioned windows and high saddleback hip roofs covered with dark slate, the Grange is very simple externally. The L-shaped block is varied by a gable over the chapel, a separate hip roof over the water-closet turret ("garderobe," I suppose Pugin would have called it), and a slightly projecting brick parapet over the square tower in which the circular staircase rose. The interior changes have not much affected the exterior; but the removal of the drawbridge and the placing of the main entrance on the ground floor shifts the normal approach to the house and makes it appear taller and narrower.

Nothing, it would seem, could have been less likely to bring the architect commissions for country houses. But conviction and sincerity always work wonders in architecture. It was probably while the Earl of Radnor was visiting the new house, at a time when only the library was habitable, that he asked Pugin to prepare plans for additions and alterations at Longford Castle. (These are not the Victorian additions at present being demolished since none of Pugin's proposals were in fact carried out.)

Pugin lived only some five years at St. Marie's Grange; finally, after attempting to rent it for several years, he sold it in 1841, receiving £500 for what had cost him over £2,000 to build. In his first years there he was busy with the designs for the Westminster New Palace competition and was doing very little other architectural work. His principal private client was Lord Shrewsbury for whom he was making designs for the decoration of his Staffordshire seat Alton Towers. This was a Late Georgian fake castle that had been built for the 15th Earl of Shrewsbury, the uncle of Pugin's patron. At the time of the 16th earl's accession in 1827 Alton and its remarkable gardens were far from complete. The original designer had been Robert Abraham (1763–1850), better known as the architect of the Westminster New Bridewell prison and of the County Fire Office behind Nash's façade in Piccadilly Circus. But Fradgley, an architect from nearby Uttoxeter, seems to have been employed by the younger Shrewsbury on the completion of the interiors up to the time he made his first contact with Pugin in 1832—appropriately enough while shopping for Gothic furniture in Wardour Street.

Long ago gutted, Alton Towers is now being demolished. But Pugin's work of the 30's there, although of some interest originally, was overshadowed by what was added—or at least only completed—later. Through much of the 40's the Shrewsburys lived in Italy where their daughters both married Roman princes. By closing down Alton Towers the earl estimated that he saved some £2,000 a year that he could donate toward the building of churches and monasteries in England. The dining hall at Alton, Pugin's most sumptuous domestic work, seems to have been completed only in 1849 after Alton Towers had been more or less deserted for eight years.

The vast projects Pugin prepared for rebuilding Garendon in Leicestershire for his other principal patron Ambrose March-Phillipps, as well as schemes of comparable completeness for William Leigh at Woodchester Park in Gloucestershire, came to even less than those for Lord Shrewsbury. March-Phillipps gave all he could toward church and monastery building. Leigh, with whom Pugin was in close contact in 1846, probably gave up his plans because of a bad building situation: "The price of labour is excessive—the men have struck on every job I have in hand . . . ," Pugin wrote him in May of that year. At Chirk Castle the alterations undertaken for Colonel Robert Myddleton-Biddulph (about 1844) included little new work except an outside corridor along the east side.

Most of Pugin's commissions from Catholic landowners were merely for private chapels of which several were mentioned in Chapter III. Only a few houses include secular construction by Pugin of much interest; the most important of these are Scarisbrick Hall, near Ormskirk in Lancashire (Figs. VIII 2, 3); Bilton Grange, near Rugby in Warwickshire (Fig. VIII 13); and his own later house, the Grange, on the West Cliff at Ramsgate (Fig. VIII 14). All three, moreover, were begun during the busy five years following 1837 when he was most active at church building and before he began working again with Barry on the New Palace in 1844.

Charles Scarisbrick belonged to an old Catholic family and was an extremely rich landowner whose father had drained the nearby Martin Mere in 1783. He was also an eccentric recluse of whom Nathaniel Hawthorne wrote when he was living nearby at Southport in the mid-50's: "He might be an interesting person to know; but, after all, his character turns out to be one of the commonplaces of novels and romances." The old 16th-century Scarisbrick Hall, a half-timbered house, had fallen into decay long before his time. The father first considered rebuilding it completely on a new site from designs by Humphrey Repton (1752–1818) and his son John Adey Repton (1775–1860); then in 1814 Charles' older brother had it partially restored by some Liverpool architect. (It is uncertain whether that architect was John Foster 2 or Thomas Rickman; but at that time secular work by the Gothick Rickman would not have differed much from Tudor work by the Grecian Foster.)

Pugin's problem at Scarisbrick was a difficult one: He had to incorporate some real medieval fragments whose integrity had been seriously compromised twenty years earlier while drastically rebuilding a feeble Late Georgian mansion consisting of a central block and two projecting wings. Pugin's first drawings concerning Scarisbrick (for ornamental details only) are dated 1836; the decision to rebuild on a large scale probably was not made until 1837. But construction proceeded very slowly and in quite as piecemeal a fashion as the work for Lord Shrewsbury at Alton.

The parsimony that inhibited Early Victorian landowners from building new mansions outright must have been profoundly exasperating to their architects. At the same time there were compensations. The extreme prolongation of the building campaigns—and the practical certainty that more and more of the old work would seem too shabby to preserve as the new work went up—made country house commissions as dependable a source of professional income as hypochondriacs provide for doctors. Landowners were richer in income than in disposable capital; moreover, they generally expected to utilize in their building operations local (and presumably seasonal) labor as well as predominantly local materials. Hence they hesitated to commit themselves at any one time to large lump expenditures and preferred to avoid the importation of the numbers of workmen that would have been necessary to complete extensive building operations within a short period. Building conditions in the country being still semifeudal, the methods of production were rather more authentically Late Gothic than the style in the case of most Early Victorian manors.

The Scarisbrick incomes from Lancashire landholdings were presumably increasing through the 40's. Even so, when Pugin died in 1852 his not very extensive plans for remodeling Scarisbrick Hall had by no means been completely carried out. Later, when Scarisbrick's sister inherited the estate at the age of 72, she brought in Pugin's son E. W. Pugin to finish the work. He not only elaborated the treatment of the whole east wing but carried up his father's tower at its end to a perfectly fantastic height; for this elderly patroness, who knew she did not have long to live, was ready to spend her money more rapidly than her brother. Pugin's work at Scarisbrick, therefore, is almost inextricably entangled with the earlier elements he merely touched up and also with the later emendations of a son who had little of his father's talent (Fig. VIII 3).

From drawings, and from paintings and carvings inside the house, it is possible to get some idea of what Pugin's Scarisbrick was intended to be. The present west wing, of course, with its pipe-like octagonal corner buttresses, is clearly work of 1814 little modified by Pugin. The balancing east wing, as he left it, was much more plausibly 15th century in character but is now quite buried under Edward's French Flamboyant frills. Only the great hall (whose completion is dated 1842 by an inscription on the arch of the south porch) and the contiguous links which connect it with the two wings are as Pugin left them. Pugin used much ingenuity to bring light into these links by providing skylights over the first-storey corridors running east and west and treating these as galleries half the width of the corridors on the ground floor.

Even if some earlier work was incorporated in the central block it probably looks today much as he wished it. The significant thing, and what most distinguished Scarisbrick from earlier Tudoresque manor houses, is the way the great hall is the heart of the plan in the true medieval way even though it is only 43 feet long (including the "screens") and 25 feet wide. The entrance porch on the north front leads into the screens passage at one end of the hall and the private apartments lie beyond the dais at the opposite end. The paired bay windows are unusual but, as in the case of Moffatt's Russell mansion in London a few years later, the secular Late Gothic vocabulary encouraged a vast extension and massing of the window areas.

The richness of the window tracery and the paneled crenellations atop these bay windows and over the porch contrasts rather too sharply with the simplicity of the side wings. In part this was doubtless intentional and considered characteristic of the period Pugin was emulating. The relatively short history of the reconstruction of Scarisbrick, although including work of two generations active between 1810 and 1870, is almost as complicated as the vicissitudes real medieval manor houses passed through in several hundred years; that history explains and justifies the lack of coherence and consistency in design. Here, as in many 19th-century houses, this pseudo-organic variety is the most truly medieval quality that a succession of more or less assiduous Gothicizers were able to produce.

The clock tower here, in its original form, provided the prototype for that on the New Palace as redesigned in the late 40's or early 50's. (Probably this tower was actually built; in any event the 1837 sketch (Fig. VIII 2) and more detailed drawings dated 1839 indicate that the conception was fully worked out and in existence in graphic form before 1840.) The tower has now been replaced by his son's, as has been said; that is doubtless why so few have noted the evidence its design offers of an important and positively architectural, rather than merely decorative, contribution Pugin most probably made at Westminster (Fig. I 1). Gladstone noted the resemblance of the Westminster Clock Tower to that of Scarisbrick, preferring the earlier version of the design; this seems to prove that it was in existence in the 50's when the Westminster tower was being completed.

By 1868, when the *Building News* described Scarisbrick, some £85,000 had reputedly been spent on it. Much of this is accounted for by the elaboration of the interior decoration under E. W. Pugin's direction by Hardman, Farmer, and Wall. But the elder Pugin's work was solidly executed in local Scarisbrick stone with trim of Longridge stone, and both white Carrara and black Derbyshire marbles were used for interior arches and door jambs, probably by him rather than by his son. In the great hall most of the carved woodwork is medieval Flemish; this was acquired by Charles Scarisbrick in Belgium and incorporated in the new structure by Pugin. On Scarisbrick's death more than £23,000 worth of detached works of art were sold at Christie's.

With Scarisbrick Hall may be contrasted Scotney Castle. This was built for Edward Hussey in Kent by Anthony Salvin in the years 1837–40, a remarkably short building campaign for so considerable a country house. But Salvin, as we have seen, was having his own troubles with ambitious country gentlemen building out of income at Harlaxton where construction ran on well into the 50's. Thirteen years older than Pugin and himself a member of the land-owning class, Salvin's career as a country house builder had begun at least a decade earlier. He was considered a great archaeological expert on castles and much consulted by the government on the preservation of the Royal castles. He was also the chief fake-castle builder of the age which was, however, rather less addicted to that expensive sport than the Late Georgian had been. But Salvin can hardly have regretted his client's decision at Scotney to leave the old castle as a ruin at the foot of the garden, in the earlier Romantic way, and to proceed expeditiously with the building of a new house.

Scotney has much less period flavor than Scarisbrick; it could almost have been built at any date during the successive Victorian decades; for there is very little fussy ornament and no elaborate traceried oriels or dominating clock tower (Fig. VIII 4). The planning also is sound rather than archaeological, with the principal reception rooms compactly grouped around the great hall (which also serves, in the manner of the period, as a billiard room) and the service quarters surrounding a court at one end of the main block. (Actually some Elizabethan plans for small country houses approach this sort of compact near-regularity, but more articulation and formal symmetry were generally characteristic of the late 16th century.) A certain regard for symmetry appears here in the placing of the principal staircase on axis with the garden entrance. Two of the chief rooms, moreover, are of unbroken oblong shape, with regularly spaced windows, doors, and fireplaces quite in the 18th-century way. On the other hand an evident regard for the picturesque determined the placing of the square tower to the left of the main entrance and suggested also the range of cross gables that surround the main roof; yet neither the symmetry nor the picturesqueness is forced.

The materials, random ashlar walling with a rather restricted use of freestone trim, were for the most part local in origin and simply and naturally handled. If the harshness of the wall surfaces and the cold quality of the moldings indicate how little traditional craftsmanship had yet been revived, Salvin nevertheless contented himself with straightforward stone-mullioned windows, plain parapets and gables, and walling masonry that was neither exaggeratedly rustic nor yet mechanically regular.

The differences from similar Late Georgian work are really rather slight, and in the next few decades innumerable houses of this sort were built that do not differ much from Scotney. As long as the practical needs of the country house client changed little the changing whims of fashion produced only superficial modifications in design. Ordinary "county" landowners were probably less influenced by aesthetic fashions than most other groups in the Victorian community, except of course the very poor. Yet it was from this relatively stable root that a new domestic architecture eventually began to grow in the 60's under the guidance of Eden Nesfield and Norman Shaw.

Salvin's country house practice was already extensive before the new reign began but much of it always consisted of alterations and restorations. Old work, fortunately, was rather less ruthlessly handled by him and by other good country house architects than by the ambitious church restorers of the period. Through the 40's, as has been said, a considerable number of architects were designing houses similar to Salvin's as their principal professional activity, and there were few architects who were not ready to turn their hands to Tudor country house work when occasion demanded. But in the late 30's Salvin's chief rival as a country house architect was undoubtedly Blore. He was a much less careful designer with far less feeling for materials; but he had a certain professional prestige because of his succession to Nash at Buckingham Palace and, rather more relevantly, to Wyatville at Windsor Castle in the early 30's. That will presumably explain why he was employed by Count Worontzow-Dashkow to design a mansion while the count was Russian ambassador in 1836.

This curious edifice, at Alupka in the Crimea, is half oriental and half Tudor (Fig. VIII 5), like an amalgam of Nash's Royal Pavilion at Brighton and Wyatville's work at Windsor. (Curiously enough Winston Churchill was housed there during the Yalta Conference.) Worontzow's palace rose from Blore's designs, under the direction of a clerk of the works he sent out, between 1837 and 1840. This remote and belated echo of the tastes of George IV, although exceptional in Blore's work, indicates how superficial and essentially decorative was his approach to neo-medieval design. He generally favored, as a stylistic vehicle, neither the late Elizabethan of Salvin's Harlaxton nor yet the Anglo-Italian of Barry's Highclere but an earlier Elizabethan; his houses were usually even more irregularly massed than Pugin's or Salvin's and plastered over with a confusion of Italianate and late Perpendicular detail.

Ramsey Abbey in Huntingdonshire, built for Lord de Ramsey in 1838–39, is little larger than Scotney Castle and rather similar in plan, but there is nothing at all modest about its design. In the first place it is three storeys tall instead of two and raised on a high basement (Fig. VIII 6). The low-pitched main roof is mostly masked by a balustrade but a high gable comes forward over the projecting hall bay. There are also two corner towers, one large and one small, and a profusion of ornate chimneys and corner turrets to enliven the skyline. The walls are irregularly broken by two- and three-storey oriels, buttresses, and porches, obscuring the essentially rectangular outline; the Elizabethan detail is positively turgid. One feature of Elizabethan architecture effectively exploited here is the tremendous banks of mullioned and transomed windows occupying the greater part of the wall surface. As at Scotney the service wing, very modest in relation to the main block, runs off to the left of the principal tower. Once more it may be noted that nothing at Ramsey is really outside the range of Late Georgian design in this vein although the planning is looser than would have been acceptable before the 20's and the composition somewhat more irregular.

Blore's great opportunity came at Worsley Hall but he did not make much of it. This enormous mansion, which is in the parish of Eccles some seven miles from Manchester and close to the beginning of the Bridgewater Canal at Worsley Bridge, was designed for Lord Francis Egerton in 1839 and built over the years 1840–45. As a younger son, Lord Francis needed an entirely new mansion and, as the principal heir of his grandfather the Duke of Bridgewater, he could afford to build one on a scale rivaling the seat of his brother the Duke of Sutherland at Trentham which was just then being so much extended by Barry. The main block of Worsley is essentially symmetrical like the more characteristic mock-Elizabethan mansions of Late Georgian times (Fig. VIII 7). Except for the mullioned bay windows Blore took much less advantage of the practical advantages of late 16th-century design here than at Ramsey Abbey. Although executed throughout in Hollington stone, the detail is mean and hard, the walling textureless. But for splashes of strap-work here and there, a form of ornament that had not been extensively revived before the late 30's, the architectural embellishments do not differ much from what had been standard in secular Gothic work since James Wyatt's time. In the keep-like tower, set at one corner of the main block where the rather rambling service wing is attached, Blore attempted to provide a dominating asymmetrical feature like Barry's loggia towers. Doubtless it served the same practical purpose of holding the water supply for the interior plumbing, but it is hardly so effective a compositional feature.

Fake-castle building, so popular with Late Georgian landowners, was by the opening of Victoria's reign mostly an amateur pastime. Hadlow Castle in Kent, building through the 40's from the designs of its owner William Barton May, is understandably known as the "Fonthill of Kent" because of its very tall and slender polygonal tower, so much more appealing than Blore's Worsley keep. But the extremely delicate and ornate detail on this tower, and even more the much less literate tracery on the main block, is actually almost pre-Wyatt in character. The extensive enlargement of Ravensworth Castle in County Durham was initiated by Nash; but the Hon. Henry Thomas Liddell, eldest son of the owner Lord Ravensworth, was apparently responsible for completing the work in Early Victorian times, adding the principal front and possibly the great hall which is 100 feet by 40 feet and 50 feet high. Ravensworth is a considerably more plausible castellated edifice than Hadlow, but it also rather resembles certain contemporary prisons. Wray Castle on Lake Windermere is more modest in scale but extremely heavy handed, owing all its charm to the romantic site and the rich growth of creeper on the walls (Fig. VIII 8). It was built for a Colonel Dawson by Horner of Liverpool in 1840–47 and was admired by no less a man than Wordsworth (who lived, of course, just across the lake).

Professional architects were now becoming too conscious of "correctness" to be willing to build castles that were purely pictorial exercises in the way of the early 19th century. But few clients were yet ready to accept the drastic modifications in planning and the sacrifices in fenestration that plausible imitation of real castellated architecture demanded. The new seriousness, extending from church architecture into all fields where medieval forms were used, was reducing castle building to the personal hobby of a few belated post-Georgians. But the prestige of such architectural hobbies was much diminished now that architecture was becoming so much more professionalized; and the professionals tended to specialize. If Pugin was not, like Salvin, particularly a castle specialist, he was nevertheless an expert on all the architecture of the Edwardian Age around 1300 when the medieval English castle (much more certainly than the medieval church) had arrived at maturity.

Alton Castle, on the rocks above the village of Alton, was rebuilt by Pugin for Lord Shrewsbury more as an archaeological exercise than for residential purposes. Because of its superb cliff-top site it is extremely picturesque; but the actual edifice is very simple, even matter of fact, as real castles must have been in their own day (Fig. VIII 9). There is little of that play of turret against tower in a pile of cubic and cylindrical masses which makes such an earlier fake castle as Gwrych (Fig. II 7) a rich romantic decoration against its hanging wood and which still motivated the designers of Ravensworth or Wray. Yet Pugin's Alton is in function little more than an ornamental "fabrick" in the landscape as they are not.

St. John's Hospital (now occupied by French nuns as the Couvent de l'Assomption), contiguous to the castle, is one of Pugin's most considerable semi-secular constructions. Built in 1840–44 but never completed in its entirety, a chapel, school, warden's lodging, and cloister are there grouped about three sides of a quadrangle. All of stone and quite vigorously detailed, this is more picturesque than the red brick clergy houses and convents he was building at Birmingham and Derby and other places. But in assessing Pugin's secular work these things merit more attention than they have generally received. They are perhaps more significant for the later development of domestic architecture along medievalizing lines than are the large castles and manors of the 40's. Surely Butterfield was aware of these edifices when he designed his Coalpitheath vicarage (Fig. V 13).

The Derby presbytery, although rather jammed in beside St. Marie's, is solid, straightforward, and not lacking in vigor. The local red brick is happily used, with a minimum of stone trim, and looks much more cheerful than the gritstone of the church (Fig. VIII 10). The Convent of Mercy in Hunter Road, Birmingham, larger and less begrimed, is even more attractive than the Derby presbytery (Fig. VIII 11). This convent has also a small church of its own which is one of the best maintained of all Pugin's ecclesiastical edifices. Built in 1840–41, the establishment was largely paid for by John Hardman, Pugin's associate in many fields, and by Lord Shrewsbury. It cost only £3,000, that is, the original convent for some twenty sisters; the somewhat later church was not consecrated until 1847.

When Pugin was designing his own second house, the Grange at Ramsgate, begun in 1841, Trappes-Lomax suggests that it may have been the influence of his second wife, who had suffered from the eccentricities of St. Marie's

Grange, that led him to adopt a more convenient plan; but his experience with clergy houses must have stood him in good stead also. The Ramsgate Grange is not, properly speaking, a country house; yet it is little smaller than Scotney Castle and much more considerable than his own earlier house near Salisbury. As at Scotney the principal rooms are arranged around a hall. The hall here is not very large but it rises the full height of the house to an open-timbered roof and contains the main staircase leading up to a cantilevered gallery from which the various bedrooms are reached. This modest and practical adaptation of the medieval great hall to the principal needs of communication in a moderate-sized 19th-century house was to provide an important element in the Late Victorian stage of the prehistory of the modern house. Barry was developing the idea at monumental scale in rebuilding Highclere; Butterfield would soon use it in his vicarage at Coalpitheath; yet it never became characteristic of Early Victorian house planning. That generally remained rather hidebound as if the many innovations proposed in the preceding Picturesque period had been too much for either architects or clients to digest.

The drawing room at the Grange occupied the west end of the house on the ground floor and the dining room faced the sea to the south. The service accommodations were not in the basement, as at St. Marie's Grange, but contiguous to the hall and the dining room at the east end of the main block of the house. Had Pugin planned more such houses of moderate size his influence on domestic architecture might have been considerable.

Built of rather dreary buff brick, the Grange is not particularly appealing from the outside; but the molded stone trim of the mullioned windows is well cut and the gables are few and ornamented only with plain bargeboards (Fig. VIII 14). Beyond the main block of the house, to the east, rises a very plain tower with the simplest possible crenellations. Neither in this nor in the plain brick chimney stacks, which are set diagonally, is there much attempt to enrich or elaborate the silhouette. The interior trim was also extremely simple, although there was some carving above the stone fireplaces and stenciled patterns once covered the walls. Characteristic of Pugin's surprisingly practical approach to 19th-century domestic architecture at this time was the use of plate glass in the lower portions of the windows toward the sea; elsewhere small leaded panes and inserts of armorial glass were keyed to the rest of the interior decorative treatment.

The very small private chapel, attached to the base of the tower on the east, was used by local Catholics after its completion in 1843. As we have seen, a few years later Pugin began his church of St. Augustine but that, although contiguous, is really quite independent both in the fine materials of which it is built and in its standard Decorated style. Both house and church are now occupied by a monastic order and rather well maintained; for Pugin

232

is now considered a great man by English Catholics, however dubious the hierarchy may have been about so cantankerous a convert in his own lifetime.

Bilton Grange, near Rugby in Warwickshire, was built for Captain J. H. Washington Hibbert, the brother-in-law of Lord Shrewsbury. Begun about the same time as the Grange, it was completed externally by 1846. Considerable extensions, made to accommodate a boys' school, now confuse the original scheme which was shown in a drawing at the Royal Academy Exhibition of 1849. On the entrance front a large square tower projects above a carriage porch that is open on three sides. The high pointed roof of this tower, rising above crenellations and terminating in an open lantern, resembles rather more the crowning feature of the Clock Tower on the New Palace than it does anything of the Tudor period.

The garden wing, running back at right angles from the original narrow front block, has a series of four identical two-storey bay windows; a fifth bay window is set against the gable at the rear end (Fig. VIII 13). Above the bay windows on the side are ranges of small gables with tiny coupled lights. The regularity of the scheme was such that the effect, even in perspective, is not at all picturesque. The red brick walls are diapered occasionally with dark brick and the stone trim of the windows is crisp and straightforward. There is none of the variety of Scarisbrick—in any event not altogether intentional—and the whole effect is harder and more mechanical, if pleasanter in color, than the Grange. The roof of the great hall, which has curved principals and curious Y-shaped rafters between, is more vigorous and structural than most of Pugin's church roofs. The oak screens and wainscoting are also simple and unornamented.

It may seem at first thought surprising that Pugin, whose churches established the mode of irregularity and free massing in Early Victorian ecclesiastical architecture, should have rejected Picturesque composition to such an extent in his domestic work; but on further consideration it will be evident that he was only being consistent with his own particular brand of functionalism. The articulated functions of his churches were vigorously expressed by Pugin in the articulated masses of their exteriors. The cellular character of domestic architecture seemed to him rather to demand a more regular, though not necessarily a symmetrical, sort of expression. Later English Gothic, which Pugin rejected for church architecture because of its secular character, was ipso facto appropriate for modern secular work. Pugin knew old secular work of the Tudor period well enough to realize that its spirit was one of regularity even though that regularity was freely broken for particular functional needs.

Willful picturesqueness was to Pugin's mind as arbitrary as absolute symmetry. However much Blore's, and even Salvin's, Early Victorian country houses may have developed out of those of the previous Georgian Age, Pugin turned away from the earlier Picturesque way of using Tudor models for houses quite as in his churches he rejected the Georgians' formal way of using Gothic models. The pronounced visual differences between his neo-Gothic churches and those that preceded them expressed real changes in the supposed needs of sacred edifices; in his domestic work the visual differences were rather slight because country houses remained much what they had been for several generations as regards their functions.

Although merely a major interpolation, as it were, in the rather shapeless earlier house by Abraham, Pugin's great banquet hall at Alton Towers had real scale and grandeur of effect. The tremendous oriel at the end, from which all the light entered, rose as high as three full storeys of the wing to the right (Fig. VIII 12). Since it also extended almost the full width of the hall it already provided a sort of window-wall like those so prophetic of 20th-century architecture to be found in Eden Nesfield's Combe Abbey and his Cloverley Hall of the early 60's. Although presumably planned and even begun considerably earlier, this room was not completed apparently until 1849 after the Talbots had been living abroad almost continuously for many years. Once the most magnificent of Pugin's interiors, it had been so gutted before its demolition that it was hard to appreciate what it was like originally. The great bay window, the richly carved fireplace, and the open timber roof were notable features, and the tall proportions provided something of the "sublimity" of his best naves.

Burton Closes, near Bakewell in Derbyshire, was a manor house of considerable size and elaboration by Pugin. Unfortunately it is now in process of demolition; but it was never perhaps as significant as the group of his houses that have been described and illustrated, being much closer to the contemporary work of other, less intransigent, architects.

Two large and completely new Tudor mansions of the late 40's by such architects deserve particular mention among the host of remodelings, additions, and alterations which represented the typical activity of the time in the country house field. One of these is Aldermaston Court, near Newbury in Berkshire, built in 1848–51 for Daniel Higford Davall Burr by P. C. Hardwick (Fig. VIII 18). Aldermaston was the younger Hardwick's first important country house commission, but he had already had relevant experience at this sort of design when working as his father's assistant on the Hall and Library at Lincoln's Inn in London earlier in the decade (Figs. X 12–13). The materials he used here, red brick with Bath stone trim and some diapering in blue brick, are exactly the same. Instead of the clear functional expression of the Lincoln's Inn buildings and the rather hard dry treatment of the detail there, Aldermaston is even more elaborately ir-

234

regular in its massing than Blore's houses and quite dripping with rich 16th-century detail. (Curiously enough, it was bought by Blore's grandson C. E. Keyser in 1893.)

Aldermaston represents a characteristic Early Victorian attempt to achieve splendor by mere profusion. Such attempts naturally worked best when the old styles imitated were originally dependent more on quantity than on quality of visual interest both in general composition and in detail. In this period late Elizabethan and Jacobean detail was more plausibly handled in this redundant sort of way than any kind of English Gothic. Yet it can hardly be doubted that men of the early 16th century would have delighted in such houses as Aldermaston; but for the development of the 19th-century house such riots of Late Romantic picturesqueness are less relevant than the simpler if less beguiling Tudor of Salvin's Scotney Castle or Pugin's Bilton Grange.

Tortworth Court, Cromhall, near Charfield in Gloucestershire, is far more interesting and significant than Aldermaston. It was built in 1849–53 for the Earl of Ducie by S. S. Teulon. Executed in local stone with Bath stone trim and using earlier and less profuse detail, Tortworth is not so prettily pink and cream and lacy as Aldermaston; it has instead a characteristically Victorian seriousness. Yet Teulon, though primarily a church architect, was not even in the later 40's quite a standard Camdenian.

Born in 1812, Teulon was of exactly the same age as Pugin. After being articled in his youth to George Legg, he was working in the office of George Porter of Bermondsey when he won a competition for the Dyers Almshouses in 1840; this good fortune allowed him to set up for himself. His career was still only getting under way at the time he undertook Tortworth. It was in the late 50's and 60's after his work had become characteristically, and at times even brilliantly, High Victorian that he attained prominence. But of the boldness of his most mature churches and houses there is at first sight little trace here. Aristocratic clients were not yet ready to sanction conspicuous originality in their mansions. Judging from Teulon's lately erected St. Paul's, Bermondsey, of 1845–48, a quite conventional Early Decorated edifice with a fairly good southwest tower, Lord Ducie need have expected nothing unusual from his architect when he decided to spend some £30,000 on a new house—eventually it was to cost him at least half as much again.

The plan of Tortworth Court is almost perfectly symmetrical, with a stair-hall at the center rising up into a tremendous square lantern tower (Fig. VIII 15). This tower dominates rather effectively the many gables and turrets of the periphery. The garden façade is both more plastic and more centralized than Blore's at Worsley Hall. There are three great mullioned bay windows the middle one of which rises two full storeys to form a strong vertical accent under a taller gable than those on either side. The service portion of the house, arranged around a narrow court behind the central tower, is more closely coordinated with the main mass than was usual in neo-Tudor planning.

A small gatehouse, with the disarmingly middle-class inscription "Welcome" in large letters, leads into a forecourt enclosed by a low stone railing. Immediately opposite the gatehouse is a one-storey carriage porch set against a three-storey tower to the right of the end gable of the contiguous garden façade. Flat roofed, with corner finials, this tower does not compete with the tall central tower behind which crowns the whole pile. That central tower ends in a traceried lantern stage covered by a pointed roof broken by cardinal and diagonal dormers below an octagonal belfry; thus its silhouette is more spectacular even than that of Pugin's tower at Bilton Grange. To the right of the modest entrance tower the house rambles away indefinitely: First comes the dining room, with a large oblong one-storey bay; then there is a stair turret terminating in an octagonal domed roof; next a small wing projects forward containing Lord Ducie's own room. The gable and second-storey oriel of this wing very nearly balance the gable that rises to the left of the entrance near the front corner. Farther to the right an orangery masks a minor service court and the house finally ends with another projecting wing equipped with a modest stair turret.

Neither archaeological considerations of correctness nor the established conventions of planning and designing neo-Tudor mansions controlled the organization of Tortworth. Instead Teulon attempted to articulate the exterior as expressively as possible. The prominent central tower indicates where the core of vertical communication lies. The symmetrical garden front makes plain the arrangement of the main reception suite which consists of morning room, drawing room, and library, all effectively the same size. The central unit of the composition echoes the tower behind. Each of the many towers and turrets represents something definite—the central hall, the entrance, the subordinate staircases, etc. Along the entrance front the gradations of height and treatment build up, as it were hierarchically, toward the great tower. By its central position, its height, and the elaborate plasticity of its roof, this tower was expected to pull together the distracting diversity of the subordinate masses, and so it effectively does.

Teulon's aesthetic aims were surely no more than half conscious; even in his bolder High Victorian work of the next two decades there are many hesitations and confusions. But Tortworth Court does represent an approach to secular neo-medieval design closer to that of the best church architects than Pugin's in his country houses. By providing a continuous suite of main rooms along the garden front Teulon satisfied as well as did Blore or Hardwick one of the sounder existing conventions, established a generation earlier, for large 19th-century manor houses. But in the disposition of the multiple minor elements of his composition he approached a sort of symbolic functionalism parallel to, although by no means identical with, that of the church architects.

Tortworth is built of a fine gray laminated limestone with Bath stone trim; the construction is businesslike and solid but quite without charm. Hard and cold, the intellectual interest of the plan and the general composition is not maintained in the uninspired execution, as is too frequently the way with Early Victorian manors.

The much smaller country house which Teulon designed just as Tortworth Court was being finished, Enbrook near Folkestone in Surrey, is altogether more satisfactory. Still building in 1854, it is at the furthest limit of the Early Victorian period and its virtues belong in part to the new High Victorian period then opening. Erected for the Hon. J. D. Bligh, a son of the Earl of Darnley, who was then minister to Hanover, it replaced an older house on the site. The compact squarish plan of the main block of the house includes a stairhall that is also a living hall (Fig. VIII 17). The library and drawing room along the garden front, both articulated by bay windows and nooks, are joined by a wide opening. The dining room, also with a large bay window, is contiguous to the service wing which is masked by a large but simple conservatory.

Externally the house is pleasant and unassertive, the local ragstone of the walling being trimmed with rather crisp and simple quoins and mullions of Caen stone (Fig. VIII 16). Only the window-wall of the staircase and the oriel over the porch show any particular elaboration of detail. The massing is compact though varied as regards the roof treatments of the projecting elements. The relatively low cost of the house, some £7,500 compared with Tortworth's £45,000, is partly explained by its much smaller size; but it is equally due to the efficiency of the plan and the lack of gratuitous elaboration. Despite the noble origins of the owner, the approach is middle class in the best sense, with no trace of the Georgian magnate's love of display. Such a house prepares the way, like Butterfield's Coalpitheath vicarage, for the later middle-class Victorian domestic architecture of Webb and Nesfield and Shaw.

Very different from both Tortworth Court and Enbrook is the first really fine Victorian fake castle. Peckforton Castle, near Bunbury in Cheshire, was designed in 1846 for John Tollemache by Anthony Salvin and completed by 1850. Crowning a 300-foot wooded hill above the Cheshire plain, it looks from a distance no less feudal than the ancient ruins of Beeston Castle that top a nearby hill (Fig. VIII 20). In its superb adaptation to the site and in the wonderful views provided by that site in all directions Peckforton more than rivals the fake castles of an earlier day. Unlike them, however, it was designed by an architect who knew intimately the castles of the great English age of castle building under Edward II at the opening of the 14th century. As an archaeological exercise it is much more considerable than Castell Coch in Wales as rebuilt for the Marquess of Bute by Burges more than twenty years later. In the superb scale of the pink random ashlar stone masonry at Peckforton, and in the avoidance of all but constructive detail, Salvin displayed a craftsmanship definitely superior to Pugin's (Fig. VIII 19).

Around an irregularly polygonal court are set the various plan elements along the hilltop's edge. A circular keep rises at one corner; beside it on the left is the *corps de logis*. The modest chapel stands to the right of the extremely businesslike gate tower, and the stables are also inside the court to the left (Fig. VIII 21). Linked together by the continuous curtain wall, this is all most convincingly plausible in arrangement. Unfortunately, however, from the point of view of persuading the observer that he is seeing an ancient edifice, the very hard sandstone is still as fresh as the day it was quarried, the chisel marks in the interiors still showing white. Even where lichen has thrown a pale green bloom over the pink stone on the eastern walls the effect, although curiously attractive, seems like the intentional coloring of a contemporary of Turner, not the result of nature and of time.

Victorian visitors, who had no reason to expect on a new structure the patina of age, were understandably much impressed. Moreover, the view published by the *Illustrated London News*, in 1851, was so patinated by the wood engraver that the castle appeared almost like a deserted and romantic ruin. "It seems," reported the *News, 18*, 323, "to exhibit the peculiar beauties of Carnarvon Castle, without its inconveniences. It surpasses Raby in the magnitude of its rooms, and it exceeds Warwick in feudal grandeur. Mr. Salvin, the accomplished architect, has proved by the arrangement of the different rooms that comfort and luxury are perfectly compatible in a castellated building" designed in the style of that Edwardian period accepted as the best for church architecture. This Edwardian style of Peckforton, of course, had a prestige that the Tudor, still currently used for most country houses, had long lost in aesthetic circles.

Butterfield was turning toward earlier forms of secular Gothic also at St. Augustine's College, Canterbury, and (in association with Cundy) in the schools and clergy house of St. Barnabas's, Pimlico, at just this time (Fig. V 28). This turn was soon to have important results. The pretty fussiness and the hard wiriness of much of the earliest Victorian secular Gothic seem rather ironically characteristic of the new materials country house builders abjured as shams. These qualities now begin to give way to an aggressively structural sort of expression, simple to the point of crudity and extremely stony.

Here at Peckforton windows are somewhat more frequent in the outside walls than in real Edwardian castles; but they have plain bearing arches (usually segmental pointed) over them and the individual lights are covered with unmolded lintels on simple brackets in the most uncompromisingly businesslike way (Fig. VIII 19). The mullions and the crossbars in the larger windows are merely chamfered; but the evident hardness of the pink sandstone, which is used for the trim as well as for the walling, clearly justifies the lack of additional finish. Such a lack of finish was now beginning to be relished as peculiarly "real" because of its evidently structural character. The windows of the great hall have simple plate tracery, and the large polygonal bay window projecting from the upper end of the hall is equally solidly treated, even to being capped with a stone roof. Thus the bold scale of the large quarry-faced blocks of the random ashlar walling is maintained throughout the detail of the openings.

The picturesqueness of the composition derives—more convincingly than at Tortworth but perhaps less consciously—from the articulation of the various masses within the surrounding curtain wall, not from elaborately ornamented features. The easy, almost haphazard, inclusion of the chapel and the stable buildings within the court, like the domination of the main block to the north by the round keep and its square turret, is of course chiefly a matter of following real Edwardian precedent. When this sort of structural detail and this sort of functional composition were adapted to structures much smaller in size and more compactly planned, however, this new and more sophisticated emulation of castellated architecture was to prove stimulating to new creative developments.

The "comfort and luxury" of the interior were on the whole of a pretty feudal order. Far removed from the all-over-upholstered Royal railway carriages that really represented the ultimate ideal in contemporary comfort and luxury was the "baronial hall" at Peckforton. This was 60 feet long and 40 feet high, all lined with the same sandstone as the exterior but smooth cut and regularly laid, under a ribbed and vaulted roof of stone. "Massive shields of armorial bearings, all simply wrought in stone," were rather ascetic substitutes for the carved mottoes and stenciled diapers with which Pugin ornamented his interiors. The dining room in the keep (36 feet in diameter and also rib vaulted) was even more monumental than the 55-foot-long drawing room; that at least had oriel windows in its corner towers as well as plenty of the rather slot-like openings that were used throughout the other rooms of the castle. Yet out of this retrospective asceticism (tempered here in fact by voluminous plush hangings) more of interest was to come in the next two decades than out of the extremely "viable" Tudor manors of the 40's that continued a more latitudinarian attitude toward Gothic.

239

Other castellated work of the late 40's and early 50's was less archaeological and less ascetic. It consisted mostly of additions and alterations to real medieval work, however. Hornby Castle in Lancashire, for example, received an extensive remodeling at the hands of Sharpe and Paley, beginning in 1849. But its new garden front, with large banks of casements and two-storey bay windows set against the corner towers, is hardly more plausible than Wyatville's garden front of Windsor Castle of a quarter-century earlier even though the detail is more correct. Salvin's very extensive work at Alnwick for the Duke of Northumberland belongs to the mid-50's and need not be described here.

For obvious connotational reasons castellated mansions tended to be erected, in the 19th century as in the Middle Ages, in the Welsh, Scottish, and Irish marches of Anglo-Saxondom rather than in England itself. In Ireland English landowners might even expect that the sturdy defenses of their fake castles would be useful in case of a native uprising; today some 19th-century castles show evidences of their occupation by Irish forces in one or another of the recurrent "troubles." Never was the state of Ireland worse than in the 40's; not surprisingly, therefore, the new mansions that were built there in the mid-century gave up the urbanity of Georgian times for a grimness that is businesslike in a quite authentically feudal way. The largest, though not the most distinguished, example of Victorian castle building in Ireland is Lismore, which was restored and effectively rebuilt over the years 1850–57 by the 6th Duke of Devonshire. This Whig magnate was almost as rich as the Duke of Sutherland and more important, indirectly at least, to the history of architecture because of the gardener Joseph Paxton (1803–1865) who was his protégé and friend.

Paxton's importance to Victorian architecture is so great that much needs to be known about him—much more, unfortunately, than can be learned from the biography *Paxton and the Bachelor Duke* (1935) written by his granddaughter Violet Markham. But as he was only incidentally a castle builder—or indeed a builder in masonry at all—it is better to concentrate such biographical information as is available in the chapters (XV–XVI) which deal with his work as a designer of edifices of iron and wood and glass. In 1850, the most important year in his life, Paxton had been head gardener at Chatsworth for 24 years. When he undertook the restoration of Lismore, which proceeded concurrently with his most famous achievements, the two versions of the Crystal Palace in Hyde Park and at Sydenham, he had the assistance of his architecturally trained son-in-law George Henry Stokes, who presumably had a relatively free hand on this job. Paxton was not so much an architect to the duke as a Minister of Works, executive officer for all the Cavendish interests, from organizing expeditions to bring back horti-

240

cultural specimens from beyond the seas to watching the duke's investments as an active director of the Midland Railway.

As with other architectural work in masonry for which Paxton was responsible—at least nominally, but with the important assistance of Stokes—it is hard to know what to think of Lismore. Were Paxton not involved, it would not be too difficult to ignore these things as most historians have so far done; but to do so is to oversimplify this phenomenal gardener's relations to the Victorian building world. Granting that Paxton's position in relation to Lismore was that of an intermediary between client and actual designer, one cannot deny him all credit (or discredit) for what was erected in his name. Detailed research must one day fill in the many serious gaps in his granddaughter's account of Paxton's life and his relations with his employer including such questions as the degree and the character of his responsibility for Lismore. For the present this Irish seat of the Cavendishes may be discussed merely as what it certainly is, one of the largest and most striking of Victorian castles.

Lismore is by no means so defensive in character as the seat of the Tollemaches in peaceful Cheshire. The site had originally been fortified by a Norman baron, John of Montaigne; when Henry II first conquered Ireland it had belonged to Sir Walter Raleigh and had then come down through the Boyle line to the Cavendishes along with Chiswick and other estates of the famous Earl of Burlington. (It had, however, never been the subject of the latter's enthusiastically Palladian activities.) The site and its historic connotations, as well as 19th-century Irish conditions, clearly justified that any extensive additions to the modest structure the 6th duke had inherited should be castellated if he were to make of it, from time to time, his principal residence on his Irish estates.

Outside the town of Lismore, in what is described as "the soft luxuriance of the Lismore valley," the extensive pile of the castle crowns a height above the river. It is most happily seen in relation to an arched stone bridge in the foreground also by Paxton and Stokes (Fig. VIII 22). Although the general plan of the castle forms a fairly regular rectangle, unlike the polygonal circumvallation of Peckforton, the silhouette is very varied above the high solid base. The outer ranges provide one, two, and even three habitable storeys, all continuously crenellated and recurrently accented with machicolated towers and turrets. Some of these are large enough to contain good-sized rooms while others only contain subsidiary staircases; but all except the smallest, which merely provide access to the tops of the larger towers, are square in shape. With the squareness of all the masses small and large go the businesslike ranges of plain mullioned windows. These are relatively large though set high enough above the ground to foil attackers, and for the most part they are quite regularly disposed. Thus they reveal, as in Late Georgian castel-

241

lated mansions, the existence of continuous suites of good-sized rooms running all along the curtain wall, not concentrated in a single *corps de logis* as at archaeologically correct Peckforton. Oriels here and there further reduce the effect of feudal grimness although they also are rather straightforward and unromantic in design. At one corner a very tall tower, with round corner turrets and boldly machicolated galleries between them, forms the principal accent. It probably also provides for water storage as do Barry's Italian Villa towers.

Thus Lismore proves to be a very much more typical Victorian edifice than one might suppose from a distant view. It is as sensible as a fake castle can be and moderately "correct" in its medieval details without any archaeological asceticism. Yet it is also an "eligible object" in the landscape picture according to the 18th-century ideal to which Paxton, as the heir of the great landscape gardeners, still subscribed. He who could design and erect the last of the enormous rockeries in the fake Alpine mode, on a scale and with a plausibility the Georgians never approached, could also realize (like Vanbrugh at the beginning of the English landscape development) the visual charm of a many-towered structure in such lush scenery as the Lismore valley offered.

One seeks in vain here for any hint of the better known Paxton, the designer of the glass and iron Crystal Palace. Like Eiffel in the next generation, the great innovator in edifices for expositions was content to build houses in the ordinary masonry modes of his day. The supposed architectural revolutionary was in much of his work more conservative than Pugin or Salvin; for they found in medieval archaeology, on the plane of theory at least, a new gospel of functional expression in architecture. But, like Barry, Paxton had common sense and an unfanatical willingness to oblige his Whig duke, himself a great Victorian but in many ways still half a Georgian also; for the duke remained a good Evangelical and steered clear of the intense Tractarians. It was the duke's scientific interests, also in the 18th-century tradition, that made him a significant figure in the Victorian Age; naturally it was in the housing of the duke's horticultural specimens, and not of his person, that Paxton initiated his great innovations in building technique.

Mentmore in Buckinghamshire and Ferrières in France are two mansions built by Paxton and Stokes for the Rothschilds in the 50's. Mentmore, near Cheddington in Buckinghamshire, built for Baron Meyer Amschel de Rothschild, was based on Wollaton (Fig. VIII 24), to which extravaganza of an Elizabethan coal magnate it may even be preferred. When the design was shown at the Royal Academy Exhibition in 1854 (No. 1165) the construction had been under way for a year or two; but it was several years more before the sumptuous interiors were completed. Variously François I, Louis XIV, Louis

XV, and Louis XVI—what the French call in furniture *les hautes époques*—these were partly executed by Paris decorators like the interiors of the Hope mansion in Piccadilly; but the finest of them, such as the dining room which comes from the Hotel de Conti in Paris, consist of real 18th-century *boiseries*. The plan of Mentmore is extremely regular and rather closer to Wollaton than is the exterior. Externally the house is all of Ancaster stone and the casements throughout are of copper; internally the provision of hot-water heating throughout, with arrangements for artificial ventilation in all the rooms, reminds us that this mansion is by Paxton the greenhouse builder. The arcaded great hall, really a covered court, has a ridge-and-furrow roof of the characteristic Paxton type carried on riveted wrought-iron girders. To these are attached the molded walnut ribs supporting the inner ceiling of specially made plate glass. Less original than Highclere, Mentmore is not unworthy of comparison with it. Certainly this is one of the finest of Early Victorian houses and an exceptional example of the Jacobethan Revival at its best.

The design for Ferrières, for Baron James de Rothschild, was shown at the Royal Academy Exhibition in 1856 by Paxton and Stokes. Somewhat like Mentmore in its four-towered scheme, it is larger and more ornate. Because of its slightly later date and its foreign location it may be considered beyond the boundaries of the Early Victorian period. It was illustrated in the *Illustrated London News*, 3 January 1863, on the occasion of a visit there by Napoleon III. The gardens are still particularly extensive and magnificent.

More significant of changing tastes around 1850 than Lismore or Mentmore, although perhaps not so attractive to modern eyes, is a Welsh castle at Ruthin in Denbighshire building at much the same time. Ruthin Castle was relatively modest in size, costing only some £12,000. Designed by Henry Clutton for Frederick B. West, M.P., it was completed in 1853. Like Salvin at Peckforton, Clutton used a local red sandstone but he attempted no such correct imitation of an Edwardian castle. Ruthin is frankly a modern castellated mansion, full of large windows like Lismore but much less elaborately picturesque in composition (Fig. VIII 23). The most feudal feature of the L-shaped block is the octagonal keep on the outer angle from which rises a taller polygonal turret. Otherwise the house is surprisingly matter of fact despite its crenellated parapets.

Three ranges of rather regularly spaced mullioned windows occupy most of the wall space, interrupted here and there by two- and three-storey bay windows. Pointed arches in the individual lights and drip molds carried well down the sides of the windows, with a few stringcourses, provide the only ornamental details. Thus the general effect is rather cold and mechanical though not thin and papery. By contrast the curious treatment of the

243

entrance front is all the more surprising. The ground storey is completely unbroken except for a deep-sunk segmental-pointed entrance arch set at one side; the heavy drip mold over this terminates in two winged heraldic beasts, large in scale and ornate in their convolutions. On the upper storeys prismatic oriels project from the wall. A simple narrow one occupies the center and two others much more complex in plan are carried around the chamfered corners at either side. Between these vertical accents, so striking in their sharp crystalline forms, are broad wall surfaces as plain as those below. Two triple chimney stacks rise above the parapet which follows the broken line of the oriels. Chamfered in a way that echoes the prismatic character of the corner windows, these stacks form prominent terminal accents in syncopation with the oriels below.

Already, as with the over-all composition of Teulon's Tortworth or Salvin's boldly "structural" detailing at Peckforton, Clutton's treatment of the entrance front of Ruthin indicates the opening of a new period. The design of this curious façade was determined not by archaeology, nor by convenience, nor yet by a desire to emulate the casual picturesqueness of earlier castellated design. It is really an original composition based on principles of abstract order and consonant geometrical forms. Aesthetic experimentation of this sort belongs to the new High Victorian style-phase just being initiated while Ruthin was being built (see Chapter XVII). After Ruthin most of Clutton's work as a country house architect is hard and dry in the most barrenly conventional Jacobethan way. Only his churches develop the High Victorian promise of this exceptional castle.

Paxton at Lismore made no serious attempt to follow an Irish version of the castellated mode nor is Ruthin especially Welsh. In the great Edwardian period of medieval castle building the Royal outposts in Ireland and Wales had been metropolitan, even cosmopolitan, in style. In Scotland conditions in the Middle Ages were different and now in the 40's a special national variant of the castellated mode flourished in country house work there. The Sutherlands had their Italianate mansions at Trentham Park in Staffordshire and at Cliveden in Buckinghamshire by Barry, but we have already seen that the duke was not satisfied with what his distinguished architect proposed for Dunrobin in Sutherlandshire. With local professional assistance Dunrobin was executed in a rather ambiguous style, more castellated than any other project with which Barry was concerned, and yet French—around the edges as it were—in an early 16th-century way (Fig. VII 5). Dunrobin is hardly a characteristic example of what is known as "Scottish Baronial," but since it has already been discussed at least briefly it may serve to introduce that curious Caledonian mode. The Scottish Baronial is more typical, almost, of the Victorian Age than the Jacobethan and generally rather more

244

original; like the Jacobethan, however, it was rarely capable of meaningful development. Royalty, and not the Leveson-Gowers, gave it considerable prestige, a prestige which lingered on through the rest of the century.

On three early visits to Scotland Prince Albert had found himself enchanted by the Highland people. The Royal doctor Sir James Clark advised, moreover, that the air—which the Prince said acted "like a tonic to the nerves"—was right "for the peculiar constitution" (physical not political!) of Royalty. In 1848, therefore, the Queen decided to have a Highland estate and bought the reversion of the lease of Balmoral Castle, near Ballater in Fifeshire, from the trustees of Sir Robert Gordon with the idea of eventual purchase of the freehold from the Earl of Fife. The house had been lately built from the designs of William Smith of Aberdeen and he was immediately bidden to make plans for additions as soon as the Queen and the Prince reached their new home in the Highlands.

On their festal progress thither the Royal couple had seen various Scottish mansions, old and new, in the Baronial mode. Although their own "castle" and its grounds are said to have exceeded their expectations, the superb site in the Dee Valley was certainly more appealing than the relatively modest house (Balmoral *I*, let us call it) which was then in existence (Figs. VIII 26, 28). That was rather similar in appearance to Sir Walter Scott's Abbotsford, as built by William Atkinson (1773–1839) in 1812–15 and enlarged after 1819, and was not much more ample in the accommodation it provided. Both picturesque and rambling piles, modestly gabled and turreted, Abbotsford and Balmoral I were generically like innumerable modest English country houses of semi-manorial, semi-castellated character that had been built in the previous thirty or forty years. But certain elements gave them both what was supposed to be a definitely regional or "national" flavor. This flavor strongly appealed to the Queen and to the Prince; for their romantic souls had been charmed by the Gaelic cheers "Gu mairrionach" and "Neish, neish" that greeted them along their Highland way and by the fact that they were passing through the actual scenes of *Waverley* and near the fount of inspiration of their friend Mendelssohn's Scottish Symphony.

The house was just as it had been left at the death of Sir Robert Gordon. The principal rooms were a dining room on the ground floor and, in the Scottish way, a drawing room above. These had wall coverings, upholstery, and curtains all of the same chintz—a treatment more "cottagy" than baronial. There was also a library—with the books removed—and a billiard room, as well as a modest conservatory. All the rooms, large and small, in the wings had to be occupied as bedrooms in order to put up the Royal attendants; but at least the Queen's room, over the library and entrance hall, was large and also chintz hung like the contiguous drawing room. The nurseries were papered and curtained with white dimity. Although the taste was Sir Robert Gordon's, not Their Majesties', it is evident that the baronial note of the exterior hardly penetrated beyond the carved *Salve* and the *Cave Canem* set in Dutch tiles at the entrance.

The leasing of Balmoral focused national and international attention on the Highlands and the historic architecture of its lairds, just as Osborne House had done for the towered Italian Villa mode two years earlier. The rebuilding of the castle on a more princely scale was begun only in 1853, although additions doubling it in extent had already been made by Smith in 1849 to provide adequate accommodations for guests and servants (Balmoral II one may call that stage). An account of Balmoral III had better await its proper chronological place in a more general account of the Scottish Baronial.

By the time Balmoral III was designed the standard treatise on the subject, the four volumes of *Baronial and Ecclesiastical Antiquities of Scotland* (4 vols., Edinburgh and London, 1847–52) by R. W. Billings (1813–1874), had appeared. As usual, the serious archaeological investigation of ancient models had followed well after casual imitation of those models became widely popular. For the Scottish Baronial of the Late Georgians and the Early Victorians was almost as much an imaginary creation as their Italian Villa mode. Like that, this Caledonian genre had some precedents in actually existing structures; but the living mode was an artificial amalgam of features found in various earlier periods within a certain area—like the various kinds of American "Colonial" (Dutch, Cape Cod, Williamsburg, etc.) of the 20th century. These were selected for their pictorial and connotational appeal and freely combined according to current visual ideals.

Some of the very earliest fake castles had been built in Scotland in the mid-18th century, among them the seat of the Dukes of Argyll, Inveraray; but Scott's Abbotsford was the first highly publicized example which is recognizably Scottish and not just generically Baronial. The setting in which Sir Walter lived was good enough for any Scot with a single *t*; north of the Border, at least the mode was off to a headstart long before Victoria came to the throne. Sir Walter himself had also revived the ceremonial wearing of the kilt and the plaid of tartan cloth for the visit of George IV to Scotland in order to encourage the transference of Scottish sentiment for Royalty at long last from the Stuarts to the House of Hanover. The Scottish Baronial of Victoria's time certainly had overtones and undertones that were more significant than those of the Italian Villa mode. But visually it takes its place as a subcategory somewhere between the Edwardian Castellated and the irregular Jacobethan Manorial in the broad range of Victorian modes based on the architecture of preacademic periods.

Civil unrest having continued longer in Scotland than in England, as all

246

Sir Walter's readers know, a defensive residential architecture had lasted there well through the 17th century. Towering keeps bristling with crenellations and capped with corner turrets like pepper pots, drawbridges that drew up, and bare stone halls where the laird and his feudal retainers drank usquebaugh together to the sad threnody of pibrochs remained in use down into Georgian times. (Equivalent architectural forms and ways of life had of course been obsolescent in England and on the Continent almost since the 15th century. Some of these features were even being revived by Vanbrugh for their picturesque effect before they had entirely gone out of current use north of the Border.) The romanticism of the Gaelic temperament and the addiction of the Scots to linguistic as well as musical archaism suggest that this prolonged retention of feudal ways of living and of castellated architectural forms, like the habit of wearing short arms, was at least partially nostalgic even in the 17th century. Of course such medievalizing became widely fashionable everywhere after the mid-18th century, if in less extreme forms.

Late 16th- and 17th-century architectural detail in Scotland was usually more or less Italianate, however, and even specifically Mannerist, although mingled with rather clumsy and crude Gothic (or perhaps even Romanesque) elements long out of fashion south of the Border. Certain continental characteristics, mostly of French origin but characteristically including stepped gables with a Low Country look, lent a picturesque air to massing that was still feudal. The cosmopolitan eclecticism of the means confirms that the picturesqueness was something consciously sought for, at least in the more elaborate mansions. Ordinary houses of course were generally small and often very plain.

In its revived form the Scottish Baronial was always evocative of Scott's romantic novels. A whole iconography of literary and patriotic figures could be associated with it, and Scottish sentimental and aesthetic nationalism has always had a tremendous appeal to Anglo-Saxons. Kilts and bonnets for children's wear; the generally abused heraldry of tartans; the Highland peasantry of Wilkie and the Highland animals of Landseer; above all, the poetry of the ballads old and new: Many popular Victorian fashions joined to support the Scottish Baronial theme in architecture. Outside the heart of Edinburgh and Glasgow—the Athens and, I suppose, the Sparta of the North—it had certainly come to be considered the Scottish national mode by 1845. Hence it was the only suitable one for the residences of Royalty or of British magnates during their visits to Scotland. Local lairds used it when they could afford to rebuild their ancestral eyries, and so did professional men—lawyers and publishers and such—when they moved to the country or even to the outer suburbs. Whole streets of it rose even in Edinburgh itself in the 50's, and critics jeered at turreted warehouses built by English architects in Glasgow.

The Scottish Baronial, combining the feudally romantic picturesqueness of the Castellated with the muddled Mannerist detail of the Jacobethan, was an almost perfect Early Victorian stylism. More cosmopolitan than the Tudor it yet subordinated its foreign elements of detail within a native frame. The Scottish Baronial lacked, moreover, those rigid paradigms which made the Italian High Renaissance palace or the Edwardian castle so awkward to adapt to inherited Georgian conventions of planning. The wonder is, therefore, that the Scottish Baronial was so little used below the Border. But by the 40's most Scottish architects, despite their continued use of Grecian forms in public work, had become adepts at exploiting its sentimental and visual appeal.

William Burn, a pupil of Sir Robert Smirke, who returned to Edinburgh to practice about 1820, was the first specialist in the genre. After Burn moved to London in 1844 his former pupil and partner David Bryce (1803–1876) continued on his own as the leading local practitioner, beginning his country house work with Carradale, built for Robert Campbell in that year. Ling, Cloth, Incharine, Glenesh, Ardarroch, Balfour—a Gaelic litany of place names—were all built or remodeled by Bryce in the Scottish Baronial before Victoria and her Consort acquired Balmoral. His most conspicuous work in the genre is, however, Fettes College, built outside Edinburgh in the 60's, perhaps the masterpiece of the revived Scottish Baronial but definitely High Victorian in flavor.

Burn, in his English country house work, followed as often the Jacobethan as the Scottish Baronial. The main blocks of his larger mansions were usually formally planned and symmetrical in expression, even though dominated by tall entrance towers and punctuated with pepper-pot turrets. Burn's work, therefore, is closer in its mixed character to that of Blore than to that of Salvin, his chief rivals as Early Victorian country house builders to the upper aristocracy.

Beaufort Castle, Inverness, which Burn built for Lord Lovat in 1834, was castellated but not Scottish Baronial. Perhaps Buchanan House, built in 1852 near Glasgow for the Duke of Montrose, is as fair a specimen as any of Burn's enormous and rather dull mansions in his mature vein. The essentially Jacobethan character of the main block is moderately "Scotticized," as it were, by the stepped gables and the pepper-pot turrets on the corner pavilions (Fig. VIII 29). As in Barry's ducal mansions, a private suite occupies a separate wing extending out to one side; but the elaborate service facilities are grouped about subsidiary courts in line with the main block, somewhat as at Teulon's Tortworth. Balentore, a much smaller house, is

248

more strictly Scottish Baronial; for it is a small compact block, with very little carved detail, but it breaks out at the top into a profusion of conical roofs, stepped gables, and scrolled dormers of a rather French sort (Fig. VIII 33). Fonthill, near Hinton in Wiltshire, the enormous mansion built for the Marquess of Westminster in the late 40's close to the ruins of Beckford's Abbey, exceeds all the rest in complexity; yet it retains an essentially academic regularity in plan and in the principal elevations despite the pretentious turreted keep tower above the entrance (Figs. VIII 30, 31).

In the estimation of his contemporaries Burn excelled as a planner; so much so that he avoided publishing his houses for fear of cribbing! So enormous are they, however, that the 20th century can hardly estimate their probable suitability to the nearly Royal *train de vie* his clients maintained in the mid-century, often at several houses in different parts of Britain. Robert Kerr (1822–1904) in his compendious treatise *The Gentleman's House* (1864; 2d ed., with supplement, 1865; 3d ed. 1871) included Burn's plan of Buchanan House (identified only as a "Modern Scotch Model") as an example of the fact that "the most convenient houses in the kingdom have for many years back come from the hands of certain Scotch architects" (Fig. VIII 29). "The name of the late Mr. Burn," he continued in a text added in the 3d ed., "has long been celebrated in connexion with this circumstance. The merits of this school make but modest pretensions to be of artistic order, but they turn closely upon practical usefulness; an unswerving adherence to the common comforts of residence, a strict and careful attention to the minutiae of the habits of the gentry, and an avoidance of every sort of ostentation [*sic*], are the guiding principles." In comparison Kerr found Somerleyton amateurish in planning (which it is); Mentmore, on the other hand, he characterized as a "grand classic plan" although he makes some minor complaints about an excessive dependence on skylights for lighting interior corridors. Kerr was a High Victorian, not an Early Victorian; but these sidelights on "functionalism" in the design of country mansions in the mid-century are most revealing. Burn owed his tremendous success with the aristocracy of his time not to his standing as an artistic designer, which was never very considerable, but to his reputation as a convenient planner which is so difficult for us to understand today.

In Ireland, as has been remarked in discussing Lismore, a defensive country house architecture seemed more than justified by the "unfriendly" attitude of the Irish peasantry toward English landowners. There a somewhat simpler and more medieval variant of the Scottish Baronial, supposed to be specifically "Irish," was occasionally employed. Clonghanadfoy Castle in County Limerick, built by the York architect G. Fowler Jones for the Misses Gascoigne, is a characteristic—even a rather superior—example. It was completed in 1850 (Fig. VIII 32). Here the Jacobethan detail on the exterior is restricted to the pierced parapet of the terrace although the interiors were completely in that mode. There are no pepper-pot turrets but even the chief tower, which is incorporated in one corner of the main block, has a stepped gable. The Irish stepped crenellations on the tower and over the entrance porch give a consistently vigorous, even a brutal, character to the silhouette. The mullioned windows are simply treated and on the more castellated entrance front, if not along the garden front, they are restricted in size and number. The oriels, as at Lismore, are in the upper storey only and have a prismatic plan like those at Ruthin. Where arches are used, as in the entrance porch and over the door in the center of the garden front, they are segmental pointed, as at Peckforton or in Lamb's work, and deeply sunk in two orders between markedly battered piers.

The plan of Clonghanadfoy provides a central stairhall with the principal rooms carried around three sides of the main block and thus rather resembles that of Tortworth Court although it is on a much smaller scale. As at Tortworth and Buchanan House, the service and stable court is to the rear. The material is hard Old Red sandstone, found on the estate, which undoubtedly discouraged elaborate carved detail. (The openwork panels in the terrace parapet, as well as the griffins on the piers, were cast in Portland cement.) It is interesting to note that the roof structure was of cast and wrought iron under the Killaloe slates.

Earlier models, the use of a hard local stone, and a scale less palatial than that of the English and Scottish ducal seats produced at Clonghanadfoy a Victorian castellated residence which shares some of the virtues of Tortworth, Peckforton, and Ruthin. The organization of the mass is simpler and more coherent than at Tortworth; unlike Peckforton, the house is clearly a residence, not a fortification (or, for that matter, a private palace like Burn's bigger mansions). If there is no such brilliant and original disposition of "abstract" elements as on the entrance façade of Ruthin, the composition as a whole is interestingly varied yet consistently scaled throughout. Like the other castles of the mid-century with which it has just been compared Clonghanadfoy is transitional to the High Victorian. Actually the Scottish Baronial in High Victorian guise was to be more widely popular in the late 50's and 60's than in the 40's.

Even more than at Osborne, when the time came to rebuild Balmoral Prince Albert made the project his own, although the original architect William Smith of Aberdeen who made the enlargement in 1849 was professionally responsible for the design. Albert was always happy among the Scots, who reminded him of the Coburgers, while the idea of a castle in the hills recalled the happiest period of his childhood at Rosenau. The Queen and he, both Evangelicals, were also more at home as Presbyterians in Scotland than as Anglicans in England; the Calvinistic seriousness of their neighbors appealed to them as much as did the Gaelic romanticism of both lairds and peasants. But Balmoral was only a vacation spot from which duty perpetually recalled them to the south; and the earliest plans for rebuilding the castle had to be put aside for a while because of the political troubles of the mid-century. Except for Smith's extensive service wings of 1849, the principal new construction at Balmoral before 1853 was actually more in Paxton's Crystal Palace mode than in the castellated mode of his Lismore. In 1851 the Prince had erected beside the house a prefabricated iron ballroom by E. T. Bellhouse of Manchester, having been much impressed by the similar structures Bellhouse exhibited at the Crystal Palace as houses for emigrants (Fig. XV 54).

Two years later, early in 1853, the contracts were entered into and the new castle really begun; by that summer the Queen could report in her diary that it was "up one storey." In the circumstances the design cannot be very precisely dated, for the Prince must have been mulling over the plans for five years, with William Smith always ready to come out to the castle from Aberdeen for consultation. The designs for the contract were prepared, in all probability, at least by the fall or winter of 1852, just after the freehold estate was finally purchased from Lord Fife. Although the Crimean War followed the year after construction began, the castle proceeded to completion by 1855; the Prince even undertook its interior decoration before the war was over as a diversion from the cares of state.

A large squarish quadrangle, with modest corner towers of varying design and stepped gables between, provided the rather unimaginative layout of the new Balmoral (Figs. VIII 25, 27, 28). The new house was entirely built of a light-colored granite found on the estate as its predecessor presumably had been also. Laid up in regular ashlar, this cold material is necessarily harsh and mechanical in effect. Kerr remarked in the *English Gentleman's House*, p. 433, of the plan of Balmoral III which he published (Plate 18) together with that of Osborne (Plate 17) that "the superiority . . . is apparent at a glance; there is a certain familiar [familial, he probably meant] character which is in fact the quality of home comfort." Although he compares it rather with that of Lord Sudeley's Toddington, a Late Georgian Tudor pile designed by its owner, the plan of Balmoral is somewhat more similar to that of Burn's Buchanan House, to which Albert (if not William Smith) might well have had access in 1852 through its ducal owner despite the jealous secrecy of the architect. The granite restricted the amount and character of the ornament, the moldings and other carved features being simply "axed" to an approximate finish, not (in the technical sense) "polished," that is, smooth cut. Heavy corbeling was freely used, however, and a horizontal drip mold continues all around the block above the first-storey windows. There is also a certain amount of rather heavy-handed ornament, mostly rope and ribbon patterns, in a 17th-century peasant-Mannerist vein.

The two principal exterior features are the entrance porch at one corner and a sort of keep, which stands well out from the main block at the end of a two-storey wing (Fig. VIII 25). The entrance porch has elliptical arches between octagonal corner buttresses, and corbeled crenellations are carried around its flat terrace roof. Behind the porch the corner gable is flanked by two pepper-pot turrets with slotted openings. Similar turrets flank the central gable on the garden front also.

The keep is the only really impressive thing about Balmoral. Rising some six storeys, it appears from certain angles to be freestanding; for the wing attaching it to the main block is hardly more than a storey and a half high, with the segmental window tops of the main storey forming half-dormers against the roof. On one corner of the keep a round tower rises two storeys higher to carry the Royal banner and provide access to the terrace on top. This terrace is surrounded by a crenellated parapet on deep machicolations with large pepper-pot turrets corbeled out at the three corners. These accents are echoed not only in the turrets above the entrance and on the garden front but also by larger turrets rising from the ground at two other corners of the main block. (One of these, however, being octagonal above its square base and also domed, is more of a sugar-caster than a pepper pot.) Although the windows in the main block are mullioned and transomed in a Tudorish way, those in the keep and in the wing leading to it are sashed and have plain architraves around them. Similar rather academic 17th-century notes are the rusticated ground storey of the keep, the arched windows set in that and also in the center of the third storey, and the balustrade on top of the round stair tower. As with the Italian Villa, the Scottish Baronial usually pretended to tell a story of accretion over several centuries.

The Queen and the Prince, for all his dabbling in design, got no better than they deserved since they refused as at Osborne to employ any of the leading architects of the day. But the interiors at least are a quite direct and appealingly quaint illustration of the Royal talent for decoration. The very carpets and linoleum were of tartan; a new and synthetic "Balmoral" pattern which the Prince had worked out was used in some rooms, but in other rooms the poplin and silk hangings and the upholstery materials were in the more gorgeous Royal Stuart weave. Stuffed heads of Highland beasts were the other recurrent theme vying with the same beasts painted in their native habitat by Landseer—a positive natural history museum in effect.

One of the most intelligent ladies in waiting, a daughter of Lord Elgin, who had presumably been brought up to admire only Greek art, was indiscreet enough to set down her private opinion of all this. Lady Augusta Bruce (later the wife of Dean Stanley) wrote that it was "all highly characteristic but not equally *flatteux* to the eye." With which understatement—fair enough for more plausible examples of the Scottish Baronial than Balmoral—we may well leave the subject.

The later history of Balmoral deserves a few words only. Victoria's heir, who disposed of Osborne House for a school for naval cadets as soon as his mother was dead, held on to Balmoral, and so have his descendants. One of her great-grandsons has lately reported that Albert, in complete Highland regalia and carved in white marble, cast a most disapproving eye on the first preprandial cocktails served at Balmoral. Even so I think one can agree with the Royal family that Balmoral is more appealing than Osborne, though one should not judge all Victorian architecture by its obvious deficiencies—and one may at least hope that Edward VIII's cocktails were Rob Roys.

Barry in his enlargement of Canford Manor and in his association with Dunrobin had occasion to approach the castellated and even the Scottish Baronial; but the virtues of those modes (which were more a matter of dimly hinted potentialities for the future than of actual Early Victorian achievement) are remote from those of the Italian and the Anglo-Italian paradigms with which he was most sympathetic. Around 1850 neither Barry's influence not yet Pugin's seems dominant in country house architecture. Moreover, although Salvin's work best exemplifies the new tendencies in several ways and Burn was extremely productive, neither of them can properly be considered a leader. The maturity of Clutton and Teulon still lay well ahead, and their best work was always ecclesiastical.

The dichotomy between the archaeological intentions of the period and a really direct and complete satisfaction of post-Georgian visual tastes for articulated mass composition and rich but expressive detail was never entirely resolved by any of the Early Victorian country house architects. The lead toward a more original and coherent program of design was being taken, around 1850, more in church architecture than in country house architecture (Chapter XVII). So nearly High Victorian a castle as Clonghanadfoy is something of a fluke in the late 40's. Perhaps only a provincial English architect, without the pretensions of a Salvin or a Burn and working in the wilds of Ireland, could have synthesized so successfully the immanent aspirations of the mid-century.

For contrast one should turn to a formally designed country house of the same period such as Bylaugh Hall in Norfolk. (Bylaugh belongs to the Anglo-Italian category of Barry's Highclere and might as well have found a place in the previous chapter.) This was built in 1849–52 by Robert R.

Banks, Barry's former chief assistant, in partnership with Barry's son Charles. It provides a perfectly coherent example of the Barry tradition in country house design and is still wholly Early Victorian. Erected near East Dereham in Norfolk for Edward Lombe at a cost of £29,389, no earlier house had to be taken into account here as was the case with almost all Barry's own country house work. The plan is very clear and straightforward—Kerr calls it "one of the best sort of Classical plans"—a square block with a central saloon rising the full height of the two and a half storeys. This is lighted from above through panels of cut glass set in a richly decorated elliptical vault. The saloon, with its arcaded corridors on two sides, is a much reduced adaptation of the central hall of the Reform Club house and Bridgewater House and probably the immediate prototype of Paxton's much larger hall at Mentmore.

From a richly ornamented porch in the center of the entrance façade a hall leads forward into the saloon. The main staircase rises rather inconspicuously out of a side corridor, quite as Barry himself would presumably have handled it. This arrangement is in sharp contradiction to the general tendency of the time to make the principal means of vertical communication a major element of the plan (and sometimes, as at Tortworth, of the exterior as well). A dining room, a billiard room, a library, and a drawing room occupy the four corners of the main block, each with a very large projecting bay window of rectangular plan. The two latter rooms run along the garden front and are linked by a large anteroom with French windows opening onto a terrace. Subsidiary rooms and staircases fill the spaces between the corner rooms on the other two sides. The service wing is at a lower level, continuing the line of the entrance façade to the left. Thus the kitchen is placed, with a convenience rare in English country house planning of any period, contiguous to the dining room and the breakfast room, although on a different level. The far end of the service wing connects with one corner of a large stable complex brought forward to flank the left side of the entrance court.

The house itself is of the same Anston stone that had been used for the New Palace, but the stable buildings are of the "white" Holkham brick that Kent had used a hundred years earlier at nearby Holkham Hall. Terraces surround the house on all sides. These are outlined by a simple pierced balustrade and serve to raise the house well above the flat Norfolk terrain. The layout of these terraces and of the extensive formal gardens was the work of W. A. Nesfield, the garden architect with whom the elder Barry always collaborated in his own country house work.

The exterior treatment is more like Barry's Anglo-Italian at Highclere than plausibly Jacobethan (Fig. VIII 34). Rusticated members, like pilasters but without capitals, articulate the wall surfaces vertically; continuous entablatures and stringcourses at the level of the ground- and first-storey window sills band them horizontally. The central bays of the entrance and garden fronts, wider than the rest, rise to form attics; the rest of the block is covered with a sort of curb roof from which a stone dormer projects over each bay. Rather stumpy obelisks rise between the dormers in line with the rusticated elements of the wall surface. At the corners of the main block and at the breaks in the side elevation, as well as over the central attics, the "pilasters" are coupled and rise well above the dormers.

Between the corner motifs, on the central attics, and above the centers of the side bays on the garden front are carved panels with scalloped tops. Inscriptions ornament the friezes of the entablatures of the entrance porch and of the bay above it; elsewhere, in the friezes on the front and sides, there are merely occasional spots of carving. On the garden front, however, the friezes of the attic and of the side bays have continuous bands of carving. Various alternatives to the plain rusticated bands used elsewhere increase the decorative richness of the "pilasters" on the front attic, the garden bays, and the porch. Curious spurs projecting from the sides of the window frames line up with the rusticated bands on the piers. An academic mind has evidently been busy trying to organize, none too logically, the various Mannerist features of design.

Compared with Highclere, the wall surfaces at Bylaugh are more plastic; but the scale is also coarser and the reticulated pattern is much less even. This is particularly true of the garden front where the two great rectangular bay windows are quite independent of the regular rhythm of the other façades. The clock tower in the stable court is too low, too simple in treatment, and too remote to play any part in the composition of the main block. Compared to Somerleyton Hall (Fig. VI 18), by that other close associate of Barry's the sculptor John Thomas, this considerably more modest mansion is better planned and more coherently designed. But it cannot be considered to represent any significant development of the Anglo-Italian mode. Down to the 70's, at least, the future lay in quite a different direction. Although more or less regular Jacobethan country houses continued to be built through the late 50's and 60's, they may properly be considered as late examples of an Early Victorian mode like most of the towered Italian Villas and Tudor manor houses of those years.

Contemporary with Bylaugh and rather more attractive, if much less "serious," is Vinters, near Maidstone in Kent. This is a Georgian mansion redecorated externally by C. J. Richardson in 1850. In the light of his detailed knowledge of the Jacobethan, the almost Rococo fantasy of the cresting over the windows and above the parapet on this house is certainly somewhat surprising (Fig. VIII 36). The general proportions and the window spacing of the original house were not changed. The elaborate embellishments were mostly executed in Caen stone, but the frilly lintels over the windows are of cast iron. The added features have the dainty prettiness of contemporary interior ornamentation in papier-mâché and a comparable stylistic ambiguity. This kind of "modernization" provides a link between the more ambitious mansions, to which this chapter has been largely devoted, and the modest detached villas of the day in which something of Late Georgian frivolousness often lingered.

In the various fields of Early Victorian architecture the relatively great significance and the comparable statistical predominance of certain stylistic modes must be noted. In the country house field the Italian, the Anglo-Italian and the regular Jacobethan, the Castellated and the Scottish Baronial are conspicuous. But most ubiquitous of all is, of course, the Tudor in all the gamut from 15th-century Manorial to irregular Jacobethan. Yet occasional clients found architects to build for them in styles that were markedly unfashionable. For instance, St. Margaret's at Isleworth near Richmond was built for the Earl of Kilmorey in 1850–52 by Lewis Vulliamy in a rather Wren-like style. This mansion was of brick, mostly light colored but with red brick quoins; the window and cornice trim was in Portland stone eked out with Portland cement. Not surprisingly, the design of the house did not long please, and it was remodeled almost beyond recognition in the late 60's.

Grittleton House near Chippenham in Wiltshire, still incomplete in 1853, had then been some years in building for Joseph Neeld, M.P. It is remarkable not only for its almost unique use of a sort of Romanesque style but also for the fact that it was largely of fireproof construction, like Osborne House, with arched floors of hollow brickwork carried on cast-iron girders. James Thomson, the architect of Grittleton, was a pupil of J. B. Papworth. His earliest work, when he was in his 20's, had been Cumberland Terrace in Regent's Park, where he probably followed sketches made by Nash. His obituary states that the work at Grittleton continued from 1840 to 1860; but it seems unlikely, because of the fireproof construction, that the actual erection of the mansion really began before the mid-40's. (He was then also building for Neeld the Chippenham Cheese Market.) The character of the design is rather like other Romanesque work—most of it ecclesiastical—of the early and mid-40's.

The plan of Grittleton is very poorly arranged. Extremely regular and nearly symmetrical, it provides a multiplicity of large dimly lighted rooms. These are separated by endless ranges of interior vestibules, lighted from above in the worst way of Somerleyton, and by quite unnecessary blind corridors. Along the end façade, completely masking the drawing room and the state dining room, is a large glass and iron conservatory, quite as at Somerleyton, although it is not so gargantuan in size (Fig. VIII 35). This is rather gracefully covered with Paxton's ridge-and-furrow roofs bent to a cloister-vaulted shape as on the Chatsworth Conservatory (Fig. XV 29). At the front of the wing at this end, which projects slightly farther than the nearly balancing wing at the other end, is a complex two-storey bay window. Halfway between these wings on the entrance façade the carriage porch is set against a taller pavilion. Behind that pavilion a square tower rises over the central hall at the crossing of the two main axes of the plan. The corners of the end wings are masked by little arched pavilions with pyramidal roofs, rather like corner turrets; as a matter of fact, the treatment of the composition throughout suggests contemporary Scottish Baronial or Jacobethan design with nominally 12th-century detail substituted for that of the 16th–17th centuries.

Neeld had a large collection of paintings, and his enormous rooms and top-lighted vestibules were primarily intended as galleries for the display of his Old Masters and his contemporary English pictures. Hence Grittleton is less a country house than a private museum. Both architectural effect and domestic convenience were intentionally subordinated to the client's rather special requirements. Since Bridgewater House was quite as much a private art gallery, Barry's superiority as an architect appears in the brilliant contrast of his commodity in planning and his elegance in design with this extremely amateurish effort. It is even hard to believe that the author of *Retreats* (1827; 2d ed. 1840), with its elegant Grecian designs for small houses, could ever have fallen so low. Probably a good deal of the blame in this case does lie with the client.

Private architecture in city or country offered few major challenges to Early Victorian architects. When novelties were incorporated, such as iron and glass conservatories, glass-roofed central courts, or fireproof construction, they either appear as irrelevant appendages or are quite invisible. The gamut of fashionable stylisms is much the same as in the Late Georgian period. If certain modes became obsolescent, such as the Grecian, they did not entirely die out in the deep country of the minor squires who built little in any event. The significance of the best work is less for itself than for its influence in other fields of building. Were this book concerned statistically with the architecture of the first fifteen years of Queen Victoria's reign, it would be desirable to follow the patronage of the land-owning class from the manor house into the village and see how the Italian, usually in its asymmetrical "Villa" guise, the Jacobethan, both regular and irregular, and the Tudor—though not the Castellated or very often the Scottish Baronial—were scaled down for use in schools, almshouses, hospitals, and other charitable institutions. But the character of all this Early Victorian country building was already implicit in the designs offered in pre-Victorian times by the authors of cottage and villa books.

The Early Victorian period away from cities and towns has a certain grace in good part because there were so few real novelties. Architectural energies were concentrated elsewhere. Curiously enough, though for good and sufficient reasons, the English countryside revived economically soon after the mid-century; but agricultural distress sufficiently explains the doldrums of country building in the 40's.

CHAPTER IX: ROYAL AND

STATE PATRONAGE

Under George IV the state had been the chief patron of public architecture. For this the enthusiasm of the sovereign, first as Regent and later as King, was in considerable part responsible. Already under William IV the tide of opinion was turning against state expenditure on public monuments; the new Sovereign's personal interest was negligible, even in the completion of Buckingham Palace. In the England of the 40's Royal and state commissions did not, as generally on the Continent, play much part in signalizing professional leadership, not even to the extent that they had in the Georgian Age. As has been said, Victoria seems to have had no particular personal enthusiasm for architecture; and her taste in artistic matters generally was rather more confused than that of most of her contemporaries. Both temperament and policy led her to dissociate herself as completely as possible from the tradition of architectural patronage of her spendthrift uncle the Regent.

Prince Albert had a much broader education than his wife and possessed a more than conventional knowledge of the arts of the past. The established German precedent of princely intervention in architecture, so brilliantly illustrated by Frederick William IV of Prussia before and after he came to the throne as well as by successive Wittelsbachs in Bavaria, was much publicized in the 40's. It naturally influenced Victoria's earnest consort. He would have liked to play a part in determining the character of public buildings, if not perhaps to commission new palaces. The projects with which he was most concerned, however, the rebuilding of Osborne House and Balmoral Castle, were hardly on a princely, much less a Royal, scale as we have seen. The Whig oligarchy—in particular the Leveson-Gowers with their inherited Bridgewater Canal fortune and their agricultural incomes from vast estates in England and Scotland—far outshone their sovereigns in the splendor and extent of their architectural patronage.

Perhaps because Albert liked to dabble in design himself—to what practical extent it is difficult, as always with Royalty, to tell—he saw that hacks and nonentities received the private commissions of the Royal family. Blore, not quite such a nonentity as William Smith of Aberdeen, was already installed as Architect of Buckingham Palace and Windsor Castle under William

IV in succession to Nash and Wyatville, respectively. He therefore continued in the 40's to make such modifications as were needed at those principal state residences.

The story of Blore's work at Buckingham Palace under William IV, after his selection in 1831 by Lord Duncannon, the First Commissioner of Woods and Forests, to take on the architectural problems of Nash's uncompleted structure, is given by Christopher Hussey in the introductory chapters of H. Clifford Smith's book on *Buckingham Palace* (1931). By May 1837 Duncannon was finally able to report that the building was ready for Royal occupancy; but within a month William was dead and his niece had succeeded him. On 13 July, three weeks after her accession, she moved there from Kensington Palace. Her first act was to command Duncannon to provide a Throne of State, but that august piece of furniture need hardly concern us here. In 1841 some changes were made in the private apartments in preparation for the Queen's marriage. The first remodeling of any intrinsic interest was the adaptation of Nash's southern conservatory—the northern one had already been carted off to Kew—as a chapel. The small octagonal apartment on the south side which had seemed a sufficient religious appendage to the original Royal client and his architect was quite unsatisfactory for the pious family prayers of his niece and her official family.

The new Buckingham Palace Chapel, as converted by Blore in 1842–43, could hardly have been more remote from the Camdenian ideals for Anglican church architecture that were crystallizing at this very time. Paired with the ancient Royal Chapel of the Savoy, it might well have provided a most striking piece of graphic propaganda for Gothic design had Pugin been able to include it in his *Contrasts*. Externally the chapel retained the Greek temple form of Nash's conservatory. Internally the roof was raised and the original cast-iron construction elaborated. Very attenuated colonnettes, fluted and provided with Composite capitals, provided the structural support of the room rather in the spirit of the imaginary architecture seen in certain Pompeian wall paintings (Fig. IX 3). The crossbeams were also of a Pompeian elegance, their cast-iron plates pierced with five circles of varying size and ornamented with wreaths and scrolls in low relief.

The wall treatment lacked the interest of the iron structural members. At the rear of the very shallow chancel the Mosaic Tablets of the Law flanked an arched east window filled with large diagonal and rectangular panes of colored glass; the same colored glass appeared in the side windows within very simple pediment-topped architraves. Across the west end the Queen's Closet was supported on Ionic columns brought from Carlton House. The interior coloring was white and off-white, with crimson upholstery; and the contemporary phrase, used to describe the chapel in the *Illustrated London*

News, "chastely elegant," must have applied perfectly when the edifice was consecrated by the Archbishop of Canterbury on 25 March 1843.

The chapel arranged for the Queen by Blore at Windsor was Gothic, at least nominally, but even more remote from the new standards of Victorian church architecture. The chosen apartment had earlier been George IV's music room at the northeast corner of the upper ward. An irregularly squarish room roughly 36 feet wide and 45 feet high with one large rectangular bay window, it would have made an even more striking Puginian "contrast" with the magnificence of the nearby St. George's Chapel than Buckingham Palace Chapel with that of the Savoy. The Perpendicular paneling on the walls and ceiling was Wyatville's; Blore's emendations consisted only of blocking off the lower portion of the bay window with a paneled screen behind the communion table and adding a Queen's Closet, 12 feet above the floor, in a square-headed recess across one side of the odd-shaped room.

Somewhat more interesting intrinsically than these makeshift religious accommodations was the ornate "Chinese" summerhouse erected in the gardens of Buckingham Palace in 1843–44; but this belated Georgian garden fabrick was of real significance only for its interior murals. These were by Landseer, Etty, Eastlake, Stanfield, Maclise, Uwins, and Sir William Ross. This venture, which belongs to the history of Victorian painting and not to that of Victorian architecture, has lately been admirably discussed by John Steegman in his *Consort of Taste* (1950). He also provides a colored frontispiece taken from one of the lithographic plates in the sumptuous contemporary publication by Lewis Gruner, *Her Majesty's Pavilion in Buckingham Palace Gardens* (1846). In that the iconographic analysis of the various lunettes illustrating Milton's *Comus* was by no less an authority than Mrs. Anna Jameson.

The first major new construction undertaken at the Royal couple's official London residence coincided in date with Thomas Cubitt's private work for them at Osborne. But the new front wing that Blore then added across the entrance court of Buckingham Palace, completely hiding Nash's palace from the public gaze, was intended more to provide additional accommodation for the growing family of the Queen than for public display (Fig. IX 1). The new wing revealed its primarily domestic purpose too, for it was hardly as monumental as the new residential terraces of nearby Belgravia or of Bayswater across Hyde Park (Fig. XIII 6).

There had long been general agreement that Nash's "Pimlico Palace" was a mistake in almost every way. The Queen wrote a letter to the prime minister Sir Robert Peel early in 1845—a mother with no place to house her growing family was the touching note she stressed—to urge that something be done and soon. Blore began to prepare plans for the east wing sometime between

261

then and May 1846 although Peel advised waiting before making application for funds to a legislature about to vote the income tax. Nearly a year passed before the government actually applied to Parliament; even then the members were persuaded to provide the money—at first only £20,000 out of the £150,000 estimated by Blore as the total needed—only on the grounds of practical necessity. The rest was obtained later by the sale of the Royal Pavilion at Brighton.

With the bitter and even scandalous memory of George IV's last venture in palace building still warm, Parliament would have been extremely unlikely to vote the much more considerable funds necessary for a completely new palace. Nor, one guesses, would they have supplied a penny to any architect who seemed to be a personal favorite of Royalty like the Regent's unlamented friend Nash. The instinct of everyone concerned—Queen, Prince, prime minister, Parliament, and even Blore—was undoubtedly to make the best of a bad job. The only serious alternative proposed was the adaptation of Buckingham Palace for some cultural use, such as a seat for the Royal Academy, and the building of a new palace elsewhere. That was much too ambitious a project for the 40's which feared bankruptcy and revolution almost equally. Blore's plans included in addition to the new east wing some modifications to the existing south wing and the addition of new kitchens and a ballroom on that side. The kitchens may have been built at this time; the ballroom had to wait for five years when Pennethorne was given the job.

A leader in the *Builder* for 28 August 1847, when the new work was under way, remarked that "the design does not pretend to grandeur or magnificence, scarcely to dignity [but that] the architect was probably right in attempting, in the present instance, little more than an ordinary piece of street architecture in stone instead of stucco." Including the mezzanine and the attic, there were five storeys as in the big new commercial buildings of the City and the terrace houses of Bayswater; the composition, however, is in three storeys only, with mere slots at the top of the rusticated ground storey to light the mezzanine and other similar slots between the brackets of the frieze for attic windows (Fig. IX 1). Yet the new front rises most awkwardly above the side wings of Nash's palace and reduces even the dome in the center of the old garden front to insignificance, not to say invisibility, as Blore and his clients probably intended it should. (The refacing of Blore's front by Sir Aston Webb (1849–1930) in 1913 did not change the proportions. That explains the curious alternation of tenses in this account, some things being still as true today as when Blore completed his work.)

Christopher Hussey reports that bolder alternative projects by Blore exist among his drawings at the British Museum. What he built justified most of the severer judgments on Early Victorian architecture. The rhythm of the openings is, for example, extremely confused, the three windows in the end pavilions being set much closer together than the windows of the main block, while the elaborately be-garlanded windows of the central feature were jammed in between two projecting bastions ornamented with giant paired pilasters. The main entrance arch, rising into the mezzanine, was flanked by oblong openings with trim just like that on the ground-storey windows. Two slightly lower arches are centered between the axial block and the end pavilions, while the doors in the pavilions were merely accented with richer trim and crowning pediments. The upper ranges of windows were pedimented in the first storey throughout and, at the end and in the center, in the second storey as well. This treatment did give the façade a certain conventional dignity; but the skyline above the cornice was broken up more incoherently even than that of Wilkins' National Gallery which had been so much criticized during the preceding ten years since its completion.

Although a balustrade with urns was carried over most of the front, this was interrupted in the centers of the end pavilions by high plinths, supporting groups of sculpture, which rose in front of the visible, though rather low, roofs. Over the central pavilion no roof showed, for two massive podia set back behind the balustrade carried seated figures of St. George and Brittania by the sculptor Ternouth, and between them a taller arched niche culminated in a wreathed Royal cypher and the date 1847 (Fig. IX 2). Except at the top and in the center, the whole façade was rather flat even though shallow balconettes projected in front of all the first-storey windows.

Blore, born in 1789, was nearing 60. His competence, such as it was, lay in Gothic and Jacobethan design. The task he undertook at Buckingham Palace was at best a thankless one. Yet nothing illustrates better the deterioration of taste in the mid-40's than the contrast between this rather vulgar Victorian palace front and the Georgian work by Nash that it masks (which is in fact not very good of its kind). There are here no compensating new values such as distinguish the best churches of the time, the "palaces" of Barry, and even some of the Early Victorian manors and castles by Pugin and Salvin.

Pennethorne, a better architect than Blore, was later called on to do additional work at Buckingham Palace. Although this work is less conspicuous, it is of much greater independent interest and still extant, except for the interior decorations. Sir James Pennethorne (1801–1871) was the principal government architect of the Early Victorian period and his characteristic commissions were of public rather than palatial character. However, there is a certain propriety in presenting him first as one of the architects of Buckingham Palace; for he was the principal pupil of Nash who had rebuilt Buckingham House for George IV, and was also Nash's successor as architect to the Commissioners of Woods and Forests as well as his adopted son.

Pennethorne was reputedly born at Worcester in 1801, the third of a family of five children whom Nash later adopted. But there is a great deal of mystery about all of Nash's private affairs. He probably had no children by his first wife. His second wife Mary Anne Bradley was the daughter of a London coal merchant of Worcestershire origin. With Nash's marriage to her in 1798 his financial and professional affairs began to brighten notably, and it has been at least hinted that she was a close friend of the Regent. Were some or all of the children Nash adopted, born between 1800 and 1808 and identified only as Bradley kin from Worcestershire, possibly illegitimate cousins of the Queen? Or if not, was it suspected that they were?

However that may be, the young James Pennethorne entered Nash's office in 1819, just when the Regent Street campaign was at its height. He stayed there four or five years; then he spent the years 1824–26 traveling in France and Italy. On his return he became within a year or two his aging master's chief aide in all his work. Before going abroad he had exhibited a water color of the Quadrant at the Royal Academy in 1823 showing the very colonnades he himself was to remove a quarter-century later. In Nash's office the elder Pugin had been his chief mentor and he must have learned rendering, if not much about Gothic design, from him.

In Rome he had worked on a paper restoration of the Forum, appropriate training for one who was to be the chief English urbanist of his generation. But Pennethorne's most serious and relevant early experience began only in 1827 when he supervised the rebuilding of the west end of the Strand and the erection of the houses in Carlton House Terrace, as well as some improvements in St. James's Park. He probably had, as was the way in the Nash office, considerable autonomy in design; but his diary indicates that Carlton House Terrace at least was entirely the work of the 75-year-old Nash. The tenants of the grand mansions there were of such political importance, however, that his mere association with them as Nash's assistant must have been valuable to his later career—they ranged from the Duke of Bedford's heir to William Huskisson (1770–1830) who was then leader in the House (and shortly to be more famous as the first victim of a railway accident).

In 1832 Pennethorne was first directly employed by the Commissioners of Woods and Forests. Nash also gave him in that year additional responsibilities, including some tedious negotiations with Blore who had just undertaken the completion of Buckingham Palace. Then in 1834 Nash left London for good and turned over his entire practice to Pennethorne. Just after Nash's death in 1835 he built Christ Church, Albany Street (whose interior later underwent the indignity of two successive Camdenian "restorations," one by Carpenter and one by Butterfield). His Holy Trinity, Gray's Inn Road, of 1837 has already been mentioned. It was not till 1838, the year after Victoria's accession, that Pennethorne's own career properly started. He was then appointed one of the two Surveyors to the Woods and Forests Board to carry out extensive improvements in St. Giles and Bloomsbury and also in Spitalfields; the other was Thomas Chawner (1775–1851) as in Nash's time. In 1840 came another public appointment for Pennethorne, this time as Surveyor of Houses in the Law Revenue Department; and in 1843, on the retirement of Chawner, he became sole Architect and Surveyor to the Commissioners of Woods and Forests. Within the purview of the Commissioners came the care of the official Royal residences as well as many other quite miscellaneous responsibilities.

No hypothetical relationship to the Royal family is necessary in order to explain Pennethorne's receiving the commission to add a new wing to Buckingham Palace in 1852. But one cannot forget, because it seems so out of character, that the Prince Consort, only too familiar with scandalous behavior in his own family, named his bulls at the Windsor Home Farm for his wife's uncles, and that when he ran out of avuncular nomenclature he often used those of their better known bastards. With a sense of humor of that order he might well have been amused to employ a possible namesake of one of his heifers. Whatever the reason, it is certainly fortunate that Blore's ballroom wing of 1846 was left in abeyance and new plans obtained from Pennethorne.

The Prince was throughout his life a fairly active amateur of painting as Steegman has lately made evident in *Consort of Taste* (1950). When he failed to persuade the government to buy the Oettingen-Wallenstein collection of Italian primitives for the National Gallery, he acquired them for himself, and after his death the Queen gave 22 of them to the Gallery. He commissioned "The Eve of the Deluge" from John Martin and aided Frith in the organization of his best known work "Derby Day" (or so the obsequious artist later declared). When Pennethorne began designing the new south wing of Buckingham Palace, it was to be expected that the Prince would insist on elaborate pictorial decoration. Abstract patterns in tartan might do for Balmoral, but in London nothing less than Raphael compositions could satisfy Albert. Where this idea came from is only too obvious. The 19th-century revival of mural painting had its headquarters in Germany, most particularly in Munich; but, when Stüler and Hesse completed the Orangerieschloss at Potsdam for Frederick William IV in these same years from 1851 on, the principal interior was decorated not with new compositions but with copies of Raphael frescoes.

If the inspiration for the interiors of the new wing of Buckingham Palace was German, the exterior (at least in its best features) has more relation to contemporary French work, as does much of Pennethorne's other government building. This point should be stressed, for some critics have loosely implied that Victorian architecture was imported from Germany by—or along with —the consort. Actually, there was very little German influence; it may even be a pity that there was not more, since at the beginning of the reign the Prussian architects Schinkel (who died in 1841) and his pupil Ludwig Persius (who died in 1845) were probably the best in Europe.

The new south wing in Buckingham Palace consists of a ballroom and a supper room, as well as related accommodations for entertaining, and has its own entrance from Buckingham Gate. (Unfortunately both the big rooms were redecorated in 1902 and no early photographs of them have come to light.) The ballroom itself was structurally complete by 1854; but contemporary views of the wing were not published until 1856, after the elaborate decorations had been installed late in the previous year. Such was the conservatism of taste of all those involved, Pennethorne as well as the consort and the Queen, that there was very little in the new wing to indicate its late date. Like Balmoral III, built and decorated in the same years, it belonged in spirit completely to the 40's.

The great arched doorways at the ends of the low entrance block facing Buckingham Gate have real distinction of a rather French order (Fig. IX 5). Broad flat archivolts are set between flat rusticated piers under spandrels filled with crisp ornament in low relief. One could almost suppose them to be the work of the aging Fontaine or of Henri Labrouste (1801–1875) and executed a good ten years earlier. The height of the wing rising behind the entrance block is excessive; from the gardens it towers above Nash's low façade in a rather insolent way. But this awkward juxtaposition was perhaps inevitable if sufficient height—actually 45 feet—were to be obtained to provide good proportions for the enormous ballroom, which is 60 feet by 110 feet with additional recesses at the east and west ends.

Sumptuous as was the interior treatment of the ballroom, it peculiarly justified that favorite Early Victorian term of praise "neat" (Fig. IX 4). Despite its great size there was no monumentality of effect because of the flat though broken treatment of the walls. The relief of the ornaments was kept very low and all decoration was confined within rectangular panels except around and under the big arches of the recesses at the two ends. Between the clerestorey windows (which were lighted by gas from outside at night) Professor N. Canzoni of Rome painted "figures of the Hours taken from sketches by Raffaelle," according to the contemporary account in the *Illustrated London News*. In the lunette over the reception recess "a copy from Raffaelle's Parnassus" was intended ultimately to replace an allegorical composition of "Britannia sanctioning Peace" which was first installed in reference to the current termination of the Crimean War. The spandrels of the great arches "contain four cupids from Raffaelle's frescoes at the Farnese Palace" (by which presumably the Farnesina was meant).

The lower walls were covered with a silk fabric woven with the national floral devices—roses, thistles, etc. Over the doors on the north side were sculptures by Reed set in the oblong spaces between the paneled architraves and the cornice running around the room below the clerestorey. Mirrors filled identical architraves below matching reliefs on the south side. Above a modest cove the ceiling was subdivided into square panels separated by double beams crosswise and by single beams lengthwise. From the center of octagonal recesses in the panels descended glass gas lustres made by Osler of Birmingham.

The clear reticulated pattern of the ceiling (which was changed in 1902) probably corresponds with the actual structural beams above; these would be of wrought iron or possibly some sort of trusses combining cast and wrought elements. But this pattern was not related to the treatment of the walls below the cove by any vertical elements which might have suggested support for the beam ends. The whole scheme of the interior, and notably the daintiness of the stucco enrichments of the ceiling, belonged in the realm of domestic decoration, not of large-scale interior architecture. Even the mural paintings and the reliefs might almost as well have been wallpaper panels in a suburban drawing room.

The supper room is nearly a square, 58 feet by 65 feet, and 45 feet high like the ballroom; but it was rather happier both in its wall decoration and in the more architectural handling of the cubic volume of space. A shallow dome, decorated in the Late Antique way as a velarium of blue with gold stars, enhanced the spatial effect notably (Fig. IX 6). The ranges of marbleized panels of the lower walls, executed by Moxon, were dignified and architectural in scale. On the north and south sides there were friezes in relief, "taken from Raffaelle's 'History of Psyche,' to which Mr. John Gibson, the Royal Academician [not the architect but the sculptor, of course] has made some additions, the whole having been modelled and executed by Mr. Reed" (not Reed but William Theed, according to Christopher Hussey).

Similar elements decorated the Promenade (now East) Gallery and the Royal Corridor by which the new rooms are approached from the main block of the palace. The East Gallery retains its original segmental skylights and frieze, as well as the rich door frames, but the walls are now plain instead of marbleized.

As an indication of the thoroughness with which the Consort and his German adviser Professor Lewis Gruner (in England 1841–56) worked out their

267

pastiche of Raphael's decorations—in the result so unlike the actual decorative ensembles of Raphael and his school—it should be noted that "in order to study the effect of various combinations of colour, and to determine on the decorations to be adopted, careful drawings in outline of the sides and ceilings of the various apartments were lithographed, so as to afford any number of copies for experiments." Not surprisingly the results had rather the look of feeble contemporary chromolithographs.

With buildings not intended for Royal occupancy the State could do somewhat better, although very little was in fact being built in the 40's and early 50's except Westminster New Palace. For many reasons this stands by itself as one of the chief monuments of the age. Although the design had been chosen before the new reign began, it was continually modified before and during construction; and its construction was by no means complete even when the Early Victorian period came to an end in the mid-50's. In size, in elaboration, in prominence, and even in structural significance only a few other buildings of the day can properly be compared with it; yet stylistically it has little connection with the dominant architectural currents of the day.

The New Palace, primarily the seat of the two chambers of the national legislature, differs in function from all other government buildings of the period. Moreover, like the new front and the new south wing of Buckingham Palace, it was almost without influence on the architects who were regularly employed by various government departments. Barry, as we have seen, did little other government work, and what he did was of a quite different character. Pugin, naturally, did none. Pennethorne, as Architect and Surveyor to the Commissioners of Woods and Forests, was in effect the principal government architect; but he had few opportunities for new construction before 1850 when returning prosperity finally loosened somewhat the government's pursestrings; and only in the Record Office did he echo the mode of the New Palace.

The Palace was the subject of a series of violent controversies fed by speeches in both Houses and usually accompanied by outside pamphleteering. The question of how the two chambers should be heated and ventilated, otherwise than by the vehemence of their members, provided the subject of the bitterest and most recurrent row. But from the preliminary arguments about choice of style and choice of materials, through the problem of obtaining a suitable clock, down to the still unresolved question, arising after the death of both the commissioned architect and his principal collaborator, as to whose was the prime responsibility for the design, almost every question concerning the Houses of Parliament seems to have had several sides. Only a large monograph, with multiple appendices, might hope to do the subject full justice. I must hazard here many statements which one or another interested party has at some time violently (and even plausibly) contradicted; worse, I must do so without always giving the opposing parties adequate hearing. But most of the important literature is fairly accessible and a list of the principal contemporary sources has already been provided in Chapter II.

The attempt of the unsuccessful competitors to upset the decision in favor of Barry's design was settled in the House of Commons by Sir Robert Peel in 1837. Barry was commissioned; but the successful architect was warned in ominous Latin: "cui mortifera est victoria"—early enough in the year, however, to avoid any suggestion of a tasteless pun. (Actually it is Pugin's death, not Barry's, that can be indirectly traced to the strain of working on the New Palace.) The first funds were appropriated on 3 July 1837. At that time only the embankment along the Thames, which reclaimed a considerable area on the east side of the intended site from the existing mud flats, was actually begun, not any part of the Palace itself. On the advice of the engineer James Walker this embankment foundation, consisting of 12 feet of concrete, was protected by the pilings of a cofferdam against the wash of the tide. After the foundation had set, the piles were sawed off at the dredged level of the river bed. On top of the concrete base the embankment wall itself was erected and faced with large blocks of Aberdeen granite.

During the two years this preliminary work was going forward a commission headed by the distinguished geologist Henry de la Bêche, after visiting various quarries in 1838 and 1839, recommended a magnesian limestone from Bolsover Moor. Inadequate supplies of this material forced the substitution of Anston stone, then considered to be of the same general character; this was a most unfortunate decision as became evident long before the building was completed and is even more plain today. But the error was the experts', not Barry's (as many have supposed).

On 27 April 1840 the first stone of the superstructure was laid privately by Barry's wife in that section of the eventual river front which was to contain the Speaker's House. Loosely, but only very loosely, it may be said that the over-all construction of the enormous complex of the Palace proceeded from this lower northeast corner to the top of the Victoria Tower at the southwest corner, which was finally completed in the mid-60's after Barry's death. Some such general sequence can be read from the successive dates on the leaden heads of the downspouts in the various courts of the building.

Early in 1841 a strike among the masons employed by Thomas Grissell (1801–1874) and S. Morton Peto, whose firm held the first contract for the superstructure, slowed down the work for a while. But far more disruptive of progress had been the appointment in January 1840 of a special heating and ventilating expert, Dr. David Boswell Reid (1805–1863), with authority independent of Barry's. Barry's controversy with Reid, unlike the strike, continued for more than five years and then broke out anew in the early 50's. The Lords—as they would again after the destruction of the House of Commons in the blitz—had generously loaned their old quarters, which survived the 1834 fire, to the lower House. Since the peers were as a result settled in very inadequate temporary accommodations, it was they who exerted pressure for the rapid construction of the New Palace. In 1844 they set up a Committee of Enquiry to obtain an explanation from the architect for the many alterations from the original plans already made. In defending himself before the committee Barry stated that these were either changes in detail only or, if of more consequence, that they had been necessitated by new requirements having the "direct or implied" authority of the Board of Works. But the censure of Barry in this report was soon balanced by a report from a Committee of the Commons which supported him. Just the same he was spurred on by the investigation to complete the Lords' chamber as soon as possible.

Reid's schemes for ventilating and heating the building would have required about a *third* (italics Alfred Barry's in his life of his father) of the whole cubic contents of the building. Acting like flues in case of a fire, moreover, the conduits of the system would, according to Barry, have seriously increased the danger of a major conflagration. The controversy came to a head finally in 1845 when an arbiter selected by the government, Joseph Gwilt (1784–1863), decided in Barry's favor and Reid passed out of the picture for some years. In 1846 Barry selected Michael Faraday (1791–1867)— a scientist rather better known to posterity than Reid—to advise him on the heating and ventilating systems that he actually used. The other controversies did not reach their climax until much later.

Pugin in 1835–36 had all but certainly made *some* material contribution to Barry's designs for the exterior of the Palace, as we have seen in Chapter II. As regards the interiors in the original project, insofar as they were then developed in detail, his contribution was presumably even more important. But that Pugin's early work had consisted chiefly of the elaboration of schemes already matured in Barry's office seems very nearly an established fact. If Barry actually obscured from his own office force the extent of his dependence on Pugin at that time, as has been charged, the fact would surely be very suspicious. Pugin's sons and others have offered, indeed, a curious story that rough sketches made by Pugin at St. Marie's Grange on the basis of plan and elevational measurements sent him by Barry were produced in the office as Barry's own before being worked up in further detail there by Pugin in sight of the office force. This sounds a most unlikely mystification. The relationship between Pugin and Barry rapidly became uneasy in any event. Sometime late in 1836 or early in 1837, just about the time the actual foundations for the embankment began to be laid in fact, Pugin broke with Barry and for the next seven years they held aloof from one another. These were, of course, the very years within which the greater part of Pugin's own fantastically prolific architectural production was concentrated (see Chapter III).

Whether or not Barry ever attempted earlier to obtain Pugin's assistance again, their collaboration was not actually renewed until 1844. "I am in a regular fix respecting the working drawings for the fittings and decorations of the House of Lords, which it is of vital importance to me should now be furnished with the utmost despatch . . ." Barry wrote to Pugin on 3 September, his son reports, under the pressure of the Lords' Committee of Enquiry; "I know no one who can so thoroughly relieve me of my present troubles of mind in respect of these drawings as yourself. . . ." After repeated appeals of this sort Pugin agreed to assist, but with the proviso that he should be paid, not as before by Barry, but directly by the government.

Why Pugin accepted is not clear. Of course his governmental salary as Superintendent of the Works (and some £500 a year which Barry in fact paid him in addition) was soon being spent on the construction of the one and only church in which he expected to fulfill at last his ambitions as a Gothic architect, his own St. Augustine's beside his new house at Ramsgate. Informing Pugin of a payment into his bank account in November 1845 Barry wrote, "I have no doubt I shall be able to appease your mind and put it in a fit state to proceed with your holy work at Ramsgate with fitting composure and Christian resignation" (even though the church was actually not begun until the next year). Thus, as Trappes-Lomax points out in quoting this letter, did the shrewd and worldly Barry bend the pious Pugin to his will.

However much Pugin may or may not have contributed to the early project of 1835–36, for everything designed for or executed at the Palace between 1844 and his death in 1852 he had a real if strictly limited responsibility. He made drawings not only for interior wall treatments and for large items of decorative art, such as stained-glass windows, but also for all the incidental fittings and furniture from throne chairs down through lighting fixtures to umbrella stands, inkstands, calendars, and bellpulls; and he was continuously supervising their execution as well. In modern slang one may therefore say that he "styled" the interiors with a completeness few architects except geniuses usually have the time, the patience, and the energy to carry out in such a large building. All this fussy work he could hardly have done, it would seem, had many major architectural decisions been in his hands also.

Pugin at the New Palace was essentially a super-decorator, both exterior and interior, and also an "industrial designer," as he had long been in the field of ecclesiastical wares. At the very most Pugin *might* have made a contribu-

271

tion to the architectural character of the building as a whole somewhat comparable to Sullivan's in his masterly façade of the Gage Building in Chicago which provides the only visible exterior of a structure otherwise completely designed and executed by Holabird and Roche. But it seems rather unlikely that Pugin's contribution at the New Palace was at all of the order of Sullivan's even in those sections that were entirely developed and carried out between 1844 and 1852.

Suspicions as to Pugin's possible responsibility for major features of the design are undoubtedly increased by extrinsic facts, however. For instance, Barry's letters to Pugin dating from the years 1835–37 "fell into the fire" when they were left overnight in Barry's hands by Pugin's son in 1858, just at the time Ferrey was preparing to write Pugin's life. Yet in the later period of actual construction, as in the earlier period of preliminary designing, stylistic analysis is more likely to approximate the truth than thrashing over again the heated controversies of the late 60's and reassessing accumulated gossip. Certainly the building that began to rise in the 40's differs markedly from the designs of 1835–36; the changes which make it different *must* be primarily due to Barry's reconsideration of various aspects of the complex in the years 1837–44. Hence the executed principal front along the river, as it has been known for a century and more (Fig. I 1), owes its character even more surely to Barry than does the original design for this façade discussed in Chapter II (Fig. II 25). This is the more true for 20th-century eyes which have learned to see this aspect of the building with the vision of the French Impressionist and Post-Impressionist painters. Few now pay much attention to the minutiae of the Perpendicular details which produce the reticulated web of the surface. Grime, decay, and spotty replacement of individual stones, moreover, as well as our different vision, make the ornament over which Pugin slaved nearly invisible now to most observers.

In 1843 Barry had the approaches to the river front much on his mind. At that time he projected a Thames embankment that should extend back toward the City and also new Westminster and Lambeth bridges to cross the river at either end of the Palace. He even proposed a monumental river front above an embankment for the Surrey shore across from the Palace. The bridges and the façades across the river were all to be Gothic (or more accurately Perpendicular) so that this whole section of the river might become an enormous forecourt harmonious with the Palace.

The next year he turned his attention to the other side of the complex. There he proposed that the Law Courts should be rebuilt as two wings enclosing New Palace Yard and extending along the west side of Westminster Hall to connect with St. Stephen's Porch. At the northwest corner, where the two wings would join, there was to be a monumental entrance pavilion, set diagonally, with a tremendous arch and a very high roof. To this idea Barry returned in 1853; but unlike the ultimate ordering of the Surrey river front—in a very un-Gothic spirit—nothing ever came of it. The Law Courts were of course eventually built in the 70's in the Strand on an alternative site—a site which Barry had, as a matter of fact, also suggested in 1845. The Surrey river front was embanked and lined with the monotonous wards of Currey's St. Thomas's Hospital, effectively blocking any axial approach from the south.

Two principal differences should be noted between the 1835–36 design for the river front (Fig. II 25) and that executed in the early 40's (Fig. I 1). One concerns the skyline, the other the wall treatment. High roofs were added behind the parapets both over the main curtain walls and on all the towers. The walls above the ground floor lost their great arches resembling those of the Birmingham school (Fig. II 26); instead they are completely paneled with rectangular tracery. This tracery incorporates the mullions of the windows and also extends over the buttresses. The latter are without steps and are triangular in section; thus they are much more metallic looking than those first proposed. The larger octagonal buttresses, which now flank the terminal towers as well as the towers at the ends of the middle section, have paneling all over them.

A treatment rather like this, possibly worked out by Pugin, had been proposed in the early design for the shaft of the great keep-like tower, it will be recalled (Fig. II 22). Except for the absence of buttresses and the pairing of the narrow windows in each bay, this treatment was also closely approximated in the original design of the curtain walls at the north and south ends of the Palace (Figs. II 22, 23). Since the over-all pattern of reticulation of the river front in its essentials had thus been set down on paper before 1837, it may perhaps be considered to go back indirectly to Pugin.

But the general handling of the river front resembles even more closely the wall treatment of Highclere Castle despite the difference in nominal style (Fig. VI 19). The fact that the continuous verticals at Highclere consist of Renaissance orders or of chains of rustication, while the broader and richer horizontal bands are provided by entablatures and dadoes, is certainly not particularly significant; the vocabulary may be different but the syntax is the same. As we have seen, Barry was the sort of eclectic who readily translates desired effects from one stylistic repertory to another. The increased animation of the skyline of the New Palace as executed, with the heavier finials above the buttresses and the parapets rising to enclose gabled niches at the middle of each bay, can also be paralleled at Highclere in various terminal features that are actually more conspicuous there because of the absence of a high roof behind. Whatever the precise dates of the construction of Highclere the design for it seems to have existed by 1840 before the final drawings for the river front at Westminster were completed.

The high roofs give plastic depth to the long front facing the Thames. This is certainly a notable change from the screen-like treatment of the top of the façade in the early project. A high roof sounds more Gothic than an invisible one; actually, however, the character and the effect of this roof are closer to a French mansard than to a medieval gable. Medieval roofs in England, moreover, had generally come down to a very low pitch by the Perpendicular period. The inspiration for the high roofs, if hardly at this date likely to come from contemporary France, would yet seem more continental than English; Victorian commentators sometimes noted the resemblance of the executed design to the rich Late Gothic town halls of Flanders. But Barry's reasons for raising the pitch of his roofs may well have been more largely technical than stylistic. Their all-iron construction was one of the greatest innovations Barry introduced in attempting to make the New Palace fire resistant.

As every one knows, the actual House of Commons was destroyed in the early days of World War II by a fire started by an incendiary bomb. There was, however, a particular reason for the vulnerability of that chamber. Unlike the outer blocks of the grid, the Commons had a wooden ceiling below the outer roof—actually not one but two—thus providing plenty of fuel for the bomb after it penetrated the iron plates above. Later, well-organized fire watching saved the building from any further serious damage by incendiaries. But that was only possible because Barry had used the best fire-resistant construction he knew throughout the whole building. Most novel to contemporaries among his various fireproofing devices was the all-iron roof.

No functional reasons required the use of an interior iron skeleton here, such as had first been introduced in textile mills in the 1790's and was soon to be accepted for all sound commercial construction. The partition walls were of solid masonry throughout since these did not incommode the organization of the plan in narrow blocks around internal courts. The floors, however, were of cast-iron or wrought-iron joists carrying brick jack-arches leveled off on top with cement. This by no means novel construction can be seen clearly in the attics beneath the roofs. (The later improvement which substituted wrought- for cast-iron joists had not yet come into use when the river front was roofed but can be seen in other sections of the Palace.) The underside of the floor construction was generally protected by plaster ceilings from the heat of any fires that might start in individual rooms. Throughout the building the interior fittings, including (in the principal rooms) decorative wooden beams in the ceilings, were inflammable; but so they are still in many supposedly fireproof modern buildings. Barry's roofs, however, were really fire*proof*, not merely fire resistant, since they provided no fuel whatever for flames whose heat might have weakened and twisted the cast-iron members until they collapsed.

John Weale's *Quarterly Papers on Engineering*, Part 5 (1844), includes an account of the earliest roofs at the Palace which the *Builder*, 2, 581, copied. A considerable quotation may well be given:

But beyond the use of iron in forming the principals of his roof [which was of course no real innovation by this time], Barry has ventured a further step, of which those unacquainted with the experience he is cognizant of might not fully understand the wisdom, but which is thoroughly appoved by all practical and scientific persons who have examined the subject minutely. We refer to the covering of the roofs with cast iron plates of a thin section, and galvanized by a process now admitted to present the best yet discovered means of protecting iron work exposed to the air and weather from their otherwise injurious effects. . . . The cast iron plates, being cast of sufficient size to span the distance between each adjoining pair of principals, dispense with the necessity on any kind of boarding whatever, thus saving not only a great expense, but also diminishing the chances of damage by fire, which would by destroying this boarding, leave the slates without sufficient support, thus making the whole roof liable to be broken in by their derangement, or, in the case of lead covering, the fire from the boarding communicated to the lead, would speedily reduce it to a liquid state, and create most disastrous and fatal consequences. [The fact that the heat would also weaken and twist the iron itself was perhaps not yet realized.]

Again, the cast iron plates allow the formation of ornamental rolls on the exterior, and parallel with the rafters, at the same time having vertical joints beneath their rolls, which together with the horizontal joints, are so continued as to be perfectly impervious to the admission of water—the architect being thus enabled to communicate an architectural character to the very roof, which cannot fail to be highly esteemed when seen in connection with the striking features of the masonry below, when the edifice is completed. . . . The corners of each plate being firmly secured by screws and snugs to the rafters on which they lie, a greater degree of lateral strength is attained than can be had with any other kind of covering; in fact, the whole roof, principals, and covering become one piece of framework, well-knit and secured together at all points by metal connections, so that the longitudinal tie-rods introduced at the intermediate points are very much lighter than would otherwise have been advisable and yet are abundantly sufficient for their purpose. . . . [Comparisons of cost, durability, and weight with roofs of slate and lead, all of them very favorable to iron, then follow.] But the many valuable peculiarities belonging to iron for the purposes required, and at some of which peculiarities we have above glanced, should be held thoroughly decisive as to its employment in the erection of an edifice of which not only the architect in the present age, but the nation for many centuries, should be justified in feeling proud.

This roof is, however, considerably less bold an engineering feat than that which Baron and Martin had provided over the vaults of Chartres Cathedral in the previous decade. When inspected from inside it even has a makeshift air as if the iron members, and particularly the tie rods, had been cut to fit with giant shears. Yet this iron roof (whose characteristics were later much refined in those sections of the Palace built in the 50's and 60's) makes evident once more how remote was the architectural world of Barry from that of Pugin. As in designing the kitchens of the Reform Club, Barry always sought the best and most up-to-date technical advice. What he learned he incorporated in his buildings as a matter of course with no archaeological or ethical prejudices against new materials or new methods of using them.

But Barry was also determined that technical innovations should, when possible, contribute positively to the visual effect of his building. This desire to "communicate an architectural character to the very roof" presages, more than do high gabled roofs of the sort most Gothic Revivalists used in the 40's, the plastic massing so characteristic of the High Victorian modes of the later 50's and 60's. Gothic roofs would then rise even higher than the mansards that were borrowed from France.

By the end of 1844 the whole river range of the Palace complex was complete as regards its masonry walls and covered with the earliest of Barry's iron roofs. The corner towers and the end walls were carried up and roofed in the next year, as well as one side of New Palace Yard and the ground storey of the Victoria Tower. Since many of the pinnacles and turrets were not yet in place, these and much of the ornamental detail of the exterior stone paneling, such as the armorial bearings which fill so many of its rectangles, may well have been refined in their design by Pugin after the renewal of his association with Barry in 1844.

Yet the river front as everyone knows it (Fig. I 1), that endless reticulation of mullioned lights and carved panels in stone, accented by spire-like buttress tops and crowned with high iron roofs, should be considered as much Barry's as the original elevation of the 30's (Fig. II 25). For the relative solidity and the larger, more irregularly scaled, elements of the first design—recalling, as we have seen in Chapter II, both the fake castles and the Gothick churches of the previous age—Barry had substituted a treatment which expressed much more frankly the actual use of this part of the complex. What is this front in function but a range of offices in several storeys extending for some 600 feet? The windows, therefore, were made larger and more frequent than they could have been in either an Italian or a Decorated scheme that was "correctly" proportioned. But the all-over reticulation merged windows and piers into one continuous pattern in low relief, rhythmically phrased by the buttresses and the stronger vertical accents provided by the towers. This reticula-

276

tion seems curiously protomodern in its quite coincidental similarity to the continuous glass areas and the slight structural members of Paxton's Crystal Palace or to later metal skeleton buildings of the 90's and our own day. Yet it was derived by Barry from the architecture of the medieval past. Its origins are to be found not merely in the Late Gothic mode of Northern Europe in general, moreover, nor even in the usual Perpendicular and Tudor of England; this panel work in stone, with frequent inset lights, comes quite specifically from the Perpendicular of the Royal City of Westminster itself.

Very dry all-over stone paneling, interrupted by rectangular mullioned and transomed windows, is the prime characteristic of the exterior walls of Henry VII's Chapel which faces the New Palace from the east end of Westminster Abbey. But in the slightly later cloisters of St. Stephen's College, within the actual area of the New Palace itself to the east of Westminster Hall, Barry (or perhaps it was Pugin originally) had noted a more richly plastic and better scaled mode of treatment which could be developed for the New Palace walls (Fig. IX 7). There the bays consist of nothing but screens of mullions and tracery set in square-headed frames between buttresses and crowned by paneled and carved parapets. Nowhere more than at Westminster could the elaboration and extension of this wall treatment be so thoroughly justified by both historical propriety and a laudable desire for harmony with existing work. Moreover, there are those who believe today that the actual cradle of the Perpendicular, England's most original medieval style, was not at Gloucester but at St. Stephen's Chapel, later the original House of Commons, back in that Edwardian period Pugin vaunted as England's Golden Age.

It was in order to expedite the completion not of the exteriors of the Palace but of the Lords' Chamber that Barry sought and obtained the renewed assistance of Pugin in 1844. This House was therefore the first part of the complex to be made available for use. In February 1847 the peers transferred themselves there, without ceremony but with real relief to be out of their temporary quarters after a dozen uncomfortable years. In this House, which exists little changed today, there is every reason to recognize one of Pugin's most elaborate and complete achievements as a decorator (Fig. IX 8). One might well suspect that he was largely responsible for the basic architectural concept also, were it not for his own statement in a letter sent to the *Builder* in 1845 and published on 6 September. There he clearly stated the limits of his responsibilities as he then saw them.

I think it incumbent on me, in justice to Mr. Barry, to state that I am engaged by him, and by him alone, with the approval of the Government,* to assist in pre-

* This does not seem to agree with the fact that he received a direct governmental salary as Superintendent of the Works as well as payments from Barry.

paring working drawings and models from his designs of all the woodcarvings and other details of the internal decoration, and to procure models and drawings of the best ancient decorative work of the proper kind, wherever they are to be found, as specimens for the guidance of the workmen in respect of the taste and feeling to be imitated, to engage with artists and the most skillful men that can be procured in every branch of decorative art, and to superintend personally the practical execution of the duties of my office. *I do not do anything whatever on my own responsibility; all models and working drawings being prepared from Mr. Barry's designs, and submitted to him for his approval and alteration* [italics mine] previous to their being carried into effect; in fine, my occupation is simply to assist in carrying out practically Mr. Barry's own designs and views in all respects.

Even if a conspiracy to hide Barry's dependence on Pugin in 1835–36 is conceivable it would have been quite impossible psychologically to renew it after Pugin's return to collaboration in 1844. The letter is so categorical, as if written verbatim to Barry's dictation, that I suppose some sort of blackmail *might* lie behind it; but despite the burning of the letters by Barry later (a melodramatic act, if it was intentional) such an interpretation seems altogether too lurid an explanation. It must be assumed that Pugin meant what he said. Even on the decorations of the House of Lords (and presumably in other parts of the interior as on the exterior) he was no more than what we would call Barry's chief draftsman, not his designer. He was not, perhaps, as Frank Lloyd Wright has expressed his relation to Louis Sullivan in the early 90's, merely "the good pencil *in the master's hand*"—for Pugin was in no sense a disciple of Barry—yet he was but a superlatively "good pencil" here, no master in his own right, at least according to his own disclaimer.

The House of Lords, it will be recalled, lies deep in the grid of the New Palace, between the central Octagon and the south end. It is on the principal- or first-storey level and it rises through the full height of the second storey to an open timber roof below the external iron roof. It is approached along the main north and south axis from the Octagon through a corridor which leads to the Peers' Lobby, a square chamber whose paneled walls, loaded with armorial carving, resemble the richest portions of the river front (Fig. IX 9). Buttresses flank the great arches in the four walls and lead up through heavy curved brackets to the principal beams of the flat ceiling. At the intersections of the four beams, which are elaborately molded and enriched, hang bold carved pendants. Between the beams the ceiling is divided into small square panels by molded joists, each panel being decorated with one of the Royal floral badges surrounded by painted foliage. The treatment of this lobby announces the theme of panels-within-panels, of articulation both

278

structural and decorative, which was carried over into all the principal interiors from the reticulated pattern of the exterior walls.

The scale and spacial amplitude of the Upper Chamber itself is considerably greater than that of the lobby, of course, but the treatment is consonant (Fig. IX 8). Here the arched brackets supporting the principal beams of the flat ceiling rise not from buttresses but from piers set between the great arches around the sides. These arches contain clerestorey windows at their tops along the east and west walls of the chamber and enclose panels for tall murals at the two ends. The beams divide the ceiling into squares; these are then subdivided into smaller squares filled with panels grouped around central lozenges. The curved brackets are pierced with quatrefoil tracery; the beams are enriched with carved inscriptions; but the bosses at the intersections of the beams are much less bold than the pendants in the lobby. The consoles of the brackets rise out of the canopies of niches set against the heavy piers not out of solid buttresses. In the niches life-sized statues are set, repeating (probably by accident) a curious feature of old St. Stephen's Chapel. Thus the general effect is quite different from that of any part of the exterior as then executed, or even the contiguous lobby.

The rather high polish of the dark brown oak overhead, although picked out with color and gold, seems to extend upward the crispness of the wainscoting that lines the lower walls. By the extreme hardness and tightness of its forms the woodwork suggests that it might be of cast iron. Actually the only visible metalwork is the very open iron railing of the narrow gallery, which is carried around the chamber above a paneled cove, and the monumental brass candelabra that flank the throne.

The benches for the Lords, running down the sides in rising tiers, consist merely of plain back and seat cushions upholstered in buttoned leather; the historic woolsack in the center is equally simple in character. The chief feature of the interior, part furniture and part architecture, is the throne which rises against the south end (Fig. IX 10). On a low platform are set three chairs. The center one, with high gabled and crocketed back and a finial crown, was for the Queen; on either side two more modest and mobile chairs, with rounded backs of almost Empire design, were for the Prince Consort and the Prince of Wales.

Behind the Queen's chair rises a sort of secular reredos with the Royal arms and supporters carved within an arched central panel. There is much use of the monogram V.R. and of crowns in the surrounding panels. Projecting forward over this, like a peculiarly elaborate Perpendicular choir loft, is the throne canopy. This has a sort of pelmet of tracery below its lower edge and statue-filled niches above. The whole is spiked with buttress-like members which project upward as pinnacles and downward as narrow pendants.

Arched brackets carry the canopy well forward over the Queen's chair of state. The side wings are quite similar but lower and less projecting. These have paneled coves beneath the projecting upper portion of the canopy rather than a flat ceiling like the central bay.

At the time of the opening only one of the mural paintings, that just above the throne, was in place. Now, alas, all the panels are filled; for these are not happy testimonies to Albert's activity as chairman of the commission appointed in 1841 to advise on the decoration of the New Palace. (The recommendations were accepted by Parliament in 1847; the first appropriations finally followed in 1850.) Perhaps the commission should have confined the artists to copies after Raphael(!) or else imported the much admired contemporary mural painter Peter Cornelius from Germany.

Disagreement with the commission's recommendations in general, and more specifically with the plan for "reviving" the art of fresco painting by New Palace assignments to various contemporary English painters, must have been the cause of greater anguish to Barry—himself not a member of the commission—than were Dr. Reid and his ventilating systems; for no Gwilt could arbitrate with Royalty. Fortunately several of Barry's powerful Whig friends and private clients were members of the commission and could take his part, at least *in camera*. But this curious episode belongs more to the history of Victorian painting than to that of Victorian architecture. Steegman's account in *Consort of Taste* (1950), pp. 129–138, is fresh, informative, and by no means unsympathetic.

Behind the throne was the Victoria Lobby where the Queen halted to be appropriately robed before her first entrance into the House of Lords (Fig. IX 15). The Victoria Gallery beyond and the real Robing Room at the south end of the Palace were not completed until several years later. In the Victoria Lobby the wall and ceiling treatment was again of articulated and paneled character like that of the Chamber and the Peers' Lobby but without curved brackets to support the beam ends. A rather plain rectangular-windowed Perpendicular clerestorey along the sides provides excellent light. Above the carved wainscoting, and also higher up in the clerestorey zone, panels were left vacant for the ministrations of the commission's mural artists. The straightforward rectangular organization of the walls and ceilings of this room set the standard for most of the less monumental interiors of the Palace.

With the larger wall panels above the wooden wainscoting filled with Pugin's flock wallpapers of brocaded 15th-century design rather than with academic murals, and with the plain quarries of the window glass enlivened by his colored armorial vignettes, these interiors are in their way as successful as the exterior of the Palace, and for much the same reason. Of course both merely extend and elaborate the theme of paneled construction and design peculiar to the Perpendicular style. But the Perpendicular was much more suited to the emergent structural methods and the mechanized detail of the Victorian Age than were the cinquecento Italian or the English Decorated which were Barry's and Pugin's preferred vehicles of stylistic expression. The New Palace is considerably more "modern" in design than it well might have been, considering its authors.

The exteriors of the Lord's wing, rising along the sides of the contiguous interior courts, are of smooth and severe random ashlar and almost without paneling or other ornament, except for the battlements that crown the walls and a few modest stringcourses (Fig. IX 11). The traceried windows are sunk into the wall and the few buttresses are flat and matter of fact in character. In these interior courts—and they are all much alike, except for the restored Cloister Court—the smoother masonry, although of the same Anston stone, has survived better than the elaborate molded work and the carving of the outer fronts. Of frankly 19th-century character, the court façades are manifestly sound in construction and almost starkly straightforward in design.

When the House of Lords, with its lobbies, was opened early in 1847 it could hardly fail to be generally acceptable to contemporary opinion. Diehard enemies of the Gothic were still about; but on the whole a limited eclecticism now permitted a varied range of architectural modes with no strongly partisan rancor against one or the other. The New Palace was not in one of the fields of building currently conceded to the Gothic; yet its architect was recognized as the principal non-Gothic leader in the profession. On the other hand, with Pugin in charge of the Gothic detail, its "correctness" was undeniable even if it was admittedly anywhere from fifty to two hundred years too "late" in style. Enriched with painted polychromy according to the latest ecclesiological fashion by the master decorator who had introduced that fashion, the interior of the House of Lords offered a bouquet too colorful to be adversely criticized, at least for several more years.

Despite the inadequacy of the murals, of which one only was in place at the opening, the House of Lords (so far as one can tell today) realized better than any of Pugin's churches except St. Giles's, Cheadle, his polychromatic aspirations. Certainly the carved and polished oak is even today very agreeable, for all its mechanical hardness of finish, compared to the stained and varnished pitchpine with which most Early Victorian church builders had to content themselves. The plates in Pugin's *Floriated Ornament*, moreover, abstracting as they do his pure sense of pattern from his usually somewhat excessive use of it, indicates that he was no unworthy predecessor of William Morris in this field of decoration in flat color. To modern eyes, moreover, the paintwork and the gilt have gained more than they have lost by the mellowing of a century. Doubtless the rather heavy, muted tonality is not

281

very medieval or really quite what Pugin intended; but the glitter and the sharp contrasts that contemporaries originally admired would probably seem harsh or garish to us now (as for that matter would most real Perpendicular polychromy if we knew it in its original state).

On the exterior of the river front a more pre-Victorian feeling was, and still is, evident; yet the softening of the carved detail, due to the erosion of the Anston stone, has provided to later eyes a rather plausibly medieval aura. Except perhaps for the river front, however, the New Palace as a whole, and not merely the House of Lords, may be considered rather characteristic of the mid-40's. Visually (if not perhaps from the point of view of physical maintenance) it has aged better than many edifices that were considered at the time to represent a higher or a "purer" artistic achievement. If a single date need be chosen to represent the precise "period" of this vast and slowly built structure in its most significant aspect, that date should be c. 1845. But of course it must be remembered that only a portion of the Palace was actually complete at this time; many changes in the general design would be made during the score of years that passed before the work finally came to a close.

The next major date in the history of the New Palace after 1847 is 1852, when the House of Commons was officially opened. This date coincides with the death of Pugin, which followed rapidly on his madness and was due in part to overwork on the endless details of the Palace. Frequently 1852 is incorrectly considered to represent the time of the whole building's completion. That is partly because the Commons are thought of as being "Parliament"; once they were housed the Westminster job might seem to have been done. But it is also partly because of the dramatic irony implicit in Pugin's death at this point. The knighting of Barry in 1852 evidences official recognition that a significant milestone had been passed. With the main portions of the building finished, moreover, the continuing stages of construction leading up to ultimate completion necessarily seem somewhat anticlimactic.

The events between the opening of the Upper House and of the Lower should now be sketched in some detail before the Lower House itself is described. In 1848 the central Octagon was proceeding to completion, the many elaborate bosses of the lierne vault then being carved *in situ* by Grissell's workmen. Like all the sculpture on the Palace these bosses were executed according to models that John Thomas prepared from Pugin's working drawings. On the exterior the Victoria Tower was now well above the roofs of the rest of the building. Its ultimate height was not determined even yet, however; hence the intended design of the upper stages must still have been fluid. But the cathedral-front character of the lowest stage, as first designed in 1835–36, and the broad proportions of the paneled upper storeys had given way to elevations that are at once more homogeneous and more authentically Perpendicular than before. The new design was neither ecclesiastical nor keep-like in character.

Despite its great size, the Victoria Tower as executed is rather a close relative of the collegiate towers of the 15th century. Heavy paneled corner turrets, octagonal in plan, flank the arches on the west and south sides of the bottom stage (Fig. IX 12). These arches are deep sunk and many ordered because of the enormous thickness of the walls at this level. Tracery filled with armorial achievements occupies the great spandrels; while the multiple orders of the arches themselves are divided by a rich band of pierced carving that rises to the Royal arms, supported by angels, set at the peak of the arch. The armorial and foliate carving, which at first sight seems so characteristic of the 19th century in its crispness and hardness, proves on comparison to be little more mechanical or repetitious than the similar Tudor ornaments across the road at Henry VII's Chapel, or in King's College Chapel, Cambridge.

Perpendicular England had prefigured certain aspects of 19th-century England. A highly centralized architectural bureaucracy together with efficiently organized carving shops had induced a mechanistic—almost a prefabricated—approach toward design on the part of the Royal architects. Henry Yevele need not have been ashamed of the work of his 19th-century successors at Westminster. Hugh Herland should have approved Barry's iron roofs; the medieval master carpenter might well have used iron principals for the magnificent roof of Westminster Hall had foundries of 19th-century scale existed to supply him.

Above the entrance arches of the Victoria Tower comes a solid stage completely occupied by paneled niches filled with statues. Next above this is a very tall stage, just rising in the late 40's, with three great windows, each divided by a central mullion. But the final completion of the tower still lay a long way ahead, and discussion of it must be put off awhile.

The revision of the design of the lower and middle stages of the tower must have been initiated by Barry in the early 40's although it was probably further refined—and doubtless much improved—by Pugin after 1844. The sumptuous interior of the porch under the tower, however, with its ranges of statue-filled niches set between the door arches and the wall arches and the elaborate lierne vault above, should be quite definitely Barry's; for its design must have been determined before the construction of the base of the tower began and yet would hardly have been completely detailed in the drawings of 1835–36 on which Pugin first worked.

Late in 1849 the House of Commons was structurally complete in the form seen in a wood engraving published by the *Builder* in January 1850

(Fig. IX 13). The interior was very similar in its main lines to that of the other House. The same clerestorey extended along the sides, with a very narrow gallery below, and the ceiling was divided by heavy beams into great squares which were themselves paneled with smaller squares. The coupled clerestorey windows were more domestic in scale and had Tudor four-centered arches; the very modest curved brackets at the beam ends rested on engaged columns which were set on consoles above the wainscoting behind the galleries. A modest canopied chair for the Speaker stood forth from the north wall; this took the same place as a visual focus of authority as did the elaborate throne and canopy in the House of Lords. Like the peers, the Commons were to sit on rising tiers of plain leather-upholstered benches facing one another across a central aisle, quite in the way they had always done since they first settled at Westminster.

This peculiar disposition, unfamiliar in republican legislative chambers, deserves further comment. (A fuller account will be found in Maurice Hastings' "The House of Commons," *Architectural Review, 108,* 161–176, and in his book *Parliament House* [1951]). St. Stephen's Chapel, which the 1834 fire destroyed, had been for centuries the traditional home of the House of Commons. In origin this was the Royal chapel of the medieval New Palace to which a college or religious brotherhood of St. Stephen had been attached after 1348. The college occupied part of the precinct of the Palace including the cloisters which were to be restored by Barry as the Cloister Court. At the Reformation the Crown took back the college buildings as it did all other properties of religious orders, and the chapel became from the mid-16th century the regular seat of the Lower House. Later the chapel was remodeled into a sort of Queen Anne meetinghouse, with a flat plaster ceiling below the old Gothic vaults and handsome wainscoting designed by Wren. But the original narrow shape of the edifice could not easily be changed and the seating retained its earlier collegiate arrangement. From the rising tiers of benches on both sides Georgian Whigs and Tories had long faced one another across a neutral strip over which the Speaker presided, like a contemporary parson, from a high-backed chair at one end. Narrow galleries—supported on iron columns, it is interesting to note—provided only the most exiguous accommodation for visitors.

This disposition, which allowed great intimacy of debate and stressed the relatively even balance of Government and Opposition forces, was absolutely insisted on for the new House; so Barry was firmly instructed, again and again, by all the leading officials whenever he proposed to change any particular. The general effect of the "advice" he received was "greatly to diminish the dimensions originally proposed, both for the accommodation of the House and the public," his son informs us. As to ladies (for whom a separate

284

gallery was eventually provided after 1870, a significant date), according to Hastings Lord Brougham had only been willing to admit that he "liked to see them in their proper place," which in his estimation was *not* attending Parliamentary debates. Lord Lansdowne added more sternly: "Ladies are not mentioned in this Report, and, so far as I can prevent it, they never shall be!" The Early Victorians might be ruled by a Queen but they were no feminists. (Curiously enough, abbesses and such had regularly sat in pre-Reformation Parliaments.)

The postwar rebuilding of the House has maintained the principles of the traditional layout with only a minimal increase in the accommodations. (But the ladies, of course, had broken most of the barriers set up against them, except in the Smoking Rooms, long before 1941.) As the *Blue Book* in which the debates and decisions of the Commons in this matter were reported after World War II makes evident, the new House is in more than one sense an example of legislative architecture. The architects of the Ministry of Works were required to execute the job according to a plan whose dimensions were laid down by legislative vote and with even less leeway than Barry was ever allowed. Gilbert Scott's grandson Sir Giles Scott, playing the part of Pugin, was only hired to spray on timid Gothic detail, while one nonprofessional member even provided a drawing of his own for a chamber like a Jacobean great hall.

The Victorian Lords, earlier more intransigent than the Commons toward Barry, seem to have been quite pleased with the comforts provided in their House after being released from a dozen years of makeshift accommodation. But the Commons, long snug enough in the old House of Lords, first entered their new chamber somewhat reluctantly in 1850 and at once became extremely critical; two years more passed before the changes they demanded could be made and the House finally opened for use. More accommodation in the galleries and surrounding corridors was first of all requested, something which Barry easily supplied (perhaps with a muttered "I told you so"). Since the members believed the low ceiling of the old House of Lords explained its superior acoustics, the Commons also insisted that Barry must lower the ceiling of the new chamber. This change he made very grudgingly, not because it would increase the fire hazard (as seems to have been proved a fact in 1941) but because a lower ceiling would (in his estimation) ruin the proportions. Whether he was right in this it is too late to judge now; however, after the clerestorey windows were cut to less than half their original height the light that entered through them was certainly much reduced (Fig. IX 14).

The new up-sloping paneled roof with its central flat had a carpenter-like directness about it that was not unpleasing. For all of Pugin's rich stenciling in the panels, the total effect was intimate, even domestic, in scale in contrast to the monumental grandeur of the House of Lords. The oaken colonnettes that carried the widened galleries on crossed brackets at their top, despite very Gothic detailing, had something of the lightness of Wren's cast-iron supports in St. Stephen's Chapel. Moreover, the great metal gasoliers hanging down from the intersections of the roof beams indicated how well Pugin could cope with the new needs of the 19th century when he was forced to do so.

The objections to Barry's new House were functional rather than aesthetic —the members even brought back briefly the truculent Dr. Reid in an effort to improve the ventilation. Yet I think their objections also reflected some dissatisfaction with the frank expression of articulation and the consistent repetition of similar elements which to modern taste might seem the chief visual virtues of the Lower Chamber. Just the qualities that made the Commons a more satisfying 19th-century work to 20th-century eyes than the less businesslike House of Lords were undoubtedly what Victorians really disliked about it. There can have been few members in the early 50's other than Beresford-Hope who knew exactly what they would have preferred to have different about the new House; yet a change of taste, almost as drastic as the one that had come ten years before under Pugin's leadership, was definitely occurring at just this time (Chapter XVII).

To anyone who had read Ruskin's *Seven Lamps*, which had appeared in 1849, or the first volume of his *Stones of Venice* when that came out in 1851, it must have been at once evident that the new Parliament House did not manifest the true "Spirit of the Gothic." The cloven Renaissance hoof of Barry was not, for Ruskin's readers, disguised by Pugin's surface polychromy and carved ornament. That decoration might follow medieval models with meticulous accuracy; but it was certainly not executed by pious workmen freely exercising their own fantasy; therefore the "feeling" could not be right according to Ruskin.

One doubts that the Queen had as yet read the architectural criticism of the brilliant young "Graduate of Oxford." Her Consort, moreover, had been busy in 1850–51 with a building even more obnoxious to Ruskin, the Crystal Palace. The Royal couple will not have been disappointed in the Palace they did not live in; it was at least more up to date than their own London residence. (Technically the Queen might not enter the Lower House; but I suspect she arranged to see it incognito. Certainly Albert knew it intimately, since he was involved in arranging for the murals.) When the Queen, on Albert's arm, started up the Royal Staircase once more from the Victoria Porch to open Parliament in 1852 there was much to impress her (Fig. IX 16). The Robing Room and the Victoria Gallery, unavailable five years before, were now gratifyingly ready for her use. At this time the chief decorations of the Victoria Gallery were on the ceiling which was of the usual cross-beamed type. The beams had carved inscriptions along their sides, and their curved brackets rested on engaged octagonal columns between the paired clerestorey windows (Fig. IX 17). Albert doubtless pointed out to her how much more edifying this and all the other interiors would be when the large paintings for which his commission was arranging were finally in place. If she had a surreptitious view of the House of Commons she must have recognized in its smaller scale and less monumental character a proper subordination to the prerogatives of the Lords.

The central Octagon was now complete and must have pleased the Queen (Fig. IX 18). Archaeologically speaking it is one of the most successful interiors of the Palace, suaver and less experimental than the bold medieval octagon at Ely if also much less of an engineering feat because of its smaller dimensions. The elaborate mosaic of Minton tiles on the floor is one of the largest examples of a peculiarly Victorian art-manufacture. The gold mosaic by Salviati in the vaulting compartments had not as yet been installed.

While Victoria had to follow a prescribed Royal route into the Palace, beginning at the porch under the tower which was named for her, the public method of entrance was and is actually much more dramatic. Arriving in New Palace Yard at the north end of Westminster Hall (whose low-gabled façade had by 1852 been rather clumsily adjusted to the richly reticulated walls of the Palace on the left), one advances down the whole empty length of the Hall under the wonderful hammerbeam trusses of Herland. Ahead a noble flight of steps rises through a tall arch into St. Stephen's Porch (Fig. IX 21). The south side of the so-called porch, immediately ahead, is a tremendous window-wall under another wide arch; here the line of advance changes direction sharply to turn onto the central east and west axis of Barry's new complex.

Since the Porch is symbolically the main west entrance to the New Palace, marking externally this central axis, it will be well to halt a moment to consider what it looks like from the outside. Because the Porch had to terminate the old Hall at its south end, the principal front faces south toward Old Palace Yard, with only a narrow façade on the west, and the composition as a whole is normally seen from the southwest (Fig. IX 20). The main feature is the great south window; this is necessarily set high because the interior of the Porch is on the principal or first-floor level of the Palace well above the low ground level of the medieval Hall. This window appears internally as a great oblong area of glass subdivided by mullions and transoms and terminating at the top in tracery under a flattened arch. Externally it forms the center of an elaborate composition almost like that of an entrance portal.

Above the window rises a tall paneled gable and on either side, at the east and west corners of the Porch, are turrets of considerable size. These turrets open out at the top in two traceried stages of almost spire-like elaboration under S-curved terminal features. Additional pinnacles at the peak and base of the south gable and also of the narrower west gable produce a general silhouette that is at once plastic and confused. This plasticity and this confusion are curiously out of character with the treatment of the wall of the main block, at right angles to the porch, which continues along the west side of Old Palace Yard to the Victoria Tower. This treatment, while more elaborate even than that of the river front, is also more mechanically regular, while the design of the Porch can only be described as turgidly picturesque.

On whom should this turgidity be blamed, Barry or Pugin? Only the large mullioned window and the paneled gable over it go back to the early design of 1835–36. The general architectural effect, with which the flatness and regularity of the reticulation of the window and the surrounding walls is hardly consonant, seems a conscious attempt to meet the new taste of the mid-century. Someone—could it have been Barry's son Edward?—was apparently seeking to emulate the bolder and more irregular handling of Gothic forms in Butterfield's first London churches, rising at just this time (see Chapter XVII). The result is nothing like Butterfield's work, of course; but it is even less like anything Barry or Pugin had ever done before; in many ways it suggests a young and inexperienced hand.

Returning to the interior of the Porch and turning to the left, one next comes into St. Stephen's Hall (occupying the original position of St. Stephen's Chapel) and through that to the central Octagon where the ordinary visitor's path joins the Queen's. The Hall agrees very well in design with the Octagon (Fig. IX 19). There is the same highly competent lierne vaulting, and the tracery in the great side windows is even more "correct" in its Perpendicular design. G. F. Bodley need hardly have been ashamed to design this Hall in the 70's; while American architects in the 1920's were still trying to do the same sort of thing at the leading universities. Of the present dreary population of statues, looking like petrified lobbyists, only a few were in place by 1852; they were always even more out of place than the top-hatted Victorians who admire them in contemporary views.

Closer in character to the House of Commons itself are the libraries and the refreshment room of the House of Lords, all in the range along the east front, which were completed and opened in the early 50's. In the two libraries, well lighted by their many mullioned windows facing the river, the general effect is particularly warm and rich (Fig. IX 22). The dark oak woodwork, not excessively elaborate in detail, frames very pleasantly the shelves filled with handsomely bound books that line the walls. Above the bookcases a frieze of square panels contains some of the most agreeable of Pugin's armorial achievements; these are quite like engraved book plates in design and colored with real heraldic vigor. Like the stenciled patterns in the panels of the ceiling, they were executed, as was all the color work in the Palace, by the decorator J. G. Crace after Pugin's designs. The patterns are smaller in scale here and more wallpaper-like than in the large interiors; but in their rather domestic way they have something of the charm of the plates in Pugin's *Floriated Ornament*. As has been said, the furnishings in these rooms, down to the very calendars mounted on the inkstands, are all from Pugin's designs turned out under tremendous pressure in the very last year or so of his life. Such things are touchingly illustrative of his conscientiousness. More objectively considered, they are also preferable to the ecclesiastical metalwork then being made to his designs in Birmingham.

The refreshment room for the Lords is simpler than the two libraries. A handsome flock wallpaper in a brocaded pattern designed by Pugin covered the walls below a curious diagonal cove of traceried panels running around the edge of the paneled ceiling. The other refreshment room, for the Commons, is simpler still. The heavily pelmeted curtains suggest that Crace, the decorator, had a fairly free hand here, for they seem more typical of Victorian upholsterers' taste than of Pugin's.

There is of course no end to the corridors, lobbies, and committee rooms that fill the vast grid of the Palace. Some of the more modest interiors, with carved oak wainscoting at the base of the flock-papered walls and lightly paneled wooden ceilings, are very agreeable in the way of the libraries and even more unpretentiously domestic. But the consistency and thoroughness with which the decoration was carried out is really astounding. In general the effect is fairly acceptable to modern eyes, just because of that Early Victorian "neatness" which made the work retardataire when it was executed in the 50's.

By 1855 the Victoria Tower had risen another stage. A second row of tall windows now appeared above those that had just been begun in 1849. Still its ultimate height had not been decided. By this time also a light open lantern, rising high above the Octagon, clearly marked the actual center of the Palace without competing in height or solidity with the two great end towers (Fig. IX 23). Largely of metal and looking very metallic, this shows none of the desire apparent in St. Stephen's Porch to meet the more advanced tastes of the time; instead it rather resembles that iron central spire of Rouen Cathedral which Ruskin so much abominated.

289

The Clock Tower is certainly the most widely known visual symbol for the entire Palace; like the sound of "Big Ben" which hangs there, it even stands for London and at times for the whole British Empire (Fig. IX 23). This feature was the cause of as much trouble to Barry as the House of Commons (which he in fact disowned after he had to obey instructions and lower the ceiling). From the first the north tower had been intended to carry a great clock. Early in 1844 Barry, on the instructions of the Board of Works, accepted an offer from Vulliamy of Pall Mall, a well-known clockmaker, to make a design for this clock. Two years later, however, the government decided to hold a competition for the clock, and E. T. Dent of London and Whitehurst of Derby, as well as Vulliamy, were invited to enter. Since Vulliamy believed that the Astronomer Royal, who was to be the referee, was already committed to Dent, he refused to enter; in fact it was to Dent that the Astronomer Royal recommended in 1847 that the commission for the clock should be given. Vulliamy did not give up hope, however, but continued preparatory work on his clock, undoubtedly with Barry's private encouragement. The next year Edmund Beckett-Denison, a prominent member of Parliament who was an amateur horologist, entered the scene on the side of Dent. Eventually in 1851 the Chief Commissioner of Works requested Beckett-Denison and the Astronomer Royal together to prepare specifications for a clock which should be built by Dent.

The tower had been begun in 1843 and the shaft had already reached a height of 150 feet when it was suddenly realized that its internal dimensions (11 feet by 8½ feet) were too small to allow the Dent clock to be hoisted up into place at the top. Since the shaft could hardly be enlarged without rebuilding the tower, the outer dimensions of the clock had to be reduced. In the new Tory Ministry of 1857 Lord John Manners became Chief Commissioner of Works. He proposed a new set of referees in the matter of the clock, of whom Barry was to be one. Correspondence of an increasingly heated nature was flying in all directions and Lord John had suggested that Robert Stephenson, the great engineer, should be made an additional neutral referee when Dent, to the dismay of his supporters, inconsiderately died. Dent's heir claimed that the contract had descended to him. Fortunately for him the Tory Ministry had by that time fallen and Sir William Molesworth, the new Liberal Chief Commissioner, accepted the Dent claim. The younger Dent completed the clock in 1858. Then it was discovered that the clock could not be installed until after the bells had been hung above it, and it was not finally set up until the next year. Big Ben, the largest and best known of the bells, was first cast in 1856; twice it cracked, occasioning quite unjustified attacks by Beckett-Denison on Barry; but finally it

290

was perfectly cast and put in place to provide what has come to seem almost the necessary equivalent in sound of the famous tower in which it hangs.

Trying as the clock controversy was for Barry, more trying really than that with Dr. Reid, its details should help to determine when and by whom the tower was designed. In the 1835–36 project the two tall end towers are the only parts of the whole vast complex that can be attributed with any plausibility, as regards their over-all design and not merely their ornamental details, to Pugin (Figs. II 22–23). But by the time the construction of the Palace actually started in 1840 the whole scheme of the north front, as of that on the south, had been changed by Barry during the years when Pugin was in no way involved with the Palace. No longer were the corner pavilions to be two towered; while the section of curtain wall between the northeast corner pavilion and the Clock Tower was now to be treated very similarly to the river front. When the Clock Tower began to rise in 1843, the year before Pugin returned to collaborate on the Palace, the new design used for the shaft must also have been all Barry's. Ten years later, however, toward the end of 1854, when the greater portion of the clock cage had been completed, it became evident that the silhouette of the tower would be most unusual, for the walls of the clock stage already overhung the shaft below. It is this bulbous termination which gives the tower its rather special character.

Negotiations for the clock between Barry and Vulliamy began, as we have seen, early in 1844. At any time in the eight years between the fall of 1844 when Pugin began to assist Barry again and Pugin's death in 1852 he could have supplied Barry with a new design for the unbuilt upper stage of the tower; and this he almost certainly did. Since the difficulty about the excessive size of the Dent clock in relation to the internal dimensions of the shaft of the tower became evident only in 1851, the necessity of enlarging the clock stage itself may not have been considered earlier than this. But there would still have been time, before Pugin's ultimate madness in 1852, for him to make the final drawings. What seems to clinch the matter is that the termination of the tower, as it was finally executed in the mid-50's after Pugin's death, is almost identical (as has been remarked in an earlier chapter) with that of the clock tower at Scarisbrick Hall before its elaboration by Pugin's son Edward (Fig. VIII 2). Thus for the design of this prominent feature of the Palace—which must certainly be considered a matter of architecture and not merely of decoration—Pugin seems to deserve more credit than Barry. His name can properly be attached, I believe—as in justice it should be—to the most familiar element of the whole complex, even though he never saw even the beginning of the construction of the section above the shaft. The heavy internal iron frame used to carry the bells in the belfry stage and the completely metal construction of the roof are as certainly Barry's idea (Fig. IX 25). The way this roof curves up in two slopes separated by an open stage to a spire-like point is peculiarly Puginian, however; thus the curiously cast-iron bent of Pugin's talent found expression finally in the material which he so incontinently scorned.

Of most other aspects of the Palace as it came to completion little need be said. The already mentioned façade toward Old Palace Yard (Fig. IX 20), however, with its alternation of tall oriels and flat bays divided by rectangular paneled buttresses, is the most interesting section of the exterior in some ways being almost as much a continuous window-wall as one finds in certain manor houses of around 1600. (Phoebe Stanton states that sketches for it by Pugin exist even though this portion of the Palace was not built for nearly a decade after his death.) The regular undulation of the wall plane forward and backward is most original; it is also curiously premonitory of Holabird and Roche's treatment of the Tacoma Building, built in Chicago in 1887–89, the first skyscraper to take advantage of a supporting metal skeleton in the design of the exterior; or even of Burnham and Root's more completely glazed Reliance Building of 1890–94, where the spandrels are all paneled with Late Gothic tracery. Considering this similarity, and noting the internal iron skeleton construction Barry used not only in the Clock Tower but also in the upper part of the Victoria Tower, a curious thought presents itself: Several of the essential ingredients of the skyscraper were already present at Westminster in the 50's! Rising altogether a dozen or more storeys to a height actually greater than that of the earlier American skyscrapers, the masonry walls of the Victoria Tower presumably could not stand firm against wind pressure except for the reinforcement provided by the metal skeleton inside. Barry and Pugin thus came very close in the latest portions of this vast masonry monument to both the structural and the visual characteristics of some of the first skyscrapers. Only in the 60's and 70's, and then very sporadically, was the logic of their separate thinking linked together by a few English commercial architects, most of them entirely unknown. The true skyscraper story begins across the Atlantic just as the New Palace was finally being brought to completion in the mid-60's.

Between the traceried finials of the octagonal corner turrets of the Victoria Tower a tall iron roof rises. This is partially masked by an elaborate pierced and battlemented parapet of stone and capped by a crown of open metal arches. As executed this is all somewhat fussier and less massive than what Barry, in 1858 at least, seems to have intended (Figs. I 1, IX 24). But the termination reveals (fortunately rather inconspicuously) that the Palace was finally finished not by Barry but by his son Edward.

The Speaker's House, opened early in 1859, was probably the last important section of the Palace entirely completed before Barry's death. The handsome large reception rooms here have a broader scale than the earlier rooms that Pugin decorated; but they are almost equally remote in their calm dignity from what High Victorians were demanding by this date. The crypt of St. Stephen's Chapel under St. Stephen's Hall, restored in the early 60's by the younger Barry, is the only part of the New Palace where heavy architectural membering—actually mostly original but nevertheless much emphasized in the restoration—and loud polychromy cater to the tastes of the generation that took Ruskin and Viollet-le-Duc for its prophets.

To summarize: Westminster New Palace, although first designed before Victoria came to the throne and not completed until the mid-60's, is stylistically an Early Victorian monument of the 40's. It is all but completely the work of Sir Charles Barry, its commissioned architect, and of A. N. W. Pugin, his collaborator in decoration, to whom the design of its most idiosyncratic architectural feature, the upper part of the Clock Tower, may properly be attributed. Even though Barry and Pugin were the two leading English architects of the period, the Palace is by no means characteristically Early Victorian, nor is it characteristic of the best work of either Barry or Pugin. Yet it is not improper to consider the Palace the most conspicuous single monument of the Victorian Age, or even its prime symbol, provided Barry's masterly organization of the plan and of the external façades as well as his little-appreciated and largely invisible use of iron are recognized to have equal significance with Pugin's carved and painted embellishments.

English architecture would have been the poorer had not Barry's iron roofs and the devoted attentions of fire-watchers protected the Palace from destruction during World War II. The portion which was burned in the blitz, the House of Commons, has been memorialized as a ruin by the distinguished painter John Piper; but it had been disowned by its architect long ago and was the least loss the edifice could have suffered. The form in which the House of Commons has been replaced does no honor to 20th-century architecture. The building as a whole, on the other hand, continues to serve admirably the principal purposes for which it has proved, through a century now, to have been so well designed. Those purposes were and are symbolic as well as practical. Barry was not afraid to accept a national responsibility and to build, with Pugin's help, a national monument.

We must now turn to other government commissions of the Early Victorian period. Even though none of them approaches in importance the Houses of Parliament, they are more typical of the general stylistic developments of the 40's.

Pennethorne's projected London improvements of 1838 were in the realm of city planning rather than of government architecture. But supervising them occupied most of his time, particularly after 1843 when he became sole Architect and Surveyor to the Commissioners of Woods and Forests and gave up private practice entirely. He also did some actual building in the New Oxford Street he was laying out; that will be referred to later in the chapters (XI–XII) devoted to commercial architecture. In addition to opening up various other new streets, Pennethorne was also responsible in the 40's for the layout of Victoria Park to the east of London and of Battersea Park to the southwest. His first actual public building and his finest work, the Museum of Practical Geology with façades in Piccadilly and in Jermyn Street, was very slow in taking form. Projected in the mid-40's, and possibly even earlier, construction began only in 1847. The building seems to have been largely complete by the next year when the director Henry de la Bêche received a knighthood; yet it was not actually opened until 1851. Before describing it, the general character of earlier 19th-century museums in London should at least be recalled.

The National Gallery had been designed by William Wilkins, who won the commission in a limited competition; it went forward slowly to completion over the years 1832–38. But this museum for paintings met with so little contemporary approval that ambitious Victorian architects were always preparing projects either for replacing it or for hiding it away (like Buckingham Palace) behind a new façade. Through most of the 40's Sir Robert Smirke was proceeding with the British Museum, but with no stylistic modification of his original Grecian design of the early 20's. The familiar southern colonnade was completed only in 1847, although the King's Library on the east had been begun as far back as 1823. The gradual completion of the exterior and the opening one by one of the various galleries were greeted with no particular enthusiasm by the Early Victorians. But the building, less conspicuously located than the National Gallery in any event, was so austere and dignified that it aroused no such malicious criticism as Wilkins' Gallery in Trafalgar Square. It was, moreover, manifestly much better planned for its mixed use as a library and a museum of varied antiquities than was Wilkins' edifice for showing paintings.

Pennethorne's Geological Museum was the first cultural monument of the Victorian Age to be sponsored by the State, and it met with not unjustified approval. On the Piccadilly side the two-storey façade of stone rose well above the neighboring four-storey houses, just as the new banks and insurance buildings in the City were doing in the late 40's (see Chapter XI). The ground floor formed a continuous chamfered arcade with deeply recessed windows between semioctagonal piers; the entrance was in the rear façade in Jermyn Street. The very plastically articulated lower storey toward Piccadilly was firmly framed by rusticated bands at the ends and by an entablature above (Fig. IX 27). The upper storey was treated rather as a solid palace front, with six large windows capped with pediments below a wide expanse of plain wall. Rusticated quoins at the corners and a bold cornice crowned with a plain parapet completed a composition remarkable for breadth of scale, regularity, and dignity.

The Jermyn Street façade was less happily proportioned, partly because the lower street level made it very tall and partly because of the wide spacing of the openings—here only five in each storey instead of six (Fig. IX 26). The walling on this rear façade was of pale gauged Colchester brick, superb technically but too flat and too similar in tone to the Anston stone dressings to provide much interest of texture or color. The high podia under the first-storey windows overemphasized the excessive storey heights, while the enormous brackets under the ground-storey sills introduced a boldness of relief not matched elsewhere on the façade except in the crowning cornice two storeys above. Had the bronze doors which Alfred Stevens designed for the Museum been executed, their rich sculptural interest might have made up for the excessive severity of the rest of the façade. As with most other attempts to utilize the great talent of this fine sculptor, the project fell through because of governmental parsimony.

The ground storey was mostly occupied by a horseshoe-shaped lecture theater in the center. Behind that, and lighted by the pseudo-arcade in Piccadilly, were the library and the offices. Two lines of Doric columns carrying very flat segmental arches divided the entrance hall on the Jermyn Street side. Here various British marbles were handsomely displayed.

The upper storey consisted almost entirely of a single enormous gallery (Fig. IX 29). This was surrounded by case-lined bays that opened onto the main floor and the two ranges of upper balconies. The whole space was covered by a semielliptical roof carried on cast-iron beams, with ranges of skylights set in shaped sashbars of wrought iron running down the center and around the haunches (Fig. IX 28). No major elements of structural ironwork were visible: The skylight openings as well as the intervening panels were conventionally surrounded by heavy plaster moldings, and the vertical supports were sheathed to make them appear like clustered pilasters. Nevertheless the interior did illustrate a remarkably frank articulation of interior structure; and the light iron balconies, with their delicate ornamental railings, at least suggested the particular material which made the treatment possible. Although the result represented a compromise, it was closer to the adventurous iron and glass court of Bunning's contemporary Coal Exchange (Fig. X 14) than to the heavy trabeated interiors of Smirke's British Museum.

The construction of the other important government edifice which Penne-thorne projected in the 40's, the Record Office off Chancery Lane, was even more delayed than that of the Geological Museum. But this building was closely involved in various unexecuted schemes for new streets in that part of London. Partly in deference to the medieval origin of the earliest records and their then location in such medieval monuments as the Tower of London and the chapter house of Westminster Abbey—but more, doubtless, because of the stylistic character of the New Palace—a Gothic or at least an Elizabethan design seems to have been in Pennethorne's mind as early as 1847. (Even before that, in 1844, he was building Jacobethan houses nearby.) By the time the Record Office was actually begun in 1851 the technical requirements of the fireproof construction, with wrought-iron girders carrying brick jack-arches, and the arbitrarily determined dimensions of the internal depository cells, each 15 feet tall with an iron mezzanine gallery, chiefly determined the external expression. As a result the exterior is more completely and regularly articulated than that of any other contemporary monumental building— or any commercial building either, for that matter (Fig. IX 30). Iron-mullioned and transomed lights in each of the three tall double storeys fill the entire width of the bays between the buttress-like vertical piers.

The way the piers are linked above the top-storey windows by segmental-pointed arches is rather clumsy, almost suggesting the heavy hand of E. B. Lamb. The extreme weight of the plain wall above the arches, coming so far forward of the sash-plane, is hardly relieved by the paneled parapet that ornaments the top. Although the façade toward the proposed new street on the north should have had a considerable grandeur, flanked as it was to be by pairs of towers like the river front of Barry's Palace, the Record Office as executed is actually more like a huge warehouse than a monumental public building. But it quite lacks the distinction of fine materials, finely put together, which the best Manchester warehouses of the day had (see Chapter XII). Instead of the red brick that Pennethorne had originally intended to use here, as on his earlier Jacobethan houses, Kentish ragstone was substituted, providing horrid crumbly rubble surfaces such as are to be seen on most of the Early Victorian churches of London. The Anston stone trim was very coarsely treated also, with none of Pugin's metallic elegance. This rather unsuccessful exploitation of a Late Gothic theme in near-commercial work may well have discouraged others from developing a similar type of design for ordinary warehouses. Construction went forward very slowly down to Pennethorne's death. The west end toward Chancery Lane, which is all anyone generally notices today, was erected by Sir John Taylor (1833–1912) only in the last years of the century.

After the mid-50's Pennethorne's activity as a government architect increased with the general revival of building in London. But at least in date, if not very consistently in style, his work of the later 50's and 60's belongs to the succeeding period. One more London work of his that was entirely completed as early as 1851 may be described here. Despite its modest size, this edifice, which was merely an addition to the Ordnance Office in Pall Mall, illustrated a far higher level of Early Victorian accomplishment than the bold and ingenious but quite graceless Record Office. It also had an originality that is quite lacking in Pennethorne's additions to Somerset House on the west (begun in 1852) to house the Inland Revenue Office; for these additions quite properly continue (and with considerable success) the eclectic late 18th-century mode of Sir William Chambers' vast complex. The Ordnance Office was a three-bayed Italian palace design of great severity, but not at all in Barry's familiar vein. Four storeys high, with rusticated bands at the corners and a simple but heavy cornice below the visible roof, the most unusual feature was the treatment of the basement windows (Fig. IX 31). Very heavy continuous archivolts linked three low arches in an almost Syrian way. The wall surfaces were of finely laid pale-colored brick as on the rear of the Geological Museum; but the stone trim was simpler and bolder in relief. This façade made its mark in the Street of Clubs by the clarity and the breadth of its design.

Pennethorne's Office of the Duchy of Cornwall in Buckingham Gate, across from his ballroom entrance to Buckingham Palace, is a rich and yet rather tawdry example of palazzo design. There seem to be too many edicular windows in the principal storey; and the entrance, in a broad diagonal bay where the street turns a corner, is much too elaborate and fussy. Here, as in the ballroom itself, Pennethorne was doubtless influenced by the taste of his Royal patrons more than at the Ordnance Office.

Although no more than an added room, the new Sorting Office at the General Post Office was a remarkable piece of metal construction not intended to be seen by the public (Fig. IX 32). The floor, which was above a portion of the original building built by Sir Robert Smirke in the 20's, was hung by iron rods from tremendous arched trusses of iron in the roof. The architect was Smirke's brother Sydney. Such new post-office construction as was exposed to the public gaze continued for the most part to be Grecian. The few provincial post offices that were actually built in the early and mid-40's are as coldly austere as if they had been designed twenty years earlier—and of course they may have been. Unusual for the excellent advantage taken of a blunt street corner and for the elegance of its detail is Wightwick's Devonport Post Office of 1849. Italian rather than Grecian in design, this has a refinement that Pennethorne's somewhat similar Duchy of Cornwall Office, built only a few years later, had already lost.

Another addition by Sydney Smirke to one of his brother's great Grecian monuments might properly have been introduced here to bring this chapter to a dramatic conclusion. But the Reading Room of the British Museum (Figs. XVI 40–41), proposed by the librarian Panizzi in 1852 and erected by Sydney Smirke in 1854–57 in the form of a domed rotunda entirely fabricated of metal, is so nearly an independent edifice and so signal a monument of the advanced use of metal in the mid-50's that it deserves a more detailed discussion in Chapter XVI, which will be devoted to the culminating episodes in the story of the Victorian use of iron. The Reading Room in Bloomsbury is not unworthy to be compared in boldness, if not in elegance of design, with Henri Labrouste's contemporary reading room and stack room in the Bibliothèque Nationale; but Bunning's Coal Exchange, a corporate and not a State-sponsored structure, is the real London rival of that great mid-century Parisian monument.

CHAPTER X: CORPORATE ARCHITECTURE

The corporate authorities of the City of London and of the rising commercial towns, rather than Royalty and government, became the great patrons of monumental public architecture in the Victorian Age. The class that controlled these urban entities also provided the clients for a new architecture of commerce almost equally monumental in character (see Chapters XI–XII). Proud of their growing wealth and their rapidly expanding towns, Victorian businessmen naturally sought to create symbols of urban magnificence both public and private. Fine exchanges, markets, town halls, and the like had frequently been built in the Late Georgian period; the Early Victorians built many larger markets in the 40's and 50's without producing any comparable in architectural quality to those designed by Charles Fowler for Charing Cross and Exeter in the 30's. But the central location, great size, and sumptuousness of the new town halls and exchanges make them peculiarly prominent among Victorian monuments. They are also most characteristic of the ambitions of the period. The extent to which they overshadowed the public works of the state reflected very clearly the rapid rise of urban capital as a new and dominant power in the land. Government buildings hardly caught up with civic buildings in magnificence before the early 80's when the Victorian Age was already drawing to a close.

The account of civic building may well begin somewhat before the new reign started with the initiation of the Birmingham Town Hall in 1832. This peripteral Corinthian temple, rising above a high rock-faced podium of Anglesey marble, was designed by the young Joseph A. Hansom and his then partner Edward Welch (1806–1868), who won the commission in a competition. The completion of this quite typical Late Georgian monument, the chief example in England of the direct imitation of a Classical model, was destined to drag on throughout the 40's. Inside, the enormous auditorium rises from ground level. It is approached through entrance passages in the podium and surrounded higher up by galleries set under windows which open behind the peristyle. The decorations are mostly Victorian in date and somewhat Victorian in style, although not very interestingly so. The Birmingham Music Festivals date back to 1768; but it was in 1846 that Mendelssohn's

Elijah had its first performance here, consecrating the hall as a principal center of Victorian musical activity and setting a pace for other cities with comparable musical ambitions.

Already by the end of the 30's in London and in Liverpool new municipal monuments had at least been projected which completely outranked in size and complexity this Late Georgian predecessor in Birmingham. Both were dependent, moreover, on vast Classical porticoes for external architectural effect, although they were by no means such direct imitations of Greek temples as Hansom's Birmingham structure. In other towns no civic monuments comparable to the Royal Exchange in the City or St. George's Hall in Liverpool were immediately planned; but the erection of vast halls and exchanges, continuing and increasing in the 50's and 60's, was soon to be as symbolic of the cultural rivalry between the various 19th-century British cities as cathedral building had been in the Middle Ages. Smaller cities followed suit, although necessarily on a more modest scale. Even in the more prosperous county towns, whose wealth in the 40's and 50's was less directly the result of new commercial developments, municipal monuments were built of surprising size and richness of decoration, usually from the designs of local architects.

In addition to the halls and exchanges sponsored by municipalities or by corporate aggregations of the commercial community, comparable architectural monuments quite as expressive of civic pride rose to the order of private individuals and limited companies. To this class belong the major provincial railway stations, such as that which George Hudson, the railway "king" who was then also Lord Mayor of York, provided in 1841 for that capital of his realm, and another later one at Hull which was the city nearest Hudson's country house. (But railway stations and comparable constructions are better dealt with in Chapters XV and XVI because of the prime importance of their structural innovations.) Clubs, athenaeums, and institutes were generally less monumental in scale, as we have seen in an earlier chapter, and of course the purposes they served were social, philanthropic, or educational rather than commercial. Yet these buildings were also intended to be urbane civic ornaments in contrast to those architectural symbols of aloof otherworldliness the Camdenian churches.

More comparable in scale with the new town halls and exchanges were two university museums with whose design C. R. Cockerell was connected, one at Cambridge, the other at Oxford. Cockerell completed the Fitzwilliam Museum in Cambridge only after the death in 1845 of Basevi who had prepared the original plans (Fig. X 5). The Taylor Institute at Oxford, of 1842–45, is entirely of Cockerell's design but unfortunately not one of his best works (Figs. X 9–11). Even so, his is perhaps the most important single name in this field because of these edifices and his work on St. George's Hall at Liverpool (Figs. X 6–8, 37–39).

Other architects whose active careers hardly extended (in two cases at least) beyond the initiation of their major works were more particularly responsible for the three most considerable public or semipublic monuments with which the new age opened. These architects were Tite, Elmes, and Basevi. George Basevi, born in 1794, was a cousin of Disraeli and, more relevantly, a pupil—even a favorite pupil, according to John Summerson—of Soane over a period of six years (1810–16). After he left Soane he spent the next three years in Italy and Greece before beginning practice in 1819. He died in 1845 when his only other considerable building besides the Fitzwilliam Museum, the Conservative Club house in London on which he collaborated with Sydney Smirke, was also incomplete. His most important work, however, was in Belgravia, where he had much to do with the layout and design of Thomas Cubitt's terraces, and in Brompton, where he designed Pelham Crescent and probably several terraces.

Harvey Lonsdale Elmes, twenty years Basevi's junior, survived him by two years, dying of tuberculosis in 1847 in Jamaica whither he had gone in the hope of recovering his health. He was a son of James Elmes (1782–1862), well known as the chronicler of the architecture of Late Georgian London, and he had worked in H. E. Goodridge's office in Bath through the years 1835–38. The younger Elmes' only other large work was the Liverpool Collegiate School in Shaw Street for which he won the competition in 1840.

Sir William Tite was knighted late in life and not, one gathers, for his architectural achievements. Born in 1798, he was apprenticed in due course to David Laing (1774–1856), the architect of the Custom House. Edward Irving's reduced York Minster of 1827 near Regent Square, mentioned earlier, was his first work; it would be a poor start for any architect's career. Tite was later associated with Cockerell in designing the London and Westminster Bank in Lothbury in 1837. He did not die until 1873; but after 1855 he was primarily active as member of Parliament for Bath and in banking, having quite retired from the actual practice of architecture though not from real estate operations in the City. A stuffy reactionary in his attitudes, he remained prominent in the affairs of the Royal Institute of British Architects, of which he was twice president, almost until the end of his life; by then the academic ideals he supported were looking up again. In the 40's Tite was very busy as an architect of railway stations, both in England and in France; such employment he owed in part to his important financial connections which were at once hereditary, marital, and personal. These connections had evidently stood him in good stead also in obtaining the commission for the Royal Exchange out of a muddled succession of competitions. That

301

was, in fact, a real professional scandal as the results of so many architectural competitions for public monuments were (and still are).

Basevi's Fitzwilliam Museum at Cambridge, designed in 1837, is above all an architectural *monument* and at first sight an extremely Classical one (Fig. X 5). But if the Fitzwilliam is compared with Smirke's south front of the British Museum, probably designed little earlier and at this time not even begun, it will be found to belong to a totally different order of expression. Not only are the columns not Grecian but the calm clarity of Smirke's work, often boring in its complacent superiority, has given way to an almost Baroque concentration of force. This is certainly very exciting architecture—even if it does excite some critics to anger. The building is a square block containing a high monitor-lighted range of picture galleries above a low basement. In the basement are a large library and other rooms for the display of small objects, all well lighted by wide groups of windows. The monumental stairhall, only a small portion of which is available for the display of sculpture, actually occupies nearly a quarter of both storeys, and more than a quarter of the total volume since its complicated vaults rise well above the coved ceilings of the galleries around it. This disproportionate emphasis on the least useful portion of the structure was further increased by Cockerell's heavy decorations and finally exaggerated to the point of caricature by an enormous and elaborate staircase. This feature, which was introduced by E. M. Barry in 1875, seems to flood the lower floor like a marble cataract. The result is almost the most fantastic of the useless monumental staircases to be seen in so many 19th- and 20th-century art museums; but Basevi need not be held responsible for its present state.

Basevi's main galleries are rather satisfactory except for their excessive height; but the intention, of course, was to hang the pictures four and five rows deep. The rooms are unusually well lighted by their monitors; and the rich ornament, all high up above a plain ceiling cove, is quite out of sight when one is looking at the paintings. The walls are quite unbroken, except for the necessary doors, and therefore provide continuous hanging space for pictures. The doorcases themselves are somewhat elaborated as axial accents; but the continuous Panathenaic frieze in the principal gallery and the continuous upholstered benches around the walls in that and several of the other galleries—both features proposed by Basevi but not carried out by Cockerell—would have provided a calm enframement for the ranks of paintings on the walls. The small corner galleries have shallow glazed domes on pendentives. In them the walls are too much articulated by pilasters to provide satisfactory hanging space although their rich and delicate decoration makes them elegant anterooms. They might well have been used for the display of sculpture or for cases filled with small *objets de vertu;* in Basevi's drawings, however, they are shown hung with small pictures clumsily grouped between the pilasters.

To this museum edifice the overpowering façade provides a quite irrelevant frontispiece (Fig. X 5). The tremendous Roman Corinthian order, raised on a high podium, belies the two-storey arrangement of the interior. The massive corner pylons not only suggest a broader structure but also block diagonal views of the building from Trumpington Street. These would reveal the unrelated but functionally expressive treatment of the sides with their completely blank first-storey walls above ranges of grouped ground-storey windows. The high rectangular attic behind the central portico hides the multiple domelets of the tall entrance hall and serves no other purpose whatsoever.

In an age whose favorite cant, by no means limited to Pugin and the Camdenians, was the detestation of "shams," this façade was the most complete sham possible. But architecture, particularly monumental architecture, *can* be conceived as large-scale sculpture—whether it should be is another matter. As an abstract plastic exercise this façade is really bold and impressive even if it lacks the subtle and efficient use of slight projections of which Cockerell was elsewhere a master. The vigor of the projecting portico is not lost as in the recessed south court of the British Museum; the strong corner accents terminating the colonnade are held down firmly by the solid blocks on top of them almost in the way medieval buttresses were loaded with pinnacles; the attic composition is sculptural, not linear.

Basevi's early plans show that the breaks at the outer edges of these pylons, which seem to extend the plane of the main colonnade to the left and the right, must be Cockerell's emendation (Fig. X 5). The complex massing of simple elements in the attic, with the plain blocking course shorter than the pediment below, may well be Cockerell's idea also. Even apart from such modifications of the original design, the bombastic Late Roman spirit of this front seems completely alien to that of the suave and elegant interiors. The Fitzwilliam, completed externally in 1847, makes evident how bored Early Victorian architects had become with standard Grecian design and explains the lack of contemporary enthusiasm for Smirke's south front of the British Museum. (This was erected in much the same years, 1843–47, from a final design that may date as late as 1837.)

The even more precisely coeval Victoria Rooms at Bristol (built in 1838–42 by Charles Dyer [1794–1848]), although considerably less original, have proved more acceptable to later taste largely because they are less restively post-Georgian. Blank walls flank the projecting Roman Corinthian portico there and a taller blank mass, housing the main hall, rises to the rear. (This hardly shows in the front view.) But the plastic composition is not merely a representational screen. Even if the portico is but an honorific convention

303

of monumental architecture, it is one that had already survived several changes of style during the preceding two centuries. In general the articulation of the exterior masses expresses the interior articulation of the plan. The Victoria Rooms are not very Grecian in spirit in the way so much Scottish monumental architecture was to remain Grecian down into the 50's; yet Dyer's design does maintain, in a way Basevi's does not, some living contact with the academic decencies of the Georgian Age.

The façade of the Fitzwilliam may not be indecent, but it is certainly very brazen in its Late Roman way. Far more than Smirke's British Museum, moreover, or such German museums of the early decades of the century as von Klenze's Glyptothek in Munich or Schinkel's Altes Museum in Berlin, the Fitzwilliam is the prototype of a new mode for cultural edifices. Architects who designed museums, art galleries, and comparable university edifices long maintained its bombastically Late Classical spirit, quite as other more precisely definable Early Victorian paradigms for churches, for clubs, for country houses, etc., were to be continued down almost to our own day. If the consistent denial of most of the practical needs of a building can be considered, even paradoxically, to be functional at all, this columnar museum mode is another instance of a symbolic sort of functional expression adumbrated by the Early Victorians for a particular type of cultural edifice. Fortunately, even before the decade of the 40's was over, James Pennethorne in the Geological Museum in London (as we have already seen) had indicated another and a better approach to the problem; but that building was, of course, a museum of "practical" or "economic" geology, not of art (Figs. IX 26–29). It was therefore more related to the world of commerce than to the world of humanistic culture. Barry's later Hunterian Museum of Anatomy at the Royal College of Surgeons, added in 1852–54, is of comparable interest with its four narrow balconies carried around the walls on iron brackets under a vast plain skylight. Larger, taller, and better lighted, this still follows very closely his earlier gallery for the Hunterian, completed and opened in 1836 before the new reign began.

Well into the 20th century the art gallery or museum, when considered a monument of culture, has tended to follow Basevi's rather than Barry's or Pennethorne's line. The immensely "practical" ideas of Sir Henry Cole in the next decade concerning the housing of art collections as well as their use were from the first condemned by the press. Ultimately, in 1871, his functional South Kensington galleries of 1856 were removed to Bethnal Green and hidden by J. W. Wild by a brick shell nearly as monumental as that of the Fitzwilliam. But that story—or at least the beginning of it—belongs to Chapter XVI.

The most comparable major monuments designed around 1840 to serve

304

other public functions than exhibiting works of art are Tite's Royal Exchange in London and Elmes' St. George's Hall in Liverpool. Elmes was a much younger man than Basevi, his opportunity at Liverpool was greater, and his taste was purer. Tite was an opportunist, and he played for attention in his competition design even more boldly than Basevi. These two buildings by Tite and Elmes are both very conspicuous and known to almost everyone but the Royal Exchange, once its first novelty wore off, has usually been noted as a major work of the period and then largely ignored by critics and historians. St. George's Hall, on the other hand, has always been most thoroughly discussed. When one considers the central location and the size of the Royal Exchange, the lack of attention it has received from posterity is rather surprising. Even Sir Herbert Baker's skyscraper, rising above Soane's Bank of England across Threadneedle Street, cannot suppress it; if anything, Baker's neo-Georgian pretentiousness enhances the relative dignity and integrity of Tite's Exchange. At least the Exchange can be considered Tite's best work and a real ornament to the City of London, if without the relative coherence and distinction of Basevi's and Elmes' comparable monuments.

The old Royal Exchange burned in 1838 and a new edifice was obviously needed. In Victorian England, and particularly in London, the continuing feudal complexity of overlapping public authorities was such that the means for obtaining a new exchange were not what one might expect. Many of the most obviously public structures, imbued with civic and even with national interest, were not maintained directly either by the state or by the City Corporation. In this case a body known as the Gresham Trustees, who had long controlled the Exchange, were primarily responsible for its rebuilding, not the City of London nor yet the state, although the national Treasury was to provide the funds. Both the City Corporation and the Mercers' Company were also involved in the matter. It was the Gresham Trustees, however, who held the competition for designs for a new building, with the requirement that it be fronted with stone and in the "Grecian, Roman, or Italian style." The program also stated that neither their own retained architect nor any of his pupils should enter the competition. Considerable difficulty at once arose about the membership of a professional jury to advise the Trustees since Barry, the most obvious candidate, declined to serve. The jury ended up as a group of three older professionals: Sir Robert Smirke, Joseph Gwilt, and Philip Hardwick, all men of long-established reputation and conservative taste. After the jury had evaluated the entries, William Grellier (1807–1852) was given the first prize of £300 by the Trustees; Alexis de Chateauneuf (1799–1853), a German from Hamburg who had entered in association with the obscure City architect Arthur Mee, the second prize; and Sydney Smirke (a brother, of course, of one of the jurymen) the third. The project of T. L.

305

Donaldson was considered to have deviated too far from the program to rate a prize; yet confusingly enough his entry was "given first place as a design" (as Katherine Esdaile has put it in her account "Battles Royal: No. 1" in the *Architect and Building News*, 9 January 1931, pp. 47–49, where the various designs are all illustrated).

The Treasury then turned down Grellier's project as too expensive but failed to approve any of the others. In the midst of the hurly-burly of cross-accusations that followed Donaldson and de Chateauneuf each published his own design. The former's had a tremendous octostyle Corinthian portico, even larger than that of the Fitzwilliam, set against an unbroken cubic block of masonry; this was almost exactly what a young Frenchman might have entered at the time in a Rome Prize contest, somewhat in the manner of C. N. Ledoux but two generations late. The German's design, to speak only of the front, was a tremendously enlarged version of the Florentine Loggia dei Lanzi, at least twice the height of the very similar Feldherrenhalle in Munich that was to be erected by Friedrich von Gärtner (1792–1847) a few years later at the head of the Ludwigstrasse. This arcaded portico was flanked by two rather mean towers in the more quattrocento version of the contemporary German *Rundbogenstil*. With Mrs. Esdaile, one may well regret that this attractive design was not executed—preferably without its towers.

The point of the next professional skirmish was to fix on *some* design that could be executed within the £150,000 the Treasury was ready to provide; Cockerell came out of this the temporary victor. Soon, however, a sort of limited second competition was being proposed in which the three jurors (!) and also Tite and Barry were invited to compete. After that rather unethical idea proved abortive, even more unethically Cockerell and Tite alone were then asked to send in new plans. Finally in May 1840 the Gresham Trustees decided to recommend the latter's design to the City Corporation, the Mercers' Company, and the Treasury.

Whether it is a misfortune, as Cockerell's admirers insist, that his project was not executed is not easy to decide. Certainly he had no more right to the commission than had Tite: It should have gone either to Grellier or to Donaldson, provided one or the other so reduced his scheme that it could be built with the sum fixed by the Treasury. Cockerell's four corner lanterns, with their tiny domes, were as unhappy as de Chateauneuf's towers. The tremendous freestanding columns on the front, with the entablature breaking out over them to support giant statues against an attic, has a bold Late-Imperial air. It is not very happy as David Bryce used it on the British Linen Bank (1850–52) in St. Andrew's Square, Edinburgh, but might have been more effective in Cockerell's own hands. The long side colonnades were to be flanked by solid bays which maintained the same external plane. This façade treatment, which goes back via J. N. L. Durand (1760–1834) to E. L. Boullée (1728–1799) in late 18th-century France, doubtless influenced Cuthbert Brodrick in his Leeds Town Hall, designed in 1855, and there the result is certainly magnificent. The court in Cockerell's design was to be lighted by a clerestorey and also by a tremendous round opening cut in the center of a flat roof. To have carried out this roof in 1840 would have represented a considerable structural feat. That fact may have been sufficient to discourage the committee from selecting Cockerell's project. (It was, indeed, to be more than a generation before the court of Tite's Exchange was finally covered with an iron and glass roof.)

Tite's design perhaps suffers no more than Cockerell's—or most of the others, for that matter—from the disparity in treatment between the main front and the other three sides. It also offered both more and less real novelty than did Cockerell's (Fig. X 1). The octostyle Corinthian portico, wider in relation to the whole façade than Donaldson's, is both conventional and overpowering. But Tite added rather anomalous "ears"—presumably coupled chimneys—above the corners of the pediment, recalling de Chateauneuf's towers and Cockerell's lanterns a little. (Fortunately these are not visible in a close view.) At the far end is the tall tower traditionally required to carry a clock and also Sir Thomas Gresham's grasshopper weathervane. This clock tower rises above four giant engaged columns carrying broken entablatures, a motif somewhat resembling that of Cockerell's front façade. The composition of the east end is therefore much too bold and tall for the narrow Freeman's Place (now called Exchange Buildings) on which it fronts (Fig. X 4). This eastern façade also terminates rather weakly at either end since the giant order is entirely omitted on its curving corners. The order is, however, repeated in the form of pilasters along the south side and also in the central bays of the north side.

The most effective aspects of the exterior are the long north and south façades. That on the south has the unbroken range of giant pilasters just mentioned, and both carry a balustrade above the entablature, with higher attics replacing the balustrades over the central five bays (Fig. X 2). The panels in the outer bays of these attics are brought forward and those in the three center bays recessed; this treatment provides a not ineffective echo of Soane's varied skyline on the Bank of England across Threadneedle Street but at many times the original scale. The openings on all three sides except the front are large and boldly handled. Wide rusticated arches on plain imposts provide for continuous ranges of shop fronts (an idea which was soon borrowed and refined by Edward I'Anson in his Royal Exchange Buildings across Freeman's Place [Fig. XII 2]). The upper-storey windows throughout have broken segmental heads of a rather Baroque character with richly carved

307

architraves. These are linked to the entablature above, on the south side by disproportionate scrolled keystones, and on the north by projecting carved panels.

The three central arches, of which only one in each façade opens through to the court, are carried on bracketed imposts. By this rather clumsy device the entrances were made wider than the regular arched shop windows that flank them. On the south side the sills of the three windows over these central arches project even farther forward than in the rest of the range, while fat garlands loop down from them to fill the spandrels. The window frames above are scrolled in section as well as in elevation in order to link them plastically with the projecting sills. The frames are also capped with segmental pediments of considerable relief carried on bold brackets. Such a handling of minor architectural features is of course not even remotely Grecian, nor is it Roman or cinquecento; it is rather in the continental Baroque tradition, although not without parallels in Late Stuart work by Wren and Archer. Apparently it was too full of movement for Early Victorians to find acceptable. Not before the mid-50's does one find a comparable elaboration of relief in the handling of wall planes, least of all in Tite's own rather restrained railway station façades (Figs. XV 4, 10).

The four court façades of the Exchange are equally plastic, although less unified in effect (Fig. X 3). If the open arcade of the ground storey had been repeated on the upper story there would have been hardly any space left for offices in the side wings. Tite therefore used deep niches in each bay sunk between engaged Ionic columns, each niche corresponding with one of the rusticated arches between engaged Doric columns below. Within these niches the window frames are projected forward to the wall plane in the form of pediment-topped edicules. Fantastically complex as is this treatment, it provided very deep and rich shadows in the paneled niche heads and between the imposts and the edicule frames.

The interiors of the Exchange are dull and heavily detailed. The broad ceilings of Lloyd's Commercial Room and Lloyd's Subscription Room are divided by wide paneled ribs rising from broad paneled piers along the walls. The central areas have either flat skylights or monitors above coves.

Begun in 1841 and completed in 1844, the Royal Exchange is a completely Victorian structure, for all its temple portico. Everything of Georgian grace and ease has departed; nor has it any of that personal sophistication of proportion and ornament that distinguishes Cockerell's precisely contemporary Sun Insurance Offices (Fig XI 4) diagonally across Threadneedle Street to the northeast. In its coarseness, its confused eclecticism, and its complex orchestration of plastic effects the Exchange is more typical of the 50's or even the 60's than of the 40's. Tite had neither genius nor even serious talent, but he did

308

have a real temperamental affinity to the great financial epoch of the mid-century. He therefore offered in the Royal Exchange a sort of preview of High Victorian financial architecture, not perhaps at its worst but certainly at its least suave or original. In justice to Tite's reputation, which is at present rather dim, this premonitory character of the Royal Exchange should be recognized, as also the fact that his railway stations, so much less interesting, are quite standard and hence rather sounder examples of Early Victorian architecture.

Tite is not a sympathetic character; born for worldly success, he set out to achieve it by any means to his hand. The machinations that brought him the Exchange commission were perhaps justified in that he provided the City with a monument that remained "high style" for a generation. The Exchange also served its practical purposes well enough during that period. But when Tite found other methods of action than architecture which brought larger and quicker results in wealth and power in the City his defection from the profession was no loss.

Elmes was a pathetic, even a tragic, character, and his life provides an ironic contrast to Tite's. Winning in his mid-20's three large-scale competitions, his professional career began as early in his life as Pugin's and with even more éclat. Yet when he died less than a decade later, worn out by work, the major edifice for which he was responsible, St. George's Hall, was still far from complete. Since the supervision of the other considerable building he designed, the Liverpool Collegiate School, was denied him, he received from that only the competition premium of £250. Worse than that, his fee of 5 per cent on St. George's Hall was based on the original estimate of £92,-000, not on the £145,000 that it had actually cost down to the time of his death. He therefore left his wife and child quite without financial provision. For them it can have been little recompense that his unfinished hall was already recognized as one of the masterpieces of the age.

St. George's Hall is much more prominent than the Royal Exchange (Figs. X 6–8). From its high position in Lime Street, opposite Liverpool's main railway station, the enormous edifice dominated the city from the first. Later the clearing of the area behind it and the erection of a range of more or less harmonious public structures to the north made it the center of one of the most impressive open spaces created in Victorian England. Even today, when Sir Giles Scott's cathedral rises far above it on a much higher hill, St. George's Hall must seem even to casual visitors to Liverpool the chief monument of the city. Vying successfully in scale with the great dockside warehouses and shipping offices, the solidity of its blackened masonry bulk emphasized the fragility of the 20th-century steel-frame structures, gutted by the blitz, across from the Adelphi Hotel. St. George's Hall is surely one of the finest of all 19th-century British monuments; it has generally also been classed, there-

309

fore, along with two completely disparate edifices, the New Palace of Westminster and the Crystal Palace, as one of England's three greatest achitectural contributions in the Early Victorian period.

But is St. George's Hall, in the way of the Royal Exchange or even the Fitzwilliam, properly to be considered a Victorian monument at all? Symbolic of its curiously isolated historical position is the fact that it was a would-be monumental painter whom the new period also left behind, Benjamin Robert Haydon (1786–1846), who persuaded the young Elmes to enter the competition in 1839. This first competition was merely for a hall comparable in purpose to the one Hansom was building in Birmingham but rather larger in size. Neither Elmes' Ionic project for this hall nor the Doric scheme with which he won a second competition for the Liverpool Assize Courts the following year is outside the established canon of Classical design in the 20's and 30's. In the latter the long front and end colonnades terminate in solid bays; but these do not project like the bold bastions that flank the Fitzwilliam nor does the hexastyle central portico dominate the long range of Grecian columns along the main façade.

After winning the first competition and before entering the second, Elmes went to Munich and Berlin to study the new monumental buildings of von Klenze and Schinkel. The successive parts of the *Sammlung Architektonischer Entwürfe* of Schinkel had appeared over the years 1828–40; the plates of this, as well as firsthand study of Schinkel's buildings in Berlin, seem to have influenced Elmes when he was instructed to combine the St. George's Hall project and the Assize Courts project into a single enormous structure. Yet the relentless axiality of the plan, with the great hall placed lengthwise in the center and the court rooms balanced at either end, is French rather than German (Fig. X 7). (The present slight differentiation in plan between the two ends of the hall caused by the semicircular rostrum at the right was an emendation by Cockerell related to the introduction of the great organ in the 50's.)

The tremendous vaulted roof of the great hall was executed in hollow bricks after Elmes' death by his engineering associate Sir Robert Rawlinson (1810–1898) who supervised the construction of the edifice between 1847 and 1849. This vault was certainly suggested by the restorations on paper of the Roman Baths of Caracalla published by the French architect G. Abel Blouet (1795–1853) in 1828, but the Liverpool vault is actually slightly larger than its ancient prototype. The great engaged columns of polished Aberdeen granite with bronze capitals are particularly Antonine in character. The decoration of this hall and the much more effective decoration of the elliptical Concert Room in the upper storey at the north end were the work of Cockerell who finally completed St. George's Hall between 1851 and 1856 (Figs. X 37–39).

These decorations are naturally considerably more Victorian in character than such parts of the work as are entirely Elmes'. Perhaps those parts should not be rated as Victorian at all since they are so closely related to much that Schinkel did earlier in the century. If St. George's Hall is not so similar to characteristic Grecian work done in Britain in the preceding decades it belongs nonetheless, like Smirke's British Museum, to the international mode of Romantic Classicism in a way the Fitzwilliam and the Royal Exchange do not.

The south end of St. George's Hall is quite conventional and rather resembles Donaldson's project for the Royal Exchange (Fig. X 6). Except for the superior proportions and the splendid pile of steps at the base (by Cockerell)—which rise, however, much too abruptly from an exiguous terrace along St. John's Lane—this porticoed and pedimented façade is, in fact, not very different from Tite's at the Exchange. The north end is not identical but has a semicircular projection housing the Concert Room in the first storey. The different treatment of the two ends hardly counts as asymmetry, for the structure is so long that the two ends are hardly ever seen at once either from the east or from the west. The extreme severity of the rounded north end is quite out of accord with the new visual tastes of the Victorian Age for sharpened accents and complex rhythms (Fig. X 7). The podium below is barely broken by the simple frames of the two entrance doors; the parapet above is absolutely continuous and unornamented. Thus there is no central focus of interest and nothing to distract attention from the even half-circle of giant engaged Corinthian columns.

The unbroken length of the east portico is surmounted by an equally unbroken attic masking the vault of the main hall. Thus the effect is even more severe (Fig. X 6). Ranges of square pilasters, freestanding for two-thirds of their height, are used here along the side wings. Such pilasters also rise like an open screen in the projecting middle section of the west front. These novel members provide a very interesting kind of structural articulation recalling the more original aspects of Schinkel's Classicism as much as the long east portico does that of his more conventional Altes Museum. Though the tremendous scale of the composition is new to Britain, the spirit is still that of the classical rationalism which dominated the end of the 18th century. The great scale and the general severity reflect the dreams of French architects like Ledoux and Boullée in the Revolutionary epoch, dreams that were codified by Durand in his *Précis des leçons d'architecture donnés à l'École Polytechnique* (1802–05) and thus transmitted to a later generation. Behind and between the columnar and pseudo-columnar elements which dominate the façades the wall surfaces are rather flat. The relief of the various panels articulating these surfaces and that of the rare window frames is very low. Windows are completely suppressed on the south and the east fronts; the moldings throughout,

311

the low council room (with the octagonal clerestorey of the vestibule showing above); and finally the gable end of the library with its elaborately traceried oriel and corner turret. The total effect is most picturesque without being rambling (Fig. X 12). As the clarity of the plan indicates, the picturesqueness is not arbitrary except for such minor accents as the hall lantern and the turret on the library gable. The articulation of the masses, emphasized by the high roofs of the two chief interior volumes (the hall and the library, running at right angles to one another), clearly expresses the complex functional articulation inside in a way the massing of Cockerell's Ashmolean fails to do.

The contemporary description of the Lincoln's Inn buildings in the *Illustrated London News*, 1 November 1845, pp. 275–282, notes correctly that the "east or garden front is, however, by far the most picturesque in effect; the line is less uniform than in the western front side; besides which, it is set off in contrast with the classic insipidity of Stone Buildings on the opposite side of the Garden." The interest in this comment does not lie in the initial statement, which is based on the placing of the main entrance in the southeast tower and the introduction of an additional low gabled porch between the library and the drawing room visible only from the east. What is significant is the association of the quality of "insipidity" with the "classic" design of Stone Buildings and the implied approval of the strong contrast which "sets off" the new work. The appearance of this comment in a periodical of general circulation indicates how common such critical reactions were becoming by the mid-40's.

The secular Late Perpendicular of the time of Henry VIII was not selected by the Benchers and their architects because of the opportunities it provided for functional articulation but on account of its connotations. These were intended to suggest the historical antiquity of the Inns of Court. Morover, the earliest extant buildings in Lincoln's Inn were in fact of 16th-century date, and in the 17th century Inigo Jones was supposed to have used Perpendicular vaulting in Lincoln's Inn Chapel out of deference to local tradition. But once such antiquarian considerations had sanctioned the emulation of a medieval style there could be frank delight in the visual disharmony between the new edifice and most of the surrounding structures. This delight is highly characteristic of the Early Victorian period which enjoyed dramatic contrast in its cityscapes as much as in its novels.

It may seem a paradox that the Lincoln's Inn Benchers should have chosen Philip Hardwick as the architect of their Gothic building. He was then (and is still) best known for his giant Doric propylaeum at Euston Station; this Lincoln's Inn edifice and the Wycliff Chapel in Birmingham, begun the same year, are actually his first Gothic works of any consequence. But the Benchers were at least as well served by Hardwick and his son as if they had commissioned any of the men whose Gothic style had been formed in Georgian days. To have selected Pugin, a prominent papist, to design buildings for an important secular institution—or even one of the new Anglican church architects just coming into notice—would have taken at this time a courage and a fanaticism unlikely among lawyers of any period.

The Hardwicks had no such instinctive feeling for medieval construction as did Pugin, but they chose their materials well and saw that they were handled in a workmanlike way. The red brick of the walls—and it was *red* brick, not buff stocks—is flat and hard, but it is very well laid; the stone trim is thin, but it is crisply modeled. Moreover, the elaborate timber roofs of the great hall and the library are sturdy in structure and competently molded, surpassing those so far provided in neo-Gothic churches both in solidity and in plausibility. The Hardwicks were at least as "correct" in their archaeology as Pugin and the Camdenians at this time. The conscientious pursuit of accuracy in the handling of detail according to some established norm of "high style" was characteristic of the phase of the Greek Revival in which Philip Hardwick, like so many of the Early Victorians, had begun his practice. In Grecian work this was already giving way to a pursuit of novelty in detail (for example, Cockerell's "Bassae" order at the Taylor Institute) and also to the exploitation of less regular and more bombastic compositional effects (at the Fitzwilliam and, to some extent, at St. George's Hall). In Italian work the parallel stage of free modulation had hardly been reached by 1843. For neo-Gothic a new standard of accuracy had only just been established by Pugin, a standard which Anglican church architects in these very years were still striving to reach. The Hardwicks' Lincoln's Inn structure illustrates this stage in secular Gothic building. The Benchers, almost as a by-product of providing for their own complex needs, also produced the first prominently located London monument in which the piquant possibilities of articulated Gothic composition were made strikingly evident. Thus the Lincoln's Inn Hall and Library have a significance in the story of Victorian architecture beyond their intrinsic interest—which is admittedly not very great since the Hardwicks' talents were always modest.

The choice of red brick for so prominent a building is of historical interest also, even though it can be paralleled in Pennethorne's model houses in New Oxford Street that were being erected at this time, and also in Edward I'Anson's new Royal Exchange Buildings. The monochrome rule of Bath or Portland stone in pretentious architecture, just being accepted for the more monumental private buildings in the City under Cockerell's leadership, was already sharply challenged here. Beyond the contrast of red brick walls, intermixed with dark headers, and warm-tinted Bath stone trim the only polychromy is provided by the traditional Tudor use of a diaper of dark bricks on the towers. Despite Wild's prophetic banded arches and diapered friezes at Christ Church, Streatham, the possibilities of a more original sort of polychromy in brick were not to be further developed before the end of the decade. The armorial glass in the windows, rather richly calligraphic in design, reached a higher level of quality than most figural windows in the churches of the time. This glass illustrates well a rather pleasant phase of Early Victorian minor art that has been insufficiently appreciated because of its utter lack of archaeological plausibility.

The next prominent public monument built in London in the 40's is so different from the preceding edifice that it seems to belong to a different world. The Coal Exchange in Lower Thames Street was begun in 1846 and completed in 1849 to the designs of the official City Architect J. B. Bunning. Bunning's clients, the men who made up the Corporation of the City, did represent in effect another world from that of the Benchers of Lincoln's Inn. That world, rising in financial power, was increasingly ready to express its new wealth in monumental architecture; but it had no more interest in the connotations of the Tudor national past, which appealed to lawyers for so many reasons, than in the meticulous antique references found in Cockerell's Grecian detailing, which meant so much to philologists at the universities. The leaders in the City were "modern" men, and to them "modern" meant the Renaissance as opposed to the Middle Ages or Antiquity. These sentiments included also some respect for Wren. That respect Cockerell also shared, which is perhaps one reason why he was so superior an architect when he worked in the City. City men, moreover, were by no means averse to the use of new materials when their practical advantages were evident.

The Coal Exchange expresses most effectively the tastes of its sponsors. Far more than the Royal Exchange, it is the prime City monument of the Early Victorian period. The commercial adaptation of the Italian palace was not more boldly and brilliantly illustrated in the City before the 50's than in its exteriors (at least by any other architect except Cockerell); the use of an interior iron skeleton received nowhere so completely integrated an architectural expression as in its glass-domed court (Figs. X 14–16). The striking disparity between the exterior and the interior even dramatizes the dichotomy in the two attitudes of the period toward structure. Externally the Coal Exchange is articulated into two solid masonry blocks extending at a sharp angle on either side of an almost freestanding circular entrance tower; internally its court is unified as a single birdcage-like volume defined by metal ribs. The exterior must be studied in relation to its contemporary context to be appreciated at all; the court is a monument for the ages, one of the very few which the Early Victorians produced.

Unlike St. George's Hall, the Coal Exchange is unequivocally an Early Victorian monument. It would have been as impossible for a Georgian architect to have designed and built it as for a Victorian of any later generation than Bunning's. Yet it stands somewhat apart from the characteristic production of the period. The other monuments of the 40's that have so far been considered have been not merely Early Victorian but Early Victorian Gothic, Renaissance, or even Classic. To derive a common denominator of Victorian style in its early phase from them requires a complicated intellectual process. Here, although the façades of the building are clearly related to the palazzo paradigms of Barry and the general composition to the Italian Villa mode, the total edifice, if considered with its remarkable court, is quite without precedent. That court above all, even though some of its decorative detail derives from Jacobethan strapwork, was never intended to be in any particular style of the past; yet it is quite as remote from what might be considered "mere" or "pure" engineering.

The engineering means are used here not solely for practical ends but quite consciously for expressive ends as well. If the character of the decoration was by no means solely deduced from the character of the materials or from the functional purpose of the elements, that character is nevertheless peculiarly appropriate to both and was freely and consistently developed, not as a mere afterthought or surface embellishment but at the heart of the designing process. The detailing of the ironwork, for example, is as much the result of fully architectural thinking as is the proportioning of the spacial volume and the organization of the skeletal structure (Figs. X 14, 17, 21–24).

The career of James Bunstone Bunning, the architect of the Coal Exchange, certainly does not explain why he, almost alone in the 40's, was capable of such an approach to the use of new materials; nor does his other work provide much that is of related interest. Later investigation may well prove that some articled pupil in his office—one who died young, perhaps, or soon lost heart after starting practice on his own—was really responsible for designing the court of the Coal Exchange. But as far as is known today Bunning himself was responsible for the court as well as for the exterior of the building. He therefore deserves—as much as Elmes and more than Tite, who were also effectively men of a single monument—that recognition as a leading Early Victorian architect posterity has thus far denied him.

Bunning was born in 1802, the son of a surveyor for whom he first worked on leaving school around 1815. He was next articled to George Smith (1783–1869), who built the Grecian Corn Exchange in Mark Lane in 1827–28 and was Surveyor to the Mercers' Company and the Coopers' Company as as well as to the Gresham Trustees. Thus Bunning grew up and received his professional training in the world of City surveyorships. After beginning to practice on his own he soon became Borough Surveyor of Bethnal Green, where he later built the Union Workhouse (about 1841), and also Surveyor to the Foundling Hospital. By 1837 he had completed his first work of consequence, the City of London School, in a dry and timid Late Georgian Gothic. Always ambitious, Bunning entered the competitions for the New Palace in 1835 and for the Royal Exchange in 1839. He built the Receiving Home of the Royal Humane Society in Hyde Park in the late 30's. Yet on the whole he continued to accumulate more professional appointments than actual commissions for building; he was a very active man just the same even if much of his work was of a modest nature.

As Surveyor to the London Cemetery Company from 1839 on he laid out Nunhead Cemetery and made considerable alterations to Highgate Cemetery. If the "catacombs" there are his work, as seems possible, he deserves high credit, for they constitute a romantic masterpiece in cemetery design— not architecture, perhaps, but macabre landscaping in a mood that is worthy of an 18th-century expert in the "horrid." As Surveyor to the Haberdasher's Company he developed their estate at New Cross; there he built (about 1840–42) the Five Bells Hotel, the Railway Tavern, and Hatcham and Albert Terraces, as well as many streets of smaller houses. As Surveyor to the London and County Bank he did building and remodeling at their properties in Canterbury, Chatham, Brighton, and Leighton Buzzard. He was also Surveyor to the Thames Tunnel and to the Victorian Life Assurance Company, as well as Architect to the Chelsea Waterworks! Such a profusion of appointments kept him busy at maintenance work, but it provided few opportunities for designing and erecting new buildings in conspicuous locations. He built or remodeled a few large mansions in and around London, however, notably Baron Vaughn's in Regent's Park.

On 23 September 1843 Bunning was elected "Clerk of the City's Works," the twenty-first in succession to hold the office. The title was changed in 1847 to "Architect" when Bunning's salary was also increased. All told he was responsible for £750,000 worth of construction for the City before his death twenty years later. Examined before the City Corporation Commission in 1854, Bunning explained at some length the character and the remunerations of his official position (*Builder, 12*, 45).

I am architect and surveyor to the Corporation and have been so since 1843. . . . I am solely employed by the City for all the operations which are carried on at their desire. When I was appointed in 1843, the salary which I received was £1,600 a year, out of which I had to pay office expenses. In 1847 the salary was raised to £2,500 a year, out of which I had to pay office expenses, amounting at that time to £1,000 a year; but my present salary is £2,500 a year with the addition of £1,000 a year for office expenses. The salary is made up in this wise:—£1,300 from the

318

city's cash, £600 for attending to the Bridgehouse estates, £500 from the Finsbury Estate, £50 from the Coal Fund, an estimated amount of £50 for preparing plans of any property that may be leased, and £50 from the Conduit Mead Estate. My income, on the whole, is less than that of my predecessor, and I am not permitted to engage in any private practice.

My duties are very multifarious. I have to attend the Court of Aldermen and the Court of Common Council when required. For the former I have to watch all ruinous and dangerous buildings within the City. I have also to attend the committee of aldermen in respect to the prisons, and I have recently erected a prison at Holloway. I also built the Coal Exchange and Billingsgate Market. I prepared an amazing number of plans for a new cattle market, when it was proposed to build it on the present site, but these plans are now all abandoned.

And so on and on, with all the familiar woes of the bureaucrat. Worst of all, though Bunning was forbidden private practice, there was yet no assurance that he would as City Architect receive the commissions for important new City buildings when they might be needed. "In the case of the Royal Exchange designs were advertised for from various architects" in his predecessor's time, Bunning explained, "whether it would be desirable to adopt this plan in all cases it is not for me to say: I can only hope it will never be done while I am City Architect . . ."

The great City street improvements have . . . been conducted under my care. On the Lord Mayor's day also I have to prepare the hall for the banquet. I have to attend, moreover, to the Guildhall, the courts of law, the officers' residences, the Monument, the Sessions house, and the public stairs, which are very numerous. I have to do with London Bridge . . . I have also to survey the City Estate, which consists of 6,084 houses, to survey dilapidations, to assess the rents, and to report to the City Lands Committee. The Bridgehouse Estate (of about 6,000 houses) in like manner comes under my care. I have also to attend the Coal, Corn and Finance Committee, and under that committee I built the Coal Exchange. I have to fix the boundaries under which the coal duty becomes payable. I attend the General Purposes Committee, and under them the Mansion-house comes within my care. [He redecorated the Egyptian Hall there in 1844.] I attend the Markets Committee and have the management of the markets, and execute any repairs that are required. I have also to attend to the police stations—six in number—and the chief commissioner's house, the city schools, and the Small Debts Court.

Multifarious, indeed, were poor Bunning's duties. When one thinks of him watching all ruinous and dangerous buildings (of which there were certainly then a great many in the City), preparing the Lord Mayor's hall for banquets, attending to the "very numerous" public stairs, surveying the dilapidations of over 12,000 houses, not to speak of fixing boundaries for the coal tax, and attending the meetings—even if only when required—

of innumerable boards and committees, the wonder is that he was actually able to design anything at all. If Bunning employed some unknown pupil on the court of the Coal Exchange, then perhaps it should be admitted that the best to be hoped of architect-bureaucrats is that they will employ designers of real talent for their major work—as J. H. Mansart, for example, did when he was Louis XIV's *premier architecte.*

Actually no other edifice of any consequence besides the Coal Exchange was designed in Bunning's office in the 40's. In the 50's official City building, like every other field of architecture, provided rather more activity as general prosperity increased. The Holloway Prison (Fig. VII 1) and the Billingsgate Market (not in its present form, however, which is due to Horace Jones), the Freemasons' Orphans' Schools and the Metropolitan Cattle Market, now known as the Caledonian (not to say Flea) Market, were completed by Bunning in 1852, 1853, 1854, and 1855 respectively, thus rounding out a not inconsiderable *œuvre* (Figs. X 25–28). Rather unexpectedly, Bunning was among the many Early Victorian architects who had the honor of signing themselves F.S.A. (Fellow of the Society of Antiquaries; not quite as honorific as a fellowship in the Royal Society but still today a real honor for architects and historians of art). No real antiquarian, he was needless to say not a member of the Ecclesiological Society.

City "improvements" primarily occupied Bunning, like his opposite number in the West End, Pennethorne, during the mid-40's. In 1845 he designed a new street to run from the west end of Cheapside to Carey Street; on this Pennethorne's Record Office was supposed to face. The next year he first planned and surveyed New Cannon Street; and in 1846 he widened Threadneedle Street, to mention only the most important of these urbanistic activities. All proceeded very slowly because of the general parsimony and lassitude of the period in such matters. It was the ultimate opening of New Cannon Street in the early 50's, however, that eventually initiated an important period of building activity in the City.

After even a summary examination of a Victorian City Architect's duties, the volume of architectural production of a Pugin or a Scott is considerably less impressive. But the Coal Exchange was for Bunning really the first opportunity his official position had offered to build a conspicuous monument—the designing of the towers for Brunel's Hungerford Suspension Bridge was a minor matter—he might well have feared it would be the only one. Into it he put everything he had to offer (or so one must suppose).

The two identical blocks of the exterior (Fig. X 16) may be favorably compared as façade compositions with the Sun Assurance Office by Cockerell (Fig. XI 4) and the Brunswick Building in Liverpool by the brothers A. and G. Williams (Fig. XII 1), to which we will come in succeeding chapters, not to speak of Edward Walters' warehouses in Manchester (Figs. XII 14, 16), the finest and most characteristic commercial buildings of monumental pretension erected in the 40's. Less severe than Cockerell's building, less derivative than the Liverpool block, Bunning's façades are also less turgid and overemphatic than many of Walters'. If either of the blocks of the Coal Exchange stood alone in a more central part of the City—or in Liverpool or Manchester, for that matter—it would be recognized as representing the highest class of attainment in Early Victorian commercial architecture. But the blocks do not stand alone; the two are linked together with a quadrant portico half their height, over which a circular tower rises in three stages in the re-entrant angle (Figs. X 15, 16).

This portico and tower are conventional enough in their treatment as individual features; but the plastic relationship of the telescopic cylinder of the tower to its projecting portico, which links the front planes of the side blocks at their base, and also to the ends of the blocks, from which it stands free higher up, is of the boldest possible order. The result is not altogether successful; yet the composition should not be denied credit for real originality merely because most of the component elements are familiar. These elements, moreover, are not actually so conventional as they at first appear. No detailed analysis of the way the window frames are linked vertically and of the curious effect of syncopation produced by the handling of the wall planes is perhaps necessary; but it should be noted how the surface of the wall is brought forward in the form of a range of articulated piers between the lower windows and then set back between the frames of the windows above (Fig. VII 16). That is a device "Greek" Thomson was to elaborate with remarkable effect a decade or more later in the upper storeys of his finest commercial façades in Glasgow. Bunning's feeling for such Mannerist subtleties of composition is very evidently greater than Walters'—almost equal to Cockerell's—among his own immediate contempories.

The heraldic animals that rise in front of the deepest voids on either side of the tower have a liveliness lacking in most ecclesiastical sculpture of the time; the linked rope circlets of the balustrade between introduce the rope theme that dominates the decoration of the interior.

In this building whose principal interior is all of exposed iron, iron plays as little part on the exterior as in other commercial monuments of the day. Yet in execution, though not in the original design, iron supports were introduced under the heavy keystone-centered lintels of the ground-storey windows in order that they might be made exceptionally wide. But the emphasis on the masonry character of the lintels accords ill with the delicate scale of these metal supports; thus they appear too much like the casual afterthoughts they probably were in fact.

Since the top of the dome over the central court barely appears behind the tower and between the visible hip roofs of the front blocks, the Coal Exchange offers no external expression of the existence of a large circular volume of space within. Even in the Early Victorian period, when the relationship of external expression to interior planning was (except in Gothic work) rather generally ignored, this represented an extreme case. But no matter how the exterior might have been designed, it could hardly prepare the visitor for the interior so long as the one consisted of bearing masonry walls and the other of an open metal skeleton.

The circular court of the Coal Exchange, the actual locale of the exchange operations, is 60 feet in diameter and rises 74 feet to the top of the dome (Fig. X 14). Around it on the ground floor and on three upper galleries are arranged the offices of the coal factors. These continuous ranges of offices are broken, at the entrance and in the three other axial positions, by semi-hexagonal wells with glass skylights over them. The 32 ribs of the dome and the 32 stanchions rising from gallery level to gallery level which support them are not evenly spaced; every fourth pair, on either side of each of the wells, was brought closer together (Fig. X 19). The dome ribs were cast by the founders (Dewers of Old Street) each in a single piece 42½ feet long and weighing two tons (Fig. X 21). The brackets supporting the galleries are integral with the stanchions; the floors of the galleries consist of cast-iron slabs bolted to the brackets (Fig. X 23). Between the stanchions the office fronts consist of glazed doors surrounded by glazed sash in simple, although unnecessarily heavy, wooden frames. Above a range of solid panels the segments of the dome were filled with ground plate glass, two panes to a segment. The oculus inside the iron ring to which the ribs are joined at the top was originally filled with amber-colored glass.

The dome ribs are remarkably delicate in section. The stanchions are much heavier, but they are so placed that their largest dimension is radial and thus they also appear quite light when seen from the center of the floor. All the iron members are today painted cream color and may always have been; this pale tone certainly increases the general effect of lightness and delicacy. The ironwork has almost no unmolded or undecorated areas; but the ornamental treatment is richest on the lower levels, where the stanchions are heaviest, and most delicate in the dome ribs and the members which encircle the dome (Figs. X 21–24). The stanchions and brackets are not solid but pierced, a treatment which is technically advantageous in making large castings. The holes are surrounded by a pattern of intertwined ropes on the two lower levels but merely with flat strapwork on the third. The moldings are very heavy, and the continuity of their lines is broken by frequent cross ribbings, bold on the stanchions and more delicate on the dome members. The undersides of the gallery floor slabs are likewise ornamented with intertwined rope patterns arranged around anchors and coal balances as alternating central devices.

The rope pattern is peculiarly well suited to the casting process. The ribbing which this ornament provides strengthens the various members more effectively than would merely thickening them. A further example of what would today be recognized by engineers—if not by doctrinaire architects dominated by a misunderstood "machine" aesthetic—as intelligent industrial design is the treatment of the bolt holes. Wherever the members are joined by bolts heavy bosses are provided, which is the best engineering practice with cast metals; but these bosses around which the moldings are carried are also visually exploited for the bold accents they provide in the decorative pattern. The moldings are all "fat"; sharp arrises (convex corners), which are hard to cast perfectly, and small "radii" (concave corners), at which cracks are likely to start in stressed castings, are both consistently avoided. There is, in other words, real refinement of technical design within the capacities of the ferrous material and the particular process used for its fabrication.

Especially elegant is the tangential relation of the integral stanchions above the top gallery to the curved lines of the dome ribs themselves (Fig. X 21). The way in which the relatively broad fascia of the horizontal members above the office fronts on this level is scaled down by moldings on the surface to accord with the reed-like treatment of the front edge of the ribs is also ingenious technically and of great charm visually.

The gallery railings are cast as loops of rope enclosing the City arms which are painted white and red. An inscription cast on the underside of the gallery slab at the entrance records the opening of the Exchange by Prince Albert in 1849, the whole being surrounded by a scrolled rope border. The cordage motif is rather excessively ubiquitous and led to contemporary witticisms about architects who hang themselves with too much rope. But this particular motif was chosen as symbolic of the ropes used in the coal mines and on the colliers that brought the coals from Newcastle and the other northeastern coal ports. Undoubtedly its suitability to cast iron influenced Bunning also. The earliest English cast-iron objects of any size, tomb slabs of the 14th and 15th centuries, have rope moldings, and often only rope moldings, for ornament. The motif should therefore have had Pugin's sanction.

The anchor motif on the gallery slabs likewise refers to the coaling ships and not, as with the Camdenians, to St. Clement. So also does the elaborate compass pattern in wood marquetry with which the entire floor was inlaid (Fig. X 19). But these represent only the small change of a coherent iconographic treatment which is one of the most interesting features of this interior.

In the solid panels at the base of the dome are painted a series of the tree ferns that originally made the coal deposits, each with its Latin name in gold and black on the crossbar above (Fig. X 17). Melhado from Bunning's office made the drawings, basing them on fossils in the British Museum; they were then executed in encaustic by Sang, the chief decorative painter of the 40's and 50's. Although the colors have sadly darkened, the outlines of Melhado's ferns are well scaled to the iron ribs; the surrounding frames, however, consist of arabesques that would be more suitable on a lithographed title page than in the dome of a large public building. In the eight narrower panels the trophies of miners' tools are a delightful industrial variant—almost a parody—of the panoplies of arms and the *trophées d'église* of the 17th and 18th centuries.

On the various gallery levels the narrower panels—every fourth—are decorated with rather conventional arabesques by Sang; but in the midst of the ornament are inset several series of little pictures. One series consists of unbelievably jolly miners (Fig. X 20); another of sailing colliers; and a third shows the chief towns then associated with the coal industry, Durham and the three ports of Newcastle, Sunderland, and Shields. The most interesting of all are the panels that show various unidentified collieries, charming early pictures of Victorian industrial scenes (Fig. X 18). In the corresponding positions on the ground storey the arabesques are executed in glazed tile (Fig. X 23). These have therefore preserved their (not very happy) color, while the encaustic panels have unfortunately all turned dark and brownish. (Doubtless cleaning off the old varnish could bring back, as with paintings on canvas, their pristine freshness.) The tile panels with their conventional allegorical figures of various abstract virtues (presumably no monopoly of even a nationalized coal industry) are so irrelevant iconographically that they may well be later replacements. Such tile decoration was certainly more popular later in the century, and stylistically these might well date from the 70's or early 80's.

Billingsgate Market still lies directly across Lower Thames Street from the Coal Exchange (Fig. X 28); but Bunning's market structures of 1850–52 were later rebuilt by his successor Sir Horace Jones (1819–1887). In Bunning's version two square Italian pavilions, with open loggias below and rather top-heavy bracketed cornices, were linked together by an arcade toward the river; in the center of this stood a tall clock tower with an arcaded stage at the top. The whole rose above a stepped stone embankment along the water's edge. Bunning's Billingsgate must have been pleasanter than Jones' market which succeeded it, but it was in no way distinguished.

The Metropolitan Cattle Market, although not actually carried out on its present site in Copenhagen Fields until the early 50's, presumably incorporated in the individual structures as much as Bunning could salvage of the "amazing number of plans" prepared earlier for the original site. The market included some fifteen acres around a central edifice that once contained no less than twelve banks and a telegraph office with a very tall clock tower on top (Figs. X 25–26). Accommodation was provided for 34,980 sheep, 6,616 bullocks, 1,425 calves, and 900 pigs. Open shelters on iron columns were provided to protect the farmers' carts. The total cost was £300,000, of which £10,000 went for roads and 15 acres of granite paving.

In addition to the central structure there are two taverns with a fountain between them: the Queen's Arms and the City Arms—and perhaps the Teetotaller's Arms. There are also several public houses, one at each corner: the Lion, the Lamb, the Black Bull, and the White Horse; with a fifth, the Butchers' Arms, at the corner of Maiden Lane. The taverns and public houses are all four storeys high and very similar in character, although the taverns are two bays wider than the public houses and therefore better proportioned. All are built of "white" Suffolk brick with generous Portland stone trim (Fig. X 27). Rusticated bands outline the corners, and there are bracket-supported cornices and segmental pediments over the arched windows of the first and second storeys. They therefore appear at first sight rather sober and Wren-like in style. But below the projecting iron balconies the ground storeys consist (except for corner piers of stone) of rows of light metal stanchions with integral balcony brackets not unlike those at the Coal Exchange; between the stanchions are glazed doors and windows. Despite the concealing shadow of the balconies the effect is rather disturbing, like the solid house fronts above continuous shop fronts seen in so much contemporary street architecture.

The central structure combines masonry and iron more gracefully (Fig. X 26). At each of the twelve corners of the one-storey range of banks and offices there is a solid rusticated stone pier; between these are five delicate iron archs carried on iron columns. Above this substructure the clock tower rises to a considerable height. Its walls are rusticated around the big clock faces; it is crowned with a loggia and below is a projecting iron balcony supported on cornice brackets. From loggia and balcony the supervisors could keep an eye on market operations.

In an attempt to link the rather slender tower with the very broad base provided by the shops Bunning introduced wide-spreading scrolled buttresses which project above the shop roofs. The effect of these is startling yet perhaps not altogether unsuccessful, even if such very Baroque features seem rather out of key with the sobriety of the taverns and public houses. The style of these—so unlike that of Victorian "gin palaces"—may have been intended to influence for the better the deportment of hard-drinking cattle dealers. Unfortunately Bunning's market was never much of a success, descending rapidly to its 20th-century status as a rival of the Parisian Marché aux puces.

At Smithfield in 1845 the younger Boulnois covered in a portion of the grounds for the Prize Cattle Show with a light iron tension-truss roof. This was carried on double ranges of iron columns in order to support also the internal galleries at the sides. The result was of technical interest only and without positive architectural character. Sir Horace Jones, as Bunning's successor after his death in 1863, was responsible for most of the London markets in use at Smithfield today.

In general the Early Victorian markets in provincial cities did not approach the high standard of Fowler's Exeter Lower Market which had been completed in 1836. If they were comparably monumental they were usually overpretentious. Not before the return of prosperity in the mid-century were most municipal authorities ready to sponsor expensive structures for this purpose. Only the Bolton Market deserves mention, chiefly because it prepared the way for the enormous covered markets of the later Victorian decades. Designed by G. T. Robinson (1828–1897), who won the commission in competition in 1851, the Bolton Market occupies an area 218 feet by 300 feet and is entirely covered with wrought-iron roofs supported by ornamental cast-iron piers, brackets, and girders. A wider "nave" and cross "transepts" break the regularity of the plan, which otherwise consists of three equal "aisles" on either side of the nave. Around this vast covered area a masonry screen is carried with little or no reference to the skeleton construction of the interior. In the center of the front, rising to the full height of the nave, is a giant Corinthian portico set in front of a wider rusticated block. A great entrance arch pierces this block, and on either side of the portico there are arched windows in both the upper and lower storeys. This Vanbrugh-like treatment is echoed in the simpler and lower corner blocks. The coherent functional expression and the simple dignity of Fowler's pre-Victorian markets has gone, but the scale of the architect's effort is nevertheless rather impressive.

Smaller towns often combined their town halls and their markets in single structures. These provide pleasanter, if more modest, examples of municipal architecture than Robinson's enormous market. The town hall built at Kingston-on-Thames in 1840 has four corner loggia lanterns. With its very simple Italian detail, it is still almost domestic in scale and suggests some of the designs in the villa books of the 20's and 30's. Much more sophisticated, and altogether a very superior example of Italian design, is the town hall with market below in Truro. It was built in 1846 by Christopher Eales (1809–

1903) of fine local stone and is remarkable for the pleasant variation in the random ashlar walling and the sharp precision of the cut-stone trim. On the front the whole ground storey is rusticated and has five tall, broadly spaced arches (Fig. X 30). The quoins of the imposts, the voussoirs of the arches, and the quoins that enframe the rather smooth walls above are all vermiculated. The five windows of the upper storey have heavy consoles supporting their sills—a favorite device of the mid-40's. Pointed and segmental pediments on scrolled brackets alternate over the window tops. Above a very bold cornice, carried on simple scrolled modillions, an open lantern rises in the center. The corner pilasters on the lantern are linked to the wall plane of the façade by modest scrolled consoles; clock faces set above light metal grilles fill the openings in the sides. Four pediments are rather arbitrarily added at the top, presumably to increase the three-dimensional effect.

The simpler rear has side wings lower than the central block. Plain rusticated quoins and voussoirs edge the main block here, the side wings, and the five arched openings of the ground floor (Fig. X 30). The central arch is set in a slight projection framed with rustication. This terminates at the first-storey sill level, and over it three narrow arched windows are grouped. These windows, and the two over the side openings in the main block, have the same rusticated voussoirs as the ground-floor arches; the smaller windows in the side wings have simple molded architraves carried on somewhat clumsy imposts.

Even more modest, and very similar, is the market house at Ashburton in Devon, built by Alfred Norman (d. 1893) of Devonport in 1850. Here there are three widely spaced rusticated arches below and a range of seven arched windows above, with molded archivolts and a continuous impost. A tiny lantern on the left front corner, with another one-storey bay beyond it containing a wide rusticated arch, lends a certain informality to the composition; but there is no very strong asymmetrical emphasis. These buildings, in which there is no dichotomy of structure between exterior and interior, indicate how satisfactorily the Italian manner could be used in the 40's to provide dignified representational character without the pompous porticoes that more Classical modes required. The spell of the latter, however, was by no means yet exorcised in county towns, as the Lincoln Corn Exchange of 1847 by William Adam Nicholson (1803–1853) conspicuously illustrates.

Despite the confirmed addiction of the Scots to Grecian forms, which lasted in general through the 40's, the Edinburgh Corn Exchange is Italianate. It was built in 1847–49 by David Cousin (1809–1878), the City Architect, who was a pupil of Playfair. The façade is of palazzo type, like those of the principal financial houses then rising in St. Andrew's Square (see Chapter XI); but there are projections at both ends of the front, and one of these rises to form a tall tower (Fig. X 29). Although intended to hold a clock rather than to provide a belvedere, this asymmetrically placed tower recalls those on Barry's country mansions. Such a feature is as exceptional at this time on a monumental urban building as the more elaborate corner tower of Bunning's Coal Exchange. The detail is heavy and of late 16th- or even 17th-century character. For example, the Doric columns of the projecting entrance porch are broken by square rusticated blocks; and the attic windows cut across the lines of the architrave and frieze of the main cornice, the molding between being split to provide ornamental frames. This front block provided banking and general office space, with a granary in the attic above; hence it closely resembled in its functions as well as in its architectural treatment the larger commercial premises of the day.

As at the London Coal Exchange, the actual exchange area is completely masked by the masonry block in front. But the construction of the exchange itself is mixed: Iron columns, with capitals at once functionally and decoratively articulated, support wooden trusses over the broad, high nave and the lower, narrower side aisles (Fig. X 29). The queenpost trusses of the nave carry a flat ceiling flanked by sloping sides roofed with patent glass tiles. The clerestorey sash could be opened for ventilation. This is honest, straightforward construction with very little arbitrary decoration; but it lacks the consistency of such all-iron interiors as the court of the Coal Exchange or the multiple aisles of the Bolton Market. Except for the rather interesting forms of the capitals, Cousin made no attempt to develop a decorative treatment expressive of the new materials and the new type of skeleton structure he was using.

The somewhat exceptional Commercial Hall and Custom House at Ipswich (1843–45), for which J. M. Clark won the commission in a competition, has a rather Jones-like air (Fig. X 31). The Tuscan portico is raised over a semicircular niche in the rusticated basement storey and approached from the quay by reversing flights of stairs. The extreme projection of the very flat modillioned cornices of the pediment on the portico and of the hip roof of the main block were certainly suggested by those of St. Paul's, Covent Garden; the windows of the first storey, with their pediments above eared architraves, are also Palladian in the way of the 17th, not the 18th, century. The heavier and more complex frames of the end windows have segmental pediments filled with shell motifs. These are more closely related to standard Early Victorian Italianism. The clock tower, set at one of the rear corners, reveals by its asymmetric location how little true sympathy remained for the academic styles of the past.

The first important revival of later 17th-century English architectural forms was at the Royal Naval College which the younger John Shaw built at Deptford in these same years 1843–45. The larger buildings there are not particularly Wren-like; but as H. S. Goodhart Rendel has pointed out in a paper on "Rogue Architects of the Victorian Era" read before the Royal Institute of British Architects and published in the *R.I.B.A. Journal*, Ser. 3, *56*, 251–258, "the resemblance between the style of its chapel and that of Wren's church of St. Benet on Paul's Wharf is very striking." Equally striking, however, is the placing of the tower in one of the re-entrant angles of the cruciform plan, thus providing the asymmetrical silhouette characteristic of a towered Italian Villa. Hence the chapel fits better into the Early Victorian scene in fact than any labeling of its style as "Late Stuart" might lead one to suppose. The heavy character of the larger and more utilitarian edifices at the College can readily be matched in various hospitals of the 40's and early 50's—Hawkins' vast extension of Guy's Hospital in the Borough High Street, for example, or St. Mary's Hospital, Paddington, begun by the elderly Thomas Hopper in 1845. More than a decade would pass by, however, before Shaw or anyone else made a bolder gesture in this direction.

The great supporter of Wren's reputation in the Early Victorian period was C. R. Cockerell. He even exhibited in 1838 at the Royal Academy "A Tribute to the Memory of Sir Christopher Wren, Being a Collection of His Principal Works." Cockerell can hardly be considered to have imitated Wren's style in his public work or even in his big banks and insurance offices in the City (see Chapter XI); yet by his choice of monumental scale and of Portland stone for these prominent edifices he clearly set out to renew—or to continue—the architectural distinction which Wren's churches had first given to that central part of the metropolis. When he rebuilt St. Bartholomew's, Moor Lane, in 1847, however, he followed the models provided by Wren's City churches rather closely; he even piously preserved the original Wren fittings which an outraged fanatic in the *Ecclesiologist* asserted should have been burned forthwith!

The next year there appeared the first part of a monumental treatise on the architecture of Wren (*The Works of Sir Christopher Wren* [1848–49]). This was dedicated to Cockerell by John Clayton, the author, since the measurements of 8 of the 46 churches ultimately included on the 60 very large lithographed plates of the whole work had been supplied by the older architect. Later, in 1852, Clayton presented many of the particulars of the City churches in a paper before the Royal Institute of British Architects—at the same meeting, curiously enough, at which von Klenze received the Royal Gold Medal. Thus, by the early 50's there was available for use in architects' drafting rooms—as there had not been in the 40's—the sort of precise documentary material which had been since the 16th century an increasingly essential concomitant of any mutation in architectural taste. When architects in the 50's took up the "restoration" of the City churches no lack of relevant visual data justified those Byzantinoid aberrations by which Gilbert Scott and others tried to draw these great works of the 17th century into the outer orbit of the High Victorian Gothic.

The "destructive" restorations of Wren churches along approved ecclesiological lines are only too familiar and lie well beyond the limits of the Early Victorian period. In 1852, however, the well-established Hardwicks (and it may be significant that it was they) restored quite differently the interior of Hawksmore's St. Anne's, Limehouse, after a serious fire. The fashion in which this was done has been much criticized in modern times; yet the Hardwicks did show real sympathy with the work of an architect still later —and hence less respectable to Victorians—than Wren. But even the Hardwicks built no new non-Gothic churches as late as this, nor did any other Anglicans of consequence.

When a church of "Roman or Italian style" was proposed as the subject for the Soane Medallion competition in 1850 there were only six entries, no one of which was considered worthy of a prize. Yet in 1850 John Weale published a measured drawing of Inigo Jones' Banqueting Hall by the young Octavius Hansard. Even though interest in Jones was much less lively than in Wren, it was paralleled at this time by a surprisingly late—or perhaps surprisingly early?—interest in the 16th-century Italian academics who had been Jones' models. At the Royal Academy Arthur Ashpitel (1807– 1869) was exhibiting in 1850 a plate of "Selections from Palladio"; while Samuel Angell (1800–1866) provided not only a composition called "Palladiana" but also a plate of the "Works of Vignola." This he followed with a paper read 4 February 1850 before the Royal Institute of British Architects "On the Life, the Genius, and the Works of Vignola." Later in the year Wyatt Papworth (1822–1894) presented a paper "On the *Peculiar* Characteristics of the Palladian School," perhaps an ambivalent title—at least with my italics. Since Palladio and Vignola remained dead, as far as direct influence on English architecture goes, for more than a generation longer, these instances are perhaps historically irrelevant and at this time merely evidence private antiquarian interest on the part of a few individuals. The Liverpool Architectural Society's competion of 1853 for a church "in the style of Palladio" did not interest the younger men at all, even in the home of "Liverpool Venetian," any more than had the Soane Medallion subject in London three years earlier.

For all his prominence and his frequent pronouncements on architectural matters Tite had effectively ceased practice by the 50's. The "Composition of the Works of Inigo Jones," imitating Cockerell's Wren tribute, which he exhibited at the Royal Academy in 1854, need not be taken very seriously.

Much more important historically is the grandiose academic project for a
"Wellington College" with which a young Scotsman in Burn's office (who
was also a pupil, more significantly, of Cockerell at the Royal Academy)
had won the annual Gold Medal the previous year (Fig. X 33). The young
Scotsman's name was Richard Norman Shaw and he was destined to be
England's leading architect of the late 19th and early 20th centuries. Shaw's
student design, known to posterity by the happy accident of its publication in the *Illustrated London News,* may be no more premonitory of what
was to happen to English architecture a half-century later in Edwardian times
than the early projects of other gifted and long-lived architects could we
have access to them. But it is surprising that his biographer Sir Reginald
Blomfield, who so deprecated Shaw's long apprenticeship to the Gothic
Revival (at this point not even begun), failed to note this startling evidence
of an early predilection for Vanbrugh-like monumentality. Shaw approached
this sort of design again only toward the end of his long career, at the time
when Blomfield (misguidedly, I believe) considered that he did his finest
work.

More important here is the fact that two years later another Shaw, the
younger John, designed the real Wellington College, the one actually built
at Sandhurst in 1856–59, in an avowed and not unplausible imitation of
the style not of Vanbrugh but of Wren, like his Royal Navy College of 1844
(Fig. X 34). Several historians and critics have in the last few years called
attention to this vast complex of buildings, little remarkable though it is
in intrinsic quality. They have rarely attempted, however, to relate Wellington College to the climate of Victorian architectural opinion of the time concerning non-Gothic work. The actual design—and above all the execution
—of Wellington College lies beyond the limits of the Early Victorian period
as it is loosely defined in this book; but some further evidence concerning the
climate of opinion in the 50's is not irrelevant, even though the discussion
must be rather arbitrarily cut off just before it begins to deal with important
new developments in British architecture.

At the end of 1853 a proposal was made to demolish no less than 30
churches (23 of which were by Wren) in the City of London in order that
the Establishment might increase its funds by the sale or lease of their sites.
As is often the way, the threat focused attention on what was threatened.
The *Builder, 12,* 43, published a hurriedly prepared and rather inaccurate
"composition" of the 30 churches—but the churches themselves were of
course readily accessible to any architect or interested layman in London.
The complete list, with addresses, was given in the *Builder,* as well as the
dates of their construction and the names of their architects presumably
drawn from Clayton's book. The *Builder's* editorial, published 14 January

1854, was followed by a flood of letters to the press, and thus all 30 churches, which included several of Wren's finest, were saved for the time being. It was perhaps purely coincidental that two anonymous articles on "The Dark Age of English Taste," published also in late 1853 and early 1854 in the *Builder, 11,* 91–92; *12,* 15–16, placed the onset of that "dark age" surprisingly late. Only with the reign of George III, approximately a century before the writer's time, was it now supposed that taste had seriously declined (at almost the very time when many modern scholars consider the "rule of taste" to have been finally established, it is ironic to note).

The first moderately conspicuous new building of the 50's in London in which one may assume that there was a return to, rather than merely a vague continuance of, the sort of design that immediately preceded the Georgian "dark age" was probably the St. Giles and Bloomsbury Public Baths and Wash-houses erected in 1852 by Baly and Pownall. But this was neither particularly plausible archaeologically nor much calculated to appeal to the new High Victorian taste, then just crystallizing (see Chapters XVII–XVIII). The size and the national purpose of Shaw's Wellington College, as well as the sumptuousness of its avowedly Wren-based architectural forms, made it the most significant example in the 50's of what was still hardly more than a fluke of Victorian eclecticism.

When the design was first mentioned in the *Builder, 12,* 406, it was described as similar in architectural character to the Naval School at Deptford by the same architect, being in "the style of Queen Anne, perhaps it may be called." This is a very early, if not the earliest, use of Queen Anne's name to designate the architecture of the Late Stuart period just before and after 1700. A detailed description of Wellington College would be out of place here, although an illustration of the original design, which was somewhat modified in execution, may be provided (Fig. X 34). Neither as designed nor as executed is the vast complex at Sandhurst to be considered a particularly distinguished or original monument. Yet when compared to the work of half a century later, when such design became only too common, it has—if one may be so inelegant as to say so—the guts (*victorianice,* "go") which are so positive a characteristic of its period. How little that period appreciated the college (although its presumed closeness to the Royal hearts seems to have protected it from contemporary critical attack) is evident from the fact that Gilbert Scott was allowed within a few years to attach to it a chapel of wholly unrelated Gothic design. But one may nevertheless assume that by the time the college was finished a few younger architects were able to look at it with real sympathy. At least Norman Shaw may be supposed to have noted it with favor; and even more surely his partner-to-be

Eden Nesfield whose Kinmel Park near Abergele ten years later first took up the "Queen Anne" to more creative purpose.

Yet Wellington College was not entirely alone in the 50's. A rather earlier and simpler Late Stuart manner, owing more to the school of Jones than to Wren and not without some kinship in materials and proportions to the less pretentious work of the earlier Georgians, makes an occasional appearance in institutional work such as the London hospitals which have already been mentioned. The first building for the City of London Hospital for Diseases of the Chest located at Victoria Park, moreover, to which Paxton proposed adding a remarkable air-conditioned exercise pavilion (Fig. XVI), has a dignity and serenity of massing and fenestration that are only slightly corrupted by the clumsy and very plastic clock tower and the rather Gothic colonnette-mullions at some of the windows. Both here and at Sandhurst a 20th-century eye cannot but note the saving grace of the relatively small windowpanes; yet this was increasingly an archaism in the 50's, particularly for schools and hospitals, now that large sheets of glass were readily obtainable. Begun in 1851 by F. W. Ordish, the hospital at Victoria Park actually preceded not only Shaw's college but also Baly and Pownall's baths in St. Giles; but it was neither so conspicuous nor so likely to be visited. Above all, few of its features quite convince one that the architect intended to return to Jonesian formulas or that his clients and colleagues would have recognized that he was doing so.

In most fields of secular architecture the Jacobethan of the early 17th century was vastly more popular than the academic manner of Jones or Wren, however much that might be corrupted by picturesque ideals or simplified for utilitarian purposes. As we shall see later, even railway stations were often Jacobethan (see Chapter XV). Yet few public or semipublic edifices were erected in this mode. St. Martin's Hall in Long Acre, erected for Hullah's Singing Schools by William Westmacott in the years 1847–50, may be mentioned chiefly because it is an exception (Fig. X 32).

More characteristic of Jacobethan work of the period are various large schools and hospitals. Only one, perhaps, need be described and illustrated as representative of a very considerable number. These edifices vary in the amount and character of the detail and the degree of archaeological plausibility achieved, but not very much in their visual interest. The Kneller Hall Training School at Whitton, near Hounslow Heath on the edge of London, rose in 1849–50 on the site of Sir Godfrey Kneller's early 18th-century mansion. Intended for the education of male schoolteachers, the project was sponsored and at least in part financed by the Committee of the Privy Council on Education; thus, like Shaw's two colleges, it was more an example of the somewhat oblique support of education by government in this period than of corporate building. The architect was George J. J. Mair (1810–1889), and his avowed model was stone-built Wollaton Hall though the material used here was red brick with Portland stone for trim (Fig. X 35). More interesting than the Jacobethan design of the exterior, so like that of many country houses of the period, was the mechanical equipment. A three-horse-power steam engine pumped the water, worked the machinery in the laundry department (including a mangle), and provided—just how is not clear—the heat for cooking. Hot water was supplied to the baths, and hot-air furnaces in the basement warmed the ground floor and the staircases. Water mains for protection against fire were also installed throughout the building.

The group including the Corn Exchange, Market Hall, and Bank in Lichfield is much less scholarly in design than Mair's school. Built by the local architects Johnson and Son in 1848–50, this is "Tudorbethan" rather than Jacobethan in its details, as was also the Brompton Consumption Hospital in London, begun in 1844. G. H. Simmonds' Town Hall for St. Matthew's Parish, Bethnal Green, completed in 1852, was of a still earlier 16th-century Tudor. Despite the use of red brick and the dissimilarity in height and width of the side wings, this has the papery stiffness of most Late Georgian work in this vein. Public and institutional Tudor and Jacobethan continued, however, to be more exceptional than private work in either vein.

Articulated massing and functional asymmetry, whether or not associated with medieval styling, were also exceptional in public monuments of the Early Victorian period and rarely handled effectively. Despite a few corner towers, regularity and dignity were still the accepted rule; as we shall see in the next chapters, this was also true of commerical architecture. Although the main Classical tide rapidly receded after 1840, basic academic traditions were likely to be halfheartedly continued in one guise or another well into the 50's. More than conscious revivalism, it is this cultural lag that explains the various apparent reflections of 17th-century modes.

When Bradford came to build its St. George's Hall in the years 1851–53 F. H. Lockwood and his partner Mawson, the Hull architects who won the competition, maintained the Classical standards of St. George's Hall in Liverpool relatively unadulterated, but at the expense of not being particularly up to date either in their nominal style or their visual effects. But Lockwood was an able architect, well trained in Grecian design, as his handsome Great Thornton Street Chapel in Hull has already illustrated (Fig. IV 12).

The detail on the Bradford Hall is less severe than Elmes' at Liverpool. The basement has a range of rusticated piers, and rich carved garlands hang between the brackets that flank the mezzanine windows (Fig. X 36). On the main front the entrance arches have vermiculated voussoirs and enormous carved heads on the keystones. Unfortunately this part of the building has been whitewashed by the cinema management now operating the hall; it therefore seems rather inadequate to support the heavy black masses of masonry above.

The giant order, which dominates the upper storey and suggests the height of the main hall within, is Roman in the more sober mood of Liverpool. On the front, the central five bays break forward and six engaged columns support a broad pediment. On the side elevation a similar range of engaged columns is carried almost the entire length of the building. Both treatments may seem at first sight but skimped variants of Elmes' great south and west porticoes. Yet between the engaged columns the wall surface here is completely articulated with panels and windows. Thus a rich effect of relief is provided behind the bold frontal plane of the order in sharp contrast to the flat wall surfaces at Liverpool. Across the Hall Ings front rusticated arches at the first-storey level provide external expression as well as light for the foyer within. On the Wakefield Road side the arches are carried higher so that they may rise well above the interior balconies. The imposts and lintels of the arches fill the entire width of the intercolumniations, and the giant order is really like a range of solid structural piers between the open bays. Below the side arches impost-like half-pilasters flank wide oblong windows and the subsidiary entablature they carry marks the level of the balconies inside. The side façade is in the main very impressive and dignified, except for the overornate treatment of the mezzanine with its brackets and garlands. It is the entrance front toward Hall Ings that is least successful in maintaining the standards of monumental design of the previous decade; even so the portico is considerably more effective than Tite's at the Royal Exchange.

On the rear façade toward Dale Street the rising ground reduces the height of the basement and there is no mezzanine (Fig. X 36); the proportions are therefore broader than on the front and side. The articulation of the two ranges of windows, which only light artistes' dressing rooms, is not interrupted by any giant order between the corner pilasters.

The interior has no vaulted roof; but the paneling of the great flat ceiling above the cove is dignified. The apse-like curvature of the rear wall of the platform much enriches the general spacial effect. As in the Late Georgian church interiors which this hall so much resembles, the galleries seem fragile and trivial. The rather Rococo decoration on the gallery parapets is as out of scale and character with the severe wall decoration behind as are the rich and delicate iron supports below. The influence of contemporary the-

335

aters, in the design of which architects were often rivaled by clowns and ballerinas, is somewhat evident here.* Doubtless even before St. George's Hall became a cinema lighter fare than oratorios was offered here on occasion.

Within two or three years, when Cockerell finally came to complete and decorate the elliptical Concert Room in the north end of the other St. George's Hall, in Liverpool, he illustrated much more successfully than Lockwood how an Early Victorian interior could be at once rich and delicate, refined and dignified. After the engineer Rawlinson, in the years since Elmes' death, had carried the building structurally to completion, Cockerell was called on in 1851 to complete the decoration throughout. The small hall, which is perhaps the most beautiful interior of the Early Victorian period, can apparently be credited entirely to him except for the basic elliptical shape Elmes originally planned. It was not opened until 1856, two years after the great hall.

Exquisite in color and covered with most elegant decoration in low relief, this room is above all a masterly exercise in the use of those "shams" Camdenians most abominated (Fig. X 38). The balconies are of cast iron designed to look like some sort of woven wickerwork; of iron also are the pierced ventilating grilles along the front of the stage and in the ceiling panels around the central skylight. The delicate arabesques of the pilasters and friezes are of papier mâché. The graceful caryatids, seemingly sustaining the balcony on their fingertips, must be of iron or some synthetic composition; they were certainly never carved in stone. Whether these are themselves supports or whether the balcony is cantilevered on iron beams, the real construction is completely concealed. The wall panels are not of wood but of plaster, superbly grained and varnished. Only the mirrors between the columns on the stage are what they seem; yet by a final paradox they create a faëry unreality by their repeated reflections (Fig. X 39).

The actual dimensions are modest, 72 feet by 77 feet, although the total seating capacity is 1,100; the stage is only 30 feet by 12 feet. Thus the effect of intimacy was probably already in Elmes' mind when he made the original plan; but he could hardly have achieved this delicacy of scale. All the color work is very pale and subtle, moreover, completely different from that in Pugin's bright diapers. Mostly neutral cream, gray, and gold, a rather blond orange-brown tone lights up the wide "wooden" panels of the walls. The gilding is used to touch up highlights, somewhat as on the fantastic architecture in certain quattrocento paintings.

The whole effect is icing-like in the most luscious though refined way— not like the hard plastery white icing of a wedding cake, or the rich dark

* This book includes, unfortunately, no account of Early Victorian theaters, few of which have survived.

shine of chocolate, but rather some exquisite Viennese *mocha torte*. Not since the French Rococo, perhaps, had a room so gay and so airy been designed. It is hard to think of any contemporary chamber music or vocal works really worthy of being heard in this interior. For once, in a century that the art of music supposedly dominated, music seems to have been almost incapable of matching architecture—generally, but perhaps wrongly, considered the art at which the mid-19th century was least successful. Both Mendelssohn and Berlioz seem too heavy even at their lightest; only the ethereal pianism of Chopin can rival what Cockerell achieved here.

A critic writing in 1875, when respect for Elmes' and Cockerell's architectural ideals had just passed its lowest ebb, remarked that "the one success, practically, of the building, is the small concert room which is as good for its purpose as the other, the great hall, is bad." With both comments one can readily agree. But however poor the great hall may be for music it retains much of the Roman grandeur Elmes intended it to have. Even so, it is easy to list serious architectural faults. The mode of entrance, from one side only, provides a most unsuitable approach to a space so strongly axial (Fig. X 7). Moreover, the narrow vestibule area between the portico and the hall provides a very inadequate foyer and has made impossible the introduction of any box office or cloakrooms. The gallery space was most inconveniently broken up by the tremendous piers required to support the masonry vault. Finally, in order to utilize the hall for concerts—after all its principal purpose—it was necessary to set up some sort of platform at one end or the other. The platform added by Cockerell necessarily interrupted the vista down the length of the hall from one court room at the south end to the other at the north; as soon as the enormous organ was set up, the great vista which Elmes intended to reveal his tour de force of axial space composition was lost forever.

The great hall could never have been really satisfactory even if Elmes had lived to carry out its decorations. Yet the structural shell, as completed by Rawlinson in the late 40's, the tremendous barrel vault of hollow brick with springing and bonding of Yorkshire stone, rising above the heavy piers with their giant shafts of polished gray Aberdeen granite, must have had a good deal of the grandeur of the ruins of the Roman baths which were its prototype. By the early 50's Liverpool had the use of John Cunningham's practical if unimpressive Philharmonic Hall, built in Hope Street in 1848, for its concerts. But the rich Victorian port, always enormously proud of its culture, could hardly have been expected to leave the interior of its chief public monument unadorned in the way the 20th century has up to now wisely left most of the stock-brick vaults of Bentley's Westminster Cathedral in London.

The form and character of Cockerell's decorations of 1851–54 in the great hall are not very happy (Fig. X 37). A complex and not very Roman arrangement of square and oblong panels filled with low-relief ornament extends along the main vault thereby diminishing the scale and unity of its curved surface. The tremendous winged figures in rather high relief which occupy the spandrels above the piers are even less plausibly Roman. At best the decorative scheme was confused, for the bold figures obscure the continuity of the vault at its base while the panels above are much too delicate for the heavy treatment of the substructure. The rusticated piers behind the engaged columns and the extremely plastic door frames and niches below the balcony balustrades seem to be from a different hand; most probably these elements follow rather closely Elmes' original ideas for the hall even if they were carried out only by Rawlinson or Cockerell.

Originally the color treatment was high and light in key, chiefly white with a little gold. The gray granite columns provided, both in their deep tone and by their hard polished surface, the most sumptuous note. A redecoration carried out in 1875 was intended to brighten up an interior that twenty years of gas lights and the smoky atmosphere of Liverpool had made impossibly gloomy. This redecoration introduced stronger and more pronounced colors but in a rather vulgar way. A contemporary critic wrote, "the general key and tone of the whole is in no way above what might be called 'house-decorators' work of no very refined type." The small panes Cockerell had used in the windows, with their simple ornamental patterns, were replaced by sheets of ground plate glass the full width of the windows: "Have you seen St. George's Hall since it was made into a gin-palace?" the wits asked, although there was none of that characteristic gin-palace engraving on the plain sheets of glass which Stevens had already introduced in the dining room at Dorchester House. At this time the sunken central portion of the floor was raised. This had never been a practical feature, but it was undoubtedly necessary for the particular spacial effect that Elmes intended. Thus the hall today is very far from being what Elmes designed in the early 40's or even what Cockerell finished in the early 50's.

There is no reason to assume that either Elmes' or Cockerell's design was ever really satisfactory; yet, when St. George's Hall was finally opened in 1854 with performances of Handel's *Messiah*, Mendelssohn's *Elijah*, and Haydn's *Creation* on two successive mornings, not to speak of operatic concerts in the evenings, it was hailed from all sides as surpassing any building of its kind in Europe. Perhaps it did, but the reasons given are not persuasive. The fact that the long façades and the great hall were designed to a module (of 13 feet) was taken to explain the harmony of the proportions, while the variations from this module in the south portico and in the court rooms were held, rather inconsistently, to indicate Elmes' freedom from pedantry. Rawlinson's vault was correctly adjudged a remarkable structural feat, but chiefly because it surpassed the vaults of the Romans—was it not one foot wider than the principal interior of the Baths of Diocletian and two feet wider than that of the Baths of Caracalla? The clumsy figures in the spandrels were highly praised in the *Illustrated London News* because they had been "taken from Raffaelle's compositions in the Vatican, of Temperance, Prudence, Art, Science, Justice and Fortitude" like the contemporary Raphaelesque decorations in the new ballroom wing of Buckingham Palace.

At least the rich materials of the balcony fronts between the piers, Irish black marble, Derbyshire spar, and Irish green marble, could be properly appreciated in 1854; grime had not yet begun to neutralize their colors nor had gin-palace redecoration overhead reduced them by contrast to near-monochrome. An elaborate pavement had been executed in Minton tiles from designs by Cockerell, with the assistance of Prince Albert's artistic mentor Lewis Gruner and Alfred Stevens (who might better have been employed on the spandrel figures above). Before the floor was raised, the whole pattern of this pavement lay between the higher borders of the hall like a tremendous sunken carpet and must have been one of Stevens' finest works of abstract decoration. Not surprisingly, therefore, but perhaps rather unfortunately, this Early Victorian hall in Liverpool became the model which other great provincial cities in the prosperous later 50's and 60's set out, in the train of Bradford, to imitate if not to excel.

With this account of the completion of St. George's Hall the story of public architecture in the Early Victorian period comes full circle. Only one more monument, also completed under public authority in 1854, need be discussed at any length. This chapter began with a Corinthian art museum; it could well end with an Ionic one. The National Gallery of Scotland, on the Mound behind the Royal Scottish Institute in Edinburgh, was begun by William Henry Playfair (1789–1857) in 1850. Yet it might be assumed from its design that it had been begun at least twenty-five years earlier, so cool and severe is the general effect (Fig. X 40). The various pedimented porticoes and colonnades are most competently disposed, and the restrained detail is in the highest degree literate though lacking in the more subtle and "scholarly" touches of Cockerell. Playfair had collaborated twenty years earlier with Cockerell on the unfinished Scottish National Monument on Calton Hill, which provides an apparently ruined Parthenon for Edinburgh's eastern acropolis; but thereafter their paths had separated rather widely despite a nominal identity of principle.

Edinburgh had long been proud of being the "Athens of the North"; yet even in Edinburgh Greek design of the retardataire order of the National

Gallery is an exception in the mid-century. Playfair himself was just completing Donaldson's Hospital, an enormous school for 100 deaf-and-dumb and 200 normal children outside Edinburgh, in Jacobethan style. (It had been designed by him, however, as early as 1842.) A similar but smaller educational plant in Jacobethan style near Donaldson's Hospital is Stewart's Hospital, built in 1849–53 by David Rhind (d. 1883). This has a livelier silhouette with various Scottish Baronial touches in the detail. Both are now overwhelmed, however, by David Bryce's Fettes College, in this same western district, which was begun in the 60's; that is a real masterpiece of 19th-century educational architecture, but it belongs to the High and not the Early phase of Victorian style.

Immediately behind the National Gallery, on the same axis as the Royal Institution but high up at the edge of the Old Town, rise the Tudorish towers of Playfair's Free Church College which was begun in 1846 before the Gallery (Fig. X 40). Framing the fine spire of Gillespie Graham's Victoria Hall, these are important elements in the cross-axial composition that extends over the North Loch from Prince's Street in continuation of the line of Hanover Street. Various Edinburgh architects had been working on this composition in urbanistic (if not stylistic) harmony since the time of Robert Adam. In what must be considered its culminating period urbanistically, Edinburgh provided the most brilliant example in the world of the skillful combination of disparate architectural elements; for her architects really knew how to produce out of what they inherited and what they added one single, highly conscious city picture such as the 19th century hardly approached elsewhere. The special character of Edinburgh urbanism in Victorian times deserves ampler discussion and adequate illustration; but the forward chronological limit of this book, the mid-50's, breaks off the story well short of its end. The extension and embellishment of the city was to continue, with little deterioration in quality, down into the 70s and even the 80's.

Such a complete lack of stylistic development in monumental public architecture between the 30's and the 50's as Playfair's Gallery seems to illustrate is but an exaggeration of a basic truth. It is worth while to compare the Royal Institution in Hull by Cuthbert Brodrick, completed like the National Gallery in 1854, with Brodrick's master F. H. Lockwood's chapel on the other side of Great Thornton Street. This comparison offers a more typical measure of the slight modulation of monumental Classical style that took place during the 40's. The chapel is a temple, even though the order is Corinthian rather than Doric or Ionic as it would probably have been at the height of the Greek Revival twenty years earlier (Fig. IV 11). Its archaeological purity of form is somewhat compromised by side wings, but these flank the front no more unclassically than the ones on Thomas Hamilton's fine Edinburgh High School of the late 20's. Brodrick's Royal Institution (today even worse blitzed than the chapel), built to house both the local Literary and Philosophical Society and a subscription library, is neither a unified temple nor yet an articulated complex expressive of mixed functions like Hardwick's Hall and Library at Lincoln's Inn. The façade presents a continuous giant colonnade terminating in solid projecting blocks at the ends. The youthful Brodrick did not attempt to express what lay behind this façade any more than did Basevi at Cambridge or Cockerell at Oxford; one would hardly suspect that the interior contains a gallery, a large lecture hall, and various committee rooms and laboratories for the society, as well as quite separate provision for the library, including an entrance hall, a reading room, and stack space for 60,000 volumes.

The ground-storey windows in the end bays and those in the wall at the rear of the portico do at least suggest that some parts of the building consist of two storeys. The columns in front are Greek Corinthian but they are coupled, as a contemporary account notes, "like those on the Louvre." Thus there is the usual Early Victorian reference to Renaissance or even post-Renaissance sources as well as to Antiquity, an eclectic rather than a puristic approach to academic design. But the moldings are still very sharp and crisp in the earlier Grecian way, while the details of the pilasters framing the entrance door and the windows under the portico are also Greek, at least in spirit, with something of Cockerell's scholarly subtlety (Fig. X 41). The incised pattern on their faces suggests some of the ornament of the late Greek Revival of the 40's and 50's in America as purveyed by the books of Asher Benjamin (1773–1845) rather than those of Minard Lafever (1797–1854). Above the crowning balustrade, which masks the complex roofs of the larger rooms behind, the central sculptured achievement is by contrast intricate and fussy, illustrating the new lithographic taste in ornament. The Hull building promised much for its young architect's later career in the High Victorian period, and that promise was on the whole kept; but it is not in itself any great addition to the roster of Early Victorian public and semipublic monuments.

The Early Victorians did not develop new and coherent formulas for their museums, exchanges, town halls, and other public and semipublic edifices. The use of Classical porticoes continued as a well-established convention. Even though increasingly unwilling, outside Scotland, to consider a dominating order alone sufficient ornament for an important representational structure, they seem to have been equally reluctant to relinquish giant columns and pilasters entirely. The smaller town halls and markets, as also the exchanges in large cities, were more likely to eschew the orders and to follow in their exterior design the astylar palazzo mode. The iron or iron and wood construction of the roofs of the large interior spaces in the exchanges and the covered markets was usually completely belied by the scale and disposition of their masonry façades, whether these were Classical or Italianate. Inside these spaces, however, the skeleton construction of the roofs was often frankly exposed; in the finer examples it was also ornamented with real feeling for the particular structural devices used and the visual possibilities of the materials. So also Cockerell, in an interior like that of the Music Room in St. George's Hall, was ready to use iron and papier mâché, and even such a supposedly outrageous "sham" as wood graining, with real elegance; thereby, moreover, he achieved decorative if not structural integrity in his design.

Beside the church architects even the best architects of public monuments (who were almost never the same men) seem to have been confused, both as to what their clients wanted and what their clients ought to have. A spirit of compromise, almost of opportunism, or at the least a serious lack of artistic integrity, seems to characterize the milieu of public architecture. The mood of the public architects is very, very different from that pious sense of dedication which must have made the church architects so maddening in their self-righteousness; but at least the latter had the intensity and assurance characteristic of all sincere fanatics. Except for Cockerell, the men responsible for public monuments rarely shared the serious professionalism of a Barry either. He was eclectic, obliging, and more and more ready by the late 40's to satisfy the tastes of his clients for greater richness; yet he was always convinced of, and true to, what he believed to be his own superior and carefully considered standards, just as the Camdenians were to their "church principles."

The architects who built public monuments in the 40's and 50's, unlike their predecessors in the first quarter of the century, seem to have been skeptical even of their own ability as Classical designers. They were rarely asked to use—or else they did not often persuade their clients to choose—preacademic styles such as the 16th-century Tudor or the 17th-century Jacobethan. When they did, men like the Hardwicks in England and even Playfair and Rhind in Scotland were sometimes better at modes they were just mastering, it would seem, than at those they were beginning to forget. Yet such men rarely showed themselves to be much more than apt students producing what Beaux Arts jargon later called "archéos" when using early forms —even the Hardwicks' Lincoln's Inn buildings do not have the assurance of Scott's St. Giles's, Camberwell, although they are perhaps more appealing to 20th-century eyes. When architects in public work tried to remold their basically academic conventions toward greater piquancy and bolder plasticity, they began to borrow right and left from the succession of post-

Renaissance styles, often with frivolous lack of consistency. The relatively infrequent use of asymmetrically placed towers and the almost total lack of functional articulation of mass, except in work based on avowedly pre-academic models, indicate how much Classical training inhibited the exploitation of the bolder compositional devices already almost *de rigueur* in church architecture.

There was therefore no coherent group of late "Classical Revivalists" in Early Victorian times to form a solid counterpoise to the group of "Gothic Revivalists," even though critics like A. E. Richardson or Reginald Turnor, whose approach is basically anti-Victorian, would like to assume such. The ideas of the Gothicists controlled in church architecture and, on the whole, in country house work and in much school building as well; but no similarly programmatic Early Victorian mode crystallized for public architecture. As a result Georgian taste, as reflected in monumental work, seems to have cracked up very slowly; no new Victorian taste matured before the mid- or even the late 50's.

There are no great individual architects whose reputations depend primarily on their work in Early Victorian public architecture. Cockerell was the most competent because his training and his integrity were comparable with Barry's; but he was at once more cranky and more pedantic. His Taylor Institute is an unhappy edifice despite its thoroughly individual character. His elegant Music Room in St. George's Hall, unlike his earlier Branch Bank and his later insurance office in Liverpool, is something of a sport in his general production. But then most of his public work was too much a matter of completing other men's projects to allow a fair estimate to be made of his innate capacity as can readily be done from his extensive commercial work (see Chapter XI). Considered in relation to the rest of Bunning's production the court of his Coal Exchange is almost a miracle, but it does not by itself make him a great public architect. The nice little West Country town halls owe most of their distinction not to their obscure architects but to the fine local stone and the sound traditional training of the local masons; fortunately these men were called on chiefly to execute detail little removed in character from that of the 18th century.

It is the stonework also, almost always turned dead black by the smoke of a century, that gives impressive dignity and craftsmanlike integrity to the finest Early Victorian public monuments in the large cities. Their architects did not stint on external masonry, however happy they were to experiment with papier mâché and various synthetics inside. As a result these are the stoniest buildings erected in England since Vanbrugh's. No stucco, and very little external brickwork, diminishes the solidity of these man-made cliffs. In that fact lies their characteristically Victorian solemnity; for their detail is often coarse if not illiterate. Today they have the macabre pomp of a first-class French funeral. It is even hard to realize that they were ever new; like many of the later Victorians, with their full beards, the town halls and exchanges seem to have been born old. But beards, like grime, are not really Early Victorian; possibly all these buildings, unlike those of the next period, ought to be sandblasted to give them back their youth.

With their present rather elderly look, the buildings discussed in this chapter are not so much characteristic of the 40's and early 50's as of the Victorian Age as a whole. The lightness—one might almost say the light-heartedness—of the finest interiors, such as the court of Bunning's Coal Exchange and Cockerell's Music Room in St. George's Hall, makes evident that Victorians before the mid-50's were not yet so consistently serious as they would be later. The ultimate architectural expressions of Victorian serious-ness have very great force; the seriousness of the public monuments in the Early Victorian range, running from the Fitzwilliam to the Hull Royal In-stitution, still has an experimental quality. Yet these edifices should not be considered merely transitional, however much stylistic analysis reveals in their design elements from the Georgian heritage; rather are they primitives of the oncoming High Victorian, as premonitory in a positive way as they are retardataire in a negative way.

Crude, confused, prematurely solemn in the vein of an undertaker's ap-prentice, few Early Victorian public buildings deserve very high rank for intrinsic architectural merit. Compared with continental work of the time they are likely to seem devoid of suavity and rather incoherent; compared with American work they lack freshness of vision and directness of approach. The aims, the ambitions, of the Victorians were high. In the 40's public purses were slim; but what was built was built solidly. The Early Victorians were never content in their public monuments with a "depression architec-ture" or, in those long decades of peace which extended from Waterloo to the Crimean campaign of the mid-50's, with either a postwar or a prewar parsimony and asceticism.

CHAPTER XI: BANKS AND

INSURANCE BUILDINGS

In *Georgian London* (London, Pleiades Books, 1945; New York, Scribner's, 1946), p. 252, John Summerson writes: "The subject of commercial architecture could be considerably elaborated towards the end of the Georgian period when the beginnings of the general commercial patronage of architects becomes visible. Private banks and insurance companies, brewers and manufacturers and shop-keepers were beginning to employ architects of repute." Yet it was not in fact until after the beginning of the new reign that commercial architecture began to be produced in any quantity. From 1840 on not only are architects of general repute frequently given commissions for banks, insurance offices, and business premises both in the City and in the provinces; new architects of considerable ability appeared who specialized in such work in much the same way other men were beginning to specialize in the more socially and aesthetically exalted field of church design.

There was also much business building done entirely by engineers but most of this can more properly be considered industrial than commercial. Georgian architects had often designed dock warehouses, factories, and other large constructions to which the general public had no direct approach; these now belonged rather in the realm of engineering, which was becoming quite sharply set apart from architecture. Such work lies off the main streets of commerce and was not usually recognized as "Architecture" by Early Victorians. Yet most of the technical innovations made by engineers in industrial structures were taken over almost at once by commercial architects and the two lines of development remained very closely linked.

This chapter and the next are concerned with commercial building in the City of London, in the shopping streets of the West End, and in the area between; it is still more concerned with that in comparable districts of the other large British cities, and even a little with more modest work in the market places of county towns. Almost all such construction now began to have some architectural pretension. Pretension, moreover, is just the right word. The usual restraint of the Georgians in such work was due in part to the fact that business in their time still lacked prestige; hence a sort of economy of cultural effort placed the housing of business low in the hierarchy of building activity. But there was perhaps also, if only unconsciously, some sort of functional asceticism involved a little like that of the mid-20th century. This attitude changed rapidly in the 40's. A desire for lavish public display, as advertisement for the proprietor and his wares, increasingly dictated the elaborate character of the new façades in Early Victorian business and shopping streets.

In church architecture the breakup of Georgian taste was signalized by a rather rapid, and on the whole quite coherent, stylistic development. But neither in large commercial buildings nor in ordinary street architecture was there any such clearly definable change of surface style in the 40's. An architect of the late 18th century—Sir William Chambers, say—would not know what to make of typical Camdenian churches of the mid-century they are so utterly different in intention and in visual character from the decorative (but not Decorated) "cathedral" that Chambers had the German medievalist Müntz design for him as an embellishment of the Royal Gardens at Kew. Emotionally Chambers might be partially prepared for Tractarian intentions in architecture, but only in the way a parlor magician is prepared for the magic of an African medicine man, his professional cynicism encouraging intense technical admiration but no sharing of the faith. Actually Chambers might well have taken such churches for real medieval work, his own archaeological knowledge being presumably insufficient to make him skeptical of what Victorians produced in the way of plausible forgeries.

Yet in front of the chief banks and business houses of the 40's, as also in many Early Victorian squares, Chambers might have felt quite at home and capable of expert professional criticism. He should have been pleased by the renewed use of his own *Treatise on Civil Architecture* (1759) for the proportions and details of the orders. The long Grecian interlude, during which the books of his scorned contemporaries Stuart and Revett provided Athenian paradigms for all and sundry with such success, was evidently about over. But he would surely have deprecated a great deal of what he saw because of the hurried sloppiness of the designing and the uneasy extremes of severity and of over-richness which were so often juxtaposed. Chambers' own relative eclecticism of taste might, even so, have made acceptable to him many of the new cinquecento variations from the inherited 18th-century academic modes. At the very least he could not have failed to be impressed by the tremendous extent and the very considerable (if superficial) indications of upper-middle-class affluence in the "better" districts of most cities. In his own day such indications had been restricted to a few very small enclaves in most British towns other than the fashionable watering places. Like an admirer of modern architecture visiting for the first time Miami Beach or Parioli, Chambers might well have been so surprised at the amount of large-scale new work as not at first to notice its tawdriness, its lack of finish, and its chaotic stylistic inconsistencies.

The reasons for the general continuance of some sort of post-Georgian style through the 40's and even the 50's were not the same in commercial building as in urban residential construction but rather reversed. Terrace houses retained their traditional patterns because their functions and their structure had been little modified; the very laws which defined their classification tended to discourage technical innovations (see Chapters XIII–XIV). Commercial architecture, on the other hand, now served functions that were in effect quite new because of the increased scale and rapidly developing specialization of business activity. In the 18th century shopkeepers and even bankers had for the most part operated in an adapted portion of their own dwellings, quite as they had been doing since the Middle Ages. Middlemen were few and business activities, such as those of insurance companies, which required large suites of offices for paper-work were relatively few in number and generally small in size.

The new or, more accurately, the deeply changed functions of the Early Victorian church provided strong extra-aesthetic reasons for a sharp turn away from the established Georgian types; and the expression of these changed functions was early given new form by an equally sharp change in the preferred stylistic models. But in commercial architecture there were no equally established types from which to turn away except, in a sense, those of ordinary Georgian domestic building. Inertial forces led Early Victorian Nonconformists, when they began to build ecclesiastical edifices of any size and elaboration, to follow the Greek temple model. That was not only hallowed by more than two decades of employment by Anglicans but was commonly in use for public architecture of a secular order. In a similar way Early Victorian businessmen, when commissioning banks, insurance offices, and business buildings in general—and hence the architects who principally worked for them—were inclined to stick to the new stylistic modes that had been introduced for secular use just before the Victorian Age began. As we have seen, Barry's Italian palace mode was one of the most popular of these; certainly no other ancient models existed that need be considered *more* appropriate for commercial work. There had never before been any considerable amount of architecturally ambitious commercial building; and the Renaissance cities of Italy seemed to provide the most impressive architectural results of the patronage of a rich merchant class, at least until the picturesque Hanseatic cities of northern Europe began to be studied and emulated in the 50's.

The influence of new (or, in fact, old) concepts of structure was considerable on Early Victorian church architecture as soon as the actual ways of building of the Middle Ages began to be carefully and sympathetically studied; but that influence was in the main a reactionary one. The new materials, notably iron, that were eventually to be freely used in commercial buildings, if well after they had been introduced in industrial work, might have been expected to revolutionize design as well as structure—and actually they did so later in the century. But conventional aesthetic considerations, dominating the thinking of Early Victorian engineers and technicians quite as much as they did that of architects, made it unlikely this should occur as early as the 40's. Only creative genius of an order comparable to Soane's could have accomplished such an architectural revolution; and architects even of near-genius were extremely unlikely to specialize in the commercial field at this time. The most talented, Cockerell, was at least as much of a Greek archaeologist as Pugin was a medieval one. If his archaeology influenced his work less than did Pugin's, he was nevertheless hardly the sort of man to lead a revolution, even though his architectural thinking (as we know from his lectures) was of an evolutionary order long before *The Origin of Species* gave topical value to that much abused term. Not surprisingly, new modes of expression in commercial architecture developed only very slowly and discontinuously—as regards architecture much that was "unfit" in evolutionary terms manifestly continued to survive, as it has done ever since.

If new functions and new materials led to no very expressive new modes of design in commercial work, yet practical considerations gradually modified stylistic expression. The modulation was confused and sometimes inhibited by contradictory tendencies because of the tastes of the period for irrelevant visual connotations and complex compositional devices. The multiple functions of the increasingly ritualistic churches encouraged articulation of internal volumes and external masses, thus justifying extra-aesthetically the picturesque irregularities and asymmetrical accents so sympathetic to the eyes in the 40's. The expansion of commercial functions, on the other hand, rather encouraged regularity, both in plan and in design, while the increasing use of iron elements in the interior construction positively required it.

The period admired monumental solidity as a symbol of dignity in architecture. Church windows could properly be reduced to screens of stone tracery filled with stained glass because of a parallel emotional preference for "dim religious light." Darkness was not at all inappropriate to the new and more sacramental ritual. In commercial buildings, on the other hand, the need for a maximum of light was obvious, and new materials and new structural methods soon made it easy to provide. Large and unbroken windows, gutting the solidity of the masonry walls, with no sort of traceried infilling and preferably glazed with large panes of clear plate glass, were therefore demanded by clients and provided by architects. But the struggle between the strong aesthetic craving for solidity and the sensible desire for almost continuous windows was never satisfactorily resolved in commercial work of the 40's; only the mid-50's saw the rise of a High Victorian commercial mode that was at once practical and monumental.

The arbiters of taste in church architecture were more or less sophisticated aesthetically. They generally insisted that their delight in solidity, in elaborate plastic effects, and in rich ornamentation should be satisfied by sound traditional materials wrought with whatever pseudomedieval craftsmanship the period could revive. Patrons of churches, moreover, were usually ready to pay the necessary costs. Otherwise, if the materials were well-laid random ashlar and heavily dimensioned timber, the most sophisticated could appreciate studied simplicity for its own sake; at least many preferred good bread to meretriciously iced cake, without denying that fine cake was more desirable when it could be afforded.

The ordinary patrons of business architecture were not themselves at all cultivated or subtle in this sense. It behooved designers to satisfy their clients' avid desires for gaudy architectural pastry as well as they could with the limited funds available. Plaster moldings may have been anathema to the leading church architects as soon as they had read Pugin's *True Principles;* but most commercial architects were frankly pastry cooks in plaster, as well as in stucco, cement, "compo," and papier mâché. A good part of their interest in new materials in fact was concentrated on synthetic materials which could provide elaborate ornamental work at a much lower cost than carved stone. But for reasons of prestige, in the highest class of commercial buildings which were those erected for banks and insurance companies, the expensive reality elsewhere represented by cheap substitutes was also in demand. For such clients a display of solid and not ersatz wealth was obviously the best advertisement; on their buildings an increasing profusion of stone carving was therefore likely to be used. For this carving John Thomas, busy though he was with Pugin's Tudor ornament at the New Palace of Westminster, was often called on to provide the models (the work was executed, of course, by ordinary stone carvers). The carved ornament on important commercial edifices is often better executed than that on contemporary churches, moreover, since it was designed with more reference to the Georgian training of the carvers.

Such a superb block of offices as Cockerell's Bank Chambers in Liverpool of 1849–50, standing in Cook Street behind his Branch Bank of England, will have been appreciated by few at the time. More than Georgian in its dignified simplicity, it is wholly executed in freestone with no carved detail at all (Fig. XI 1). If this be the finest commercial edifice of the 40's—as I think it is—it is by no means a representative one. Rather it is more exceptional than Wild's Christchurch, Streatham, among Early Victorian churches or Cockerell's own Concert Room in Liverpool among interiors for secular use. Cockerell is the first Victorian commercial architect whose work requires discussion in some detail not so much because of his Liverpool chambers as on account of his famous banks; for these early established a recognized standard even though that standard was rarely maintained by others.

Charles Robert Cockerell, after 1833 Soane's successor as Architect to the Bank of England, is an architect at least of Pugin's or Barry's stature, if not of their historical importance. Born in 1788, he was the son of an excellent Late Georgian designer, Samuel Pepys Cockerell (1754–1827), who was Architect to the Foundling Hospital and Surveyor to the East India Company. Young Charles grew up to become for some years a principal assistant to Sir Robert Smirke; he began his own practice in 1817 after a brief but highly productive archaeological expedition to Rome and Greece. Thenceforth a recognized authority on Greek architecture, Cockerell was without question one of the best trained and most original of the younger men who accepted the Greek Revival program. In 1819 he was appointed Surveyor to St. Paul's Cathedral. He was also officially associated with his father in the surveyorship of the East India Company according to the usual semihereditary practice of the City Companies. Moreover, the uncle for whom Cockerell had been named, Sir Charles Cockerell, was a retired nabob with important connections in the company. (It was for Sir Charles, incidentally, that Repton Indianized Sezincote, the principal prototype of the Brighton Pavilion.) Much later Cockerell, at the age of 45, was appointed Architect to the Bank and his real career began.

Cockerell's earliest commercial work of consequence dates from the reign of William IV although at the Bank of England itself he did nothing considerable until much later. His Westminster Insurance Office in the Strand, built in 1831–32, was an important early instance of the employment of an architect of distinction by a private company for its principal seat. (The Bank of England and the East India Company were, in prestige and through their close governmental connections if not yet in legal fact, public institutions.) His important work at the Universities and at St. George's Hall in Liverpool has already been discussed in the previous chapter. That work makes plain why his architectural reputation is principally that of a continuator of the monumental tradition of the Late Georgian period. But it was his succession to Soane at the Bank and his various City surveyorships which must chiefly have recommended him to ambitious private banks and insurance companies, not the particular mode of design of which he was a recognized master. Cockerell's first Victorian bank was the London and Westminster head office in Lothbury on which Tite was associated with him.

Cockerell was by 1837 a leader of the profession, favorably known for his own buildings as well as for his archaeological research in Greece. (His study of the temple of Jupiter Olympius at Bassae had appeared in the supplementary volume of Stuart and Revett's *Antiquities of Athens* in 1830.) In 1836 he had already been elected a Royal Academician and soon he was to be the Academy's Professor of Architecture. His marriage at 40 to the daughter of the great engineer John Rennie symbolized his distinguished position in the professional upper middle class. But both at school at Westminster and on his travels in the East he had made many friends among the aristocracy. Probably he inherited considerable private wealth from his uncle. Not only was he older and more established, both socially and professionally, than Pugin at the opening of Victoria's reign, he represented a rather different type of Victorian. Serious and earnest, but in a somewhat donnish way, he was not a fanatic about styles. Although not really interested in medieval forms, except as he was generally interested in all architectural history and theory, he had yet been ready to design St. David's College, Lampeter, in Gothic in the late 20's. Unlike Smirke or Wilkins he was no doctrinaire either in his use of Greek forms or in his considered opinions on architecture.

Because of his important official appointments, his early membership in the Academy, and his intense study of ancient architecture, Cockerell's "public form" resembled closely that of his French contemporaries. He must have resembled them also in private character, as well as in his outlook on professional matters, more even than did Barry. He had formed an early friendship with the French architects Majois, A. N. Caristie, and A. F. R. Leclère (1785–1853) while he was a youth in Rome. They and various German scholars who had accompanied him to Greece remained his correspondents on archaeological matters throughout his life. Not surprisingly, therefore, Cockerell's architecture seems frequently more continental than English; for it is more characteristic of the general European academic line in the 30's and 40's than of peculiarly English developments. Cockerell, for example, felt the importance of continuity with the past of the two previous centuries, while Pugin and the Camdenians felt only the need for a sharp break with English postmedieval tradition. From the first they abominated the name of Wren; while in 1838 Cockerell prepared the elaborate drawing of Wren's principal works which was mentioned in the previous chapter. (To this, of course, Pugin's plate of his own churches was intended as a boastful counterblast [Fig. III 10].)

Cockerell was admirably suited by training and temperament to give a new dignity to the housing of banks and insurance offices. He felt no need to *copy* Wren any more than he did to copy the so obviously unadaptable temples which he had measured in Greece and Sicily. But he was anxious that the new commercial architecture of the City should be worthy, in its scale and in its materials, of Wren's churches which were the earliest monumental works remaining in the area. But the dignity and directness of trabeated design at which he aimed was more analogous to the work of the ancient Greeks than to that of English architects of Late Stuart times. His moldings and his orders (when he used them) are Greek; but they have a personal flavor based on exceptional examples he had himself discovered and measured. Thus the general character of his Victorian work is far removed from the conventional English Grecian of the preceding decades and closer to what the French were soon to be calling *néo-grec*. While Pugin and the Camdenians illustrate what was actually the dominant attitude of the new epoch in their increasingly meticulous archaeology, after 1837 Cockerell moved away from the close imitation of ancient models in a direction quite his own. The Gothic church builders hardly began a comparable movement before 1850 (see Chapter XVII).

The façade of the London and Westminster Bank, across Lothbury from the Bank of England, was as original a composition as Soane's Bank Houses (built 1807–10), across Prince's Street on the other side, but it already belonged to a wholly different world (Fig. XI 2). What Cockerell may have thought of Soane as an architect is unimportant; but his personal vision of classicizing design was wholly at variance with the delicacy and the fantasy of Soane's most characteristic work. (When he got the chance Cockerell even regularized the ingenious but fussy liveliness of Soane's skyline over the Threadneedle Street façade of the Bank.) Where the Prince's Street houses were domestic in scale, with smooth flat surfaces and incised linear ornament, Cockerell's bank in Lothbury was monumental, firmly articulated in terms of trabeated masonry structure, and strongly plastic; it was also very simple and direct in its handling. From a high base, broken only at the central entrance, broad pilaster-like members, horizontally rusticated, rose through two storeys. The piers at the ends projected slightly, isolating the bank from its modest domestic neighbors. They also supported, above the cornice which broke around them, seated statues representing "London" and "Westminster" —tyches, Cockerell doubtless considered them. (These were by William Grinsell Nicholl [1796–1871], who also did the pediment sculpture on the south end of St. George's Hall in Liverpool and possibly the caryatids in the Concert Room there.)

The central opening at the entrance was broader than those at the sides; the ground-storey windows filled the full width of the spaces between the piers, each being divided in three by delicate bronze members (like the shafts of ancient candelabra, contemporaries found them, although they actually seem almost devoid of reminiscence). Inner jambs, delicately carved with fasces and similar symbols, reduced the width of the windows in the storey above. These recessed frames, suggesting a plane behind that of the rusticated piers, much increased the plastic effect of the whole façade. The seven attic windows were small and architrave surrounded; the wall between was less boldly rusticated than the piers below and with vertical as well as horizontal channels. Against the sky a tall balustrade masked the roof. The chimneys at the ends were set far enough forward to echo the terminal accents of the projecting end piers below.

All in all this was a refined and carefully studied composition of the most sophisticated academic character. Depending for accent upon a minimum of carving, it had nonetheless a real richness of effect. Thus it was expressive of solid wealth, as the banker-clients must have wished it to be, while it was in no way brash or insistent except for its firm rejection of the modest domestic scale of its 18th-century neighbors. Before its demolition in 1928 the façade had been much extended so that it had quite lost its original proportions and its characteristic rhythms. Unfortunately no photographs of the original front before extension seem to remain; the later state may be seen in A. E. Richardson's *Monumental Classic Architecture of Great Britain and Ireland* [1914], Plate XXXVII.

Inside the bank a corridor 38 feet long led through the front block on the street to the main banking room at the rear. This was 34 feet by 50 feet and no less than 59½ feet high. Tite, not Cockerell, was chiefly responsible for its design. Two Greek Doric columns on each side supported a continuous balcony around the walls. Overhead, a domed roof on pendentives, all of masonry, carried a smaller glazed dome which admitted light from above. Two arched windows below the pendentives on the north and south brought in additional light from the sides. Thus the interior was considerably less original than the façade and much less novel in character than Soane's shallow tile vaults and floating lanterns inside the Bank of England across the street. But the effect was dignified and the treatment skillfully handled to make the most of an enclosed site.

In the provinces in the late 30's the Greek Revival was still in its heyday. Such banks as received any serious architectural treatment were for the most part provided with Grecian "pilasters." Such edifices usually form an agreeable part of the Late Georgian urban scene in a way many of the contemporary "Early English" churches distinctly do not; but they are rarely marked by any individual distinction in design. Rather an exception to this is the Royal Bank of Liverpool (now the Queen Assurance Buildings), at No. 10 Dale Street in Liverpool, built in 1838. Here Samuel Rowland, breaking with the extreme severity of John Foster's Greek, attempted to cater to new tastes without breaking with the basic Grecian conventions. He did so, however, in a much less academic and restrained way than Cockerell. Complexity of composition, boldness of surface relief, and above all a rather coarse fantasy and profusion in the use of rich scrolled ornamentation produced an effect more like that of late Greek Revival work in America than anything else in Britain.

A more conventional financial building of the same date is the nearby Norwich Union Insurance Office at No. 27 Castle Street. This has four Grecian Corinthian columns and a wide pediment above filled with bold scrolled carving somewhat like that on Rowland's building. Small balconies carried on scrolled brackets project between the column bases at the first-storey level. Thus there are some concessions to the rising taste for richness and plastic elaboration; but the giant order still controls and unifies the composition as in so much public architecture of the time.

In London, insurance companies were beginning to demand more novelty but they did not always obtain it from the rather conservative architects they employed. The Globe Insurance Office, built by Philip Hardwick in 1837, had a bowed front facing Cheapside with a Doric order and was still quite in the Regency vein. J. Davies in the Marine Insurance Office nearby and Thomas Hopper at the Atlas Fire Office at No. 92 Cheapside (still standing but badly damaged in the blitz) made tentative use of the Italian palace mode, which was just then receiving its most conspicuous embodiment in Barry's Reform Club house in Pall Mall. Hopper was a considerably older man than Hardwick or Cockerell and had never become a convinced Grecian, so that his Atlas Office has, not surprisingly, a rather 18th-century air. Although Chambers would probably have thought the walls unduly congested by the edicular treatment of the first-storey windows between the pilasters, he would certainly have recognized the architectural vocabulary. Hopper's contemporaries, while admitting it to be "a handsome ornament" to the City, were very critical of various details. But their Classical-functional arguments (so to call them) against the use of decorative engaged columns and blind balustrades hardly express directly their essentially Victorian *malaise* with the more than semi-Palladian character of Hopper's façade. Such multiple elaboration of surface, with both orders and edicules, was hardly to return to fashion before the mid-50's; then High Victorian architects would use it with a plastic bombast quite lacking here.

At about the same time Hopper was building another conspicuous assurance office, this time for the Legal and General Life Company at No. 10 Fleet Street, which was more advanced in style though less palatially monumental (Fig. XI 3). A Doric order divided the large ground-storey windows whose sash were set well behind the columns. On the first storey a continu-

354

ous arcade linked the windows; on the second there were edicules. But the vigorous articulation seems un-Victorian because of the severity of the detail, as a comparison with its taller neighbor, built nearly two decades later by the elder George Aitchison (d. 1858), makes very evident.

The new Victorian pace was not really set before Cockerell built the Sun Assurance Offices at the corner of Bartholomew Lane and Threadneedle Street (Fig. XI 4). Fortunately that is still extant although considerably modified. The design was carefully studied in 1839–40 and the building executed in 1841–42 at a cost of £18,500. The irregular shape of the site is skillfully handled by cutting off the corner and placing the main entrance there. The total frontage runs to some 150 feet and the height is 56 feet. The four storeys are reduced in effect to three by joining the second storey and the attic behind a single order. In each of the two façades this order is set in a shallow recess between solid end bays. The whole composition is unified by the continuity of the rather heavy modillioned cornicione at the top. Above that the chimneys provide inconspicuous terminal accents at the ends of both façades.

The entrance on the corner is turned toward the main avenue of approach; therefore Cockerell concentrated on this corner most of his ornamental features. A pair of Doric columns provides a slight porch before the door. Above, in the first storey, comes the only found arch on the whole exterior richly elaborated by a carved garland. Over this arch two engaged columns flank a large architraved window. Below this window is a curving slab balcony; above it appears the symbol of the insurance company—the Sol Invictus of antiquity, derived from the ancient coins Cockerell knew so well. In a way, therefore, this very academic building is as much designed in perspective as are Pugin's and Scott's contemporary churches with their elaborate corner towers; it even has a touch of special erudition in the ornamentation to match the sacramentality of Durandus!

The plastic articulation of the walls is much greater than on the London and Westminster Bank (Fig. XI 2). Above all, the rhythms are more complex, both horizontally and vertically, because of the way the terminal bays enframe the four more open bays between. On the ground floor these central bays are completely articulated structurally. The haunched-segmental arches (which probably represent the first appearance of this favorite Victorian form) rest on plain square piers with molded imposts. Rustication at this stage is restricted to the arches and the corners. The storey next above received little emphasis since Cockerell wished to shift the focus of attention upward to the crowning double storey. Except for the continuous architraves around the windows, which are recessed in the central bays and brought forward in those at the ends, the treatment is very like that on the

Westminster Bank. Behind the terminal colonnade the second-storey and the attic windows appear to be set in a continuous articulated stone frame. In the end bays the windows have pediments carried on scrolled brackets; these project well forward of the wall, which is in the same advanced plane as the front surface of the colonnade. Just as the consoles of the balcony at this level on the corner deflect the observer's interest to the garlanded arch underneath, so in these end bays of the side façades similar accents are set below the top-storey windows primarily to attract the eye downward since their practical function is merely to support very light balcony slabs.

Although the orders are Grecian and the moldings also have a Grecian refinement, this composition recalls in spirit Italian Mannerist work of the mid-16th century—that later cinquecento with which Victorian architects seem to have had a real aesthetic affinity. But above all, this is a highly personal and even original building. It was skillfully planned for contemporary business needs (or so we are assured by writers of the period), incorporating the offices of two related companies and residences for their managers; it was superbly executed, moreover, in fine Portland stone. The Sun Offices once dominated their surroundings as much by the coherence and plasticity of their design as by their relative bulk. The façades also provided a model of commercial monumentality considerably more suggestive to other architects than the rather austere front of the nearby Westminster Bank. They still readily put to shame Sir Herbert Baker's Bank of England, as rebuilt in 1925–39, and most of their other neighbors.

Cockerell designed only one more insurance building, and that in the years 1856–58 rather beyond the end of the Early Victorian period. The Liverpool and London Office in Dale Street, Liverpool, at the corner of Exchange Place is a large and complex block (Fig. XI 5). The main façade in Dale Street is articulated in much the same way as the two façades of the Sun Offices. Although there is more carved ornament, it is still of a cold *néo-grec* order, somewhat like Henri Labrouste's in France but rather more plastically treated.

Before turning to Cockerell's work for the Bank of England, the small Savings Bank in Bath completed from the designs of George Alexander in 1841 should be recalled. Only three bays wide and three storeys tall, this building quite overshadows in scale the contemporary post-Georgian terrace at whose end it stands. It is a solid Bath stone cube, with very plastic door and window enframements, and crowned with a bold cornicione (Fig. XI 6). It was here in Bath rather than in London or any of the larger cities that Barry's paradigm for the Early Victorian clubhouse seems first to have been adapted to financial uses by totally ignoring the symmetry of the exterior in the interior disposition. A modest monument, this is therefore also an important one historically. Despite its small size it is not unworthy of comparison with its great rival in Pall Mall.

For a long time Cockerell had little new work to do for the Bank of England beyond the modest Dividend Warrant Office behind the western end of Soane's south front. This was opened in 1835. In 1844, however, his position as Architect to the Bank bore fruit in concurrent commissions to provide four splendid daughters for the London Old Lady, branch banks at Plymouth, Manchester, Bristol, and Liverpool. All rather similar, these are definitely semipublic monuments; they were certainly quite consciously intended to overshadow other local banks as completely as the Bank of England, the central banking system of the Empire, overshadowed all British private bankers.

The Manchester branch bank in King Street is the least advanced in style and the least interesting. Four engaged, unfluted Greek Doric columns in the center are echoed by an additional pair near the ends of the rather broad façade. But even so this is anything but a conventional Grecian design. Great arches rise two storeys in the three center bays to mark the chief banking room. The pediment, moreover, is not carried on the entablature over the engaged columns but raised higher above a plain attic. Cockerell's characteristic "displaced accents" make their appearance in the first-floor window balconies of the end bays. The rusticated wall surfaces, however, seem rather flat in the old Late Georgian way; and the boldly projecting columnar motif is stretched too wide to be really effective.

Despite its pinched site in a narrow street, the Bristol branch bank façade is a much finer and more concentrated composition (Fig. XI 10). As at the Westminster Bank in the City, projecting piers are used to isolate it from the neighboring buildings. Attached to the inner side of these piers low entrance portals project, overlapping the narrow rusticated side bays in elevation. The two engaged Doric columns in the center are boldly fluted. Behind them, even more than at the top of the Sun Offices, the frames of the ground-floor and mezzanine windows seem to be merely members of an open stone screen. Above, a rather flat second storey rises in the plane of this stone window screen below. This storey contains three very large plain arches and carries a plain pediment above.

There is little or no ornamentation, less actually than at Manchester, but the linking of the elements is very subtle and produces an effect of great plastic richness. The side piers end at the level of the top-storey imposts. The advanced plane of the two portals is carried across the front as a simple iron railing on a stone base. The projection of the lower storeys in front of the upper is emphasized by a slightly more elaborate iron railing on the outer edge of the main cornice. Despite the extreme severity of the detail, this

357

remarkable exercise in plastic organization forcibly recalls Roman Baroque church façades. Cockerell was the best sort of academic eclectic like Chambers in the previous century. On the basis of a real knowledge of European architecture since the Renaissance, as well as of Roman and Greek antiquity, he knew how to utilize compositional suggestions from various disparate sources, at the same time cleverly disguising their origins. Thus he not only modulated Baroque concepts to conform to his own personal taste, formed on Greek temples, but protected himself from contemporary critics who would have condemned anything overtly Baroque in origin.

The Liverpool branch bank occupies a corner site where Cook Street joins Castle Street. It was not necessary, therefore, for Cockerell to concentrate all the plastic interest on a single elevation. The Castle Street front, however, is richer than the one at Bristol—even too rich, perhaps—so that it is less satisfying than the side façade to modern eyes (Fig. XI 9). There are boldly rusticated corner piers and even carving on the Doric capitals, as well as in the frieze, not to speak of a boldly bracketed cornicione above the second storey. The small Ionic columns flanking the central window of the second storey and the arched drip mold (for such it amounts to) above the rather shallow niche in which this window is set cannot but appear somewhat petty. But the projection of the characteristic first-floor balconies into the plane of the colonnade on the front, and well out from the wall plane on the side, is both striking and effective. Three great rusticated arches rise from the ground floor on the side façade in Cook Street, defining clearly the height of the main banking room within (Fig. XI 9). These are really impressive; but the diagonal view of front and side together was certainly not considered so successfully as at the Sun Life Offices where the main entrance was placed at the corner.

The interiors of the branch banks, although of course not due to Tite's cooperation as in the London and Westminster, are hardly up to the exteriors, at least as one sees them today. The fireproof construction is entirely hidden under neutral plaster surfaces with rather inexpressive molded membering. The lithe grace of Soane's interiors at the mother bank had been forgotten; the rich delicacy of Cockerell's later Music Room at St. George's Hall is hardly foreseen. Yet these interiors are certainly solidly designed even if they do lack that integrity of expression of structure and materials which gives distinction to the masonry exteriors.

In the treatment of masonry Cockerell achieved a standard of precision the previous century had hardly known. There is surely no decline in basic craftsmanship in these edifices, as the extreme simplicity of the Bank Chambers, standing immediately behind the bank in Cook Street, makes still more evident. It is well to realize that it was not necessary, as Pugin and the Camdenians believed, to revive medieval methods of building in Early Victorian times in order to obtain good craftsmanship. On the contrary very few of the leading church architects' buildings of the 40's were as well built in the first place or have survived as well physically as Cockerell's.

Cockerell's patrons were of course very different from those who supported the Gothicists. Hardheaded bank and insurance authorities were ready (at least when they employed so serious an architect) to pay high prices for good materials and expert workmanship—at the Liverpool bank some £23,-000. Such men probably knew better than aristocrats like Lord Shrewsbury and Beresford-Hope whether they were really getting their money's worth in sound materials and construction even if their visual tastes were unsophisticated. The masonry of the walls of the Liverpool branch bank is of the hard Derbyshire gritstone which comes from Darley Dale; the plinth of gray Aberdeen granite. The superbly simple, polished red Peterhead granite fascia surrounding the entrance door is an early example of this favorite Victorian material used as a color accent, and one of the finest of all.

Cockerell's clients in the 40's already wished to have their new business buildings monumental and complex in design, but they were still conservative enough to prefer dignity to display. Symbolic functionalism demanded that a bank—and above all a branch of the Bank of England—should be solid, not flashy. Down into our own time vestiges of this attitude remain. That explains why the basic stylistic character established for Early Victorian banks has continued as a tradition of eclectic practice quite as long as has the stylistic character of the Early Victorian church. Some sort of architectural effect not unrelated to that of the Liverpool bank is still, to most laymen, as much the accepted symbol of serious finance as some derivative from Camdenian church models of the 40's is the symbol of respectable religion. Even modern architects like Howe and Lescaze and Pietro Belluschi have reflected such an attitude when working for banks and insurance companies, showing a renewed predilection, indeed, for Cockerell's polished granite as a luxurious embellishment.

In the Early Victorian period the British upper middle classes were working out for themselves a set of new architectural symbols. This is a cultural activity of which our own age is only just beginning to realize the need. They met perhaps with wider success in establishing types of expression for buildings to serve activities not entirely new but merely changed in scale or in emphasis, such as banks and churches, than in structures such as railway stations in which absolutely novel functions required expression. Yet, as we have already seen at the court of the Coal Exchange, when new structural systems were architecturally exploited to serve new purposes the results are far more exciting (see Chapters XV–XVI).

359

The Early Victorian methods of half-conscious symbol creating in architecture and the continued acceptance of those symbols explain why even the earliest examples in which the symbols were given material form so often strike us today as lacking freshness of invention. Like certain quotations, various formulas of design have since been so recurrently repeated—and often, alas, so irrelevantly—that the relative novelty and suitability of the Victorian originals can only be realized by an imaginative effort on the part of the observer. Studying early examples such as Cockerell's banks in their contemporary context can help to reveal their unique qualities. Here at Liverpool the Grecian conventionality of the slightly earlier Norwich Union Office next door in Castle Street effectively emphasizes Cockerell's positive originality in the design of his branch bank; while the Bank Chambers behind illustrate even better how devoid of excessive architectural elaboration his best commercial work could be on occasion.

Cockerell, though he continued in practice a decade after Pugin's death, is like Pugin an initiatory figure. Since he was an older man whose own tastes had set before the new period began, Cockerell had less influence on the direction monumental commercial architecture took in the 40's and 50's—even in London and Liverpool where he chiefly worked—than did Pugin on church building throughout Great Britain. The effect of Cockerell's Royal Academy teaching was not apparently progressive in effect despite his real erudition and the generosity of his theoretical ideals. Norman Shaw, one of the latest of his pupils, is perhaps the only architect of consequence who owed him much. That debt is most ambiguous; its ultimate repayment was not even a Victorian episode. The new academicism of the Edwardian period, which Shaw did so much to initiate and which led directly into the neo-Georgian of the period of George V, goes back in part to Cockerell. Neo-Georgian architects such as Professor Sir Charles Reilly or Professor A. E. Richardson at their best were disciples of Cockerell even more truly than of the earlier Georgians. This, Richardson's enthusiastic—perhaps rather over-enthusiastic—account of Cockerell's work in his *Monumental Classic Architecture of Great Britain and Ireland* [1914], a great folio volume in which that work is best illustrated, clearly reveals. (Even John Summerson a generation later named one of his triplets Charles Robert!)

In Scotland the chief bank built in the mid-40's was the Commercial Bank of Scotland (1844–46) in George Street, Edinburgh, which was designed by David Rhind. This is distinctly less original than Cockerell's Westminster Bank in London or his branch banks in the provinces; it is also much more ornate and expensive looking (Fig. XI 7). Set back in a row of very severe Georgian houses of post-Adam date, this large structure has at first sight a somewhat 18th-century air, at least until the hardness and metallic crispness of the detailing is fully apprehended. Actually Rhind was not in the least Palladian. As A. E. Richardson has remarked, he was evidently inspired here by Playfair's more characteristically Grecian Royal College of Surgeons which had been built in 1830 south of the Old Town.

Over the tall Corinthian portico of the Commercial Bank the heavy pediment is loaded with figure sculpture. The wall of the building behind the portico, extending one bay beyond on either side, is articulated by rather slender antae not by conventional Corinthian pilasters. The wall plane itself is rusticated and just visible as an edging around the ground-storey openings; the upper-storey openings have arches with very thin archivolts carried on narrow imposts. At the base of the upper-storey windows, above an ornamented stringcourse, a balustrade is threaded across the façade between the actual wall plane and the plane of the projecting antae. Another balustrade masks the roof above the main cornice at either side of the pediment.

Like Cockerell, Rhind employed here a very unorthodox sort of Grecian design, freely introducing arches and balustrades. But the Commercial Bank is quite without the coherent personal taste which gives distinction to all of Cockerell's banks. In Scotland generally, and to some extent in the North of England also, similar though smaller banks with giant porticoes are almost as characteristic of the 40's as in America. There an even purer Greek taste continued in financial circles than in the "Athens of the North." The revived Greek temple had made its earliest appearance as a bank in Philadelphia almost a quarter-century earlier. This was designed by William Strickland (1788–1854) rather than as was long supposed by Cockerell's professional "brother" B. H. Latrobe (1764–1820) who had been a pupil of S. P. Cockerell.

The most prolific of all Victorian bank architects, John Gibson, was making his first professional mark in Scotland at this time. One of his earliest and least characteristic works, the Romanesquoid Baptist chapel in Bloomsbury, has been mentioned in an earlier chapter; but banks were to be his life work. Gibson was born in 1819 and had been employed in Charles Barry's office from 1835 to 1844, in the later years effectively as chief designer. He was therefore singularly well prepared to use Renaissance forms with taste and authority. His National Bank in Glasgow, however, the commission for which he won in competition, was not very advanced in style. It had a much more deceptively Palladian look than Rhind's Edinburgh bank.

Pilaster orders divided each of the two storeys into bays, with paired engaged columns flanking the central bay (Fig. XI 8). The wall surfaces, of Binnie stone from near Edinburgh, were completely rusticated, and the archivolts of the ground-storey openings were broken with ornamented quoins. The first-storey windows carry pediments on scrolled brackets with enriched architraves rather than Barry-like edicules surrounding them. The Corinthian frieze of the first storey was richly garlanded, and decorative carved urns above a blocking course corresponded to the pilasters below. Above the central projection of the entablature rose an elaborate armorial achievement flanked by two seated females, the work of John Thomas. The whole exterior was therefore very ornate in contrast with the Grecian severity of Cockerell's banks. Though better proportioned it had a good deal of the spuriously 18th-century air of Hopper's Atlas Fire Office in London.

The great central banking room, which received no external expression, had a high coved ceiling above a Corinthian pilaster order. In the center of the flat ceiling a dome, glazed with stained glass by Ballantine and Allan of Edinburgh (who had executed the windows of the House of Lords), floated between flat panels. The whole interior effect was broad and open but completely without structural character. Obviously much iron was needed to sustain this ceiling but there was no visible evidence of its use. Gibson achieved a certain dignity and order in the disposition of the decorative elements and added to it richness with the warm colors of the real and simulated marbles; but the whole interior effect must have been rather specious and lacking in individual flavor. (The decorator was Bennett, of Boyle and Company, a local firm.)

Gibson in his first maturity represented Early Victorian architecture at its most complacent, content to avoid solecisms and to achieve sumptuous effects by controlled elaboration of inherited modes. Soon—very soon, indeed—such an approach was to seem positively reactionary as more exotic models and greater plastic vitality were demanded. So much more difficult was it to handle successfully this new and bolder vein that Gibson's conservative work often appears worthy by contrast merely because of its relative restraint. He came into his own only with the 70's when restraint once more began to be fashionable; thus eventually he appeared to be a leader, not the laggard he had actually been throughout most of his middle life.

The Royal Insurance Buildings in Liverpool begun in 1846 by William Grellier (who had won the first competition for the Royal Exchange in 1839) not only offer an excellent counterbalance to Gibson's Glasgow bank but also a more significant document in the history of Victorian taste (Fig. XI 12). Quite like Cockerell's Sun Offices, this edifice was a four-storey block pierced by many windows, but there the resemblance ended. Grellier's model was still doubtless Italian—no longer the Farnese of Barry's Reform Club house but rather some North Italian palace of the late 16th or 17th century if, indeed, he bothered to seek specific authority for increasing the ornateness of a widely accepted model. Sophisticated critics of the time were quite aware of the massiveness appropriate to design in the Italian palace manner, as also, more specifically, of the wide wall spaces, both between storeys and between the windows in each storey, which Renaissance precedent demanded. But such pedantries concerning "correctness" were boldly ignored by Grellier in the large size and the close spacing of his openings as also in his frankly four-storeyed treatment. As in the case of Hopper's Atlas Office and of Gibson's Glasgow bank, the resultant congestion of the façade was more noticeable than the considerable actual increase in the window area even though no Palladian pilaster orders hemmed in here the boldly projecting window frames.

The high base was not solid but broken by wide windows. The ground storey consisted of rusticated piers quite unrelated to the palace façade which began with the storey above; the Doric order at the entrance in North John Street rose straight from the ground. The rhythm of the front was highly conventional with the central accent the entrance provided carried up by the large first-storey window and the second-storey balcony above. Three windows, evenly spaced, flanked the central bay in each storey. The heavy armorial trophy in the broken pediment of the entrance rose in front of the central window of the first storey; this knot of plastic interest was evidently expected to focus the whole diffuse composition. But the curved and segmental pediments of the other first-storey windows, being carried forward on richly carved brackets, were almost as conspicuous; while the coarse rustication at the corners was insufficient to control so much activity on the intervening wall surfaces.

The attic, which appeared like an afterthought, positively crawled with ornament. This ornament was more delicate in scale than that below and was placed between, instead of around, the window openings. Even a contemporary critic in *The Builder, 6,* 618, remarked that the "attic is a little overdone." The façade terminated in a rather underscaled balustrade topped by two inadequate urns. Therefore the vigorously bracketed main cornice below the attic could not bind the façade together any more than did the vermiculated quoins on the corners.

The contrast of this commercial palazzo with the great, simple, red-brick warehouses Jesse Hartley (1780–1860) was building along the new docks at the same time is shocking to modern eyes (Fig. XI 11). But to the Early Victorians such things were merely not "Architecture"; moreover, the men who built them usually called themselves engineers, not architects. In 1844 Liverpool had over £2,000,000 worth of such work under construction; before the end of the Early Victorian period it rose way above that sum. Much of it fortunately remains, particularly at the north end of the docks.

Hartley was the engineer responsible for all the work at the docks; but

of course building warehouses was but a minor part of his activities compared
to the excavation and the embankment of the various slips and basins, with
which we are not concerned here. For ten or fifteen years, from the beginning
of the Albert Dock (1842–46) through the completion of the Stanley Dock
(1852–56), Hartley's "style" changed very little; it is, in fact, more properly
to be considered post-Georgian than Early Victorian. The interiors have
a purely industrial elegance. Inside the vast edifice of the Albert Dock warehouse, measuring 99 feet by 88 feet, very shallow brick arches were supported on iron beams above the widely spaced iron columns. The exteriors
of all the dock warehouses had slightly more pretension, with their endless
ranks of cast-iron Doric columns and occasional great elliptical arches along
the basin's edge. But it is the fine red brickwork, carefully spaced windows,
and modest brick cornices that give the design of these warehouses its essential character as engineering-achitecture of a very high order (Fig. XI 11).
Curiously enough, in his smaller dock constructions Hartley used stone,
generally in a smooth-surfaced rubble of most distinctive character and
with overtly medievalizing features like those seen on contemporary prisons
(Fig. XI 13). But the swinging curves of the outer walls and the subtly
sculptural shaping of the copings and gateposts have an elegance that suggests the Art Nouveau of the 90's. For much of his detailing Hartley seems
a saner rival of Victor Horta (1861–1947) or Antonio Gaudì (1852–1926),
but one working a generation earlier than they without benefit of aesthetic
or professional pretension.

It remains to defend such ornate work as Grellier's Royal Insurance Buildings in comparison with the simplicity and directness of Hartley's docks
and warehouses. The latter are built of red Lancashire stock brick, which
is impressive en masse from a distance but coarse when seen at close range.
The insurance building was all of hard gritstone, less superbly worked than
the stone of Cockerell's bank, perhaps, but well able to stand up under the
smoky climate of central Liverpool. Since this stone was destined to turn
a deep charcoal gray in a generally gray climate, the exaggerated projection of all the features was justified to provide effects of relief that might
be expected to endure. The fussy elaboration of the carving would soon
be reduced to a lithographic pattern of blacks and dark grays; less turgid
detail would hardly have been seen at all after a few years—five only,
contemporaries declared, in Leeds.

Without the site, what Grellier built cost some £18,000, nearly as much
as did the branch Bank of England; the warehouses alone at the Stanley
Dock four years later were contracted for at £127,978. Considering the great
difference in dimensions however, the cubic cost of Grellier's edifice works
out much the higher of the two. This block should not therefore be considered

tawdry like the contemporary work in stucco and other synthetic materials of which a great deal was still going up in Liverpool (Fig. XII 12). Since its façades would necessarily be seen at closer range than the dock warehouses and were intended to serve as an advertisement for the financial strength of the company, an effect of richness and solidity was most desirable. The windows had to be enlarged and brought closer together in order to provide adequate light for the offices inside; therefore only great boldness in the relief of the window frames could be expected to provide a monumental exterior effect—or so it seemed to most other Early Victorian commercial architects as well as to Grellier. With the resolution of the dilemmas of design and construction and function once partially accomplished, a truly Victorian sort of monumental business architecture did eventually arise. The Royal Insurance Buildings were almost as much a primitive of the High Victorian as certain early churches by Butterfield (see Chapter XVII). Hartley's docks, even including their extraordinarily abstract curved detail, are an aftermath— or else perhaps a delayed climax—of Late Georgian engineering-architecture.

In every way more literate, but also much less forward looking, was Gibson's Imperial Assurance Office at the corner of Old Broad and Threadneedle Streets in London beside Moxhay's Hall of Commerce. This was completed in 1848. As on Cockerell's nearby Sun Offices, the awkward angle was given special treatment, but this angle did not include the main entrance which occupied instead an ordinary bay in the side façade (Fig. XI 14). Only three storeys tall rather than four like Cockerell's and Grellier's insurance offices, the Imperial's façade was more correct academically.

The ground-floor openings were covered with round arches ornamented by vermiculated rustication and by carved heads boldly projecting from the keystones. The arches were no wider than the trabeated first-storey windows above; thus they did not constitute an arcade. The frames of the first-storey windows were Barry-like Corinthian edicules set in a flatly rusticated wall. The attic windows, with segmental tops and carved architraves, were linked by a stringcourse below and a carved frieze above. The ground and first storeys were equal in height; but the surface richness was made continuous on the former in order to provide a solid base, while it was concentrated at the edicules on the latter. As a concession to interior needs, the attic storey was made relatively too tall and its windows were much too large for correctness. But the spacing of the windows throughout all the storeys was as relentlessly regular as on a real Italian palace.

In contrast to all this conscientiousness of proportioning, with the whole façade carefully executed in Portland stone and the details neatly carved in rather low relief, the treatment of the corner accent appeared the more strikingly turgid. On the quadrant, which was slightly inset, Doric columns banded with rustication flanked a ground-floor arched window of normal height and width. On the first floor the conventional edicule was broadened by extra pilasters and also linked by rather meaningless scrolls and arabesqued spandrels to an elaborate armorial achievement filling the attic above. All this complication was confused and even irrelevant since the building was not designed in perspective and the main entrance was not at this angle. Moreover, the carving was all executed in Portland stone which does not stand up to the acid air of London in the way gritstone does to the smoke of Liverpool. Inevitably the façade must rapidly have lost the rather timid elegance it possessed when new; yet on the whole the Imperial was definitely more advanced in treatment and more skillfully composed than Gibson's earlier Glasgow bank.

Well into the next decade the correctness of Gibson's Imperial rather than the boldness of Grellier's Royal was generally preferred by most bank and insurance companies. Although Gibson himself rarely repeated the formula he used here, the prestige of his master Barry's Reform Club house —and by the end of the decade of his Bridgewater House—continued to suggest that something resembling a West End clubhouse or a West End mansion provided the most proper symbolic reference for the seat of a distinguished financial institution. There are many characteristic examples of the financial palazzo, richer than Alexander's Bath Savings Bank but not as ornate as Bridgewater House, which date from just before and just after 1850.

A carved frieze, shell-filled arches above the ground-floor windows, and a projecting pedimented porch elaborate, for instance, the Western Bank (now occupied by the Scottish Widows' Fund) which was built in Edinburgh at No. 9 St. Andrew's Square in 1848. In St. Andrew's Square and along George Street in Edinburgh are various other versions of the Reform Club house dating from the 50's, 60's, and even the early 70's. Some of them, such as the Scottish Provident Institution at No. 6 St. Andrew's Square, the New Town branch of the Royal Bank of Scotland, built by Peddie and Kinnear in the late 50's at No. 101 George Street, and the Union Bank of Scotland, built by David Bryce at No. 62 George Street as late as 1872, have real Barryesque quality. Bryce's earlier British Linen Bank in St. Andrew's Square, with its attached giant order, was already outdated by the palazzos on the south and the west of the square by the time it rose on the east side in 1850–52.

In Glasgow the Commercial Bank by Rhind, in Gordon Street between Buchanan and West Nile, begun in 1854, followed intentionally the Farnese Palace. Clarke and Bell's Caledonian Insurance Office was also Italianate, not Grecian, when it was built the next year. The Bank of Scotland, built by J. T. Rochead around 1860 in George Square, Glasgow, is comparable to the best Edinburgh banks although considerably richer as regards the carved work. There is shell carving over the ground-storey windows as at No. 9 St. Andrew's Square in Edinburgh, while atlantes support a projecting entablature over the central entrance, which is loaded with a heavy armorial achievement. Tripled brackets in the cornice and richly draped urns above the crowning balustrade further illustrate the increasing tendency, even in Scotland, as the mid-century wore on, to elaborate the established formula without essentially modifying it.

Thus the Reform Club house, as well as Cockerell's banks, provided as important a Victorian model for the use of the financial world as Pugin's St. Oswald's, Old Swan, did for the religious. Indeed it was Barry rather more than Cockerell who set the pace here as in so many other fields of secular architecture; moreover he did so, as it were, inadvertently since he himself built no banks or insurance buildings. Characteristic of such a situation is the fact that Gibson, who had learned the formula from Barry himself, rarely stuck to it very closely. Others, however, who had no contact with Barry continued to use the palace mode for a decade or two without significant development, just as Pugin's basic models remained in general use well through the 50's and even beyond.

In the later 40's private banks of distinguished design, some of them very modest in size, were being erected in many of the larger cities; not all of them followed Barry very closely. One of the finest is Sir Benjamin Heywood's (now Williams Deacon's) Bank, in St. Ann's Square in Manchester, which was built in 1848–49 by J. E. Gregan (Fig. XI 16). The main block is of Halifax stone, all laid up on its natural bed with the exception of the columns. This masonry is superbly cut and as sharp in detail as the day it was completed, though smoked now to a broadcloth-like blackness. The rusticated ground storey is broken by three arches toward the square; surprisingly, three Palladian windows are introduced along the side toward St. Ann's Street. In the storey above, the windows are all edicular, with one triple window at the narrow end and another in the middle of the long front. The attic windows are flanked by very long, shallow consoles beneath the bold cornicione. The corner of the building is cut off on the diagonal, but with no opening at all on the ground floor; and all the wall edges have crisply rusticated quoins. In comparison with Grellier's Royal Insurance Buildings, or even with Gibson's Imperial, the effect is remarkably cool and discreet. It may not be particularly original but this bank of Gregan's shows even more personal refinement than his Barryesque institute.

Even quieter is the rear block of the bank in St. Ann's Street. This is linked to the front block by a one-storey bay; here the main entrance is set in a superbly profiled niche. Above this, one plain wreath is carved in the tympanum with single word "Bank" immediately over the door. The rear block itself is of red Lancashire brick, carefully selected and immaculately laid, with all the quoins, architraves, stringcourses, and cornices of Halifax stone. The five flat-topped openings are all wide and admirably spaced; the first-storey windows are emphasized by cornices above the architraves and by plain molded panels between the stringcourse and the continuous sill moulding. Gregan's work, like Cockerell's, can enforce belief in the valid after-life of the Georgian academic tradition. But it was exceptional in its day and really rather inexpressive of Victorian Manchester compared with that of Walters (Figs. XII 14, 16).

In small cities the banks are likely to be rather less distinguished. At North-ampton, for example, there is an Early Victorian building, now occupied by the Royal Insurance Office, at No. 6 in the Market Square which is hardly more than an elaborate post-Georgian dwelling. This is three bays wide and four storeys tall like a terrace house; the upper storeys actually provided a residence for the bank manager. Edmund Francis Law (1818–1882), a local architect who was County and Town Surveyor and eventually Mayor, employed a single Palladian window in the center of the rusticated ground storey between two narrow arched doorways, an obvious but rather awkward arrangement (Fig. XI 17). The first storey has three edicular windows evenly spaced. The attic windows utilize the cornices of the second-storey win-dows below as sills. This treatment creates a series of vertical accents in contradistinction to the more usual horizontal linking of top-storey openings. The whole front is framed by rusticated quoins and by a bracketed cornice with a frieze of rosettes. The result is respectable, dull, and even rather pathetic because of the considerable deterioration of the nicely colored local stone in which the front was executed.

Although Law had lost the competition in 1849 for the Corn Exchange which was to be built in the Square beside the bank he generously accepted, with a proper respect for the general urbanistic effect, the main horizontal lines of the Exchange façade which the competition winners George Alex-ander and his associate on this commission, Hall of Northampton, were erecting. The happy professional cooperation between the winners and the losers in a competition here, and between a public and a private client, shows Early Victorian urban building in its most civilized and agreeable aspect, even if hardly at its most technically advanced or its most boldly original.

Other banks in county towns, such as the Gloucester Savings Bank built also in 1849–50 by the local architects Hamilton and Medland, were likely to be even more laggard in their simple astylar treatment and less friendly in their relationship to their neighbors. If rarely positive ornaments, how-ever, they were yet almost never blots upon the various market squares and high streets in which they were built.

Back in the mid-30's the new Law Life Assurance Offices in Fleet Street beside St. Dunstan's-in-the-West were described as being an admixture of "bad Italian architecture with some of the characteristics of the pointed Style." This early use of what was evidently Jacobethan design for an insurance building was loudly protested. Curiously enough, Jacobethan design, so popular for country houses and for various sorts of institutions in the 40's, was emulated only very rarely in Early Victorian banks and insurance offices. As has already been remarked, this was also true of public buildings. At Lichfield the Corn Exchange and Market Hall, built in 1848–50 by the local firm of Johnson and Son in Elizabethan style, has been mentioned as an exception; that group also included the local savings bank, which was even more of an exception.

More characteristic of the local banks built in the late 40's and well through the 50's in small towns is the two-storey edifice of Italianate design in the main street of Bakewell, Derbyshire. Usually freestanding, as here at Bakewell, and rising well above the surrounding houses because of their greater storey heights, such typical Early Victorian banks often have real dignity and a sort of monumentality that seems the more acceptable because it is so modest. Executed in good stone with highly competent local workmanship, the few conventional elements borrowed from the 16th-century palace formula display as little originality as do the Decorated features of the churches of the period. Yet they fit into the existing townscapes with infinitely less awkwardness and deserve, therefore, more respect than they have generally received.

By the late 40's the day for modest repetitions of Barry's Reform Club formula was already over in the larger cities. Only perhaps in Edinburgh and Glasgow did an inherited restraint control, well through the 50's and even the 60's, the architecture of financial palaces. In London, particularly, architects were much less hidebound after 1850. If the edifices designed after the mid-century are generally less well proportioned and less solidly built than the earlier examples, they nevertheless show some positive influence from the Westminster Bank and the Sun Insurance Offices in which Cockerell first set a new standard for Victorian financial building in the City. Sancton Wood (1814–1886), for the Queen's Assurance Company at Nos. 42–44 Gresham Street on the King Street corner, and Henry Baker, in the Bloomsbury branch of the London and Westminster Bank, perhaps followed most closely Cockerell's precedents, although without his dignity of scale and his scholarly discretion in detail.

The Queen's Assurance and Commercial Chambers (to give the structure its full name) were faced with Portland stone even though they cost but £8,000 (Fig. XI 15). The entrance is at the King Street angle; above it, in the first and second storeys, there projects an awkward segmental oriel wholly unrelated to any other features of the façade. This provides a poor substitute for Cockerell's corner treatment on the Sun Offices or even for Gibson's ornate corner feature on the Imperial's building. But the composition is now really designed in perspective around this chamfered angle, for the terminal bays in both Gresham Street and King Street are set off by pilasters in the same way that this angle bay is set off and neither side façade is symmetrical as both were at the Sun and the Imperial.

Segmental arches provide, as in Cockerell's insurance building, for wide ground-storey windows except in the corner and end bays. The engaged columns used for supports in this arcade produce an effect that is richer but less plastically solid than that Cockerell achieved with his plain square piers at the Sun. The way the rusticated basement arches rise up below the ground-floor windows destroys, moreover, the effect of continuous support below the arcade that Cockerell always provided. The arched windows of the first and second storeys are large and closely set; the alternately curved and pointed pediments above the first-floor windows indeed all but cover up the intervening wall surface. The paneling between the imposts and the continuous podium between the sections of balustrade across the base of the windows seem to suggest that Wood was attempting to achieve a continuous articulation of the wall. This is rather opposed to the essential solidity of the palazzo formula but definitely premonitory of later developments. Raphael's Pandolfini Palace in Florence provided for it an obvious precedent, moreover. The attic range of square, architrave-surrounded windows is set in a continuous band of rusticated wall; this and the bold modillioned cornicione above are rather more conventional in character than the main storeys below. The contract cost of the building in 1851 was £4,973, doubtless considerably exceeded during construction. Wood showed the design in the Architecture Room at the Royal Academy Exhibition in 1853.

Sancton Wood was primarily a railway architect and in his stations, several of which will find a place in Chapter XV, he attempted similar compromises between Italian formulas and new functional needs with somewhat more success; or so it has seemed to a posterity which has thus far largely ignored his commercial and residential work.

Henry Baker's Westminster Bank (Bloomsbury Branch) in Holborn was built in 1853–54 at a contract cost of £7,676, later increased to some £10,000. This is more sober and conventional in general effect than Wood's Queen's building, even though the ground-storey windows in the three central bays were made very much wider (Fig. XI 18). The windows in the upper storeys, however, are smaller and hence more broadly spaced, with the frames of those in the end bays and of the one in the center slightly elaborated. Chains of rustication flanking the end bays and continuous stringcourses at the second-storey sill level and below the attic windows square off the design in a rather dull way. Contemporary critics excused both the general lack of relief on this façade and the extreme openness of its bottom storey on the ground that the building had to face north. They noted with approval that the entire façade was of Portland stone.

The use of isolated cast-iron supports inside was most notable here, for this made possible a large banking room on the ground floor under the multiple offices of the first storey. Nonbearing partitions curved in plan created a curious keyhole-shaped interior space for the banking room which must have been extremely effective (Fig. XI 18). In general, however, the iron supports and beams and the brick jack-arches that were consistently used in these financial buildings in order to make them fire resistant had little positive effect on the interior planning and almost none on their design.

The obscure Henry Baker won the commission for this branch of the mother house in Lothbury in a competition which H. E. Kendall, Samuel Angell, and T. H. Wyatt (as well as two unidentifiable Smiths) also entered. It is worth noting that, except for Cockerell, few architects known for their work in other fields, as were Wyatt and Kendall, ever had much success in obtaining commercial commissions.

At the head office of the Westminster Bank very considerable interior alterations were also undertaken in 1852 to the tune of £5,984. Cockerell was not consulted and Tite, who was employed alone, removed the dome that had been the principal feature of his original banking room when it was first built fifteen years before. Tite was now ready to avail himself more fully of the large spans which could be supported with wrought iron trusses in order to avoid masonry vaulting altogether; but he did not have the wit to take positive advantage of this in the organization of the plan as did Baker in the Holborn branch bank.

Banks and insurance offices played a very important part in the Early Victorian urban scene. Rising above their domestically scaled neighbors, either by actual extra storeys or merely by the increase in their storey heights, they dominated street architecture until, in the later 50's and 60's, ranges of office buildings of comparable scale replaced generally the earlier Georgian dwelling houses. Built almost always of stone, the financial houses set a pace of solidity and expense with which other commercial architecture could not immediately catch up. The functional needs could be fitted into the palazzo formula without much adjustment, and the continuing demand for dignity and prestige rather discouraged for a time further innovation after that formula had once been accepted. Although few other commercial agencies vied with the financial houses in the prominence and elaboration of their principal seats before the mid-50's, it was in other branches of "street architecture," such as wholesale warehouses and commercial chambers (of which Wood's Gresham Street building already represents an instance, at least in part), that the boldest steps were being taken in the mid-century. In shop fronts all inhibitions of solidity and dignity were early thrown aside. In them the technical possibilities of wide expanses of glass made possible by light iron supports and the many opportunities for ornate detail provided by various other new materials were enthusiastically exploited from the first.

CHAPTER XII: COMMERCIAL

STREET ARCHITECTURE

Against the street architecture of the preceding Georgian Age the Early Victorians had many complaints. They found it intrinsically monotonous, deadly dull, and lacking in expression; they denounced it as tawdry in the choice and handling of materials; worst of all, it was archaeologically implausible! Regent Street, Nash's magnificent West End development built up around 1820, was the particular object of their detestation; on the last two counts at least it certainly merited criticism. But what seemed to Victorians the tedious monotony of Regent Street seems to the 20th century a most desirable consistency of character, the more surprising in that it was achieved by many different builders and by several architects only loosely controlled from the Nash office. Even the individual buildings hardly strike modern eyes as dull when they are studied in the contemporary engravings after T. H. Shepherd's drawings that are so prolifically provided in James Elmes' *Metropolitan Improvements* (2 vols., 1827–31). Their lack of strong individual expression appears to us the desirable result of tactful cooperation.

Although the Early Victorians intended in theory to leave Regent Street behind, they were singularly incapable of doing so in practice. The same stucco and cement coatings, so loudly attacked as shams by the critics, continued in use not only in London but in most provincial cities. The rather slapdash handling of conventional Greek and Roman decorative elements —implausible archaeologically but controlled by a general discipline—gave way to an equally slapdash imitation of Italian Renaissance (or occasionally of Jacobethan) models for which there were as yet no accepted traditions of adaptation. Even where there was some general architectural control in the designing of whole streets the diverse sources of inspiration which were nearly equally acceptable to Early Victorian taste made consistency of character an almost impossible achievement for the various individual designers. Although the separate structures may have (at least superficially) more positive individuality as a result than did those of Regent Street, the different modes of stylistic expression were so totally unrelated to any underlying sense of function and structure that the surface variety has become, at least to our later eyes, only a meaningless masquerade. The slight variations of scale and proportion that gave a pleasant diversity of character to the buildings of Regent Street seem to have been more interesting and more truly individual in the best sense of the word. What, for example, could have had more personal "style," within the general frame of accepted Regency styling, than Soane's terrace of shops and houses built for Mr. Robinson on the east side of the street in 1820?

Curiously enough, many of the sins of Regent Street had already been corrected in the 30's when the new streets in Newcastle were laid out and built up by the entrepreneur Thomas Grainger (1798–1861). There the local architect John Dobson (1787–1865) set the pace, and the designers in Grainger's building office were quite ready to take from Dobson their models for such ranges of buildings as he did not design himself. The streets of Newcastle, and particularly Grey Street, brought to completion in the first years of the new reign, are in some ways the finest commercial streets ever built. Although the local stone was of a dreary brownish color, now turned nearly black, there is here no tawdry construction of the Nash order. The slope of the streets and their curving sides avoid monotony; the skillful handling of the skyline gives a remarkable variety to the massing; yet the scale and the character of the detail provide consistency throughout. By varying the placing of the Corinthian and Ionic pilasters, engaged columns, and porticoes, certain individual structures were made to stand out. Public and semipublic structures are thus clearly differentiated from their less representational neighbors. Furthermore, the detail throughout is of a purity and correctness unknown in Nash's designing. In any event the hard stone discouraged the frivolous sort of purely superficial ornamentation that was so easy and so cheap to execute in stucco.

From such a peak of achievement, the culmination in several respects of Georgian urbanism, a decline was naturally to be expected. Despite their ambiguously late date there is no reason to consider any of the good streets of Newcastle to be Early Victorian; for the tide of new construction initiated in the mid-30's ran out within a very few years after the new reign began. Dobson continued to practice in Newcastle until his death in 1865, but his Central Station is almost alone worthy of his earlier work. In general the local architects of the next generation were markedly inferior not only to Dobson but to their contemporaries in other provincial cities.

It is interesting to speculate what a Cockerell or a Barry might have accomplished in the 40's had he had the backing of a Grainger in some provincial city. Cockerell was certainly a more sophisticated designer than Dobson, and his handling of masonry was equally solid and considerably more subtle. Actually, however, no provincial city in the 40's or early 50's built up a whole new commercial district so completely as Newcastle did in the 30's and early 40's. In London the new streets, for various reasons, are particularly inferior. One of the chief reasons, of course, was the lack of an inexpensive building stone or even of a visually satisfactory local brick, a problem still unresolved a century later.

Banks and insurance offices, as we have seen, were the first commercial edifices to seek individual monumental expression. The characteristic business structures in Early Victorian streets were still of a hybrid character as they had been in the Late Georgian period, with shops below and residential floors above. Houses they were called, and houses they remained in design, even though they were lifted arbitrarily above shop fronts in which increasingly large plate-glass windows occupied nearly the full width of the ground storey. The old Georgian window tax restricted the number of openings in the upper storeys while the usual brick walls, whether or not stucco covered, restricted their size. But behind the plate glass of the ground storeys the entire weight of the floors above was often carried on light cast-iron supports.

Contemporary critics approved the continuing solidity of the upper-storey walls because it provided approximately the proportion of void to solid sanctioned by academic tradition; but they recurrently deprecated the apparent lack of support below—one must admit that it can sometimes be disconcerting even today. Structural articulation of the ground storey with masonry piers and arches, as on Cockerell's Sun Insurance Offices, did not appeal to shopkeepers. It restricted the width of the shop windows and set their openings too far back from the pavement. In practice, therefore, the shop front went its own way and must be considered as a separate entity. (Whether it ought properly to be one or not is an issue which is, after all these years, not yet decided.)

According to Edward I'Anson (1812–1888), perhaps the ablest London commercial architect from the early 40's down into the 70's, the first building designed expressly and solely for use as offices was built at the Lombard Street end of Clement's Lane in 1823 by an otherwise unidentified Mr. Voysey. I'Anson's own first office building, still including dwellings above, was built in Moorgate Street in 1837 among the severe post-Regency "houses" with which Robert Smirke had just lined that new thoroughfare. (It had been cut through from Lothbury to Finsbury Pavement in the mid-30's.) Large blocks of "commercial chambers," to use the contemporary phrase, comparable in scale to insurance offices but more generalized in the types of business served, did not appear in any considerable numbers either in the City or in the provinces before the late 40's.

Warehouses in the centers of cities were still essentially utilitarian structures until the Manchester cotton merchants in the late 40's began to demand for them a representational character as impressive as that hitherto reserved for banks and insurance offices. That was because these cotton warehouses were not mere places of storage but the principal seats of their wholesale business to which clients came from all over the world. But the Manchester cotton warehouses—and the wool warehouses that served similar commercial purposes in Leeds and Bradford—are thenceforth in a different category from the dock warehouses in ports such as London and Liverpool and Bristol. The latter, throughout most of the Victorian Age, are properly to be considered works of engineering rather than of architecture.

London had always been a divided city. On the one hand there was the aristocratic and governmental West End. That district required no specialized offices for its professional men as yet. The government's civil servants, if any new provision at all were made for their increasing numbers, had quarters in what were still public monuments rather than government offices. On the other hand there was the City. A source of wealth but not of prestige, the City was on the whole still content to leave architectural splendor to the other end of town, except for its principal financial houses.

Farringdon Street North, on the site of the old and noisome river Fleet, represented an ambitious City "improvement" of the mid-40's which replaced the old Fleet Market and the horrid shambles that had surrounded it (Fig. XII 5). Yet the new buildings which went up there in the early 40's were duller and more monotonous than anything Nash ever built; and Bunning, although he was City Architect from 1843 on, does not seem to have been responsible in any way for their design. Three storeys of stucco ran along the street above continuous shop fronts, the endless upper walls varied only by the most modest and conventional of embellishments. A wide pediment covered five bays in the near center of a block that was some forty bays long. Plain oblong architraves surrounded the first-storey windows; arched windows were introduced only in the storeys above. Although there were continuous stringcourses at all the sill levels, no cornice crowned the top of the wall; there was merely a flat parapet half masking the dormered mansard behind. Wider corner bays, with triple windows linked vertically and an elliptical oculus in the third storey, broke up but hardly enlivened the general pattern. Concerning such street architecture, far more than concerning Regent Street, all the strictures of Victorian critics hold firm.

Individually designed new buildings, such as the depot of the Religious Tract Society in Paternoster Row (perhaps not a typical commerical organization even in the Victorian Age), were little better and not even very different. The Tract building had the same architraves over the first-storey windows, here capped with very flat segmental pediments; and there were the same triple windows in the center and end bays, with arches in the three bays between. The fourth storey was reduced to an attic above the modest main cornice. But beside the dirty brick houses in the rest of the street the clean stucco of this façade must at first have stood out. Like the banks and insurance buildings, the greater number of the storeys and the greater storey heights also gave it a temporary advantage in scale. The ground-floor order and the trim of the central windows above were executed in Portland stone although the total cost was only some £12,000. The building was built on ground leased for 61 years from the City Corporation; this fact, which would be equally true of many commercial edifices (although the actual ground landlords would be various), helps to explain the evident avoidance of unnecessary expense in buildings intended to last at the most for only two generations. But poverty of invention in design and entirely conventional detail too often produced façades that seem rather cluttered in spite of their relative simplicity. The architect of the Tract Society's depot was John Young, earlier a designer for Thomas Cubitt at Eaton Square and in Pimlico. Later he (or perhaps his son) was to be a bold designer of commerical buildings when the firm name became John Young and Son in the 50's.

The antiquity of the Inns of Court and the general use of brick in their medieval and later buildings discouraged the introduction of so definitely modern a material as stucco. The new buildings erected in these legal purlieus, whether for representational purposes like the Library and Hall at Lincoln's Inn or for ordinary use as lawyers' offices, are all of brick. The 90-foot block of chambers at Staple Inn built by Wigg and Pownall in 1842–43 was Jacobethan like the Law Life Offices of 1834 (Fig. XII 3). The style encouraged the use of many large stone-mullioned windows but the composition was much bedizened with scalloped gables, chains of rustication, and strapwork cresting; the resultant elaboration was of the fussy order so very popular already on country houses and on many institutional buildings outside the cities; it was certainly not at all businesslike in the way of so much real Jacobethan work. The walls, moreover, were not ruddy but pallid in color, being of "white" Suffolk brick; and the trim of Portland stone was rather pinched looking for all its profusion. Thus the effect had none of that archaeological plausibility so frequently found in the best Jacobethan work of the 40's, whether all in stone or in good red brick with rich stone trim.

It is not in London but elsewhere, in cities whose only prestige was commercial, that the first blocks of chambers seem to have been built with something of the monumental pretentions of the contemporary banks and insurance offices. The Brunswick Buildings at the corner of Brunswick and Fenwick Streets in Liverpool (Fig. XII 1), erected by A. and G. Williams in

377

1842, was an Italian palazzo almost as impressive as the Reform Club house itself (Fig. VI 5) and much larger than Alexander's slightly earlier Savings Bank in Bath (Fig. XI 6). Three storeys high and seven bays wide, with a high base below and an extremely bold cornicione above, the block of the Brunswick Buildings had a massive plasticity. The wall surfaces, moreover, were markedly plastic also, for the ground storey and the broad corner quoins were boldly rusticated and the pediments of both the first- and the second-storey windows came well forward on scrolled brackets. A Doric frieze at the top of the ground storey and a carved band below the cornice completed the enrichment. The three arches in the center of the ground storey contained two portals, each filled by a richly grilled metal door, with a small window set between them.

Despite the elaboration of the detail there was great dignity in this design: The bays were equally spaced, the proportions of the storeys nearly equal, and only the curious arrangement of the entrances appeared somewhat makeshift. Although the plain wall surface was minimized in favor of the framing elements, both those of the block as a whole and those of its multiple openings, there was none of the exaggerated boldness evident in Grellier's Royal Insurance Buildings erected a few years later here in Liverpool (Fig. XI 12); there was also little of that diffuse and meaningless richness which was to clutter and confuse the composition of Gibson's Imperial Insurance Office in London (Fig. XI 14).

On the other hand, there was also none of Cockerell's originality. The Brunswick Buildings were rather what Barry himself might have designed had he been called on to carry out an important commercial commission. They were novel (at least in relation to the conventional modes of the previous generation) and completely literate, serene rather than striking, and not at all tawdry or cheap. It might perhaps have seemed that such a suave new mode of commercial design would have little future in the Victorian Age. Actually innumerable office blocks not very dissimilar to the Brunswick Buildings, but much inferior in quality, were to be designed well into the 60's; more significantly, some of the finest urban architecture of the mid-century was to develop rather directly from this commercial version of the Italian palace formula.

The mid-40's saw several new business streets cut through Bloomsbury and St. Giles by Pennethorne under the Improvement Act of 1839. The somewhat undefined authority of the Commissioners of Woods and Forests, who had been responsible earlier for Regent Street, was rather more limited under Victoria, in fact at least if not in law. Although Pennethorne nominally had as much power as his master Nash, the results were in general notably inferior both because his collaborators were feeble men and because the

378

speculative building fever of post-Waterloo days was now largely focused on railway construction.

The extension of Coventry Street as a 60-foot thoroughfare into Leicester Square and its continuance beyond as Cranbourne Street (with a width of 54 feet) was but the beginning of a very considerable new artery which was intended to continue northeastward across Holborn to the Foundling Hospital. For this very ambitious further extension the supervising architect was to have been Barry; but the work in the short new streets that were actually executed between 1843 and 1845 was all by very obscure men such as Charles Mayhew; Herbert, Archbutt and Company; and Burton and Dent.

Mayhew's block in New Coventry Street was quite an extraordinary object, a terrifying example of the apparent lack of support in heavy buildings raised above continuous glazed shop fronts (Fig. XII 6). On top of the shop windows, with their very light iron supports and wide sheets of plate-glass, tremendous pilasters with no bases whatsoever rose through three storeys. These members were single on the ends and coupled between the bays in a perverse reversal of the normal scheme of things. Between their broad surfaces, made heavier and more pier-like by horizontal rustication, the first- and second-storey windows extended the full width of the bays and were subdivided by light metal supports. In the top storey small coupled arches under an embracing arch introduced a feeble suggestion of Romanesque tracery. To add further to the top-heavy effect there was a broad and elaborately ornamented frieze below the cornice; while above the cornice a high arcaded balustrade was interrupted over the pilasters by pedimented edicular niches—presumably disguising chimneys. The curious rhythm of this façade, with the single pilasters at the ends flanking the narrow chamfered corners and a double bay in the center, was as illiterate as the extraordinary ornamentation. So crude and clumsy is the whole effect one rather grudges giving Mayhew credit for the clarity of his first- and second-storey window treatment. This is as far a cry from the pinched dullness of Farringdon Street as from the dignified Renaissance archaeology of the Brunswick Buildings. It was to be a decade and more before the High Victorians would begin to design façades as bold but with more coherence of structural expression.

The work of the other men farther on in Cranbourne Street was perhaps more closely controlled by Pennethorne; in any case it was much less startling. For the most part the regular pattern of windows in the three storeys above the shop windows was as continuous as in Farringdon Street; at the top a plain parapet, masking the roofs, provided a continuous level skyline in contrast with the peculiar balustrade-*cum*-edicule treatment of Mayhew's block. One building, however, had towers at either end rising above the parapet. Marked off from the walls below by vertical bands of ornament these features provided happy accents in the general monotony of the street. All this work in Coventry and Cranbourne Streets seems to be gone today.

There is less monotony and a generally higher standard of design in New Oxford Street which was built up chiefly between 1845 and 1847. Most of the original construction here lasted down to World War II and a considerable amount survived the blitz. Nos. 36–42, with heavy rusticated pilasters, might well be by Mayhew, but the rhythm of the bays is more satisfactory than in his Coventry Street block. The vertical loading is also less because the top storey is treated as a mere attic above the main cornice. Nos. 75–77 (once part of a larger unit) are very much more elegant but also less original (Fig. XII 8). The pediments of the first-storey windows rest on engaged Corinthian columns, and there is excellent ornamental detail on the stringcourses below the top-storey windows and also in the cornice. These might well be from Pennethorne's own designs.

Most characteristic of the general level of New Oxford Street is the range numbered 93–105 (Fig. XII 4). In this group the corner house is emphasized by triple windows in the first and second storeys linked together by a narrow balcony. The pairs of houses are separated by recessed bays which provide a rather less subtle rhythmic scheme than that of the range numbered 36–42. There are no pediments or engaged columns on the first-storey window frames here such as are used on Nos. 75–77. The attic with its small round-arched windows and the frieze and dentil course of the wide entablature below them provide the only ornamentation. The arched windows offer a premonition of Pennethorne's Ordinance Office in Pall Mall and suggest that these houses were at least designed in his office.

Nos. 44–50 are the severest and the best designed. Rusticated piers set off the end bays and also each pair of windows in between (Fig. XII 7). Plain panels link the tops of the first-storey windows to the plain stringcourse at the second-storey sill level. The guilloche frieze is restricted to the width of the sunken panels between the rusticated bands. These features, as well as the general care for proportion and rhythm, are distinctly reminiscent of Cockerell. All the more surprising, therefore, is the clumsy attic with its little panels set above the chains of rustication and tiny arches opening between them. Could this attic have been a later addition?

All these façades are executed more or less competently in stucco. Their equal four-storey height, despite some variation in the location of the main cornices, gives real continuity of design to the whole street. Yet there are marked differences in scale and in relief, notably between those groups of

380

houses in which the first- and second-storey windows are linked vertically and those in which each storey receives independent treatment.

The present-day shop fronts in New Oxford Street—few of them are original—are no worse related to the solid façades above than were those of the period when the street was new. Because of the plasticity of the upper wall treatment, the lack of apparent support below is very noticeable. As far as one can judge from views of Regent Street when it was new, however, the general effect of New Oxford Street is not markedly inferior to the ranges of earlier buildings in the West End where Pennethorne obtained his earliest professional experience. As with all stucco-fronted buildings in dirty cities that effect depends a great deal, of course, on frequent and harmonious painting of the wall surfaces. New Oxford Street represents about the top level of London commercial building in the mid-40's. Any superior quality that modern eyes may seem to recognize in other work of the period is usually just evidence of stylistic retardation.

In the heart of the City only one new structure of great prominence was really worthy of comparison with the Brunswick Buildings in Liverpool. The Royal Exchange Buildings occupied the full length of Freeman's Place (now *called* Royal Exchange Buildings, confusingly enough) and faced the east front of Tite's new Royal Exchange. They were designed by young Edward I'Anson, an exact contemporary of Pugin's, who down through this time was still working with his father. The commission may well have come direct from Magdalen College, Oxford, which was the ground landlord.

In the Royal Exchange Buildings the rule of stucco was broken but without recourse to an expensive all-over facing of Portland stone; such facing was still reserved for banks and insurance companies. The walls here were of fine red brick and the trim was executed in Portland cement (Fig. XII 2). The ground storey, occupied by various shops and railway offices, rather resembled that of the buildings lining Percier and Fontaine's Rue de Rivoli in Paris, as begun in 1811 and as it was being continued down through this period. But there was no open portico though the broad arches, resting on square piers, were fully glazed. Where doors were needed they occupied half the width of a bay and were barely distinguishable from the rest of the window sash, quite in the mid-20th-century way. The ground storey was therefore very open in design, regular in rhythm, and monumentally scaled, even in relation to its enormous neighbor the Exchange.

As the storeys above were to be occupied by miscellaneous offices there was no need for I'Anson to break up the continuous rhythm of the upper windows in order to mark off separate dwelling units. The storey heights, moreover, were of the new "financial" height. Therefore the whole building rose well above its old four-storey domestic neighbors and overshadowed them also in the scale and the ordering of the design. Yet the façade consisted of only three storeys and an attic. The low windows of the attic with molded garlands between them suggested a continuous frieze below the cornice rather than an extra top storey.

The first- and second-storey windows were remarkably large; but they were not closely spaced nor were their frames particularly heavy. Consoled pediments on the first storey, alternately segmental and pointed, and consoled cornices at the second-storey level provided moderate accents of relief; additional consoles below the windows carried balconettes in the first storey and merely supported the window sills of the range above. The sill lines were marked by continuous cement stringcourses of sufficient breadth to link together these balconettes and consoles. There was really no principal accent. But on the curving bay at the right end of the façade a shell motif filled the first-storey pediment while a keystone served as an oversized console for the balconette above. Rusticated quoins enframed the ends of the composition. Starting above the ground-floor piers, and crossed by all the horizontal stringcourses, these were the only vertical elements.

In its extreme severity this long business block was in marked contrast to the houses of New Oxford Street. It suggested, as does much of I'Anson's later City work also, that he had knowledge of and respect for the work of contemporary (and even of rather earlier) French architects. But the use of red brick, although out of fashion in London for a century, was purely English. This provided a somewhat premature prophecy that color would eventually return to City architecture; but of the polychrome extravagances of the mid-century there was, of course, no real suggestion as yet.

In the provinces the still quite monochrome extravagances of crude Londoners like Mayhew and his fellows were generally avoided. Although stucco was much used through the 40's, and even into the 50's, the elephantine detail and the strange syncopations of rhythm seen in Coventry Street and to some extent in New Oxford Street seem to have had less appeal. In part this was due to conservatism of taste. Variations on Greek themes lasted longer in provincial public architecture, as we have seen, than in the metropolis; hence there was less demand for novelty in commercial architecture.

The relatively exclusive character of the architectural profession outside London was probably chiefly responsible for the superior quality of commercial design. There were in Early Victorian London, as there had been in the 18th century, many builders who set up as architects with no professional training at all. Below Cockerell, Barry, Pennethorne, and I'Anson, therefore, came many levels of architects, often self styled, of less and less competence. But in the large provincial cities, whose great expansion mostly dated from this period, there had often been in Late Georgian days but one out-standing architect, such as Foster in Liverpool or Dobson in Newcastle. The advice of such leaders had long been taken on all architectural problems of any consequence. In their offices the men of the new generation coming to professional maturity in the mid-40's had almost necessarily received their training. That training must usually have been rather inhibiting because it was so limited. Yet there was less hurry and scurry in the provinces, always the curse of any metropolitan architectural scene, and undoubtedly a sounder technical tradition survived in a provincial building industry little cor-rupted by Nashian flimflam. For these reasons the Early Victorian com-mercial architecture of the other British cities is both solider and less strik-ingly novel than that of London. Today it merges almost unnoticeably with what remains of Late Georgian work and is usually quite overshadowed by the flood of new commercial building that began with the mid-century.

A block of buildings erected by James Wylson (1811–1870) in Queen Street, Glasgow, in 1847 was a fair specimen of recognizably Victorian provincial work—much building of the 40's and even later is not recog-nizably Victorian at all. Yet Wylson's commercial terrace lacked both the "novelty at all costs" of men like Mayhew and the suave Italianism of I'Anson (Fig. XII 9). The three upper storeys rode uneasily on the light metal arches of the shop windows even though piers were placed under the projecting corners of the end and center pavilions. The first storey was rusticated and had arched windows. Above the imposts of the arches in the three pavilions brackets supported balconettes before the second-storey windows. The archi-traves and cornices of these windows, however, are quite simply treated. Only the top-floor windows, with their rounded upper corners and eared architraves, were particularly novel in character or unacademic in propor-tion. Yet the very close spacing of the windows and, above all, the uneven-ness of the rhythm indicated how far the Georgian sense of academic order and proportion had been corrupted. The arrangement of the parts was not even strictly symmetrical although it was presumably meant to appear so. Here, as with Mayhew's bolder work, it is not altogether unjust to speak of architectural illiteracy even though Wylson's contemporary reputation was high.

There are individual structures in various other cities far richer and often much finer than this particular sample of Glasgow street architec-ture. In Birmingham the East India and Colonial Export Warehouses at Nos. 1–6 Horse Fair, although half destroyed in the blitz, still provide a hand-some specimen of Early Victorian stucco dating from the mid-40's (Fig. XII 10). Along the ground storey is a series of rusticated arches, and the conventional first-storey windows have alternately segmental and pointed pediments carried on consoles. But the top storey, rather originally, consists of ranges of three little arches in each bay enclosed by square panels. As on many of these commercial buildings the name, in large sans-serif relief letters, provides a fine ornamental band in the frieze. Like much contemporary work in America, still in general considerably more Grecian in style, these stucco façades often have a curiously title-page-like character because of the papery flatness of the wall surfaces and the woodcut-like or lithographic character of the ornamental features.

Also badly blitzed is the more advanced stucco façade at Nos. 43–46 New Street in Birmingham, probably also of the mid-40's. Here the four bays of the first and second storeys have big triple windows while the attic windows form a continuous arcade that is very delicate in scale. Against this arcade rich armorial achievements with cherub supporters are set above the second-storey windows. There is, however, no straining for a bold plastic effect that would be unsuited to stucco. The whole design, although rich in a sort of typographic way, is very refined, almost "refeened," in feeling like the pages of a contemporary *Keepsake* or ladies' yearbook.

Larger and less refined, and also contrasting sharply with the cold sobriety and the superb material of Cockerell's Bank Chambers in Cook Street (Fig. XI 1), are the Atherton Buildings at No. 19 Dale Street in Liverpool. Although but seven bays wide this façade rises a full five storeys. The windows of the principal floor are not only pedimented, they also carry rich foliate ornamentation. As in the more monumental Brunswick Buildings there is more than one entrance. A continuous balcony at the first-storey level (now mostly destroyed) and balconettes at the second-storey windows give some plastic relief; a balustrade on the top, with corner urns, enriches the skyline above the bold inscription that gives the name of the building. This was at least an attempt to rival in stucco Grellier's Royal Insurance Building. But as long as such façades continued to be executed in stucco, as economy demanded, they necessarily had a transitional air. The traditional training of plaster-workers, as well as their plain common sense, led them to flatten and refine all the detail, thus diminishing the bold relief at which Victorian architects now increasingly aimed. The Boote Buildings, in Elliott Street between Charlotte and Rose Streets, built in 1846, illustrate this point rather well (Fig. XII 12).

As the general rebuilding of the City of London did not begin until the 50's and was then so extensive as to sweep away much work done in the 40's, good examples of Early Victorian commercial façades, either in stucco or in stock brick, are hard to find there; very many must also have been destroyed in the blitz. Because of its very unusual use of exposed iron, a small warehouse at No. 50 Watling Street deserves more attention than it has yet received from critics and historians (Fig. XII 13). The windows in the upper two storeys of both façades of this corner building are separated only by delicate iron columns; the crowning *cyma reversa* cornice is likewise of iron patterned with honeysuckle ornament. All the lintels are of iron also. Only the corners of the building and the "spandrels" between the lintels and the sills are of brick. The date of this building should be previous to 1844 because of the tightening of the London building code in that year. The style, moreover, is still almost Grecian in a delicate Regency way, which suggests an early date. The quite uncharacteristic openness, simplicity, and refinement of this warehouse is rivaled in another larger and doubtless somewhat earlier one at Nos. 5–9 Aldermanbury (Fig. XII 11). There the upper-storey windows form continuous bands, with extremely light supports (iron? or wood?) between them and very delicate detailing. The façade here has obviously been extended either to the right or to the left at some time, probably before 1844 for the reason given above.

To a 20th-century eye such exceptional things suggest that a commercial architecture of glass and iron, such as actually appeared in America around 1850, ought to have been imminent as well as immanent. But there were good reasons both technical and aesthetic—and after 1844 legal as well— why the English commercial development actually took a very different line in the mid-century. On the technical side it was already widely realized that unprotected iron supports were not safe against fire, something Americans seem to have ignored down to the time of their great urban fires in the early 70's. On the other hand, so open a façade treatment contradicted too blatantly the long-accepted academic rule that solids should outweigh voids. The somewhat contradictory conviction that monumental effect in street façades depended on a maximum of relief was as yet unformulated. Eventually arcades would provide both plastic modeling and a maximum of penetration, but that came only in the mid-50's and without benefit of visible ironwork on the exterior.

It is far from obvious to 20th-century critics that street architecture should aim at providing monumental effect in individual structures. But advancing Victorian taste stressed, as we have already seen, the expression of the single building over the harmony of the group. Any sort of façade treatment that minimized the possible introduction of strong plastic accents, even in quite unpretentious structures, was therefore deprecated. Stucco as a medium was still in fact condoned, particularly in London, because of the expense of bringing in stone for masonry; but it was nevertheless scorned by critics as being a "sham." The delicacy of treatment to which stucco naturally lent itself seemed to Victorians not refined but vulgar. The same was of course even more true of the slender scaling of the isolated metal or wooden supports in the two London façades that have just been illustrated.

Partly because of the increasing availability of superior materials in Manchester and partly because of the concentration of the local architects on a special commercial type of edifice, it was the wholesale warehouses of "Cottonopolis" that set the pace for commercial building in the late 40's. The principal clientele consisted of merchants of rapidly growing wealth in a town where there was no overshadowing aristocratic tradition. Their patronage was solid if not inspired by much aesthetic flair. The familiarity of both the local architects and their clients with the metal-skeleton construction long used in cotton mills was certainly important also; its direct effects are usually not easy to check but they can often be deduced from the particular character of the exteriors.

George Godwin (1815–1888), the editor of the *Builder,* writing about Manchester in 1848, referred to it as "this immense capital of our manufacturing enterprise—this vast mart of active wealth—this hive of stirring industry." With fewer clichés, he goes on to say that "there is less bad *building* in Manchester than in London. Brick work is usually very well and soundly executed there, and would put to shame much of it that has been, and is being, done in and around the metropolis." The accuracy of this statement will be evident to any Manchester visitor whose eyes are sharp enough to see anything at all through the murky local atmosphere. The hard, dark-red Lancashire bricks, generally without the sort of grayish bloom they acquire in the sea air of Liverpool, are not very sensuously appealing under the thick coat of grime Manchester's smoky air so soon provided. But they are firm, regular, and always well laid, with sound bonding and fine pointing. Perhaps that was because they had never been regularly covered up with stucco in the way London's yellowish stock bricks had generally been for a generation and more. Together with this red brick, more and more stone trim was used from the mid-40's on. Hard Yorkshire and Derbyshire building stones were readily brought in by the new railways and soon became almost as cheap as brick. But the characteristic Manchester warehouses, whether all of stone or of the more usual brick with stone trim, were always solidly built. This was primarily because their owners were ready to spend very considerable sums and even wished to make them as far as possible fireproof, like the big new cotton mills in the surrounding area.

"Fireproof" is a term of somewhat indefinite meaning, but the fire-resistant interiors of cast- and wrought-iron structural elements that Sir William Fairbairn (1789–1874) was perfecting in the Lancashire cotton mills were early emulated in Manchester warehouses. Edward Taylor Bellhouse (1816–1881), a leading Manchester iron founder, had even developed by 1848 a fireproof hoist on which baled goods were lifted from one floor to another. The extreme inflammability of cotton textiles was only too well known; the close-packed siting of the warehouses in the main streets of the city increased the hazards of conflagration. The familiarity with the use of iron in mills has already been mentioned; but it was perhaps even more because the merchants' own offices were in the same warehouses as their inflammable goods that Manchester so rapidly and generally accepted "fireproof" construction.

These cotton warehouses, rather than the local banks or insurance offices, were here the characteristic seats of wealth. That fact certainly encouraged the development in Manchester of a special architectural expression early recognized by contemporaries as superior in dignity and integrity to the commercial architecture of London and most other Victorian cities. The leading local architects specialized in warehouse work; of these the best known and the most distinguished is Edward Walters.

Walters was born in 1808 and was a nephew of the elder Edward I'Anson; thus the best of the new, strictly commercial architects of London, the younger I'Anson, and he were first cousins. (Could this close Manchester connection explain the use of red brick by I'Anson on his Royal Exchange Buildings?) After working in the office of the leading London builder Thomas Cubitt and then in that of Lewis Vulliamy, Walters was employed for a while by John Wallen, a London commercial architect who made early use of interior metal-skeleton construction. He was then sent to Turkey in 1832 by the engineer Sir John Rennie (1794–1874), Cockerell's brother-in-law, to supervise an ordnance plant that Rennie was building there. Returning through Spain, Italy, and France, the young architect had a chance to study Renaissance palace architecture; for the days of exclusive preoccupation with the antique were already over and those of exclusive preoccupation with the medieval had not yet begun. The many water-color sketches he made at this time were to become the principal sources of his mature inspiration. He also made valuable friends on his travels. One was the well-known engineer William H. Barlow (1812–1902), for whom he later designed the stations on the Midland line between Manchester and Ambergate; more important was Richard Cobden (1804–1865), then the first citizen of Manchester.

Because of his acquaintance with Cobden, Walters settled in Manchester in 1839 and built his first warehouse for him at No. 16 Mosley Street. In the early 40's his practice was still general, consisting chiefly of private houses and Dissenting chapels. (The relative importance of his Cavendish Street Independent Chapel of 1847, one of the first Dissenting churches to follow closely the Camdenian models, should not be forgotten even though

Walters had no personal flair for Gothic design.) His real career as a warehouse architect began in 1845 with the building of the S. Schwabe Warehouse; it was to continue all through the 50's so that his later warehouses belong in date to the High Victorian period.

It seems to have been the success of Waterhouse's Gothic design over his own Italianate one in the Manchester Assize Court competition of 1859 that discouraged Walters, when he was only a little over 50, from continuing actively with his practice. He had then been for over a decade the leading Victorian commercial architect of Britain, equaled in distinction and in reputation only by his cousin Edward I'Anson in London. Although Walters' style finally matured only about 1850, his early warehouses and those which his local rivals Travis and Mangnell and J. E. Gregan were building in the late 40's and early 50's are among the most impressive Early Victorian monuments; to them all that has so far been discussed except Cockerell's and I'Anson's work may be considered but a preface.

The Schwabe Warehouse of 1845 at Nos. 46–54 Mosley Street is of brick with a generous use of stone trim; in fact the entire ground storey is of stone (Fig. XII 14). The windows are large and much more closely spaced than academic convention allowed. But recesses in the façade enclose the first- and second-storey windows in order to provide vertical continuity in the design and to phrase the considerable array of similar openings. The moldings were consciously made very bold so that they might remain visually effective in the smoky atmosphere of Manchester. No earlier commercial work in London could be compared with this in solidity and dignity except I'Anson's Royal Exchange Buildings; there, of course, most of the trim was merely of Portland cement, not of stone. Of the more sumptuous and monumental financial buildings, only Cockerell's are in the same class; and the particular example of Cockerell's banks then building in King Street in Manchester was not his happiest. In the provincial cities Liverpool had its stone Brunswick Buildings but other large towns were still mostly content with stucco; in wool towns such as Bradford warehouses were still almost completely utilitarian in character although they were usually all of fine Yorkshire stone.

The Italian cinquecento palace model had been early illustrated in Manchester, and with particular authority, in Barry's severe Athenaeum of 1837. After nearly a decade of exposure to Manchester grime the appearance of that nearby edifice in Mosley Street would have made evident to Walters that bolder detail and smaller plain wall areas than Barry had used were requisite under the local atmospheric conditions. The need for more light inside from larger, more closely spaced windows and the possibility of emphasizing the architectural detail both by contrast of materials and by heavier relief were not evident to Walters alone among the Manchester commercial architects. For example, there was Travis and Mangnell's slightly later Gardner Warehouse in Bond Street. This was taller than Walters' with a high ground storey in the form of a continuous stone arcade on molded imposts, brick being used only for the spandrels. Above, brick piers separated the bays of arched windows in the upper three storeys; but these piers were crossed by continuous stone stringcourses at the sill levels. The imposts of the window arches were also of stone as was the continuous cornice that crowned the façade. In the top storey two small arches were coupled under the main arch in each bay.

Somewhat similar to the Gardner Warehouse, though with less vertical continuity and no stone basement, is Ashton Hoare's Warehouse which still stands at the corner of Portland and Charlotte Streets. On this the windows are coupled in the lower storeys and the attic range consists of triplet arches, but the whole edifice is rather weighed down by a tall paneled parapet. In many more warehouses the designers or their clients were content with plain red brick walls broken only by the stone architraves of the windows and crowned by heavy stone cornices. These can be somewhat dull and monotonous externally, but the standards of their internal construction were extremely high. Usually they have brick-arched floors on wrought-iron girders carried by cast-iron columns; sometimes there were from the first water cisterns at the top connected to an interior system of fire hose.

The warehouse built at the corner of Portland and Parker Streets in 1850 by J. E. Gregan was of more considerable interest than most in its design although the floor beams there were still of wood, not of iron. The plan well illustrates the freedom of interior disposition made possible by the use of isolated iron columns; only the exterior walls and those around the hoist, the staircase, and the light-well are load bearing (Fig. XII 18). Light partitions subdivided the first storey into offices and sample rooms with perfect elasticity, while the storage floors did not need to be subdivided at all. As this warehouse was built for a firm that had considerable dealings with America, one of the upper storeys provided special suites of offices for the free use of transatlantic clients while in Manchester. As in modern skyscrapers, various offices could be thrown together or partitioned off at any time without affecting the load-carrying interior supports of metal.

The exterior walls were all faced with Yorkshire stone, the trim being more smoothly cut than the walling (Fig. XII 18). No attempt was made to disguise the height, perhaps because Manchester merchants were long used to factories five storeys and more in height. (Well before Manchester warehouses were being designed by competent architects, a visitor in 1838 had commented not unfavorably on their imposing height.) But what was most remarkable about the design was Gregan's handling of his batteries of windows. They had to be much more closely spaced than convention sanctioned, both because of the need for admitting all possible light and also on account of the narrow aisles between the lines of columns inside which required that the bays in the outer walls should be narrow also. In the three main storeys Gregan accented the alternate windows by means of simple frames and pediments; those between he kept mere holes in the wall. Thus in the perspective of a narrow street a more conventional sort of window spacing was strongly suggested without recourse to actual trickery.

There was no cinquecento ornament of a Mannerist order on this severe block; but the way in which the accents are alternated recalls a characteristic mid-16th-century compositional device. Although all the features are very simply handled, the fashion in which every other bay of the ground storey is narrowed and recessed, as it were in syncopation with the accents of the projecting window frames above, is even more specifically Mannerist. Otherwise Gregan made little attempt to embellish his façade, using merely chains of broad rusticated quoins at the corners, rather plain stringcourses at each floor level, and a very modest cornice and parapet. The rusticated entrance, not even centered, is considerably more severe than that on his contemporary bank (Fig. XI 16). The resulting effect of the whole composition was most businesslike, yet not at all dull. Unfortunately this warehouse was entirely destroyed in the blitz.

The next prominent warehouse in Manchester, that built for James Brown, Son, and Company in 1851–52 nearby at No. 9 Portland Street, is still extant. The 75-foot front toward Portland Street is much more elaborate and was considered in the 50's to have opened a new stage in warehouse design (Fig. XII 16). Actually Walters' façade scheme is considerably less expressive and original than Gregan's; but in the great richness of its detail this warehouse vied for the first time in Manchester with the newest insurance offices of London and Liverpool. The windows are huge, but they are still rather widely spaced. There also appear to be only four storeys, although the building is 62 feet high with individual storey heights of 11 feet. Actually, however, the basement (which is considerably taller than that of Gregan's warehouse) is so handled that it seems to be merely a part of the ground storey, while the attic storey is completely masked by the entablature, the cornice, and a tall crowning balustrade. (The present range of good-sized rectangular attic windows along the 115-foot side façade in Aytoun Street was inserted later.)

The main entrance is marked by a wide rusticated arch set in a deep recess rather like that on Gregan's bank. The narrower side windows are also arched but between them the rustication rises only to the imposts; the spandrels over the windows are separated by pairs of curious flat brackets somewhat like stumpy pilasters. The first- and second-storey windows are segmental arched; they are also linked vertically by scrolled brackets supporting the second-storey sills in a way that recalls the end-bay treatment on Cockerell's Sun Assurance Offices. The bold curved pediments of the first-storey windows similarly rise up to the sill level of those in the third storey and in perspective actually overlap them. But the vertical movement upward is stopped by the rather flat archivolts of the third-storey window arches beneath the broad and unbroken frieze of the main entablature.

The cornicione and frieze, together with the broad bands of rustication at the corners—unbroken by any stringcourses above the ground floor—surround and confine the rather restless pattern of the heavy window enframements. In order to continue upward the central emphasis of the entrance arch in the ground floor Walters made the frames of the middle windows on the first and second storeys somewhat broader and bolder than those of their neighbors, loading them also with carved enrichments. In the third storey a central pair of arches rather awkwardly interrupts the even window rhythm. The balustrade masking the attic becomes a solid parapet above the three center bays, and heavy urns at either end provide terminal accents against the sky.

This façade, supposedly inspired by the Italian palaces which Walters had studied before settling in Manchester, is actually rather remote from any 16th- or even 17th-century originals. The Brown warehouse is as rich as Grellier's Royal Insurance Buildings in Liverpool and as boldly plastic but it is also considerably more coherent and sophisticated. The Yorkshire stone is superbly cut with many subtle differentiations of texture, but all of it is today black as a stove; the building, moreover, faces north. The lack of any play of light and shade due to this orientation, and the certainty that within a few years the exterior would be solidly black, were taken into account by Walters, however. Just as on his earlier warehouses he consciously exaggerated the relief of his detail. The result seems to justify the means he employed.

The black-begrimed stone soon came to have a rich velvety surface like broadcloth, an appropriate expression of the sober merchants who worked within. The ornament, seen almost as black on black, has a quite lithographic depth of tone. Beside Walters' detail, Barry's and Gregan's more correct High Renaissance forms on the Athenaeum and on the Mechanics' Institute appear somewhat thin and cold; much of the refinement of their design has actually become invisible in this murky atmosphere. Structurally, however, Walters' warehouse is no more advanced than was Gregan's across the way on the Parker Street corner; for only the interior columns are iron, the floor beams being still of wood.

The warehouse that stands two doors away to the left at Nos. 3–5 Portland Street was also built by Walters in the 50's. Unlike his somewhat later Kershaw, Leese, and Sidebottom warehouse in between, this has not been modified. Towering over its neighbor on the left, the Queen's Hotel (which Walters had built only a decade earlier), the four tall storeys of strongly modeled black stone contrast sharply with the smooth painted stucco and restrained trim of the hotel. Nothing could indicate more clearly the development of taste during that decade. The ground-storey arcade, subsuming a high basement as at the Brown warehouse, has coupled pilasters and scrolled keystones. Walters' favorite motif, *nèo-grec* wreaths, decorates the spandrels in all six bays. The entrance is placed, with no special emphasis, in the second bay from the left.

The first-storey windows at No. 3–5 have segmental arches with scrolled keystones. The second- and third-storey windows are not only set in recessed vertical panels as at the Schwabe Warehouse, they are further linked by the high placing of the segmental pediments over the second-storey ones as at the Brown warehouse. But the top-storey windows are not arched and therefore they do not seem so overpowered by the strong horizontals of the bracketed cornice and the balustrade above them. The lack of central emphasis makes this warehouse somewhat less individually monumental than the Brown warehouse or the one between. As the Manchester streets filled up with buildings of the new Victorian scale architects were beginning to think again in terms of over-all street composition, particularly when they were called on, as Walters was here, to build near earlier examples of their own mature work. Beyond the frequent use of crowning balustrades and urns, moreover, Walters never attempted to individualize his façades by elaborately broken skylines.

Retail architecture in Manchester was not usually so remarkable as the great wholesale warehouses. Gregan's Falkner Building in Bridge Street had three storeys of Palladian windows executed in stone set in the red brick wall; when it was built in 1846 this set a pace comparable to Walters' Schwabe Warehouse in Mosley Street of the previous year. Two shops in Market Street, built in 1851 by Starkey and Cuffley, were of even more interest (Fig. XII 17). All of stone, this double façade was very open in design even though the shop doors and windows on the ground floor were separated by fairly heavy rusticated piers. On the upper floors three arched windows, separated only by small, closely coupled columns, occupied the full width of each of the two "houses." Projecting coupled columns of larger size rose at the ends of the two houses and between them; these were linked only by the cornice at the top. Sharply broken by projecting entablature blocks in the center and at the ends, this cornice formed a feeble crown to the composition; nor was it much improved by the pierced balustrade above and a range of rather silly urns silhouetted against the sky.

For all the restless multiplicity of nearly identical parts here, the actual extent of the window area was extraordinary, coming very close to that in the famous building of 1848–50 in New York by James Bogardus (1800–1874) of which the fronts were entirely of cast iron. No other English commercial work was yet so open in design. Within a few years, however, this completely arcaded scheme of design, reducing the wall to an articulated screen of columns and arches, was to become the basis of much of the finest High Victorian commercial work. Although the composition is more remote from the Carlton Club house than were most commercial palazzos from Barry's Reform, the debt to Sidney Smirke's still unfinished façade in Pall Mall is evident (Fig. VI 7). Within a few years influences from earlier Italian styles would give the arcaded commercial façade a more coherent and vigorous character; but in the Early Victorian period the cinquecento club-houses of London remained the chief sources of inspiration for ambitious designers of business buildings.

Beside the commercial work of Walters and Gregan in Manchester, even beside the rather less sophisticated work of Travis and Mangnell or Starkey and Cuffley, most London street architecture between 1848 and 1852, when the effects of mid-century prosperity were finally felt in the City, seems both timid and tawdry. In Regent Street Pennethorne was called on in 1848 to remove Nash's colonnades in the Quadrant in order to bring more light into the shops and houses (Fig. XII 15). In patching up the façades he also elaborated the surface treatment. Although the shop fronts remained very simple their mezzanines were ornamented by arabesque-covered pilasters with molded panels between; above, a balustraded balcony on scrolled brackets was carried along at first-storey level to provide a continuous horizontal line. Not content with these embellishments, primarily intended to mask the point where the roof of the colonnade once joined the façade, Penne-thorne also reframed the first-storey windows more heavily and linked their cornices to the frames of the second-storey windows by means of scrolls. All this new decoration was of course executed in stucco.

In New Oxford Street Henry Stansby designed in 1848 a row of houses with exposed brick walls and Jacobethan detail (Fig. XII 19). It is surprising that Pennethorne's earlier suggestion of using Jacobethan design for London houses, once illustrated by a small group he built when New Oxford Street was first opened, was so little followed otherwise. No visual documentation of these houses by Pennethorne seems to remain. They were probably not dissimilar to Stansby's and perhaps even more like Wigg and Pownall's chambers at Staple Inn (Fig. XII 3). Doubtless London builders had difficulty in obtaining bricklayers to execute satisfactory exposed brickwork so long had the rule of stucco lasted; good red bricks, which had to be brought from a considerable distance, were certainly more expensive than the usual yellow London stocks; when bricks were brought in from a distance the pallid Suffolk "whites" were still generally preferred in the metropolis.

Stansby's shop fronts projected out from the plane of the house fronts above and were crowned with strapwork parapets. Richly rusticated pilasters separated the shops; the windows in the upper storeys were grouped in three's in the individual house-fronts with molded mullions between. They were also linked vertically by ornamental panels between the first and second storeys. An entablature set off the top storey as an attic with a scalloped and pinnacled gable rising through a balustrade over each vertical group of windows. The façades were articulated plastically by projecting the principal window bays. These projecting bays were narrow in the middle of the group and broader toward the ends, and all were clearly outlined by rusticated stonework on their edges. The stair bays at the ends, flat with the actual wall plane, had only a single window in each storey.

The evident advantages of the Jacobethan as regards fenestration were only very mildly exploited by Stansby. Hardwick Hall suggests how naturally the English mode of the late 16th century lent itself to the incorporation of very large and closely spaced windows. Through the 50's and 60's, moreover, Jacobethan continued to be more exceptional in street architecture than in public architecture, almost as exceptional as was Gothic, which had as yet hardly been utilized for commercial buildings at all.

In one of the better examples of the dominant Italianate mode, a range of "houses" that were also built at this time in New Oxford Street, the ground-floor arcade of I'Anson's Royal Exchange Buildings, was borrowed in order to provide a plausibly structural frame for wide shop windows (Fig. XII 27). But the curious treatment of the upper storeys here, with arched niches over the piers and one heavily pedimented window above each shop arch (not to speak of an alternation of windows and architraved panels in the attic), produced a curious effect of Mannerist syncopation. This was quite without the dignity and restraint of Gregan's Manchester warehouse, however, and almost as disconcerting to the observer as Mayhew's top-heavy building in Coventry Street. Executed in stucco, such design must be considered somewhat frivolous; but the heavy seriousness of the Victorian Age, already so evident in Manchester's business streets, was still largely lacking from the flashy commercial areas of London. A contemporary writer in the Companion to the *British Almanac* for 1851, p. 229, nevertheless praised these novel façades for their "reality," echoing rather stupidly the new critical cant of the day.

The problem of relating shop fronts to the buildings of which they formed the base was usually quite ignored in the main West End shopping streets. Regent Street was barely completed before individual shopkeepers began to open up the lower storeys of their premises with huge windows and to enframe them in all sorts of ornate ways with little regard for their neighbors. In 1837 W. H. Leeds in the *Architectural Magazine* singled out for praise a Grecian shop front in Bond Street designed by one of the Inwoods; undoubtedly this was attached to the base of some plain 18th-century dwelling house whose character it quite ignored. The next year the editor of the *Magazine*, J. C. Loudon, in summarizing the progress of architecture, was already mentioning (and with approval) the use of "the Louis XIV style"—which might mean various things then, but usually some sort of Rococo—for shop fronts in Bond Street and Regent Street. "In combination with the immense plates of glass now used for shop windows and accompanied by rich gilding on a pure white ground, it has a striking and most magnificent appearance," according to him. (It sounds rather like an early Lyons!) A particularly elaborate shop front was added to the building that formed the corner of the quadrant and Tichborne Street in 1840 (on the left in Fig. XII 15). The arched windows were filled with single sheets of glass, Ionic columns projected between, and every available surface was covered with low relief ornament executed in some sort of synthetic composition. (Probably this was called Louis XIV, although it is actually more Henri II, not to say Louis Phillippe.)

A year or two later on Mr. Fair's house in Prince's Street, Hanover Square, even more meretricious "exterior decoration" had spread over the entire four storeys of the house front, the whole terminating in an almost unbelievable armoral achievement high above the parapet and capped by a figure waving a flag (Fig. XII 22). But that was an exception; the characteristic Early Victorian decoration of fashionable shop fronts was generally restricted to the ground floor, or the ground floor and mezzanine, as it is today. Since the shop front itself frequently projected slightly from an earlier house front, the shop window and its enframement provided the real architecture of the street for the passer-by. And shop fronts may perhaps properly be considered almost as independent of the buildings against which they are set as the large shop interiors on the ground floor are unrelated to the broken-up plans of the residential or office floors above them.

The L. T. Piver shop front, executed in 1846 by an obscure French architect named Cambon, was a characteristic example of the most expensive and elegant sort of West End work (Fig. XII 26). It also illustrates very well what the Early Victorians meant by the "Louis XIV style." Another somewhat later perfumer's shop in Piccadilly was even more ornate. The door on the left leading into the house above balanced the shop door on the other side of a broad plate-glass-filled arch (Fig. XII 24). It is hardly possible to suggest a plausible name for the nominal style of the window enframement here. The rich and intricate "compo" work, with its sentimental busts and its hanging trophies, belonged in spirit not with the serious architecture of the period but with its characteristic book decoration. Many of the richest contemporary display types actually seem to derive from painted letter forms first developed for use on the fascias of shops. Here on this shop front the curious flowing plasticity of the ornament, interrupted occasionally by sharply linear elements, has much similarity to the handling of ornament on stamped cloth book covers and elaborate title pages of the day.

In the Early Victorian period shop fronts were on the very boundary line of the field of architecture. Along with interior decoration and furniture they belonged to the field of the minor arts connected with architecture as they have on the whole continued to do until quite lately. Except in the rare cases where they were designed integrally with the whole of the façade, they are an architectural bypath. This statement is as true of the severe and dignified mahogany fascias with which the conservative shopkeepers of Edinburgh once framed their wide show windows when adapting 18th-century dwelling houses in Prince's Street and George Street for commercial use as of the ornate "Louis XIV" of London's West End.

The Early Victorians did not precisely invent commercial architecture; but its development was so considerable and so rapid that commercial architecture became for the first time a field of primary significance in the 40's. Within fifteen years from Victoria's accession monumental scale and monumental design, not to speak of the most solid and permanent of building materials such as hitherto had been restricted to a few insurance buildings, became accepted as proper for all commercial premises of any consequence. Although in London the worthy examples were still few, Liverpool, Manchester, Edinburgh, Glasgow, and other cities already made a brave showing. The general introduction of iron into interior construction behind the masonry façades was also proceeding much more rapidly than in the cognate field of urban residential building.

The Early Victorian period was in most things preparatory, and nowhere more so than in the field of commercial architecture. As in other fields the most characteristic achievements (if achievements they were) seem to have been the establishment of new and higher standards, as regards both materials and methods of construction, and the general acceptance of certain post-Georgian modes of design quite unrelated to the latter. The implications of the new structural methods were not fully exploited, and no very direct expression of new functional needs really became acceptable before the mid-50's, largely because commercial architecture was controlled—perhaps one should say inhibited—by the arbitrary conventions of borrowed modes, most particularly the formula of design derived from the Italian Renaissance palace.

This stylistic vehicle, even when very freely handled, was only accidentally appropriate—if, indeed, it were really appropriate at all—to the new practical needs of business and to the new structural possibilities deriving from the use of internal metal-skeleton construction. Unlike the characteristic modes of almost "functional" design used for more strictly industrial buildings such as textile factories or dock warehouses, in which the new metal construction had first been introduced so long before, the palazzo paradigm as used in the commercial field was not a Georgian inheritance even though Barry had first introduced it at the Travellers' Club house as early as 1829–31. The palace mode is rather to be considered one of the prime Early Victorian stylistic symbols of functional expression, more comparable to the contemporary Decorated church pattern than to the quite special Classicism of Cockerell's banks. This is true both in regard to the range of that mode's influence on Victorian architectural development as a whole and as regards its influence on architecture outside Britain. The English 14th-century parish-church pattern as codified by Pugin and the Camdenians satisfied the contemporary need for symbolic functional expression peculiarly well because the services of the Anglican Church during the 40's had been completely reformed by a parallel liturgical revival. Connotation therefore approached denotation in the minds of contemporaries when they saw an Early Victorian church. But the connotation of the Italian palazzo mode of the High Renaissance was rather remote in its application to any 19th-century needs except for such actual private palaces as Bridgewater House and Dorchester House.

It was true, as Victorian writers never tired of stressing, that Italian palaces had in the Renaissance frequently been the direct architectural expression of new commercial wealth. Moreover, as is sometimes forgotten today, the business needs of merchants in Florence and Venice had actually been served by the large rooms on the ground floors of their monumental town residences. But the storage and office requirements of a Florentine wool merchant were very different from those of a 19th-century textile magnate in Manchester or Bradford. The Italians had really lived upstairs in their palaces most of the year as City merchants were just ceasing to do at the time the new strictly commerical palaces began to be built in quantity. Manchester merchants such as Richard Cobden or James Brown, when they employed Walters to build their business premises in Mosley or Portland Streets, were likely also to be employing him to design residential villas in Victoria Park whence they would "commute" daily to their business in town. The country residences of the Florentine and Venetian magnates at their villas at Fiesole and on the Brenta were primarily summer places, even though their families stayed in them a larger part of the year than the men of affairs could conveniently do themselves—just as the families of businessmen who have houses in the country often do today.

The Italian analogy, dubious as it was in many ways, nevertheless provided a widely accepted model that architects were expected to follow in pretentious commercial work. Fortunately their clients did not cultivate the study of ancient palaces in the way churchmen cultivated ecclesiology; thus the commercial architect's freedom to adapt was much greater than the contemporary church builder's. The precedents of Florence and Venice sanctioned the idea that a merchant's principal place of business, not his private residence, should offer the chief public expression of his accumulating wealth and his growing prestige. In this latter idea there was perhaps some analogy also with the established concept of the English country house; for that had always been, in some sense, the aristocratic landowner's principal place of business. There, rather than in his West End residence, convention had long dictated that the rich Englishman should display the architectural and other cultural evidences of his position, his wealth, and his taste. Important country houses built by new commercial and industrial magnates in Victorian times, however, are likely to indicate their effective retirement from business and a consequent shifting of their capital into the ownership of agricultural land, even though such a shift was generally rather uneconomic before the 50's.

Another rather curious Early Victorian connotation of Italian palace design appeared in a statement in the *Civil Engineer and Architect's Journal*. This was quoted in the *Illustrated London News* as a comment on Gibson's Imperial Assurance Office. "What the club is to the street architecture of the West-end, the assurance office is to the City; and the edifices devoted to the more useful purposes of life, it is pleasing to see, are not inferior to those which are only the appendages of luxury. Indeed, the range of assurance offices in London constitutes in its architectural, as well as in its moral [*sic*] aspects, a characteristic of which England may be proud."

Rather tentatively in the Travellers' Club house, then more boldly and conclusively in the Reform at the very opening of the Victorian Age, Barry had firmly established the Italian palace mode as the preferred stylistic vehicle for a new club architecture that rapidly and completely superseded the earlier Grecian mode. The Reform Club, moreover, celebrating by its very name the passage of the Reform Act in 1832, was the symbolic headquarters of those members of the Whig aristocracy who had opened the way to upper-middle-class participation in public life. Naturally, therefore, the very style of its clubhouse had prestige for the rising financial and mercantile magnates who were the clients for the new commercial architecture.

Barry himself had introduced the palace model to Manchester at the Athenaeum somewhat before local architects were much called upon to design monumental warehouses. In the City, Henry Flower's Gresham Club (built in 1844 in King William Street) followed Italian models. "The idea of the east end was suggested by a recollection of the pontifical palace at Florence, while the central motif derives from a palace on the Grand Canal in Venice," the *Builder's* contemporary description carefully explained. Rendered in Roman cement, this City clubhouse was of course already outshadowed by Cockerell's Sun Assurance Offices which were entirely faced with Portland stone. More definitely than this businessmen's clubhouse, the insurance buildings of the 40's were the City equivalents of the West End clubs in splendor and prestige, as the writers in the press recognized, and the earliest were almost precisely coeval with them.

The absolute acceptance of the limitations imposed by ancient models in the design of Early Victorian churches was carried to the point of avoiding all materials and methods of construction not found in the originals; it is as much this fact as anything else that gives consistency and integrity of character to the best of them. Through the 40's such proscriptions effectively discouraged all but unconscious originality in design. The more remote and indirect connotations that served to fix the Italian palace as the most suitable prototype for commercial monuments fortunately permitted the incorporation of new features; for the use of plate glass and iron columns in business edifices did not present the same semiethical dilemmas as in church architecture. Even in the 40's, therefore, novelty in adapting the palazzo mode was not entirely discouraged. But real originality is actually not much more frequent or more striking than in church design before the early 50's.

The semi-functional, semi-Renaissance canons of commerical design definitely discouraged elaborate articulation of mass, asymmetrical accents and, above all, the picturesqueness provided by broken outlines. Since it was such things that particularly appealed to the abstract visual and plastic tastes of the time Early Victorian commercial buildings could never provide so satisfactory a vehicle of contemporary aesthetic expression as did the new churches of the 40's. Victorian architectural standards were dichotomous. On the one side was an ecclesiastical or high-aesthetic wing, on the other a secular

399

(not to say worldly) wing, the greater prestige residing of course with the former. Urban secular building, including housing, as we shall see in the next chapters, followed a line that may be loosely called cinquecento even though the stylistic models used might range all the way up the centuries from High Renaissance Italian to the "Louis XIV" favored for shop fronts. The designers of schools, charitable institutions, country houses, and isolated country buildings in general, as has been said, tended rather to follow the Anglican church architects in accepting an at least equally broadly interpreted English trecento.

That there was a basic and accepted dichotomy of taste is evidenced by the fact that men like Gibson and Walters among the leading commercial architects built churches in medieval style even when they worked for Nonconformists. If Gilbert Scott in the 40's built no Italianate commercial buildings that was doubtless because he was not asked to do so. His Gothic principles would certainly not have stood the strain of a large commission for which Gothic was proscribed (as we know from the most famous episode in his later career). But he probably had as yet little idea how medieval forms might be plausibly adapted for use in commercial edifices.

That Carpenter and Butterfield also built no City palaces is less surprising; as consecrated "church architects" their Camdenian principles would have made it prostitution for them to accept such employment. Pugin had a broader and deeper sense of the universality of ancient Gothic architecture and even published one semicommercial design in 1843 (Fig. XII 23). In this "house" front, broad segmental-pointed arches at the base provided adequate display windows for a grocery shop; above these the large mullioned windows of the domestic upper storeys were freely grouped under a plain gable. This project of Pugin's was of course only ordinary "street architecture" like the new "houses" in New Oxford Street; it is in no way functionally comparable to the great banks and insurance blocks of the City or the commercial palaces of Liverpool and Manchester. But no one in the 40's would have thought of employing the dedicated Pugin even for such modest urban work. Nor did other architects try to follow this intelligent suggestion until G. E. Street began to exercise his critical acumen—if not his own equally dedicated designing talents—on such secular problems in the early 50's (see Chapter XVII).

Street architecture sank generally in the 40's well below the extraordinarily high level to which Grainger and Dobson had carried it in Newcastle in the late 30's though it was rising again just at the end of the decade when prosperity began to return, particularly in the Northern cities. But the Early Victorian period in commercial architecture did establish an important new field of architectural activity with its own particular conventions. As with church architecture, professional specialization in the commercial field developed rapidly. This specialization was probably bad for English architecture as a whole since it restricted the talents of an active-minded group in the profession pretty much to their own urban bailiwick. Yet specialization also laid solid foundations for bold achievement in the next two decades. In the versatile career of a Cockerell the banks and insurance office he designed exceed in historical significance—and perhaps even in absolute quality—almost all his non-commercial work. A Gibson, an I'Anson, a Walters are quite new phenomena. The full harvest of their early pioneering came only in the late 50's and 60's and from less well-known—often even quite unknown—hands.

In commercial architecture the production of the 50's was to be somewhat ambiguous in character. On the one hand, after the middle of the decade, new formulas of design more and more succeeded the palazzo mode in the work of the bolder architects. On the other hand, the palazzo mode itself, increasingly hybridized and enriched, continued indefinitely in use well into the next decade. Here we must attempt to bring the Early Victorian story to an end, if somewhat more arbitrarily than in other fields, around the year 1855. Yet it would be improper to break off the account without looking forward a little at what was to follow in the late 50's and 60's. (In my article "Victorian Monuments of Commerce," *Architectural Review, 105,* 61–74, the story is carried on, and amply illustrated, with no such break at 1855 as the plan of this book makes necessary.)

The arcaded mode of design, for example, which opened up masonry fronts until they were articulated skeletons of narrow piers and wide arches with no solid parts but the spandrels, was responsible for many of the finest commercial edifices of the High Victorian period. This mode was initiated almost precisely in 1855 although there were certain significant premonitory steps that go back to the late 40's. The Northern Schools of St. Martin's-in-the-Fields in London built by J. W. Wild in 1849–50 offer, for example, the first completely arcaded front (Fig. XII 21). But that building was not intended for commercial use; it had only three storeys of which the topmost was an open trabeated loggia; and it has always been hidden away in a narrow alley in Soho. The significance of its Italian Gothic character and the reception which critics gave its arcaded design can be better discussed in the last chapter of this book where the comments of Ruskin, who praised it in a general way, and of Street, who recommended it as an especially sound model for commercial work, will be considered.

Starkey and Cuffley's Manchester shop fronts of 1851, which have already found a place in this chapter, were less noticed by contemporaries and are at best unimpressive since their arcading is bound in by thick party walls at the ends and in the middle (Fig. XII 17). Arcading, on the whole, was to belong more to the Gothic than to the Renaissance side of Victorian architecture in the mid-century. And it was not much before 1855 that the newer Gothic ideas of Butterfield and of Ruskin were brought to bear on building generally. Only then did regular commercial specialists begin to feel any real kinship with the highbrow church architects who were already transforming the Victorian Gothic.

Even the earliest commercial examples of a more elaborate sort of arched articulation in façade design, following the Sansovinesque formula Sydney Smirke introduced in his project of 1847 for the Carlton Club house, seem to date from just after the time work was resumed on that clubhouse in the mid-50's. Despite the frequent use of arcading in the ground storey from the time of Cockerell's Sun Life Offices onward, and the occasional extension of the theme—usually in a very superficial or tentative way—into the first storey in the late 40's and early 50's, the completely arcaded commercial façade is not an Early Victorian achievement.

A possible candidate for a date before 1855, the warehouse at No. 12 Temple Street in Bristol probably designed by W. B. Gingell, may be illustrated (Fig. XII 28); but the chances are that its resemblances to the basement of his Bristol General Hospital built in 1853–57 (Fig. VII 19) are to be explained by a date corresponding to the latter part of that relatively prolonged campaign. It is even more possible that this admirable façade may be still later and date only from the 60's; certainly the phrasing of the arches into triplets tends to be a late rather than an early characteristic of arcaded fronts.

A remarkable commercial structure was built in Glasgow in 1855–56 at the corner of Jamaica and Argyle Streets. Even more definitely than No. 12 Temple Street, this has to be considered an early step in the High Victorian rather than a climax of the Early Victorian, that is, if any break at all is to be made in what was a rather continuous development. The façade is arcaded throughout the three upper storeys; it is also entirely made of iron. The arches are obviously not bearing ones but purely decorative (or at most a way of reinforcing the reticulated metal frame). The basic importance of the scheme of design initiated here lies rather in the width of the bays between the principal iron piers—bays which the arches merely subdivide—and in the particular material which made such wide bays possible. In other words, this is better considered as a horizontally articulated façade than as an arcaded one. The extreme delicacy of the detailing is much more suitable to iron than the characteristic American imitations in cast iron of the solid forms and proportions of Renaissance masonry arcading. Yet at this relatively late date the Jamaica Street warehouse can hardly be considered epoch making if James Bogardus' all-iron building of 1848–50—already so well publicized in Britain—is remembered and the many other American

402

iron façades which followed it in the next few years. No architect's or even builder's name is given for the Jamaica Street warehouse and it is probable that the designing of the façade as a whole, as of the details of the components, was undertaken in the foundry of a man named McConnel who took the contract to supply his own patented girders of wrought iron with cast-iron distending frames. (For illustrations and a more detailed account of the Jamaica Street warehouse and other Glasgow façades largely of iron, see my article "Early Cast Iron Façades," *Architectural Review, 109,* 113–116.)

It is tantalizing to read in the *Builder* the remarks of a Belgian architect, Servaas de Jong, who came to London to visit the Great Exhibition in 1851, concerning an earlier façade at No. 76 Oxford Street which he describes as being entirely of iron and glass. The remark that he preferred its "mauresque" detailing to the "architecture in cordage" of the Corn Exchange court suggests that the designer may well have been Owen Jones since he was the principal Victorian expert on Islamic decoration as well as an associate of Paxton's at the Crystal Palace (see Chapter XVI). Jones, moreover, was certainly responsible a few years later for the Crystal Palace Bazaar in Oxford Street. Of this the magnificent interior, arched in iron and glass, was shown in the *Illustrated London News* in 1858. (This cut is repeated in my above-cited article in the *Architectural Review.*) Here also, according to the accompanying account, the narrow side façade in Great Portland Street was all of glass and iron.

As with all-over arcading, so also with other schemes of open articulation of the façade, whether all of exposed ironwork or with the iron members covered with thin masonry, significant development seems to have begun only in 1855 whatever No. 76 Oxford Street may really have been like. Cockerell's Westminster Bank at the very beginning of the Early Victorian period was vertically articulated in design. But this compositional device was evidently so closely associated with Grecian "pilaster" treatments in contemporary estimation that it was little adopted until after 1855. The occasional linking of one storey with another under a single tall arcade was almost always in the 40's a superficial ornamental treatment as on Walters' Schwabe Warehouse (Fig. XII 14). Any other use of continuous vertical elements in Early Victorian work must be considered rather a retention of Late Georgian ideas than a forward step toward the over-all vertical articulation which was to come to maturity in the 60's.

There is, however, a remarkable façade in Mosley Street in Manchester which must date from before 1851 since it appears in an extensive view of the street published by the *Illustrated London News* in that year. This is in several ways exceptional (Fig. XII 20). The four storeys are linked in pairs vertically by tall colonnettes—of Classical design but not of Classical proportions—ranged in two superposed orders. To judge from the modest scaling of all the members, there must have been considerable iron used in the construction of this façade but in the present state of the building just *how* much is difficult to determine. Technically advanced as this edifice almost certainly is (and curiously premonitory in design of the vertical articulation of the 60's also), to the eyes of the 40's and early 50's it would have appeared merely retardataire—Grecian actually, and badly proportioned Grecian at that. It certainly had no influence in Manchester where iron and glass walls were reserved longer than elsewhere for the supposedly unseen rears of the great commercial buildings.

Articulation of a horizontal sort follows a slightly more continuous, or at least recurrent, line through the Early Victorian period than does vertical articulation; the distinction between vertical and horizontal articulation, however, is a somewhat arbitrary one. Both ultimately tend, for technical reasons, toward over-all reticulation of the exterior wall, with neither the horizontal nor the vertical elements strongly emphasized except insofar as a priori ideas of design have decided otherwise. Nevertheless the two lines of development, before the mid-50's, would seem in fact to be quite separate, largely because the Georgian backgrounds of these alternative approaches to complete articulation were so distinct.

The use of wide groups of windows for workrooms in the top storeys of silkweavers' houses in Spitalfields was well established in Georgian London. Georgian factories of modest height frequently had their windows grouped in three's between brick piers, moreover, with the long lintels supported on light intermediate mullions of wood or iron. Of this treatment an excellent example was the Snell Factory at the Grosvenor Basin, designed by J. B. Papworth in 1831. Before the imposition of the more rigid London Building Code of 1844, in certain exceptional commercial buildings in the City already mentioned in this chapter the upper storeys were of course opened up even more drastically (Figs. XII 11, 13).

In the principal section of the building at Nos. 5–9 Aldermanbury the windows are grouped three, one, and three, with only very narrow pilasters —presumably of iron but possibly of wood—separating them. In what seems to be a mere extension of this façade to the right, four windows are thus grouped. The continuous entablatures which run the whole length of the façade above these groups of windows in the first and second storeys increase the effect of horizontal articulation. At No. 50 Watling Street the use of iron lintels and of slim iron colonettes between the windows allowed the width of the openings to be very much increased. As the ironwork is all visible, the upper storeys practically have an exposed iron skeleton. The end piers and the "spandrels" between the storeys remain of brick, however, and the shop windows have stone cladding on the supports and bressumers of pilaster and entablature character.

Although entirely of bearing masonry construction the superb façade of Cockerell's Bank Chambers in Cook Street, Liverpool, built in 1849, may almost be considered an example of horizontal articulation also, so wide are the windows (particularly in the first storey) and so narrow the masonry piers between them (Fig. IX 1). The segmental window tops are not arches, it should be noted, but merely an easing of the bottom line of the broad and obviously structural lintels. The piers are laid up in large blocks without vertical joints so that the construction is almost as monolithic as the "skeleton" façades in granite introduced to 19th-century America by Alexander Parris (1780–1852) in the early 20's around the Quincy Market in Boston, Massachusetts.

In prefabricated metal buildings for export, such as the industrial warehouses E. T. Bellhouse sent to San Francisco in such quantity in 1849, the horizontal shapes of the large windows and the two-storey galleries that were often carried across the front indicated clearly the width of the bays of the light iron frame. A striking example of this, but commercial rather than industrial, was provided by the long buildings, each with eight shops below and eight flats above, which were sent to Melbourne in 1853 by Samuel Hemming of Bristol (Fig. XII 25). Here also the porch columns in the two storeys corresponded with the internal bay structure, and the wall bays on the ground storey were completely filled with sash. The large-paned windows and their wooden shutters in the storey above gave an almost equal effect of open horizontality, in the tradition associated with the West Indies which seems to have been imported there from India in the 18th century.

In England, however, various circumstances combined to discourage the horizontal grouping of windows in the late 40's. On the one hand, the window tax made double or triple windows correspondingly expensive and they were usually restricted to axial or terminal positions where they could serve as accents in the composition. On the other hand, in the designing of the more ambitious new buildings, the conventions of the astylar palazzo mode reinforced inherited academic ideas of the proper relative proportion of window opening to solid wall. The general taste for the visible solidity of massive stone construction, moreover, which developed in reaction to the light and fragile stucco planes of Late Georgian architecture, established at least as powerful an inhibition against any increase in fenestration.

The lifting of the window tax in 1851 was gladly received by all commercial architects who were without great pretensions to art; such men were little committed to the plausible imitation of the solidity of cinquecento palaces. The Smith Building at Nos. 188–192 Strand, as rebuilt by H. R. Abraham in 1852, appeared to a contemporary writer in the *Illustrated London News* "to proclaim the abolition of the tax; the triple fenestration no longer imposes triple penalty, and Palladian forms of window emancipated from the tax seem to rejoice as they gaily reflect the broad light from their ample surfaces" (Fig. XII 29). In each of the four bays of the first and second storeys of this façade the windows were grouped in three's and divided vertically only by the entablatures of the pilaster order that formed the frames and mullions. As on certain houses in Prince's Gate (then Terrace), built by an architect named Johnson in South Kensington two years earlier, where the front windows are similarly grouped without thought of expense (Fig. XIV 15), the familiar Palladian arches over the central windows of the groups were omitted even in the second storey. But over the entablatures both at Prince's Gate and in the Strand there are segmental pediments, borrowed probably from the end bays of the garden front of Barry's Bridgewater house (Fig. VII 10), to take the place of arches. The building in the Strand was built for W. H. Smith, the bookseller, on the Duke of Norfolk's land for some £9,000. In the much larger building which H. R. Abraham built some years later for Smith at No. 184 Strand he reverted to the conventional palazzo mode with the windows single and broadly spaced, even avoiding the use of large shop windows in the ground storey. But within a year or two after 1852 large windows in pairs and triplets had become a commonplace of commercial architecture in the City, although it cannot be said that the device was ever much used by careful architects or that it led directly to any new formula of commercial design.

By the mid-50's a basic change in the architect's approach to the designing of the exterior shells of metal skeleton buildings was at hand even though the palazzo mode—with or without modification—was still to remain popular for many more years. To draw the line at 1855, and to say that what precedes is still Early Victorian and what follows represents a later style-phase, must necessarily be arbitrary, as has already been remarked. There is no act of legislature such as there was to be in the case of workers' housing, no change in the urban building codes to signalize that year as especially epoch making (see Chapter XIII); nor was there any such critical attack on a prominent structure as that with which George Godwin denounced the "Brompton Broilers" as they rose in 1855 (see Chapter XVI).

Late examples of the commercial palazzo, examples often intrinsically finer than those built before the mid-50's, can be educed in quantity to indicate how vigorously this characteristic Early Victorian mode throve for at least another decade. It long remained the favorite vehicle of conventionally trained architects, just as a comparable Early Victorian type of terrace design was continued even longer in the practice of unambitious and untrained builders. It would be tempting to include some of these later palazzos in this account, despite their late date, because of their great intrinsic interest. (For illustration and discussion of some of the best examples, many of them unfortunately undated and insecurely attributed to known architects, see my above-cited article in the *Architectural Review, 105.*) In various more or less subtle ways, as in the tendency toward hybridization of the palazzo with arcading or else with some other sort of vertical or horizontal articulation—or merely in the use of richer, later, and more eclectic detail—the best and most characteristic examples of the commercial palazzo after the mid-50's really cease to be Early Victorian in character. The special flavor of the Victorian urban architectural world—hitherto proud but restrained; concerned with good urbanistic manners; a little student-like and docile; preparatory, even—underwent a general change around 1855 when articulated, and more particularly arcaded, types of design began to come generally to the fore. The façades that were still essentially of the palazzo type, moreover, were usually elaborated plastically in one way or another to compete with them in boldness of effect.

The conscious assimilation by certain commercial architects of Ruskinian ideas, as also the increasing rejection by many others of the suave Barryesque sanctions of design inherited from the 40's, becomes evident almost precisely in 1855. Henceforth such edifices as remain characteristically Early Victorian in design must be considered retardataire. As the next chapters devoted to housing will indicate no really comparable *stylistic* line can be drawn in the field of domestic architecture; but the Housing Act of 1855 and the even more important collapse of the housing boom of the early 50's the year before, presumably because of the Crimean War, provide even stronger reasons for bringing the account of Early Victorian development to a close in that year.

CHAPTER XIII: THE BEGINNINGS
OF VICTORIAN HOUSING

The rapid development of commercial architecture in the Early Victorian period offered new opportunities to architects. In the field of domestic building, on the other hand, both in the cities and around their suburban fringes, trained architects were less employed, at least proportionately, than in Late Georgian times. With the rising standards of professional ethics architects were less likely to be directly involved financially in estate development in the way of the Adams at the Adelphi. In any event the 40's saw a general decline in house production from which recovery came only in the early 50's. This rule applies rather equally to all types of residential accommodation from new dwellings intended for the homeless poor to mansions designed for magnates. Too many houses had been built—or at least planned and partially completed—in the years after Waterloo; it took some time to catch up with and absorb the expansive undertakings that had been initiated in the 20's. Two detailed case histories concerning this flood of Late Georgian house production and its aftermath are provided in John Summerson's *Georgian London* [1945] and in Anthony Dale's *Fashionable Brighton 1820–1860* [1947].

The word "housing" in modern parlance is usually restricted to the provision of dwellings of one kind or another for those whose low incomes require philanthropic or state assistance of some sort if they are to be adequately housed at all. The concept is an old one, of course; but the activity as we now know it became an important element in political and social economy only toward the end of the Victorian Age. This chapter and the next are not primarily concerned with what is best called *public* housing although much that is important in its early history will be included. But the word "housing" may properly be extended to cover all types of multiple residential construction planned and built by single operators whatever the incomes of the tenants and purchasers or the actual methods of financing the project. In Victorian times almost all housing was a field of rampant "private enterprise"; even when philanthropic agencies entered the field they expected (and often received) returns on their investment which the stockholders in a uranium mine would hardly dream of today.

408

For the most part in the Victorian Age the ways of financing the development of urban and suburban land for residential purposes remained much what they had been in the 18th century. Housing for the urban poor was just beginning to be recognized as a social responsibility. Evangelical Tories, particularly the young Lord Ashley (later 7th Earl of Shaftesbury, 1801–1885), were leaders; Dickens was an active propagandist and also the advisor to Angela Burdett-Couts, heiress to a great banking fortune, in her benefactions; while an American financier, George Peabody, was eventually to be the principal "angel" in the field after the Early Victorian period had come to an end. But all this new activity, motivated by the dreadful urban conditions which the Victorians had (at least in considerable part) innocently inherited from the Georgians, hardly got under way until general prosperity returned after the hungry 40's; indeed nothing of much statistical significance happened before the 60's. What can properly be covered in this book is therefore largely preliminary to the real story.

In general throughout the Victorian Age, groups of residential units—whatever the size of the group or the pretension or lack of pretension of the individual units—were built by speculative builders on leasehold land; this had been the London practice since the days of Nicholas Barbon in the late 17th century if not, indeed, ever since Inigo Jones built the first London square, the Covent Garden Piazza, for Francis, Earl of Bedford, under Charles I. The builders' product reached the ultimate consumer, often enough, only through a maze of intermediate leases and subleases between the ground landlord and the tenant. (See Summerson, chaps. ii, iii, vii, xii, and xiv.)

The layout of an area was usually controlled at the outset by the ground landlord through his estate architect or surveyor. Estate architects might design a few houses to serve partly as a "come-on" and partly as models for the builders who would take larger or smaller parcels of lots on which to build more. Carcasses—that is, the bare brick shells of houses and their structural floors and roofs—were as often as not first erected by one speculator and then sold off to be finished later, either singly or in groups, by other operators. In the 40's many such carcasses stood incomplete for years and years. They would ultimately be surfaced with stucco and made habitable internally by men quite other than the architects or builders responsible for the layout of the district or the construction of the earlier houses there. But usually houses would be finished to some rough approximation of the appearance of their already completed neighbors. (Dale gives the best documented accounts of this process.)

Responsibility for the design of any built-up area, whether urban or suburban, was therefore generally extremely diffuse, not to say confused. A

409

basic layout, with a few model houses designed by the architect or surveyor of the estate, may (or may not) have provided a frame which the builders who first took up leases on the various sections respected and which set a pattern for the character of those builders' houses. The first builders involved may (or may not) have employed their own architects—usually not —and they may (or may not) have completed extensive ranges of houses in an initial campaign. If they disposed of portions of their lease to other builders, with or without carcasses, the latter may (or may not) have built groups of additional houses—or even have completed the existing carcasses—in a way that maintained the standards of the estate architect or the first builders involved in the area. Worse: This chain of devolution might descend through many more steps and continue over several decades.

Thus the attribution of the design of urban or suburban housing to particular architects is extremely precarious. Even if a certain man was definitely involved in the original layout, he is not particularly likely to have had anything to do even with the first houses built, much less with those filling out the scheme with houses finally erected, or at least finished, twenty years or so later. Even if the original builders who first took up large leases in the area happened to employ architects, ranges of carcasses may have been the chief result of their initial campaign with only a very few finished houses. The intended design of those houses might be largely ignored by later builders (or their architects) when the carcasses were finished later or when more units were built.

For the same reasons housing floats in time; the really rapid building up of large areas within a few years was certainly much less common than it appears to have been in retrospect. A certain continuing consistency of anonymous character—consistency even with work of pre-Victorian times —was not really broken off before 1870, and in housing for lower income levels hardly even then. This consistency quite disguises even for the expert the long periods over which the actual construction stretched out in some areas, unless some sort of documentary evidence—which is usually rather hard to come by—can be unearthed. (Summerson has had access to the records of the Cubitt firm; from these he should eventually be able to provide masses of precise information.)

The conditions under which 19th-century speculative building proceeded in towns and in suburbs were very, very different from those in rural areas; yet the results, as regards both determinable responsibility for design and accurate or even meaningful dating of complete complexes, are more like those that are familiar in earlier villages and their groups of cottages. Over them, indeed, the control of the local landowner was more absolute than in the cities although architects were only most exceptionally employed at any period for such work. It is extremely difficult to accept, with the known circumstances of the 19th-century building industry, any concept of an organic or group vernacular for urban housing in Victorian times such as rural villages, at their best, had provided well through the 18th and into the early 19th century. The very boundaries of such housing entities as might be considered definite organisms would be but the accidental boundaries of freehold estates, or more usually only of such portions of them as were developed in a short time or in closely related building campaigns. These entities are extremely vague, visually as well as functionally, except for the squares that formed the usual core of urban developments of any social pretension and the wider streets immediately contiguous to them.

Housing provided by row houses built with party walls in "terraces" or by rows of paired residences called "semidetached" was conventional in Victorian cities. For such housing it is the successive norms, that is, the standards that were widely accepted over considerable periods for particular types of tenants, that would be most important to define. Yet these norms are often best illustrated in areas whose filling-up can neither be closely dated nor definitely associated with the names of particular designers or groups of designers. Accurately datable groups, whether or not the work of known designers, therefore have their own extrinsic importance. Conspicuous exceptions to the norms, moreover, are significant and frequently more interesting intrinsically than most run-of-the-mill work. Sometimes also the exception of one decade supplied the basis for a new norm in the next; more often, admittedly, exceptional work had little general effect. Certain architectural fashions that were very strong in other fields caused only a ripple of novel detail to flutter briefly across the drafting boards in builders' offices or are perhaps also illustrated by two or three architect-designed houses. The true norms of housing of the Early Victorian period can be defined almost better by noting what fashions were *not* exploited by builders than by attempting a detailed description of those vague norms themselves.

Where urban housing followed continental models (as was very rarely the case in England itself), with large blocks subdivided not vertically into houses of two to five storeys but horizontally into flats or apartments, the situation as regards dating and individual responsibility for design—if not usually the quality of the design—is rather more satisfactory. Whether such blocks of flats were built by philanthropic agencies to house the "worthy" poor—the "unworthy" Victorian poor might as well jump in the river if they could not get themselves into a comfortable workhouse or gaol—or speculatively for rental to those of higher income level, they were almost all architect designed; they were also more likely to be completed within relatively short periods of time. Few architects, except Henry Roberts, showed any distinction or even any special "know-how" as designers of blocks of flats.

Special laws in Scotland, providing for what would now be called co-operative ownership of blocks of flats, created a very different situation there. In this book, which pretends to cover all Britain but is necessarily English centered, it is impossible to go into this interesting subject.

The erection of houses that were individually designed by architects for particular clients, whether country houses, mansions, or detached villas, played a considerable part statistically in Victorian house production but must largely be ignored in this chapter. Country houses and urban or sub-urban mansions, whether they are of special interest as the work of architects of serious pretension or merely characteristic examples of the period, have already been dealt with in Chapters VI–VIII. The villa architects of the Late Georgian period, some of whose more proto-Victorian designs were discussed in the first chapter, either continued to practice or had very similar successors in the 40's and early 50's. Most villa work tends to fall into place as part of the suburban operations of speculative builders. The Picturesque modes of the 20's and 30's were in general corrupted and standardized by builders of the 40's, not creatively developed. Cottage and villa books deteriorated in quality and even, it would seem, decreased in quantity. Designing small individual houses as paper projects seems no longer to have appealed to creative architectural minds; perhaps it did so earlier because Late Georgian architects found so little actual building to do in the two decades before Waterloo and then went on for some twenty years afterward producing villa books chiefly from a sort of inertia. Only in parsonages built by church architects is minor domestic work of much interest in the Early Victorian period (Fig. V 13).

Blocks of flats remained exceptional types of residential construction in England throughout much of the Victorian Age. As they were therefore always "news" in their day, flats offer a well-documented subject for the architectural historian even though they lack any particular visual interest for modern eyes. It has been noted that flatted housing had long been a usual norm in Scottish cities right through the centuries from the Middle Ages; the introduction of the genre in England was a characteristic new development of the 40's. The acceptance of flats even by the lowest classes was gradual and grudging though it might seem that the poor had little choice but to take what was offered. Already, however, the lower classes had some curious power of appealing to the sentimentalities of their "betters" when it came to the virtues of individual householding and private garden plots.

The last is of course a highly prejudiced statement. Since the poor rarely have much direct opportunity to call the tune in architecture, reports of their desires prepared by others (whether philanthropists or bureaucrats) are largely suspect—my own, or Charles Dickens', pro-flat opinions are more than equally suspect, I hasten to add. Since in 20th-century Britain the power of the lower classes has become political the subject deserves serious study. But it is basically sociological rather than architectural and can only be touched on in this book.

The very slow and halting acceptance of "luxury" flats, even by the more sophisticated members of the upper classes who did not disdain other aspects of continental living, would require a novelist for its proper presentation. The nearly absolute refusal of the middle classes to occupy flats—always associated in their minds apparently either with charity or with cosmopolitan immorality—is even more notable. Some understanding of the curious mixture of motivations which led the middle class to reject flats helps also to explain why the great bulk of the terrace houses and semidetached villas offered for sale or lease by speculative builders shows so little advance, either functional or stylistic, beyond Late Georgian standards in the 40's and 50's. The point is worth developing although necessarily with too large a proportion of surmise to have much evidential value.

The home was certainly no place for "art" in the estimation of solid Victorian citizens. Even the wealthy in the cities, at least before the 70's, were generally shamed by the classes just below them into keeping any startling aesthetic novelties they might fancy well hidden behind sober and monotonous street façades. As to improvements in technical equipment, these could only strike the bourgeois as unnecessary, or even status lowering, since they seemed chiefly designed either to ease the lives of the servant class or to reduce their numbers. "Hot-and-cold running chambermaids," as they have been called, might not have been available in the plural to families in the lower reaches of the middle class and the upper reaches of the artisan class; but there was always at least one slavey to carry the heavy scuttles filled with coals to the various individual fires in the living rooms and the brightly polished brass containers of hot water to the bedrooms three and four flights up from the kitchen. Any inconveniences there might be never fell upon the men of the family, moreover; however high a pedestal was now placed under woman in the abstract, Victorian England was after all peculiarly a man's world.

To the middle classes, flats were respectable only for men living alone—"chambers," as they were called. Arranged and run almost like college residences, such were the traditional abodes of London lawyers in the semi-collegiate Inns of Court (Fig. XII 3). Flats were also not unsuitable for men's

413

XIII

playthings, that is, kept women. Yet these women, having their own special status to maintain, are reputed to have preferred the discretion of a detached villa in St. John's Wood even though their wicked Parisian odors certainly continued to hang about blocks of luxury flats well into the 20th century.

Blocks of flats continued to be news as late as the 70's, whether they were built in a slum or in Kensington Gore, while the standard types of Victorian house production were generally taken for granted. But the relative paucity of contemporary published data, particularly visual data, is not serious when so large a part of the production is still extant; it certainly remains more extensive than the human mind can ever hope to grasp except through a sampling technique.

A serious difficulty in attempting to deal fairly with Victorian housing lies in the fact that so much of it seems but an epilogue—if a mammoth and labyrinthine one—to a story begun in the 17th century and already at its climax by Late Georgian times. Less than in commercial architecture is there any clearly recognizable change of character in the late 30's. Yet decline in house production and increasing financial timidity on the part of speculative builders seem gradually to have been leading to a real reduction in the small sums spent earlier for architectural advice. Negative conditions of this order controlled most work of the 40's but naturally they do not characterize it with much definiteness. Even with the return of prosperity and the resumption of large-scale building activity in the early 50's the weight of inertia—both in design and in technical matters—remained surprisingly heavy. Not before the late 60's was there any considerable bulk of new housing, at least in urban areas, that ceased to be Late Georgian in essential character as well as in external appearance. By then, however, the heyday of the upper-class terrace house was already over. For poorer tenants in town and in the shabbier suburbs terraces or rows of semidetached houses using Early Victorian designs little modified from Georgian prototypes were built even later. Until one recalls the proto-Victorian designs that had been published in the villa books of the first third of the century, many of which were discussed in Chapter II (Figs. II 1–16), it may seem to the casual observer as though the outer and more open suburbs had been Victorianized more rapidly than the inner residential areas; actually the lag there was quite as great but the Late Georgian traditions that lingered on were rather different.

The almost indefinite continuance of what might be called post-Georgian modes in housing did not have the same background as the slow Early Victorian formulation of a new commercial architecture—that process, in any event, was to speed up markedly in the 50's to a peak of High Victorian achievement in the early 60's. If terrace houses, and to a somewhat lesser extent detached and semidetached villas built in series, continued to ex-

414

emplify long-established patterns of design, there were several causes that did not apply in other fields of architecture. Neither the function, the structure, nor the economic organization of the production of ordinary houses really changed very much during the Early Victorian period. The representational or status values houses offered to owners and tenants also remained much the same.

How different was the hotel story! Railways focused the streams of travelers in numbers too great for the traditional inns. First the railways themselves, later new joint-stock companies, provided capital for building huge and increasingly complex edifices. In these new urban hostelries all the novel luxuries of America and the Continent began to be included from as early as the opening 50's, as the Great Western Hotel makes evident (Fig. VII 16), even though the peak of quantity and quality in hotel building came only in the mid-60's. In flat-building, on the other hand, a conservatism comparable to that evident in terrace housing controlled well through the High Victorian period. Whether the intended inhabitants were the metropolitan poor or relatively well-off members of Parliament seeking London accommodation for part of the year, the amenities of flats improved very slowly from the early 50's down to the 70's. The few blocks built or planned in the 40's were still quite tentative and even experimental.

The Victorian housing story is by no means *merely* an epilogue as previous writers have tended to present it (if indeed they touched on so dubious a subject at all). At best it is an important sequel to the Georgian story, although like most sequels markedly inferior in interest. The finer episodes, moreover, are likely to be remembered as belonging to the earlier volume, just as Alice's better adventures through the looking glass are often credited to her earlier visit to Wonderland. To be just to the Early Victorians the line between the wonderland of Georgian housing—for a wonderland it has usually seemed to the present generation—and what went on behind the looking glass after 1837 must be drawn as sharply as possible. Up to now whatever has been admired in Victorian house production of the 40's and 50's (and even in some cases of the 60's) has too often been loosely attributed to the preceding Georgian Age or more precisely, but even less accurately, to that short post-Waterloo period which is labeled "Regency." A tremendous wave of house building did *begin* while George IV was still Regent but it also continued to gain momentum almost as long as he occupied the throne. In the less affluent 30's, moreover, there were some important realizations of urban schemes which had first been proposed rather earlier even though they had barely been started when George IV died. Dobson's magnificent work at Newcastle may be mentioned in this connection, although it was mostly commercial and monumental, not domestic, and continued well after 1837.

In general, house production began to decline under William IV leaving many ambitious projects far from complete. Large areas, for which we give credit to the Regency, must therefore still have looked rather like Florida after 1929 at the very beginning of Victoria's reign. Throughout the 40's a great deal of urban residential building merely filled out ambitious layouts initiated a decade or two earlier. In Edinburgh, for example, the areas extending north, east, and west from the late 18th-century "new town" remained unfinished well into the 50's although the general scheme for their development dated from the 20's. Most of the section of Playfair's original plan running north toward Leith on the low ground below Calton Hill was never built up according to his magnificent ideas at all. One is readily deceived by names like "Carlton," "Regent," and so forth as to the real date of construction of particular terraces in various cities. Such names were often assigned in the original layout in the 20's although many of the houses were not built for almost a generation. There were certainly still many gaps in the terraces with these distinctly "Regency" names around the east end of Calton Hill in the 50's. In late houses the real date of construction is evident in the character of the interior treatment as well as from their omission from early maps. Sometimes the unbarred window sash give a clue even to the casual passer-by.

Kemp Town at Brighton is generally considered to be, after Nash's Regent's Park terraces, the largest, grandest, and most homogeneous of "Regency" developments. (I owe all my facts here to Dale's previously cited work.) It actually dates, of course, no further back than the late 20's in its origins by which time the Regent was King and had already left Brighton for good. When the 6th Duke of Devonshire, Paxton's friend, described his own house in Chichester Terrace in 1845 it was still "surrounded by . . . shells and carcases of . . . houses." By 1834 only 36 out of 105 houses had been sufficiently finished to be inhabited; more than ten years later, when the duke wrote, the number had risen only to 71. Later still, after Cubitt took up again the extension of Chichester Terrace westward to balance Arundel Terrace on the east, the work was finally carried to completion by his trustees only after his death in 1855. Kemp himself, the overambitious founder, had left England a broken man as early as 1837.

At the other end of Brighton in Hove there operated Baron Goldschmid. Being a financier, he was not dependent like Kemp on an agricultural income and the proceeds of estate development for capital. Yet he waited until 1849 before he began to build up the western half of Adelaide Crescent of which the original layout is clearly dated by the name of William IV's queen. Only after that did he even lay out Palmeira Square at its head, while the building of the terraces there ran on into the 60's, well beyond his death.

The wonder is not that the houses in this square are inferior to those Decimus Burton had first designed when Adelaide Crescent was begun a score of years and more earlier but that they are any good at all.

Yet in many essentially Late Georgian developments completed after such long lapses of time a surprising homogeneity of quality makes it difficult to distinguish, at least from the outside, the latest built houses from the earliest. This is the more remarkable because the tastes and standards of architects during the late 30's and 40's, at least in church building, had undergone a total stylistic revolution; in various other fields of construction an equally drastic technical revolution had taken place. An absolute decline in the competence of the craftsmen employed in the building industry has generally been *assumed* but not proved. It should already be evident from earlier chapters of this book that this is most unjust, at least as regards stonecutting and bricklaying, in many fields of building; I am not sure that it is necessarily true even of the stucco-covered work of the house builders. (Present-day English architects assure me they generally find Victorian houses solider than Georgian ones when they are called in to do remodeling.)

When in the 50's the curve of house building turned sharply upward again a great many more heads of families could aspire to the amenities of a three- to five-storey house in a "good" residence district than in Georgian times; what they expected of a house in plan and section had, however, changed very little. The enhancement of social status they sought could best be assured if the new houses were as similar as possible to those built in the previous boom period. This was a consideration builders naturally recognized and whose importance for sales or rentals they probably exaggerated. Such new amenities as might be in demand—for the most part mere gadgets—could be readily incorporated without any modification of traditional plans and structural methods. Builders, seeing a chance for profits once more, were not likely to introduce the costly fireproof floor construction that was coming to be standard in commercial work and even in some portions at least of expensively built urban mansions and country houses.

The deterioration of established building techniques from Georgian standards that *may* have taken place in Early Victorian times has certainly been much exaggerated by modern writers, if only because the worst Georgian jerry-building had already collapsed before the 20th century opened. Yet poor construction could best be disguised by retaining an established framework of design and using a smooth outer coating of stucco as the house builders of the 40's generally did. Nash—as was well known to the Victorians and thoroughly confirmed by the blitz—had hidden all sorts of structural shoddiness under his stucco; only the skin of paint seems over the years to have held together the houses in his famous Regent's Park terraces. The vio-

lent critical attacks on stucco in the Early Victorian period were not therefore likely to be heeded by speculative builders; their clients did not bother
to look below the nicely painted surfaces nor did they worry about "shams."
The renewal of the paintwork permitted recurrent freshening up of terrace
housing. The dreariness of unpainted houses for several years after World
War II reminded many how exceptional the lack of paint had previously been
in the West End of London.

Most terrace houses were built by large-scale operators on "spec" for lease
or for sale. The organizations and methods of such operators had long been
established and their experience often went back to the 20's. Such men had
little interest in the soul-searchings of the architectural profession, whether
technical or stylistic, being anxious to unload their product on the unwary
as quickly as possible. As in much 20th-century private housing the vagueness of the relationship between builder and client also tended to favor both
conservatism and eclectic uncertainty. A few saleswords covered a multitude
of slightly modified versions of established types of design—like "Ranch
House," or somewhat earlier "Cape Cod," in 20th-century America.

When building for himself a particular man may well want a house that
is *different* from those of his neighbors and one to which therefore some precise stylistic label can be plausibly applied; on the other hand, a speculator
building for undetermined clients only too rightly assumes that marked differences in the styling of his product from what is already familiar are not
going to be pleasing to any considerable number of lessors or buyers. The
modern market analyst would certainly confirm the Victorian builder in his
stylistic timidity; moreover, real novelty whether technical or aesthetic always tends to cost more in building. Ecclesiastical and commercial clients,
being less anonymous, could insist on higher standards of quality in both
materials and design. Mid-Victorian ladies, moreover, who were the ones
chiefly to suffer from deficiencies in house planning, probably really liked the
"neat" painted stucco and the conventional designs which the house builders
usually offered. They obviously had little influence on church design and
none on commercial building in the 40's and 50's, which was perhaps just as
well. Eventually a none too happy feminizing influence spread from domestic
architecture into many other fields in the Late Victorian period after 1870.

Next we must consider the matter of "representation," not to say frankly
snobbery. The yearning for status was at its most intense in the middle classes
although not inoperative upon the tastes of either the rich or the poor; this
yearning was also probably more intense in the women than in the men of
the period. Most families who moved into Victorian terrace houses were out
to better their social standing; hence, quite as in the 20th century, they had
a strong preference for house types long associated with assured social posi-

tion. Just as the retired industrialist was quite likely to build his country house in the form of a castle or a manor, so the members of the urban middle classes, male and female, wanted houses not too unlike the Georgian houses of the older portions of the West End and the comparable districts in other cities. The urban habitations of English aristocrats had long presented a rather middle-class front to the world since individual magnificence was generally reserved for their territorial seats. The new middle-class oligarchy which the Reform Act had established in power quite naturally accepted the aristocrats' well-established convention of group display in town residences with little or no individual differentiation of individual houses from their neighbors.

In London, as in other cities like Edinburgh and Brighton, the Early Victorian period saw a great deal of filling in of ambitious earlier schemes. Through the 40's many houses in Belgravia (Fig. XIII 32), planned and partly built in the early 20's, were still waiting for purchasers. John Summerson in *Georgian London* [1945] notes that Royalty in the person of the Queen's mother settled at No. 28 as late as 1845, acquiring the house directly from the builder. Edward Thomas Delafield, a rich brewer, also moved there soon afterward, paying £1,095 a year for his house and stables. Nearby Eaton Square was not entirely built up until 1853. To the south the less pretentious development of the Pimlico portion of the Grosvenor Estate also advanced but slowly toward the river. Warwick Square was already laid out in 1843; but one side of St. George's Square was still occupied by Cubitt's workshops in 1851 after the other side was filled with houses in the previous year.

A grander development north of the Park, on the Bishop of London's Bayswater Estate, had been laid out by George Gutch (d. 1875) under William IV (Fig. XIII 32). John Crake's Hyde Park Gardens, designed in the most massive manner of the Late Georgian period, went up there in 1836–38. The magnificent urban scenery in the squares behind Hyde Park Gardens must date from the late 30's and early 40's, at least as regards the general scheme. Oxford and Cambridge Squares were being formed in 1837; Hyde Park Square had at least been begun by then. The great engineer Robert Stephenson, well representing the newer type of wealthy men who filled up the Bayswater squares, moved ten years later into No. 34 Gloucester Square, one of the center houses ornamented by a three-storey engaged Corinthian order (Fig. XIII 6). But he was certainly not the first tenant in the square or possibly, even, of that particular house. The houses at the ends of Gloucester Square are by George Ledwell Taylor (1788–1873), John Summerson informs us. Was Taylor also responsible, then, for that rather breath-taking view (now ruined by rebuilding) through the open northwest corner of Hyde Park Square diagonally across Gloucester Square (Fig. XIII 1)? Presumably

Gutch, in his original layout, had at least envisaged it; for he could feel assured that when finally built the terraces in this latest westward salient of the rich bourgeoisie would be tall and boldly composed.

Far to the northeast, surprisingly enough, near-suburban Islington saw in the late 30's and early 40's some rather impressive terrace building also. This was done handsomely and to the designs of known architects but the houses were certainly intended for tenants on a somewhat lower economic level than those in Bayswater. Whether because of or despite that fact, these Islington terraces are more novel in their stylistic character. Milner Square, built in 1841–43 by Gough and Roumieu, has façades of exposed stock brick with cement trim (Fig. XIII 2). The continuous articulation of the entire square by tall pilasters, with no center or end accents, produced an almost Martinesque monumentality. (I refer to the painter John Martin [1759–1854] but do not imply these were abodes either of Belshazzar or of Satan, the subject matter of two of his better known pictures. John Summerson finds something rather hellish in the insistent rhythm, and the effect is admittedly grim rather than grand.) Milner Square lacks the picturesque charm that the overscaled order of Gloucester Square rather surprisingly provides when seen through a screen of trees from Hyde Park Square (Fig. XIII 1). The long narrow plan of the Islington square, with its continuous façades curved at the corners, is perhaps more properly urbanistic but the pictorial drama of Bayswater, improving in some respects upon Nash, is quite absent.

Nearby, R. C. Carpenter had already designed his terraces around Lonsdale Square in 1838 (Fig. XIII 3). Carpenter was, of course, destined within a few years to operate at the very heart of the ecclesiological world, but the ground landlords employing him here were the Drapers' Company who were certainly no Camdenians. At that date his domestic Gothic was not at all like the "correct" 14th-century Decorated of his later churches but rather a pleasant Late Georgian kind of Tudor. The walls are of stock brick; the trim, which is very simple, is of painted stucco. (For this youthful sin he doubtless paid later by hours of ecclesiological penance.) The mullioned windows are large and freely disposed in the façades. Although the whole square is most solidly executed it looks back to the flimsy Gothic terraces, rare though they were, of Regency times rather than forward to the characteristic Early Victorian Gothic of the church mode at which Carpenter was so soon to be one of the most conscientious, if uninspired, virtuosos.

Percy Circus in Clerkenwell was also begun in 1838, though not completed until 1853, probably after a long hiatus. It is rather dramatic because of the way the rather conventional houses climb its steep slope. Some of the Early Victorian circuses on the northwesterly slopes of the Edinburgh New Town are similar in character. Severe in design and solidly built in stone, their design appears to be pre-Victorian but they were in most instances not executed until well after the new reign began.

To the northwest of Belgravia between the Brompton Road and Knightsbridge, Montpelier Square, modestly "Regency" in the character of its small houses, was laid out just about 1837. Its very name recalling earlier watering places, this remains a demure oasis very different from the brash stucco cliffs of Bayswater (yet one understands that its demure look was at one time rather deceptive, like that of so many St. John's Wood villas). Victoria Square, off the northeast end of Ebury Street on the other side of Belgravia, is another such oasis dating precisely from 1837. Prettier and more varied in treatment than the dark gray terraces that surround the big Pimlico squares, it is not very typical either of the period or of the district in its modest but genuine charm.

Even the grandest of the London terraces of the very opening of the new reign look tawdry beside those of Clifton. Clifton had been an independent watering place rather than part of Bristol; it was now becoming the principal residential suburb of that great western port. Yet even today the steep slopes between have retained for Clifton a separate character. Linked in its beginnings with the end of a more famous Georgian tradition in nearby Bath, Clifton offers the largest and most distinguished array of very early Victorian housing, the ready availability of Bath stone encouraging the continuation of a dignified and sophisticated resort architecture.

The most impressive thing in Clifton is the terrace known as the Royal Promenade on the north side of Victoria Square (Fig. XIII 4). This dates, as the name of the square implies, from 1837 (that is, the original design; the execution may have continued over some fifteen years before the terrace was entirely completed). Despite the sober and extremely literate character of the Royal Promenade its Early Victorian date is suggested by some of the incidental features. The minuscule arcade above the principal cornice, linking the attic windows together, and the rich continuous scrollwork of the pierced balustrade below the first-storey windows are not quite Georgian in effect. The presence of the Royal arms, set against the pilastered attic of the central block, presumably gave rise to the local legend that the central house was intended for the new Queen's occupancy on an early visit to Bristol. Certainly the whole long range of more than a dozen houses has a distinction of proportion and material more suited to a Royal residence than the tawdry new east front Blore erected in 1847 for Buckingham Palace (Fig. IX 1).

Many more terraces at Clifton of rather similar character presumably belong to much the same period. The last houses in Worcester Terrace, which resembles the Royal Promenade very closely, were not completed, however, until 1851–53 (Fig. XIII 5). Evidently there was a considerable hiatus in terrace building at Clifton in the mid- and late 40's. But with the return of prosperity the thread seems to have been taken up again at much the same point at which it was dropped.

Hamilton Square in Birkenhead is named for Thomas Hamilton of Edinburgh who laid it out and built the first houses in 1844. Also of stone and very large, it is rather more dour as befits its Scottish architect and its location; for it was planned as the center of a new port town, not as an ornament to a resort. Another Edinburgh architect, Gillespie Graham, may have been involved in preparing the general plan of the town (Fig. XIII 35). In Plymouth, where stucco was as ubiquitous as in London, Wightwick had built the delicately detailed Esplanade along the Hoe in 1836. The simpler and more heavily membered Athenaeum Terrace and Leigham Terrace, as well as those in Mulgrave Street and Lansdowne Place, are presumably slightly later and hence technically Early Victorian (Fig. XIII 7).

Still simpler in detail are the terraces in smaller county towns, but they are not without their own excellences. Remarkably bold in articulation are two contiguous terraces of two-storey houses in Eastgate Street in Winchester, for example. One of these (Nos. 4–8) is in effect a range of small villas juxtaposed around a curve, each with two semicircular bay windows (Fig. XIII 8). The other (Nos. 10–20) is so "functional" in expression, in the modern phrase, that it can only be compared with the cottages in Joseph Gandy's book of 1805 (Figs. II 4, XIII 9).

To find anything positively Victorian in the work thus far mentioned, except perhaps the great height and heavy membering of the Bayswater terraces or the bold scale of the tiny Winchester houses, is difficult. The few real innovations in design represent individual quirks of taste rather than the adumbration of new norms for terrace design. These novelties hardly compare in interest with the peripheral instances of highly individualized design which the first third of the century so frequently provided (see Chapter II). In less expensive work the differences from the norm established for "fourth-class" houses in the 18th century are so slight as almost to defy recognition. Peacock Terrace, Liverpool Grove, facing one of Soane's finest churches in the South London district of Walworth, obligingly carries the date 1842 and its name on the parapet (Fig. XIII 10). But for the consonant character of the lettering one might almost assume the inscription was a late insertion and the houses at least a quarter-century earlier.

In the Late Georgian period architectural novelties seem often to have come up the social and economic ladder from the villa and the cottage, but that is hardly true of Early Victorian terrace building. The more modest the terrace and the smaller the tenants' means, the surer it is to be laggard in style by a generation or more. In terrace design Clifton did not set the pace of fashion for the 40's in the way Bath had done a century earlier, much less commercial Plymouth or Birkenhead; the new Victorian norms eventually made their first appearance in the West End but they had not yet done so in the earliest years of Victoria's reign.

Several new professional journals covering the related fields of architecture, civil engineering, and estate surveying appeared in the opening years of the Victorian Age but they devote surprisingly little attention to terrace housing. Some factual information on new housing estates is given in the editorial text; it is through a perusal of the advertisements of estates being developed and the tenders for preliminary civil engineering work, for carcasses, and for finishing houses that the statistical importance of this branch of the building industry can best be sensed, however. Illustrations of terrace-house plans and elevations are actually rarer than maps of estate layouts. This fact emphasizes the subprofessional rating of terrace design, for which architects were now very little employed. When builders' draftsmen wished to refresh or vary the repertory of stock forms that were to be (quite literally) plastered over stock-brick house carcasses, they seem to have done so merely by picking up ideas in the streets or else by casually adapting features from the published illustrations of more pretentious architect-designed work.

Outside the Gothic and Jacobethan fields, the handsomest new architectural books were likely to be foreign ones, such as those of Percier and Fontaine and of Grandjean de Montigny and Famin, not to speak of Letarouilly a bit later. These were certainly the best sources for Italian Renaissance precedent but they would have seemed much too expensive to ordinary builders. Moreover, the builders' draftsmen would have had little access to the few libraries where such books might have been currently available. A monograph like W. H. Leeds' on a prominent London monument by a recognized professional leader, his *Travellers' Club House* of 1839, was less costly and more generally accessible. It seems to have proved particularly useful in providing "crib" material for detailing house fronts. The repeated ranges of edicular windows on terrace houses built in various parts of London in the 40's and even later make evident that this was an important source of current ideas.

Ordinary builders, as in the 18th century, were more usually content with what are called "builder's books," often in fact with new editions of those their grandfathers had cherished before them. Paradigms for the orders were as readily available as they ever had been, but the use of the orders at large scale was going out of fashion now (despite Bayswater) and they were in any event awkward and expensive to execute in brick and stucco. Furthermore, the codified Late Renaissance versions of the orders, as generally accepted down through the time of Chambers' *Civil Architecture* (1759), had been upset by the invention of personal variants by such architects as Adam and Soane, and even more by the increasingly general substitution of Stuart and Revett's Grecian models for the earlier Roman ones.

But the special character of the Greek orders as used by a great academic architect like C. R. Cockerell who had the advantage of personal study of idiosyncratic types in Greece itself was now shaking the authority of the Grecian norms. With the breakdown of all accepted standards for the orders, long the core of academic discipline in architecture, there disappeared likewise any general rules of thumb concerning the proper forms for cornices, stringcourses, quoins, and all the other small change of architectural design. These minor features were, of course, even more important in the builders' repertory of detail than the orders had ever been.

After more than a generation of nearly continuous employment, moreover, workers in stucco and cement had undoubtedly developed ideas of their own about detail. But habits induced by the nature of the material and the easiest way of using it were generally bad habits from the point of view of correct academic design. Gothic theorists, on the other hand, were coming to realize that achievement of high quality in revived medieval detail would ultimately depend on just such a development of special habituation among the workers in the various building crafts. The craftsmen who executed old medieval buildings were now thought to have had what is pedantically called a *habitus* dependent on their materials and on their tools. This habitus was thought to owe something to their piety, according to Pugin; or to their happy sense of individual expression, according to Ruskin a few years later. Between the Early Victorian stuccoworkers' impious and lazy habitus and the sort of prayerful or joyful craftsmanship the Gothic Revivalists wished to revive there was certainly no viable bridge in the 40's.

Looking into an Early Victorian edition of the *Carpenter's Guide* by Peter Nicholson (1765–1844) one finds, in addition to geometrical diagrams, many miscellaneous plates of detail of the most diverse origin. (The Nicholson bibliography is incredibly complicated, but certainly in its origins the treatise goes back to the 1790's; the dating of individual plates is more significant than the dating of editions and issues.) Such a book also provides illustrations of quite a number of individual buildings by important achitects, both British and American. These examples range from Decimus Burton's Grecian Athenaeum Club house and the great Corinthian temple that Thomas U. Walter (1804–1887) built for Girard College in Philadelphia, both shown complete, to door and window details at large scale taken from Sir Jeffrey Wyatville's Gothic work of the 20's at Windsor. Most of the specimens shown were about twenty years old by the mid-40's. The one brand-new terrace elevation will be discussed later (Fig. XIII 34). The inclusion of models for urban houses

424

is relatively rare, and this offers a most valuable precisely dated example of one stage of Early Victorian terrace design with the architect's name given, which is most unusual.

T. L. Walker's *Architectural Precedents* (3d ed. 1841) included complete plans, elevations, and even some sections, as well as full specifications, for a pair of "second-rate" semidetached houses (Fig. XIII 12). Even though this material was offered by Walker for its presumptive technical value rather than as a model for designers, it was closely followed by many suburban builders. Inspiration for particular features of design came more often from cottage and villa books, usually ones of much earlier date. Although designs for terraces had always been rare in such works, various elements of detached villa elevations could readily be applied to ranges of row houses. The production of these books was now well past its peak, but the proto-Victorian ideas in the compilations of the Late Georgian period—to which attention has been called in chapter II—continued to be imitated from copies retained in builders' offices. Many of them must have been bought in the boom of the 20's to supplement the more conservative Late Georgian repertory of forms and details provided by "builder's guides" like Nicholson's; apparently they were consulted on and off for a generation or more until they finally fell apart.

The plates dated 1839 in a remarkable book by S. H. Brooks can no longer be called *proto*-Victorian. (*Designs for Cottages and Villa Architecture* carries no imprint date but probably appeared in 1840.) His so-called "Grecian" and "Swiss" villas, variants on the asymmetrically towered Italian Villa, provided details of an oddity that builders were hardly ready to incorporate in terrace façades or even in semidetached work much before the late 40's (Fig. XIII 11). Richard Brown's *Domestic Architecture* (1842; later ed. 1852) is more typical of the sort of book that builders' draftsmen leaned on in the 40's for ideas. The appearance of another edition of this as late as 1852 indicates that a demand for this sort of material continued through the whole Early Victorian period. Extremely ambitious in size and architectural pretension, Brown's proposed designs would hardly have appealed to such Early Victorians as were in a financial and social position to erect them; for mansions of this scale architects would surely have been employed. But Brown's elevations were full of curious details for the use of cribbing designers in builders' offices.

Tudor, Jacobean, Mannerist (though called Florentine and based, according to Brown, on Petrarch's villa at Arqua, Fig. XIII 13), Pompeian (an irregular Italian Villa), Flemish (castellated), Venetian (with oriental verandahs), Swiss, French, Egyptian, Grecian, Roman, Anglo-Grecian (actually rather Soanic), Anglo-Italian (a towered villa), Persian, Chinese, Oriental,

Morisco-Spanish, Norman, Lancastrian, and Plantagenet: Such a listing of the titles of Brown's designs sounds almost like a parody of the villa books of a generation earlier. But there had been a surprising deterioration since the beginning of the century in the technique of presentation, both in the general pictorial quality and in the care with which the details were rendered, though Brown's plates were still engraved, not lithographed or cut on wood. All the charm and the precision of the earlier books had gone. With such visual material about, the wonder is not that the detail on builders' houses deteriorated through the Early Victorian period, but that it retained any relation to the standards of architect-designed work at all. The continuance of a certain circumspection in detail must be credited to the very inertia and conservatism of all the forces acting upon the house building trade.

A much superior publication of the 40's is the "Third Book" of Charles Parker's *Villa rustica*. The rather archaeological way in which his Italian Villa designs, based for once on real edifices in Italy, were presented in the earlier "First Book" and "Second Book" of 1832 and 1833 has been mentioned in chapter II (Fig. II 11). In this "Third Book" (issued in 1841 and reissued, together with the other two, in 1848) Parker offered a range of projects for National Schools all in a very personal Italian Villa manner. These were mostly presented in firm outline with no vagueness about details (Fig. XIII 14). The walls are strongly articulated with broad flat bands of relief. The similar bands which surround the openings are varied, not only with rectangular ears, but frequently with curved elements of a rather peasant-Baroque character. The low-pitched projecting roofs are tile covered and supported on chunky consoles; while the chimneys and open belfries which still further enliven the roof lines of the boldly broken masses are heavily corniced and sometimes even gable capped.

Parker's Italian does not have the distinction of Barry's: He was only the poor man's Barry. All the same, many professional colleagues borrowed effectively from his stock of ideas; while the simplicity of his lively effects and the bold scale of his details provided various piquant ideas for builders' draftsmen to emulate. They might profitably have made still more use of them.

John White's *Rural Architecture* was published in 1845 in Glasgow. North of the Border a consistent lag in stylistic development is evident through most of the Victorian Age. Villa books in Scotland, like monumental Grecian design, tended in the 40's to preserve pre-Victorian qualities rather longer than in England. Yet the character of White's designs is closer to the general norm of builders' production in the Early Victorian period, even in England, than is the very advanced plasticity of most of Parker's National School projects or the fussy picturesqueness of Brown's mansions. White offered several moderate-sized Grecian mansions and a variety of Tudor houses of different

426

sizes. But his irregular Italian designs are the most interesting. As is so often true of Scottish work, these have a very American look (Fig. XIII 15), not because they were especially influential across the Atlantic but rather because the cultural relationship to metropolitan London architecture was so similar in the Northern Kingdom and in the former colonies. Yet Gervase Wheeler and Calvert Vaux (1824–1895) in America, both English born, must surely have known this work, as many of the designs in their books of the 50's make evident. So doubtless did the Scottish-born Philadelphia architect John Notman.

Bracketed eaves, quoined corners, small grouped arches, all more delicate in scale and in relief than Parker's similar features, characterize these designs by White. Bay windows are freely used and a simple tracery sometimes fills the window arches. Thus the Italianate effect is mildly eclectic and well domesticated—one can hardly, in the circumstances, say well "Anglicized." White also offers some simple semidetached cottages of a single storey with cross gables of low pitch. His plans are unusually free in the disposition of the rooms; hence the exterior massing is likely to be asymmetrical. But it is never assertively so since there are no tall loggia towers to provide emphatic off-center accents.

White shows one very elaborate Jacobethan mansion in great detail; but the Mannerist extravagances of its profuse ornamentation were generally beyond the aspirations of ordinary builders in the penurious 40's. The gusto of the urns and other decorative features on this mansion, lithographed in outline with no refinement of rendering, contrasts with the still rather Grecian crispness of the molded work on his Italianate houses (Fig. XIII 16). White's Jacobethan plates also served to complement as well as to "interpret" for builders' draftsmen the more accurate original documents provided earlier by Henry Shaw and C. J. Richardson. Such plates were certainly not without effect in the builders' world. When they were shown to the stuccoworkers as models, they helped to loosen the tightness of form that resulted from early Grecian training. It is rather curious that White offers no Scottish Baronial designs. But that mode seems rarely to have descended to the suburban builders' economic level in Early Victorian times, however popular "Balmoral" was destined eventually to be as a designation for detached and even semidetached villas.

For the use of builders also, and perhaps as much as a decade later in date, is a book of *Designs for Villas, Parsonages, and Other Houses . . . from £200 to £5000* (n.d.) by Samuel Hemming of Birmingham. In this many of the plates are lithographed in two or three colors. The book has additional value because of the detailed and very businesslike set of specifications provided with each design. The £200 houses are shown as a single pair only;

but they are really terrace houses since the solid ends are evidently party walls (Fig. XIII 17). Designs for these tiny houses are as close to the bottom of the Victorian urban builders' stock as anything one can find in published plans and elevations. Various changes may be noted since Peacock Terrace was built in Liverpool Grove in 1842 (Fig. XIII 10). Scrolled brackets flank the glazed transoms over the entrance doors; smaller brackets, economically grouped in three's over the upper windows, support the main cornice. No blocking course masks the roof and the chimney tops are clumsily corniced.

In other words, even in these minimal cots there was some attempt to increase the general effect of plasticity and to vary the skyline in the Parker—or for that matter, the Barry—manner. At Peacock Terrace the windows still have nine-paned sash; here the sash have merely a central bar. This must be considered a technical improvement since it introduced the upper-class luxury of large panes of rolled glass. It is certainly an indication of late date—how late in the case of such inexpensive work I do not know precisely, but undoubtedly after 1851. This sash division also quite de-Georgianizes the elevations, as everyone must realize it would do from noting the blank look of earlier houses that have lost their small-paned sash.

The plans of these houses might seem to require no comment; but as plans of "fourth-class" houses of the Early Victorian period are hard to come by they may well be analyzed here. A large front room serves as a parlor; behind is a smaller living-kitchen; the side hall is widened out at the rear in order to allow room for the stairs which lead up to three bedrooms above. In a rear wing is a pantry and scullery; the outdoor privy and the dustbins open on a paved back yard which is surrounded by a wall and equipped with a pump as well as a central drain. The ground coverage is, in a sense, practically 100 per cent; at least their is no proper garden space at all.

A more elaborate pair of semidetached houses shown by Hemming were to cost £520 each. Since these would need to occupy more land they were necessarily intended for a suburban site. Their style is very modestly Jacobethan, with curved gables and even a bit of carving in the spandrels of the Tudor-arched doorway. Doors and window openings are quoined and mullioned in stone against the plain red brick walls. At long last painted stucco trim had gone out, at least in Birmingham, even for very low-cost work; but terra cotta had not yet come in.

A plain "Italian" house shown by Hemming is asymmetrical in its fenestration but completely cubic in mass (Fig. XIII 18). The two-columned porch at the door adds both convenience and prestige; all the windows have cornices carried on scrolled brackets and the corners of the house are ornamented with paneled quoins. This house, costing £670, is intended as a detached parsonage house—presumably for a very Low Church parson. It could easily be built in pairs, however, or even in a continuous terrace, since the end walls are solid.

In a pair of houses costing £750 each, simple polychromy in red and white brick was introduced, reflecting one of the most popular new ideas of the early 50's (Fig. XIII 19). There is nothing Gothic about the design, however, nor yet is it all Italianate. The segmental arches used throughout are purely and frankly structural in character. Yet the front is made quite plastic by an ingenious grouping of the two porches and the flanking bay windows under a continuous penthouse roof. This rather original treatment of materials and forms would probably not have been acceptable to Victorian builders and their clients in this price range much before the mid- or late 50's.

A stuccoed villa (Design 7) whose estimated cost rose to £1,080 is much more conservative and might have been built more than a generation earlier, except for its large-paned sash and the off-center location of the entrance. Two others, at £1,550 and £1,800, are closer to the usual norm of respectable Early Victorian villa design. Both are symmetrical and three broad bays wide. The more sober and correct one (Design 9, which was also the dearer) suggests, despite its modest size, a conscious emulation of such London mansions as those in Kensington Palace Gardens designed by Barry's associates and imitators (Figs. VI 13, 21). The trim is rich and rather well scaled; chamfered quoins bind the corners and there is a rusticated plinth, all intended to be executed in cut stone. A plain stringcourse below the first-storey windows and a frieze of circles below the modillioned cornice were also to be executed in stone. Continuous architraves, slightly eared on the ground storey, surround the windows; scrolled brackets of excellent proportion support the cornice over the door. In this project there is no variety of silhouette and practically no arbitrary ornament except for the curious little scrolls that flank the base of the first-storey architraves. In building such a villa suburbia would be aping the restraint of Early Victorian plutocracy a decade late.

The other villa, costing £1,550, is less restrained (Fig. XIII 22). On this, rustication covers the entire ground storey, and the middle section of the façade projects, although only very slightly. But the triple windows in this central section give a richer and busier effect to the whole façade. Their cornices are supported on deep scrolled brackets and they also have curved pediments over the wider central windows. This treatment was probably suggested by the windows in the end bays of the garden front of Barry's Bridgewater House, designed in 1847 (Fig. VII 10). It was a motif London terrace builders took up about 1850 when the feeling for continuity in terrace composition, inherited from the 18th century, began to yield to a contrary desire to give emphasis to each individual house.

The plan of this £1,550 house is superior to those of the general run of

Hemming's villas (Fig. XIII 22). The entrance is placed on one side so that the front façade may be regular; but the symmetry toward the street was not allowed to restrict the free grouping of principal rooms of varying size. The service wing and the stable yard ramble off to the rear and side with real functional ease. The upper storey has an open gallery at the rear intended, apparently, for the children of the family.

Many of the books which help us to understand the terrace builders' milieu float as vaguely in time as do the urban and suburban housing developments. The recurrent editions of Nicholson, for example, although they do usually carry dates of publication, include individual plates from various earlier issues. From their dates it would seem that these plates continued to be issued until they wore out. Books such as Hemming's are likely to be quite without dates of any sort, on title page, preface, or individual plates. And even in books like his, as in the periodicals of the time, actual designs for terraces— particularly for upper middle-class terraces—are rarely provided. Production of terrace houses was evidently even more standardized and unvarying over the years than that of semidetached houses or freestanding suburban villas so that new designs were not much in demand. The terrace builders were doubtless so complacent by this time in their subprofessional "know-how" that the architects and others who compiled books of house designs hardly thought it worth while to offer them direct suggestions even to the modest extent they had done in Late Georgian times. Yet these books offer the best historical clues there are in the foggy climate of design and technical knowledge Early Victorian terrace builders seem to have worked in, just as comparable 18th-century books do for their Georgian predecessors.

The analysis of samples of this literature in the preceding paragraphs has brought the story well forward into the 50's. But we must not forget that a continuing Late Georgian background was provided for the housing industry all through the 40's by the gradual finishing up of various major developments initiated in the 20's and 30's; and builders as well as architects were capable of maintaining established standards surprisingly well—as at Birkenhead by Thomas Hamilton and by various architects and builders at Clifton—when they continued to follow norms that went back to pre-Victorian times. Against this almost unchanging background the more advanced designs in the villa books of the 40's, whether or not they were actually intended to be used for terrace houses, chiefly suggest what the more popular stylistic novelties would be when building generally revived around 1850 rather than what was being commonly erected much before that date. Such designs also help to explain, because they parallel exceptional executed work and sometimes even derive from it, the more positively post-Georgian ambitions of a few

430

ambitious builders, even from the very early 40's. But they must not be permitted to distort the true statistical picture of Early Victorian terrace housing which is far more one of coherent continuity than of cumulative change and increasing variety.

From such a fog of vagueness it is a relief to be able to turn to one particular terrace built at a known date by a known architect. This terrace in Lowndes Square in London has the further interest that it probably initiated the first important new Victorian mode of terrace design. The publication of the plans and elevations by the *Surveyor, Engineer and Architect* in 1841 while the houses were in construction surely indicates that their significance as examples of a more sophisticated and up-to-date sort of terrace design than the overscaled post-Georgian of Bayswater was immediately recognized by professionals (Figs. XIII 20). These plates also made the design readily available as a model for other terrace builders to follow if they wished. The prestige of a Belgravian location and of their builder, if not so much of their architect, would have had a good deal to do with the unusual recognition accorded these houses by the press, as also with the presumptive interest of other builders in emulating them. Before describing the Lowndes Square terrace, the general building situation south of the Park around 1840 should be summarized.

In 1842, as John Summerson noted in *Georgian London* [1945], T. L. Donaldson in his inaugural lecture as Professor of Architecture at University College "held up Belgravia as the most honourable specimen of speculative building and awarded it a special encomium." Whatever may have been the responsibility of Thomas Cundy II, the Grosvenor Estate architect of the period, for the general layout or of George Basevi for either that layout or for the design of the actual terraces in Belgrave Square, it was the great builder Thomas Cubitt whom Donaldson specifically praised. Already in the late 20's Cubitt had employed his brother Lewis to design some houses in Eaton Square. The more modest terraces in outer Belgravia itself and those in Pimlico to the south seem, however, to have been designed in Cubitt's own office—many of the latter, at least, by John Young before he established his own practice, according to his obituary in the *Builder*. These terraces are on the whole respectable if dullish examples of post-Georgian design suited to the rather unfashionable clientele for which Pimlico (unlike Belgravia) seems from the first to have catered.

The building up of the Grosvenor Estate in Belgravia was far from complete—although largely off Thomas Cubitt's hands through subleasing to other builders—when in the mid-30's he obtained from a man named Lowndes, the ground landlord, the lease of a narrow tract of land lying be-

tween Wilton Crescent and Sloane Street beyond the northwest edge of the
Grosvenor lands and just east of Hans Town on the Cadogan Estate which
had been built up to Henry Holland's designs as early as the 1770's. In 1836–
37 Cubitt laid out on the Lowndes tract a long and narrow square. This square
is more like Montague and Bryanston Squares on the Portman Estate north
of Oxford Street which date from around 1810 than like the great quadrilat-
eral of Belgrave Square or the wide mall of Eaton Square; but it is also less
regular than they or than Gough and Roumieu's somewhat similar Milner
Square in Islington. Lowndes Square was not entirely built up until 1849;
but the short terrace of five houses at the south end was erected in 1841–43
to the designs of Thomas' brother Lewis. This is the terrace of which the
Surveyor published the designs in 1841.

According to Beresford Chancellor in *The History of the Squares of London* (1907), Lowndes Square was in the 40's supposed to have been built
up "with greater regard to architectural effect" than any other then existing
in London. (For this or other reasons Sir William Tite was one of the rich
and prominent men who took a house in it.) Two short streets enter the
square from Knightsbridge on the north; on the south there is only one exit,
at the lower left corner. One end house of the terrace on the south side
therefore stands almost free, with a low projecting entry along its open side;
the other end house, at the closed corner of the square, has no such appendage. But this slight asymmetry in the layout is minimized in the elevation; for the two end houses stand forth equally from the main range of the
façade between (Fig. XIII 20). Despite the five irregularly spaced doors in
the ground storeys of the houses, the composition suggests a single palazzo
with the strong end emphasis that Barry liked so much. There is no central
motif at all such as had long been usual in pretentious terraces, particularly
those running along the sides of squares. The definite reflection of Barry's
ideas of façade composition is undoubtedly one of the chief reasons contemporaries were so impressed by the new terrace. Many terraces hitherto had
been without orders merely because they were modestly designed but none
had hitherto been "astylar" like these in the particular sense of Barry's cinquecento clubhouses.

In another way also Lewis Cubitt broke with Georgian convention. On
earlier houses more than three storeys tall the principal cornice had generally
been placed below the attic storey; here the terminal cornice was at the top,
with the third-storey sill line marked only by a modest stringcourse. The
square attic windows, with their eared architraves, form a sort of broad
subfrieze as on Barry's palazzos. Such specific motifs as the treatment of
the attic windows here or the modest quoins of the end houses and the quiet
cinquecento architraves of the second- and third-storey windows are quite

close to Barry in general effect even though they lack his sure sense of proportion.

In some elements of the detail another influence is obviously present, that of the "poor man's Barry" Charles Parker; yet this influence is by no means so strong here as in the screen of the Bricklayers Arms Railway Station which Cubitt began the next year (Fig. XV 24). The bold cornices on the chimneys and their ornamental chimney pots, although they are used in a Barry-like way, are more willful in their picturesqueness than Barry himself would have approved at so early a date. The arched windows of the first storey, with their paneled imposts and their rusticated archivolts, are less definitely Parkerian. But the balustrade below them is made up of pantiles—a rather rustic Italian note—and the boldly scrolled brackets at the tops of the entrance doors, while rather small in scale, have something of the plastic gusto of Parker's characteristic peasant-Baroque detail (Fig. XIII 14). The stucco coating is not an imitation of Bath stone ashlar like Nash's on the Regent's Park terraces; it is rather a frank over-all plastering of the wall surface, close to the true Mediterranean stucco tradition and very like Barry's treatment of the stable court at Trentham.

The asymmetrical layout of the south end of the square was not entirely ignored; the projecting entry at the left calls definite attention to the side façade in Lowndes Street. More subtly—if less dramatically—than in the case of the diagonal vista from Hyde Park Square into Gloucester Square (Fig. XIII 1) Cubitt was trying out new picturesque possibilities in terrace design: As far as the dignity of Belgravia would allow he made a sort of Italian Villa composition of his terrace even if he eschewed any strong asymmetrical accent in the way of a tall loggia-topped tower.

There is nothing remarkable about the house plans (Fig. XIII 20). Almost as in the little slum houses published later by Hemming, the narrow hall widens toward the rear to make room for the stairs. Therefore the library behind the dining room is long and narrow, with a smaller "Gentleman's Room" opening off it behind the stairs. A "gentleman's room" in the modern sense, a ground-storey water closet, is approached by a tiny lobby which leads back to the hall under the stairs. On the first storey the principal drawing room runs across the whole front of each house; from this a large secondary drawing room extends to the rear of the house. Because of the wide opening between them the two form a characteristic L-shaped reception suite which is practically one big room occupying most of the principal floor. In the basement the kitchens extend well beyond the rear of the main block of each house. The left corner house is somewhat more amply planned; and various projections and balconies increase the picturesque effect of its Lowndes Street façade, particularly as seen in perspective.

433

The *Surveyor's* remarks accompanying the plate (Fig. XIII 20) seem curiously muddled but they deserve to be quoted, at least in part, for they are quite diverting.

This building contains five mansions of ample size, and fit for the accommodation of the higher classes of society; but the taste of the architect, Mr. Lewis Cubitt, has so managed them, that, even at a very short distance, they appear as one magnificent palace, richly, yet tastefully ornamented and greatly superior to anything that has previously been erected in the vicinity of London. They are, in fact, the first houses in which the chaster part of what is called Elizabethan [*sic*] architecture is harmoniously blended with Tuscan; and the result is rich, chaste and classical—at least in the proper sense of the term, and not confining it to the merely pillared or pilastered structures of what are usually termed the classical nations and ages. . . . In a dwelling house, even of the most costly description; and more especially if civic or suburban, columns and pilasters are quite out of place, in such a climate as ours. . . .

And so on, with a repetition of all the arguments for astylar design that Leeds had marshaled in his introduction to the *Travellers' Club House* monograph in 1839. But Cubitt's discretion, the *Surveyor* noted, was also shown in his restrained use of ornament: "Even though the mansion be large, it should not be overlaid with ornaments, because that makes it look like a porcupine, or a lady furbelowed, flounced, frilled, gaffered and padded all over, till she looks like a hen careening before the wind on an April day" —an enchanting if rather complex architectural metaphor.

Whether Thomas Cubitt considered his brother's architectural services too expensive or his craftsmen found difficulty in executing the Mannerist or Parkerian elements of ornament—which I suppose represent "the chaster part of what is called Elizabethan"—the builder does not seem to have employed his architect brother again on London houses. In the two great mansions he built the next year between Knightsbridge and the Park, facing each other across Albert Gate, Thomas was content, as we have seen, to have his draftsmen apply a more sedate cinquecento dress to their five storeys (Fig. VI 14). Before the entrances, moreover, are set just such Belgravian porches as Lewis dispensed with in Lowndes Square, although these are of unusually noble dimensions.

In watering places, quite naturally, Parker's picturesque suggestions for broken massing were more boldly exploited than in London. Lyppiat Terrace in Cheltenham is probably by the local architects W. C. and R. Jearrad who seem to have come into much of J. B. Papworth's practice there even before the latter's death in 1847 (Fig. XIII 21). This terrace provides a striking Italian Villa composition even though the repetition of the loggia towers at both ends actually makes it symmetrical. Bold cross gables break up the

434

total length into five parts; their low-pitched roofs projecting on brackets are certainly very Parker-like. But the narrow grouped arches of the windows in the towers and the bay windows are more like those on White's quieter Glasgow villas (Fig. XIII 15). Much of the other detail, moreover, seems a little too delicate for the bold relief of the bracketed eaves and balconies.

A two-towered double villa nearby, known as Lansdowne Villas, is definitely pre-Victorian in its refinement; this is definitely by the Jearrads but presumably some years earlier in date. Various coarser versions of Lyppiat Terrace, probably a decade or more later in date, are also to be seen around Cheltenham. Lyppiat Terrace itself is one of the most delightful specimens of Early Victorian design in a town best known for its supposedly "Regency" architecture. As at Lowndes Square, the new ideals of the 40's for terrace houses are here effectively epitomized. Above all, it is an agreeable contrast to the Jearrads' pretentiously porticoed Queen's Hotel with the completion of which the new reign started at Cheltenham (Fig. XV 18).

After being introduced in Belgravia by Lewis Cubitt, elaborate astylar terrace design next appeared in London north of the Park. The district behind the Uxbridge Road and west of the earlier Bayswater seems to have been first laid out, at least roughly, before the Great Western Railway decided in the late 30's to bring its tracks into town in this area (Fig. XIII 32). Brunel's original 1838 station for the Great Western was no more than a temporary accommodation arranged in the arches under the Bishop's Road viaduct (Fig. XV 15); but the land between Eastbourne Grove and the Paddington spur of the Grand Junction Canal, which then extended south to the line of Conduit Street East (now Praed Street), was pre-empted from the first by the railway for an eventual terminus intended to rival that of the London and Birmingham Railway at Euston Grove. Eastbourne Terrace was therefore built up with rather modest houses whose inhabitants presumably could not afford to complain of the railway yards in front of them; these houses have little interest although they are mostly still extant, and thoroughly begrimed, today.

Still farther to the west, with a protective mews between, Westbourne Terrace, running north from Westbourne Crescent, was actually a great mall as wide as Lowndes Square extending all the way to the Bishop's (now Bishop's Bridge) Road and in narrower form even beyond the railway bridge. Parallel to Westbourne Terrace on the west ran Gloucester Terrace. For some years this formed the outermost edge of the tide of terraces which had been moving inexorably westward ever since Inigo Jones laid out Covent Garden Piazza under Charles I. Westbourne Terrace, if not its less pretentious appendage Gloucester Terrace, is without much question the finest flower of the urbanism of the 40's. The architect who set the pace for the district would seem to have been R. P. Browne; at least he accepted a tender for six house carcasses in Westbourne Terrace in 1844. He was also making alterations and finishing four houses that same year in nearby Sussex Gardens within the older section of Bayswater along the southern edge of the grand new development.

The long rows of good houses on both sides of Westbourne Terrace are set back, like the Regent's Park terraces and crescents, behind gardens and approached by inner drives (Fig. XIII 24). Half hidden by the trees in their gardens, they face each other across the broad road while at the end, a little to the left, there appears the tall spire of Cundy's Holy Trinity. That is no masterpiece; but its delicate silhouette, seen between the rows of great trees, forms a fine accent to the long vista; most other London churches of the 40's (and perhaps particularly Cundy's in Pimlico) are horrid excrescences in the formal squares whose centers they occupy.

The central groups of houses in each of the longer individual terraces here are still brought forward in axial blocks, Georgian-wise, yet this is hardly noticeable because of the very steep perspective views the long ranges of houses enforce; moreover, the continuity of the several successive terrace compositions is quite broken up now by the big trees in the front gardens. Many of the prominent corner houses offer a real suggestion of Italian Villa composition (Fig. XIII 23). Their attics, ornamented with a frieze of round windows below a bold cornice, rise almost like the tops of massive towers above the plain and regular four-storey houses that constitute the norm for these terraces. Yet everything is very dignified, much more in the mood of Barry than of Parker. The round three-storey projections toward the side streets vary pleasantly the cubic forms of these corner houses; the consistent tripling of the windows in their façades, in contrast to the endless unvarying rows of standard oblong openings in the ordinary façades between, provides a "chaster" version of the Italianate grouped arches of Lyppiatt Terrace.

In the northernmost terrace on the east the effect is more picturesque still because of the introduction there of what Summerson has called "quasi-semidetached" houses (Fig. XIII 25). Here the separate pairs of houses, each only three storeys tall (as in the cross streets leading east and west out of Westbourne Terrace), are separated yet linked by the lower wings set back from the frontal plane of the main blocks. Although the detail is very restrained in character, with correct pediments on scrolled brackets over the principal windows, the plastic variety of these façades is considerable. Curved bay windows in the ground storeys, recessed porches before the set-back wings, and a further recession of the attics above the wings make the mass composition quite complex. The slight stepping upward of the

436

pairs of houses due to the rising ground enhances most effectively the general picturesqueness of the perspective composition.

Many of the smaller two-storey houses in Gloucester Terrace are also quasi-semidetached (Fig. XIII 28). These eschew academic trim in favor of coupled arched windows. Such features are introduced over the rounded ground-storey bay windows and also in the recessed wall plane above the entrance doors. The flat trim suggests Parker rather more than does that of the Jearrads' terrace at Cheltenham, but the scaling is very delicate. This simple and rather pretty formula was repeated with variations west of Gloucester Road in what was called Kensington New Town, south of the Park. That area was being built up modestly—and a little prematurely— at about the same time as the Westbourne Terrace development.

In Kensington Gate, at the head of Gloucester Road, are two larger and more ornate Italian Villa terraces (Fig. XIII 27). Their skylines are enlivened by pairs of corner towers, and one detached house on the south at the Gloucester Road end even has a round tower on the front capped with a dome. The published report of an accident in connection with the building of these houses indicates that their architect was named Bean and that they were still in construction in 1851; but the terrace may well have been designed and begun several years earlier. By 1851 more ambitious South Kensington developments had already begun to the north and east of this area (see Chapter XIV).

Elsewhere in London there seem to have been few attempts to introduce Italian Villa towers in terrace design. Gloucester Crescent, on the Camden Town side of Regent's Park, has one or two of them; but the stock brick walls of the houses are so dreary today and the cement trim so conventional that they appear picturesque only at night. In most views of the street the towers do not show (Fig. XIII 26). These houses in general resemble the respectable but very dull ones with which Harrington, Ampthill, and Oakley Squares were being built up on the other side of Camden Town. These squares are on the North Bedford Estate in an obviously undesirable district, cut through by the tracks approaching Euston Station, which was first laid out in 1843–45. In London the Italianate mode seems to require all-over stucco to be effective; it depends very much on proper maintenance for its fresh, pretty look, moreover, something hardly to be expected in rundown, train-ridden districts.

After the blitz the beautiful, almost irridescent, colors to be seen on the stucco fronts in Hereford Square, mostly built by John Blore in 1846, were partly due to discoloration by fire. But these richly composed terraces (described, goodness knows why, as "small and regular houses of quasi-oriental design" by contemporaries) had evidently at some time, and more probably early than late, been painted in various other colors than the ubiquitous pale cream that had been established by Nash as standard for London. In Pimlico the dark gray of the stuccoed walls of the terraces probably maintains approximately the original hue; perhaps even the rich reds and blues of many of the porch columns, so pleasant a contrast to the endless cream paint of fashionable Belgravia, may also be original. (Postwar rehabilitation, in order to make more respectable the upper edge of Pimlico as the district of Victoria —so-called for the station, not the Queen—has unfortunately brought in a good deal of cream color now.) These few examples of stronger color seem to be exceptions to the general rule of pale and monochrome paint treatment for stucco through the Early Victorian period, but obviously it is a matter about which it is hard to be certain. One may guess that there was more variety of color than has survived, since the pull of Georgian prestige tends to substitute cream for other colors in all upper-class districts.

Nineteenth-century London stock bricks, above all when framed with cement trim, have not yet aged so gracefully as those of the 18th century partly because they are rarely so completely blackened. But the smooth heavy trim, whether or not it is painted, increases by contrast their shabby appearance (Fig. XIII 26). In terrace architecture of the Early Victorian period the omission of a stucco coating usually represented an economy, not a reflection of the current critical attacks on "shams." Even the superb ashlar of such residential towns as Clifton and Cheltenham seems, in a curious way, almost like a substitute for the still fashionable stucco of the West End and Brighton. There unstuccoed houses in supposedly "Regency" terraces are both late and, properly speaking, unfinished as Dale has shown in *Fashionable Brighton 1820–1860* [1947].

As one moves eastward in London there is less and less Early Victorian stucco and the cement trim is of a crisper and more Grecian order. The fine quasi-semidetached houses in Lloyd Square and Holford Square in Clerkenwell and such a modest range as College Terrace, Stepney, contrast in their geometrical severity with the softer and lusher work in Paddington; even the brickwork is still almost up to a Georgian standard of excellence—and of grime (Fig. XIII 29). At least two "third-rate" houses in Holford Square were built as late as 1844 by James Harrison. This does not, of course, establish the date of the design; the other terraces mentioned may have been earlier.

In the suburbs Italian Villa types of design were more frequently exploited than in town, and with greater boldness. Thus in the late 40's Roumieu initiated the development of Manor Park, Streatham, with an Italianate lodge to which was attached an observation tower no less than 70 feet tall—a veritable Lansdowne Tower of suburbia. But this, like the general layout of the estate with houses of "various styles" set around an open landscaped central area, belongs to another aspect of Victorian town planning. Before turning to that other aspect the occasional use of "various styles" in more urban areas must be discussed.

R. C. Carpenter's Tudor terraces at Lonsdale Square have been mentioned (Fig. XIII 3); at Cheltenham just one terrace of similar design seems to date from around 1840. Tudor or other Gothic modes are still more exceptional for terraces built later in the 40's. At the Royal Academy in 1847 the elderly Samuel Beazley (1786–1851) exhibited "a crescent of residences in castellated Gothic style"; but these were intended for erection on Castle Hill in Dover and a stylistic reference to the castle was not unnatural. Remembering the castellated towers of Telford's Conway Suspension Bridge twenty-five years earlier, one may almost consider such a reference characteristically Late Georgian rather than Early Victorian since Beazley himself had matured in Regency days.

In London itself, far to the west of Westbourne Terrace on the Norland Estate beyond Notting Hill, 48 houses were contracted for in 1847. These included (presumably) the row of Tudor houses with asymmetrical plans and round-arched Elizabethan porches known as St. Ann's Villas (Fig. XIII 31). St. Ann's Villas are not a terrace but consist mostly of semidetached pairs; yet, in the absence of circumambient foliage, the effect is definitely urban, not suburban, even though such a variegated effect is most unusual in Early Victorian London. The material is red brick, with all-over diapering of blue brick and Bath stone quoins, window mullions, and porch detail. This coloristic combination can hardly be matched in the London of the 40's except on the Hardwicks' new buildings at Lincoln's Inn, frequent though it is on neo-Tudor and Jacobethan work in the country. The multiplicity of tall-finialed gables and two-storey oriels, with occasional square-battlemented towers, produces a continuously varied silhouette quite unlike the regular though alternating rhythms of such streets as are lined with Italianate semidetached or quasi-semidetached houses.

Another curiosity of this obscure region is Norland Gardens. Here two facing terraces of modest two-storey houses are entirely built of cut stone, something almost unknown at this time in the fashionable parts of the West End. The design, moreover, is still quite Palladian. These houses and the even smaller—"fourth-class," actually—stone houses in Boxmoor Street, alongside, must represent the artistic or economic idiosyncracy of the landowner, not the usual pinchpenny tactics of London builders. The name of the street suggests the source of the stone; possibly the owner had some personal connection with the Boxmoor quarries.

439

Far less surprising than St. Ann's Villas is a terrace on the Ascot Road at Windsor which was built by S. S. Teulon of Tudor red brick. For this project, exhibited at the Royal Academy in 1849, the exalted sponsorship of Prince Albert may perhaps be assumed. A range of Gothic houses and shops, built in Trumpington Street in Cambridge near St. Michael's Church in 1851, also had a distinguished sponsor in Whewell, the Master of Trinity. Since Whewell was something of an authority on Gothic, he probably designed them himself.

The West End embargo on Gothic housing was generally maintained elsewhere well into the 50's. Even seaside resorts, following what has been called the "Belgravia-by-the-Sea" tradition of Brighton, usually aped the terraces of London, picking their models according to the wealth and social status of the presumptive clientele. Llandudno, on the Mostyn Estate in North Wales, for example, was projected in 1849. Almost at once the builders began to wall off the ocean with endless ranges of three-storey terraces consisting mostly of boardinghouses even from the first (Fig. XIII 30). It would be a compliment to refer to this Welsh resort as Pimlico-by-the-Sea since its visitors came mostly from even less distinguished districts in various Midland cities. Wehnert and Ashdown—who were architects though very obscure ones—showed at the Royal Academy in 1855 a drawing of the "improvements" then being carried out there and perhaps had general supervision of the town in the early years. The *Builder* condemned what was displayed as having "details generally and a cement coating in the worst style of Brighton and other south coast towns." But the Llandudno architects and builders lacked the solid traditions of Thomas Cubitt's organization, which continued building at Brighton well beyond his death, and the houses are much inferior to those in the older resort, even the ones of this very late date.

Belgrave Place at Brighton dates from 1846 and so do some of the houses on the west side of Eaton Place there—names, of course, that fully justify the term Belgravia-by-the-Sea. The northward extension of Brunswick Town at the Hove end of Brighton by Baron Goldschmid and his son continued into the 50's, and even later, in the form of solid ranges of terraces. S. Morton Peto's Lowestoft development on the East Coast may also be mentioned even though it is in very poor shape today; indeed by 1855 hardly a coastal town in England had failed to acquire along its front more or less competently designed terraces to mask the sea view and create a citified atmosphere. Only rarely was an open layout attempted such as seems to Americans the most natural pattern for a seaside resort.

Before turning to the Early Victorian estate layouts of an open sort which differ markedly from the characteristic terrace-lined squares and streets of the London West End, several especially attractive entities in the metropo-

440

lis should be mentioned that are neither conventionally urban nor yet in the Picturesque tradition of the Georgian model hamlet. The Boltons on the Gunter Estate in West Brompton was laid out at the end of the 40's by George Godwin at the time he began St. Mary's there. (Godwin, best known as the energetic editor of the *Builder,* was to continue for more than twenty years as surveyor to this estate.) His undistinguished church, St. Mary's, completed and consecrated in 1850, is of cruciform plan with a central tower; built of the favorite Kentish ragstone rubble of the period, it is now in a state of advanced decay.

This edifice is set down, most surprisingly, in the center of an oval, or double crescent, surrounded by rather large and formal semidetached houses of richly embellished Italianate character. One such pair was built as late as 1859 by Thomas Burton for £3,150; but the first were probably of Godwin's own design and some ten years earlier in date; in any event they are all nearly identical. Widely spaced and separated by lush shrubberies, these houses nearly convince one of the viability of the semidetached formula for semiurban rather than outright suburban housing. In size they are almost comparable to the sumptuous villas—some of them also double—in Kensington Palace Gardens; this places them more in the class of mansions than of ordinary Early Victorian semidetached work, which is generally rather pinched and drab in character.

As with most other types of group housing, the origins of "semidetachery" (if one may so call it) are Georgian. As far back as 1794, Summerson informs us in *Georgian London* [1945], the original layout plan for the Eyre Estate in St. John's Wood, north and west of Regent's Park (which, of course, did not then exist), showed nothing but paired houses set around the square, the crescent, and the circus, as well as along the ordinary streets. Although much smaller, the Boltons might even be considered a sort of realization, more than half a century later, of the projected Eyre Circus. In the Late Georgian period St. John's Wood gradually began to fill up. If little trace of the splendidly coherent project of 1794 was retained, yet the houses were almost all either semidetached or independent villas, each in its own modest grounds. This local tradition lasted right through the Early Victorian period and even beyond.

Whatever the date of the individual houses, the building up of the St. John's Wood district, including also Maida Vale on the west and extending up toward the Hampstead slopes on the north, must be considered—almost as much as the later terrace building in Belgravia or at Brighton—the realization of a pre-Victorian ideal; for it represented the development of an earlier scheme according to the particular Late Georgian mode of urbanism already firmly established in the area. Only in certain streets, such as St. John's Wood

441

Park and Cavendish Road, does the heavy pomposity of some of the houses make evident how long and how late the process continued here. A semi-detached scheme, with the pairs of houses visually insulated by planting, naturally does not inhibit stylistic variety in the individual units in the way a terrace layout does. Even if a few (or indeed a great many) houses in a terrace have to be filled in later, the work must still be done more or less according to the design of the earlier ones or utter visual chaos results—as, of course, it often did in Late Victorian times. Here in St. John's Wood the considerable variety of design in the separate villas seems pleasant and natural, particularly to American eyes.

The development of the Norland Estate as a whole, which did not begin until the late 40's and continued through the next decade, had somewhat similar characteristics to that of St. John's Wood. The layout is more compact, however, with less greenery—today at least—and a high proportion of "third-class" terrace houses; while the earliest and most interesting houses there, St. Ann's Villas, are not "Regency" either in date or in character. Just to the east of the Norland Estate is the finest Early Victorian layout in London in the semi-urban manner, Thomas Allom's Ladbroke Grove. This development is so important as to require extended discussion, difficult though it is to recover many of the details of the story (Fig. XIII 32).

"After 1850," wrote Summerson in *Georgian London* [1945], "it is rare to find an architect of any reputation meddling with estate management. . . . One of the chief factors in the decline of Paddington, Chelsea and Islington, where a less prosperous type of client was anticipated . . . was the loss of status of the architect in his capacity of surveyor for estate developments." Thomas Allom's reputation today rests chiefly on his sketches of earlier architecture in Britain and abroad, which were so frequently engraved and published, and also on his work here as surveyor of the Ladbroke Grove Estate. But he was not a professional nonentity, however uninteresting one may find most of his individual buildings today with the exception of the Hull chapel he worked on with F. H. Lockwood (Fig. IV 11). His status —if one is to be snobbish about it—was probable higher in his day than Lewis Cubitt's and certainly above that of R. P. Browne. (Summerson's general remarks nevertheless hold true for most of London.)

The significance of Ladbroke Grove does not lie in the quality of the individual terraces and semidetached houses with which it was built up. Whether or not Allom designed many, the best are those least recognizably Victorian and even they are really very dull. Architectural grandeur was costly and it was largely restricted in the 50's to Paddington and South Kensington. Even architectural piquancy was likely to be expensive, at least when carried out as the professional conscience even of estate archi-

442

tects now began to require—at St. Ann's Villas, for example—with real materials rather than with stucco icing (Fig. XIII 31). Piquancy was therefore left to the outer suburbs and in the London area is mostly High Victorian in style as well as in date. What Allom offered at Ladbroke Grove was a new type of housing development, the culmination in many respects of Early Victorian urbanism, at least in London. Provided the land was not too dear, such a layout was not necessarily extravagant and its basic amenities have remained appreciable to this day.

As with the Royal Promenade in Victoria Square, Clifton, rumor conveniently linked Royalty with the early reputation of Ladbroke Grove. The altitude and breeziness of the district—psychologically, if not actually, healthier than the West End even today—might well have suggested to Early Victorian physicians that a villa here would be a desirable change from "Her Majesty's Pimlico Palace" for the Prince of Wales when a youth. How important they considered height and air is evident from the origin of the Royal *villégiature* at Balmoral as a sort of psychosomatic medical prescription. But probably the rumor was manufactured just to draw eligible tenants this far west of the frontier of fashion in Westbourne Terrace; the intervening area was mostly of "low," or at least socially indeterminate, character around 1850.

St. John's Church in Ladbroke Grove had been built in 1844–45 by Stevens and Alexander and is one of their better works. But it was not until 1853 that Allom showed at the Royal Academy a view of a "Crescent, Terrace and Gardens Now Building" in the northern part of the Notting Hill district. The actual date of the layout by Allom must lie somewhere between 1845 and 1853, therefore, and probably later rather than earlier. If the church was built, as churches usually were, in connection with a scheme for developing the area, that original scheme—probably not by Allom—must have died and been revived later as was true of so many real estate projects antedating the mid-century. The church is clearly an existing building incorporated into the new scheme, not its true focus. A tender for 21 houses in Westbourne Grove West in 1848, along the main approach to this district from Paddington, and the building activity on the nearly contiguous Norland Estate, which was under way by 1847 at least, suggest a *terminus post quem* some few years later than the consecration of St. John's in 1845.

The area Allom laid out is a large one bounded on the east by Kensington Park Road and on the west by Clarendon Road. It begins on the south with Ladbroke Gardens, the largest "square" in London. This is two streets north of the main western artery that extends out from the north edge of the Park, here still called the Uxbridge Road at the time, now partly Notting Hill Gate and partly Holland Park Road. The northern side of that portion of the road had already been built up with semidetached houses of distinctly Regency character, mostly Grecian in style like those that originally lined Maida Vale. These were probably then not more than a decade old, if indeed there were not still many gaps in their close-set rows. The great urbanistic virtue of this area, though one rarely appreciated by speculative builders in any period, was the relatively high altitude of the terrain and the rounded slopes by which the land fell away to the north and west.

The principal street north and south, always called merely Ladbroke Grove, is broad and straight. It rises gradually between rows of trees from Holland Park Road to the crest of the hill by the church; then it turns down more steeply until it crosses Blenheim Crescent at the northwestern edge of the estate. Ladbroke Gardens, extending east from Ladbroke Grove along the southern edge of the estate, do not constitute a square in the ordinary sense of the word nor is the name a mere euphemism for an ordinary terrace-lined street. The "gardens" are really a good-sized urban park with regulation terrace houses facing it on the south from across another street; that side was apparently not controlled by Allom or else, as early maps suggest, he intended to build semidetached houses there for which a continuous terrace was later substituted. On the north the private gardens at the rear of the terrace houses in Kensington Park Gardens open directly on the more public area of Ladbroke Gardens. Set far back from Ladbroke Grove, and with extensive gardens behind, another short terrace faces the west end of Ladbroke Gardens.

North of this terrace comes the church, set in its own little open plot but not confined, as usually in the West End, by the solid walls of a terraced square; the picturesque and rather rural character of its design is therefore partially justified. A short terrace of tall houses to the north—not the church —forms the real center of Allom's plan. (The small and rather dainty modern block of flats by Maxwell Fry at its southern end somewhat confuses the focal effect today.) Behind this tall terrace, to the west, lies a convex crescent, if one may so put it, of semidetached houses. Additional rows of semidetached houses run parallel to Ladbroke Grove in Lansdowne and Clarendon Roads on the western slope of the estate. The northern half of Lansdowne Crescent, facing the semidetached houses behind the church, consists of two concave terraces. Concentric with this and facing on the curved continuation of Lansdowne Road, as also in Elgin and Blenheim Crescents, are additional ranges of concave terraces. These are separated by wide strips of planted space running along the northwestern slopes between their rear gardens. (Again early plans suggest that semidetached houses were originally intended here.)

East of Ladbroke Grove four similar terraces, all straight in plan, continue the lines of the upper four terraces to Kensington Park Road. On the

444

east side of Ladbroke Grove, facing the short focal terraces of tall houses, the scheme seems to have been out of Allom's control. Early maps show rows of semidetached houses; but the two extant short and irregular terraces of unequal length, terminating a group of semidetached houses of various sizes, were very likely built at the same time as the church, before he made his layout. Behind these lies Stanley Crescent, lined on the west by a long convex terrace. On its other side short terraces separated by open garden areas run eastward to Kensington Park Road.

As the plan makes evident, most of the irregularities were not intentional but are rather to be explained by the location of the existing church, and doubtless also of a few earlier individual houses and even one or two short terraces. In the main Allom succeeded in combining a maximum orderliness with optimum exploitation of the slopes of the terrain. With a generosity that was perhaps impossible nearer the West End where land was so dear, he balanced his solid terraces with large open areas in a fashion foreshadowing much 20th-century theory concerning the use of tall, widely spaced housing blocks. The standard terrace-house accommodations—"second class" for the most part in contrast to the "first-class" houses of the better sections of Bayswater and Belgravia—were varied with still more modest semidetached houses in the St. John's Wood tradition. It is quite probable that Allom originally intended to use many more of these as the none-too-accurate maps of the 50's and early 60's suggest. Economic pressure may have suggested later a relative increase in the number of terrace houses as the scheme was carried out, a process that could easily have continued over ten or twenty years with little control by Allom.

The finest effects in the Ladbroke Grove layout derive from Allom's masterly handling of the cross views. These effects are something no plan can makes fully evident, although the openness west of the church and Lansdowne Crescent and east of Stanley Crescent is surely clear enough even on paper. The operatic grandeur of Bayswater gives way here to something richer, more varied, and more humane.

The architectural insipidity of the various terraces and villas is fortunately irrelevant to the general impression; on the other hand the mature character of the planting (after nearly a full century of growth, it must be remembered) is most important. Here, it must seem, Allom created the masterpiece of Early Victorian planning, retaining the most vital elements of the Georgian tradition and at the same time vigorously renewing it.

Along Manningham Lane, in the suburban residential area outside Bradford, there is a somewhat similar layout. The terrain here is less interesting but the character of the architecture is much superior. Rather short terraces, all of stone, ranged along the higher side of the principal thoroughfare face semidetached villas and even small mansions grouped around short descending culs-de-sac now almost completely masked by heavy foliage (Fig. XIII 33). The treatment of the houses varies from a sort of post-Georgian academicism to rather sober Yorkshire reflections of more definitely Victorian modes. The dates of construction may extend well down through the 60's although the layout probably belongs to the early 50's. One dramatic view up from the Lane to the rear of Mallinson and Healy's St. Paul's (Fig. V 18) might suggest that this church of the late 40's, so superior to St. John's, Ladbroke Grove, had been built in relation to an already formulated scheme of extensive development in Manningham. Yet the history of Bradford in this period—rather a small town until the 50's—makes so early a date rather unlikely.

Indicative of the smallness of Bradford is the modest size of the terrace houses here—they are mostly "third class" in London terms. Significant also is the rapidity with which these taper off into rows of mere workmen's cottages as one approaches the great monumental complex of the Manningham Mill which dominates the area visually as well as economically. Leading Yorkshire textile magnates such as the Bradford alpaca king Titus Salt did not continue to reside very long in town once they grew rich; instead they hired, bought, or built country houses in the neighborhood. Hence in these northern cities aristocratic terraces of the Westbourne Terrace or Lowndes Square order were not needed even in the days of great Victorian prosperity in the late 50's and 60's.

Allom's Ladbroke Grove layout provided in its openness and its free use of semidetached houses a happy variant to the standard formula for housing the London middle classes at the end of the Early Victorian period. This variant was certainly not unrelated in concept to the widely spaced ranges of very expensive mansions built on Crown land in Kensington Palace Gardens. Activity there, stalled in the late 40's, was reviving in the early 50's. But quite a different variant from the London norm is often found in such arteries of the West End as were becoming regional shopping centers. Many of these were actually in succession to the "high streets" of suburban villages developed considerably earlier at the edges of London. Only now were these agglomerations swamped by the main Victorian building tide pushing westward.

Perhaps it is rather arbitrary to include here, rather than in the chapters on commercial architecture, the blocks of shops that were built in such arteries, even though above the ground floors the three or more upper storeys were regularly occupied as dwellings. Such dwellings were not normally leased by status-conscious members of the middle class any more than were the dwellings over shops farther east in New Oxford Street. Yet

446

a pretentious terrace-over-shops, such as that the builder Isaac Wilkinson contracted to build for a Mr. Phillips in the late 40's to the designs of the architect Frederick R. Beeston, obviously had a West End character (Fig. XIII 34). Located in St. George's Place, Knightsbridge, beside St. George's Hospital and facing Hyde Park, this was to cost £2,017. When this terrace achieved the honor of inclusion in John Weale's 1849 edition of Nicholson's *Carpenter's Guide,* an honor maintained in several later compilations of plates from this work, all the other buildings similarly presented were of a more monumental order. These included, as has already been noted, Burton's Athenaeum Club and Walter's Girard College, edifices that were still considered major public ornaments despite their Grecian styling. The only other commercial material found worthy of illustration in this edition of Nicholson were a few of the more fashionable shops in Regent Street, Mount Street, and Elizabeth Street, Cavendish Square. Beeston was evidently determined to outshine Cubitt's houses in Lowndes Square and Browne's in Westbourne Terrace and was rewarded for his pretension by this contemporary recognition.

The shop fronts below with their conventional wide windows may be ignored in most respects; but these windows did make cast-iron bressumers necessary and must also have encouraged the use of cast-iron beams and even a few cast-iron interior supports, structural elements not ordinarily found in Early Victorian houses, whose construction was still almost completely traditional. The increasing desire for fire-resistant floors, which was already leading in the more expensive country houses to considerable use of iron, had affected terrace builders' methods hardly at all as yet.

The complete specifications for Beeston's houses are given by Nicholson. These cannot be considered so typical of Early Victorian practice in builders' housing as those provided by Walker in his *Architectural Precedents* (3d ed. 1841) at the beginning of the new age or by Hemming in his *Designs for Villas* at (or even beyond) its end. It is chiefly the design of the terrace that is important. This is the most advanced of the late 40's in London. Beeston's ideal is evidently the same as Barry's at Bridgewater House, rising in St. James's at this same moment, and in his other work of the 40's: a richer and more plastic version of the cinquecento. That ideal was soon to be widely shared by ordinary house builders even if they rarely exemplified it as notably as Beeston was able to do in this terrace.

The extension upward of the attics of the end houses well above the main roof level certainly echoed Barry's Board of Trade without rivaling the more picturesque Italian Villa towers on the Jearrads' Lyppiat Terrace in Cheltenham. In the end houses here the first-storey windows are rather conventionally edicular, as on Barry's clubhouses and later on Cubitt's Albert

Gate mansions farther out Knightsbridge. On the other hand the quoins with scalloped ends that break up the architraves of the other first-storey windows are piquantly Mannerist; the eared segmental architraves of the windows above even have a vaguely Baroque air. Such things, one feels, would have shocked Barry. The arched top-storey windows and, above all, the paired windows in the attics at the ends are not at all Barry-like; indeed, one might as well call them "pure" Victorian. If these windows are not quite so cranky as the crotchets of the ascetic Butterfield (see Chapter XVII), they are nevertheless closer to E. B. Lamb than to Charles Parker. Because of the relative novelty of their treatment at this time, moreover, Nicholson provided a large-scale plate of details for all the world to copy. That surely explains the frequency with which this and comparable motifs were echoed by builders of houses in England and America through the 60's and even into the 70's.

It is rather ridiculous, perhaps, to analyze such motifs in historic terms; but some analogies from the past will help to characterize the aesthetic climate in which they first appeared and soon grew so popular. Thus the curious molded frame which is continued around the two close-set windows but not carried down between them might recall an element often found in the Early Christian architecture of Syria were it executed in heavily scaled stone. Yet the outward curve at the ends of this ornamental band and the ears at the springing of the arches, not to speak of the exaggerated keystones breaking up through it, rather suggest Mannerist or even Baroque precedent.

Merely silly (if not outright disgusting) as the treatment of this window must appear today, its special character did not result from architectural illiteracy or the casual designing practices of builders' drafting rooms. Beeston was a properly trained architect and must have been conscious that he was innovating here or, at the least, giving an intentionally "Victorian" slant to borrowed elements. Designers in builders' offices were hardly yet ready to use details so extreme on terrace houses; only on suburban villas, and more particularly on those designed by architects, is this drastic sort of corruption of Barry's cinquecento in the spirit of S. H. Brooks' or E. B. Lamb's designs of the 30's to be found in the mid-century. It is well to recall again that such ideas preceded as well as followed the introduction by Barry of the standard Renaissance mode.

Now a wholly different system of 19th-century development from that common in the Early Victorian West End deserves to receive extended comment, even though by its very nature the system rarely produced complexes with a coherent architectural character. The proto-garden-suburb—to give it a very clumsy name—had its origin in the landscape gardens of the 18th century, not in Georgian urban planning. Its earliest examples are the Pic-

turesque hamlets certain country landowners, urged on by critics in the name
of both taste and philanthropy, built for their rural tenants before and after
1800. Of these pre-Victorian hamlets the one by Nash at Blaise Castle near
Bristol, dated 1811, is one of the best still extant. At the opening of the Victorian Age the 6th Duke of Devonshire was providing for the rehousing of his
tenants, farther away from Chatsworth than the old village he had just demolished, the new model village of Edensor in this 18th-century tradition. Edensor, indeed, is a sort of anthology of Picturesque cottage designs compiled by
John Robertson of Derby from the books of the previous decades. (Jeffrey
Wyatville was still working at Chatsworth itself down to his death in 1841
and he provided the designs for the two disparate gate lodges near the village
in 1837 although for some reason did not receive this interesting commission.)
In its rather skillful general grouping and its fine clusters of trees Edensor
must owe a good deal to the duke's gardener Joseph Paxton. The church built
by Gilbert Scott in 1866–70 for the 7th duke finally provided the culmination of the composition, tying the group together in one perfectly Picturesque
whole. Most of Edensor was carried out in the years 1839–41 but it was
designed and begun at least a year earlier.

A decade before Edensor was rebuilt Nash had developed in a comparable
way some extra building land on the Crown's Marylebone Estate. Along the
edges of the Regent's Canal, behind the already completed ranges of the
Regent's Park terraces and north of the markets and the contiguous working-
class district, he laid out in the late 20's and shortly began the two Park
Villages, East and West. These consisted of various Tudor and Italianate
villas, both detached and semidetached, all loosely grouped along winding
roads. The individual houses were completed (and probably in fact largely
designed) by Pennethorne under William IV as Nash gradually retired
from practice.

Barry's Queen's Park for Thomas Attree at Brighton, although only the
proprietor's own villa was ever built, represented a parallel but more advanced scheme dating from 1829–30. There the group of villas of varying
design was to have been set around an open park. Decimus Burton's development of the Calverly Estate at Tunbridge Wells is quite similar. It provides
today probably the finest extant example of what was definitely a Late
Georgian, not a Victorian, realization of the idea; for these middle-class
developments represent only a transformation and an enlargement of the
earlier rural hamlets into loose groupings of individual villas arranged around
an open park.

The principal inland watering places, such as Clifton, Leamington, and
Cheltenham, maintained more generally the urban terrace-house tradition
of Bath. Resorts on the coasts, hoping to rival Brighton, naturally followed

that prototype in their layout as closely as they could, regardless of the terrain. All of them, however, had some peripheral villa-dotted roads planned before the new age began, even if these were usually no more consistently carried out in the end than was St. John's Wood. Later terraces in resort towns, moreover, were often short and isolated like Lyppiat Terrace at Cheltenham; such groups of houses were generally designed with an eye for varied silhouette, like extensive super-villas, rather than as a continuous wall about a square or along a street in the West End way.

When Benjamin Ferrey in 1836 faced the problem of developing the Jervis Estate on the broken cliffs and deep chines of Bournemouth, his decision to lay it out with no long straight urban streets or large regular squares must have been largely determined by the terrain. But his open layout was, we can now realize, no Early Victorian innovation even though no town had as yet been so planned in its entirety. The phenomenal later success of Bournemouth as a resort has rather obscured the positive pictorial values of Ferrey's original scheme of 1837–40. The curving streets, now intermittently built up with shops and miscellaneous structures of various dates, are for the most part merely awkward to navigate and visually muddled; nor do early views help one to envisage clearly what must have been at first a rather charmingly diffuse picture.

Once the detached villas of varying design would have been seen so dramatically across the bold chines that their pathetic Tudor and Italian Villa stylisms, even if distinguishable amid the rich foliage, would have been readily forgiven as irrelevant incidents in the ever-changing coastal scene. During the late 30's and the 40's Ferrey's skillful planning successfully subjugated the terrain to domestic use without destroying its natural wildness and irregularity, or so we may believe. But Ferrey's Early Victorian Bournemouth is now all but lost in a way that earlier and more urban resort layouts have not been. If Bournemouth's churches make it almost as worthy of the attentions of the student of later Victorian architecture as is Brighton, its character as a whole is now totally undistinguished, with few traces even of work of the 50's, much less of the 30's and 40's.

Birkenhead represents a very different sort of Early Victorian venture in town building from Bournemouth. Here the sea was to bring not health but wealth. In the 40's Birkenhead appeared destined for great commerical success; but rich old Liverpool across the Mersey successfully used against its young rival the foul tactics of a later epoch of capitalism. After a merger of interests had been skillfully worked out in a joint Mersey authority the Liverpudlians who dominated that authority saw that most of the profits flowed into their coffers on the west side of the river wherever the ships might actually dock. Little is left of early Bournemouth because the Jervis venture so signally succeeded. The ambitious projects of the citizens of Birkenhead, on the other hand, after having been sufficiently realized to make their distinctive character clear, remained largely intact because the town had no comparable later growth (Figs. XIII 35, 36). These realized projects still provide most impressive ornaments for a city that is on the "wrong side," not of the railway tracks, but of the river. Jersey City and Hoboken, across the Hudson from New York, are not more pathetic; but they can offer nothing like the solemn grandeur of Birkenhead's principal square, so properly named "Hamilton" for its Scottish architect. Nor do the New Jersey satellites provide suburban areas comparable to Birkenhead Park, the principal achievement in the planning field of one of the greatest of all Victorians, Joseph Paxton, until one gets as far out as Downing and Davis' Llewellyn Park in the Oranges.

When in 1847 a portion of the Birkenhead Docks was opened, the *Illustrated London News* gave full, and even lyric, coverage to the new town:

> Where on it stands
> The vacant winds did whistle and laugh of sunshine
> Sported in wild freedom,

the account began. Birkenhead, like Liverpool itself a hundred years earlier, had been but a fishing village a few years before; now, like its elder rival across the Mersey, it had become in the writer's proud words "one of the finest examples on record of the brilliant results of unfettered British enterprise. Anciently, the settlement and consolidation of a town was the work of generations, now thanks to steam, they spring up and prosper with all the rapidity of the famed ice palace of the Queen of Russia."

When the first plan for developing the Wallasey Pool on the east side of the Mersey estuary took form in the 20's the Liverpool Town Council bought up the surrounding lands in order to avert the danger of a nearby rival to their own profitable docks. But in 1843 a new company was formed under the leadership of the great Birkenhead shipbuilder John Laird to which the Liverpool Corporation (rather surprisingly) sold those very lands. A Parliamentary act authorizing the construction of the Birkenhead Docks was passed in 1844 and the excavation of the docks and the building of the new town started at once. An unlucky thirteen years later, in 1857, a new act of Parliament, engineered by the Liverpudlians, set up the Mersey Docks and Harbor Board to hold authority over the docks on both sides of the river. The independent development of Birkenhead as a planned entity then stopped even though the town did not entirely cease to expand (in a rather tawdry way) as an adjunct to the great port across the estuary.

Laird and his associates in the mid-40's did not limit their activities to building vast docks and warehouses around the Wallasey Pool. From the first they envisaged a balanced, one might almost say a model, city (Fig. XIII 35). While the docks were building, the solemn central square also rose near the Mersey's edge; much farther back, leaving room for a great deal of lower-class housing between, Paxton was invited to lay out the park around which the residences of the rising local magnates were to be built (Fig. XIII 36). That these men should have turned to the gardener of the Duke of Devonshire for the layout of this park suggests their ambitions. What is not clear is how much previous experience Paxton can have had to prepare him for undertaking a project so different from anything that was needed at Chatsworth. Yet he was already the duke's general advisor, actually a sort of Commissioner of Works to the Cavendish Estate as has been said, and so he may already have had some part in the plans for the development of Eastbourne on Cavendish land on the south coast as a rival to Brighton and Bournemouth or with similar Cavendish ventures elsewhere. Paxton's activities as a planner surely deserve more detailed investigation than they have yet received. Once more the failure of his granddaughter to realize the variety and the scale of his achievement seriously obscures his remarkable stature as a leader of the age. (Violet Markham does not even mention Birkenhead Park in *Paxton and the Bachelor Duke* [1935].)

Birkenhead Park, considered purely as landscape architecture, is not particularly distinguished despite its 180 acres and its two lakes (Fig. XIII 36). This was not a period of creative development in landscape design, as the 18th century had been, and Paxton's landscape work is no real exception to the general rule. What is significant is the way Nash's original intentions for Regent's Park were merged with the patriarchal ideal of the Picturesque rural hamlet in the manner of Edensor to produce a new entity more along the lines of Barry's scheme for Queen's Park at Brighton. A "belt," such as the poet and landscape gardener Shenstone had introduced a century earlier, runs inside the roughly rectangular area of the park at its upper end. But in this case it was widened out into a real carriage road along whose winding length residences of various sizes and styles are casually placed, with here and there a short isolated terrace. These circumambient edifices are widely spaced and do not wall in the park like the Regent's Park Terraces; yet they are not lost in the heart of the park as are the isolated villas there. Instead, they are rhythmically grouped like the houses in Nash's two Park Villages, though much more loosely. But the many breaks in the continuity are quite arbitrary, not determined by accidents of terrain as in Ferrey's Bournemouth layout.

Some of the individual houses are doubtless original as their rather deli-

452

cate Tudor detail, quite like that on St. Ann's Villas, suggests; but more of them are later by at least a decade, including particularly those grouped in terraces. One advantage of such a scheme, of course, is that it permits a gradual building up of an area over a period of years without leaving the very evident and unseemly gaps that unfinished squares or straight streets lined with incomplete terraces display. Another advantage, or so it seemed to Victorians, was that considerable variety in the style and character of the individual buildings was feasible without excessive disharmony, as has been noted of St. John's Wood. Here the various villas and short terraces are even more thoroughly insulated visually from one another by foliage as in American suburbs. Even if Paxton had, at the first, some sort of general supervision over the style of the houses, it must have come to an end very shortly. Only the three lodges, contracted for in 1844, seem certainly to represent his taste. Designed by Lewis Hornblower of Liverpool and executed by a builder named Stone with extremely refined and delicate detail, these are all towered Italian Villas (Fig. XIII 38). Paxton's own house at Chatsworth is so similar that it was probably built at this time, and from the designs of this same architect, out of the ample proceeds of Paxton's (first?) important outside commission. The southern end of the park is stated not to be of Paxton's design; perhaps, therefore, the heavy and complex Ionic gateway, providing the main entrance from the city and set awkwardly across one corner of the park, need not be blamed either on him or on Hornblower. This entrance was nevertheless already completed by the time the docks were opened in 1847.

Developments of similarly mixed character, but usually much less comprehensive, characterize increasingly the extension of Victorian towns in the late 40's and 50's. The relationship of the villa-lined streets to public parks is generally less close; often there is no real park at all, merely a tangle of winding streets. In 1844 Scott and Moffatt won a first prize for designs for detached villas to be used for the development of White Knight's Park, near Reading. The extensive upper-class development around Victoria Park, Manchester, had begun as early as 1837; but the building up of the area with mansions for the great cotton magnates continued for decades. Roumieu's Manor Park, Streatham, more definitely in the tradition of Barry's Queen's Park project and of Birkenhead Park, was laid out (as has been noted) in 1849. The Duke of Devonshire's estate at Carlisle, for which Paxton was presumably responsible, was planned at least by 1850 when "a building plan [had] been started for the erection of handsome streets, crescents, plantations, two parks, a good central site for a church and detached villas." This actually has a layout more like that of Ladbroke Grove than that of Birkenhead Park and occupies the rising land called Stanwix across the river Eden from the old town. Much later, in 1862, Paxton laid out the Westbourne Estate for the Scarborough Corporation as an "ornamental" park, with space for about forty separate villas, at the foot of Oliver's Mount and skirting it on the east, north, and west.

The West End Park at Glasgow, of the early mid-50's, is also definitely of Paxton's design, although in the conservative Scottish way it is surrounded chiefly by flatted terraces and crescents, not by detached or semidetached villas. But farther out of the city Roseheath on the Firth of Clyde had been laid out in 1849 as a villa-community on an estate belonging to the Duke of Argyll. In 1851 a suburban district of villa residences at Queen's Park, Chester, was initiated by the local architect Harrison. Dartmouth Park, near the Forest Hill railway station, was developed by Lord Dartmouth as a villa estate, beginning in 1849. The great popularity of the Sydenham area south of London dates only from 1852 after it was known the Crystal Palace would be re-erected there. Yet building ground at another Forest Hill estate in Sydenham was offered to be let by the elder George Aitchison in 1853. In the same year, moreover, George Godwin, who laid out the Boltons, prepared a plan for the Haywood Estate at Ashford in Kent—46 acres on which only detached and semidetached houses were to be built, except for two terraces near the church. (In 1851 Samuel Beazley had laid out at Ashford a new town for the South-Eastern Railway; it is not clear whether Godwin's scheme was a realization of this or a neighboring development.)

With the widening of White Ladies Road in Clifton, first at the inner end in 1854 and then beyond Gotham Road in 1858, the end of terrace building seems to have come in that finest of Early Victorian residential areas, for the road is mostly lined with semidetached houses. Because of the clean cream-colored Bath stone of which they are built these illustrate more pleasantly than usual the rather meaningless current variations of design in this increasingly popular middle-class type of suburban dwelling (Fig. XIII 37). Contiguous open park land and meandering streets provide a more park-like setting for the larger detached mansions—some earlier and some later in date—which fringe Clifton on the other side toward the Downs. In 1864, after the opening of Brunel's famous suspension bridge, Leigh Wood across the Clifton Gorge began to be taken up as sites for even more extensive villas. But these really occupy small private estates, of which "Alpenfels" in Bridge Road, with a large Swiss chalet designed forty years after Robinson's projects of the 20's, is perhaps the most interesting. Such later developments take us well beyond the end of the Early Victorian period.

The story of Early Victorian housing is so complex that a single chapter cannot cover it entirely. There is no real chronological sequence between this chapter and the next nor any clear separation of topics. On the whole, the following chapter deals with the housing of the lower classes, and more specifically with the early beginnings of philanthropic mass housing, down to the time when the state first began to give the movement some sort of assistance—at the start barely more than recognition of its existence. But it will also return in a cyclical way to describe the most advanced upper-class urban housing developments of the early and mid-50's.

In almost every other field of design there came a definite change of stylistic phase sometime around 1855 but this is not true of housing; even in the later 50's one seems to have advanced hardly beyond the point where the story began in the 30's. Despite the general lack of real development the story is nevertheless not without its attractive—or at least its diverting—episodes. Frequently these attractions—and certainly most of the diversions—are literary rather than visual. But to point them out should suggest there can be variety and relief in British residential areas generally considered as monotonous and dreary as a calm ocean on a gray day. Beneath the barely rippled surface rising and falling swells can often be clearly apprehended provided one looks for them with sufficient historical awareness.

CHAPTER XIV: HOUSING IN

THE MID-CENTURY

Urban London is an ocean whose rising Victorian tide spread outward in all directions, even in the unprosperous 40's. The previous chapter made some attempt to chart this process. Relatively too much time was doubtless spent among the frothy waves at the water's western edge, where the tide was split in two by Hyde Park, and too little on the inexorable rise of flooding brick and stucco in the areas to the north and south and east. Fortunately a more conscientious oceanographer of London, John Summerson, promises eventually to continue through Victorian times the tale his *Georgian London* [1945] has carried so brilliantly from the days of Charles I to those of William IV.

Suburban London, on some of whose villa estates the last chapter has touched, is not an ocean but rather a jungle. Here I have had the good fortune to make many safaris with Summerson, as expert a tracker as he is an ocean-ographer. But I must confess that I have brought back alive few of its strange denizens, the speculative builders and the architects belonging to what Summerson has called the "Lower School." The reading of their spoors is confused by various factors. Many suburban developments, for example, the initiation of which at a definite date is recorded, lay dormant after the building of a few sample villas and perhaps a church; such areas were filled up only some years—or even several decades—later with houses of a much cheaper sort than were originally intended. These will naturally have little or no visual relationship to the stylistic character of the original villas; even recognizable traces of the original layout are often hard to find. Much of the most characteristic work of the earlier villa builders seems significant therefore only in terms of the individual houses. In their present physical context most Early Victorian villas in the suburbs are but the lowest layer in an architectural deposit accumulated over two generations or more. Any tenuous organization deriving from the tradition of the Picturesque village, with the houses strung out perhaps in a Shenstonian belt around a park, has usually disappeared as the suburbs decayed. The various elements in the scene are often barely identifiable today as the deposits of successive decades but appear to be all of much the same age.

The newer, more isolated, type of housing that was increasingly the successful rival to the urban terrace as the Victorian Age advanced has already been mentioned and some indication of its Georgian ancestry provided. But it was in America that the suburb made up of detached houses reached its richest 19th-century flowering. Even in the Early Victorian period the genre had already taken firmer root there than in Britain; many cities would never know any other pattern of upper-class housing. Somewhat later a millionaires' resort like Newport would really be but an expanded example of the same convention, even though the individual mansions are often as large as country houses in Britain.

The more sociological types of multiple housing, to which the term is generally restricted nowadays, are very unappetizing in Early Victorian examples; but these are extremely important as the beginnings of a major development. Most of the urban poor in Early Victorian times were lucky if they were able to rent, when newly built, such fourth-class houses as Hemming illustrated in his book (Fig. XIII 17); yet his models are typical enough of what was being built in most towns, even if always in grossly insufficient quantity. The visual character of these urban "cottages" varies a good deal according to the available building materials of different districts. The red brick with white headers of the Oxford slums, prefiguring Butterfield's Keble College of the late 60's and 70's, is much preferable to the stock brick of London. In the Yorkshire wool towns, although good stone was readily available, the houses are usually as depressing today as those in the East End because of the grimy deposits they share with the local public monuments. Yet they seem more solid and less down at heel than in towns where the usual building material was stock brick of whatever color.

Plans vary from city to city, reaching their nadir in the back-to-back houses of Leeds and the "courts" of Liverpool. But these vicious plan formulas had been developed in the previous century, not introduced in the 1840's. So much did such planning increase the rental yield of slum property that reformist Victorians sought in vain for their condemnation; some, I fear, remain in use even today. The refined detail of the wooden trim in certain Leeds slum areas—the Georgian vernacular at its simple best, one might heartlessly say!—gives evidence that the Victorian Age should not be blamed for bad planning inherited from the Age of Enlightenment.

Unlucky Victorian workers usually had to house their families not in newly built houses specially designed for their occupancy but in a room or two—perhaps even a basement room—of a house built earlier for the middle class. Statistically a large majority must have been thus "unlucky," and slum conditions were certainly almost beyond belief in most cities. Foreigners like Friedrich Engels and Gustave Doré inveighed against them in the 40's and 50's with text and picture. Dickens also fulminated; and

George Godwin, in his articles in the *Builder* and in his caustic treatises, was perhaps the best informed and the most effective of all the antislum crusaders. But the slums such men attacked were mostly the result of the physical deterioration and the overcrowding of Georgian or earlier houses —their pre-Victorian date might almost lead today to their preservation as historic or artistic monuments, had not the much abused Victorians as far as they could replaced them. The Victorians may be accused of building new slums of their own—for slums many of their lower-class housing estates very soon came to be—but they never built any so bad as those they inherited. Victorian middle-class housing, intended for single-family occupancy with plenty of servants, has perhaps deteriorated more, especially when sloppily subdivided for multi-family occupancy, than the fourth-class workers' houses of the 40's and 50's whose modest accommodations now seem so spacious to a heavily taxed bourgeoisie. Indeed, third-class Victorian houses near fashionable districts, if not fourth-class ones, are today perhaps the most desired of London residences.

By far the greater part of new lower-class housing in the Early Victorian period was speculative. Builders' decisions as to the class for which they would, in any particular district, erect terraces were principally determined by their sense of social topography. Relative proximity to Hyde Park and to the older residential areas of the West End decided the social rating of most urban estates. Yet the West End had always had its own minor streets occupied by tradesmen and retainers—even its bits of real slum property —and the newer developments north and south of the Park carried on this tradition. The principal squares and streets were supplemented by more modest terraces behind them, like Gloucester Terrace behind Westbourne Terrace, where those concerned with ministering to the ruling classes, or those who sought a "good address" at bargain rates, could be accommodated. Sometimes this would be over the shops in the shopping streets of the district. The chief indication of a cheaper street is frequently no inferiority in the design of the terraces but merely the presence of shops or even of a public house. The public house usually constitutes the end unit of a terrace and aims at slightly more architectural display than the houses adjoining (Fig. XIV 1). But Early Victorian "pubs" are very dignified in the West End, often less remote from Barry's Pall Mall standards than such relatively fashionable houses over shops as Beeston's in Knightsbridge.

Even in the poor streets insulating the principal strongholds of the rich from the impertinent new railways, the "pubs" have what the French call *tenue* to flatter the respectability of their clientele of solid tradesmen and upper servants. Surprisingly enough the Percy Arms near Lloyd Square in Clerkenwell, a district whose social character was already deteriorating, was considered so distinguished in design as to be included among the plates in Weale's reissues of Nicholson's *Carpenter's Guide* from 1847 on. To the usual paraphernalia of rusticated quoins and modillioned cornices were added handsome shell-topped windows borrowed straight from the garden front of Barry's Travellers' Club house. But the Percy Arms, like most urban pubs, was in a sense the local club; why should it not ape, twenty years later, the elegances of Pall Mall? Like the church the pub was usually a focal, and indeed a public, monument in Early Victorian London. In the poorer districts it often reflected as visibly as the church new stylisms that hardly affected the design of the ordinary row house at all; for pubs like churches were generally built from the designs of architects or of men who called themselves such (although Weale does not, in fact, reveal the name of the designer of the Percy Arms).

Workers' housing in cities flowed out of the builders' offices—if the more modest builders ever had proper offices—without benefit of any sort of serious designing. It was therefore something of a vernacular product like the country cottages of the Middle Ages, although the analogy is one that must not be pushed very far. A designer was needed only for the general layout, if even for that. Where workers' housing was not built as a general speculative activity but for a particular client, such as a millowner who wished to house his hands near the plant, a more positive estate entity usually resulted from *someone's* conscious design. Yet the units of which the entity was composed were usually standard—or for that matter, often substandard—and the layout itself little superior to that provided by speculative builders working for themselves.

For various reasons Early Victorian mill housing in Britain never had the functional virtues or the visual qualities of that in New England. At the expense of possible objection from sociological historians of housing, the project of Robert Owen (1771–1858) for New Lanark and the Fourierist scheme of James Silk Buckingham (1786–1855) for a model town of Victoria (presented in his *National Evils and Practical Remedies* [1849]) may be ignored here. One may readily agree with Owen and Buckingham that the ultimate solution of the problem of workers' housing would necessarily be related to some deeper social or economic mutation; but the basic fact of the Victorian housing story is that no improvement of consequence, at least before the 80's, came as a by-product of such theoretical reactions as Owen's and Buckingham's against the laissez-faire economy and the stratified capitalist society other Victorians were so busily building up. A rather feudal sense of responsibility for their tenants had been reawakened in landowners by agricultural reformers in the 18th century and was to some extent shared by industrial employers in the early and mid-19th century. But essentially selfish motives best explain most of what the Early Victorians actually accomplished in the field of working-class housing in the 40's and 50's. The dreams of the highly imaginative proto-Socialists had little influence until toward the end of the Victorian Age.

Upper-class sentiment was recurrently stirred by bathetic presentations of the horrors of existing slums, horrors almost too great for 20th-century minds to believe. On occasion such sentiment spurred into action many well-meaning men, including some leading manufacturers. But more frequently manufacturers and great corporations like railways were forced to build new towns for their workers not out of sentiment but merely because their plants were in areas where no housing accommodation existed. If speculative builders were unable to finance the building of workers' houses in quantity, the bigger industrial entrepreneurs had to undertake such (not at all unprofitable) ventures for themselves. The propaganda of sentiment, to which factory owners and railway directors were as much exposed as anyone, undoubtedly re-enforced the natural tendency of the energetic entrepreneur to *entreprendre* whatever no one else was going to do for him—particularly if he need lose no money thereby. To these mixed motives should be added also the successful Victorian businessman's pride in the general architectural setting of his manufacturing operations. This was particularly strong with the Yorkshire wool magnates who were far less content than the cotton men in Lancashire to have their growing wealth and culture represented only by palatial warehouses in the center of town.

At the most famous industrial town of the Victorian Age, Saltaire, all these considerations, and particularly the last, were certainly operative. Titus Salt had built up a new branch of the woolen textile industry using alpaca fibers from South America. By 1850 he had decided to move out of congested Bradford to a vacant site some distance away on the Aire River. The new community, which he proudly named for himself, was from the first destined to be a complete entity. Moreover, his heirs continued down until they sold the whole property in the present century to extend the original scheme. For his mill Salt obtained the advice of the greatest millwright and consulting engineer of the age, Sir William Fairbairn, who was responsible for all the technical aspects of the mills, both mechanical and structural, including of course the internal iron skeleton. He had for some time in his Lancashire practice been improving on the methods of internal metal construction developed since the Strutt mills at Derby and Belper were built in the 1790's.* (Externally the walls were naturally of local stone, in the tradition of such

* The story of mill building in Early Victorian Britain is less significant or visually interesting than in the preceding Georgian period or in the America of the second quarter of the 19th century. It is therefore barely touched on in this book.

earlier Yorkshire industrial work as the Akroyds' fine Copley Mill, dating from the mid-40's, in its lovely valley outside Halifax.)

To design the exterior of the mill Salt commissioned Lockwood and Mawson. They were Yorkshire men and had just won the competition for St. George's Hall, the great new public building with which expanding Bradford was attempting to rival Liverpool. From them Salt certainly expected a design of equally monumental character. The original mill, 540 feet by 56 feet and six storeys high, with 10,000 square yards of one-storey weaving sheds attached, is indeed a major Victorian monument in its own right just as Salt wished it to be (Fig. XIV 2). But in its villa towers and rusticated corners it echoes Barry and Parker, like the most advanced terraces of the 40's, rather than the already outdated columnar mode of St. George's Hall (Fig. XIV 3). Later extensions preserved in the main the original style although there was some increase of piquancy in the detailing; for even in Bradford "Italian" came to mean "Italian Gothic" rather than cinquecento within a very few years after the mill was first built.

There were no houses at all in this part of the Aire valley, and Bradford was too far away for Victorian commuting facilities. Salt therefore planned to build in the first year, that is, in 1852–53, six or seven hundred cottages in terraces, and also a chapel since he was a Congregationalist like so many of the wool magnates. He furthermore planned from the first for a building to contain commercial baths and a laundry; for a lecture hall; and finally for some larger detached and semidetached houses for his foremen. By 1854, the year after manufacturing began at Saltaire, only 150 cottages had actually been completed. These run in continuous terraces along the modest streets that rise up a steepish slope at right angles to the mill and the stream. The names of these streets—Titus, Caroline, William Henry, George, Amelia, Edward, Annie, and Herbert—suggest rather touchingly Titus' devotion to his own family.

The houses are all built of the same quarry-faced stone as the mill and have simple Italianate coupled windows and bracketed cornices. They rather resemble the modest Parkerian houses in Gloucester Terrace and Kensington New Town then being built on the edges of the West End; but they are really superior to those stucco rows because of the excellence of the ashlar walling and the plain dignity with which the detail is executed. (Admittedly, now that the stone has turned grimy, they are not superficially as appealing and look like nothing at all in photographs.)

Toward the west the houses are more barren in design, as if architect or client had decided to carry the work forward more cheaply in the late 50's. But no expense was spared on the Congregational Chapel when that was built in 1858–59. This confronts the office block of the mill with a handsome circular porch of giant Corinthian columns over which rises a tall open lantern. Although in a mode that was more than ten years out of date even in most Dissenting circles, the chapel indicates that even as late as this Lockwood and Mawson's ability to handle monumental Classical forms was little impaired.

In 1866 a new major building campaign began. To that period must belong the more elaborate, and definitely High Victorian, houses that line the main street and run along the high road at the upper edge of the town; 81 additional houses were contracted for at this time. The Methodist Church of 1866–68 is still conventionally Italian in composition but richly eclectic in its medievalizing detail; the Salt Boys' High School of 1867–68 similarly illustrates the multiple sources characteristic of much High Victorian design in the middle range as does also the Saltaire Institute and School of Art of 1867–71. By 1872 there were in all 820 houses at Saltaire; thus within two decades Salt had effectively completed the scheme as it was originally envisaged. Lockwood and Mawson continued to design all the additions to the mill, the later public buildings, and the terrace houses. Their control of the whole town is almost unique in history.

Beside Saltaire, Copley Village, which was laid out for Colonel Edward Akroyd contiguous to his somewhat earlier Copley Mill near Halifax in 1853, seems modest in size, having only 112 houses. But the isolated site, so near the big wool town and yet so remote from its congestion, with the hanging wood on the hill behind, provides a more attractive setting than the shallow valley of the Aire. At the edge of the wood W. H. Crossland's St. Stephen's, built in the 60's, eventually provided a very plastic Gothic accent to balance the severe, almost Grecian, mill. (Crossland, when a young man in Scott's office, was probably responsible for the whole of Copley village too. See next paragraph.) Copley undoubtedly offers a more idyllic glimpse of the Victorian industrial environment at its best than does Saltaire where the local stone was always rather bilious in tone and is now gloomily begrimed. Here the stone is lighter in hue and the whole atmosphere seems cleaner and closer to nature. The crisp Tudor of the Copley terraces encouraged the use of larger windows; it also seems somehow more "real" than the Italianate detail at Saltaire, even though it was certainly less original.

Other Yorkshire manufacturers were moved to emulate Salt in the 50's; William Black, for example, designed in 1855 90 houses on the Eastwood Estate at Rotherham in connection with the new Effingham Works. But it was Akroyd who carried out the most ambitious project. Gilbert Scott was building the church of All Souls, Haley Hill, in the mid-50's for him beside his own mansion, and it was from Scott that he obtained the original plans for a large development to be called Akroydon. Akroydon was not actually begun until after 1860, however, by which time Crossland had definitely taken over as Akroyd's architect. (Scott was then after bigger game in Whitehall where his struggles with Palmerston over the Foreign Office commission were at their height.) The Akroydon layout is not particularly distinguished and must date at the earliest from after 1855, several years later than the layout of Copley. The terraces themselves are more varied in design than those at Copley and their ranges are broken by the moderate slope of the terrain, with a view down a steeper slope into the industrial valley below. In character the houses are not without some resemblance, because of their simple use of late medieval vernacular elements, to the "reality" of Philip Webb's first houses built at the end of the decade, although the material is of course not brick but Yorkshire stone. The execution of the various terraces at Akroydon, which began only in 1861, places the finished work, quite as much as Webb's houses, beyond the limits of the Early Victorian period; but the spirit of the project belongs to the mid-50's when it was first conceived.

In 1851 the census revealed, for the first time in any large country, that more than half the English population lived in cities. More and more towns, new and old, were now becoming relatively large cities with all the housing vices mere size seems to induce. In these cities the poor formed an amorphous mass of unskilled labor quite unlike the skilled operatives who worked for the wool magnates of Yorkshire and were so well housed by Salt and Akroyd. Large-scale amelioration of ordinary workers' housing by employers was hardly to be expected and had to await state action. This began only as the Early Victorian period drew to an end and was rather ineffective before the 80's.

The provision of residential quarters for proprietors and managers over their own business premises in the center of town was now less and less frequent. The commercial middle classes were rapidly moving out like their "betters" to purely residential quarters and to the suburbs beyond them. In the City of London the upper storeys of great warehouses and office buildings often provided lodgings for clerks and salespeople still. Employees might thus "live in" like other "servants," if they were unmarried, and were expected to do so by some bosses. Many single workers in the City (and presumably in other large towns) accepted partial control over their non-working hours by employers just in order to have such accommodation. And from contemporary literature it would appear that the stuffier employers' regulations for their clerks' behavior were often as arbitrary as they were hypocritical. Decent private lodgings for single young people aspiring to middle-class respectability—and how could they hope to rise in the Victorian world without pretending at least to such an aspiration?—were evidently very difficult to find. Lodging houses were therefore as proper a field for philanthropic activity as dwellings for families in London and were naturally as paternalistic in their administration as the rule of employers over clerks housed at their business premises.

Lodging houses built in cities to accommodate single people were naturally many storeyed. Land costs in Victorian times would hardly have permitted, in any district convenient to urban places of work, the building of groups of individual minimal dwellings such as constitute so many of the almshouses of the pre-industrial period. The charitable foundations which controlled the funds of older institutions of the almshouse type frequently rebuilt them on a large scale in the 40's and 50's, but usually well outside the centers of the towns. Various corporate bodies also established new almshouses in the suburbs for their superannuated pensioners, such accommodations being in principle only for the use of the "decayed" whose days of economic livelihood were over. The relative luxury one finds in Early Victorian almshouses reflects at least a remnant of the piety inherent in all medieval charity since the harsh new sociological theories of the Utilitarians and their successors played very little part in modifying this form of charitable housing. Such housing was too small in quantity to be of much statistical consequence, however.

The members of the Society for Improving the Condition of the Laboring Classes, as their ponderous title indicates, had a broader social purpose than the old charities. In 1845 they first undertook, in the Clerkenwell area of London east of Gray's Inn Road, the building of "a certain number of houses as models of the different kinds of dwellings they would recommend for the industrious classes in populous towns." The operative words here are "model" and "dwellings." The two tiny terraces, forming a short cul-de-sac street, were not in themselves expected to alleviate London conditions, of course; nor could they even be considered superior to what was currently being put on the housing market by the better sort of speculative builder (Fig. XIV 5). The project was merely intended as an exemplar of a new semipublic kind of housing. The Society hoped that other similar societies, generous private individuals with capital, and even a few well-intentioned ordinary builders might be encouraged to follow the model they provided; thus more low-cost dwellings might be made available than the economics of the housing market seemed to make profitable in a laissez-faire world.

The *Illustrated London News*, 7, 244, gives an excellent account of this first project of the society with the long name. That account may well be quoted, but with considerable interpolation of comment to make it more intelligible. "They have taken, on reasonable terms an eligible plot of land, on the estate of Lord Calthorpe, and thereon they have erected a model street." The location, north and east of Gray's Inn Road, is referred to sometimes as Clerkenwell, sometimes as Pentonville, but the same project was meant, the two districts being contiguous. The prison connotation of Pentonville seems unhappy but is not without irony; as has been said, Pentonville Prison itself was doubtless the most comfortable Early Victorian lodging house! Lord Calthorpe was also a large Birmingham landowner and the patron of S. S. Teulon in much of his best work.

"In the arrangement of the buildings, the object has been to combine every point essential to the health, comfort, and *moral habits* of the *inmates* [italics mine]; reference being had to the recommendations of the Health of Towns Commission, particularly with respect to ventilation, drainage, and an ample supply of water." This reference to the governmental reports of 1844 and 1845 on the Health of Towns indicates how much even the first steps in the amelioration of workers' housing in the larger Victorian cities owed to the diagnostic investigations of public officials in the Benthamite tradition. Sir Edwin Chadwick and Sir J. P. Kay-Shuttleworth in the Civil Service, as well as such doctors as John Simon, then medical officer to the Corporation of London, were in some sense the Gabriels of Early Victorian housing. But government had as yet no powers to implement positive action; positive action by government, moreover, would have been false to the "advanced" economic principles of the time.

The Committee of the Society, in a circular of recent date, show the importance of their design, by reference to the exceedingly bad, and exorbitantly dear accommodation for the poor in houses let out in lodgings. The lower-priced apartments are for the most part positively unwholesome, from the want of drainage and ventilation, and frequently from positive dampness and exposure to the weather. The rent usually demanded in such unhealthy situations . . . compels the mechanic to be content with one [room] . . . in which parents and children, boys and girls . . . not only dwell during the day but sleep during the night. So common is this practice, that in the closest contiguity to some of the principal streets of the metropolis are courts and lanes, the houses of which are filled with mechanics—six, eight, or even ten of whom sleep in one room nightly!

In their two Clerkenwell terraces the Society provided dwellings of several different sorts. Even the nine largest, of three rooms each, were rather smaller than the considerably later Hemming plan described in the previous chapter (Fig. XIII 17). There were also 14 still more minute houses, of only two rooms each, and one lodging house containing 30 rooms which were intended for widows and other single women. (Single men of the poorer classes were apparently considered too rowdy to be coped with in the initial stages of the Society's experiments.) "Minimal" is certainly the word for these model dwellings, although several of them do have the unusual contemporary luxury of indoor privies; but backyards were either nonexistent or reduced to a few

465

square feet, so that most of the privies *had* to be indoors. If these "model" blocks of dwellings had been repeated in contiguous streets the ground coverage would have approached the 100 per cent of the notorious back-to-back housing in Leeds.

No architect's name is given. But the Honorary Architect to the Society from the first was Henry Roberts (d. 1876), to whom credit was definitely given for the designs of the Society's next project; that makes it all but certain he was the author of the first Pentonville terraces. Henry Roberts, as the first English housing architect, deserves more attention than he has yet received; but the Pentonville Model Lodging-houses would hardly lead one to suppose so. Even the respectable but conventionally Grecian character of his most conspicuous building, the Fishmongers' Hall beside London Bridge built in 1831–33, gives only a limited idea of his attainments as a designer and a technician. A pupil of Charles Fowler, the distinguished market architect of the 20's and 30's, Roberts was brought up in a rather special tradition of Italianate functionalism, if one may so put it. This was quite different from the Italian Villa mode of the cottage-book architects or the palazzo mode of Barry and provided the real basis of his later approach to the design of housing projects.

The very different character of Fishmongers' Hall is explained by the five years from 1824 on that he had spent as assistant to Sir Robert Smirke, the most academic Grecian of them all, at that time principally engaged in building the British Museum. The Hall is really secondhand Smirke, although Roberts made the most of his riverside site in a way Smirke might not have dared to do and the interiors are lighter and gayer than those at the Museum. The first London Bridge Railway Station of 1844 owed its architectural character to Roberts too, although he only assisted the responsible engineers on the design. No more personal in design, this is not Greek but a rather academic Italian Villa with a tall tower at one corner of the façade. After this station, although he built St. Paul's, Dock Street, East Smithfield, in 1846 and enlarged the National Scotch Church in Crown Court, Covent Garden, and its schools in 1848 in a Romanesquoid mode, Roberts was primarily occupied with housing as the technical collaborator of the Society's head Lord Ashley. At a time when better known architects were abjuring financial rewards on occasion for love of the Catholic or the Anglo-Catholic Church, Roberts' devotion to the cause of housing was as single minded and as self-sacrificing. To later housing architects he should be more of a patron saint than Owen or Buckingham.

Lord Ashley was an Evangelical Tory who led all movements for improving the lot of the industrial working classes in the face of the rising tide of laissez-faire economics. Ashley was the principal mover in the Society, as significant a figure in the latest and most ambiguous stage of Romanticism as his ancestor the 3d Earl of Shaftesbury had been at its very first stirrings when he published his *Characteristics of Men, Manners, Opinions and Times* (1711). But the Tory peerage shared Ashley's ideals up to a point. The flood of interested visitors who came to examine the new Clerkenwell buildings included the Marquess of Cholmondeley, the Dowager Marchioness of Westminster, Earl Fitzwilliam, five viscounts, as many other lords, two bishops, "and other distinguished persons." This indicates how more than respectable, how positively fashionable, the cause of philanthropic housing was soon to become in the Victorian Age. (Most bishops, of course, were busy with "higher" things in the frenzied ritualistic controversies of the time; it is surprising that even two found time to inspect edifices so unecclesiastical in purpose and in style.) "The result has been such unqualified approval of the design, as . . . will induce the Committee to commence their [next] projected work of the same kind, in the very heart of St. Giles," according to *Illustrated London News, 8, 244.* What there was for contemporaries to approve in the "design" it is hard to say, but the word as used here presumably had no exclusively visual meaning. Even entrance arches and blocking courses are lacking and neither Italianate nor Gothic elements make any appearance. All there was to appreciate were exactly such basic qualities of simple proportion and straightforward use of ordinary materials in the post-Georgian tradition as were most rapidly going out of fashion in the mid-40's, however much they may have returned to fashion since.

The Society's next venture, the five-storey model lodging house in George Street, St. Giles, was designed even more soberly, perhaps with the hope of inducing sobriety of behavior in the single men who were to be allowed to live there (Fig. XIV 4). The account in the *News* continues:

The Society in building a *Model Lodging House for Single Men,* has been influenced by a consideration of the awful disclosures made in the Report of the Health of Towns Commission—painfully confirmed by members of the Society, who have inspected the condition of the existing lodging houses in the metropolis. In many of these dwellings members of the laboring classes are crowded together, without regard to sex, in the same low, dark and noisome room, without provision for ventilation or drainage, nor any supply of water for the common purposes of cleanliness. Whilst some of these houses are frequented by the depraved and dissolute, the majority of the lodgers are hardworking people, who are doing their utmost to support themselves by the exercise of lawful occupations. It is on behalf of this much neglected and deserving class, and with a view to showing how they may be rescued from the discomfort and contamination to which they are at present (through no fault of their own) so injuriously subjected that the Committee decided on purchasing from the Commissioners of Woods and Forests a piece of freehold ground in George Street . . . a street chiefly occupied by lodging houses.

George Street lay between High Holborn and Pennethorne's New Oxford Street near his newly opened Endell Street; in a sense it was part of the "improvements" the Commission was sponsoring in this notorious slum area.

The building was 80 feet long, with kitchen, wash-house, bath, stove, and storerooms in the basement. The ground storey provided a common living room, 33 feet by 23 feet, as well as the superintendent's office and his private apartment. Each of the four upper floors contained two dormitories with a fireproof stone staircase and "washing and waterclosets" on each floor between them. The dormitories, 10 feet in height, "will lodge 104 inmates and are partitioned in the height of 6 feet 9 inches, so as to place each bed in a separate compartment." For the new lodging house £2,000 more was then needed out of a total cost of £4,200 for land and building. Fortunately the earlier venture in Clerkenwell was already providing "rents remunerative to the Society though lower than are ordinarily paid by the laboring classes." It was therefore expected that the new project would soon become self-supporting and might thus serve as a financial as well as a technical model for imitation in other densely populated localities in Britain.

At this time César Daly in the *Révue générale de l'architecture* devoted several plates to the "private architecture of the English proletarians." In these the individual dwellings are shown for the first time grouped horizontally as real "flats" such as the French were accustomed to. They rose to a height of four storeys and were even plainer externally than those the Society built in Clerkenwell and St. Giles. It is not clear just where they were built; they were not necessarily in London and may even have been in Scotland.

Considering the ambitious projects at Birkenhead for the housing of the upper classes, it is not altogether surprising to find that flatted blocks of workers' dwellings, comparable to those Daly published, were already being built there in 1846. These blocks have a few positive features of Victorian style about them (Fig. XIV 9). Rusticated quoins decorated the corners and arched windows were introduced in the second storey on the long elevations. Ornamental gateposts flanked the entrance to the "courts" separating the blocks one from another; but these courts, if less confined than in the Liverpool slums, were narrower than the blocks themselves so that the light and air that entered their narrow chasms, four storeys deep, must have been minimal. The Society's standards for flatted dwellings were to be rather higher when they finally began to build such structures.

468

At the annual meeting of the Society in July 1849, according to a contemporary account, Prince Albert from the chair

made a speech which spread with electrical rapidity over the kingdom, quickening good impulses, inducing kind feelings, prompting noble acts. . . . "To show how man can help man, notwithstanding the complicated state of civilized society, ought to be the aim of every philanthropic person; but it is more peculiarly the duty of those who, under the blessing of divine providence, enjoy station, wealth and education. Let them be careful, however, to avoid any dictatorial interference with labour and employment which frightens away capital, destroys that freedom of thought and independence of action which must remain to everyone if he is to work out his own happiness, and impairs that confidence under which alone engagements for mutual benefit are possible."

From the Queen herself (undoubtedly primed by Albert) had come two years earlier a recommendation that Parliament should enact legislation based upon the conclusions of Chadwick's Commission on the Health of Towns. The Prince had also just learned from the experts that the drains at Buckingham Palace were in a shocking state and had immediately had them improved. In the 1849 speech the Prince Consort brilliantly presented a theoretical balancing of the opposed doctrines of British Tories and Liberals (always so inappropriately phrased in French as *noblesse oblige* and *laissez faire*) that dominated the social thinking of the time. In the Society's activities, to which Albert lent his sponsorship, the Tory code of obligation did not yet conflict seriously with the Radical devotion to free enterprise. In 1850, for example, Henry Roberts was actively urging the abolition of the brick duties and the window duties as being absolutely necessary before any "great real advance will be made in the sanitary movement" because only such action could reduce the cost of building for the poor. (This was in a speech at Exeter Hall published in the *Builder*, 8, 121.) Thus he was asking for specific political action in order to accomplish a desirable economic and social effect, but his demand was apparently not considered "party" in its implications. As we know, both taxes were in fact very shortly removed.

The Society had taken in 1848 the somewhat backward step of remodeling three tenements in Charles Street, Drury Lane, into a lodging house for men and one at No. 76 Hatton Garden into a smaller lodging house for women. These projects were intended to show "how old and ill-arranged buildings may be renovated and fitted up," and the Hatton Garden house proved shortly to be the "most profitable of their undertakings." It is the completely new block of flats built the next year in Streatham Street, Bloomsbury, which indicates how much higher Roberts was soon able to persuade the Society to raise its technical standards. Here the standards were actually well above those of the builders who were erecting houses for the upper middle classes in the fashionable areas north and south of the Park in these mid-century years, both in the solidity of the structural methods employed and, to our present taste, in the soundness of their design (Figs. XIV 6–8).

The structure of this four-storey block in Streatham Street, which went up in 1849–50, is entirely fireproof with arched hollow-brick floors set in cement and tied with iron. Although there is some variation in the plans, the ordinary apartment has a living room, a kitchen with scullery alcove, and two bedrooms (Fig. XIV 8). Each apartment has its own entrance from the open galleries that run along the west side of the interior court. The exterior treatment is still what can be called post-Georgian and extremely restrained in character (Fig. XIV 6). The linking of the two lower storeys with rusticated piers of brick and the heavy cornice on chamfered blocks at the top provide a conventional but dignified architectural effect. The incised sans-serif inscription over the door, "Model Houses for Families," has a certain masculine elegance. These features give a breadth of scale and even an interest of relief that is quite lacking in Roberts' earlier work for the Society.

The court galleries are carried on piers that rise in two tiers of two storeys each to support very flat segmental arches of great breadth and vigor (Fig. XIV 7). The intermediate storeys are served by iron balconies with plain iron railings. These articulated façades have a functional directness and a care for proportion that is in the sturdy tradition of the Late Georgian engineers rather than the dilute post-Georgian vein of the speculative builders. This is, in fine, one of the most distinguished works of the Early Victorian period despite its almost total lack of recognizably Victorian character.

The cost of these remarkable dwellings (which are still extant and serving their original purpose better than many built fifty years or more later) was £7,370. The extra expense of the fireproof construction had been "only £42 or about 12 shillings per hundred pounds." At the same time another architect, William Beck, was building a still larger block of workers' dwellings in Spicer Street, Spitalfields, to the east of the City, at a cost of £9,379.

The philanthropic housing movement was beginning to spread outside London too. Lumsden's Model Dwellings in Glasgow, by James Wylson, were completed in 1850. But of course housing in freehold flats had always been common practice in Scotland; even the local aristocracy had only moved out of the towering tenements of the High Street and the Canongate in Edinburgh after the New Town was begun in the 1760's. Patrick Wilson's "Improved Dwellings for the Working Classes" in Leith Wynd, off the High Street, replaced in 1851 a group of middle- or upper-class 17th-century tenements that had become noisome rookeries. These dwellings were expected to provide the "charitable" return of 7¾ per cent on the investment, actually a very modest yield for the period. Ashley Buildings were built at the head of the Canongate in 1852 and named for Lord Ashley, to mention one more Edinburgh example.

The advantages of the flat system were stressed by William Wigginton in his book on *Sanitary Reform—Model Town Dwellings for the Industrious Classes* (1850). In that same mid-century year Roberts also brought out *The Dwellings of the Laboring Classes; Their Arrangement and Construction,* which ran to three editions by 1853. This provided various plans and elevations of blocks of flats for others to follow. Beckett-Denison, perhaps as a respite from his struggle with Barry over the clock for the New Palace, at this time set about converting existing lodging houses in Leeds into what he considered model ones. Emissaries of the Prussian Government were consulting Lord Ashley about housing reform in Berlin; Ashley was also taking some justified credit for the generous action of Louis Napoleon, then Prince-President of the French Second Republic, in contributing £2,000 toward the study of such matters in Paris.

Roberts' Thanksgiving Buildings, in Portpool Lane off Gray's Inn Lane, cost £6,865 in the early 50's. They were rather badly hit in the blitz but their fireproof construction then proved its worth. Roberts' best known housing venture, curiously enough, is a tiny block of four flats to be seen today in the open setting of Kennington Park. With Roberts' position as Architect to the Society, of which the Consort himself was patron, it was naturally he who was chosen to design "Prince Albert's Model Houses." These were first erected beside the Cavalry Barracks off Knightsbridge in Hyde Park in connection with the Great Exhibition. (Another model structure was exhibited by the Society inside the Crystal Palace in Class 27; this Roberts also designed.) Prince Albert's Houses look like nothing so much as a semidetached pair of cottages but they actually consist of flats paired on the two storeys. In theory, moreover, they could either be carried much higher or extended horizontally into a sort of flatted terrace.

The sober engineer's Late Georgian of Roberts' Holborn and Bloomsbury work was seriously compromised in the design of this housing exhibit (Fig. XIV 14). The ending of the tax on bricks in 1850 stimulated innovations in their use; a new sort of bold polychromy executed in brick was already being startlingly illustrated in the slowly rising walls of Butterfield's All Saints', Margaret Street. Roberts' patent system of hollow-brick construction was extended in these houses of 1851 from the floors to the walls, a technical advance; but he also indulged in the new polychromy, using straw-colored bricks from Aylesford for the walling and red ones from the Buxley Works near Esher for the window trim and quoins, a dubious stylistic "advance" toward the High Victorian. Two sorts of glazed bricks were also introduced in the open entranceway, gray ones made of North Devon clay by Mr. Seagram in Vauxhall and very light-colored ones—later to be chiefly associated with municipal "conveniences"—from the Potteries.

The springers of the hollow-brick arches were of cast iron with brick cores and the tie rods were of wrought iron; but these metal elements of interior construction did not affect the design of the façades. Since the circles that crown the two end bays contain the initials V and A, it is probably just to attribute to Albert's own taste the unhappy combination of straw-colored and red bricks, the unstructural flat-pointed arch that covers the entrance way, and the silly Jacobethan scallops that mask the flat roof. As always, Albert was a sounder patron of technical innovation than of advanced architectural design.

These houses were rebuilt after the Exhibition in Kennington Park and there they can still be studied. What a pathetic example they are of the combination, thus early in the history of workers' housing, of advanced technical ideas with cheap echoes of a current architectural fashion! It is hard not to believe that the architect of the Streatham Street court façade, if uninfluenced by Albert's uncertain taste, could have produced a more dignified design, even one incorporating bricks of several colors.

Much later than this, in 1856, Hunt and Stephenson built a row of lodging houses over shops on the Duchy of Cornwall's Estate in Vauxhall Row, Lambeth. These were intended to be income producing, not philanthropic or exemplary, and they retained considerable post-Georgian sobriety in the plain rustication of their ground-storey piers and the flat trim of their windows with no Victorian piquancy at all. Evidently the Prince's taste was not allowed to influence the handling of the Royal family's Duchy of Cornwall investments.

The plans of the Prince's houses are very ample. Each flat has three bedrooms in addition to a living room, a kitchen, and a little entrance lobby; there was also a scullery and an interior water closet, something which was beginning now to be considered a minimal necessity. The inset entranceway and stairs provide a direct approach to the upper flats which is fairly well protected from the weather. The next year Roberts executed the equivalent of this quadruple unit as the center of a longer block built for the Windsor Royal Society at Windsor. This Society was a joint-stock company with a capital of £6,000. The capital was raised in 10-shilling shares and a dividend of 5 per cent was guaranteed. Of the five blocks in the scheme, the other four consisted of ordinary two-storey cottages arranged in pairs and in groups of four. (Here in the country the water closets were still placed in the rear yards.) These cottage blocks, suited to a relatively open terrain, are the prototypes of much 20th-century council housing—even, I fear, as regards

472

their plumbing facilities in some cases! One and a half acres, between the Long Walk and the Cavalry Barracks, had been purchased from the Commissioners of Woods and Forests for £287, a price which is in great contrast to the land values in central London where Roberts had previously built his workers' housing. But workers' housing was proving a good investment for the various societies at the end of the Early Victorian period whatever the land cost.

In 1854 a sanitary congress held in Brussels devoted most of its attention to workers' housing. (Uncle Leopold was evidently helping to make nephew Albert's philanthropic interests international.) For this congress Henry Roberts prepared a report on "The Pecuniary Result of Model Houses for the Laboring Classes" which includes most revealing figures. The first model lodgings, those built in Clerkenwell, had returned an income of about 4⅓ per cent on the cost of the buildings and 4 per cent on the cost of the land; the George Street lodging house had done as well on the land and better (5 per cent) on the buildings. The Streatham Street Houses for Families were on leased land and the return to the Society was 5¾ per cent of the total cost. As the washing establishment and the "Huxters' Depot" (whatever that may be) were not in full operation at Thanksgiving Buildings in Holborn, their eventual yield could not then be determined. But the best investments of all were the remodeled buildings, as has been said. That in Hatton Garden for single women returned 7½ per cent and that for men in Charles Street, Drury Lane, 17 per cent. Thus was noblesse oblige happily reconciled with laissez faire.

When philanthropy in workers' housing could be so financially painless it is not surprising to find a powerful rival society appearing in the London field in 1853. This was the Metropolitan Association for Improving the Dwellings of the Industrious Classes, a title that in its unction recalls the Société pour l'Amélioration de la Race Chevaline which runs the races at Longchamps across the Channel. The new Society did not employ Roberts; their favorite was another and much inferior architect, H. Alfred Darbishire (1839–1908), who was destined later to become a sort of Gilbert Scott, or more accurately an Alfred Waterhouse, of Victorian housing. The first Metropolitan projects were the Victoria Lodging Houses and Wash-house in Francis Street off the Vauxhall Bridge Road in Westminster (54 dwellings for married guardsmen) and a giant block of 108 dwellings begun the same year in Nelson Street, Snowfields, south of the river. The latter was built at a contract cost nearly three times that of any of the older Society's projects.

Henry Ashton (1801–1872), an architect more prominently associated with flats for the upper classes, showed at the Royal Academy Exhibition in this same year 1853 a block to be built in Ashley Place, Westminster (which was named, needless to say, for Lord Ashley), backing up to his "apartment houses" in Victoria Street which will be discussed shortly. In these modest workers' flats the open staircases of Henry Roberts' Thanksgiving Buildings were again used. In the same year Beckett-Denison was carrying the housing gospel from Leeds to Doncaster in a vigorous lecture; while a committee of parishioners, shocked by the interstitial slums of aristocratic Mayfair, hired Mr. Newsom, a builder, to put up a small block of eight two-room flats in Grosvenor Mews, Berkeley Square. The next year Charles Lee began a block of 60 dwellings for the Metropolitan Association; and in Lisson Row, Marylebone, the Habershons built model lodging houses costing £1,228 for the local Marylebone Association (MAFIDIC as we might abbreviate its long name today) along the Metropolitan's lines.

In Liverpool the Prince Consort's model flats were repeated in twenty dwellings in Upper Frederick Street this year also. At about the same time R. R. Rowe in Vicar's Buildings at Cambridge seems for the first time seriously to have attempted more up-to-date styling in workers' housing. With molded bricks and bands of red and white he emulated some of the bolder innovations of the opening High Victorian period, with which the terminal chapter of this book will deal in some detail, more happily than Prince Albert and Roberts in their 1851 dwellings.

The lifting of the brick and window taxes in 1851 seems, as Henry Roberts had prophesied, to have stimulated the construction of workers' housing very considerably and not merely to have encouraged more lively wall treatments. But the Parliamentary Act for Facilitating the Erection of Dwellings for the Laboring Classes was not passed until 1855. This did not apply to Scotland and went no further than to allow the incorporation of companies under the Act "for the purpose of providing dwellings . . . with or without private gardens, or with or without common gardens, or places of common recreation for the use of the inmates of such dwellings . . . The regulations as to drainage, ventilation and water . . . to be approved of by the General Board of Health, whose officer is at all reasonable times to inspect the dwellings erected under the Act and authorizing the imposition of fines if the dwellings are not kept in a proper condition." The act was a feeble and, it might appear, almost meaningless gesture toward the aspirations of Lord Ashley and his friends; yet it initiated the whole body of housing legislation which reached its culmination in the programs voted by the National Government during World War II. Its special character also helps to explain why responsibility for all British housing outside Scotland remained until a few years ago seated in the Ministry of Health. The original General Board, the Victorian ancestor of the 20th-century Ministry, was in 1856 so small and feeble a government organ, however, that it was expected to require only

3,000 square feet of office space against the 51,000 proposed for the new War Office.

In 1855 in the *Builder* a certain William Chambers (an obscure Victorian, not the Georgian knight returned to action), calling like Wigginton on Scottish precedent, repeated the earlier pleas for the erection of blocks of flats not only for the "humbler" classes but for "other" classes as well. The account that has been given of working-class housing in flats should be balanced by some reference to the rare Early Victorian blocks of flats that were built in England for these "other" classes; in Scotland such blocks continued to house a large proportion of the urban middle class, as they had always done, and there was really no significant new development at this time.

Flats in the form of "chambers" for professional men, essentially for consultation with their clients but in which they often lived if they were bachelors, were an old tradition of the Inns of Court and almost of monastic origin. But chambers were not necessarily restricted to lawyers. In 1839 Decimus Burton built a luxurious block of "club" chambers in Regent Street at a cost of £26,000, imitating the new palazzo mode of Barry's clubs which had already superseded that of his own Grecian Athenaeum. Others of a similar order were built in the West End in the next few years. Flats for the use of English middle-class *families*, on the other hand, seem to have remained almost unthinkable well into the 50's.

The *Builder* might emphasize in 1849, in replying to the query of a correspondent, that in Paris even the nobility were happy to live in apartments in *maisons de rapport;* the fact was stressed, moreover, that respectable Edinburghers, and not just immoral Parisians, preferred their "houses" piled up in horizontal layers to the "London higgledy-piggedly style of middle-class dwelling." "If any city in the world demands a thorough reform [of its middle-class housing habits] it is London," the *Builder* continued. "The time has now arrived when the expansion and growth of this city must be *upward* in place of *outward*—when 'houses' must be reared above each other, with all their paraphernalia of pavements, landings, outer doors and inner, lobbies, kitchens, and closets, instead of straggling miles farther and farther away from the centre."

The activities of the Westminster Improvement Commission, created by acts of Parliament of 1845 and 1847 to lay out Victoria Street from Westminster Abbey west to Pimlico, seem to have been modeled on Parisian precedents, although the great day of boulevard building in France under Baron Haussman still lay well ahead. Emulating Rambuteau, Haussman's predecessor as Prefect of the Seine under Louis Phillippe, the Commissioners had by 1849 opened nearly the whole length of the new street to a width of

80 feet and had also obtained control of the building land on either side to a depth of 60 or 70 feet. Two years later the entire street was finally opened; but three years after that—just a decade after the first act of Parliament which set up the Victoria Street Corporation—the whole scheme collapsed into insolvency.

In 1852–53, when the new street was already completed as a thoroughfare, interest in all things French was generally increasing thanks to the flashy beginnings of the new Second Empire under Napoleon III. His tremendous plans for modernizing Paris were already being discussed although even the construction of the New Louvre had then barely been begun. It is not surprising therefore that those years and this Victoria Street area, whose particular residential or commercial character still remained to be established, should have seen the construction of the first actual upper-class flats in London. Perhaps one might better say "apartments" in the American and continental way; such a verbal trick, if exploited at the time, could have helped to distinguish the new blocks in Victoria Street from the flatted workers' dwellings provided by the various philanthropic housing societies and associations, including those being built nearby in Ashley Place as part of the same scheme. (Actually they were sometimes referred to as "club chambers.")

Back in 1849 the *Builder* had already published a scheme for middle-class houses divided into apartments. Their modest Italianism suggests a conscious emulation of Browne's houses in Westbourne Terrace and they might readily have been mistaken, on the garden side at least, for conventional Paddington terraces (Fig. XIV 10). The suggested inclusion of shops on the ground floor in the Parisian way and the resemblance of the open access galleries to those of Roberts' Streatham Street Houses (published by the *Builder* earlier in the same year) might have been expected to damn them for upper middle-class use. The individual flats were extremely modest in their accommodations, moreover, providing no more space than fourth-class houses. Hence they would have appealed, if to any tenants at all at this time, only to those who were close enough to the bottom of the middle-class heap to resent the accusation that they were living in glorified "model lodgings." The idea of flats had eventually to be taken over by the middle classes from their presumed "betters" if it was ever to become acceptable.

Mackenzie, the entrepreneur who asked Henry Ashton to design the first London apartment houses (if I may so call them), avoided many of the mistakes of the 1849 project. Ashton, for example, gave to the design of his buildings a definitely continental character, although one recalling Vienna or Berlin more than Paris. The undomestic scaling and the foreign look might help to make more palatable the fact that there were shops below. These shops were not modest sales premises in the West End manner, like those Beeston

476

was providing below his terrace in St. George's Place, with all the visual emphasis focussed on the house façades above. Rather Ashton provided a great range of wide-arched shop windows, with a mezzanine above in each arch, quite in the grandest manner of the new banks and insurance offices in the City. Prince Albert, we are informed, inspected some of the apartments in 1854 when they were available for letting and "was pleased to express his approbation of them architecturally."

Mackenzie's project included a long multiple block between Carlisle Place and Howick Place on the south side of Victoria Street, with two additional smaller blocks to the east and the west. The multiple block backed against the lodging houses Ashton was building at the same time in Ashley Place to the south. Presumably it was the latter that the Prince, as patron of the principal housing society, was most interested in; but his approbation of Ashton's work seems to have extended to the more luxurious blocks which faced north on Victoria Street. In a view published late in 1854, two appear completed and a third beyond Howick Place is still partly under scaffolding; but other apparently similar blocks resulting from the activities of other entrepreneurs and their architects can be seen in construction across the street (Fig. XIV 11). Discussion may well be confined to the central and largest of Mackenzie's three blocks, about which the most information is available, since all the blocks are quite similar. This one, in actual fact, was built not as a unit but as four attached "houses," each with its own staircase. The façade, however, was treated as a continuous composition like a terrace.

The arched ground storey and mezzanine were broken by four rusticated and pedimented doorways that provided the entrances to the apartments above, as well as by wide rusticated piers between the bays. Above there are four storeys, each containing within the over-all length of the multiple block eight apartments arranged in pairs on either side of the four staircases (Fig. XIV 12). At the front of each apartment was a drawing room 15 feet by 21 feet; into this there opened through a wide door a dining room 15 feet square. These reception rooms were approached by an interior hall from the entrance lobby which was entered from the stair landing. To the rear there were three bedrooms in each apartment, one very small, while a fourth bedroom opened off the hall in front. A kitchen 13½ feet by 15 feet was accompanied by a small scullery and a water closet as well as by a servants' bedroom (practically without light or air but apparently not very small—until one notices where the apostrophe is placed). The master's water closet and a storeroom, as well as a separate servants' stair, opened off the passage that led from the hall to the kitchen; while a large closet (in the American sense of hanging cupboard) was also provided off the main corridor. It was a poor plan but fairly ample in its accommodations, comparable perhaps to

477

a third- or a modest second-class house. The grandeur of the principal stairs, supplemented by a hoist for heavy weights, hardly made up for the tiny interior courts from which the halls of the apartments might obtain a little light and air.

The cost of each "house," that is, each group of apartments on a single stair, was £16,700. The construction was fireproof throughout, with iron girders carrying brick jack-arches and solid stone stairs. One of the houses was entirely hot water heated; all had provision for cooking with gas. The shops, each with its own basement and mezzanine, were rented at £150 a year; the flats ranged from £200 down to as low as £80.

Mr. Mackenzie's hopes for this ambitious venture crashed in 1855, presumably because of the Crimean War. The crash may have induced the insolvency of the Victoria Street Corporation from whom the land was leased, but doubtless in wartime other lessors were also unable to fulfill their contracts. In any event one apartment house, somewhat smaller than that just described, remained in carcass for more than a decade. It was finished only in 1867 when the nearby building activities in Grosvenor Gardens seemed briefly to suggest that something of Belgravian glamor might eventually radiate beyond Victoria Station. This block was probably not a Mackenzie-Ashton project but rather the venture of someone else imitating them—perhaps of Henman who showed a design for a Victoria Street apartment house at the Royal Academy Exhibition in 1853. Or for that matter the completed structure may have owed its executed form entirely to H. S. Legg, the titular architect of the Freehold Investment Company which put some £45,000 into completing it in the mid-60's.

The long rows of windows in the upper storeys of Ashton's first block are not unlike those of ordinary terraces, but at the center of each "house" a great Palladian stair window, rising from the first into the second storey, interrupts their regular rhythm in a quite monumental way. In its scaling the façade resembles the big commercial palazzos of the period more than the usual terraces of the West End. The cornice is extremely rich and bold, as were once the shop arches below; yet the general effect is dreary and regimented like Berlin, not urbane and sophisticated like Paris or Vienna. Doubtless high rentals, unfamiliar planning, and poor communication with the West End and the City discouraged prospective tenants from taking the new apartments in Victoria Street. But the uncertain social rating of the area and of the type of dwelling, as well as the very continental appearance of the buildings, must have played some part at least in their early failure.

As long as the blocks remained clean and new, and before both sides of the street were built up solidly with never a tree or an open space in sight, the effect was doubtless much less grim than it is today; but over it there seems

478

always to have hung an air of failure. However that may be, at the time Victoria Street and this experiment in housing the London middle classes were hanging in the balance in the mid-50's, Arthur Ashpitel and John Whichcord (1823–1885) renewed the propaganda for apartment living in a pamphlet called *Town Dwellings—an Essay on the Erection of Fireproof Houses in Flats* (1855). This treatise stressed the various technical aspects in which Ashton's blocks were so unmistakably in advance of the practices of the terrace builders; yet London builders after a brief wartime halt continued on their busy way with no real change in their methods. Good-class blocks of flats continued to be built only in Scotland, and even there the Edinburgh New Town was rounded out to the northwest with terrace houses little inferior to those of a generation earlier. (In 1856 it was reported that the completion of Melbourne Place at the corner of Victoria Terrace would finally fill the original layout as planned by the Improvement Commissioners even before George III died). At the same time a "city of villas," as it was described by the *Builder* in 1856, rose to the far south in the Greenhill, Morningside, and Merchiston district, with other similar ones to the north in Trinity and Granton. The best villas in the new southern suburbs are up to White's standards or even superior.

In London a great new wave of the housing ocean was pushing forward, first south and then north of the Park, along the old familiar lines in the early 50's (Fig. XIII 32). The principal wholly new development was now in South Kensington between the Park and the New Brompton Road. Contiguous to this district on the east lay the simple Late Georgian distinction of horseshoe-shaped Brompton Square. South of that several stucco terraces, the finest in the form of crescents, had been designed by Basevi and were even more definitely pre-Victorian in style and in date. These had long bounded with modest elegance the rather confused area north and west of Henry Holland's Hans Town. This area on the western edge of the Cadogan Estate had itself been filling up little by little in the 40's from the south or Chelsea side with poor terraces of third- or even fourth-class houses.

Considerably farther out, to the north of the New Brompton Road, the Boltons soon stood by themselves, all the houses being indicated as present in maps of the early 50's, although some must have remained mere carcasses down to the end of the decade. Nearer Sloane Street, Ovington Square and Ovington Gardens were already laid out on the site of Grove House south of the Brompton Road. L. Elliott finished two houses in Ovington Square in 1852 for £1,642, indicating that the carcasses were already built several years earlier perhaps, and the layout must have been earlier still. The square and the neighboring "gardens" were now rapidly filling up with large houses as presumably were Beauchamp Place and Beaufort Gardens nearby. Thurloe

479

Square and Onslow Square farther west, and most of the terraces lying between them, date from this period as well; but Thurloe Square was still open on the north and Onslow Square on the west. Most of this terrace building south of the Park before the mid-century was a sort of side-wash of the tide, pushing into pockets that had not been filled earlier and making only timid sorties beyond, rather than a concerted advance of the upper middle-class front beyond Sloane Street.

It was the decision made in 1850 to place the Crystal Palace on the south edge of the Park, facing Gore House, whence Lady Blessington and D'Orsay (who made it so famous) had long since departed, that made the fortunes of South Kensington or, more accurately, of Old Brompton as this region was still known. In 1852 the Commissioners of the Exhibition purchased with a part of the proceeds of the Exhibition (so much larger than had been expected) a tremendous tract of land between Kensington Gore and the New Brompton Road; in this transaction they were assisted by the pious prayers of Prince Albert that they might get a good bargain. The tract included 21½ acres of the Gore House Estate, bought for only £60,000, and 47½ acres of the Harrington Estate to the south, costing £153,500, indicating that Heaven heard Albert's appeal. Here in the Brompton Groves, famous for their fine old trees and still the resort of metropolitan sportsmen after feathered game, the great educational institutions proposed by the Prince as a permanent memorial to the Exhibition would be built. (Even a new National Gallery, to be built facing the Park on the Gore House property, was included in the early plans.)

Originally it was assumed that much of the area would not be built over at all, and at first only two main streets were planned (Fig. XIII 32). The one on the west, parallel to Gloucester Road, was then called Albert Road (it is now Queen's Gate). The other at right angles to the first, running out of the Brompton Road westward by the edge of Thurloe Square to Gloucester Road, was later named Cromwell Road. The holdings of the Commissioners south and west of these roads were advertised for lease to builders in 1853 to provide an income from the investment for the support of the various institutions shortly to be set up in their own new buildings nearer the center of the tract.

Even before the Commissioners acquired their South Kensington property Sir Charles James Freake (1814–1884) had begun a new development on the northeastern border of this area facing the Park between the outer end of Knightsbridge and Kensington Gore. Prince's Terrace was evidently completed there by the summer of 1851 since it appears in bird's-eye views of the Crystal Palace across the road on the southeast. (Fig. XVI 5). Freake's houses, designed by an architect named Johnson, opened a new cycle of terrace house design, superseding the modest Italianism of Lowndes Square and Westbourne Terrace with something richer and more pompous, if hardly as attractive (Fig. XIV 15).

No longer does the whole terrace form a unified composition. The centralized grouping of the windows in each of the house façades emphasizes instead the individual dwellings as repeating entities. A projecting porch of the old Belgravian order at the side of each house syncopates awkwardly with the triple windows in the center of the upper storeys. Engaged columns decorate these windows and there is a curved pediment over the central one in the second storey. As has been remarked already, this pseudo-Palladian motif was probably suggested by the windows in the end bays of the garden front of Barry's Bridgewater House (Fig. VII 10). The panels between the window groups have a slightly Parisian air further enhanced in the third storey by the segmental arches over the windows. The fourth storey is mansarded, perhaps in emulation of the new Hope house in Piccadilly (Fig. VII 17); but the roof is inconspicuous, being partly masked by a balustrade above, and the small attic windows are quite unornamented.

On the rear façades large bay windows in the first storey of each house, decorated with arches and engaged columns, break up even more the unity of the terrace as a whole. Above the bay windows the spacing of the upper-storey windows is quite irregular (Fig. XIV 15). Although a minor matter, it is perhaps worth pointing out that the published elevations show single panes in the sash of the front windows, central sashbars in the two lower storeys on the rear, and nine-pane sash of Georgian character in the upper windows on that side. This distribution certainly offers no infallible guide to dating houses by means of the size and type of the window sash! But the specific locations do indicate the relative prestige of different kinds of sash in 1850. As with Lewis Cubitt's houses in Lowndes Square, it is significant that these designs were published when new. Unfortunately nothing seems to be discoverable concerning Freake's architect Johnson. If certain drawings at the Royal Institute of British Architects by H. L. Elmes (and hence prior to his death in 1847) are actually studies for these houses, Johnson may merely have corrupted in execution Elmes' more refined ideas for individualizing terrace houses.

In cities where stone was used for terrace building, superposed orders such as were introduced here proved too expensive to execute. Builders in the provinces tended in the 50's rather to copy in freestone the less advanced terrace house models provided by such architects as Elliott in Ovington Square or R. H. Moore in Queen's Terrace in Queen's Road, Primrose Hill (he finished four houses there for £940 in 1852). Above fine ashlar walls, however, the heavy modillion-supported cornice of St. Aidan's Terrace, Forest Road, Birkenhead (probably built at the same time as T. H. Wyatt's nearby St. Aidan's College in 1853 and just possibly by Wyatt), appears less clumsy than do the similar cement cornices on London houses of unstuccoed stock brick (Fig. XIV 17). The horizontally rusticated ground storey at St. Aidan's Terrace, imitating the stuccoed ground storeys of many London houses otherwise all of bare brick, breaks out into a range of bay windows like those on the rears of the Prince's Terrace houses. The windows here have central sashbars to belie the lingering Georgian character of the over-all terrace composition with its center and end projections. But this is a very superior terrace all the same, curiously isolated in a villa district well south of Paxton's park.

Where the local brick was red and where stone rather than stucco trim was used, as in several provincial cities, the general effect even of rather modest terrace houses of the early 50's can also be quite superior, even though London houses of similar size would be but third class. The terrace on the south side of Woodhouse Square in Leeds, a city otherwise poor in terrace architecture of any period, is a good example (Fig. XIV 13). The peculiar sash divisions in the windows of this terrace resemble some of those to be seen in Westbourne Terrace; in the provinces such windows probably indicate a date for the houses in the early 50's rather than the mid-40's.

Within a year or two a Mr. Elger seems to have succeeded Freake as the active entrepreneur of a more extensive Prince's Gate development. As early as 1854 he had already sold off all but two of the houses in Prince's Terrace; but a change in the design of the house fronts reflects the change in control before the group was finished. (The two that J. P. Morgan bequeathed to be used as a residence for the American ambassador, as well as their immediate neighbors, fail to conform to the designs published in 1851.) Elger was also operating to the south of Prince's Gate. Here he had leased two fields from the Earl of Listowel and, to the irritation of the established residents of contiguous Brompton Square, had cut off by a brick wall the right of way from the round head of the square to the Park. In this roughly oblong area he proceeded to lay out Prince's Gardens and Ennismore Gardens, providing fine private grounds for the use of the individual householders. The treatment is somewhat along the lines of Allom's contemporary planning at Ladbroke Grove, but more enclosed. Quite exceptionally the terraces in Ennismore Gardens were all built of freestone. As in the stone-built cities of the provinces, the houses lack the opulent decoration of those facing the Park and what is now Exhibition Road to the west, but they have a solid dignity almost unique in London. Their plainness and tremendous height make these stone houses appear prison-like, however; and they are also very gloomy in hue since they never receive the fresh coats of paint that banish grime temporarily from stuccoed houses in London.

A Mr. Jackson had begun by this time to build up the outer side of the great boulevard along the western edge of the Commissioners' Estate. This remained incompletely filled on the inner side, however, well into the 70's; then it became the scene of Norman Shaw's bold attack on the lingering traditions of coherent terrace architecture. (The J. P. Heseltine house at No. 170, built in 1875, was his first bombshell.)

But interest in unified terrace design had not entirely disappeared by 1855; for there is an unusually handsome terrace at Nos. 113–127 Cromwell Road on the south edge of the Commissioners' Estate where building only began about that year. Moreover, just as Early Victorian terraces owe most of their visual virtue to the endurance of sound Late Georgian traditions, so later terraces, even into the 60's, usually owe their attractive qualities to the continued use of types of design first introduced in the 40's even if little exploited before the 50's.

The really positive new stylisms of the 50's, High Victorian Gothic and Anglicized Second Empire, obtained no early hold on terrace design. Scott's conspicuously Gothic houses of 1853 in Broad Sanctuary, Westminster, for example, had no influence in London or elsewhere before the late 50's. In South Kensington, indeed, the Early Victorian and the Late join with almost no intervening High Victorian of any sort. But there was more variety in the provinces where terrace-house design was less stabilized.

Facing the early terraces already mentioned in Eastgate Street in Winchester, and executed like them in stucco, is a later terrace of five houses—Nos. 70–74 (Fig. XIV 16). In this the ground-storey doors and windows are linked into a continuous arcade as much Romanesque as Gothic in character, while the first-storey windows (now mostly replaced with oriels) are great glazed squares set under continuous segmental-arched architraves. These are simply molded with some feeling for the quality of the plastic surfacing material also evident in the detailing of the arcade below. The date is uncertain but perhaps about 1850.

In Liverpool a range of contiguous row houses, Nos. 27–37 North Bedford Street, makes a suave and original use of red brick with modest stone trim, including some discreet Gothic touches. Despite their simplicity these are so eclectic as to defy analysis, not to speak of accurate dating. The tendency of the last few years to pursue in the jungles of London suburbia and in provincial towns chiefly the more fantastic architectural fauna of the mid-century has led to a neglect of the quieter and more urbane things which also exist in some quantity. Even so, these little Gothic terraces in Winchester and

Liverpool are distinctly exceptions because of their originality and high quality of finish.

North of the Park in London as well as south, but apparently more slowly, a new housing wave began to roll forward in the early 50's; for now the considerable districts nearer the West End whose development had been initiated in Late Georgian times were really being filled up. For example, the last house in Belgrave Square, No. 49 at the northeast corner, was built in 1850, apparently by P. C. Hardwick, and Eaton Square was finally completed in 1853. The new projects of the 40's, all much more modest in extent than those of the 20's and 30's, were soon filled to saturation by the rising prosperity of the early 50's.

As a control on the newer developments in South Kensington and Bayswater (to which we will come shortly) it may be interesting to see what was happening in the older portions of the West End to satisfy those whose particular social aspirations turned eastward toward earlier aristocratic centers rather than westward toward the new upper middle-class frontier. This will illustrate that snobbish brake on taste, holding back the acceptance of new fashions in terrace housing everywhere to the west, which was undoubtedly provided by the continued prestige of Georgian Mayfair.

Grosvenor Square was probably laid out under George I. The terrace built on the east side about 1730 was, according to Summerson in *Georgian London*, the first instance of the use of center and end blocks to compose a row of separate houses into a single grand elevation. The square filled up gradually in the next twenty years or so. I suppose it was the falling-in of the original 99-year leases, one by one, that led to so much piecemeal rebuilding of the individual houses in the 1850's.

H. Harrison, rather than the Grosvenor Estate architect Thomas Cundy II, rebuilt No. 37 in 1853. But Thomas Cundy II refronted and remodeled, if he did not entirely rebuild, Nos. 19 and 19a in 1855, the contractor being Kelk and the cost £12,845 and £7,137 respectively, figures which suggest rather extensive operations. Edward I. Mason was responsible in 1856 for alterations and additions to another house which cost only £2,156; and in the same year John Dwyer, working on No. 30, was refused permission to build a "portico" (presumably a Belgravian porch) by the Board of Works. Three houses on the south side, whose fronts at least are probably all by Cundy, indicate best the dignity and severity of style of these rebuilt or refaced mansions of the mid-50's.

Two are of "white" Suffolk brick, and the third may possibly owe its all-over stucco coating to a still later refurbishing (Fig. XIV 19). They are four storeys high and equipped (I suppose by permission of the Board of Works) with conventional Belgravian porches placed below one or another of the first-storey windows. All the ground storeys are stuccoed in the usual pattern of flat horizontal rustication, while a broad vertical band of the same pattern sets off each house from its neighbors. These are possibly 18th century to the left; but the ones between the fronts that we are discussing are presumably of the 70's and 80's when far more of Mayfair was rebuilt than in earlier Victorian times.

The four windows in each front are evenly spaced and ornamented with modest architraves. The tall windows of the first storey alone have pediments; those of the third storey are square and underlined by a stringcourse. Except for the porches and a balustraded balcony continued across each façade on the line of the porch balustrade, only the cornices, with molded frieze, heavy dentil course, and modillions, provide plastic relief. On one of these houses, that near the center of the south side of the square, the balustrade is broken above the cornice by paneled blocks and a carved terminal ornament.

Such houses came close to satisfying the conventional taste of the early 20th century for Georgian sobriety, which probably explains why they have been allowed to survive through another ninety-nine years. The restraint of their design was equaled in Lord Rothschild's enormous stone-built Piccadilly mansion, beside Apsley House, which was built by C. O. Parnell a few years later; but such dignified severity was more than any but the very richest and most determined social aspirants could swallow in these midcentury years. Perhaps it was not unnatural that aristocrats (who usually remodeled their country mansions in an approximation of whatever might have been the original Late Medieval style) should have rebuilt or refaced their town houses with some suggestion of the Georgian façades they were replacing. No such discreet architectural bait, as we have seen, was being used by Freake and Elger and Jackson to tempt the upper classes generally to take the new houses in South Kensington. North of the Park, beyond Gloucester Terrace, even richer dishes were now being provided in what was soon recognized as the characteristic new residential quarter of London.

During the 50's the entire district between Gloucester Terrace in Paddington and the Kensington Park Road at the eastern edge of the Ladbroke Grove Estate filled up rapidly, mostly with terraces but partly with semidetached villas, engulfing earlier and more sporadic settlements (Fig. XIII 32). As usual it is not easy to date the individual terraces and groups of villas; I shall mention only those that were probably initiated at least before 1855. Along Porchester Terrace and Inverness Gardens much remained of a considerably older villa colony, although the modest semidetached houses on the east side of the road were now being replaced by a continuous terrace of tall row houses. Two other villa colonies, more picturesquely laid out along curving streets, were probably still being built during the 50's. One of these, Westbourne Park Villas, lay to the north along the Great Western tracks which have since absorbed the greater part of the area. Another colony constituted by Clifton and Pembridge Villas fanned out below the western end of Westbourne Grove. Many of the original small houses here have lasted into our own time. Perhaps the somewhat earlier rows of villas along Westbourne Grove itself were already giving way in the 50's to a new shopping street. In the northern half of this district, between the Westbourne Grove and the Westbourne Park rows of villas, long terraces of rather modest houses were built in the early 50's; these are of almost no visual interest but they illustrate well the considerable range of incomes for which the builders catered in this area. Many small terrace houses in the area between Brompton and Chelsea, probably somewhat later in date, are quite similar.

The most impressive parts of Paddington and Bayswater as built up in the 50's are to be found farther east in the triangular tract between Gloucester Terrace and Porchester Terrace and also in the contiguous squarish area bounded by Queen's Road on the east and by Hereford Road on the west just south of Westbourne Grove. Between the Moscow Road and the Bayswater Road (Uxbridge Road then) is a rather confused area which had been built up well before 1850, partly with modest terrace houses and partly with villas. At the core of this lies Orme Square where the earliest terraces are quite Belgravian in character and probably date from the earliest years of Victoria's reign.

In the above-mentioned triangular section to the east, near its northern apex by the Bishop's Bridge Road, is the trapezoidal Cleveland Square which must be almost exactly contemporary with the Freake-Elger development around Prince's Gate. Indeed there is a certain similarity in the planning to that of Prince's and Ennismore Gardens behind Prince's Terrace as well as to that of the so-called "gardens" in Allom's Ladbroke Grove layout which must date also from the early 50's.

The familiar London "square" has its ultimate origin in the Italian piazza, something which the first of them, Inigo Jones' Covent Garden Piazza, proves by its very name. But the surrounding Italian arcades disappeared as soon as the piazza scheme became Anglicized and domesticated. At Covent Garden the church, with its dependencies, lies on one side of the square, and a public market occupies the center. By Victorian times new churches, if built in squares at all, were generally placed in their centers amid naturalistically planted foliage—Cundy's dreary churches in Pimlico, for example, or Godwin's at the Boltons. The asymmetrical composition and inappropriately rustic materials of these edifices, however embowered

486

in trees and shrubs, make the sharpest and most unpleasant contrast with the regular design and the painted stucco or plain stock brick of the surrounding terraces—almost a caricature of *rus in urbe*. By 1850 G. E. Street was proclaiming the unsuitability of such designs and materials in towns; but after that date fewer town churches were built in squares in any event.

The best High Victorian churches of the later 50's and 60's are usually to be found in congested slum districts where they could serve a missionary purpose. London squares, although surrounded by public carriage roads, were fenced and treated as communal gardens for the use of the adjacent householders. Tenants in the grander and more pretentious contiguous streets, who also attached the name of the square to their street address for prestige's sake, had access also. Locked gates preserved the privilege of entry to those who had keys, and the care of the grounds was either a responsibility of the owner of the freehold or else rated to the surrounding householders.

Regent's Park was somewhat different because of its great size and the fact that the related terraces were set well back from the surrounding carriage road; a large part of the park itself was open to the public, moreover. A new formula for communal gardens, closely related to the handling of the front gardens of the Regent's Park terraces, was already established by the beginning of the Victorian Age. At least it had by then been most splendidly illustrated in Crake's Hyde Park Gardens, a grandiose terrace designed in 1836. There the houses were set back from the Park even farther than the Regent's Park terraces and entered from a carriage road on the north side. Therefore the planted area between the "rears" of the houses and the Uxbridge (now Bayswater) Road along the Park is directly accessible from the houses without crossing any public street. Something rather similar but less expansive was done in front of the houses in Westbourne Terrace.

This new urban planning formula may best be called simply "gardens," although that pleasant name was soon also used euphemistically for terrace-lined streets of a quite conventional order with no open space at all. "Gardens" are most brilliantly illustrated in Allom's layout at Ladbroke Grove in the early 50's; but there the formula is almost semi-suburban. It was behind Prince's Terrace in South Kensington and more boldly still in the newer parts of Paddington that the "gardens" layout was most generously exploited in a thoroughly urban area at this time.

Between Cleveland Square and Cleveland Gardens (which lie to the north) a tremendous block of eight five-storey houses stands free and actually divides the square from the gardens. This block was begun shortly after 1851. On the north or entrance front the houses are entered through coupled porches set against the three-storey projections which give a massively plastic interest to that elevation (Fig. XIV 20). Otherwise the treatment of these north or entrance façades is without much interest except for the marked widening of the edicular first-storey windows of the central houses. This is a sensible functional modification of a familiar motif; but it throws the Barryesque formula of the design rather out of kilter. On the other side—the "garden" (but not the Gardens) front—the big oblong block is broken only by the projection of the end houses (Fig. XIV 22). But on this side the ground storey of each house communicates directly with open but private gardens, a considerable strip across the northern half of the square being subdivided into plots that belong strictly to the individual tenants. The rest, which is communal but not public, is not cut off by any drive.

Conventional terraces face Cleveland Gardens across carriage roads on the north, east, and west. Those on the east continue into Devonshire and Craven Terraces which run parallel with Gloucester Terrace south to the Park. In the broader part of the triangle south of Cleveland Square, Queen's Gardens and Craven Hill Gardens are less ample versions of the "gardens" formula. The different terraces of this district vary slightly in design according to their date; but they vary rather more in quality of execution, definitely deteriorating where carcasses were taken over by later builders and finished sloppily to make a quick or forced sale. The terraces in Prince's Square and Leinster Square, a little farther west, with their entrances on the street between the two and their private gardens opening directly onto the open squares on either side, are excellent examples of the gardens layout too. They date definitely from 1856–58 which would be just after the development to the east of them was well under way if by no means entirely completed.

In Devonshire Terrace, just south of Cleveland Square, are some rather interesting houses forming a quadrant. These are probably of about 1855. Narrower than most, their very large windows are set close together in an approximation of the open design that was developing in the mid-50's in commercial architecture, but the treatment here is rectangular and trabeated rather than arcaded. A similar parallel to the increased fenestration of commercial façades, superbly executed in Bath stone in this case and continuously arcaded above the ground storey, may be seen in the terrace at right angles to the Royal Promenade in Victoria Square, Clifton (Fig. XIV 23). The single-pane sash and the bands of rustication separating the houses, as well as the fussy elaboration of the attics over the deep-bracketed main cornice, place these houses at least as late as the mid-50's. But the detail is on the whole so suave and crisply cut, for all the fantasy of the iron balcony railings, that this terrace provides a by no means unworthy complement to the still almost Georgian dignity and severity of the Royal Promenade.

488

A later and even more striking example of all-over articulation, used on a terrace of very modest two-storey houses in Strathbungo, a southern suburb of Glasgow, brings into the housing story the name of the one architect of really high distinction who seems to have designed any terrace housing in the 50's. Moray Place by Alexander Thomson is with little question the finest of 19th-century terraces, both in design and in execution, and one of the world's most superb pieces of design based on Greek precedent (Fig. XIV 21). The end houses project slightly and are articulated by two-storey antae carrying a pediment. On the ground storey in each of these houses a subsidiary order flanks the door and the two identical windows. Half-antae carry an entablature with an usually broad frieze and a very slightly project-ing cornice. Above this a low blocking course supports the sills of the first-storey windows which occupy the full width of the bays. This complete articulation, as of a peristyle glazed, is carried one bay around the ends.

In the eight houses between, the ground-storey piers are somewhat broader and without any differentiation from the plain flat ashlar that is carried across over the doors and windows. In the jambs of the openings, however, thin slices of antae are placed, echoing with extreme subtlety the half-antae on the end houses. The plain ashlar of the ground-storey wall terminates in a fascia at first-storey sill level. In the first storey a range of antae of the same size as those below forms a continuous "colonnade," six antae to a house, the narrow spaces between being completely filled with large-paned casements. The terminal entablature is identical with that on the end blocks. All the moldings are simplified and, as it were, metallized. The sharp preci-sion is that of Greek marble of the 5th century—it may even be considered *too* mechanically perfect by some.

The ornament is almost all incised, largely linear palmettos on the broad friezes and smaller ones on the cavetto molding which appears over the top cornice on the end houses only. Tiny rosettes line the architraves; and on the face of the first-storey sills throughout the central portion of the ter-race is cut a geometrical key pattern. The ground-storey half-antae have no ornament in their capital zone, although two sharply cut lines define its depth. The two-storey antae have incised palmetto bands under a vertically fluted necking and also a key pattern just below the abacus. A similar pat-tern decorates the top of the second-storey antae on the houses between.

The refinement of Thomson's study of detail was not restricted to the stonework. The single-pane casements in their delicate, presumably metal, frames under a plate-glass transom have the machine-made elegance of the mid-20th century. The five lampposts, supporting plain round gas globes before each of the front doors—the only accent that picks out the actual entrances in the range of apparently identical openings—have the attenuated distinction, and even the elaboration, of ancient bronze lighting standards.

Thomson moved into one of the end houses of the Moray Place terrace in time to be listed there in the Post Office Street Directory of 1861. Two other housing schemes of his are almost certainly earlier, although all post-date the initiation of his own practice with his brother. This occurred about 1856 after he left the office of John Baird with whom he had previously worked. Walmer Crescent, opened in 1858–59, is fine but not so fine as Moray Place (Fig. XIV 24) despite the additional interest of the concave plan and the two-storey projections between the houses. Queen's Park Terrace in Eglinton Street was begun the year Walmer Crescent was completed, just before Moray Place (Fig. XIV 25). Flatted in the habitual Scottish manner, this is wilder in its details than the other terraces and closer to Thomson's commercial work.

I owe the precise dating of Thomson's terraces of the late 50's to Graham C. Law, whose Cambridge dissertation of 1950 on Thomson represents a remarkable piecing together of one of the greatest of Victorian architects' work. (See *Architectural Review, 115,* 307–16.) Thomson's villas of the 50's are also extremely interesting but can unfortunately find no place here.

Late though they are, Thomson's terraces are almost more Late Georgian than Early Victorian—or, according to a different interpretation of his highly personal style, they might be considered High Victorian, like his fine St. Vincent Street and Queen's Park churches which date respectively from the late 50's and the mid-60's. With them this chapter may appropriately conclude—on a high point rather than a low one. The actual material provides no obvious stopping place short of the late 60's. Thomson's terraces exaggerate a general truth that has already been stated more than once: The greatest virtues of Victorian urban housing, down through the 50's, lay in the continuation and development of Georgian ideas, not in any real innovations. Yet the planning formula I have referred to as the "gardens" layout would barely be recognized for what it is but for its extensive exploitation in the early 50's. Nor, in the Late Georgian period when so much serious architecture was Grecian, did architects often approach the perfection of Moray Place, Strathbungo.

The most significant new beginning in the Early Victorian period was the introduction of flatted housing, but that was barely under way when the period came to an end. From a field of construction so laggard and devoid of positive development as Early Victorian housing it is exciting to turn to one in which almost everything was new: needs, materials, and even methods of designing. (Novelty of design, however, was often rather inadvertent on the part of the responsible engineers and architects.) But in our enthusiasm for Early Victorian metal construction we should not lose sight of the lessons, ambiguous though they are, of the housing story over the years 1835–55; nor, under the glittering glass and iron roofs of the new "ferrovitreous style," should we forget the still more metallic precision and elegance of "Greek" Thomson's Glasgow terraces. Housing *can* be distinguished in design even if it rarely was in Early Victorian Britain.

CHAPTER XV: EARLY RAILWAY STATIONS

AND OTHER IRON CONSTRUCTION

The general history of the development of iron construction is long and complex; moreover, it is essentially international. Even though the achievements of Early Victorian England provide a sort of culmination in the story of the use of iron in building—at least before the introduction of structural steel in place of cast and wrought iron around 1860—there was on the Continent and in America in the same period important activity of comparable scale and of equal technical ingenuity. In the 40's the early wire-cable suspension bridges of J. A. Roebling (1806–1869) across the Monongahela at Pittsburgh and the Ohio at Cincinnati illustrated a transatlantic boldness of attack exceeding that of contemporary English engineers. James Bogardus in his own building in New York first showed as early as 1848–50 that permanent urban structures could be successfully built of cast iron both inside and out. Likewise, in assessing the achievements of this period, many historians have considered Duquesney's Gare de l'Est in Paris superior to its great English rivals. Less justifiably, the magnificent domed court of Bunning's Coal Exchange has been ignored by most writers in favor of Henri Labrouste's Bibliothèque Sainte Géneviève. But the London exchange is, I believe, the foremost early example of the frank and elegant use of a coherent system of iron structural elements inside a masonry shell (Figs. X 14–24).

Major English achievement in iron structures did not begin with the Victorian Age. Many of the principal English contributions to the history of iron construction had been made in Georgian times. The first iron bridge was built in Coalbrookdale, Shropshire, in the 1770's, nominally to the design of Thomas Farnolls Pritchard (d. 1777), an architect, although the ironmaster Abraham Darby III was himself probably most responsible for the forms the iron elements took. (The village today is appropriately called Iron Bridge.) William Strutt, a millwright, first introduced a complete interior skeleton of iron in a calico mill in Derby in 1792, and shortly thereafter in another mill in Belper. Thomas Telford, a civil engineer who had been trained as an architect under Sir William Chambers, slung the suspension bridge which is still the longest in the British Isles across the Menai Strait in 1819–24. Well before the 18th century was over architects and builders were using cast-iron columns freely and frankly in various sorts of buildings. By the time of the Menai Bridge such columns were rising tree-like, crowned with naturalistic copper palm leaves, in the kitchen of the Regent's Pavilion in Brighton. They also appear, with less flamboyant embellishments, in the middle of several of the palatial reception rooms there, while the whole staircase is of iron in an openwork Chinese design of great elegance and ingenuity. In John Nash's other most famous works, the Regent Street Quadrant and Carlton House Terrace, the Doric columns of the colonnades consisted of heavy fluted cylinders of iron.

A still more notable development in the use of iron in internal construction ensued after the Victorian Age began. In Chapter XII the influence of the increasing use of interior iron supports on the planning and even the design of commercial buildings was discussed. Of such "invisible" technical developments the present chapter will have little to say. Some of the relevant facts have been given already in dealing with various building types; detailed development of the story can be left to Turpin C. Bannister's more technical treatment of the subject published in the *Architectural Review, 107*, 231–246. Some day this will doubtless be carried forward further into the Victorian Age.

In the chapters on public architecture some important museums, markets, and exchanges have been discussed in which iron and glass roofs cover large interior areas. As these are examples of mixed construction, their purpose is more significant than the particular materials used. In several senses railway stations are also public buildings even though the Victorian public paid for them not on the rates but as subscribers to railway shares. Stations are also usually of mixed construction; but the "sheds," the vast iron and glass roofs over the platforms and the tracks, are much the most important part. A discussion of the development of this completely new sort of edifice may properly emphasize these sheds rather than the contiguous or surrounding masonry elements of station complexes. Nevertheless, railway stations have a character of relative permanence, as well as intentions of monumentality, that contrasts rather sharply with the two chief sorts of Victorian buildings, the great greenhouses and the "Crystal Palaces" which made even more consistent and exclusive use of metal and glass.

Enormous conservatories were built in considerable numbers to house in tropical comfort heterogeneous horticultural collections of plants brought back from warmer climes. These collections illustrate a Victorian passion, at once aesthetic and scientific, deriving from the earlier Romantic cult of Nature. The small greenhouses of Georgian times which Loudon illustrated in such profusion could hardly have provided for the extensive and exotic new museums of plant material gathered together in the 30's and 40's. In even larger edifices of glass and iron still more fantastic man-made flora were displayed at expositions. The vast greenhouses were often destroyed once the passionate Victorian enthusiasm for horticulture began to pass. Of the exposition buildings few were intended to be permanent even though the most important lasted—in a revised version—down to 1936. The important distinction about these structures, however—which is in fact more or less true for any edifices of unwelded metal construction—is that they were demountable or, more significantly, "remountable." The rebuilding of the original Crystal Palace at Sydenham, with the same materials although to a modified design, first made this possibility dramatically evident.

Since British railway stations almost always consisted, except for the sheds, of solid structures of brick or stone masonry, they were not ordinarily demountable; yet (to use a more familiar present-day word) the sheds themselves were important early examples of "prefabrication." Some railway stations, moreover, were prefabricated as a whole for export. Made all but entirely of metal and wood, these were disassembled and shipped to their ultimate destinations overseas after first being assembled at the manufacturer's plant in Britain. But complete railway stations were exceptional in the Victorian manufacture of prefabricated structures. As with present-day prefabrication, the making of houses preoccupied industrialists. Lighthouses, warehouses, and churches were also important in the total production; and at least one complete theater was shipped to Australia.

This chapter will be concerned chiefly with railway stations, with the major structures of glass and iron, and with various sorts of prefabricated buildings. The development of railway stations provides the central theme because of the wealth of extant examples, and also because so many of these examples are of a quality comparable to all but the finest completely iron and glass edifices. Of the great early conservatories and exhibition buildings, moreover, only one really important example is still extant. Some who make use of Victorian stations, concerned not with history but with their own present comfort, may regret the fact of their survival; but the continued existence of these typically Victorian monuments is exceedingly gratifying to most students of architecture, at least when they are not traveling in Britain! Suggestions made to the architects and public relations officers of the "big four" railways, before nationalization, that the preservation, repair, and maintenance of these major 19th-century structures was a cultural duty were met somewhat as 18th-century deans must have responded to early "Gothick" enthusiasts. Victorian stations are preserved through necessity, not through choice.

An extensive rebuilding campaign, such as Italy has seen, appears to be ever more distant, though minor emendations will doubtless be made in much the same way that Decorated choirs, Perpendicular clerestoreys, and Georgian reredoses were added to Norman cathedrals. Stations are the real "cathedrals of the 19th century," a claim made for them at least as early as 1875 (*Building News, 29,* 133). (I owe this reference to Carroll Meeks, from whose Harvard Ph.D. dissertation "The Architectural Development of the American Railroad Station" [1948] I have been most generously allowed to take much of the factual material in this chapter.) In the meantime an awareness of the remarkable intrinsic interest of these structures does ease the discomfort of using them. Some, indeed, stepping from their train at King's Cross or Paddington across the narrow arrival platform directly into a taxicab, may in any event remember the unconscionable amount of time consumed in reaching public vehicles amid the 20th-century splendors of New York's two terminals.

Irony aside, the great Victorian stations of Britain, now carrying loads of traffic infinitely greater than those for which they were designed, are really not yet obsolete. Thus they illustrate the extraordinary architectural abilities of the various teams of engineers and architects who built them. As with Greek temples or medieval churches, the particular buildings of any period which once fulfilled their original function with real humanistic success seem assured of an almost indefinite afterlife. There are other Victorian buildings that have claims to cultural distinction of one sort or another; but the great railway stations have the surest, the broadest, and, even into the foreseeable future, perhaps the most enduring.

The 19th century was a Railway Age; it was also an Age of Iron. Railways and iron, moreover, are indissolubly linked—even in our present days of aluminum rolling stock. At the opening of Victoria's reign Railway Age and Iron Age came together to maturity. The railways, as they expanded, demanded ever more and more iron for their rails, their locomotives, and their sheds, thus continually stimulating iron production. And it was the railways that brought together the raw materials for that production, moved the semifinished products from plant to plant, and finally distributed iron members of all sorts—including various large-scale building components—all over Britain. With road and canal transport wonders had already been achieved by the iron industry in Georgian times, but the volume of production increased by leaps and bounds with the advance of the railways.

The very first railways, in actual fact, had been at the pitheads in the ore fields and even inside the mines themselves, just as the first steam engines had been designed to pump water out of the deeper workings. But the fully developed sort of railway that required a real "station," the passenger railway, appeared only in the 1830's. Nothing but fragments of stations survive, moreover, that are pre-Victorian in date. It may provide a useful frame of reference for the general story which will follow to summarize here the successive station accommodations of the earliest railway to enter Liverpool, the Liverpool and Manchester, which is in any event generally considered the first true railway in the later sense of the word.

The original terminus of this line was built well east of the town at Crown Street and opened with the line itself in 1830. Because the hills surrounding Liverpool were beyond the power of early locomotives to climb, the line at first had had to end some distance from the heart of the early 19th-century city. Passengers were transported from Dale Street to Crown Street by omnibus with a relative expenditure of time comparable to that now lost in reaching airports outside large cities. A tunnel under the hills to carry the rails farther into the town was begun in 1832. Crown Street was finally succeeded in 1836 by the first of a succession of terminals at Lime Street considerably nearer downtown Liverpool. Of its Manchester opposite number, Liverpool Street Station, a considerable portion remains although Crown Street itself is entirely gone.

The Crown Street Station in 1830 consisted of a very plain two-storey structure in the Late Georgian vernacular. This was a narrow oblong in plan and contained waiting rooms, ticket offices, and so forth, with offices or dwelling accommodations above for the station officials. This brief description is based on a reconstruction of the original plan worked out by Carroll Meeks. He believes that John Foster II supplied the design, at least for the masonry portion of the station. It seems to me more likely that George Stephenson (1781–1848), the chief engineer of the railway, or Joseph Locke (1805–1860), the resident engineer of the line, worked without benefit of architect. (Christian Barman in *Railway Architecture* [1950] assigned the station to another architect named James Franklin, but none of his reviewers has accepted the attribution.)

The entrance to Crown Street was from a vehicle court under a marquee at the narrow end of the masonry building. Along the building's right-hand side a columned porch covered the single platform. To that platform both departing and arriving trains were brought by shunting them between parallel pairs of rails, the locomotives being shifted on turntables at the city end of the station.

Over the three tracks was the "shed" consisting of a low gable roof supported on wooden queenpost trusses with a span of about 35 feet. On the station side the trusses rested on the columns of the porch; on the other side was a continuous wall pierced with unglazed openings to let in light. There was apparently no glass at all in the shed roof. Although the porch columns were almost certainly of iron, the designer (whether architect or

496

engineer) made considerably less effective and conspicuous use of the new material than had already been done in various buildings by Nash and others. It may be assumed that a fence with entrance gates preceded the vehicle court. In this modest complex most of the elements, complete or in embryo, of which Victorian stations were to be composed can already be distinguished.

At the first Lime Street Station, completed by John Cunningham (1799–1873) just before the beginning of the new reign, the enclosed block, though longer, was as simple in design as at Crown Street. But the shed was much broader (55 feet) to shelter five lines of track instead of three; moreover, a second covered platform, for arriving trains, paralleled on the far side of the shed the one that ran along the solid block, the latter being reserved for departing trains (Fig. XV 1). On both sides of the shed the diagonally braced queenpost wooden trusses were supported on cast-iron "arcades." A third arcade was carried along the far side of the arrival platform toward a second vehicle court from which arriving passengers left the station. Segmental openwork "spandrels" linked the iron columns to the longitudinal beams above. These elements formed the chief decorative embellishment of the shed which thus resembled a rather clumsy Regency verandah; the spandrels also served a practical purpose as braces between the supports. With the greater width of the shed, some glass was now introduced in the roof.

Less important functionally than the addition of the second or arrival platform, but constituting the first attempt at monumental expression in a railway station, was the two-storey masonry screen which masked the whole station complex from Lime Street. This screen was an elaboration, not by Cunningham but by John Foster (then architect to the Liverpool Corporation), of the familiar Roman triumphal-arch motif (Fig. XV 3). Toward the cost of this symbolic gateway to their town the Liverpool authorities contributed £2,000 and lent their official architect. The gesture was a worthy tribute to the railway from a rich and architecturally ambitious seaport much of whose business was coming in over the new rails from the cotton firms of Manchester. Various tall arches provided entrances to the station behind and also to Lord Nelson Street on which the station block actually faced; in the solid portions of the screen were the offices of the company. Thus the screen was more than a mere magnification of the presumptive courtyard fence at Crown Street; it represented a fairly early example of monumental commercial architecture as well as a conspicuous urban ornament paid for in large part by the municipal authorities.

By 1846 the number of miles of railway in Great Britain had risen to 2,236; traffic increased more than commensurably and Lime Street I had become inadequate when it was but a decade old. (Because of the frequent practice of building successive stations in the same location it is convenient to distinguish them by Roman numerals.) Lime Street II, begun in 1846 for the North-Western Railway as successor to the Liverpool and Manchester, was not entirely new since the original honorific screen across the front was retained. But the station block behind was much enlarged at a cost of £30,-000, receiving from the hands of William Tite an impressive if rather dull five-part academic façade toward Lord Nelson Street of Lancashire red brick and Darley Dale stone (Fig. XV 4). Tite was by this time one of the chief railway architects not only of England but of France as well and the usual collaborator of the engineer Joseph Locke in both countries; Locke as engineer-in-chief of the North-Western was responsible for the cutting back of the tunnel face in order to permit enlarging the station and also for the general disposition of the tracks. The long central section of this new block carried an attic which was entirely occupied by the ticket department; this suggests that the need for additional office accommodation was as important a reason for rebuilding the station as the increasing flow of passengers. But for the patrons' comfort a continuous covered porch was now provided facing the vehicle court off Lord Nelson Street (Fig. XV 4). The new work was done piecemeal, the station remaining in use during the four-year campaign of reconstruction.

The really extraordinary feature of Lime Street II was its shed. This was designed and executed by Richard Turner, a contracting engineer who maintained the Hammersmith Works in Dublin (rather than by Locke). Its special character was theoretically protected by Turner's patents. The new shed, not actually begun in its final form until 1849, was 360 feet long and 153½ feet in span (Fig. XV 2). Seventeen segmental girders of wrought iron, set 21½ feet center to center, rested on the walls of the station block on one side and on cast-iron Doric columns 2¼ feet in diameter on the other. The style of the supports was doubtless a conservative idea of Tite's but they were connected by the usual segmental "spandrels" of openwork iron as in the earlier shed. The sickle-like girders were trussed vertically by radiating struts of wrought iron tied by connecting bars which were attached also to the girder ends. Horizontally there were frequent purlins, curving braces, and additional tie-rods; these formed a rigid system from one end of the shed to the other. Thus, under the vault-shaped shell of the shed roof supported by its recurrent sickle-truss principals, the upper volume of the interior was crisscrossed with tenuous lines of force. They adumbrated, it would seem, a new type of spacial definition as yet beyond the aesthetic comprehension of either engineer or architect.

The outer surface of the shed roof was of galvanized corrugated iron, effectively a new material at this date, with three ranges of openings extending the full length of the station. These slots were placed asymmetrically in the width of the roof, but they all extended the full length of the shed. The long openings were filled with rolled plate glass in panes 12½ feet long, a product which at this dimension was almost as new a material as the metal sheeting around it. There were some 700 tons of iron in the shed; all of it was wrought, moreover, except for the cast-iron columns. The chief proponent of the use of wrought iron in construction, the great Manchester millwright Sir William Fairbairn, had been Turner's principal consultant on the job. Crown Street may have been either architect or engineer designed; at Lime Street I the architects still made the braver show; but now the engineering contractor Turner and the consulting engineer Fairbairn put the architect Tite completely in the shade.

After its enlargement in 1846–51, in the middle of what Carroll Meeks has called the "classical stage" of railway station development, Lime Street apparently remained adequate for fifteen years and more. The shed of the next station in succession (Lime Street III), begun in 1867, was designed by the engineers William Baker and F. Stevenson and executed over several years by George Thomson and Company. Although it was the largest in the world upon its completion, this shed was hardly more mature in its aesthetic conception than Turner's had been when originally designed some twenty years earlier. As some technical historians forget, bigger in the 19th century was not always better; by the late 60's, moreover, the great Victorian epoch of station building was really over. A new element in the station complex appeared at Lime Street III for the first time in Liverpool, the vast hotel by Alfred Waterhouse (1830–1905) which replaced Foster's arched screen in front of the shed. This formed the visible monumental front of the whole complex when it was completed in the early 70's and still does so today to the detriment of its handsome neighbor St. George's Hall.

The incorporation of a hotel in the characteristic English railway station grouping seems to have begun at York almost thirty years earlier. There G. T. Andrews modified in 1842 the original design for "King" Hudson's home station in order to provide hotel facilities above the restaurant accommodations (Fig. XV 23). These were behind the cross platform which there connected the arrival and departure platforms on either side. In the early 60's at E. M. Barry's London terminals at Charing Cross and Cannon Street the hotel blocks finally became the main façades of the stations; more than a decade before this they were already more prominent than the station facilities behind them.

Thus the history of one major Liverpool terminus over forty years epitomizes the course of pre-Victorian and Victorian station design on a single site. At no stage, however, can it be considered to have had positive virtues beyond undoubted priority at Crown Street, again at Lime Street I, and in the size of the sheds, at least, at Lime Street II and III. Most other great Victorian stations are finer in design.

Of the next important station to be built after Lime Street I, the London and Birmingham London terminus near Euston Square, somewhat more remains than of its Liverpool contemporary. The "Euston Arch" still stands, though now almost entirely hidden from Euston Square by a hotel block of the date of Waterhouse's at Lime Street; indeed, before nationalization J. L. Martin, then architect of the London, Midland, and Scottish Railway, assured me that it was the intention of his board to retain permanently this early and famous symbol of the railway station as a city gate (Fig. XV 6). Philip Hardwick's propylaeum (to give it a more accurate name than arch) seems still to stand as one of the most appropriate entrances to the Victorian Age, having been effectively completed in 1837 just as the new reign began. Yet its precise Doric detail was already considerably more retardataire than was the Perpendicular detail of Barry's and Pugin's contemporary designs for the New Palace.

After deciding to bring the rails farther in toward town than Chalk Farm, out to which trains were hauled by stationary engines up a considerable slope for some years after the line first opened, the London and Birmingham Railway acquired a large tract of land behind Euston Square. With Hardwick as collaborating architect, George Stephenson's son Robert Stephenson, the chief engineer of the railway, planned in 1835 a remarkable double station with a central vehicle court approached through a freestanding propylaeum (Fig. XV 7). The Great Western Railway directors were invited to take over the western half of the proposed group of structures; as they preferred to bring their line into London in the residential West, only the eastern half of Euston I was ever built. It was opened with the Birmingham line itself in 1837, although the complex was not really quite completed until 1839.

On either side of the Arch stone gate lodges separate subsidiary entrances, thus forming a more open screen than at Liverpool but with very handsome iron railings and gates set between the stone blocks. To the right of the central passageway one gate led into a "carriage dock." There, at the end of the tracks, passengers could disembark from their own private means of locomotion; these were then loaded—carriages and horses too—onto special wagons attached to the train. (This aristocratic practice did not long survive here or at other early stations; but it is an interesting parallel to modern "Drive-Ur-Self" arrangements at airports.) Farther to the right another gate provided a "Way Out" from the departure platform.

The stuccoed office block of the station was as plain as at Lime Street I, but it did have a one-storey colonnaded porch along the court side like Tite's at Lime Street II. The 200-foot double shed was more ambitious than at Liverpool, however, the departure and arrival tracks being subdivided by a central range of cast-iron columns and the ranges of trusses, also of metal, each having a span of 40 feet (Fig. XV 8). The ties of the trusses were of course mere wrought-iron bars, but the cast-iron supports were rather elegantly detailed, with tiny molded capitals below the segmental-arched longitudinal members. The latter were filled with ranges of diminishing circles, a quite functional sort of ornament for openwork members cast in metal. Between these light "arcades," in the best manner of the Regency ironworkers, and the massive Doric Arch there was no visual relationship whatsoever; even the long solid block, with its conventional porch along the vehicle court, and the sheds are related only by their rather precarious physical attachment. It would appear, therefore, that Hardwick's responsibility as architect was largely restricted to the entrance screen, with probably some say in the detailing of the colonnaded porch and the trim of the station block.

Euston roused the wrath of Pugin. In his *Apology for the Revival of Christian Architecture in England* (1843) he parodied it on Plate III, offering in contrast two very solid designs of his own for segmental-pointed railway bridges of stone with associated waystations covered by simple timber sheds (Fig. XV 9). For the sum (about £30,000) that was spent on that "piece of Brobdingnagian absurdity"—the Euston Arch—Pugin thought the company might have built "a first-rate station, replete with convenience . . . which would have been really grand from its simplicity." That was a particularly unjust criticism; for nothing could have been much simpler than the office block and the train sheds of Euston I; if they lacked grandeur, the Arch certainly still has it.

The other terminus of the London and Birmingham Railway, also by Stephenson and Hardwick, was at Curzon Street in Birmingham. This was so far out from the center of the city that it took a half-hour to reach it by omnibus, or so contemporaries complained. (I should say that I had made it on foot in rather less, but doubtless the intervening streets are straighter today.) Curzon Street was very similar to Euston in its layout. The arch was really an arch, this time with engaged columns. But it also contained company offices in the upper storey, like the screen at Lime Street I, and public refreshment rooms below, the first to be provided at any station. The colonnaded porch on the main station block curved gracefully around the narrow end so that there was less disparity between the pompous architectural symbol in front and the utilitarian conveniences behind than at Euston. The metal trusses of the shed had a span of 57 feet, a considerable advance beyond those of Euston although they were planned at much the same time.

Another London station, following immediately after Euston in 1837–38 just at the opening of the new reign, is that erected by the London and Southampton Railway in Nine Elms Rd., Vauxhall, south of the river. This is now the Transport Museum of the British Railways, appropriately enough, but is still usually called Nine Elms. The architect was William Tite who was already titular architect of several British railways and also of the Le Havre-Paris line in France. These new semibureaucratic appointments as railway architects were for a time as lucrative as the surveyorships of the City livery companies and the great urban landowners' estates; the opportunities they offered for new construction, moreover, were quite comparable to the official diocesan appointments held by various leading church architects of the day.

Nine Elms is conceptually closer knit than earlier English stations; just possibly it was influenced by the two early Paris stations by Eugène Flachat (1802–1873), at the Place de l'Europe and at St. Lazare, completed in 1837. An arcaded porch on the front, recessed between two small end blocks, forms the entrance to the waiting rooms and ticket offices (Fig. XV 10). Beyond these a cross platform for the first time links the departure platform on the left and the arrival platform on the right; while from the latter there is direct access to a side vehicle court. The wooden-roofed shed is wide and low, covering four lines of track; the flanking sections over the narrow side platforms form, as it were, flat-roofed "aisles." The cast-iron supports have curious undulating foliage above the little scrolled brackets which terminate the circle-pierced spandrels. Was this not very happy attempt at decorative innovation due to Tite or to Locke, the engineer of the line? It is not easy to resolve the relationship of the two; for the collaboration seems to have been closer than at other early stations. The contemporary Tite-Locke station at Southampton was quite similar, larger but rather less interesting.

As Nine Elms and Southampton were being completed the first really great Victorian station was begun, the Trijunct at Derby for the North Midland Railway and two other lines. Here the more considerable credit must certainly go to the architect, although he worked under the direction of Robert Stephenson. Francis Thompson of Derby is less well known than that prominent City figure, Tite, but a far better architect. He was once as famous, moreover, for his modest rural stations, hardly more than gatekeepers' lodges, as for his larger works (Fig. XV 13–14). Later he was also to be the worthy collaborator of Robert Stephenson on the most distinguished of Early Victorian bridges, the Britannia Tubular Bridge across the Menai Strait (Figs. XV 34, 36–38).

Derby Trijunct, like Crown Street, Liverpool, had only one platform; more accurately the arrival platforms were parallel to but set back from the departure platform. Terminal spur tracks came in from both ends and passengers could be unloaded from two different lines at once. The total length of the office block in front of the departure platform, with the screen walls at its ends masking the arrival platforms, was 1,050 feet. With this novel layout only narrow sheds were needed to protect the arrival tracks; but extending out from the departure platform were three wider sheds, the central one having a span of 56 feet, nearly equal to those at Curzon Street.

All the shed construction was of metal except for the arch-pierced brick wall on the far side which echoed the inner station wall opposite (Fig. XV 12). The cast-iron columns were extremely slim and elegant, their reeded surfaces bound with spiral bands. Above the delicate molded capitals paneled members supported longitudinal iron beams. These had the character of architraves, with no bracing "spandrels"; their continuity, however, was broken above each support by a narrow armorial panel masking the joint. As one sees this shed in a contemporary print, with the light streaming down from the broad glass panels at the apex of the roofs, the tie-rod trusses appear so airy in their linear pattern and the slender members of the substructure are so cleanly rectilinear that it seems as though Thompson or Stephenson had at least glimpsed the aesthetic possibilities of a new sort of enclosed space. The spacial volumes are not defined, except along the masonry side walls, by solid boundaries at all but merely by intersecting lines of force that provide a system of three-dimensional co-ordinates. Such an effect was hardly to be recognized as visually significant before the 20's of the present century.

The masonry portions of the station were almost as direct and elegant in expression as the metalwork of the shed (Fig. XV 11). The materials were deep red Derby brick with finely cut trim of Darley Dale or some other Derbyshire gritstone. The compositional interest of the almost endless façade was provided by the careful phrasing of the openings, arched or trabeated, in the main block. The projections of various sections forward from the rear plane of the long screen walls at the ends, as also the raising and lowering of the parapet, created a considerable degree of orderly variety in the composition. Above the tall, boldly projecting central block, and elsewhere at intervals, the skyline was accented with superbly carved trophies and armorial achievements. Enough of the original wall remains to the right of the later station to reveal the quality of Thompson's work. It is certainly comparable to that of the best engineering-architecture in masonry produced during the previous half-century.

Across the road from the station there stands, practically intact, another edifice of considerable historical importance (Fig. XV 11). Because of the many lines of track of the three separate railways that joined here, Derby

Trijunct is located unusually far—even today—from the business part of the city. The North Midland therefore built, very close to their station but not joined to it or even in axial relationship with it, a fine new hotel. This is still in its modest way one of the British Railways' show places, familiar to those who visit the town from all over the world on Rolls Royce engine business. Rather charming murals of Queen Victoria's visit to Chatsworth in 1843 were added in a prewar redecoration of the dining room. The two three-storey blocks of the hotel, once linked only on the ground storey, were later joined together through their full height. Built of fine red brick like the station, these blocks have little embellishment beyond their admirable proportions and the firm cutting of the stringcourses and other moldings of gritstone. Stylistically the hotel, like the station, is still Late Georgian in character. But the idea of the hotel as part of the English Victorian station complex was first realized here. The Curzon Street arch was early referred to as a railway tavern and even known as the Queen's Hotel; but it seems unlikely that it had complete hotel accommodations before the side wing was added in 1840 by Robert Benson Dockray (1811–1871), the engineer of the line. Of course the hotel was not yet incorporated physically with the principal structure at Derby, as it was to be a year or two later at York, but it is in itself a quite considerable adjunct.

At the same time at Derby the monumental all-stone Royal Hotel was rising to the designs of Richard Wallace, right in the center of the city. This is part of an ambitious group including an Athenaeum, the post office, and a bank, all rather in the manner of Dobson's Newcastle work. Neither of these new Derby hotels compares in pretension with the principal resort hotels of the late 30's. The Queen's at Leamington by the Jearrads (1837), for example, which has already been mentioned, has a three-storey pedimented portico above an arched base, like a distended version of a neo-Palladian mansion (Fig. XV 18). The Great Western Hotel in Hotwells Road at Bristol by R. S. Pope (1839) has crisper Classical detail and a more plastic mass composition with superposed porticoes and end pavilions (Fig. XV 19). The two Derby hotels are at least more forward looking in their respective locations and less pompous in their external embellishment, if equally conservative in style.

In 1842 Francis Thompson brought out a book of designs for *Railway Stations*—or is *supposed* to have done so, since no one in the present century has been able to locate a copy. Six of these designs, including several executed along the North Midland line, were so much admired by J. C. Loudon that he republished four of them the same year in the Supplement to the new edition of his *Encyclopedia of Cottage, Farm and Villa Architecture and Furniture*. (Curiously enough, he modified their plans in such a way that they might serve as models for ordinary suburban villas.) Those at Wingfield and at Belper are symmetrical, the one a stripped Grecian, the other more Italianate, but both in the finest sort of post-Regency vernacular (Fig. XV 13). The Eckington Station, which had an asymmetrical L-shaped plan and a round entrance tower at the corner set back between the two main blocks, was rather more advanced in its Italian Villa way. That at Ambergate was elaborately Jacobethan (Fig. XV 14). For a very long time many rural stations were conceived more as dwellings for the crossing keeper than as accommodations for the public. In Loudon's Supplement drawings for a gate lodge of Tudor design at Ravenworth Castle designed by the Hon. Henry Thomas Liddell, who also completed his father's castle (as we have seen), precede the Thompson stations; immediately after them come Wyatville's gate lodges at Chatsworth, one an Italian Villa, the other half timbered. A railway crossing-keeper was, in the estimation of the period, a special sort of lodgekeeper, working for a company instead of a landowner and controlling mechanical instead of horse-drawn traffic.

Neo-Tudor models, such as were so profusely offered by Late Georgian architects in their villa and cottage books and later anthologized by Loudon, soon became more popular than Thompson's simpler and more original Italian Villas. Even for larger stations Tudor or Italian Villa styling often took the place after 1840 of the Grecian mode of Euston and the Late Georgian functionalism of Derby Trijunct. Moreover, Late Gothic ideas influenced the structure as well as the design of shed roofs in several important stations of the early 40's. This picturesque eclecticism in the design of railway structures was as much due to the taste of the regular engineers of the railways as to that of the architects who were sometimes, but by no means always, employed.

The brilliant and opinionated engineer of the Great Western Railway, I. K. Brunel, had won the competition for the bridge at Clifton across the 250-foot-deep gorge, downstream from Bristol, in 1829. His project was for a bridge in a single 700-foot span on the chain-suspension principle, supported by piers in the form of enormous Egyptian pylons. Construction began in 1837 after considerable delay and was very discontinuous. Brunel's Egyptian cavetto cornices now crown irregularly battered piers of Pennant stone originally intended to be faced with iron; while the arches that cut through them are of a steep catenary curve, presumably intended by Brunel to be regularized when the bridge was finally finished. The bridge was eventually opened in 1863, after a long hiatus, by using the iron materials of another suspension bridge completed by Brunel in 1845. That bridge had crossed the Thames behind the Hungerford Market until the railway bridge leading to Charing Cross Station replaced it in the early 60's. W.

H. Barlow, the third engineer on the Clifton job, did not bother to cover the pylons with metal plates stamped with hieroglyphics, as Brunel had originally envisaged (Fig. XV 17). In a way this is a pity; to see an Egyptian suspension bridge one must go to Leningrad. There something very like the original Brunel project was reproduced entirely in iron at very small scale, with all the Egyptian details in place but without the Romantic context of the precipitous Clifton Gorge. Because of this superb setting, and despite the generation it took to build, the Clifton bridge properly rates as one of the great 19th-century achievements in engineering. It is, however, only accidentally Victorian in date and owes its relative simplicity and curiously expressive structural forms to accident.

Brunel did not attempt to use Egyptian design for railway stations, although W. J. Short had proposed an Egyptian station at Kennington Common in the mid-30's. (This was published by Loudon in the *Architectural Magazine* in 1836.) At Paddington, Brunel—or the Great Western Railway's directors—was actually content for nearly fifteen years with what was practically no station at all. In 1838 the waiting rooms and ticket offices were merely placed under the arches of the viaduct that carried the Bishop's Road across the railway line, well to the north of the site chosen for the eventual mammoth terminus—that was certainly an extreme instance of some sort of "functionalism" (Fig. XV 15). Even the sheds at Paddington I were extremely modest in dimension (one 30-foot span, and outside it another of 12 feet with a five-foot cantilever); they were also very modest in design (Fig. XV 16). The slender iron columns supporting the wooden trusses had only undecorated bell capitals; but a decorative wooden pelmet ran along the edge of the cantilever in the tradition of the Regency awning-verandah. This was probably the first example—and certainly one of the simplest—of what was to be a very persistent form of embellishment for small wayside stations.

The larger Great Western stations at Reading and Swindon, built respectively in 1839–40 and 1841–42, were externally in the dullest of "Engineers' Italian" without any "Villa" touches at all. But Swindon was the station where the Queen descended from the train en route to Windsor, so it had a most sumptuous Royal waiting room. This more than rivaled in its Early Victorian elaboration anything Her Majesty had by this date in her own official residences. The smaller stations along the eastern half of the line were also extremely simple and had, of course, no such Royal fittings; but their admirable cantilevered marquees are all attractively edged with scalloped wooden pelmets like those of Paddington I.

At the other end of the line, at Bristol and at Bath and also in the smaller way stations, Brunel turned to more exotic stylisms—not to the Egyptian but to the Tudor and the Jacobethan. At Temple Mead Station in Bristol the irrelevance of the turrets and battlements infuriated Pugin almost more than did the Doric columns of Euston. Still effectively extant though not in use for passengers today, this station was a remarkable terminus both in plan and in construction despite its irrelevantly castellated styling. Temple Mead I was built in 1839–40 and the similar but somewhat smaller station at Bath in 1840–41. At both stations the railway came in on a high viaduct so that it was possible to develop their plans on two levels. Tite was trying the same scheme at this time in the otherwise undistinguished Blackwall and Minories terminals of the short London and Blackwall Railway in the East End which was raised on an embankment above the swamps of Dockland throughout its length. (Some French engineer, perhaps Eugène Flachat, was also doing this rather more dextrously at the Gare de Versailles, later Gare Montparnasse, in Paris, also of 1840.)

The Temple Mead I shed has a fine wooden hammerbeam roof resting on Tudor arcades with iron columns at the inner edge of the two side platforms (Fig. XV 21). The trusses are abutted across the platforms from the buttressed walls in a rather ingenious way. This roof not only puts to shame Pugin's matchstick timberwork of the period, it actually has a span exceeding that of the greatest feat of medieval carpentry, the hammerbeam roof of Westminster Hall (72 feet to Herland's 68 feet). In other words, the engineer Brunel was here reviving the Gothic in the spirit of the Roman vault of St. George's Hall, likewise intended to exceed its ancient model in span but as yet only a dream of Elmes. The lighting from above is particularly cleverly handled; for it comes through the roof at the edges, just where it is most needed, in a most unmedieval way.

The platforms are side lighted. From them, on either side, several flights of stairs run down; those on the departure side lead to the waiting rooms and ticket offices facing one vehicle court, those on the arrival side to a sort of cloister opening on another vehicle court. A subsidiary shed, without platforms, extends well beyond the Temple Mead end of the main shed and connects with a four-storey block of the most childishly castellated order in which were the chief offices of the company. This block is flanked by gateways leading into the two vehicle courts.

Except for the lack of cross communication between the sides, such as Tite had already provided at Vauxhall, this is a remarkably mature station, superior in concept, though certainly not in design, to Thompson's Trijunct (Fig. XV 20). Unfortunately the Tudor embellishments, despite their theoretical relevance to the hammerbeam roof of the shed, give the edifice, as Pugin wrote in his *Apology for the Revival of Pointed or Christian Architecture* (1843), p. 11, the air of a "mere caricature." "Mock-castellated work . . .

507

shields without bearings, ugly mouldings, no-meaning projections and all sorts of unaccountable breaks . . . make up a design at once costly and offensive and full of pretension." Thus, and justly, did the Christian Functionalist give his verdict on what was certainly "engineer's architecture," if a far cry from the solemn engineering-architecture of the Late Georgian period.

Bath is a through station, not a terminus; but otherwise it is a smaller and simpler Jacobethan twin of Temple Mead, with the cove of the hammerbeam roof filled in and a wide skylight along the center of the top. Several other stations begun in 1840–41 deserve more particular mention. London Road I in Manchester had a very nobly scaled office block at the front. Big rusticated quoins on its corners and an enormous flat-arched symbolic entrance, rising two storeys, recalled the bold detailing of Sir John Rennie's Stonehouse Victualling Yard of the 30's in vigor and simplicity of expression. But this front block was really no part of the actual station; that was entered from the left as usual and had its arrival court on the right. This court was separated from the platform only by the iron columns supporting the edge of the shed. As at Bristol there was no cross communication at all.

The Brighton Station by Daniel Mocatta (1806–1882) is duplex in plan; that is, a departure platform originally ran down the middle of the shed, with arrival platforms on either side to serve two separate railways. The waiting rooms and so forth are placed in the front block, as at Nine Elms, and necessarily a cross platform was provided from the first. The mode is a more delicate version of Tite's Italian at Nine Elms too, with an arcade carried across the front and trabeated porches at the ends. This station still provides a by no means unworthy entrance to what is miscalled "Regency" Brighton. When it was built the Brighton that everyone knows and admires was actually just coming to maturity at the hands of C. A. Busby and the Wilds, seventeen years after George IV's departure from the town.

Instead of the stucco of Brighton, G. T. Andrews used "white" brick with stone trim for "King" Hudson's station at York. (Hudson was Lord Mayor of York at the time, as well as the leading speculative entrepreneur in the railway field.) The design is almost as hard and cold as most of Tite's work. The triple shed is somewhat like Tite's at Vauxhall also, but with the light tie trusses of Derby Trijunct. The round-ended slotting in the iron spandrels illustrates perhaps the most elegant and technically correct way to detail such openwork cast-metal members (Fig. XV 22). But the major innovation at York, as has been said, was the provision of complete hotel facilities within the main station block like those Dockray had just added beside the original arch at Curzon Street in Birmingham and Thompson had built across the road at Derby. These are in a plain, Barry-like wing rising behind the cross platform and over the refreshment rooms.

Also unusually elaborate is the duplication of the various accommodations for passengers in another wing beside the arrival platform. To this is sacrificed, however, a direct route out on the arrival side such as most other early stations provided. Although this first station at York was superseded after a generation by a later one—also very fine—the original structure remains practically intact and is still used for offices by the Great Northern division of the British Railways. There, in the engineer's office, is preserved an elevation of the principal, or departure, front toward Tanner Row (Fig. XV 23). This seems to indicate that the hotel, completed a year after the rest of the station, was an afterthought or at least that its top storey was, having been added (doubtless) in rivalry of Dockray's hotel in Birmingham; for these upper storeys appear clearly as an emendation on the drawing.

Another architect, the equal of Thompson in distinction, designed the next really important London station. Like Nine Elms, this is south of the river, as is also the London Bridge Station. (The original joint station of the Brighton, Croydon, Dover, and Greenwich Railways, completed in 1843 at the southwest end of London Bridge, was soon submerged in an enormous complex of later work almost impossible to disentangle today. It had a tall loggia tower, like Barry's at Trentham Park, at one end, designed by the architectural advisor to the engineers, Henry Roberts, as has been said.) The fine Bricklayers' Arms Station, off the Old Kent Road, was built by Lewis Cubitt in 1842–44 for the Dover and Croydon, later the South-Eastern, Railway. Cubitt's terrace of 1841 in Lowndes Square (Fig. XIII 20) is Italian Villa in a sense, as has been said, and so in a rather more marked way was this station. It was also much more positively Victorian in character (Fig. XV 24). Curiously enough the *Illustrated London News* described the Bricklayers' Arms on its completion as being in the "English railway style," to such an extent was rural Italian design associated by this time with the new railway structures, in the country if not in cities. Although quite symmetrical, the frontal screen was elaborated with the peasant-Baroque detail so prominent in Charles Parker's designs in *Villa rustica* (Fig. XIII 14). (Parker's projects, moreover, were often taken over almost in toto for small rural stations.)

At either end of the Bricklayers' Arms screen, pairs of carriage arches 22 feet tall and broad in proportion led to the departure and arrival courts. Three similar arches in the center, opposite the railheads, were closed with wooden doors. These were presumably reserved for the use of Royalty. Three large doors between the departure arches and the central group led into the first- and second-class waiting rooms and were sheltered by pantiled hoods carried on boldly projecting brackets. A balancing group of doors on the other side led out from the parcel room and the arrival platform. At the rear of that

509

platform a carriage dock like the one at Euston I was provided with its own railheads and waiting room. The disposition behind the screen was therefore not in the least symmetrical in the way of Brighton or York even though the central arches did lead directly to the cross platform (Fig. XV 25). The departure porch ran back, behind the second of the lefthand arches, along the side of the solid block of ticket offices and waiting rooms; then came three parallel sheds, the first two each sheltering a pair of tracks, the third covering the arrival platform with the carriage dock at its rear.

Cubitt had very bad luck with his shed roofs here; they crashed almost as soon as the station was opened and again in 1850. But with the design of his entrance screen he was peculiarly successful, whether the manner of design he used be called "Italian Villa" or "English Railway" (Fig. XV 24). The continuous plane of the screen, some 30 feet high, was varied as at Derby only by slight projections and recessions; even the central clock tower was visibly thin in section. On the other hand the overhanging hoods, with their red pantiles, offered vigorous relief against the stone-framed stock brick walls. In silhouette the clock tower, with its crowning belfry, provided a rich, even an ornate, accent; yet this accent was also plastic or "architecturesque," not merely picturesque in outline, because of the bold curving hood over the clock and the heavy supporting consoles at the sides. Thus it announced clearly the station's location from a distance, as justifiably advertising the railway's terminus as a steeple does a church.

A more formally Italian station, still largely extant as the Bricklayers' Arms unfortunately is not, is that at Cambridge (Fig. XV 26). This was built, together with various smaller stations on the Eastern Counties lines, by Sancton Wood in 1844–45. Wood specialized even more in station work than did Lewis Cubitt although he designed more conventionally and with less personal brilliance. The Cambridge station originally incorporated a narrow shed for one line of track under one side of the main block, quite in the manner of many early American "depots." Balancing this was a very elegant, almost quattrocento, arcade on piers across the front, which has now been partially enclosed to provide more office space. The small stations on this line, presumably by Sancton Wood also, are of a quite Late Georgian regularity and simplicity, nicely executed in the local yellow brick which is a far pleasanter material than London stocks.

Paralleling the Italianate stations by Cubitt and Sancton Wood, large numbers of medium- and small-sized stations were following the stylistic lead of Brunel's Temple Mead or Thompson's Ambergate. Most features found in "Old English" designs published in cottage books of the 20's and 30's were somewhere utilized—although thatched roofs were naturally eschewed for safety's sake. On the short Croydon and Epsom line the "atmospheric" system

510

(which moved trains by vacuum tubes) required large chimneys at the stations. Above bargeboarded and brick-diapered "Tudor Parsonages" rose tall octagonal shafts which broke into spires or crowns of tracery at the tops (Fig. XV 28). The architects of these stations (built around 1845) were, curiously enough, the Brandon brothers, best known for treatises on medieval English parish churches and their open timber roofs.

William Livock, though otherwise unknown to fame, was a much more active railway architect than the Brandons. He also followed national rather than Italian precedent in most of the medium-sized stations he designed at this period. His Peterborough station was a dry, symmetrical Tudor composition; Northampton, of red brick with stone trim in the Jacobethan vein; Thrapston had a timber-framed upper storey with ornamental plasterwork in the panels and richly carved bargeboards. All three were completed in 1845. Except for the marquees over the platforms, not always included in the original scheme, these stations and their successors for a decade or more were in appearance merely Picturesque houses belatedly set down—as it were by accident—at the track's side. Like Thompson's on the North Midland line, they might almost equally well have served for ordinary domestic purposes. Since they have no relation to the development of iron construction, such small stations may henceforth be ignored in this chapter and the next.

Even in the larger stations erected before 1845 the achievements of the railway architects and engineers in the structural use of metal were very modest. The widest span, that of Temple Mead I, was accomplished with timber and according to a traditional medieval principle. Although invisible, Martin and Baron's new iron roof above the vaults of Chartres Cathedral, executed in 1837–39, exceeds in its dimensions, if not perhaps in lightness and ingenuity, any English railway shed roof of this period which was carried on iron principals. Furthermore, the coming of the railways actually discouraged the building of iron suspension bridges since it was feared the vibration of the trains would shake them down. There are, however, many small iron bridges along the railway lines which are simple and well designed on arch or beam principles. The greatest early railway works other than stations, the viaducts, were mostly built of timber or masonry (Fig. XV 27). The superb lines of the the tall-arched masonry viaducts, rivaling the aqueducts of the Romans, illustrate the continued technical linkage of Victorian engineering with the architectural traditions of the past rather than any new step toward a metallic future. Glass, moreover, was used only very timidly in the shed roofs of stations up to the mid-40's. High cost, restrictions on available pane sizes, and limited over-all production long kept shed roofs from being really "ferrovitreous."

511

The earliest triumph of ferrovitreous construction was in quite a different field, providing for no new mode of public transportation but for the inherited hobby of a duke (Fig. XV 29). The Great Conservatory at Chatsworth—designed in 1836, begun in 1837, completed in 1840, and demolished in 1920—was the first considerable edifice to be planned by one of the most brilliant and characteristic men of the Victorian Age, Joseph Paxton, but with the assistance of the architect Decimus Burton. Paxton, as everyone knows, was not an architect or an engineer but a gardener, and more specifically a horticulturist or plant specialist. Yet his name is known as a builder to thousands who have never heard of the railway-station architects Francis Thompson and Lewis Cubitt or even, perhaps, of that once highly publicized engineer I. K. Brunel. Before his life's work was done Paxton was to be a railway director, a member of Parliament, and a knight. He had also, as we have seen, a distinguished career as a planner of parks and suburbs in an age little addicted to large-scale planning, all without losing his earlier pre-eminence as a horticulturist.

Paxton's granddaughter Violet Markham's story of his life and that of his patron, *Paxton and the Bachelor Duke* (1935), is disappointing but it is the most compendious single account of his career. Francis Thompson in his *History of Chatsworth* (1949) is also inadequate in his coverage of Paxton's work there omitting, for example, all reference to Paxton's own house.

Born in 1803, Paxton was employed as an undergardener at Chiswick when he first attracted the attention of the 6th Duke of Devonshire. Established at Chatsworth in 1826 and married the next year, he rose rapidly in the duke's service to be Head Gardener, then Forester, and finally in effect the Cavendish "Minister of Works." Close collaborator of the duke in all his ventures and interests, he was a real friend as well, as the duke himself wrote in his *Handbook of Chatsworth and Hardwick* (1845).

When Paxton first came to Chatsworth Sir Jeffrey Wyatville's building operations there were well under way. These included much work on the main block of the house as well as the construction of a long service wing with a huge loggia tower at the end. Wyatville's campaign at Chatsworth continued through the 30's, setting the pace for Barry's at Trentham Park. The gate lodges, which might well have fallen within the Head Gardener's purview, were by Wyatville also, as has been noted, while the most complete illustration of a Romantic model village, Edensor, was built by the obscure John Robertson of Derby. But the Great Conservatory was certainly Paxton's in everything that matters, despite Burton's collaboration.

The chief prototype of the Chatsworth conservatory was the Anthaeum at Hove of the early 30's. This had likewise been the project of a horticulturist, Henry Phillips of Brighton. But the advice of the supervising architect Anson

Henry Wilds (d. circa 1850) was not followed and this first great ferrovitreous bubble collapsed even before it was completed. Another Brighton architect, Charles Augustus Busby, so often the collaborator of Wilds and his father, undertook to rebuild the Anthaeum; but nothing came of the scheme, probably because funds were not forthcoming. The ruins still remained in situ until the mid-50's when Baron Goldschmid cleared the ground to lay out Palmeira Square.

The Duke of Devonshire had taken No. 14 Chichester Terrace in Kemp Town in 1828. From then on he was often in residence in Brighton, with Paxton a frequent visitor. Whether he or Phillips landscaped the slopes of Kemp Town in front of the duke's house, Paxton must certainly have known all about the unhappy Anthaeum fiasco from the beginning. The legend that he explored the crumpled remains in 1850, at the time he was designing the Crystal Palace, can hardly be true; it doubtless represents the transference in date of some inspection he made at the time of the collapse, or perhaps a few years later in the mid-30's when the Chatsworth conservatory was first being planned.

There were certainly important resemblances between the two edifices which were of nearly identical function. But the Chatsworth conservatory was oblong in plan, not round like the Anthaeum, and its roof rose from the ground not in one arc but in two, like a cusped arch (Fig. XV 29). All the ribs were necessarily curved like those of the Anthaeum, and even the ridge-and-furrow arrangement of the segments of the outer covering (of glass set in wooden sash) may well have been an echo of the pointed lobes of the Brighton dome. Those lobes, in turn, could have been suggested by the oriental domes of Porden's, Repton's, and Nash's designs for the Royal Pavilion (which again derived ultimately from the Indian buildings illustrated in Thomas Daniell's and William Daniell's *Oriental Scenery* [1795–1807]). But there is no residue of orientalism about Paxton's famous ridge-and-furrow system of roofing as he developed it at Chatsworth. The hollowing out of the wooden members at the base of the ridges to serve as gutters was his own invention, as was also the sashbar-cutting machine he patented at this time.

Of the Great Conservatory at Chatsworth there remains today only the low masonry wall around the edge to which the bases of the curved iron ribs were once anchored; but the tremendous size of the area entirely roofed by Paxton with glass—277 feet by 123 feet and thus of the order of magnitude of even the largest station sheds built before 1845—is still sufficiently evident to the visitor. The roof once rose 67 feet above the ground, undoubtedly creating an impressive effect of interior arched volume. This could be most dramatically appreciated from the light gallery carried around the sides, presumably at the level of the cusp. The staircase leading up to this gallery was romantically hidden in one of the corner rockeries. Paxton was the last great rockery designer, as the fine remaining examples of artificial rockwork in the Chatsworth gardens still make evident to such visitors as do not take them to be real.

The conventional arched and pilastered entrance doorways at the ends of the conservatory (presumably Burton's) were awkward and overscaled intrusions in the delicate transparency of the whole; but their large size permitted carriages to be driven right through, as was done with the Queen's at the time of her visit to Chatsworth in 1843. Underneath the conservatory there was a small railway to carry fuel and heavy plants—thus even here the iron rails on which the new age so generally moved forward played their modest part. The demolition of the Great Conservatory in 1920 was most regrettable; but even the Cavendishes, after a world war, found excessive the cost of the coal required to keep such a vast volume at near-tropical temperature.

The year after the Queen's visit to the Chatsworth conservatory a "palm stove" (to use the contemporary term) was planned for the Royal Botanic Gardens at Kew to accommodate the "most lofty and the most delicate of the tribe" of *Palmae.* "Under the botanical direction of Sir William Jackson Hooker, the enlightened and public-spirited Curator of the Royal Gardens," to quote the *Illustrated London News,* Decimus Burton designed a structure which seems to derive directly from the one with which he had been associated earlier at Chatsworth. The Kew Stove is little larger although it is longer (362 feet); but the central pavilion is only 106 feet wide and 62 feet tall; while the wings are 56 feet wide (the precise width of the Derby Trijunct central span) and only 33 feet high—loftier *Palmae* (and doubtless as delicate ones) could grow at Chatsworth.

The Kew conservatory, however, is much more beautiful than the one at Chatsworth can ever have been (Fig. XV 31). The smooth glass surfaces are more bubble-like, and the repetition of the curved walls of the projecting central pavilion in its own upper stage and in the end wings, as well as the complete absence of visible masonry elements, provides a more perfect realization of the ferrovitreous dream. The heating was from below, by coils of pipes under perforated cast-iron slabs, a premonition of a popular method of domestic heating in the mid-20th century.

The interior has its special visual delights. A gallery is carried around the "crossing," if one may so call it, and supported only on single piers where it traverses the "transepts" (Fig. XV 32). A large spiral staircase in a delicate vertical cage of iron is placed directly on the longitudinal axis. The glass, of which 45,000 square feet were required (less than the 70,000 at

Chatsworth because of the unfurrowed surfaces), is slightly tinged with green to temper the sunlight. This gives an agreeable subaqueous quality to the foliage-filled interior.

The ironwork was provided by Richard Turner of Dublin, who was soon also undertaking to span the considerably broader shed of Lime Street II with a different sort of curved principals tied with wrought-iron rods, as we have seen. The detailing of the cast-iron members here is remarkably straightforward; only at the top and bottom ends of the "buttresses" which brace the "clerestorey" are there conventional scroll forms (Fig. XV 33). Whether this ornamental restraint combined with real grace of expression should be credited to Turner or to Burton is not clear. What is clear is that architect and contracting engineer collaborated here more harmoniously than railway architects and engineers usually did on stations—compare Turner's work done in association with Tite at Lime Street II, for example, on the score of refinement (Figs. XV 2, 4). In the total absence of visible masonry elements, the architect was spared the temptation to overscale the design; or perhaps, like Thompson at Derby, Burton already had an inkling of the new visual possibilities of iron construction not altogether surprising in one of his Late Georgian antecedents. (He had been in practice by this time for twenty-five years, having begun very young as an aid to his builder-father by designing terraces at Regent's Park.)

The smoke of the heating plant was carried almost 500 feet from the palm stove to issue through—of all inappropriate things—the belfry lights of an Italian Romanesque campanile built of stock brick. This was the smallest and probably the earliest of the fantastic tribe of Victorian campanile chimneys. Working with metal seemed to offer architects few hints for the more original treatment of masonry design, even though they soon learned to avoid detailing iron like stone. Or perhaps the masonry contractors, in this case Grissell who was building the New Palace for Barry, were less stimulating associates than the principal contractor Turner, who worked and thought only in metal.

No other English work in iron compared as yet in scale with these two giant greenhouses. But the proposal of a Mr. Gye at this time to provide a ferrovitreous covering for the entire length of a London street at least deserves mention. Paxton was to make a similar suggestion at the height of his fame in the 50's. The great examples of covered shopping streets, however, are all continental not British, although they were often built with British capital.

If Victorian ferrovitreous architecture began with a commission from a duke, Victorian prefabrication in iron may almost be said to have begun with a palace for a king. Of King Eyambo's background less is known than of the Cavendishes', but his realm was on the Calabar River in Africa. A neighboring prince having obtained from England a prefabricated house of wood, King Eyambo applied to a Mr. Laycock of London in 1843 to send him a prefabricated iron building to house himself and his 320 wives. The unsubdivided upper floor, only 30 feet by 50 feet, must have provided none too generously for so extensive a harem (Fig. XV 30). The ground floor might be said to have an Anglo-Palladian plan, with central hall and four corner rooms. Iron verandahs surrounded the whole and the central hall rose an extra storey above the hip roof to terminate in battlements. Because of cost the construction was not entirely of iron, as the King requested, but partly of wood.

The iron prefabrication industry had significant pre-Victorian beginnings. Lockkeepers' houses along canals, made entirely of iron slabs, were known as early as 1790 (Richard Sheppard, *Cast Iron in Building* [1947]). A very considerable, if rather confused, account of early prefabrication will be found in John Gloag and Derek Bridgewater, *A History of Cast Iron in Architecture* (1948). Eventually Bannister's studies, when published, will provide a really scholarly account, of which his 1950 article in the *Architectural Review* gives a foretaste.

By 1844 a considerably greater export of iron houses is reported in the press. Wood, Weygood and Company of London, were then regularly shipping warehouses as well as houses to Africa and the West Indies. Peter Thompson of Commercial Road, Limehouse, in London was active at home with the construction of temporary churches of wood; examples were going up at Kentish Town, at Hampstead, and at St. John's Wood around London in the early 40's. He also sent a church made of metal to Jamaica in 1844; the side walls of this were framed with cast-iron pilasters which supported a framed roof of wrought iron, a relatively early example of its structural use. The cost was only £1,000 for an edifice 65 feet by 40 feet with a chancel 24 feet by 12 feet and a western tower of wood. Grissell, Peto's former partner on the first contract for the New Palace and now sole contractor for its continuance, sent a prefabricated iron building to Mauritius to be used as officers' quarters, as well as one for a hospital and another for a lazaretto.

Intrinsically more interesting were the iron lighthouses of the 40's and early 50's. One of the earliest of all may have been that completed in 1841 at Morant Point, Jamaica, by Alexander Gordon after several years' preparation. When in 1843 the contracting engineers Cottam and Hallen set up another in their yard in Southwark near Waterloo Bridge the structure attracted wider attention than Gordon's because it was so conspicuous a feature, for a brief moment at least, of the metropolitan skyline south of the Thames (Fig. XV 41). After disassembly, it was sent to Bermuda, where it was re-erected on its permanent site. The metal shell was then weighted at the base by filling the spaces between the outer casing and the inner spiral staircase with bricks and concrete. This lighthouse was 130 feet tall and tapered from a diameter of 24 feet at the base to 14 feet just below the top. Above that point the outer shell flared out again to support a gallery 20 feet in diameter, which was protected by a delicate iron paling. Over the gallery came the 16-sided glass light room which was covered with a cone-shaped roof of iron. The principal components were 135 cast-iron plates, those at the base being 56 inches square and those above diminishing in size with the taper, all bolted together through internal flanges. The upper portion had an internal casing of wrought iron.

In 1851 the United States government ordered a corrugated iron lighthouse from John Walker (probably not the same as the homonymous York iron founder, whose dates are 1801–1853) of London; and in the same year Henry Grissell sent one of cast and wrought iron to the Barbados. Sir George Grove (1820–1900), later famous for his *Dictionary of Music* (1879–90), began his extraordinarily varied career by supplying two cast-iron lighthouses for erection in Bermuda in the 40's. These are but a few instances of a rather considerable activity which continued well beyond the end of the Early Victorian period and may have started before it began.

Nor was production limited to the export trade even though few examples have survived a century of buffeting by the seas. Whether the engineer Bush meant to erect his proposed Goodwin Sands lighthouse on dry land first is irrelevant. In this elegant reverse-tapered design of 1844, with its near-Doric capital, the exterior caisson as well as the interior iron pier and the spiral steps projecting from it were certainly all to be made to specification in advance like those of Gordon's Morant Point lighthouse (Fig. XV 40). Yet of course such structures, although related to more characteristic prefabricated products, do not represent quite what is ordinarily meant by prefabrication today: They were certainly not made up from parts industrially produced in identical series.

Only around 1850 did true prefabrication of houses really reach considerable proportions, and then only for export. It will be better to consider first the railway stations and the ferrovitreous architecture in general of the short period 1845–50. Meeks, using the morphological terminology of the late Henri Focillon's *Vie des formes* (Paris, 1934), has considered the decade 1845–55 to be the "classical age" of the railway station not only in England but throughout the world. Such a major dividing line as he discerns in the mid-40's between what he calls an "experimental" and a "classical" period does not agree with the concept of a coherent Early Victorian style-phase such as this book has on the whole tried to present. It does, however, apply remarkably well to ferrovitreous construction in general, which certainly moved to a climax around 1850 and before 1845 had amounted to little. Events in the realm of technics, which is under the aegis of science, can only be organized rather awkwardly under the more humane rubrics of artistic styles and style-phases.

Technical progress—particularly to optimistic 19th-century minds as also to those today who have inherited a similarly sanguine view of science—appears as the continuous and necessary result of cumulative activity in the basic sciences. But the arts, including of course architecture, show no real progress, properly speaking, only a succession of more or less autonomous cultural entities which are identified eventually as styles or phases of styles. Therefore, only the broadest correlation between technical and artistic development, a correlation corresponding to very large historical units of time, has much real meaning. Since this chapter is much concerned with technical developments, the humanistic concept of an Early Victorian style-phase must necessarily be somewhat in abeyance here.

Commenting on railway stations in general, and more specifically on Euston where a "vast concourse" (to which we shall come shortly) had lately "swallowed up all the money and all the light in the establishment," Samuel Sidney asked in *Rides on Railways* (1851): ". . . why are our architects so inferior to our engineers?" This remark is too kind to Robert Stephenson's work at Euston I; moreover, in many cases where engineers had less unsympathetic architects than the two Hardwicks as collaborators, their structural concepts received a clarity of expression and a refinement of detail such as engineers working alone or merely utilizing subordinate draftsmen as "exterior decorators" rarely equaled. Pugin's criticisms of Brunel's Temple Mead I are not unjustified whoever Brunel's anonymous collaborator at Bristol may have been; had the great engineer's complete Egyptian scheme of decoration been carried out at Clifton, the piers of his bridge would certainly have been inferior in expressive character to the unembellished forms we admire today. The modest Italianism of the towers which Bunning, as collaborating architect, designed for Brunel's Hungerford Bridge of 1837–45 to accord with Fowler's Hungerford Market, on the other hand, was quite unexceptionable but hardly worth mentioning now that the bridge has gone.

The finest bridge of the 40's is Robert Stephenson's and Francis Thompson's Brittania. This was built to carry the Chester and Holyhead Railway across the Menai Strait near Thomas Telford's masterly road bridge on the suspension principle of twenty-five years earlier. Designed in 1845 and completed in 1850, the Britannia rivals its earlier neighbor as a structural feat and exceeds it in maturity of design, if not in visual drama (Fig. XV 34). Here Stephenson, as engineer, had the advantage of working with a very

518

talented architectural collaborator and also of employing a good sculptor. Pairs of superb lions, of the same Anglesey marble as the rest of the masonry, guard the entrances. They are charmingly described by a contemporary, Sir Francis Head, in the *Illustrated London News, 14, 24*, as "of the antique, knocker-nosed, pimple-faced Egyptian, instead of the real Numidian form" (Fig. XV 35). Each 12 feet high, 24 feet long, and weighing 30 tons, these beasts were the work of John Thomas and they add considerably to the total interest of the bridge. Moreover, they are intrinsically his best effort, superior both to his Tudor work in the New Palace and the cinquecento embellishments he designed for various banks and insurance buildings.

The engineering details of the Britannia Bridge need not concern us much here. Suffice it to say that it represented a major step in the supersession of cast iron by wrought iron as the structural engineer's favorite material. The engineer Andrew Thomson had spanned the Clyde with a malleable iron beam-bridge in 1839; and William Fairbairn, who was from the first Stephenson's technical advisor on the Britannia Bridge, had for some time been urging the merits of the "cellular self-supporting principle" of the tubular bridge. The trains were to pass within enormous hollow girders which were first assembled on shore from wrought-iron plates. The sections of these "tubes" were next floated into place between the masonry piers and then hoisted up into their proper positions. The first tube was floated in June 1849; but one of the two parallel tubes of Stephenson's other tubular bridge at Conway had been successfully floated and lifted into position the previous year (Fig. XV 37). Like Telford's suspension bridge there, this was the castellated twin of that across the Menai Strait.

Over the Menai Strait the two principal spans of 463 feet were supported on a central pier standing on the fortunately located Britannia Rock in the middle (Fig. XV 38); the total length of the bridge, consisting in all of four spans between the two entrances at either end, was 1,500 feet. The trains were carried 100 feet above the level of the strait at high tide. In the original design of 1845 curved suspension chains were intended to assist in supporting the tubes and there was some ambiguity of expression because of this mixed method of support. In the executed design everything is rectangular; even the sides of the tubes are striated vertically by the reinforcing ribs between the lapped wrought-iron panels and are framed, top and bottom, by the horizontal I-beams which strengthen the floor and the roof (Fig. XV 36).

A similar rectangularity controls Thompson's masonry detailing both on the two entrances and the three great piers, although the great height of these reflects the early intention to use them to carry suspension chains (Figs. XV 33, 35, 38). The enormous scale of the rock-faced masonry and the trabeation of all the openings may perhaps suggest a little such very early Egyptian buildings as the Temple of the Sphinx; except for the lions that precede the entrance, however, there is nothing specifically Egyptian as the "style" of the bridge was loosely denominated by contemporaries. The extreme horizontality of the cornices and the careful proportioning of the openings in the tops of the piers come closer to being a monumental version of J. M. Gandy's "functional" villa manner of the beginning of the century (Fig. II 4).

There is very little arbitrary ornament except for the lions. But the openings in the sides of the piers at the level of the iron tubes are decorated with bold carved grilles, recalling a little the Tudor portcullis and—less happily —the barred windows of a gaol (Fig. XV 38). These grilles were presumably intended to suggest, even to the inclusion of carved bolt heads, the iron construction of the tubes themselves. They are certainly most effective; by their scale and their character they successfully relate the engineer's ironwork to the architect's masonry in a way no iron detail imitating stone membering can ever do.

The Britannia Bridge, an almost unqualified masterpiece of engineering-architecture, owes its final distinction to the subtlety and discretion of Thompson's handling of the masonry work. At Conway the close proximity of one of the most romantic of Edwardian castles seemed to demand of Thompson and Stephenson, as of Telford before them, a castellated treatment of the piers (Fig. XV 37). Yet the plain oblong towers there, machicolated and flanked at the entrances by round corner turrets, have something of the severity of real Edwardian work and appear almost like outworks of the castle. They are certainly not as trivially picturesque as the battlemented cylinders of stone over which the suspension chains of the neighboring structure pass.

All the stations on the Chester and Holyhead Railway were also the work of Stephenson and Thompson. The one at Conway was of course Gothic, with a marquee over the platform carried on very delicately traceried iron brackets. But most of them were in a very simple and refined version of the Italianate "English railway style," with the marquees carried by scrolled brackets. One of the best is at Bangor. Yet there the nearby tunnel entrance, perversely enough, has an Egyptian cavetto cornice. The prettiest small station is that at Holywell (Fig. XV 39). The small square two-storey main block is of an elegance comparable to that of the contemporary villas Persius was building at Potsdam in the early 40's. This block is flanked by tiny corner pavilions; between them a flat marquee is cantilevered over the platform, rather like the concrete slab roofs of 20th-century covered terraces. The station at Abergele is similar but the marquee there is carried on a Renaissance arcade.

520

The largest station, the General at Chester serving several lines, was still "one-sided" like Thompson's Derby Trijunct. The treatment of the two sheds, which rest on a central masonry arcade between, is hardly an advance over Derby; but the introduction of various independent kiosks on the platforms was significant (Fig. XV 43). Somewhat later the shed-covered platforms of English stations were to develop thus into wide concourses with various freestanding edifices quite separate from the main office block. Almost identical with Derby Trijunct in layout, Chester General also required a façade of the same length (1,050 feet); but the composition, while symmetrical, is less axial in emphasis (Fig. XV 42).

The central block has a bracket-supported marquee that runs between broad projecting blocks on either side. These blocks are accented by corner loggia towers linked together by projecting planes in the façade. Additional low towers punctuate the long arcaded screen walls that mask the arrival platforms at either end. The detail is delicate in scale, like that at Holywell, but there is unfortunately a good deal too much of it. Pursuing a more varied silhouette, Thompson eschewed here the continuous surfaces varied only by a few bold projections which make the Britannia Bridge and the Derby Trijunct Station such admirable expressions of a post-Georgian engineering aesthetic in masonry. Station design was generally losing contact now with its Late Georgian beginnings and becoming more positively Victorian.

Chester Central was built in 1847–48, paralleling the construction of the Britannia Bridge. The structurally more ambitious operations at Lime Street II, including Tite's new masonry block (Fig. XV 4) and Turner's tremendous shed with its novel construction of sickle girders (Fig. XV 2), were carried out, as we have seen, from 1846 to 1851. Two big early Dublin stations were built in these years also. They are Sancton Wood's Kingsbridge and the Broadstone Terminus by J. S. Mulvany (1813–1870). The latter, supposedly in an "Egyptian style," is not unworthy of comparison with Thompson's Britannia Bridge. A tall solid block, containing the director's house, is set across the head of the tracks as at London Road I in Manchester. The minor stations on the Midland Great Western line to Cork and on the Great Western and Southern line to Galway, by Wood and Mulvany respectively, were opened along with the Dublin terminals in 1850 and 1851.

The most famous station of the late 40's, Newcastle Central, was likewise built very slowly. Although it was begun in 1846, the contract for the curved malleable iron principals of the sheds was let (to Abbot and Company of the nearby Gateshead Park Ironworks) only in 1849. In the three sheds of Newcastle Central the detailing, though simple, is less expressive of metal than Thompson's at Derby Trijunct (Fig. XV 46); but the reflection in the curves of the metal structure of the arcs of the railway lines is very happy (Fig. XV 45). The resultant visual harmony between the concentric bending of the sheds in plan and the elliptical-arched forms, not only of the solid spandrels of the arcades but also of the principals above, gives this station an unusual elegance and distinction. Yet its fame has derived rather from its enormous stone portico, approaching in scale the monumental foreworks of America stations of the early 20th century. Heavy screens of masonry on either side of the portico hide the expressive curve of the sheds behind, moreover. (This front is not Early Victorian in date of execution even if presumably part of Dobson's original design of the 40's.)

Euston, as enlarged late in the decade for the London and North Western Railway, was not quite as much a new station as Lime Street II in Liverpool. The two Hardwicks, and perhaps more specifically the elder, were responsible for the twin hotels that were now erected opposite the screen. Between them a passageway led to the Arch from Euston Square although this was not actually opened all the way through to the south until much later and is now covered by a later hotel block. These Euston and Victoria Hotels were quite modest in design and construction, but they were conveniently and clearly related to the general plan of the station complex of which they were detached adjuncts.

In connection with the contemporary enlargement of the platform accommodations the younger Hardwick next built a large addition to the station block at a cost of about £150,000. This is to the left of Euston I and immediately in line with the Arch. More monumental than useful throughout, as Sidney complained, the chief new feature introduced here into station design was the Great Hall, completed in 1849. Like Thompson's wide platform at Chester this was a prototype of the concourses which were to be an element of many later stations, particularly outside England (Fig. XV 49). Renaissance rather than Grecian in style (being based on the interiors of Peruzzi's Palazzo Massimi alle colonne in Rome), the Great Hall is as much an example of architectural splurge as the original Doric Arch. It is, however, curiously inferior in its materials, for the plaster walls are merely painted to simulate gray granite and the columns in the double screen at the end are only covered with scagliola to imitate red granite. These pretenses illustrate the shamming of the period at its shabbiest. The mawkish plaster reliefs in the corners of the attic, symbolizing the chief cities served by the line, are by the same John Thomas who was executing at this time the Britannia Bridge lions, but they display no trace of the beasts' stern "engineering" quality. Except for the two hotels, now all but lost in later construction, the later work of the Hardwicks at Euston II deserves its fame much less than does Dobson's Station at Newcastle.

In the new Paragon Terminus of 1847–48 at Hull, where "King" Hudson was accustomed to detrain for his nearby country seat, G. T. Andrews provided no important advances in layout over his earlier station at York. But the hotel here is much larger than that at York and much more sumptuous (Fig. XV 44). It forms a great quadrangular block about a central court, 60 feet square, covered with an iron and glass roof. Slightly projecting corner blocks, connected by pilasters and arches in the two lower storeys, give variety to a solid but undistinguished cube of what might be called post-Palladian design. It was well executed throughout in Anston stone ashlar, not in painted stucco like Euston II. But the hotel was not functionally linked to the station block (of similar style) on the left and to the rear or to the sheds at whose head it stood; it merely provided an architectural symbol of prestige like the monumental open screens of earlier stations.

The Jacobethan, in terms of connotation, might be considered still less suitable for the masonry portions of a station complex than Andrews' post-Palladian, even if that retardataire mode was in fact, quite as much as the more romantic Italian of Cubitt, Thompson, and Sancton Wood, a leading "English railway style" of the Early Victorian period. Yet the Jacobethan group at Stoke-on-Trent, designed by the otherwise unknown R. A. Stent (who exhibited the drawings for it at the Royal Academy in 1848), represents perhaps the best piece of railway urbanism of the late 40's. The station block, made elaborately picturesque by its curved gables, has an arched porch in the center and over it a great mullioned bay projecting from the stationmaster's office. This block lies along the departure platform and faces a square where a statue of Josiah Wedgwood was appropriately placed in 1863. Opposite the station on the far side of the square is the North Staffordshire Hotel, built of the same red brick and ornamented with restrained black diapering and cut-stone trim. Taller and less ornate than the station, this hotel appears at first sight not unlike many Jacobethan country houses of the period. Being on the outer edge of the town it even has large gardens of its own to the rear. The sides of the square are formed of short terraces of two-storey houses of the same materials and style. This is only one of many stations that emulate, like various institutional edifices of the time, Jacobethan country houses with surprising plausibility if with little appropriateness; but it is nearly unique in the successful integration of the station with its urban setting.

Eclecticism knew few bounds in station architecture by the late 40's. Shrewsbury and Huddersfield were both good-sized provincial stations, completed and opened in 1849 and 1850 respectively, but they could hardly be more different in appearance. Shrewsbury, out of deference to nearby medieval walls, is Tudor, although of a less frivolous order than Brunel's work at Temple Mead I. Since the railway tracks are raised here, as in Bristol, the station entrance is on a lower level, and the façade is therefore impressively tall. As no architect's name is mentioned, this may well be "engineer's architecture" like Temple Mead.

At Huddersfield the station by James P. Pritchett (1788–1868) and his brother Charles P. Pritchett is surprisingly Classical in superficial style. Like the Queen's Hotel at Cheltenham it might almost be a great neo-Palladian country house built a century earlier. A two-storey Corinthian portico projects from the pilastered main block and one-storey colonnades connect with lower porticoed blocks at either end. The Royal George Hotel here, set at an oblique angle to the station on one side of a great irregular square, is presumably also by the Pritchetts and of the same date. In any case it is a remarkably fine late example of stone-built post-Georgian, much more worthy of Dobson's Newcastle than the modest hotel he originally attached to one end of his station. (That was later swallowed up in a larger one built by William Prosser in the 60's.) The Lion Arcade, across from the station at Huddersfield, was also built by the Pritchetts in 1852–54 but in a more advanced Italianate vein. The general effect of the square is handsome but lacks the consistency of Stoke.

Two other considerable stations of this period, Tithebarn Street in Liverpool by the engineer Hawkshaw and Shoreditch II in London by Sancton Wood, have both been replaced. They were examples of the London Road I type, each having a solid block intended to contain the company offices across the front. This block was on a higher level than the street in both cases and masked the end of raised railway lines. Tithebarn Street from the front was a conventional Barryesque palazzo quite like other good business blocks of the time in Liverpool and elsewhere. Wood's Shoreditch (replacing in 1849 a modest earlier station of 1840 by William Evill) was not much more interesting, despite its raised corner pavilions, except for the excellent sheds that lay behind (Fig. XV 47). These were similar to but lighter than those at Newcastle and without their curved plan. Glass and iron clerestoreys instead of the usual roof lights flanked the higher central shed to provide illumination.

A gargantuan viaduct which was supported on a very long Roman Doric colonnade executed entirely in cast iron was added in the late 40's to George Stephenson's early Victoria (Huntsbank) Station of 1840–42 at Manchester. This should be mentioned here even though it was a mere adjunct; for with this addition Victoria had for some time the longest platform in the world. It repeated, at several times the scale and a generation later, almost the exact forms of Nash's quadrant colonnade that Victorian "progress" had just demolished. The quantitative advances of Victorian engineering are often thus associated with a total lack of qualitative or stylistic development.

524

The 40's were not a period of prosperity and building programs in many fields were, as we have seen, timid and slow. Yet these were the years of the most optimistic railway expansion and of the wildest speculation in railway shares. Gladstone's Railway Act of 1844 brought some order to the scene, so that the speculative bubble did not really burst until 1849 when the defalcations of George Hudson were discovered. "King" Hudson was in some respects the Krueger of his age; but he had been a really productive entrepreneur and the stations on his lines set a pace for other railways. After the crash stockholders in all the railways began to complain loudly of the enormous sums being spent on stations; they *had* actually been very large in relation to the expenditure on other buildings in this rather penurious decade. Yet, considered as capital investment, the expenditure of the 40's on stations has proved after a century to have been more than justified. Most of those built in that decade continued to serve their purpose for several generations; with additions and emendations many still so serve today —and quite as satisfactorily as various other buildings a hundred years old such as churches, say, of which the functions might be thought less subject to cumulative change.

Besides the stations of the later 40's not many other buildings in which iron was prominently used are of comparable scale or have continued in use in the same conspicuously successful way. What was architecturally the finest piece of glass and iron construction, the court of Bunning's Coal Exchange, has already been discussed at length in Chapter X (Figs. X 14–22). Of similar scale but much less distinguished in design is the narrow rhomboidal court of John Cunningham's Sailors' Home in Liverpool, also built in 1846–48. Immediately behind the site of John Foster II's severely Grecian Custom House in Canning Place rises this tall Jacobethan edifice, now stripped of its curved gables and always rather ungainly in proportion. Against the factory-like regularity of its five storeys of mullioned windows is set a tremendous portal topped by a carved stone trophy of more than Jacobethan symbolic fantasy. Within the actual entrance boldly scaled gates repeat in cast iron and with still greater virtuosity a similarly heterogeneous collection of maritime items set around Liverpool's badge, the legendary "liver bird" (Fig. XV 50). These gates offer a hint to the visitor of the rather remarkable iron construction to be found within: five storeys of galleries with delicate and irrelevant Jacobethan detailing leading up to a broad skylight above (Fig. XV 48). As in the similar courts of American office buildings of the 80's the effect of the upward glance is rather vertiginous; there is none of the suavity and coherence of the court of the Coal Exchange, yet the sight of all this elaborately articulated ironwork is nevertheless impressive.

525

Five storeys of interior iron skeleton construction was nothing extraordinary at this date. By 1850 James Ponsford, without benefit of either engineer or architect, was completing a flour mill in Upper Thames Street in London which was a full eight storeys tall. In this edifice rolled iron joists were carried by sockets in cast-iron girders supported on the usual cast-iron columns. But externally iron was not yet being used for industrial or commercial buildings in England any more than it was for domestic or monumental structures; indeed, as we have seen in an earlier chapter, of the various possible elements of an all-iron interior skeleton, only cast-iron columns were ubiquitously used despite the variety of available systems—some developed locally, some borrowed from France—for producing supposedly "fireproof" floors.

Modern historians give great significance to American achievement in this period. The building James Bogardus erected for his own use in New York in 1848–50, with an exterior frame as well as an interior skeleton of cast iron, was undoubtedly the first storeyed urban structure to be built, both inside and out, with a framework of iron that provided a permanent alternative to masonry; yet the dependence of the Bogardus Building on English experience must by now be very evident. Just before this Bogardus had spent some ten years of work and study in England; moreover, like other American builders of the time, he had to depend on the researches of such British engineers as Hodgkinson and Fairbairn for his technical information on the structural possibilities of metal. Precise figures on the comparative strength of various types of iron and of different beam-section patterns were then to be found only in English treatises.

It is so natural for 20th-century writers to stress the structural importance of metal that the appeal of cast iron to the Victorians as a decorative vehicle is often either ignored or deprecated. Since presentday taste in metalwork is largely based on familiarity with wrought or machined members, the perfect technical propriety to the casting process of various ornamentally plastic effects (as has been remarked in connection with the ropework detail of the Coal Exchange) is generally unrealized. Crude and bombastic as Cunningham's iron gates of the Sailors' Home may be, manufacturers of cast iron in the late 40's were becoming increasingly aware of the need for carefully considered design, particularly for products that were to be sold directly to the public.

It is not, alas, very relevant to architecture but it is of real significance in the general picture of industrial art in the Early Victorian period that Alfred Stevens, the greatest English sculptor of the 19th century, was in 1849 made director of design at Hoole and Robson's Green Lane Ironworks in Sheffield. His exquisite mass-produced cast-iron grates and firebacks are more characteristic artifacts of this moment in history than are his caryatids and other stone decorative sculpture, executed for Dorchester House, which are now so carefully preserved in the Tate Gallery. Of this particular alliance of art and industry little ever came that would affect the design of the large metal components used in building construction. The imagination can only play with the thought of a cast-iron building whose separate members might have been designed by Stevens in Hoole and Robson's foundry; actually the designers of building elements in Victorian ironworks were mostly both untrained and uninspired.

In the late 40's and early 50's prefabrication in iron rose to its Victorian climax corresponding to the "classical" moment of railway station design. The big cast-iron windows made for the palace of an Egyptian prince and exported to Cairo by M'Adam of Belfast in 1849 were, of course, merely large-scale examples of decorative detail and of no particular interest either technically or artistically. But the California gold rush in that year and the increasing pace of British emigration to Australia provided new and avid markets for completely prefabricated structures. The iron houses and warehouses produced by E. T. Bellhouse of Manchester, hitherto primarily a millwright, seem to have been sent to San Francisco in great profusion (Fig. XV 53); but the lack of building materials and of building workers there drew to the booming West Coast town prefabricated structures from all over the world and made of all sorts of different materials. Some houses even came ready built from China and New Zealand, two countries which might be thought consumers rather than producers of such highly industrialized items.

John Walker, who supplied a lighthouse in 1851 to the United States government as we have seen, was producing corrugated iron houses for California two years earlier. He also held various British government contracts for supplying iron houses in quantity for the use of emigrants to Australia. Other manufacturers, particularly in the big British ports, busied themselves with prefabrication for export, particularly Samuel Hemming of the Clift House Works near Bristol (Fig. XV 51). He had started out in the business by making a house for his own son who was emigrating to Australia. By 1854, when Hemming and the other prefabricators were forced to shift to the production of barracks for the Crimean War, Hemming's works had sent whole streets of shops with dwellings over them (Fig. XII 25), many churches and chapels, and even a complete theater to Australia. At the same time W. and P. M'Lellan of Glasgow sent out a large iron mansion for the mayor of Melbourne. The innovation-minded James Edmeston (1791–1861) produced in 1854 an ornamental clock tower whose cast-iron frame was filled with glazed terra cotta; this was for erection in the city of Geelong in Australia (Fig. XV 52). It even roused the enthusiasm of the *Ecclesiologist* as the reviewer poetically envisaged "cathedrals of porcelain" rising in the near future both in the Antipodes and at home.

Iron frames covered with corrugated iron sheets were the standard product and roofs of the latter material are still, I understand, a conspicuous feature of the antipodean scene. But wood and several metals other than iron entered into many of the prefabrication schemes; houses partly of zinc, for example, were sent to Australia by J. Middlemass of Edinburgh in 1853. Houses of glazed clay slabs set in iron frames were exhibited by Edmeston in 1852 two years before his ornamental Geelong clock tower was sent to Australia. Even C. F. Bielefeld, the papier-mâché manufacturer, whose famous catalogues display the profusion of cheap and generally rather meretricious ornament so freely used in interiors and even on exteriors in the 40's and 50's, caught the infection. He showed a project for "portable" houses with iron frames filled with panels of waterproofed papier-mâché, an early version of modern wallboard. All told, the excitement and enthusiasm over prefabrication in various materials was comparable in the early 50's to that a hundred years later after World War II.

The leaders of the Ecclesiological Society lent high intellectual and aesthetic tone to the new developments. First they persuaded Peter Thompson to accept their advice on the ritual arrangement of his temporary churches. These were chiefly of wood with brick filling but occasionally, as we have seen, of iron. In 1853 they went further, commissioning their most "correct" architect R. C. Carpenter to design a model iron church. The project proved abortive because of Carpenter's ill health and early death in 1855 as well as for another and more crucial reason: English bishops refused to consecrate iron structures as parish or district churches and such edifices could therefore only be set up for temporary use. In any event, as we shall see in the next chapter, 1855 represented a turning point in the general Victorian attitude toward iron construction.

At Balmoral in 1851 Bellhouse had set up to Prince Albert's order a prefabricated ballroom (Fig. XV 54), the Prince having been much impressed by the Bellhouse houses for emigrants shown that year at the Great Exhibition. Although some new construction in the most permanent of materials, the local granite, was already under way at Balmoral (and much more was to follow in a year or two with all the romantic paraphernalia of the Scottish Baronial), the Royal patron of the Exhibition was delighted to have this opportunity to display his intense personal interest in technical as well as artistic "progress." (One wonders whether Bellhouse's emigrant houses henceforth carried the inscription: "By Appointment.")

This brings the story of metal construction to that extraordinary edifice erected in 1850 to house the Great Exhibition of All Nations of 1851, the first international exposition and obviously one of the more climactic events of the Victorian Age. This structure was the largest example, doubtless, that the world has ever seen of prefabricated, demountable—and "remountable"—construction; certainly it is the most famous ferrovitreous monument of all time. The 1851 Exhibition Building was named the "Crystal Palace" by a clever journalist, and his happy inspiration actually played some part in the acceptance of Paxton's extraordinary project. To the complicated story of the Palace and cognate structures of the early 50's the next chapter is devoted; for the Palace and the great metropolitan railway stations which were its exact contemporaries provide several of the highest points in the Victorian architectural story, at least as the 20th century reads it.

CHAPTER XVI: THE CRYSTAL PALACE: FERRO-VITREOUS TRIUMPH AND ENSUING REACTION

The Crystal Palace was first built in Hyde Park in 1850–51 to house the Great Exhibition of 1851 and then re-erected in considerably changed form at Sydenham south of London in 1852–54. The structure is so important technically, artistically, and even (in connection with the exhibition it housed) philosophically that a volume would hardly be adequate to discuss it, much less part of a chapter. Indeed, several volumes were devoted to the Palace while it was news; and after the Sydenham Palace had been demolished by fire in 1936 a modern monograph recorded its complete history. On this book, *1851 and the Crystal Palace* (1937) by Christopher Hobhouse, I have drawn heavily in the next few pages, particularly for details of dating, personnel, and statistics. A later account is given by Yvonne ffrench in *The Great Exhibition: 1851* (n.d.) from which several amplifications and corrections of Hobhouse's facts have come. The general bibliography of works in which it has received serious discussion would occupy many pages while a list of more casual and passing references would be like a list of references to *Hamlet*. Its "iconography," that is, the pictures made of it and reproduced in every medium from photography to the various peculiar processes of Victorian art industry, would perhaps be more considerable than the bibliography.

Of all this flood of material the book called *The Building Erected in Hyde Park for the Great Exhibition of the Works of Industry of All Nations, 1851* (1852) by Charles Downes, with scientific description by Charles Cowper, is perhaps the most valuable. Although the description occupies only 45 pages the 26 plates, all folding, are lithographed with the greatest delicacy and precision from drawings prepared by Downes, or under his direction, on the basis of the original working drawings loaned by the contractors Fox and Henderson. From these plates a facsimile of the original structure could be built today. The same can hardly be said without considerable exaggeration of the published records of any other major edifice of the past.

Of more than equal value for the method of construction, in this case of as great importance as the actual design, is the running history of the building, both pictorial and literary, provided by the *Illustrated London News*.

530

The publication there of the official Building Committee's own design on 22 June 1850 (Fig. XVI 1), prepared after the announcement of the decision not to commission any of the entrants in the preceding competition, was followed by the epoch-making—and doubtless technically unethical—presentation on 6 July of an alternative design by Paxton, neither architect nor engineer, nor even an entrant in the original competition (Fig. XVI 2). This irregular publicity undoubtedly played a great part in the acceptance of Paxton's scheme. From the fencing in of the Hyde Park site in August, the progress of the construction of the Crystal Palace was illustrated almost step by step, with full explanations of the special machinery developed, accounts of the testing of the strength of the materials at the site, and even a description of Chance Brothers' glassworks near Birmingham where the sheet glass was blown in larger quantity than for any previous building. Finally, in August 1852 the *News* showed the disassembly of the structure as the components were taken down and removed to Sydenham for re-erection. Later, in the next two years, the story of the second version at Sydenham was also well covered.

Prince Albert for some time after his marriage to Queen Victoria found in the English scheme of things no real place to exercise his undoubted talents. With his appointment in 1841 by Sir Robert Peel as president of the Royal Commission supervising the completion and the decoration of Westminster New Palace his personal enthusiasm for the arts, at least, began to have a more public outlet. Thenceforth, as Royal patron of various semi-institutional bodies, he really had a sympathetic role to play in the life of his time and (as John Steegman tells in *Consort of Taste* [1950]) he played it on the whole with tact, assiduity, and even brilliance. In 1847 the Society of Arts was reorganized with the Prince as president, and the society's first exhibition of "Art-Manufactures" was held. In connection with this exhibition the Prince first came into contact with Henry Cole, a contemporary who deserves to be as well known as Paxton; the very phrase "art-manufactures" had been of his coinage two years earlier.

A civil servant employed in the Record Office, Cole had first been active in Rowland Hill's campaign for the reform of the postal service and the introduction of postage stamps. (He was personally most responsible for the first stamped envelope, which he had designed by Mulready.) Two years before the first Art Manufactures Exhibition he won a prize offered by the society for a crockery tea service of simple and even "functional" design that was much admired by Prince Albert. It was Cole, by 1847 a member of the council of the society, who organized the exhibition of that year. Similar exhibitions were held with even greater success in 1848 and 1849. Looking forward two years, Cole then began to plan for a more important exhibition to be held in 1851, undoubtedly with the approval of the Prince as president of the society. This was to be modeled on those that had been held in Paris every five years since the beginning of the century, of which that of 1849 was particularly notable despite the revolution of the previous year.

It was on his visit to this Paris exhibition with his younger friend M. D. Wyatt that the idea of making the London exhibition of 1851 international occurred to Cole as it did also to Francis Fuller, another member of the society who went to Paris. But the original suggestion seems to go back to Buffet, the new French Minister of Agriculture and Commerce, whom the English visitors met. An international exhibition would provide an opportunity, Cole and Fuller both thought, for the English to learn from the products of neighboring nations who were then admittedly superior in many branches of art-manufacture.

On 30 June 1849 the Prince first gave his blessing to the ambitious scheme for the exhibition when it was presented to him by Cole, Fuller, Scott Russell, the secretary of the society, and the Prince's builder friend Thomas Cubitt, then busy completing Osborne House. Albert also suggested that a site in Hyde Park opposite Gore House should be sought for the Exhibition rather than the modest courtyard of Somerset House, which the Office of Woods and Forests had already agreed to make available, or a more central alternative site that had been proposed in Leicester Square. The next step was a tentative arrangement with Messrs. Munday, a firm of contractors, to put up the large sums judged necessary to carry out the project. This hasty contract was superseded at the end of the year when a Royal Commission to sponsor the Great Exhibition was established by Parliament, largely thanks to Sir Robert Peel. Without such official recognition the project could hardly have gone forward successfully even in the heyday of laissez-faire.

The Commission originally included Lord John Russell, then prime minister, Peel, Gladstone, and Cobden—certainly a distinguished array of Victorian statesmen. As representatives of architecture and engineering, Charles Barry and William Cubitt, whom the Prince had already consulted about the probable cost of erecting an exhibition building in the Park, were also prominent members. Earl Granville, a cousin of the Duke of Sutherland, was as vice-president the active executive up until he became Foreign Minister the next year. Granville worked in close association with a committee from the Society of Arts whose most energetic member was Cole; and Cole (at least according to his own very plausible account) was the real brains of the whole campaign. Subscriptions flowed in, led by £50,000 from S. Morton Peto of Somerleyton, the great railway contractor, whose fortune had evidently proved immune to the Hudson crash. Within a year nearly £80,000 had accumulated. But Cole and his associates had by then rounded up English exhibits requiring, it was estimated, some 400,000 square feet; at least as much (and probably considerably more) space would be required by the foreign exhibitors. How was the exhibition to be housed and what would its housing cost?

In January 1850 a building committee was appointed by the Commission. On this the Duke of Buccleuch and the Earl of Ellesmere, both enthusiastic builders, had as professional associates the architects Cockerell, Barry, and Donaldson, together with the engineers Robert Stephenson, I. K. Brunel, and William Cubitt, a brilliant roster of constructive talents. Twenty acres of the Park, at precisely the spot first suggested by the Prince, were now definitely selected as the site and an international competition was rather hurriedly organized. Out of the 245 designs submitted in this competition 65 received mention, while 18 others (of which no less than 12 came from French architects and engineers) were singled out for "further higher honorary distinction." Two ferrovitreous projects were finally selected from the 18 for still more exalted "special mention." One was a scheme by Hector Horeau (1801–1872), who had submitted an iron and glass design for the Paris central markets the previous year; the other was by Richard Turner of Dublin, the builder of the Kew Palm Stove and the Lime Street II shed, with whom was associated his architect brother Thomas Turner of Belfast. If it had proved possible to erect either of these projects with the amazing rapidity and economy of Paxton's, and if later that edifice could have been as successfully rebuilt elsewhere, Horeau or the Turners might have won immortal fame. Rightly or wrongly, the committee decided against commissioning either the Frenchman or the Irishmen.

In Horeau's project five parallel aisles were to be covered by a single continuously sloping gable roof. Over the very wide central aisle or "nave" the roof was to be supported by curved iron girders. The outer slopes would rest on straight girders connected to the iron columns by spandrel-brackets, the latter perhaps acting as cantilevers on the principle of those in the sheds of the Gare du Nord II in Paris as rebuilt a decade later. The "nave" was to end in a tall half-domed "apse" of iron and glass, and there were also to be "transepts." The iron members were to be broadly spaced and mostly rather heavy in section, as in contemporary railway sheds; the spandrels would be filled with large open circles and scrolls of frankly decorative character.

The Turners' scheme was less prosaic. It included no less than five domes, descendants of that of the Brighton Anthaeum, the central one 200 feet high, the others 150 feet. These would rise over a rectangular super-conservatory, 1,440 feet by 1,060 feet, within which a miniature railway was proposed to carry the public around. The estimated cost was £ 300,000—a figure which doubtless gave pause to a committee that had thus far collected only £ 80,000. On the strength of Richard Turner's great works at Kew and Liverpool, the latter just being successfully completed after four years of effort, it seems not unlikely that this scheme, given a similar period of years, could have been successfully executed; but whether it could later have been demounted and the components economically re-used is another matter.

The competition program had stated that "any cheap mode of construction will be fully considered." But men as well along in years and firmly established in their profession as were the architects and engineers on the building committee often remember from their own bitter experience that novel methods of design and construction can prove much more expensive and time consuming than their highly optimistic proponents suspect. So the committee set out to prepare a design of their own. As a matter of judgment they may have been right or wrong. But since the program did not require them to employ any of the competitors they were not necessarily unethical, as many said at the time, in disregarding designs which seemed to them unfeasible of execution within the short year that remained before the exhibition was to open.

Theoretically, the committee's design was intended to combine the best ideas obtainable from all those submitted, or at least from the top 18, a synthesis to which reference had originally been made in the program as among the possible ways of utilizing the premiated competitors' drawings. Were committee design ever really effective in architecture—a recurrent illusion of which the United Nations Secretariat provides the latest dubious example—this group should have produced something extraordinary; it certainly included most of the best British brains in the architectural and engineering professions (Fig. XVI 1). Actually the design is presumed to be almost entirely Brunel's—or some say Donaldson's—and has generally been deprecated. It is not, however, so devoid of virtue as is usually supposed.

Not ineffective visually, the committee's design influenced J. D. Herholdt (1818–1902) more than a decade later in the external treatment of his splendid Copenhagen Central Station built in 1863–64. It might not even have been impractical, had there been more time to erect it and no need to demolish it within two years (as the terms of the grant of the park site required) and to recover as much as possible of the original cost by selling the used materials. But the drum of the dome alone (of 200 foot diameter) would have required, it was estimated, some 15,000,000 bricks; these bricks would have become almost valueless when the building was demolished, just rubble to be carted away and dumped for fill.

Hence, when the character of the committee's design was generally known and it was offered to contractors for competitive bidding a noisy storm of not unjustified criticism broke. As has been said, this official design was published on 22 June 1850 in the *Illustrated London News.* A lithographed pamphlet had also been prepared to present it in full detail to such contractors as might wish to make bids. But even the faith of the committee (or at least of the parent commission) in the feasibility of the project seems to have been somewhat shaken by this time. Moreover, the enemies of the whole idea of the Exhibition, led in the Commons by the revolution-fearing Colonel C. de L. W. Sibthorp of Lincoln (a brother of the vacillating sponsor of St. Ann's Bedehouses there), attempted anew to quash the Royal Commission through the establishment of a Select Committee of Parliament to inquire into its operations. Wicked communistic foreigners would flock to London, Sibthorp warned the Parliament, and probably overthrow the British Constitution. Lord Brougham was an equally strong opponent in the Upper House. Salvation came like a miracle from a quite unexpected quarter.

Paxton in the 40's had come to be something like a Minister of Works to the Duke of Devonshire. He was also engaged on various outside town-planning operations as well as on building commissions like Lismore (in which he had the assistance of his son-in-law G. H. Stokes) that were quite conventionally architectural. His most significant new construction was a special greenhouse for an enormous water lily, imported from Africa and christened *Victoria regia,* that was thriving in a most embarrassingly expansive way under Paxton's care in the Chatsworth gardens. This Lily House was relatively modest in size, 60½ feet by 46 feet 9 inches, but extremely interesting technically (Fig. XVI 3). The lily pool was enclosed by a delicate glass-filled arcade and roofed over with ridges-and-furrows. These were carried on horizontal iron girders, not as in the Great Conservatory on arched ribs (Fig. XV 29). The span of the girders was reduced by two internal rows of columns rising on either side of the pool. The idea of attaching the outer skin of glass and wood only intermittently to the supporting iron beams was suggested to Paxton, according to his own account as given in a paper read at the Royal Society of Arts in the fall of 1850, from a study of the structure of the lily plant itself; for the thin flat web of its enormous leaves was strong enough to support a "good-sized" child because of the reinforcements provided underneath by a skeleton of curved ribs tangent to the underside. The use of the hollow interiors of the iron columns to carry the water from the gutters in the wooden furrows to the ground has, I believe, no such precise botanical prototype; but many hollow-stemmed plants with which Paxton would have been familiar might have suggested the idea. From this time on "Paxton roofs" and more specifically "Paxton gutters" became common technical terms, although the gutters had first been devised for the Great Conservatory a dozen years earlier.

The possibility of adapting the construction of the Chatsworth Lily House to the needs of a building for the Great Exhibition occurred to Paxton only in June. Among the Duke of Devonshire's vast interests, in which Paxton frequently represented him, was a large holding in the Midland Railway. When Paxton mentioned his idea to Ellis, the chairman of the Railway, at the House of Commons on 11 June the latter took him at once to see Cole at the Board of Trade. The proposals for tenders on the committee's plans were to go out to contractors in about two weeks. Yet after this conversation Cole suggested (and amazingly enough the committee accepted) the introduction of a special clause in the official request for bids permitting contractors to submit tenders on alternative designs along with those they might care to make on the committee's own drawings. Certainly this was an extraordinary idea and must have indicated Cole's personal lack of faith in the committee's design.

Paxton was an extremely busy man. It was only after a visit to Llanfair, where his friend Robert Stephenson was setting in place the final tube of the Britannia Bridge, that he was able to make his first sketches. He may well have talked then to Stephenson about his ideas for the exhibition building; but it was a day or so later, while he was presiding over a committee meeting of the Midland Railway at Derby, that he first scribbled a section and an end elevation of his scheme on the blotting paper which lay before him (Fig. XVI 4). Returning to Chatsworth after about ten days he began to draw up, with the technical assistance of the engineer W. H. Barlow whom he borrowed from the Midland Railway staff, more complete sketches of his project. The extraordinary boldness and simplicity of his design may well owe something to the hurried conditions of its preliminary production. Certainly imagination and not ratiocination called the tune.

On his way back to London after the sketch project was completed Paxton ran into Robert Stephenson again on the Trijunct platform at Derby, perhaps by previous arrangement. However that may be, they traveled to town together and he readily won the great engineer's full support for his scheme. In London he went first (at Stephenson's suggestion) to see Lord Brougham and won this important enemy of the whole exhibition idea over to his side. The next day Stephenson, who had been the first chairman of the Executive Committee of the Royal Commission, took him to Lord Granville; two days later he was received by Prince Albert. The Prince had known the Great Conservatory at Chatsworth since the Royal visit in 1843 and was easily persuaded to back Paxton; indeed, he probably realized that only such a novel scheme as this could save the whole plan for the exhibition from foundering. Still the commission itself hung fire despite the Prince's and even the dying Peel's strong approval of Paxton's project. It was only after the commission had, properly enough, referred the matter to their own building committee (who were, however, the joint authors of the official design) that Paxton took the bold step of publishing his project in the *Illustrated London News* on 6 July (Fig. XVI 2). The rather justifiable fury of the committee at this appeal to the public can well be imagined; but Paxton must have known that higher authorities would condone the irregularity, even if they had not actually suggested and approved it in advance. Public opinion fortunately was highly favorable, in part perhaps because Jerrold of the *Punch* staff invented the appealing name of "Crystal Palace" for Paxton's design. (Actually the term may not have been coined until the fall when it began to receive general currency.)

Paxton, preparing to take advantage of Cole's special arrangement about alternative designs, was by this time in touch with Fox and Henderson, engineering contractors whom he knew well, and also with Chance Brothers of Birmingham, who were the only manufacturers likely to be able to supply the quality and quantity of glass that would be needed. Thus by 10 July Fox and Henderson were able to offer, in addition to their tender on the committee's drawings, an alternative tender for a design that had been hurriedly developed in some detail from Paxton's Chatsworth sketches. This "Crystal Palace," as Jerrold christened it, they proposed to erect and to remove after the close of the exhibition for £79,800, retaining ownership of the components themselves. Or, if it were preferred to leave the Palace standing as the outright property of the commission, they would erect it for £150,000. This latter offer the building committee finally accepted after negotiating for the inclusion of an arched transept. The higher transept would permit the retention on the site of a certain tall elm of which Colonel Sibthorp had become the impassioned defender—the last card he had left to play against the Great Exhibition.

Since the idea of the transept certainly originated with the committee the story that it was Barry's contribution has some plausibility despite Paxton's opposing claim that it was his own idea. However that may be, Fox and Henderson agreed to include the transept without increasing their tender, a notably generous gesture. (Actually the contract was later adjusted—by some £35,000—to cover the additional cost of the whole edifice when it had been completed.) Moreover, since the commission was not yet chartered as a corporate body, Fox and Henderson agreed to proceed on no firmer legal basis than Lord Granville's personal word that the contract would be signed in due course. Agreement finally came on 26 July; five days later, on 1 August, Fox and Henderson took over the site although the contract was not actually signed until October.

A great many pages could be—and in other books have been—filled with startling statistics about the Crystal Palace. Probably to us in the 20th century the most extraordinary fact is that from 1 August, when Charles Fox (1810–1874) began a seven-week session of 18-hour days on the personal preparation of the working drawings,* to 1 May 1851, when the exhibition opened in the completed structure, was but nine months, a period more usually associated with human gestation than with the prolonged campaigns of design and construction that have been required for the flimsy pavilions of modern international expositions. The barest dimensions may be given to indicate how great was the feat not of building the Crystal Palace at all (which was great enough) but of building it within the available time before the Exhibition was due to open. The main area covered was 1,848 feet by 408 feet, but an additional area 936 feet by 48 feet extended along much of the northern side. The main building rose in tiers, the second tier 264 feet wide and the third 120 feet, to a height of three storeys, all covered with Paxton roofs (Fig. XVI 5). High above the whole rose the barrel roof of the transept, furrowed likewise, some 135 feet from the ground at its crown. Of the amounts of materials of various sorts used, one figure will serve to give an impressive idea of the relation of the operation to the English building industry of the Early Victorian period: The sheet glass, of which Chance Brothers contracted to supply 900,000 square feet, was equal to a third of England's annual glass production less than a decade before. Beside this the more than 3,000 columns and the 200 miles of wooden sashbars seem less phenomenal. The cost of enclosing 33,000,000 cubic feet works out at a little over a penny a cubic foot. Or, considering that the space was in fact merely rented from the contractors for some fifteen months, the rental was at the rate of less than a halfpenny a year per cubic foot.

The three men primarily responsible for this marvelous feat of rapid and economical space enclosure were recognized at the time as Paxton, Fox, and William Cubitt, the chairman of the building committee; for these three, along with Cole, were knighted in 1852 for their services. Paxton without a doubt was the real designing architect-engineer despite his lack of professional status; Fox (with his partner Henderson) was the contracting engineer; and Cubitt was the engineer representing the interests of the commission as client. One other man who received no knighthood, Owen Jones, also deserved great credit. He was responsible for the minor decorative as-

---

* As the separate drawings were furnished, Henderson planned the production of each of the various components and got it under way, an equal feat of engineering prowess.

538

pects of the Palace, particularly for the color; but that is something that we can apprehend today with less assurance than the ingenuity of the construction and the elegance of the design. In this field Barry also made an important contribution; for he suggested the multitude of flags of all nations which enlivened the otherwise rather flat and monotonous skyline, still usually the happiest decoration of exposition buildings.

In Paxton's first sketch made on the Midland Railway blotter the essential principles of both the design and the construction are clearly conceived; even the ultimate arched transept is perhaps implicit in the arched trusses provided under the flat roof of the nave (Fig. XVI 4). Here, and in the preliminary design published in July, the linking of the exterior piers is definitely arcade-like as on the Lily House that was the prototype (Figs. XV 2, 3). There are even proper capitals at the springing of the arches and no vertical elements continue upward through the spandrels. In the executed design the curved members forming the spandrels are definitely braces and the stanchions continue up to the top of each storey, enframing transom panels braced with central circles (Fig. XVI 7). The arched braces terminate below in an arbitrary modillion-like curve, with a slight scrolled enrichment, against the sides of the stanchions. But the character of the executed "capitals," which are mere thickenings of the octagonal stanchion shafts at the transom level, is as clearly determined by the casting process as is the diagonal cutting off of the sharp corners at the top of the spandrel openings and around the circles in the transoms. This was done in order to avoid as far as possible the small concave radii (to use a technical term) which are a source of weakness in castings, as has been said in discussing the Coal Exchange. (Why this was not done at the base of the spandrels I cannot explain.)

There are many other parallel refinements. Note the differences of detailing, for example, between the longitudinal lattice girders, cast in one piece, that supported the galleries, and the heavier trusses, which were built up to the same dimensions and the same lattice pattern out of cast and wrought elements, that carried the great weight of the roof (Fig. XVI 9). Then there is the graceful and expressive extension of the corners of the flanges where the separate sections of the interior columns are joined together; that was to provide clearance for the wrenches when the bolts and nuts were tightened at assembly and loosened at disassembly (Fig. XVI 8). Also "neat," in a modern slang sense, are the projections to hold the horizontal girders, but neat in the Early Victorian critical sense also.

Such detailing is based on direct knowledge of the methods of producing the separate parts in the factory, and also on a long and intimate experience with assembly procedures such as Paxton hardly had. The detailing, therefore, must be considered an important part of the contribution of Fox and

539

XVI

Henderson to the design. The actual appearance of some of the various components of the Palace can be checked in what remains of the Midland Station at Oxford (Fig. XVI 10). This structure was built by Fox and Henderson, but without benefit of Paxton's collaboration, in 1851 just as the Palace was reaching completion. Their bid was so much under that of any of the other builders it is surprising that other complete stations were not built in the 50's on the Crystal Palace system. But there at Oxford is an extant sample of the original Crystal Palace construction as authentic as the great monument at Sydenham which burned down in 1936. Being modest in size, moreover, its straightforward design was not confused by any attempt to outbid the splendors of the Hyde Park original. It provides a fascinating contrast to the Ruskinian ironwork in the court of the University Museum, dating from just beyond the limits of this book, which is so familiar to Oxford visitors with a serious interest in Victoriana.

The more carefully one studies the working drawings in Downes' book the more convinced one becomes that the architectural refinements of the Crystal Palace were of a new order, despite such occasional purely decorative touches as the little scrolls below the spandrels or the rather Saracenic cresting at the roof edges, both probably contributions of Owen Jones (Figs. XVI 6, 7). These refinements in the structural membering depend not on the sensitivity of a designer of Jones' retrospective background and training but on the producing engineers' peculiar comprehension, at once thorough and subtle, of the processes of manufacture of the components and also of the most convenient and rapid methods of assembly—and of *disassembly* also, it should not be forgotten—of those components on the site.

It is by no means certain that Paxton had nothing to offer here. The ridge-and-furrow roof was completely his invention, from the large unlapped glass plates (of a size he had first persuaded Chance Brothers to produce for the Chatsworth conservatory more than a dozen years before) to the gutters scooped out of the wooden members at the bottom of the furrows by the special woodworking machinery he had developed. Above all, the comparably ingenious sashbar cutting and finishing machines, by which the 200 miles and more of wooden members were prepared to receive the glass, had been his idea and such machine tools had first been used in 1838 at Chatsworth in completing the Great Conservatory (Fig. XVI 11). The other machine tools used for drilling and punching the iron parts at the site were presumably Fox's (or Henderson's) adaptation of existing factory equipment; but their presence at the site itself indicates a most advanced and elastic rationalization of serial production toward which Paxton may well have contributed something from his Chatsworth experience.

The most extraordinary aspects of the whole operation lie in what modern

540

industry knows as "production engineering" and in what might be called in military terminology the "logistics." This tremendous edifice was built—and could only have been built within the available time—by a remarkably tight organization of the supply of materials and the sequences of assembly, an organization that was the equivalent, conceptually, of modern line-production of complicated machine products like automobiles. A succession of teams of specialized workmen followed one another along the length of the site—foundation layers, column setters, and so forth, down to the final groups of sashbar carpenters, glaziers, and painters (Figs. XVI 12–14). At the same time subassembly teams were building up on the site such larger components as the fabricated trusses for the nave roof and the laminated wooden arches for the transept (Fig. XVI 13).

These arrangements imply a very nearly perfect correlation of the sources of supply. As anyone who has been concerned with modern assembly procedures well knows, a slight shortage in one minor part—say a nut of a particular size—can bring the whole line to a stop. Direct and exclusive contracts with the major suppliers—as with Chance Brothers—and Fox and Henderson's own primary responsibility for the manufacture of the metal components (although there must have been a good deal of subcontracting) doubtless simplified the problem. But the commission had no such authority as a modern government department does even in peacetime; the mere organization of the labor forces must have required very exceptional talents on someone's part. There was, for example, only one brief strike and never, apparently, any shortage of the specialized workmen needed.

It is tempting to continue this discussion of the procedures used in building the Crystal Palace. The degree of their correlation is rarely equaled in the erection of 20th-century skyscrapers and factories; their improvisation in 1850 was of the order of Henry Ford's principal contribution to modern industrial methods. But in a book on Victorian architecture it is perhaps more important to consider their effect on the resulting edifice. The utmost standardization of parts was obviously essential to rapid erection. This standardization merely carried further the modular planning and designing implicit in Paxton's thinking from the first, but it did carry it *further*. The metal parts, at least, must require as little selection as possible in order to fit at the site without adjustment; the achievement of maximum interchangeability—even more important if the components were to be taken down and reassembled elsewhere—implied a real feat of design and manufacture. It was in fact a triumph of production engineering of an order that had been attained by 1850 with only a few small products such as clocks and small arms, mostly in America, or so Sigfried Giedion informs us in his *Space, Time and Architecture* (Cambridge, Mass., Harvard University Press, 1948). Yet the visual results of such standardization are more significant here than its rationale. Modern architects and critics are, if anything, too preoccupied with rationalization in a present-day building industry which actually uses in most types of construction a smaller proportion of factory-made parts than did the Crystal Palace.

Some special refinements of detail have been noted already, but the overall effect of the building must now be considered. It is worth while also to attempt to imagine how the linear patterns, which can be apprehended so clearly in the contemporary wood engravings, were modified by Owen Jones' much debated application of his "science of color" to the decorative painting. Of this neither the contemporary photographs nor Dickinson's or Baxter's color prints provide entirely convincing evidence (Figs. XVI 15–16). Such visual documents are certainly attractive, but can they be considered accurate in the matter of color to the extent that the black and white views, whether photographic or wood engraved, undoubtedly are concerning matters of form? There was then no panchromatic film to control the photographic recording of color values; and the color prints, even if originally fairly correct, have faded unevenly, as an examination of several of the same group makes very plain.

The predominant pale blue of the metal skeleton—a distance color—must have enhanced the feeling of uncircumscribed space more than the color prints indicate. As in a modern factory, the view down the nave—and a fortiori diagonal views on the ground level or from the galleries—would have seemed like a view in a forest. Such vistas would have been effectively unbounded by visible walls, yet measured and hence defined by the intersecting three-dimensional grid of horizontal and vertical coordinates of the ironwork (Fig. XVI 16). The exhibits were like furniture in a room or bushes in a wood—or for that matter machine tools in a factory—as the Dickinson prints well indicate. They broke up the foreground irregularly and also masked the remoter distances. The strong red on the underside of the girders, condemned by most contemporary critics, was repeated behind the railings of the gallery and in the freestanding screens against which many of the exhibits were hung. It certainly seems most effective in the color prints; for it provides a phrasing of sharp accents in the Turnerian vagueness of the general light blue of the metal work. This is otherwise relieved only by the yellow on the diagonal faces of the columns and on some projecting details. The most frequent contemporary criticism of the color was that it was more appropriate to wood than to metal. But one of the dreary or horrid alternatives suggested by hostile critics as more appropriate for the metal elements of construction was a brown-black, like rusted cast iron, with golden yellow accents, surely a rather grim alternative.

542

The Palace seems to have framed its unbelievably heterogeneous contents with more grace and ease than might have been expected. They ranged from Hiram Powers' white marble "Greek Slave," shivering in a red velvet tent, up to the largest power machinery and down to the most minute objects made of precious stones and metals. The Crystal Fountain designed and executed by Osler of Birmingham is one of the few major exhibits that seem worthy of the Palace. The carriages on display were also miracles of functional grace and elegance, easily surpassing in their perfection of form and expression the details of the surrounding metal structure which I have so highly praised. They have hardly been equaled before or since in vehicle design. Yet the new spacial effect was most fully appreciated before the contents were installed and again after they were removed. Of this effect the Midland Station in Oxford, small and low, gives no idea; but the nave of the second version of the Palace at Sydenham, entirely arched like the original transept (Fig. XVI 26), certainly gave some impression of that portion of the Hyde Park edifice, the portion most generally appreciated by contemporaries.

In Hyde Park Colonel Sibthorp's elm had given scale to the transept (and also amusing difficulties about birds in the early spring of 1851—I shall not steal Mr. Hobhouse's best story by explaining this reference). The vaults of traditional architecture, not to speak of the arched roofs of the finest existing ferrovitreous structures, had prepared the way for aesthetic apprehension of tall spaces that were semicylindrical overhead. The length was not so great but that the interior façades at the ends, with a familiar spoke pattern in their vast lunettes, provided a bounding screen to terminate the view (Fig. XVI 15). The transept was absolutely, as well as relatively, much higher than the nave; and undoubtedly extreme vertical dimensions, as in mountains, are more awe inspiring than extensive horizontals, as in plains and deserts—at least they were to Victorians, whose sensibilities had been trained in the Romantic period.

Spacially speaking, the great wartime factory at Willow Run near Detroit, which is most like the nave of the Crystal Palace, is boring to most people; while the concourse of the Grand Central Station in New York, for all the solidity of its painted sky, is not. Although the character of the space was more novel in other parts of the Palace, the success in space creation was probably greatest in the transept. That is why it would be of interest to establish whether or not the original suggestion for it came from Barry. Certainly his towered project for the second version of the Palace at Sydenham was extremely unhappy and inappropriate to the tenuous materials; but that does not prove that his architect's eye could not have imagined the fine feature that crowned Paxton's first Palace.

The detailing, down to the giant electric clock hands which utilized the twelve spokes of the lunette to tell the time, was due to the home team of Paxton and Fox and Jones, and most specifically to the last. Equally distinguished is the simple but frankly decorative treatment of the staircase and gallery railings which must also be Jones' (Fig. XVI 18). I cannot leave the edifice which is generally considered the greatest achievement of Victorian England without a final comment on the diagonal tying used in the transept bays and those contiguous to them. Never before or since has this sort of wire bracing been used with such immaculate elegance and functional expressiveness. Its almost invisible lines defined still more precisely than the heavier structural members the three-dimensional subdivision of the total interior space (Figs. XVI 15, 18).

But contemporary comment is more significant than any I can add, both because those who made it really had a chance to experience the Palace many times and because, on the whole, they were more capable of clear expression than 20th-century critics like me. We are today more befuddled than strengthened in our appreciation of the Palace by our knowledge of how inadequately its general promise has been realized in later architecture. We are also at a loss, as with any destroyed building, to determine how far our judgment of its quality is raised or lowered by the character of the available visual documents—in this case almost (but not quite) everything that the historian or critic could ask for. Even among contemporary comments mere uncritical praise is hardly worth quoting. The blanket condemnations of Pugin and Ruskin, men instinctively unsympathetic to the whole mid-19th-century industrial era of which the Palace was the finest flower, are also of little interest. Yet paradoxically Ruskin, at least, did have for such structures as the Palace and the great new railway stations some kind of approximation of a 20th-century functional aesthetic. He was ready to grant them various prosaic virtues just so long as their designers made no attempt to impinge upon the sacred realm of Architecture. There were many others, however, who could see at least vaguely how Paxton and his associates were broadening the very concept of architecture, even though these critics were quite unable to develop that broadened concept any further.

In 1851 the Royal Gold Medal in architecture was, on the recommendation of the Royal Institute, presented to T. L. Donaldson (and not in this year or any other to Paxton or to Fox, it might be noted). Relatively unproductive as an architect, Donaldson is not a major figure to posterity. But he was one of the *doyens* of the profession in 1851; he had moreover been head of the only school (that at University College, London) where anything like a professional curriculum in architecture was offered in the England of the 40's and 50's. He was also a member of the Royal Commission's building committee and seems to have shared with Brunel the onus of responsibility for the ill-fated project Paxton's had superseded. The tribute Donaldson paid to the Crystal Palace in accepting his Gold Medal is therefore the more notable. To him it was "the most successful edifice of modern times"; and he was careful to say that as much credit went to Fox and Henderson as to Paxton, as well as to mention the major contributions of Owen Jones and of his committee colleague Barry. (This last recognition is one of the things that strengthens the attribution of an idea of the transept to Barry since Donaldson must have known the facts and was relatively impartial.) He did not bring in the name of William Cubitt at all, it is interesting to note.

More definitely critical comment can well be quoted from a writer in the *Ecclesiologist*. That journal was of course the organ of a clique of fanatical specialists little likely to be even interested in ferrovitreous building—or so one might have supposed except for the Ecclesiological Society's subsequent commission of 1853 for a "model" church of cast iron. Considering the Palace as an architectural work, the reviewer repeats, but with more graciousness and balance, Ruskin's strongly negative opinion: "Lost in admiration at the unprecedented internal effects [he still found] it is engineering—of the highest merit and excellence—but not architecture," a tenable critical position even today. Yet to say, as the reviewer did, that "form is wholly wanting" indicated considerable visual insensitivity or, as is more probable, a very limited definition of form in architecture. The additional complaint, that "infinite multiplication is destructive of the Palace's claim to architectural merit," was not without perspicuity. In that point certainly lies the crux of a serious aesthetic argument concerning not the Crystal Palace alone but the claim of much of the best building of the present century to be architecture in the fullest sense. Recognizing that the Palace was a temporary structure, the *Ecclesiologist*'s reviewer finally stated that its admittedly great virtues paralleled those of architecture as might those of an oriental monarch's tent; but architecture by his definition (and by many others'—today one would perhaps rather put it *monumental* architecture) must have relative permanence.

What I have said earlier about the similarity of the spacial volume of the nave of the Palace to that of modern factories was acutely, if negatively, recognized in one aspect by the critic's remark that the Palace was not an "organic whole." He pointed out that it could be enlarged or reduced in size without really affecting its external or internal visual qualities. "Organic" has several meanings in relation to architecture; in some ways—in terms of process—the Palace is one of the most completely organic edifices ever planned and built. But visually the critic was right; the Palace was not, in the way of a Butterfield church or a Frank Lloyd Wright house, an "organic whole." Rather, like an Albert Kahn or an Owen Williams factory, the Palace was extensible or retractible without essential modification of character. It is sad that the Crystal Palace should actually have discouraged the *Ecclesiologist's* "dreams of erecting churches, or at least clerestoreys, of iron and glass" as their critic wrote. But this was only temporary, and the dreams bade fair for a moment to be realized in the next few years with Carpenter's cast-iron church.

A correspondent wrote to the *Ecclesiologist* just after this article appeared with much warmer praise of the Palace. He found the "skill, ingenuity, and talent in its construction . . . as daring, though not so enduring, as that of the most glorious mediaeval piles: the construction is almost invariably *real*, and all its beauty depends on the development of that construction." I italicize a favorite catchword of the more sophisticated critics of the day; it was probably introduced by James Fergusson (1808–1886) and perhaps indicates his authorship of the letter. Whoever he was, the writer preferred the tall proportions of the transept to the squat proportions of the nave and also regretted the roof was invisible from the exterior except over the transept. Both were understandable reactions.

He then commented with enthusiasm on the success of Owen Jones' polychromy. Over-all polychromy was a major critical excitement of the moment even though it was not yet generally accepted as desirable. Nowhere had it been employed so extensively as at the Palace. When one looks down the nave the ends seemed to disappear in a light blue fog, he noted, because of the handling of the colors. This could be considered a triumph or a failure of architectural expression according to one's acceptance or rejection of the Palace's revolutionary new spacial concept. The writer concluded that the "forte of the [iron] style is clearly not in beauty"; which is surely true enough if beauty be associated, as it had been in the 40's, chiefly with the stone architecture of 14th-century England and of cinquencento Italy. But this writer actually preferred to beauty what he called "reality" in architecture. To distinguish reality from beauty, as he did, was equally necessary in order to appreciate Butterfield's Camdenian-sponsored revolution of these same years in masonry church architecture (see Chapter XVII).

The foreigners who came to London for the Great Exhibition were, if anything, more enthusiastic about the Crystal Palace than the British. The Palace itself was for them the chief exhibit. Whereas to the British, who wanted to sell their own goods, the fact that the technical ingenuity of the Yankees and the traditional artistic taste of the French, as illustrated in the Exhibition, were showing up their best home efforts in several departments of art-manufacture was understandably disturbing. It could not but dampen somewhat their appreciation of the edifice that housed those exhibits. Reichensperger was a German ecclesiologist—or at least a learned gentleman whom the *Ecclesiologist* accepted as a colleague in that special, rather purely Anglican, "science." He was quoted as finding the "total effect of the interior magic and almost intoxicating" even though the "high sense of the beautiful" was overlooked. Paxton, he felt, had executed his task as an engineer rather than as an architect, producing a tent, not a building. (Functionally, it might be remarked, this was obviously the most sensible thing to do in providing shelter for an exposition.)

The eulogies have been sampled. Fame, the ancients' reward for virtue, assured the Crystal Palace an intangible immortality in the minds and even the hearts of men. When the end of the Palace's fifteen months of life came in the summer of 1852, the other reward of grace that it received could, for a long while, hearten pious Christians even though it eventually confirmed rather the materialistic theories of biology. After all attempts to achieve perpetuation of the Palace on its original site had failed and the original contract with Fox and Henderson to disassemble the structure had been carried out, in the years 1852–54 the components of the Palace rose from the dust of Hyde Park to physical reincarnation on the Sydenham heights south of London. Yet there was something a little unsatisfactory about this resurrection of the flesh.

The long afterlife in the suburbs, filled though it was with the soft susurration of palm trees and high adolescent voices singing the Alleluia Chorus, was increasingly inglorious. I never saw it myself, but in late photographs the Sydenham Palace suggests less a resurrected body according to Christian doctrine than an embalmed corpse. By the time the Palace was finally cremated by accident in 1936 the odor of sanctity had, I judge, given place to something distinctly mustier; but the final fiery obliteration of the physical integuments of the Palace revived its fame: Its spirit is more respected today than ever now that its body is no more.

In regard to the afterlife of the Crystal Palace the biologists have the better of the argument. Superiority of inheritance—sometimes, in this or that aspect, actual superiority to the parent—was evidenced in numerous early progeny, even though the strain rapidly deteriorated through miscegenation. Today a vast array of modern buildings claim descent from the Palace, with more or less genealogical plausibility, as aristocrats do from a Charlemagne or a Norman William. Many 20th-century architects might with more reason introduce Paxton into their professional names than John Buonarroti Papworth did that of Michelangelo. Besides descendants, the Palace also had brothers and sisters; all except the little station at Oxford were stillborn but they are interesting nonetheless as illustrating the limits of Paxton's imagination as an engineer-architect.

Paxton readily accepted the distinction his critics made between ferrovitreous and other sorts of architecture. In the church at Baslow, which he was restoring for his duke at the very moment the Palace was being erected, his respect for its original 13th-century style and his handling of the ritual arrangements met with the full approval of the *Ecclesiologist*. At Lismore in Ireland for the duke, at Mentmore in England and at Ferrières in France for the Rothschilds, he—or rather his collaborating son-in-law Stokes—accepted the most conventional standards of the age for eclectic architectural design in stone as we have already seen. But in situations where Paxton thought the articulated and translucent structure of the Crystal Palace appropriate—as it certainly was not for the restoration, however drastic, of Derbyshire churches and Irish castles or for the palatial housing of international financiers—his mind remained creative. Moreover, in these later ferrovitreous projects he was perhaps more creative architecturally than technically since the major technical problems of the new building method had now been solved.

In the wave of general enthusiasm that greeted the opening of the Crystal Palace it was natural that Paxton should be called upon to provide designs for all sorts of structures. Graciously he complied with most of these requests and on some occasions seems to have come forward with unsolicited suggestions. He submitted in 1851, for example, a project for roofing the court of the Royal Exchange with iron and glass, something actually not accomplished until much later (Fig. XVI 17). He supplied a design, never executed, for a large (200 feet by 72 feet) glass and iron exercise room to be attached to the City of London Hospital for Diseases of the Chest at Victoria Park (Fig. XVI 21). Rather overelaborate in design, this was technically remarkable for the inclusion of what we would today call air conditioning.

The elaboration of the exterior of this project may have been in response to adverse comments on the simplicity of the Crystal Palace itself. Several such were reported in the *Builder* by James Edmeston. An unnamed Dutch architect, who was also quoted in the *Builder*, claimed with some justice that ferrovitreous construction lacked surface relief and further urged that more should be made of the opportunities iron provided for adding inexpensive cast ornament to structural members. Even Cockerell, when he came to "the vast importance of iron . . . in its artistic application" in his sixth Royal Academy lecture in 1852, stated ex cathedra (and effectively in answer to Ruskin) that it was "an error to suppose the material incapable or unworthy of decoration."

Since iron casting offered endless opportunities for mass-produced decoration as well as for innovations in basic structure, the simplicity and functional elegance of the earlier ferrovitreous buildings were soon rejected for richer effects. The rising *horror vacui* of contemporary taste led to excessive elaboration of detail in ironwork as the later 50's and 60's developed a more self-assured phase of Victorian style. Moreover, the engineering line of strictly structural development and the line of architectural exploitation, conceived largely as a matter of decorative elaboration, took diverging paths.

In the years 1851–54, however, many ambitious cities in England and throughout the world were projecting and building Crystal Palaces rather directly based on the original Paxton model—New York, Belfast, Dublin, Breslau, Copenhagen, among cities abroad, and even such modest resorts as Cheltenham and Stoke Damarel at home may be mentioned. For the New York Palace Paxton sent over a design in 1851. This project proposed an edifice 600 feet by 140½ feet divided into a nave and two side aisles. The gabled nave roof was to be supported on principals of timber, not iron. Turrets were to rise at the angles, as on the exercise room project for the Victoria Park hospital; this new design of Paxton's also followed that project very closely in the elaborate detailing of the exterior. The simpler interior ought, however, to have been one of Paxton's best efforts (Fig. XVI 19). Coupled iron columns were to divide the nave from the aisles. Narrow galleries would have run the whole length at clerestorey level; and these were to be supported on spandrel brackets similar to those forming a sort of arcade over the columns. The spacial composition would have been more conventional than that of the Hyde Park Palace, but clearly conceived and nobly scaled.

Bogardus' alternative scheme for the New York Palace was bolder and a much better example of thinking in terms of "remountability." But it was not at all appropriate to the material in its detailing; for the Renaissance arcading of the exterior walls of the enormous rotunda was to consist of precisely the members then so popular in America for cast-iron commercial façades. So large was the diameter of the edifice, however, that the individual components could be straight in plan and hence readily sold to builders for use in business structures after the building was disassembled, certainly a sound idea economically. Too bold even for the expansive 50's, however, was Bogardus' idea for roofing his structure with sheet iron suspended from radial rods following a catenary curve down from a tall observatory tower in the center to the outer walls. Even today suspension principles in architecture are more talked about than exploited at such enormous scale. But with Roebling then planning to span the Niagara River with one of his wire-cable bridges, it is not really surprising that the ingenious Bogardus should have proposed utilizing a similar principle to hang a roof over an enormous exhibition hall.

The executed New York Crystal Palace in which the 1853 Exhibition was held need not concern us much. It cannot have been one of the best-favored children of the London parent, and an early holocaust precluded any detailed portraiture by photography. Two points about it are of interest, however, for they were omens, the one favorable, the other unfavorable, for the later development of metal construction. The New York structure's blazing end not only foreshadowed the ultimate destruction of the Sydenham Crystal Palace in 1936, more significantly it was a warning of those great urban fires of the early 70's in America which seemed to confirm the wisdom of the more conservative British in not emulating Bogardus' iron-fronted shops and warehouses.

A passenger lift was a principal exhibit at the New York Palace although it operated in a tall detached tower. Such elevators as they were called in America, suspended by Roebling's wire cables, were soon to provide means for reaching upper storeys without effort. They would render desirable and useful the tremendous increase in the height of urban edifices metal construction would soon make physically possible. Without vertical transportation for visitors office buildings would never have grown into skyscrapers in the way they did in New York in the 70's and in Chicago in the 80's. When the lead in metal construction conclusively passed from Britain to America it was the "elevator buildings" of New York and Chicago that prepared the way for the masterpieces of Louis Sullivan and his colleagues in the 90's.

Far finer than the New York Palace was that built in 1852 for the Great Industrial Exhibition of 1853 in Dublin. This was designed and built by John Benson of Cork who was knighted, as Paxton had been, on its completion. Benson was the winner of a competition in which Deane and Woodward, also of Cork, were second; Richard Turner of Dublin, once more out of luck as in the earlier London competition two years before, was third.

Benson's earlier Cork exhibition building, erected in 1851–52, had had wooden arches and contained little if any structural iron. For the Dublin Palace C. D. Young and Company of Edinburgh supplied cast-iron columns although Turner received the contract for the laminated-wood arched girders, which closely resembled those of the transept in the Hyde Park Palace. The plan consisted of three parallel naves 425 feet long, each ending in a half-dome. The central nave was 100 feet wide; the two at the sides 58 feet. There were also four aisles, two between the naves and two others along the outer edges. Each of these was 25 feet wide and had upper galleries (Fig. XVI 23). The vitreous element was here even more in abeyance than the ferrous; only the crowns of the nave roofs were filled with glass, while the half-domes were covered externally with waterproof cloth. Yet despite the relative solidity and opacity of the exterior the harmony of the various curved forms, particularly at the half-domed ends, seems to have given the Dublin Palace something of the bubble-like quality of the Kew Palm Stove (Fig. XVI 22). Except for the simple foliate capitals of the iron columns there was even less arbitrary ornament than at Hyde Park. But the structural diamond pattern of the arched trusses of the principal nave was agreeably echoed in the similar patterns of the gallery trusses and even in the design of the gallery railings. This great work of Irish architecture deserves to be much better known.

While the possibility still remained of retaining the original Crystal Palace on its Hyde Park site as a gigantic "winter garden" like one he had admired in Paris in the 40's, Paxton prepared a design for its enlargement of which a model was placed on view inside the Palace itself in the spring of 1852. He proposed to extend the lowest level of the building at each end in order to form vast exedras enclosing courts that could contain the largest scientific exhibits (Fig. XVI 25). Four towers were also to have been added at each end of the original edifice for ventilation and to mask the chimneys of the heating apparatus. Two would be placed on the corners of the highest tier of the nave rising two tiers more, with two others above the corners of the middle tier rising one tier more. All this would have been carried out on the existing module and with the identical vocabulary of construction and detail. Paxton evidently hoped, by thus raising the ends according to Barry's favorite compositional formula, to make the whole Palace more organic in design. One fears the additions would have had no such happy result but merely have confused the simple regularity of the original scheme.

Parliament in the end insisted that the site be cleared. A new private company was therefore formed to buy the materials from Fox, Henderson and Company after their disassembly and to erect with them a permanent exposition structure at Sydenham. The *Builder* published a project by a Mr. C. Burton for a tower 47 storeys high to be reassembled from the materials. (This was before the Sydenham site was obtained.) No man-made structure ever reached a comparable height before the Victorian period was effectively over. Yet it was stated that Fox and Henderson were convinced it could be safely erected; one may wonder how they would have braced it against wind stresses.

Actually the second Crystal Palace was to be the work of the same men who had been chiefly responsible for its first incarnation, Paxton, Fox and Henderson, and Owen Jones as advisor on decoration. (One hears no more in this connection of Sir William Cubitt.) Barry also made suggestions for "improvements" to the design; fortunately they were not accepted. His son remarks, with filial piety, that they "would have done much to redeem from ugliness a building, which has the advantage of enormous scale, and which must be a conspicuous feature in every view of the environs. The plan proposed would have had a striking and even magnificent effect, and one, moreover, unique in its kind. Few can fail to regret that, even when rejected, it was not allowed to suggest some bolder and more artistic effect than is seen in the existing building." Superior as the relative simplicity of the executed Palace must

551

seem to 20th-century taste without Barry's three pointed domes, rising where the three transepts cross the nave, and the nine additional domed turrets, which were to be placed where they would do the most damage to Paxton's clean silhouette, or so it would seem, Barry's suggestions may have stimulated Paxton to prepare a more elaborate design of his own (Fig. XVI 20). In this superb scheme three domed pavilions were to stand in front of the main line of the tall nave. The reverse-curved terminals that crown these domes, providing a piquant climax to their bubble-like transparency, seem almost like an echo of the Brighton Anthaeum. Owen Jones was to use similar oriental motifs in his projects for a Paris Crystal Palace to be built on the heights of St. Cloud and for a North London Crystal Palace at Muswell Hill, both dating from the end of the decade, which are among the finest of many unrealized ferrovitreous dreams. These later designs by Jones and his recognized position as an authority on Saracenic art suggest that Paxton in this alternative project was really influenced by him rather than by Barry. However that may be, this scheme represents the culmination on paper of Paxton's career as a designer of buildings of iron and glass.

The idea of the continuous arched roof over the nave in the executed Sydenham Palace was perhaps inspired by Benson's Dublin Palace as well as by the original Hyde Park transept (Fig. XVI 24). But the expression is less regular; for the arched lattice trusses, now of metal rather than of laminated wood, were used only intermittently along the nave and broke up the continuity of the interior volume in a rather unfortunate way (Fig. XVI 26). In the center of the building the roof of the main transept was carried still higher than those of the nave and the minor transepts at the ends. All three transept ends were buttressed by rising tiers of regular horizontal construction, a treatment which seems to parody the sort of pyramidal composition suitable for massive buildings of masonry. It was certainly not a happy arrangement for the outer web of a transparent volume. Unhappy also, as a similar parody of masonry design, were the broad bands corresponding to the main diamond-trussed arches inside which formed projecting frames like giant archivolts at the transept ends on the garden side.

Successive storms and a serious fire during construction gave the prophets of disaster cause to shake their heads, but the Sydenham Palace went up in two years and was opened in 1854. The terraces and elaborate parterres extending down the slope are perhaps the most considerable remaining example of Paxton's work as a gardener. But the eclectic virtuosity of his gardens here is inferior in interest to what he did at Chatsworth within a frame that went back to Capability Brown or in his suburban parks at Birkenhead and Glasgow. More interesting than the executed scheme was an earlier pro-

552

posal in which he included a considerable residential area to the northwest of the Palace.

The water towers at either end of the Palace, although provided with ridge-and-furrow roofs of the Paxton type, were entirely Brunel's. With their over-hanging observation galleries, these are rather clumsy in silhouette and their heavy metalwork contrasted disagreeably with the delicacy of the Paxton-Fox-Henderson membering on the Palace itself. From a distance, however, they gave a not ineffective vertical accent, and one that survived the fire of 1936.

Various "courts" illustrating the different styles of architecture were set up on the ground floor of the Palace in the side aisles. Owen Jones, M. D. Wyatt, E. M. Barry, and others were responsible for these, not Paxton. They had no connection at all with the ferrovitreous architecture around and above them; indeed, their very presence must now seem to have been anomaly. But Jones in his later projects, Wyatt already at Paddington II, and even young Barry eventually in his Floral Hall beside the Covent Garden opera house all gave evidence that they understood quite well the visual possibili-ties of Paxton's ferrovitreous "style." Hardly a glazed arcade or a covered market was now proposed at home or abroad but it was said to be of "Crystal Palace construction" or, more strikingly, in the "modern English style," the one style not represented in the Architectural Courts.

Wherever Paxton's ridge-and-furrow roofs were used, as in much railway station work, the relationship to the Crystal Palace is direct; for the device was protected by patent. Such edifices may all be considered legitimate descendants of the first generation. The Midland Station at Oxford by Fox and Henderson already mentioned and a smithy they built at the Portsmouth Navy Yard in 1852, whether or not these actually incorporated—as the latter was expected to do—actual materials from the Hyde Park structure, are sib-lings rather than children of the original Crystal Palace and actually senior to that at Sydenham.

Nevertheless, in these culminating years of Victorian activity in iron con-struction, the greatest feats and the most distinguished architectural achieve-ments—after the two London Crystal Palaces and perhaps also after that at Dublin—are railway stations. The years 1845–50 opened the "classical" period of station building, as has been said in the preceding chapter; the suc-ceeding years 1850–55 conclude it; after that the story becomes somewhat anticlimactic. Exactly corresponding in date with the two versions of Pax-ton's Crystal Palace, the two finest London stations, both fortunately almost completely intact, represent the English if not the international apogee of railway architecture. King's Cross, built in 1850–52, is in terms of its archi-

553

tectural expression earlier than Paddington, built in 1852–54, by a decade rather than by two years (Paddington, in fact, might almost be considered High Victorian). But, as has been said, it is rather irrelevant in discussing station sheds, which lie largely within the realm of technics, to emphasize contrasts between artistic style-phases which overlap as much as the Early and the High Victorian. A third station, Grand Central (now New Street) in Birmingham, exceeded both of the London stations as a technical achievement. But this seems never to have been as much an organic whole as either of the others; only a little of its original construction remains visible today in any event. Grand Central was built over practically the same years (1850–54) as the two London stations, thus more than a decade and a half before its New York namesake which was perhaps the first transatlantic station to be a really major structural achievement.

Station building was little affected by the crisis of 1849 in railway financing. With general prosperity rising, indeed, extension of the railway network in fact barely halted. Increasing traffic continued to demand large additions to existing stations, moreover, as at London Bridge where several lines were now using the joint terminus. The architect of the extensions there who began the process of burying Roberts' handsome original station in a heterogeneous labyrinth of undistinguished construction was Samuel Beazley, better known for his theaters. His Lord Warden Railway Hotel at the port in Dover, built in 1850–53, is also part of the mid-century schemes for bettering passenger communication between London and the Continent. That handsome post-Palladian block, like the Royal George at Huddersfield, is evidence of the slowness with which Victorian stylistic novelties were accepted in hotel design before the late 50's (Fig. XVI 27). Yet it was actually begun only two years earlier than such initiatory examples of the use of an advanced sort of Victorian Gothic in this field as Southerndown Hotel near Bridgend in remote—and romantic—Glamorganshire by J. P. Seddon (1827–1906) (Fig. XVI 28), not to speak of the Hardwicks' proto-Second Empire Hotel at Paddington (Fig. VII 16).

Now at last the Queen had her own Royal Station at Windsor, costing £6,970, with special resting rooms for her private use. This modest Tudor object, though on a branch line of the Great Western from Swindon, was designed not by Brunel but by Tite, dullest of railway architects. But Tite's day among the architects was coming to an end as he grew to be more and more of a City magnate. It was to another and more distinguished early station architect, Lewis Cubitt, that the next important railway to enter London, the Great Northern, entrusted its London terminus. Among the 593 miles of railway opened to traffic in 1850, the Great Northern line had in many ways the most style. Its carriages, for example, were of varnished teak, as proposed by Edward Bury, F.R.S. Thus they were much more subdued and expensive looking than the rolling stock of other British railways which was generally merely painted with gay livery colors.

For its London terminus the Great Northern acquired in 1850 the site of the old Smallpox Hospital in the New (i.e., Euston) Road near its intersection with the Caledonian Road, a point long known as King's Cross. A small temporary station was first hurriedly built north of the Regent's Canal, but Cubitt was already preparing plans at that time for the permanent station to the south. The ground for this was cleared in 1851, and King's Cross Station itself was rapidly completed in very much less time than had been required to erect the major stations of the late 40's. It was opened to the public on 14 October 1852. The great simplicity of the design of King's Cross is probably in part to be explained by the company's desire to have it ready as soon as possible after the opening of the line; but one suspects that it also represents a tacit response to the loud protests of the public—or at least of the worst fleeced investors—against the architectural extravagances preceding the Hudson crash. The Peruzzian splendors of the Euston II Great Hall were in fact never really rivaled in any later London stations, which helps to explain the frequent surprise of transatlantic visitors at their modestly utilitarian appearance.

King's Cross is the most utilitarian of stations but it is also perhaps the most expressive architecturally. Of the so-called "English Railway style," so well illustrated by Cubitt's Bricklayers' Arms a decade earlier (Fig. XV 24), only the clock tower over the plain buttress between the great arches of the front gives so much as a hint. King's Cross, as one ordinarily apprehends it, is of a stripped functionalism almost as severe as Ruskin thought appropriate to railway stations. The breadth of its scale is the most striking presentment of the great new forces of the Railway Age; yet the expression is rather more precise than that in offering a readily intelligible meaning even to casual travelers.

Two enormous arches, in four unmolded orders, built of London stock brick reveal frankly the ends of the departure and arrival sheds behind (Figs. XVI 30, 32); they also provide a principal front cleaner and bolder even than that of François Duquesney's Gare de l'Est in Paris, built over the years 1847–52. These arches are flanked and separated only by the plainest of square buttress piers topped with flat brick fascias. Under them the vast lunettes are subdivided by rectangular sash grouped between narrow vertical mullions. Under the two glazed lunettes a projecting porch, consisting of six segmental-arched openings, is bluntly terminated by the rusticated brickwork of the buttress bases.

The two other elements in the group of masonry blocks which enclose the great sheds are rather different in their scale; hence they appear almost like accidents—comparable in their apparent irrelevance to the huddle of Underground station entrances and kiosks that now defaces the area between the entrance and the Euston Road (Fig. XVI 32). Yet this very inconsistency of scale is in itself most expressive of the disparity of the various elements that make up a Victorian station even if the total compositional effect is quite inharmonious visually as a result. Quite differently than in Camdenian churches, the honest expression of the various related internal functions has led to a high degree of articulation on the exterior; if Pugin had designed a station it would presumably have been still less integrated visually.

King's Cross is one sided in plan, not two sided, nor is it provided with a head block like Euston II (Fig. XVI 29). Therefore the great arched portion of the façade is no more than an honorific screen, in principle rather like that of the Bricklayers' Arms. But no attempt was made, in the way Cubitt had done there, to mask the asymmetry of the various elements in the complex by extending the screen to the left and right of the shed ends. On the right the narrow standing space for vehicles beside the arrival platform is covered by heavy wooden trusses that help to buttress the shed roof on that side. This important plan element is represented on the Euston Road front only by its end. In that end opens a wide entrance arch with voussoirs and keystone of rusticated brickwork (Fig. XVI 30). But this feature is more or less masked in perspective by the heavy buttress tower on its left and often passes unnoticed today. The single office storey above, which is what now appears most underscaled on this side of the front, is an irrelevant later addition (Fig. XVI 32). As a mere appendage the arrival entrance was originally not too badly related to the main façade; but the same could never have been said for the larger wing on the left.

That left-hand wing, as seen from the Euston Road, represents only the relatively narrow end elevation of the long block containing the "pay office" which is now rather larger than before (100 feet by 40 feet by 40 feet high) but hardly a "concourse" (Fig. XVI 29). There are also waiting rooms and refreshment rooms within this block as well as various company offices on the floors above. As from the first in most English stations, the main elevation is quite properly turned toward the departure court running along its side flank. But this disposition does not justify, except on extremely radical functional-expressive grounds, the lack of compositional relationship between this important element of the station complex and the great arched screen of the front. This is visually more disturbing than at Euston I where the Arch and the station block were physically remote from one another.

In the detailing of this side block at King's Cross, particularly on the end which immediately flanks the great arched openings at the end of the sheds, Cubitt reverted to an almost Regency delicacy (Fig. XVI 31). This detailing may even seem earlier in its rather post-Palladian way than the fine Grecian terraces in nearby Tavistock and Gordon Squares which he had (probably) designed for his brother Thomas back in the 20's before his personal architectural career really began. As at Derby Trijunct or Huddersfield, the very plain Great Northern Station Hotel seems very loosely related to the rest of the complex. It occupies a curving block southwest of the departure court; very likely a year or two later in date, it was perhaps not even part of the original scheme.

The glory of King's Cross is its double shed, each side wide enough for seven lines of track and a full 800 feet long (Fig. XVI 31). The shed roofs were carried on laminated arches of wood. These members were fabricated on the ground like those of the Crystal Palace and then raised into position where they were firmly held by iron shoes at the haunches. The spans are each 105 feet and the arches rise 72 feet to their crowns. After the original eight-ply wooden arches began to deteriorate from the action of the steam and smoke of the locomotives below they were replaced in 1869 by arched steel girders. But these replacements were fitted into the original cast-iron shoes so that visually the sheds are little changed today. The widely spaced arches are supported on stone corbels at the top of brick pilaster-buttresses. The inner thrusts of the two ranges of arches cancel out; the wooden trusses over the cab shed, as has been said, take the thrust on the arrival side; while on the departure side the solid station block with its upper office storeys provides more than adequate abutment.

Except around the doors along the departure platform there is almost no masonry detail and little detail in any other material. But between the arches and the lower section of the roofing, which slopes out tangentially, there are cast-iron shoes forming ornamental spandrels. These are most elegantly—and almost abstractly—composed of large and small circles (Fig. XVI 33). Above the tangential slopes the roofs are entirely filled with great panes of glass divided horizontally by iron purlins. These give visual continuity to the long perspectives. Benson's Dublin Crystal Palace must have looked something like these sheds and may have derived some inspiration from them; the spans were certainly all but identical.

King's Cross has a vigor and a boldness of scale in the parts, as well as an absence of frivolous detail, that has particularly appealed to 20th-century taste. It is surely the Early Victorian climax of station shed development. It must also be in some sense a child of the Crystal Palace transept, designed just as Cubitt was preparing his plans for the station.

The directors of the Great Western Railway waited fifteen years to build a permanent London terminus; but when they finally did so Brunel provided them with a masterpiece rivaling in its richer way the severity of King's Cross. It is worth noting that the responsibility for King's Cross seems to have been predominantly the architect's, while for Paddington it was rather the engineer's. (My article on "Brunel and Paddington" in the *Architectural Review, 109, 240–246*, has rather more illustrations than can be provided here but is otherwise identical with what follows.)

Paddington introduced to London Andrews' Hull scheme of a monumental hotel block masking the ends of the sheds. The Great Western Hotel has been discussed at length in an earlier chapter (Fig. VII 16); it is only necessary to stress again that the hotel is *not* really a part of Paddington Station as unfortunately many visitors suppose it to be. Whether Brunel or his directors chose the Hardwicks as its architects, the station and the hotel are merely contiguous, not interrelated, buildings; they actually had less organic connection originally than the hotel and the station at King's Cross which at least face one another across a vehicle court.

Where King's Cross had two parallel sheds, Paddington had three (the fourth on the right is a happy 20th-century extension of the original scheme). Over the location of the original turntables, beyond the up-end of the platforms and behind the hotel, a large area now used as a concourse but then intended for shunting locomotives is covered with low Paxton roofs (Fig. XVI 35). Above these rise the vast glazed lunettes of the sheds, unframed by masonry, which are unfortunately visible only in oblique views around the ends of the hotel. Paddington had four platforms and ten lines of track to begin with. The inner platforms were reached by retractible drawbridges since there was at first no cross platform such as the modern concourse behind the hotel now provides.

The three sheds totaled only 238 feet in width so that even the large central one did not exceed in width the 105-foot span of those at King's Cross; but the elliptical (more accurately five-centered) arches are of wrought iron, 16 inches to 18 inches deep, shaped to an I-section (Figs. XVI 34, 36–39). The arches are untied and hence more striking visually than Dobson's at Newcastle (Fig. XV 46). Brunel gave his system rigidity by flaring out the bases of the cast-iron columns that carry the shed roofs and by bolting these broad bases to heavy concrete foundations. There are two 50-foot transepts for traversing frames to lift rolling stock across from one track to another. (These frames are no longer used and their technical character is not altogether clear, nor even the need for them considering the ample shunting arrangements to the south.) The transepts, which are of the same arched construction as the naves, diminish slightly the continuity of straight views, but they provide a richness of space composition and

558

a wealth of effective diagonal vistas almost unique in Victorian railway stations (Fig. XVI 34). The open area of the three roofs is narrower than at King's Cross; moreover, the skylights are not curved in section but consist of Paxton roofs tangential to the central arcs and sloping at right angles to the longitudinal axes. This is not a very graceful treatment; yet it does effectively express the difference between the glazed and the unglazed sections of the roof, a difference minimized in other sheds in favor of a unified containment of the interior spacial volumes.

Brunel employed Matthew Digby Wyatt as collaborating architect. Still very young, Wyatt was chairman of one of the committees of the Great Exhibition and had been among Cole's closest associates since their visit to Paris together in 1849. In 1852 a book of his containing 50 plates devoted to *Metalwork and Its Artistic Design* was published in connection with the exhibition organized that year at Marlborough House by Cole's new Department of Practical Art under the Board of Trade. These plates are mostly of rather small medieval objects, often of gold or silver, but they evidence Wyatt's preoccupation with designing metalwork appropriately.

Because of his reputation as an authority on Italian design, both medieval and Renaissance, Wyatt would soon be one of the collaborators on the Architectural Courts in the second version of the Crystal Palace; yet he came from the most modern-minded aesthetic milieu in mid-Victorian Britain, that connected with Cole and his Department of Practical Art. Brunel's definite instructions to Wyatt that the ornament for Paddington should be unrelated to any style of the past and suited to the new materials employed represented for Wyatt not an engineer's solecism of taste but a sympathetic challenge. The critical world of the early 50's, moreover, was ringing with attacks on "copyism" and calling loudly for "progressive developments." (Of this there will be somewhat more to say in Chapter XVII.) To these attitudes Wyatt was certainly responsive at this time; yet his decorative work at Paddington at the very beginning of his successful career is almost unique in a life more distinguished for organizational activity and educational leadership than for its very diverse and mostly quite derivative architectural fruits. (For more discussion of these see Nikolaus Pevsner's *Matthew Digby Wyatt, the First Cambridge Slade Professor of Fine Art* [Cambridge, 1950], in which the present Slade Professor at Cambridge pays tribute to the first to occupy the chair as Sir Kenneth Clark had earlier done at Oxford for Ruskin.)

Wyatt was asked by Brunel to assist as a decorator or, more accurately, an expert on ornament; perhaps, therefore, only the actual ornament is of his design. Yet there seems to be so coherent an integration between the general handling of the interior space and the detailing of the structural ele-

559

ments that a true collaboration between Brunel and Wyatt on the over-all design must, I think, be assumed. The extant drawings sent by Brunel's office to Fox, Henderson and Company for the contract include all the executed detail of the cast-iron columns. This is vaguely Moorish, but still more closely related to the overlappings and penetrations one finds in the detail of E. B. Lamb (Fig. XVI 36). Such forms were certainly novel and also very suitable to the casting process; but they are not elegant or suave in the way of Cubitt's spandrels at King's Cross, which still seem to look back toward Late Georgian models of industrial design in metal (Fig. XVI 33). There are various other bits of metal detail to be seen in the executed work; but the somewhat Alhambraic strap-iron bands that provide a purely ornamental tracery in the lunettes at the end of the shed, the pierced stars that lighten the webs of the arches, and the foliate curves of strap-iron that fill the lower ends of the main I-section girders do not appear in these contract drawings (Fig. XVI 36–39). Such ornament was probably added at the site from working drawings by Wyatt that have since disappeared. Not being an integral part of the structure like the modeling on the columns, these frills would probably not have come from Fox, Henderson and Company, or at least not as part of the basic contract for the main iron components.

Only every third arched principal of the roof is supported by a column; those between rest on heavy horizontal girders running the length of the sheds. The treatment of the juncture of the arched and the horizontal girders is rather complex; yet structure and decoration are here effectively fused in a fashion that is full of "character" and "reality," to use two of the most popular critical terms of the day. These newly desired qualities of expression, qualities many contemporary writers on architecture were now calling for with more or less vehemence, seemed to justify a great deal of clumsiness and coarseness, just as similar slogans are sometimes supposed to justify various crudities of detailing today. Such detail at this time appeared as a "manly" protest against the petty frippery of Early Victorian ornament; now similar gaucheries are acclaimed as a desirable alternative to "drugstore-modern" slickness. The mid-20th century *should* be able to understand Wyatt's work at Paddington; the mid-19th could readily see it as a parallel in architecture to the gawkiness of the new Pre-Raphaelite painters who had, in 1852, just received the public approval of Ruskin.

Although there were some island enclosures on the arrival platform, the Paddington sheds were essentially open on all sides except along the departure platform. There the wall of the waiting room and office block, visible only up to the top of the ground storey, abuts the arched principals of the departure shed. On the outside of this block a tremendous marquee detaches the elaborate decoration of the ground-storey wall from the barren storeys of company offices above which are only seen from the higher level of Eastbourne Terrace. These lower walls, both on the outer and on the inner side of the block, consist of ranges of arched openings with "pilasters" between them (Fig. XVI 37). The upper half of the pilasters is occupied by flattened brackets comparable in design to the "capitals" of the isolated cast-iron columns. Fat moldings surround the arches and the spandrels are tightly filled with scrolled relief decoration. All this detail looks like iron; if it is not iron but cement Wyatt must have consciously assimilated the modeling to the character of ironwork, something that had hardly been done before except by Francis Thompson in his carved-stone grilles on the piers of the Brittania Bridge.

At the transept ends tall second-storey lunettes of office wall become visible. Each contains three arches from under the central one of which project iron and glass oriels (Fig. XVI 39). One of the oriels is, in function, merely the glorification of the little bay windows on way stations from which humble country stationmasters look up and down the lines; but the Paddington stationmaster rules a vast and complicated spectacle and so is allowed to look down upon it from a sort of Royal box. Since Paddington was the London terminus for the Queen's frequent travels between London and Windsor, a Royal Suite was added here to the usual provision of ticket offices, waiting rooms for two classes of passengers, and refreshment rooms. Alfred Stevens was approached to provide the decorations in one of the rooms of the Royal Suite but apparently nothing came of the idea. (Correspondence concerning this is at the Victoria and Albert Museum, Nikolaus Pevsner found out for me.) Upstairs very extensive office accommodations were provided and these are still occupied by the staff of the Great Western. In the Chief Engineer's office many valuable visual documents concerning the work of Brunel are preserved.

Wyatt's ornamental drawings, which might help to explain the theory behind his fantastic detail, are unfortunately missing. His ornament reached a climax of the "Victorian" (a term somewhat later to be used as a technical word for detail not of "copyistic" character) not in the Royal Suite but in the treatment of the walls surrounding the stationmaster's oriel and its mate (Fig. XVI 39). The pilasters between the windows are covered with flat incised ornament which is repeated above on keystones curiously outlined with double cusps. (The other voussoirs of the arches have similar concave scallops on their outer ends.) Higher up, around the inner edge of each of the arched transept roofs, a sort of pelmet of pierced voussoirs, rather like the edging of lace paper found in candy boxes but very coarse in scale, provides a stiff enframement for each of the two lunettes.

These curious ornamental features, like many later and more extreme

561

examples of self-conscious "Victorianism," are less easy to accept today than is the fat, cast-iron-like character of the molded detail on the walls below. But they are certainly not imitative nor can they properly be called illiterate; for Wyatt had a wide and sensitive knowledge of past ornament as well as a conscious desire to develop at Paddington a new sort of decoration appropriate to his own age. Only later did his detail become stylistically derivative and what the early 20th century would consider "tasteful"; the ornament here is admirably expressive of the most advanced taste of the early 50's.

It is appropriate that Paddington should be the subject of one of the most famous Victorian anecdotal pictures, W. P. Frith's "Railway Station." (One of several replicas hangs in the Great Western offices, Fig. XVI 38.) This painting ought to provide accurate evidence as to the original colors used on the shed; but by 1861, the date of the picture, Paddington had unfortunately been repainted a muddy brownish-gray. Other evidence indicates that the polychromy was even at first rather timid, merely some accents of red on a gray ground. When I was asked some years ago by Brian Lewis, then architect of the railway, what color I thought Paddington should be painted in the course of postwar repairs, I answered as a historian: "Gray with touches of red." Considering the many suggestions of Owen Jones' ideas so evidently present in the detail, I would now say as a critic that the elaborate theories of the lecture he gave at Marlborough House in 1852 on the "Science of Color" might well be applied. (This was published the same year as a pamphlet with the title *An Attempt To Define the Principles Which Should Regulate the Employment of Colour in the Decorative Arts.*)

Certainly no single color, and least of all a "respectable" pale green or buff, can be expected to do full justice to Wyatt's ornament, or even perhaps to the magnificent complex of spacial volumes inside the sheds. As a compromise the old Great Western livery colors, chocolate and cream, if boldly contrasted in the detail, might be appropriate. However it is painted —and it deserves a fresh coat every few years—Paddington, like King's Cross, remains physically in excellent shape. Now state property, the preservation and maintenance of these great Victorian stations as cultural monuments has become a public responsibility; of this responsibility one trusts the members of the Royal Fine Art Commission, several of them enthusiasts about Victorian architecture, are well aware. (Victorian stations are presumably too late in date to receive the protection of the Royal Commission on Historic Monuments.)

Before turning to the third great station of these years, Grand Central, Birmingham, a more modest London station in the City should at least be mentioned. Like Tite's earlier London and Blackwall stations, Fenchurch

562

Street is the terminus of an elevated line. Therefore its platforms are approached by stairs inside the masonry block facing on the street. Designed by the railway engineer George Berkeley in 1852, apparently without benefit of architectural advice, Fenchurch Street is uninteresting in detail compared to Paddington. But the carrying forward of the cambered trusses of the shed roof over the frontal block to end in a broad segmental pediment is effective. This very expressive device had hitherto been used chiefly on American stations. The pediment is heavily handled here, however, particularly in comparison with the delicacy of the scalloped wooden pelmet that edges the Paxton roof of the marquee along the street below. That has a charming "folk art" air like those on remote country way stations. Conceptually, Fenchurch Street is one of the most completely integrated of English stations even though it lacks all sophistication of expression. The Berlin stations of the 70's were to develop this model with great success after the day of British leadership in station design was over.

As at King's Cross, so also at Birmingham, when a new central station was proposed in 1850 much nearer the center of the city than Curzon Street, architectural pretension was discouraged by the reaction following the financial scandal of 1849. But the scale of the venture alone assured grandeur. The total width of the track area to be roofed was set at 200 feet even though the authorities could not for some time decide whether to use three parallel sheds or one single span exceeding in width even that of Lime Street II. An earlier statement in this chapter, which considered these stations of the 50's as architectural monuments, noted that Grand Central was less of an organic whole than King's Cross or Paddington; yet in the functional sense the new Birmingham station was, as we shall soon see, both extremely complete in its facilities and very logically organized.

William Livock, the architect, whose earlier Jacobean and Tudor stations have been mentioned, was here required to restrain his picturesque proclivities. He seems to have been less able to give ornamental distinction to the engineer's work than Wyatt at Paddington, perhaps because his responsibilities as a decorator were less extensive and his responsibilities as an architect limited to the frontal block. However that may be, the masonry part of the station was a plain and simple sort of Italian, close to the usual manner of Tite or Andrews and almost identical with ordinary commercial palazzos of the time. As with so many of those, the façade was executed in "white" brick with heavy Portland cement trim of conventional academic design. This front portion of the Grand Central complex—of which in any event the greater part is now obliterated by an enormous later hotel to the right—can almost be ignored visually as significant station architecture. But it does have conceptual values of a high order.

Livock's planning was excellent, as was also his complete integration of a rather large hotel with regular station facilities, something no one had as yet successfully achieved. The vehicle court, now a public street, is approached by a short spur from New Street—Stephenson Place this is called today, appropriately enough. A nine-bay arcade, set under the projecting four-storey block of the hotel, received the passengers who then passed into an unusually large range of waiting rooms, ticket offices, and refreshment rooms strung out along the departure side of the shed. (To the left a separate portal led into the company offices in one of the side wings of the front block.) For the first time in England the tracks in a major station came in below the street level. Passengers descended by stairs within the masonry block to the platform level; there they found themselves inside a tremendous shed which created almost as much excitement when it was new as the Crystal Palace itself.

Boldness had won the day and the engineer E. A. Cowper was allowed to design and execute a shed with a single span of 212 feet and a length of no less than 1,080 feet. In a bird's-eye view of the time, such as the double plate which the *Illustrated London News* happily published on 19 June 1858 at the time of the Queen's visit, this shed roof seems to take up a disproportionately large part of central Birmingham. It had no rivals in the world for several decades, I believe. The shed roof was supported by sickle-trusses executed by Fox, Henderson and Company. These were more remarkable feats of fabrication than any components of the Crystal Palace itself, for the 45 ribs each weighed 25 tons and rose 75 feet above the rails at their crowns. A continuous monitor filled with fluted glass provided ample illumination from the top of the shed.

The technical problems of fabrication and construction of the shed roof were worked out by J. Phillips of Fox, Henderson and by William Baker of the London and Northwestern Railway in association with Cowper. Livock as architect presumably had little to say about the form of the sheds beyond decorating the inner wall of the masonry block with a giant order of Tuscan pilasters. These were quite irrelevant in their highly conventional design to the sickle-trusses they appeared to support. At Paddington, in the same years when this Birmingham station was proceeding to its completion, Brunel was providing retractible drawbridges to reach the interior platforms; here for the first time permanent passerelles, crossing over the tracks at the upper level of the ticket offices, carried the passenger traffic to and from the island platforms in the middle of the shed and the arrival platform on the far side.

In 1885–86 this station was much enlarged. The shed finally taken down in 1946–47 was not, therefore, the original one; but it was quite similar in scale and technical character. Many can testify that as a feat of space enclosure this station shed was one of the most remarkable, even though it almost entirely lacked the other architectural qualities that give a higher distinction to King's Cross and Paddington. Except probably in the planning, there had evidently been no true collaboration here between the engineers and the architect. Hence architecturally—perhaps one should say visually—there was no coordination between the vast masonry hotel and office block containing 122 rooms and offices, the architect's chief contribution, and the shed which was the engineers'. If a Francis Thompson could have worked on this project in the same spirit in which he worked with Stephenson on the Brittania Bridge, the finest of all Victorian stations should have resulted. Livock seems to have reserved whatever creative flair he may have had for his picturesque medium-sized stations.

A City solicitor Charles Pearson had proposed in 1851 that a Grand Central Terminus for London be built in the Holborn Valley but the government rejected the scheme in 1853. In that year Henderson made a bolder proposal for a central terminus, all of iron, to be carried on piles in the middle of the Thames. Nothing came of that brilliant idea either. (It might well be revived as an eventual solution of the London terminus problem, at least for suburban traffic.) But what must have seemed rather more fantastic urban railway projects, at least when first proposed, came in time to execution and soon required a new type of station. The original scheme for an underground railway running from Paddington along the New Road via Euston and King's Cross to the City dates from 1853; the first stations of the Metropolitan were not built, however, until 1860–63 beyond the limit of this book. In Liverpool a high-level railway along the docks was begun in 1854 and completed in 1856 with very modest halting places. It was in the new world some twenty years later that elevated station design rose in New York to real heights of Victorian fantasy to the delight still of artists, if not perhaps of most passengers.

In 1852 J. Porter supplied prefabricated railway stations of considerable size to the Rio de Janeiro Railway. But really significant serial production —if not total prefabrication—of stations for English use came only considerably later, despite the admirable model provided in 1852 by Fox and Henderson at the Midland Station in Oxford. Prefabrication in general reached and passed its peak in the early 50's. The Crimean War, which had surprisingly little effect on building production in general, deflected the energies of prefabricators from their export trade with the New World and the Antipodes. Barracks and military hospitals ordered by the War

565

Office, both for home encampments and for shipment to the Black Sea, pre-occupied the industry and had what we would today call a "priority" on materials for several years.

Before the war began one more major monumental project of iron-skeleton construction was undertaken although its completion was delayed till the end of the war. The British Museum was barely finished in the mid-century, largely according to Sir Robert Smirke's original plans of the 20's although increasingly under his brother Sydney's supervision, when it became evident that the space for books in the King's Library was already quite inadequate. Several people seem to have had similar ideas at various times for building an iron structure in the vast interior court to serve as the principal reading room and to provide additional stacks. It was only in 1852, however, that Sir Anthony Panizzi (1799–1879), the brilliant Italian Librarian of the Museum, decided on the present scheme and called upon Sydney Smirke to prepare designs for it. A tender of some £100,000 from Baker and Fielder was accepted and construction got under way although it proceeded rather slowly for the next year or two. Unlike the square reading room with isolated interior supports carrying terra-cotta domes which Henri Labrouste built a few years later at the Bibliothèque Nationale in Paris, Sydney Smirke's plan provided a vast unbroken circular area with no internal supports over which was to rise an iron-ribbed dome 106 feet high. This dome was to be lighted by a very wide oculus in the center and by 20 large clerestorey windows between the ribs, a solution that was bolder than Labrouste's but less elegant. The structure is best appreciated externally in views showing the dome in construction (Fig. XIII 40) since the stacks are somewhat awkwardly arranged in the surrounding "spandrels" of the plan instead of occupying an adequate and regular site of their own as in Paris. A model of the dome was shown at the Paris Exhibition in 1855 and the next year at the Royal Academy Exhibition Sydney Smirke offered drawings of various sectional details.

Somehow the Reading Room as executed is rather disappointing; certainly the decorative treatment lately provided by the Office of Works seems at once sparse and incoherent. (Smirke's own ambitious plans for painted and sculptural decoration were never carried out in any event.) The proportions also, particularly as seen in photographs that must necessarily be taken with a wide-angled lens, appear clumsy: The walls are too low and the expanse of almost unbroken dome surface too great (Fig. XVI 41). Comparison with Bunning's Coal Exchange (Fig. X 14) once more reveals how rarely bigger, in the 19th century, meant better. Comparison with the Salle de Lecture of the Bibliothèque Nationale indicates how much more sure academic architects in France were at this time when it came to handling metal architecturally; but Henri Labrouste in all his work was, of course, a finer designer than Sydney Smirke.

Precisely during the war years came one of the most discussed examples of iron construction of the 50's. Curiously enough this edifice, intentionally temporary, was epoch making in the story of Victorian acceptance of iron, but epoch making in a negative sense; the animadversions against it certainly signalized the end of the ferrovitreous heyday of the preceding five years. Erected for Henry Cole's Department of Practical Art as a Museum of Science and Art and located at the southeastern corner of the large tract of land in South Kensington the Commissioners of the 1851 Exhibition had bought with part of the Exhibition's profits, this was the earliest manifestation of their intention, enthusiastically supported by Prince Albert, of developing what we would call today a "cultural center" as a memorial of the Exhibition. The tremendous complex of museums and institutes between the Cromwell Road and Kensington Gore, built up slowly over the next half-century and more, all stem from this modest structure of the mid-50's.

The activities of the new department, both educational and curatorial, which were to be so significant both for artistic education in Britain and for the general development of museums of applied and industrial art everywhere, had begun in 1852 at Marlborough House. That mansion was now required as an official residence for the adolescent Prince of Wales and the department's activities were henceforth to have their own headquarters just west of the Brompton Oratory. This first edifice of 1855–56, erected on part of the site of the present Victoria and Albert Museum, was in intention as much a warehouse for the storage of the department's growing collection of miscellaneous material as an organized museum project. Doubtless because the war made monumental construction difficult, or at least unpatriotic, Cole employed no architect nor even a well-known engineer to provide the design. The Edinburgh contractors C. D. Young and Company, who had supplied the columns for Benson's Dublin Crystal Palace, were entrusted with the entire responsibility for both design and construction.

It is true that Sir William Cubitt was supposed to be concerned in an advisory capacity but he seems to have had little or nothing to say about the particular form the building took—and perhaps cared less. Cole's architect friends Owen Jones and M. D. Wyatt, so closely associated with the educational work of the department in industrial design, were also conspicuously absent as consultants on this structure. That was really unfortunate; for Wyatt's work with Brunel at Paddington and Jones' various iron-and-glass shop fronts and his ambitious ferrovitreous projects for Crystal Palaces in London and Paris indicate the serious interest both of them took in the design of structural ironwork.

The plan of the Brompton building was of the simplest: a rectangle covered by three parallel rows of arched tie trusses, with a two-storey "nave" down the center and upper galleries over the outer "aisles." The external frame of cast-iron components was filled with corrugated iron sheets (Figs. XVI 43, 47) and so were the roofs, except for the narrow monitor skylights along their tops (Fig. XVI 46). All the detail of the cast members was sparse compared to that of the Crystal Palace and had little or none of its expressive elegance. The wrought-iron members were of course mere tie-rods or plain rolled sections (Figs. XVI 42–46). The spandrels, hitherto the characteristic field for ingenious cast-iron ornament, had merely a single open circle in each; the gallery railings, with X-panels somewhat like those at Dublin, almost alone caught the eye (Figs. XVI 45–46).

Whatever may be thought of Cole's attitude toward architectural design in this necessarily pinchpenny scheme, as a museum director his attitude toward the problem of housing miscellaneous collections was so revolutionary that it was hardly approached again before the 1920's. As in the original Crystal Palace the exhibited material, artistic and scientific, was arranged with real ingenuity within the neutral, indeed almost invisible, structural frame provided by the contractors. The installation was articulated both logically and visually so that the whole effect had a certain pleasant freedom and variety. Screens were frequently used to isolate groups of major objects. Thus in theory, if not necessarily in fact, there was allowance for almost complete rearrangement with changing exhibition needs. Little of the actual installations was brilliant so far as one can tell from contemporary views; but within such a frame the exhibition techniques of the most advanced 20th-century museum practice could have been used with ease. Material of the sort brought here from the Architectural Museum, building fragments and casts, has proved rather recalcitrant to arrangements that are at once logical and attractive even in later times. The installations in many sections of the Victoria and Albert, down to the postwar reorganization under Sir Leigh Ashton, were actually inferior to those in the original Brompton building.

Externally the museum was dreary, its ranges of corrugated panels unbroken by openings of any sort; while the low camber of its segmental roofs, without the bolder lift of modern Nissen or Quonset huts, was barely visible except from the ends. The one prominent external feature, the open porch across the south end, was dry and starved looking; yet it was not so resolutely industrial in character as the plain, and therefore almost unnoticeable, side walls (Fig. XVI 47). The "prefabs" for export of the preceding five or ten years seem generally to have had better proportioned exteriors as well as more refined cast-iron detailing of their visible gallery supports (Figs. XII 25, XV 51, 53).

This edifice, conceptually comparable to much 20th-century building, was destined to suffer a 20th-century fate: Its reputation was early blasted by adverse publicity. (Physically, the demountable construction allowed it to be taken down and reassembled in 1871 at Bethnal Green; there it still stands, masked externally by a heavy brick shell designed by J. W. Wild.) Beside the Crystal Palace in the spring of 1851 a boiler house had been erected to provide steam power. This was naturally made of the same structural members as the main building; but it was largely closed in with corrugated-iron panels rather than glass since no great amount of light was required inside. This Hyde Park edifice had of course been demolished in 1852 when the Exhibition site was cleared; but now in 1856 George Godwin, the influential editor of the *Builder,* who was doing considerable building himself in this general vicinity, took one malicious look at Cole's new museum and cried: "Brompton Boilers!"

The attack, moreover, was soon followed up in detail. To the editor of an architectural journal it was unforgivable that no architect had been employed. (The gardener Paxton's triumph had been hard enough to bear.) Cole's ideas for advanced museological utilization of the untrammeled interior were too new to be clearly explained at the time, even if he himself quite understood all their possible implications; the appointed apostle of art-in-industry was sponsoring a large-scale industrial product in which all artistic considerations were ignored, or so it could be asserted by Godwin.

Whether or not one prefers today the stripped "functionalism" of the Youngs' membering to the richer effects Brunel and Wyatt had just achieved at Paddington is not the point; nobody, least of all Cole, was claiming that the "Boilers" were an illustration of a new architectural aesthetic. As Godwin refused to recognize, they were only intended to provide makeshift housing in wartime for the museum's collections and would be replaced later by a more permanent structure. But the Museum of Science and Art was the first result of the Department of Practical Art's impingement upon architecture and hence not beyond justifiable criticism.

Jerrold's happy phrase "Crystal Palace" had certainly prepared the way for the acceptance of ferrovitreous architecture in 1850–51; now Godwin's libelous nickname helped to dampen the general enthusiasm for prefabrication and a new engineering-architecture the Crystal Palace had so signally aroused five years before. Almost immediately the results became evident. On the one hand, where visible iron was used after this time in edifices of any architectural pretension, architects and fabricators vied with one another to prove it capable of elaborate decorative effects, preferably based on past styles; on the other hand, the serious critical and professional interest in matters that were primarily technical, such as prefabrication for

569

export, diminished markedly although the trade itself continued active through the 70's. Even in railway stations positive interest in the visual character of the sheds seemed to diminish and real collaboration between architects and engineers grew less frequent and less successful. St. Pancras Station, built in the late 60's by W. H. Barlow and Gilbert Scott, illustrates this particularly well when compared with a station designed entirely by engineers like York II (Friary) Station, which dates from 1871.

The contemporary photographs of the Brompton Boilers in construction have such a fascinatingly special quality—and those in which the workmen appear almost the look of an aerial ballet (Fig. XVI 42)—that present-day observers tend to ignore how extremely shapeless and ill-proportioned the exterior was, particularly as regards the entrance front (Fig. XVI 47). If one looks at that front alone and forgets the use Cole made of the interiors it is not difficult to understand why Godwin's campaign stirred up such a general reaction against iron construction. Moreover, he was crystallizing a sentiment already well developed by 1856 if thus far chiefly expressed by a few highbrows like Pugin and Ruskin.

Interest in the use of iron for building had been rising for more than two generations, reaching a climax in the early 50's. Now the architectural profession, which had never really liked a material it was not trained to use, rose in revolt against it. Even the general public grew rather bored with the sight of iron, moreover—as around 1935 the world began to grow bored with exposed ferroconcrete—unless it were very ornately treated or else quite subordinated as an incident in masonry design.

Parallel with the climax of the Victorian story of iron, as represented by the Crystal Palace and the great London and Birmingham stations, there had been developing in the early 50's a largely unrelated excitement about the problem of "style" in architecture. This excitement had its professional center in Gothic church-building circles although powerful repercussions before long influenced all types of building and all contemporary stylisms. Moreover, Ruskin, the most enthralling new architectural writer, was soon able to make architectural problems almost as much the concern of all men with pretensions to culture as they had been in the 18th century.

From the greenhouse, the train shed, and the "prefab" we must now return to the Camdenian church, from the world of Paxton back to the world of Pugin, in order to see why Early Victorian architecture ended as it actually did. Even before Pugin died in 1852 the world of the 19th-century Gothic enthusiasts began to undergo a remarkable transformation. No longer were Victorians—as at just about this time they first began to think of themselves —to be humble emulators of the 14th-century Edwardians; henceforth 19th-century Gothic was to be self-consciously of its own age yet not at all ferrovitreous; characteristically, nothing more is heard of the Ecclesiological Society's "model" iron church after 1855.

Between 1850 and 1855 the Early Victorian phase of architecture began to be wound up. If one must have a specific date, the death of Pugin in 1852 is as good as any, but only in the same coincidental sense in which the death of Sloane in 1837 marks the beginning of the Early Victorian phase. Or the end of the Early Victorian period can be associated with the Crimean War years 1854–56. In the field of construction in iron the refusal to accept the Brompton Boilers as worthy of the name of architecture— or even of halfway decent building—is as significant a negative *terminus ante quem* as the Jamaica Street Warehouse in Glasgow, of precisely the same date, is a positive one. With that somewhat paradoxical statement this chapter may well terminate—architectural periods neither begin nor end at precise moments any more than for logical reasons.

CHAPTER XVII: RUSKIN OR BUTTERFIELD?

VICTORIAN GOTHIC AT THE MID-CENTURY

The earlier chapters in this book have brought the account of various aspects of Early Victorian architecture down into the mid-50's and it must be evident that Early Victorian modes of design came to no abrupt termination. Yet, just at the moment when Early Victorian architecture, supported by returning prosperity, was rising to its greatest heights of achievement and originality at the beginning of the 50's, most of its presuppositions were already being questioned. Two men, one a critic and the other an architect, a man who never designed or built anything of consequence and a man who never wrote a book or an article, took the lead in this questioning. Both John Ruskin (1819–1900) and William Butterfield made their new positions clearly evident in the years 1849–51, before Pugin's death and while Paxton was building his Lily House and his Crystal Palace.

Thanks to the buildings Butterfield began and the books Ruskin published in those years British architecture took a very different turn than might have been expected, say, in 1848. The turn was, indeed, a turnabout after 1855; and most of the characteristic architecture of the late 50's and the 60's was the direct or the indirect result of that turnabout. It is convenient and appropriate that the architecture of the 50's and 60's, which broke so completely away from the continuance of established Early Victorian modes, should be called High Victorian.

The idiosyncratic elements of High Victorian architecture are not easy to isolate. The originality of the mode, like the flavor of curry, is due to the proportions and the blending of various architectural herbs and spices, many of them familiar enough. Yet certain specific indications of the onset of the High Victorian, above all on the Gothic side with which we are most concerned here, are clearly discernible. These indications help to particularize the characteristic new flavor, so much more acrid and pungent than the milder bouquet of Early Victorian architecture.

To writers on the Gothic Revival the most obvious evidence of a change of phase in the 50's has seemed to be the increasing use of ideas and details of continental origin. Among these the features of Italian origin have properly been considered the most important; but other elements of German or Flemish origin are certainly present, even if critics have not always recognized them. To the technically minded, on the other hand, ambiguities in the employment of iron are likely to seem more significant. The visible use of iron in a direct or "functional" sort of way was rare after 1855 in architect-designed buildings. Yet minor elements of iron both structural and decorative were very frequently incorporated in pretentious edifices; and the subtle influence of the internal metal skeleton on exterior design was even more significant for the future. Enthusiasm for the ornamental possibilities and structural economies of new materials was by no means restricted to iron. Various products both natural and manufactured, products hitherto rather costly outside the regions of their origin, were now made widely available by railway transportation.

To the period itself perhaps the most striking sign of "modernity" was the extension of the boundaries of the Gothic Revival. Modes of design at least nominally Gothic were now widely employed in fields very remote from the ecclesiastical. Even public houses designed by builders and sewage-pumping stations (including their machinery) for which engineers prepared the drawings were often Gothic.

The most important novelty, however, related in one way or another to almost all the others, was the introduction of polychromy or, to be more precise and also to introduce one of the favorite terms of the period, "constructional coloration." This was achieved by combining building materials of various hues. (The phrase "permanent polychrome" was also used, since architects and their clients had come to realize how rapidly the earlier sort of painted polychromy lost its effectiveness because of fading and grime.) Constructional coloration is by no means always conspicuous in High Victorian architecture—indeed it is often very restrained or even totally absent in the work of several of the best architects; but the earliest steps leading toward its general acceptance in the late 50's are highly significant. Moreover, the characteristic stylistic modulation of neo-Gothic in the mid-century is unusually easy to trace along this polychromatic line.

External polychromy naturally made a great impression on contemporaries when first seen. Examples were almost always commented on at length in the professional press, and critical statements favoring modern exploitation of permanent polychrome, or merely lauding ancient instances of its use, received a generous hearing. Buildings in which structural coloration played a conspicuous role and books advocating it were news in their day. Mere straws in the wind were recurrently discussed in recognizable terms while other, more subtle, evidences of stylistic modulation went unmentioned for lack of a descriptive vocabulary. This brings us to the main issue of this chapter: Ruskin or Butterfield?

573

Literary propaganda for structural polychromy was considerable from 1849 on. The literary minded have therefore tended to assume ever since that permanent polychrome, like Italian Gothic forms, was introduced by books—and more specifically by the books of John Ruskin, the first of whose architectural treatises appeared in 1849. Like most established historical theories this one is partially true but requires considerable elaboration and refinement. There had certainly been some use of constructional coloration in Victorian England well before any serious written propaganda for it began; moreover, internal polychromy of some sort was already generally, if not universally, accepted by the late 40's. But the characteristic polychromy of Pugin, as seen at St. Giles's, Cheadle, and that of the Camdenians also, was only a form of ecclesiastical interior decoration, even when it was employed in a secular edifice like the New Palace. Chiefly produced with paint, it was applied to buildings that were physically complete in their original monochrome state and rarely, if ever, to their exteriors.

But at St. Giles's a new sort of polychromy had made a tentative appearance. Glazed tiles whose colors were permanent and integral, such as were already being used here and in most other up-to-date Early Victorian churches to provide patterned floors, were carried up by Pugin to form a dado along the aisle walls. In 1848, moreover, a writer in the *Ecclesiologist* in a general article on tiles stated that "we will not scruple to recommend them" for such use. Tiles are not precisely structural, but they are integral parts of the structure of walls and floors, not something applied with a stencil and a brush like the painted patternwork of the time.

Pugin did not entirely eschew external polychromy in his secular and semi-religious work. Where his models were "Domestic Debased" (that is, Tudor) he frequently introduced a few large lozenges or simple symbolic patterns of black headers in the red brick walls. In schools and institutions designed by more frankly picturesque architects such traditional English lozenge work and even all-over diapers of black or blue headers against red or yellow brick walls were exploited enthusiastically. E. B. Lamb in some small buildings at Chequers Court had even used, with glib appropriateness, a checkered pattern of stone and brick throughout. Since the ancient prototypes for this sort of structural coloration were of so late a date, these Tudorish wall treatments never received the approval of ecclesiological purists and hence such brick polychromy was little used in churches in the 40's. Even the use of brick for churches was disapproved as a modern economy throughout most of the decade.

Another sort of structural color had been rather characteristic of the earlier periods of the Middle Ages in England. Dark Purbeck marble shafts were much used in the 12th and 13th centuries, as at Canterbury and Westminster

Abbey, against walls and piers of Caen or other light-colored freestone. Although many such prototypes were rather *too* early for Camdenians (as diapered brickwork was much too late), the greater strength of various marbles and granites had led architects to use them again in the 40's in the form of svelte colonnettes and even of slender monolithic nave columns; freestone columns, even if monolithic, had to be much more heavily dimensioned in order to carry the weight of thick nave arcades and clerestorey walls. This practice was not at first very well received by critics; in reporting on Scoles' St. Francis Xavier's at Liverpool in 1848 the *Ecclesiologist*'s reviewer remarked (not wholly unjustly) that the slender green marble shafts of the nave arcade looked like cast-iron pipes, as has been noted. In any event, native marbles and granites were not yet very readily obtainable at any distance from the quarries.

In Northamptonshire, and doubtless elsewhere in England, if freestone of two different colors were readily available, an irregular banding of dark and light courses had occasionally been used in the 13th and 14th centuries. Although necessarily regional, this practice accompanied authentic Decorated design of the most approved sort. In restoring the church at Brayfield-on-the-Green, Northamptonshire, in 1847 Derick adopted this zebraic mode of the neighborhood in his chancel for archaeological reasons. Medieval English striped work in freestone provided a most striking premonition of High Victorian structural coloration and one perfectly acceptable to Camdenian principles.

Examples of some sort of near-polychromy in brick in the 40's are more frequent and more significant, even if unblessed by the ecclesiology of the day. After the Late Georgian convention of coating brick walls with cement or other renderings was rejected as an unethical faking of ashlar masonry —and most architects of any aesthetic pretension had accepted, before the 40's were over, this proscription—a simple bichromatic treatment, with walls of red, white, or yellow brick and trim of stone or cement, became common practice for all sorts of secular buildings both modest and elaborate. In areas where fairly good building stone was available, architects made a similar differentiation in Gothic work between walling masonry of local stone set as rubble or random ashlar and ornamental trim of superior stone very carefully cut. The latter was usually brought from some distance, but whether imported or local it was used in larger blocks and more smoothly pointed even if not carved with ornament or moldings. This differentiation today is more a matter of texture and scale than of color now that both sorts of stone have weathered to nearly the same tint; yet it is evident enough that tonal contrasts were being consistently sought in the 40's rather than avoided as in Late Georgian times.

Mature High Victorian structural coloration was to be characterized by a general use of bricks of various colors in external walls, with or without the additional contrast of interspersed stone or marble courses. Still more characteristic is the way the various colors of the materials used in the wall surface were knitted together. A mere constrast between walling material and trim was not considered truly polychromatic; moreover, High Victorian polychromy was always more or less dependent on non-English—usually Italian—inspiration for the boldness of its effects if not for the particular patterns employed.

For early instances of Italianism in polychromy one must look as far back as the early 40's. Ruskin mentioned with approval only one modern English instance of structural coloration in the first volume of his *Stones of Venice* (1851): J. W. Wild's Christ Church, Streatham, built in 1840 (Fig. IV 10). There even the selection of a bright yellow brick for the walls indicated Wild's personal taste for strong color; but it was the intricate use of red and black bricks in the radiating patterns of the arch voussoirs and the rich diapering of colored tiles on the campanile roof, not to speak of the delicate Cosmati-like arrangement of various colored bricks in the cornices, that specifically suggested Italian models. Wild's ideas may well have come from a study of the lithographs in H. Gally Knight's *Saracenic and Norman Remains in Sicily* [1838]. His church, indeed, was generally disapproved at the time as too "Saracenic" and hence inappropriate for "Catholick" worship, as has been noted earlier.

In the other important Italianate church begun in 1840, Wyatt and Brandon's St. Mary's, Wilton, the coloration was less structural and entirely internal. But the fragments of real medieval colored marbles and Cosmati work that Sydney Herbert and his mother brought back from Italy provide a unique richness of permanent coloring in the elaborate fittings. By the time Wilton church was completed in 1846, the two volumes of H. Gally Knight's *Ecclesiastical Architecture of Italy from the Time of Constantine to the 15th Century* (1842–44) had provided additional visual documents on medieval Italian work with its various characteristic forms of structural coloration.

By 1848 John Woody Papworth (1820–1870), a son of J. B. Papworth, was showing at the Royal Academy a design for completing the west front of the Florence Duomo in the marble-paneled Tuscan Gothic style of Giotto's Lily Tower. (To this monument Ruskin was already paying the highest critical tribute in his *Seven Lamps* although that work had not yet appeared in print.) In the same year T. H. Wyatt's young brother M. D. Wyatt's *Specimens of Geometrical Mosaic of the Middle Ages* called attention by its rather crudely colored plates to the boldness and freedom with which Cosmati work and marble intarsia had been used throughout the Middle Ages in Italy to add brilliant detail to architecture.

Through the mid-40's the Camdenians were as opposed to foreign ideas in church architecture as to round-arched medieval forms in general. At that time the foreign architectural inspiration of the aesthetically heterodox, whether Italian, German, or French, was generally of a Romanesque order and ipso facto disapproved by the *Ecclesiologist*'s reviewers. Later the Camdenians began to grow less nationalistic. In 1847 writers in the *Ecclesiologist* were not only recommending the use of brick for church building but actually referring with approval to such foreign models as the medieval brick churches of Belgium, Germany, and Italy provided. The cathedral of Albi in southern France was also praised for the broad and bold masses of its brick walls.

When George Truefitt's *Architectural Sketches on the Continent* (1847) appeared it was received by the *Ecclesiologist* with an approval denied earlier to the Reverend J. L. Petit's enthusiastic propaganda for the "effectiveness" of continental Gothic. Truefitt was even elected a member of the Ecclesiological Society in 1848—this must seem to posterity somewhat surprising, for his later innovations in Gothic design were to be more extreme even than the mannerisms of E. B. Lamb which the Society never tired of condemning.

It was *Sketches of Continental Ecclesiology* (1848) by Benjamin Webb, one of the founders of the Camden Society, that really lifted the ban on foreign study for Anglican church architects and sanctioned a more catholic interpretation of "Catholick" ritual traditions in planning. When Lewis Vulliamy's All Saints', Ennismore Gardens, was reviewed in the *Ecclesiologist* the next year, its strictly basilican plan was forgiven on the ground that the design had been prepared in 1837 before the science of ecclesiology was born; the polychrome embellishments of the apse by Owen Jones were warmly commended, moreover, as "another triumph of the principle of decorative colour" even though they were not without a slight Alhambraic (not to say Saracenic) flavor. When Edward A. Freeman in his *History of Architecture* (1849) expressed lack of sympathy with the "narrow insular exclusiveness with which the ecclesiological movement set out," he was not unjust to the Camdenians; but he could no longer so properly complain of the "narrowness and prejudice which still exists in some quarters"—that is, if he was referring to the *Ecclesiologist*, as of course he was. His own personal preference for the Perpendicular, however, was almost unique at this time; Perpendicular remained anathema for nearly two decades longer among High Anglicans and its revival is characteristic of the Late, not the High, Victorian period.

The professional propaganda which preceded the removal of the brick tax in 1850 built up great hopes for significant innovations in the use of baked clay products, particularly in London. Tremendous enthusiasm greeted the Northern Schools of St. Martin-in-the-Fields when the design for them was shown by J. W. Wild at the Royal Academy in 1850. Wild's versatile though simple use of cut, rubbed, and molded red brick attracted more contemporary attention than the Italian Gothic character of the design (Fig. XII 21); yet it is the priority of the Northern Schools as the first instance of the Italian Gothic mode in Victorian England, as also its priority in using superposed arcades for the façade, that gives this work of Wild's its great historical importance.

In a paper read before the Oxford Architectural Society early in 1853 "On the Revival of the Ancient Style of Domestic Architecture" the young G. E. Street spoke with the highest approval of these schools, the idea for which he believed Wild had derived from a Gothic bridge at Pavia. He particularly recommended them as a model for commercial work, pointing out that adequate shop windows could readily be fitted under broader arches in the ground storey. Street even praised the completely even rhythm of the façade, claiming that the builders of the Middle Ages broke with regularity for internal convenience only, not like modern Gothicists in order to achieve arbitrarily varied effects.

Street furthermore remarked in connection with this building: "In the upper storeys [of hypothetical commercial work of this order] the continuous lines of arcades would be very grand if prolonged to any length." Within the next few years this suggestion was generally taken up by commercial architects with most impressive effect, particularly perhaps when the detail of the arcades was of a Renaissance rather than a medieval character. The *Ecclesiologist* had already officially approved the design in reviewing the 1850 Royal Academy Exhibition: "At all events Mr. Wild remembers that he is building in brick and for a town," their writer stated. In this remark the writer was echoing a protest Street had just made in an article on town churches against such urban churches and schools as were "suited only to a village green" because of their very rustic materials and excessively picturesque massing. To this important article of Street's we must return later.

No summary of the prehistory of medieval Italian influence on Victorian architecture and of the early exploitation of structural coloration would be complete without mention of the Nottingham Corn Exchange by T. C. Hine. This was completed in 1850, like Wild's schools, but was never much noted by contemporaries nor had it in fact much intrinsic quality. The mode was Italian Romanesque—more or less; the material, brick with elaborate stone trim; there was also much painted polychromy within. But the significant innovation was the introduction of specially designed encaustic tiles on the exterior. These tiles were ornamented with wheat sheaves and profusely employed on the stringcourses and around the windows. For a decade and more such tiles were to provide the small change of polychromy as they had already begun to do in church interiors several years before this.

The High Victorian Gothic properly began, however, with the building of a church, not a school or an exchange. That church was largely built, if not entirely completed internally, well before the Early Victorian period showed many other signs of coming to an end. Intended to be the model church of the Ecclesiological Society and executed over a rather considerable period of years with real prodigality, All Saints', Margaret Street, off Oxford Street in London, is one of the major works of Victorian architecture. The architect was forced to protest that he did not have carte blanche (as the press had reported); the treasurer of the building fund had to explain that the church was really not the benefaction of a single donor (as was also inaccurately reported) and that contributions were in fact sadly needed. But in the end All Saints' was completed and decorated with a sumptuousness unknown since St. Mary's, Wilton, a decade earlier and rare in any decade of the 19th century.

Two prominent London churches, All Saints' and St. Mary Magdalene's, Munster Square, were being designed in 1849 by the two leading architects associated with the Ecclesiological Society. Both edifices were intended to provide models of ritual arrangement and design superior to the London churches then most approved by the Society. Most regrettably, S. W. Dawkes' St. Andrew's, Wells Street (of which the Society's founder Benjamin Webb was the incumbent), was Perpendicular in style even though its interior arrangements were supposed to approach ecclesiological perfection (Fig. V 6). St. Barnabas's, Pimlico, just completed by Thomas Cundy with the presumed aid of Butterfield, was Early English (Figs. V 27, 29). St. Mary Magdalene's, by the Camdenians' first favorite among architects R. C. Carpenter, was completed (without the intended north aisle and tower) in 1851 and has already been sufficiently described in Chapter V (Figs. V 16–17). Crowning Carpenter's career and likewise terminating the Camdenian story in its Early Victorian phase, this church is modest and incomplete in appearance today. Discreetly polychromed internally by the decorator Crace—mostly with paint, of course, although some of the colonnettes are of colored marble—its great west window was not commissioned until 1855 as a memorial to Carpenter. Ecclesiological specialists could—and still do—appreciate its ritual perfection; but there was never much to strike the innocent eye of the layman or, for that matter, of the professional not well indoctrinated in Camdenian principles. Crace's paintwork, moreover, has all but disappeared under a century of grime. The erection of St. Mary Magdalene's was not officially sponsored by the Ecclesiological Society although its construction was observed, stage by stage, with the most enthusiastic approval; yet it may be taken to represent the normal aspirations of the High Church party at the mid-century. All Saints' is surprisingly different in almost every way.

The congregation of Margaret Chapel in Margaret Street, just northeast of Oxford Circus, had long desired a suitable setting for their elaborate ritual which included by 1847 complete musical masses. The 18th-century edifice, originally built for Deists *horribile dictu*, in which they had for some time worshipped, must have been most distasteful to them. Beresford-Hope, from the beginning the most enthusiastic of the lay ecclesiologists and one of the richest, proposed that a new church for this worthy group might be built as a model of correctness in ecclesiology such as the Society had long aspired to sponsor. With Sir Stephen Gwynne, Beresford-Hope took over control of the Margaret Street building scheme. Since the congregation insisted on staying in the neighborhood only a rather exiguous piece of land could be acquired. Onto this site a church of considerable size, not to speak of a clergy house and a choir school, was to be fitted by the Society's other favorite architect William Butterfield.

There can never have been more than one alternative to Butterfield as an architect for this model church; that is, of course, Carpenter. Unfriendly critics justly complained that only the work of Carpenter and Butterfield was regularly praised in the *Ecclesiologist* while the churches of other men were usually criticized with a strength of language often ludicrous today and always ungentlemanly, not to say un-Christian. Of the two men, Butterfield was doubtless closer to Webb, with whom he had been cooperating on the volumes of *Instrumenta ecclesiastica* for several years, and perhaps also to Beresford-Hope, even though it was Carpenter who was remodeling Beresford-Hope's country house Bedsgebury Park. Despite the published disclaimer that All Saints' was not "his" church and the large contributions made by others—some £30,000 from Henry Tritton out of a total cost of about £70,000—Beresford-Hope was nevertheless the effective client as the agent of the Society and the actual purchaser of the new site.

Professionally, Butterfield was almost as busy by this time as Pugin had been ten years earlier. His practice certainly did not rival Gilbert Scott's, but it already outdistanced—in distinction if not in extent—that of other church architects. By 1848 he had completed the restoration and enlargement of St. Augustine's College, Canterbury, for Beresford-Hope and was just beginning St. Ninian's, the Episcopal cathedral in Perth. On the recommendation of the Ecclesiological Society he had provided designs for a cathedral and related buildings in Adelaide, Australia, as well as a revised east end for that at Fredericton, New Brunswick. Various smaller churches at Epping, Pinchbeck Bars, Lincoln, and Harrow Weald were being rebuilt or drastically restored by him, as was also Dorchester Abbey in Oxfordshire, the last a major Society-sponsored project.

The basic dates for the construction of All Saints'—cornerstone laid 9 November 1850; consecrated 28 May 1859—are more than a little confusing. The church was actually completely designed by Butterfield and even contracted for in 1849. In its April 1850 number the *Ecclesiologist* announced that "the founders and architects are anxious to make it a practical example of what we are very anxious to see tested, viz., constructional polychrome." The article then went on to describe the character of the red and black brick patterning planned for the exterior and the more elaborate geometrical mosaic of marble and tile that would ornament the interior. Moreover, All Saints' was so far completed structurally in the normal two years (i.e., by late 1852 when only the murals, the stained glass, and the furniture were lacking) that the *Builder* published in its number for 22 January 1853 an influential view of it as an effectively finished building (Fig. XVII 2); two years later, in March 1855, a similar view appeared in the *Illustrated London News*.

Although neither the professional journals nor the *News* published views of the interior until after the actual consecration in the spring of 1859, the profession was certainly aware of the strikingly novel character of the exterior from the beginning of 1853 and the general public from 1855. In that year, moreover, Butterfield's own drawings for the church which were shown that year in the English section of the Paris International Exhibition provided for foreigners striking evidence that a great change had been taking place in English architecture in the few years since the Great Exhibition was held in 1851. The many who had visited London then had been on the whole rather bored by the major Early Victorian monuments they saw; henceforth, for the next two or three decades, visitors interested in architecture were to find all sorts of excitement in Britain.

Long before 1855 many whose interest was aroused by reports of the novelty of All Saints' must have visited the site when they came to London; for it was well advertised by the Camdenians as a model of their architectural aspirations and most conveniently located in the heart of the West End where visitors could readily find it. Once the walls had risen even a few feet above the ground, the startling character of Butterfield's structural polychrome had certainly become evident even to casual passers-by. The steeple, moreover, rising higher than any other structure in the London of its day and as striking for its stark silhouette as for its boldly banded walls and spire, soon provided a prominent landmark to draw the curious to Margaret Street (Fig. XVII 1). It is natural that Butterfield, operating here under a blaze of publicity quite alien to his own seclusive nature, should have been generally credited with the initiation here, at one stroke, of the High Victorian Gothic. The circumstances are such that this assumption can hardly be essentially untrue; yet to arrive at a more rounded truth one must consider—and I believe must dialectically combine with such an assumption—the opposed thesis that Ruskin is the only begetter of the High Victorian Gothic in general and more specifically of structural polychrome.

In 1848 Ruskin, the 29-year-old author of *Modern Painters* (5 vols. 1843–60) of which the first three volumes had already appeared, was spending the first winter of his *mariage blanc,* not in carrying further his interminable treatise on painting, but in writing and illustrating a new work on architecture. *The Seven Lamps of Architecture* was written rapidly between November and April and appeared early in May 1849. It was then very widely noticed both in literary and in professional journals, although more favorably in the former than in the latter. The simple matter of chronology makes it impossible for Butterfield to have been influenced in the design of All Saints' by Ruskin's *Stones of Venice,* for the first volume of that work did not appear until 1851 by which time his major design decisions must all have been made. The question therefore is: Does All Saints' show internal evidence of familiarity with the text of the *Seven Lamps?* No direct evidence of Butterfield's reading of the book is available; but the long and on the whole enthusiastic review in the *Ecclesiologist,* although belated—it did not appear until October 1849—gives ample evidence in its nine pages that the book was carefully read and pondered in the circle of Butterfield's closest associates.

The reviewer early states the *Ecclesiologist*'s official approval of the basic doctrines in Ruskin's "Lamp of Truth" even though he expresses less antipathy to the use of iron in construction than does Ruskin. Ruskin's defense of the propriety of using marble plaques over brick walls, a crucial point theoretically, is also accepted although his arguments are in fact patent sophistries. In discussing Ruskin's "Lamp of Power" the reviewer commends those passages favoring "mighty masses" and scorning walls cut up by buttresses as any friend of Butterfield's naturally would. The review also notes that Ruskin, under the rubric of the "Lamp of Beauty," finds color *"essential"* in architecture but that he deprecates its use, except with extreme discretion, in sculpture. "Instructive and eloquent" are the words chosen to characterize the book's theories on the use of color, even though Ruskin's analogies with Nature's use of color in shells and insects are found hard to follow and his dictum that color-mosaic is the only feasible modern ornament is considered too extreme.

Ruskin's high praise of Giotto's Florentine campanile is remarked on as surprising, as also the fact that a new work entirely devoted to Italian Gothic, *The Stones of Venice,* was already announced as in preparation. Agreeing warmly with Ruskin's attack on the rising clamor of the day for a new style, the reviewer approves the four old styles Ruskin suggested for universal acceptance. (These are, of course, the Pisan Romanesque, the Florentine Gothic, the Venetian Gothic, and the earliest stage of English Decorated.) Ruskin's remark that the Decorated was "the most natural, perhaps the safest choice" is naturally underlined since it represents the long-established Camdenian position.

Finally the reviewer in the *Ecclesiologist* states correctly that the book should not be considered an architect's vade mecum in practice; its aim was rather to discover basic principles and to commend them to all men's attention. Ruskin's statement that no art can be truly Christian without the guiding principles of self-sacrifice, truth, and obedience echoed the Society's own doctrines. For all the "regrettable violence" of Ruskin's attitude toward the "Unreformed Church" and his protests against the "restoration" of medieval monuments—an activity at which the Society was one of the most aggressive sinners—it is no wonder that the reviewer, speaking for the Society, says that its members "regard his volume with feelings of gratitude and admiration."

Quite different had been the reaction of most contemporary architects who rightly saw in the *Seven Lamps* a criticism of the very basis of their eclectic practice. But the *Ecclesiologist* expresses its readiness to defend Ruskin against the Philistine attacks of the profession. Ruskin was a true critic, a serious intellectual, and an exponent of high principle, not a time-serving opportunist like all the professionals except a very few redeemed architects in the Society's own group; even his Low Church views could be forgiven since his piety was unquestionable.

Thus to review the *Ecclesiologist*'s review may take the place of summarizing here Ruskin's familiar doctrines as they first found expression in the *Seven Lamps.* Of course there is no certainty that the review reflected Butterfield's opinions nor did it very specifically underline those aspects of the doctrine of the *Seven Lamps* which have usually been considered most immediately influential. Only the internal evidence provided by examination of the architect's church and the critic's text can, in the absence of information about what Butterfield was reading at this time, establish a probable relationship between the architect and the critic.

There is very little about All Saints', particularly as regards the exterior, which should be considered specifically Italianate, a point that was early noted by the perspicacious G. E. Street (Figs. XVII 1–4). Despite the boldness of the massing and the general avoidance of buttresses, the handling of form here could hardly have been derived from the recommendations given in the *Seven Lamps*. Insofar as the formal elements are not conventionally 14th-century English—the tracery, for example—they are purely Butterfieldian.

Although there is a strong suggestion of foreign influence in a few features, notably in the handling of the steeple (Fig. XVII 1), that influence seems North German rather than Italian. The suggestion tentatively broached by John Summerson (in an important article in the *Architectural Review*, 98, 166–175, reprinted in *Heavenly Mansions* [1950]) that Butterfield had studied the monuments of Siena at first hand is hardly borne out by internal evidence; it rests in any event on the most indirect sort of hearsay. But many English architects and ecclesiologists in these years were visiting and reporting on the brick Gothic of North Germany; if Butterfield had not seen German churches himself he had probably at least heard of their chief characteristics. Even so, the wooden spire is not necessarily un-English except in its bold scale and extreme simplicity; and those are of course characteristic qualities which Butterfield imposed on almost every major feature he borrowed from the architecture of the English past.

The combination of black and red brick in the walling is certainly un-Italian but not necessarily un-English; banding in brick of these two colors has, however, closer German prototypes. The stone bands in the tower and on the west front are more Italianate and hence more "Ruskinian" in a loose sense. But it is the way the black patterns are disposed, almost regardless of the architectural forms that cut across them and as gratuitously irregular in their spacing as they are coarse in scale, that seems to follow most closely what Ruskin was then recommending (Fig. XVII 3). For instance, under the "Lamp of Sacrifice" Ruskin remarks, "chequered patterns, and in general such ornaments as common workmen can execute, may extend over the whole building . . ." Carved work, on the other hand, such as bas reliefs and capitals, should in his estimation be restricted to eye level: This certainly applies to the Annunciation relief Butterfield placed low on his lone south buttress (Fig. XVII 3). It also applies to the carved work inside the church which is mostly on the capitals of the nave arcade (Figs. XVII 5–7, 9).

Under the "Lamp of Power" there are many Ruskinian dicta that All Saints' illustrates particularly well—which does not necessarily mean, of course, that Butterfield had to learn composition at this late date from Ruskin. His own well-established liking for the broad, the crude, and the tall could nevertheless have received sanction and stimulation from the critic's

584

writing, just as the similar tastes of others did when familiarity with Ruskin's ideas became general a few years later. Under the "Lamp of Beauty" also the Ruskinian requirement that one member shall always dominate the whole edifice justifies, but certainly does not explain, the tremendous steeple Butterfield raised over All Saints'.

It is in what Ruskin says further about color under the "Lamp of Beauty" that one can find the closest relationship to Butterfield's characteristic way of designing walls here and in his later work. A building, Ruskin says, should be colored (with natural materials) as nature colors one thing, say a shell or a flower or an animal. Color should therefore be independent of form and placed on broad surfaces, not on focal points of plastic interest. All of that prescription certainly applies very precisely to the color work on the inside as well as on the outside of All Saints'. Graceful carved work of elaborate form, such as capitals, should according to Ruskin be executed in plain white marble—as are Butterfield's capitals in the nave arcade (Figs. XVII 5–7, 9). Colored areas should have irregular, blotched, imperfect shapes since Ruskin asserts that color in nature is always arranged in simple and rude patterns with either very soft or very simple outlines. Of soft outlines there are none, inside or out, at All Saints'; but all the rest of this Ruskinian doctrine about color is so perfectly illustrated that Butterfield must have been following it— or so at least it must seem in the absence of any negative evidence such as formal disclaimers of Ruskinian influence by him or his close associates.

"Blotches," "zones as in the zebra," "chequers and zig-zags," "triangles, squares and circles," the very words of condemnation that generations have used to criticize the color work of Butterfield and his imitators, appear as Ruskin's specific recommendations in the "Lamp of Beauty." The critic indeed asserts that it is impossible to be "overquaint" or "over-angular" in the arrangement of the elements of architectural coloring; even Tudor paneling could be acceptable if executed in flat color—and here and there on the aisle walls Butterfield seems to follow this heretical suggestion (Figs. XVII 6–7). All Saints' bears no over-all resemblance to the Doge's Palace, to Ruskin "the purest and most chaste model he can name"; nor yet to his favorite S. Michele of Lucca, such as is frequent in later Victorian commercial architecture. Yet the lack of coordination at All Saints' between window arrangement and surface pattern exceeds that to be seen on the Venetian palace which was Ruskin's chief exemplar of over-all polychrome wall treatment; and Ruskin's recommendation of the use of simple, highly abstracted forms in color inlay as on the façade of the Lucca church is closely followed inside and out. "Sharpness and piquancy," which Ruskin so much admired in the constructional coloration of the Pisan school, are exactly the qualities that best characterize Butterfield's polychromy from this time on.

Under the "Lamp of Life" Ruskin offers a vigorous recommendation of irregularity in architecture, writing specifically in praise of what he calls the "bold 'sketchy' work of the master." This phrase seems peculiarly to sanction that rather makeshift and awkward juxtaposition of parts to which Butterfield was already much addicted (Fig. XVII 4). When Ruskin expressed the wish that modern English architects had a little of the "impudence" of the Pisan builders he picked one of the words later critics have most often been tempted to use in describing Butterfield's approach to design. When he notes with approval that there is "sensation in every inch" of the Pisa monuments Ruskin seems even more precisely to be preconizing Butterfield's mature style. The "fearlessness" of living architecture, which he likens to that of nature, the "courage" that shows itself in avoidance of logical consistency in detail, the bold use of "noncorrespondent" features, and the "quaint and uncouth forms" for which he expresses particular admiration in all the architecture of the Middle Ages—these are the familiar qualities of Butterfield's best building. "Freehand work" expresses Butterfield's basic method of design; while "variety in execution, some careful, some careless," seems exactly to define the results he rather perversely achieved by close supervision of his buildings in construction. Finally, when Ruskin came under this Lamp to conclude that "the only manner of rich ornament left to us is the geometrical colour mosaic and that much might result from our strenuously taking up this mode of design," he may even have provided the particular call that Butterfield and his sponsors were heeding in making All Saints' so polychromatic (Figs. XVII 5–7, 9, 11).

If posterity still finds All Saints' rather harsh and raw after a century, one may note—as perhaps Butterfield noted in the "Lamp of Memory"—that no building, according to Ruskin, reaches its prime till four or five centuries have gone by. Monumental architecture, Ruskin held, should therefore be designed chiefly with reference to its appearance after a half-millennium. At All Saints' three or four centuries more should mercifully reduce the frescoes (if not the murals in glazed tile) to invisibility and possibly destroy the stained glass which the blitz ironically spared. Ruskin's recommendation that Italian Gothic should be practiced only in hard materials such as granite, serpentine, and crystalline marbles certainly applies to the materials Butterfield used in his interior; while his external finish *looks* hard and permanent enough to have satisfied the Egyptians.

Finally, if we consider the main stylistic prescription of the seventh Lamp, the "Lamp of Obedience," it is evident that Butterfield accepted the discipline of the early English Decorated, one of the four styles Ruskin proposed for universal acceptance in 19th-century England. Just as Ruskin demanded, Butterfield achieved his considerable originality at All Saints' within an already established frame of style (at least as that ambiguous word was understood in mid–19th-century England, meaning a codified system of architectural forms derived from the work of some past age). "True freedom," Ruskin said, "comes from restraint under accepted rules"; it was such freedom that Butterfield sought and found. Just as Ruskin insisted would be the case, the stylistic libertarians in this decade and the next, those who attempted consciously to create a wholly new and original 19th-century style, were more shackled by the limitations of their own time.

Such considerations as the above do not really answer the question as to Ruskin's actual influence on Butterfield at All Saints'; nor can it be answered finally without discovering a direct avowal in the architect's own words (or equivalent evidence provided by close associates) of his debt to Ruskin. Those who award to Butterfield the chief credit for the initiation of the High Victorian Gothic must otherwise be more nearly right. The influence of All Saints' was immediate, unmistakable in its effect, and generally recognized by contemporaries; but the reputation, and hence the influence, of Ruskin became widespread only with the publication of the three volumes of *The Stones of Venice* (Vol. 1, 1851; Vols. 2, 3, 1853) and the appearance in book form of his more succinct *Lectures on Architecture and Painting Delivered at Edinburgh* in 1853 a year later. Direct Ruskinian influence, moreover, was reinforced, at least in its Italianizing direction, by G. E. Street's *Brick and Marble Architecture of the Middle Ages* (1855) before it became widely noticeable in contemporary architecture. In 1855 a second edition of the *Seven Lamps* became necessary to satisfy the appetite of the growing body of Ruskin's disciples, and his direct association with a major building project, the Oxford University Museum, began. Emulation of Butterfield's All Saints' can be clearly recognized as it spread through the work of the profession in the years immediately following 1850; Ruskin's doctrines, on the other hand, were for the most part being discussed rather than followed in those years and still seemed to most architects impractical and highfalutin, as indeed they often were. Only after 1855 did a more peculiarly Ruskinian and Italianizing current, readily differentiated from the earlier stream flowing from the Butterfieldian spring in Margaret Street, become significant.

To consider All Saints' primarily in relation to Ruskinian doctrine as first adumbrated in the *Seven Lamps* gives but an inadequate idea of the character of that epoch-making building. Much more is non-Ruskinian—even, perhaps, anti-Ruskinian—about the church than has thus far been indicated; moreover, its highly individual quality does not derive solely from those elements that may conceivably be Ruskinian in ultimate origin. As in the work of any architect of true originality—whatever the sincerity of his subservience to some style of the past or his commitment to revolutionary style creation—

587

it is the fusing together of elements deriving from various sources within and without the world of building, past and current, that gives idiosyncratic distinction to a masterpiece. Only the effective solution of the interrelated functional, structural, and representational problems which the particular commission and the available materials provide, not a mere illustration of architectural theory, produces the epoch-making building and initiates a new architectural style-phase capable of further development by others; this is as true of Sugar in the 12th century or Le Corbusier in the 20th as of Butterfield in the 19th.

Butterfield's not very Ruskinian choice of materials at All Saints' appealed almost at once to many other architects. He used red and black brick externally, for example, where Ruskin would evidently have preferred banding in different colored stones or else in stone and brick; within a year or so, well before All Saints' was completed even on the exterior, everyone else seemed to be using red and black brick too. Inside the church glazed tile was freely combined with natural marbles in the geometric mosaic of the walls (Figs. XVII 5–6, 9, 11). Thus artificial color and natural color were brought into the sharpest juxtaposition at the expense of tonal and textural harmony. Ruskin, who detested most 19th-century manufactured materials, must have disapproved this use of tile. Certainly such mixing of disparate hues and textures reflects Butterfield's personal war against all sorts of accepted "taste," not Ruskin's ideas. The resulting acrid flavor did not remain peculiar to Butterfield for more than a year or two; for this and many more of his personal idiosyncrasies were almost at once parodied by architects generally.

Undoubtedly a close spiritual kinship existed between Ruskin's critical "crankiness" and the more creative "crankiness" of Butterfield, but there were vital differences too. On the whole Ruskin was a pessimist, fundamentally unwilling to believe that any new architecture could be really good in the way of the old architecture of the Middle Ages. Butterfield, on the other hand, was an optimist, always full of the ambition to create for his own day. As his restorations so terrifyingly indicate, he felt quite capable of improving on the work of medieval builders. It was Butterfield's optimistic spirit and not Ruskin's defeatism that would color the High Victorian period and its characteristic architecture, at least in the 50's and early 60's. The more important and subtle effects of Ruskin's writing on architecture came only somewhat later. In the years just before 1860 sensitive younger men like William Morris and Philip Webb began, after careful study of his writings, to reject the very things—structural polychrome, for example, and medieval Italian forms—which are supposed to illustrate most definitely the impact of Ruskin's ideas on Victorian building. Ruskin was once more totally disgusted with 19th-century architecture by this time, as he had been when he began to write the *Seven Lamps* a decade earlier. After the completion of the University Museum at Oxford in 1859 he withdrew rather selfrighteously from all contact with contemporary production; but his influence then widened and began to flow through many divergent channels. Unlike Butterfield's, the later influence of Ruskin, or at least important aspects of it, has lasted down into our day. It is time now to consider All Saint's, the first masterwork of the High Victorian Gothic, for itself, never forgetting that it is precisely contemporary with Paxton's Lily House and his Crystal Palace, not to speak of King's Cross and Paddington.

In August 1849 the *Ecclesiologist* referred for the first time to the Society's model church, "which will, we trust, ere long be commenced. We take a peculiar interest in these churches [All Saints' and Carpenter's St. Mary Magdalene's] from their metropolitan locality and from the desire of their founders and their architects to embody in them those principles of church arrangement which we have always enforced, as the natural development of the catholicity of our commission." This statement evidently puts the emphasis squarely on the plan at All Saints', a major consideration in all architecture to which Ruskin in the *Seven Lamps*, and indeed later in the *Stones of Venice*, gives almost no attention whatsoever. Camdenians agreed with Palladians—and with architects of the 20th century—in finding planning of basic significance. (Ruskin, incidentally, being still an extreme Protestant at this date, must have thoroughly disapproved the "advanced" ritualistic sort of planning All Saints' was intended to exemplify.) Unfortunately for its value as a Camdenian model church, All Saints' was sadly constricted by a nearly square site only 98 feet by 108 feet. Butterfield's ingenuity was notable in fitting the various necessary elements of the complex into such a site but he had little room for any positive organization of spacial volumes (Fig. XVII 8).

Along the north side of the plot, away from the street, lies the church, with what amount to party walls both at the east end and along the north aisle. The nave is very short, having only three bays; the chancel, although it occupies two-fifths of the total length of the site, is rather inadequately "developed" for the advanced ritual demands of the period. The tower rises over the western-most bay of the south aisle, the space underneath serving as a baptistery. If the plan of a building be considered, as in modern theory, the true generator of the internal spacial volumes, this plan must be considered as poor today as it was unsatisfactory according to the highly specialized Camdenian ideals of its own time. Interior volume seems to have meant as little to Ruskin at this time as did planning; but Butterfield's usual mastery of space composition must be appreciated elsewhere than at All Saints'.

The choir school and the clergy house were pushed as far as possible to the west and to the east in order to allow an entrance court off Margaret Street on the south side of the church. Even so, these attached blocks forced the entrance porch into an awkward corner and cut off any nearby views of the full length of the church. The significant new relationship of the higher chancel roof to that of the nave is therefore hardly apprehensible from any point on the south. Views of the exterior as a whole can only be obtained now from the roofs of the tall surrounding buildings; doubtless the general external composition could more readily be seen from a distance when the neighboring structures were largely domestic and considerably lower than they are today.

Because the site made it difficult to introduce much light at ground level—and because of a natural desire to obtain grandeur of scale in one dimension when the other two were so restricted—Butterfield made his nave very tall and lighted it by a nearly continuous range of good-sized clerestorey windows (Figs. XVII 5–6, 9). Earlier the Camdenians had deprecated clerestoreys as alien to the best 14th-century English parish church models—Carpenter's St. Mary Magdalene's, Munster Square, and his Brighton churches had none. Yet somewhat later than this Beresford-Hope was to write in *The English Cathedral of the XIXth Century* (1861) that the "practised eye of 1861" felt at All Saints' the lack of a triforial member between the nave arcade and the clerestorey, a feature which would still further have increased the internal effect of height. Butterfield's proportions here are literally transitional from the extreme lowness of the Early Victorian to the very great heights favored after the High Victorian style-phase had crystallized.

The chancel arch does not rise very much higher than the nave arches. But on the tall eastern nave wall above it Butterfield lavished his most brilliant and original polychrome patternwork. Indeed, this rich field of abstract mosaic (or, somewhat more precisely, intarsia or even *opus sectile*) provides the most conspicuous feature of the whole interior (Figs. XVII 5, 9). The chancel itself is covered with elaborate rib vaulting as if to make up for its lack of depth. Externally the chancel roof has to rise somewhat higher than that of the nave to cover this vaulting; thus the picturesque, though symbolically awkward, conjunction of a long low chancel with a taller nave, so characteristic of the churches of the 40's, was here reversed with excellent if rarely noticed external effect. Internally the chancel seems too much apart from the nave and very inferior in clarity of design to the bold arch and crowning wall that precede it.

Butterfield's handling of the nave spandrels and of the interior aisle walls requires little further comment beyond that given in earlier paragraphs. The extraordinary contrasts in scale, tonality, and color between the integral mosaic work of tiles, brick, and stone at the top and bottom of the north aisle wall and the fussily figured tile murals in the zone between should, however, be specifically noted (Fig. XVII 6). Here, even more than usually, Butterfield was ill served by an artist-collaborator. The treatment of the wall areas between the south aisle windows where the plain red brickwork is varied with bands and frames of incised stone is also rather too delicate in scale (for all its crudeness of pattern) in relation to the bolder decoration above and below (Fig. XVII 7). Yet these walls provide the best example of the architect's peculiar decorative intentions, intentions which seem to approach those of certain mid–20th-century American abstract painters such as Gottlieb or Motherwell who have lately been decorating synagogues.

As always in Butterfield's work, there is in the Margaret Street church an all-over composition of decorative flat patterns and then, cutting through this as if by accident, an almost unrelated arrangement of plastic architectural forms. The very English 14th-century arcade is carried on polished red Peterhead granite colonettes clustered into piers (Figs. XVII 5–7, 9). Harmonious enough with the wall decorations in their hardness and their sanguine tint, these piers contrast too much with the tonal effect of the flat mosaics in the spandrels above because of their naturally mottled surfaces and the deep soft shadows that lie between their glittering highlights. With the form, if not the material, of the piers the character of the capitals is archaeologically appropriate. The intricately carved foliage of the capitals, wreathed under round abamuses, follows an insular mode deprecated in *Stones of Venice, 1,* by Ruskin; he rightly preferred the more organic foliage carving of French and Italian medieval capitals; and within a few years such capitals would be emulated by High Victorian architects to the point of ludicrous parody. The complex bundles of very English intrados moldings in the nave arches, loosely grouped in a suggestion of two main orders, give an effect of weight and thickness to the spandrels which the smooth marble and tile plaquage on their flat surface rather contradicts. (If not exactly Italian, Butterfield's spandrel treatment is certainly not English of any other period than the High Victorian.)

Higher up, in the clerestorey, the windows are linked together in a continuous arcade whose arches are varied in width with all the "impudence" of a Pisan architect of 1100 (Fig. XVII 6). The polished colonnettes supporting these orders are also varied in length. Even the position of their bases *seems* to be irregular in a fashion that almost defies geometrical analysis. Groups of three clerestorey windows run with each of the three nave arches below but the startling contrast in the scale of the two arcades rather obscures this simple and, probably consciously, "Trinitarian" relationship. The brackets carrying the arched principals of the roof are all set immediately over the crowns of the window arches, not over their spandrels. (There is, of course, an engineering reason for this which is illustrated in the arcades

591

of the Doge's Palace; one wonders whether Butterfield knew it or merely sensed it.) Thus the roof seems to conventionally trained eyes to repose most precariously on the clerestorey wall, just as the clerestorey wall itself seems inadequately supported by the widely spaced and rather slight nave piers— at least until one realizes the presumptive strength of their monolithic granite construction. For Butterfield this is unfortunately a dull and rather under-scaled roof. In particular the fretwork on the underside of the principals has a deceptively Tudor look somewhat like that of the flat panel work in stone on the aisle walls; generally Butterfield's carpentry was more vigorous and even at St. Barnabas's it is better scaled than here (Fig. V 29).

The choir and sanctuary are still richer than the body of the church, both plastically and in the rather barbarous use of paint and gilding over structural polychrome. (In the nave there is no paintwork except on the wooden roof.) The rich tracery in the arches on either side of the choir has a somewhat Italian look; the emphasis on open trefoils and quatrefoils also recalls a little Ruskin's avowed preference for simple and early forms—in his estimation the pattern of the openings and not the linear arabesque of the bars should be the determinant of the design, but that is not quite true here. Between the colonnettes below the tracery there is some rather ingenious strap ironwork of the sort for which Butterfield had long been particularly admired by advanced contemporaries. In the spandrels of the chancel arches a less strident and slightly more harmonious sort of mosaic patterning is introduced than in the larger nave spandrels; this is executed in brick and tile combined with various marbles and incised work (Fig. XVII 11).

The sanctuary is lined with elaborate niches of alabaster, redundantly gilded, in which are ranges of saints on flat gold backgrounds (Figs. XVII 5, 9). These were painted by William Dyce (1806–1864). The effect is rather timid and commonplace like the roof, partly because of the confused involvement of plastic and colored elements that Ruskin deprecated, but more because Dyce (though a rather fascinating landscape painter) was in his Nazarene moments such a feeble artist. Certainly his fake quattrocento refinement made him the worst possible collaborator for Butterfield.

Because of the absence of a conventional east window all the light falls diagonally from high side windows between the vaulting conoids. The surprisingly simple altar on which the light is dramatically focused is set against a plain alabaster wall, now covered by a curtain (Figs. XVII 5, 9). The vaulting overhead, with chalk severies between alabaster ribs and bosses, suffers like the reredos from redundant gilding and painting. Throughout the sanctuary, indeed, painted polychromy of the sort that had become ubiquitous in the 40's obscures the new structural sort of coloration. As offensive "hierarchically" (so to put it) as Butterfield's trick of combining cheap glazed bricks and colored mastic with real marbles, this mixture of genres remained characteristic of his work for decades to come.

The baptistery under the tower introduces no unfamiliar elements and the fittings of the side chapels, much later in date than the original campaign of decoration, also require no special comment. Of the windows, particularly the great west window by the French designer Gérente, it is kinder not to speak at all. Even the most enthusiastic contemporaries agreed that Butterfield was, to put it mildly, unlucky with his glass. (It is therefore unwise to illustrate the west end of the interior; by obscuring the strident conflicts in color tonality between glass and walls photographs flatter too much the general effect.) As with Butterfield's murals, one might most charitably assume that he cared little about his glass; but the evidence is rather that he enjoyed, like the musical composers of the 1920's, very abrupt changes in color and in scale.

All Saints' certainly represents a "very striking development" of that "application of decorative colour" which the *Ecclesiologist* early in 1850 had announced would form "an important object of the Society's study for the ensuing year." But what actual principles of color theory should it be considered to illustrate, other than those Ruskinian ones enunciated in the *Seven Lamps?* Color harmony in the ordinary sense is conspicuously lacking. Even Mr. Summerson's ingenious theory that Butterfield believed the colors of all natural materials *must* automatically go well together breaks down in the face of his free use here of glazed tiles and colored mastic, neither of which can be considered "products of nature." Nor can the gilded and painted polychromy of the sanctuary, which disguises the natural materials to which it is applied, or the tedious murals and the horrid stained glass be thus justified. I believe other explanations are more plausible.

One of these is that Butterfield, and perhaps most of his contemporaries when employing constructive coloration, were interested not in color (as we think of it today) but rather in vigorous contrasts of dark, light, and medium values. The striking effectiveness of Butterfieldian structural coloration as seen in contemporary wood engravings—which provided the only vehicle through which architects and laymen could be visually prepared for the reality—suggests that this explanation may be at least partially valid (Figs. XVII 2, 5). The other explanation (which does not exclude the first) is that Butterfield's approach to color was closely parallel to that of the most advanced contemporary painters in England, the Pre-Raphaelites. They also avoided tonal harmony consciously as an enfeebling heritage of academic taste; and the "reality" which they were seeking, with Ruskin's blessing, in the early 50's required (as regards color) the utmost intensity and independence of local hue.

Butterfield had no close contact with these younger artists; Dyce, his collaborator at All Saints', was only a timid forerunner. Moreover, their significant careers in architectural decoration began only with their work done at the Oxford Union from 1857 on. The Pre-Raphaelites achieved their first real masterpieces of decoration only around 1860, in collaboration with a younger generation of architects, after William Morris had turned his mature genius to the problem of coordinating stained glass and wall painting with architecture. Working first with George Frederick Bodley (1827–1907), after Bodley began to reject structural coloration in favor of a return to the painted internal decoration of the 40's, Morris and his associates eventually created for him and other architects admirable color churches. But these represent a reaction against, not a continuation of, Butterfieldian color theories.

To re-enforce the parallelism of Butterfield's polychromy at All Saints' with the early work of Millais and Holman Hunt and Rossetti it may be further remarked that their painting of the 50's has been better appreciated by posterity not in its orginal colors but as translated by the taste and skill of contemporary wood engravers like the Dalziels into crisp tonal patterns of black and gray and white. The weakness of both Butterfield and the Pre-Raphaelites at this period is only too apparent in the presence of the originals, for neither time nor grime has been able to mellow their colors.

There is little need to analyze the exterior of All Saints' and its flanking structures. The verticalized proportions and architecturesque irregularity, the brutal simplification of form, and the crankiness of the details, all of which constituted a novel and purely Butterfieldian idiom here, were to become generalized in the work of advanced architects within the next few years (Figs. XVII 2, 10). This process of generalization was in fact complete some years before All Saints' was finally consecrated in 1859.

During 1849–50, before the construction of All Saints' actually began, Butterfield initiated a good deal of other work. Characteristic touches of structural polychrome or cranky detail are to be found in most of it, including such important restorations as Merton College Chapel and St. Mary Ottery's, Exeter. But the two most important of his new churches, St. Matthias's, Stoke Newington, designed in 1850 and built in 1851–52, and St. Thomas's, Leeds, consecrated in 1852, alone require discussion here. Neither church is so Ruskinian, even hypothetically, as All Saints'; at St. Matthias's colored materials were hardly used at all. But both are strikingly different from the conventional churches of the day that followed closely the Camdenian formulas of the 40's. St. Thomas's was the smaller and less striking of the two and was completely demolished just before World War II. The blitz made a most distinguished ruin of St. Matthias's, a ruin which might well be left in its touching postwar state.

As in Butterfield's rather dull contemporary church of St. John Evangelist's, Huddersfield, a line of small ventilators took the place of clerestorey windows in St. Thomas's, Leeds. The exterior mass of the church therefore appeared very low and broad, although the roof slopes were not quite continuous over nave and aisles (Fig. XVII 12). Curious masonry dormers at the east end of the nave, with large traceried windows in them, created a sort of hidden transept and also provided some clerestorey lighting. The materials, inside and out, were red brick with flat bands of stone and some very simple patterns in "black" brick. Red, "black," and white bricks alternated in the voussoirs of the principal arches also. A letter writer who was quoted in the *Ecclesiologist, 12,* 69, remarked "it is no small satisfaction to those who know and feel the power of this 'art of arts' to see the bricks of a manufacturing town used with a judgment and delicacy which reminds us that Mr. Butterfield can impart an Italian hue and refinement to the coarse and disheartening vicinity of coal-smoke and mill chimneys." To later eyes the effect was not even as Italian as that of All Saints', however.

The "delicacy" that the writer stresses may seem an unlikely quality to find in any of Butterfield's work; yet away from London the patterns of his brickwork are often small in scale and the colors soft and exquisitely balanced. Here the continuous dark lozenging of the spandrel zone of the outside walls, with stone billets at the intersections, resembled in its refinement English Tudor patterns more than it did the zebraic stripings and savage tattooings of All Saints'. The plain billets of stone set between the horizontal bands lower down produce a crisp pattern suggesting abstract paintings of the 1920's. The red bricks remained cleaner here than in London, despite the general grime of Leeds, and were of a light orange-pink tone. The headers, moreover, were of a pale blue-gray, lighter than the stone bands, which the smoke of Leeds eventually dyed black. Thus there was a harmony of tone and value which contrasted with the stridency of All Saints' both outside and in.

The willful destruction of this edifice, long dismantled, removed a major work from the Butterfieldian canon. Despite the small original cost of £2,000, provided by a retired tradesman of the district, and the obscurity of its location, this small church (it held only 750) revealed, as the *Ecclesiologist, 15,* 59–60, remarked on its completion, "the hand of a master who builds *con amore* when there are difficulties and succeeds better with bricks than with other materials." Yet Dean Hook, who had been the patron of Chantrell at St. Peter's, saw in it nothing but additional proof that a true style for the 19th century was still nonexistent; to him it represented only a servile imitation of 14th-century Gothic (*Builder, 10,* 363). Hook particularly protested Butterfield's total failure to meet the wants of the "reformed" liturgy, something which Butterfield as a devout Tractarian had of course no interest in doing. It was, in fact, to be nearly a decade before a Broad Church version of High Victorian Gothic came to maturity. In Butterfield's work stylistic innovation was always combined with the most elaborate provision for the revival of an "unreformed" medieval ritual.

The chancel of St. Thomas's, Leeds, was added by Butterfield only in 1891–93 and the steeple never built, which explained the unwonted humility of its external appearance. But at Stoke Newington the tower of St. Matthias's still rises with overpowering arrogance above the ruins (Figs. XVII 14–15). The placing of a tower at the east end of the nave, except in cruciform churches, had hitherto been deprecated by all the purists beginning with Pugin. But Butterfield had already done this in the design he prepared in 1848 for completing the east end of the Anglican cathedral in Fredericton, New Brunswick. On the other hand, Pugin's original design for the tower of his modest St. Marie's, Rugby (which was shown at the Royal Academy Exhibition in 1849), provided modern precedent for the gabled capping that Butterfield used at St. Matthias's.

In the Middle Ages such a conclusion to a steeple had been little used in England, and then only as a sort of makeshift on rather modest towers. Butterfield's monumentally gabled tower has therefore a distinctly continental look, say Norman or North German. As often with him, it is more likely that he arrived at his own design by exaggeration of a native prototype than by imitating some foreign model, since he probably knew continental work only through the drawings other less insular architects brought back from their sketching tours abroad. In the original project, published in the *Ecclesiologist* in 1850, the simple silhouette of the steeple was confused by corner pinnacles; but these, as the commentator in that journal advised, were omitted in execution (Fig. XVII 13). The clumsy triplet aisle windows, set under segmental-pointed heads, were also very understandably disapproved but these Butterfield did not modify.

The other changes that Butterfield made from the early design in the executed church were of varying merit. The bold introduction of enormous traceried lights rising well up into the tower gables is most effective (Fig. XVII 15). The simplification of the buttressing to achieve broader, less broken wall surfaces was an improvement also; the really extraordinary treatment of the west front was not. The splitting of the enormous window by a central buttress rising out of the low western portal's gable was undoubtedly derived from the entrance front of Dorchester Abbey on the restoration of which Butterfield was still at work; but that makes it no less clumsy. This feature well illustrates the delight Butterfield took in borrowing the most peculiar and exceptional features he knew in English medieval architecture whenever these agreed with his own exaggerated sense of what was expressive and workmanlike.

Henceforth standard paradigms of medieval style were increasingly avoided by advanced architects; instead, unique—even accidental—solutions of special difficulties hammered out by medieval builders were snatched up with glee when the work of the English past was rifled for inspiration. For anyone with only a general 20th-century knowledge of medieval stylistic development it is often hard to believe that ancient prototypes ever did exist for many High Victorian features. "Hunt the crotchet" was a game soon to be widely played and one quite alien to the preceding Early Victorian preference for suave and consistent imitation of the more obvious medieval models. Except for a few wildmen like E. B. Lamb, Butterfield was the earliest champion at this sport; and only Street was his rival in finding strange medieval devices to enliven, often with perverse structural logic, the more familiar Gothic solutions of various problems of design.

Where Butterfield is apparently most crankily original—in his plastic forms at least, if not in his color work—he is likely to be best armed with some sort of forgotten precedent. As always when architectural style is changing, a corresponding image of the most admired sorts of architecture of the past was also adumbrated at the same time—so Robert Adam a century before had drawn the ornaments of Spalato not in their original Late Roman terms but in those of his own very personal vision before his career as an architect began.

The houses that were rising around St. Matthias's as it was being built were mostly no more than two or three storeys tall and there was plenty of land at its sides as well as the broad avenue of Howard Road approaching the front (Fig. XVII 15). Yet Butterfield designed St. Matthias's as a town church to form a dominating monument in a district that has never in fact developed into more than a very modest and shabby suburb. In the nave the high-waisted proportions of All Saints' are reversed. The aisle arcade is quite low and the tall clerestorey is lighted by very large traceried windows of the kind hitherto used in aisles. Internally the chancel and sanctuary arches that support the tower are kept very low; thus there is an even more considerable break than usual between the noble spacial volume of the nave and the rather constricted subsidiary volume of the low vaulted choir.

Externally there is no structural polychrome here, only vast plain surfaces of gray-brown stock brick quite like those of the grand contemporary engineering works in and around London (Figs. XVII 14–15). The walls are broken by a minimum of stone stringcourses, arches, and buttress weatherings, all intentionally rather crudely shaped. The keying of the stonework into the brick is most willfully abrupt and has become very con-

597

spicuous. But the exterior reveals more clearly than that of All Saints' with its distracting surface patterns the boldness and the grandeur of Butterfield's proportions as well as the great originality of his characteristic mass composition.

The inside is almost equally bold and plain despite the red brick used in the sanctuary vault between the stone ribs and the tessellated tiling of the reredos at the east end. But this masculine, even monk-like, austerity contrasts not unhappily with the pretty fussiness of earlier Camdenian interiors and also with the curiously unsensual lushness of All Saints'. At St. Matthias's Butterfield seems to have taken up again the line of Pugin's boldest and baldest churches such as St. Barnabas's, Nottingham. But he was raising this line to a height of originality that Pugin could hardly approve. Here Butterfield was certainly encouraging his younger contemporaries to be as "freehand," as "impudent," and as "fearless" as Ruskin was recommending in his books, and even more perhaps than at Margaret Street.

A writer in the *Ecclesiologist* remarked, in speaking of the schools at St. Matthias's, that a window arch with an unpierced tympanum is "an excellent idea borrowed from German Pointed." This offers another indication that it was the emulation of German rather than of Italian medieval models which was thought by contemporaries to explain most of the special qualities of Butterfield's work around 1850. But his willful originality in design was also recognized. In the *Ecclesiologist*'s account of another new Butterfield church at West Lavington, the writer pointed a deprecating finger at what he frankly called Butterfield's "whims and eccentricities." Despite this criticism from the circle of Butterfield's best friends, an anonymous architect complained in an article on "Architectural Puffing and 'Ecclesiological' Bitterness," *Builder*, 8, 507, that the Society coddled their favorite architect and condoned all his peculiarities. He was correct enough in noting the Society's almost exclusive (and a priori favorable) preoccupation with the work of Carpenter and Butterfield while the work of everyone else was likely to be harshly criticized if mentioned at all in the *Ecclesiologist*. But Butterfield's peculiarities were not always praised by any means.

At West Lavington the *Ecclesiologist*'s critic "observed a tendency to prefer stiff and quaint forms, which show some originality, to more hackneyed expressions." He also warned Butterfield that this tendency was "good and hopeful" only if done with "extreme caution and very chastened taste. We trust we may not be registering the first traces of an excessive reaction to traditionary architectural rules on the part of the eminent architect"—which, of course, was just what they were doing. Far worse than the setting of squares level within quatrefoils rather than diagonally at West Lavington—a characteristic Butterfieldism—was "a growing use of

598

Third Pointed [i.e., Perpendicular] forms—disguised of course . . . " which the critic thought he detected. Indeed, for the *Ecclesiologist's* reviewer, the design of this simple and "unaffected" village church was "deprived of much of its beauty by what we can consider little better than the *crotchets* of the author." That was stern talk from an avowed friend.

After the original design for St. Matthias's (Fig. XVII 13) had been illustrated in the *Ecclesiologist,* with the strictures on the tower pinnacles and the aisle windows already mentioned and other minor complaints, Edward A. Freeman, the architectural historian, commented tersely in a published letter: "It appears to me one of the worst designs I have seen in a long time." After noting the "hideous" clerestorey windows and the fact that the west front was in his estimation a "depraved" copy of Dorchester, he furthermore remarked, like the letter writer in the *Builder* (who may well have been Freeman also), that in the Society's publication "the productions of Mr. Butterfield do not meet with the same just severity as those of other architects." He also castigated Butterfield's "pretense" and "affectation of simplicity."

Perhaps to prove impartiality, in reviewing St. Matthias's after it was completed the *Ecclesiologist* repeated its earlier critical comment that the aisle windows were ungraceful and added that the curious combination of west buttress and west window was unhappy. Butterfield's woodwork, which was as frequently a matter for complaint with contemporaries as his ironwork was for praise, was also castigated as "positively ugly," "heavy in construction and inelegant in form, a blemish to the church." A general tendency to "cumbrous and uncouth ornamentation in the window tracery" and the excessively high glaze of the tiles in the tessellated reredos (a rather minor matter) were also protested. Yet this basically friendly critic rightly saw that most of what appeared objectionable at St. Matthias's was the natural result of a reaction against the "prettiness and frippery of much modern design," reprehensible though it was that Butterfield in his "manly and vigorous design" had reacted quite so far. The critic also wrote that it was "difficult to speak too highly of the genius and power shown [by] the distinguished architect of so remarkable a church." Thus Butterfield's position as the leading Camdenian architect was reaffirmed; it would last at least through the 50's.

Although St. Matthias's was a considerably larger church than All Saints', 135 feet long by 45 feet wide and 70 feet high inside, in its "affectation of simplicity" it cost only about a tenth as much, £7,000. It deserved, however, all the attention it and other contemporary works by Butterfield in and near London were receiving at this time. The important church and "college" he was building on remote Cumbrae Island in Scotland were never published; few contemporary architects or critics could conveniently visit them—nor, for that matter, the present author a hundred years later. The remarkable rapidity with which other architects took up Butterfieldian ideas well before All Saints' was completed (or indeed much more than begun) can be explained only by the immediate acceptance of the two London churches as worthy of study by other architects even while they were still in construction, and also by the characteristic attitude, often uncritically close to adulation, of the *Ecclesiologist's* reviews of them.

Although the reviews were never entirely without qualification, Butterfield's new churches were nevertheless the particular models that readers of the paper would naturally urge their own architects to follow; and most High Church clergymen were among the readers as were the pious laymen who sponsored or paid for new church building. Certain architects with Camdenian connections may well have had access to Butterfield's actual working drawings. It was natural—and on the whole correct—to suppose that Butterfield's "crotchets" were intimately related to his "genius." Hence many young architects were inclined to emulate him by developing crotchets of their own or, if that were too difficult, by imitating his. The exploitation of Butterfieldian crotchets soon became a major indication of stylistic change in Gothic design; quite as symptomatic as permanent polychrome, it was of more basic effect in breaking up inherited stylistic discipline.

Despite Ruskin's ultimate appeal for unity and obedience in matters of style, a docile reading of the *Seven Lamps* would presumably tend to stimulate rather than to inhibit tendencies toward what might be called Butterfieldism. Pugin and the Camdenians in the 40's had been authoritarian regarding architecture in a quite Catholic way; despite all Ruskin's inner yearning for some external authority to supplant that of his dominating parents, he was, on the other hand, a Protestant who could not help encouraging private judgment on the part of his readers. He quoted Scripture, in and out of season, to lend the weight of Biblical authority to what the cynical must always have realized were his private visual preferences, quite as much as Butterfield's crotchets were the material expression of his. Ruskin's mind was not so fanatically single as Pugin's nor was his doctrine, even in the early 50's, so coherent as that of the Camdenians had hitherto been.

Yet his remarkable aesthetic sensibilities, excelling Pugin's in subtlety and variety of response to all things seen, whether natural or man made, found literary expression in a rhetoric more memorable than his predecessor's and most eminently quotable. Reading Ruskin confirmed, or seemed to confirm, the propriety of following Butterfield's stylistic lead; it also provided the verbal ammunition for defending the results whatever they might actually look like.

Butterfield's influence was not spread through the agency of his pupils as is most often the way that innovations of highly personal talents reach wide acceptance. At this time, indeed, he had no pupils, or none of any consequence. Henry Woodyer, his only real pupil, had left the office and begun his first major work, the church of the Holy Innocents at Highnam in Gloucestershire, as early as 1847. This is the most important Anglican example of painted internal polychromy, rivaling Pugin's St. Giles's, Cheadle, but it is not particularly Butterfieldian. Gambier Parry, the client, was himself responsible for the murals. This church was almost complete by 1850 even including the elaborate decorations. Only then did Woodyer first use encaustic tiles to ornament a reredos in a small church he was restoring at Hawnes in Bedfordshire. But this minor touch of permanent polychrome need be considered no more significant than a similar reredos erected by Scott at just the same time, almost certainly with no influence from Butterfield.

Gilbert Scott was three years older than Butterfield and in 1849 he had just been confirmed as the recognized leader of the modern Gothic practitioners; for that was what his appointment, in succession to Blore, as Surveyor of the Fabric of Westminster Abbey implied. The tiled reredos Scott introduced in his restoration of St. Andrew's, Barnwell, may be considered merely a casual extension to the east wall in the chancel of the dadoes Pugin had used on the side walls of St. Giles's, Cheadle—as may Woodyer's also, for that matter. Yet it is nevertheless true that both Scott and Woodyer within a year or two began to swing into the current of the High Victorian Gothic which Butterfield had just set on its tumultuous way. The enthusiastic acceptance of the new Butterfieldian ideas by much younger men, which started even before most of them had been fully realized in execution by Butterfield himself, is what is most important historically at this point.

J. P. Seddon, for example, was only 23 when his design for a parsonage for St. John's, Long Green, was exhibited at the Royal Academy Exhibition in 1850. This already showed "some effect . . . cheaply obtained by the mixture of red and yellow bricks," according to the slightly patronizing account in the *Builder*. G. E. Street's school at Inkpen in Berkshire (costing only £250) was presumably designed in 1850 also. Its chamfered red brick arches set in flint walling and its tympana filled with ornamental tile work might in themselves seem hardly to justify much notice; yet the *Ecclesiologist* in 1851 not only described this tiny edifice in detail but underlined the fact that the bricks were *red* in order to indicate that they were introduced to give positive coloration to the walls. The reviewer also found in this school a great deal of "character"—the usual word for Butterfield's chief virtue—with none of that "exaggeration" for which Butterfield was already being

601

reprimanded, even by his friends. From such very small acorns great architectural careers often grow.

The extended review of the little Inkpen school was but one among many indications that the *Ecclesiologist* already took Street more seriously than any other young architect. And the *Ecclesiologist* was right; for Street was destined to be, after Butterfield and Ruskin, the most important architect and archaeologist-critic of the High Victorian period. He is not likely ever to be entirely forgotten, if only because of the excellence of his archaeological studies of Spanish medieval architecture and the prominence of his belated Law Courts in the Strand (first designed for the competition held in 1866 but not built until 1874–82). To a far greater extent than Butterfield's or Ruskin's, however, Street's importance as an architect and a critic has been eroded by time, largely because the Law Courts which are his best known work were built only at the very end of his long career after being redesigned several times. They give no fair idea of his talents in the best period of his production in the 50's and early 60's.

Street's career was really rivaled in the High Victorian period only by Gilbert Scott's; which might well mean that his capacities, like those of Scott, were primarily geared to the achievement of worldly success. The present-day impression of his work has generally supported this interpretation. Actually, Street was as single minded an artist as Butterfield and a more careful student of medieval architecture than Ruskin. He was, moreover, the master of most of the young men who became leaders of architectural taste in the next generation. Among his pupils are found not only distinguished architects like Philip Webb, Norman Shaw, and John Dando Sedding but also William Morris whose influence on later architecture throughout the world was to be even greater than theirs.

Street's own architectural achievement does not really rival Butterfield's; his work was both less consistent and less individual. His more extensive and more varied production, as well as his broader archaeological studies, probably made this inferiority inevitable. Yet in the field of church architecture his church of St. James-the-Less, Westminster (1859–61), and his SS. Philip and James's, Oxford (1860–62), both built at the peak of the High Victorian period, are no unworthy rivals of Butterfield's contemporary St. Alban's, Holborn (1858–63). More than any other architect of the mid–19th-century, except perhaps Butterfield or Scott, Street deserves—and an adequate picture of the architectural history of the time will ultimately require—a detailed study. (The *Memoir of George Edmund Street, R. A., 1824–1881* [1888] by his son A. E. Street is most unsatisfactory except for the inclusion of the text of his father's Royal Academy lectures.) Here, alas, only the merest beginning of such a study can be introduced within the compass of the present brief account of the inception of the High Victorian Gothic of which he was soon to be one of the three chief leaders.

Street was born 20 June 1824. He was therefore 10 years younger than Butterfield and 13 years younger than Scott with whose careers his ran parallel in the 50's, 60's, and 70's. His birthplace was Woodford, Essex, effectively an outer London suburb, where his solicitor father was then living. He was articled in 1841 at the age of 17 to Owen B. Carter of Winchester, the architect of the handsome Tuscan Corn Exchange, now the Public Library, there. Three years later Street entered Scott's office just after the latter's split with Moffatt. He was elected a member of the Camden Society in 1845, immediately following its reorganization in London as the Ecclesiological Society. The Society soon received him into its innermost circles and almost from the first his work was reviewed in the *Ecclesiologist* with a consistent approval otherwise reserved for the activities of Carpenter and Butterfield.

While Street was in Scott's office he is thought to have been personally responsible for the fine Early English tower of St. Matthew's, City Road, in London (Fig. V 7)—he afterward spoke of it with critical detachment, but that proves nothing. Before he left the office in 1848 he had built one small church at Par in Cornwall and had probably begun three others nearby at Sticker, at St. Cuthberts, and St. Mary's at Biscovery. After his departure several other Cornish church rebuildings followed immediately including SS. Peter and Paul's, Shevioke, and another at St. Merwan. He also provided a new chancel for St. Peter's, Plymouth. But soon he set up his office at Wantage in Berkshire, drawn there by the High Church leader Dr. Butler. A church at Coleshill and restorations at Sundridge in Kent and at Harley in Middlesex, as well as a school chapel at Chavey Down nearer his new headquarters, were proceeding under his direction around 1850. All this work was modest and correct enough to receive ecclesiological approval; yet to connoisseurs of the time, if not always to later ones, real individuality and character were clearly discernible.

Street was beginning to make an archaeological reputation by his contributions to the *Ecclesiologist* and he was also reading excellent papers before various architectural societies. His first important critical writing followed upon a trip to France made in 1850. The fact that so loyal a young Camdenian could take this trip at all indicated the rapidly decreasing insularity of the Society since the appearance of Webb's *Sketches of Continental Ecclesiology* in 1848. Street was possibly influenced also by reading the *Seven Lamps* which had appeared the year before he went abroad. That book could certainly encourage the cheaper excursion to see the Gothic of northern France as well as the more difficult and time-consuming tour of northern Italy. This latter expedition Street did not undertake until 1853 after an intervening trip in 1851 to Germany and Belgium which were then considered to be, even more than Italy, the homelands of brick building.

Street's important article of 1850 in the *Ecclesiologist,* "On the Proper Characteristics of a Town Church," even though it echoed some opinions that had already found expression in the *Ecclesiologist,* represents a landmark in the history of Victorian church architecture. The tall clerestorey of Scoles' church of the Immaculate Conception, Farm Street, had been approved as proper in a town church when the design was shown at the Royal Academy Exhibition in 1847, but Street's demand for clerestoreys in his article was more forthright. The *Ecclesiologist's* recommendation of brick for church building in the same year, with references to the medieval town churches of Belgium, Bavaria, and Italy, has already been mentioned; but Street's protest against the imitation of country churches in London was new. His condemnation of the rusticity of Kentish ragstone rubble was very pointed since it applied to all the town churches hitherto most highly approved by the Camdenians, including Carpenter's "model" church of St. Mary Magdalene's then still in construction. According to Street these churches should have glittered and shone with fine hewn ashlar outside and with marbles and frescoes within; but for London plain brick was at least preferable to rough walling stone.

Street's next suggestion in his article, that steep roofs were not perhaps indispensable, was heresy to most Camdenians. Even on old churches the Society had demanded, and in restorations provided, roofs of very high pitch. Street's insistence on the need for clerestoreys and his remarks on the redundancy of steeples, particularly those of the simple broach type placed in picturesque asymmetrical positions, were less novel; but such preferences did not necessarily savor of the forbidden Third Pointed as did his approval of low roofs. Height was in Street's estimation of immense importance both in the nave arcade, as at All Saints', and in the clerestorey, as at St. Matthias's. Long chancels also were even more desirable in the city than in the country, Street considered, since in urban parishes there were likely to be more considerable groups of attached clergy and larger choirs.

Street also wanted more elaborate interior decoration, preferably in permanent materials; if it could not be introduced at once, it should at least be planned as Butterfield was doing at All Saints'. In any event the initial shell should certainly be grand even if it had to remain unadorned for a long time. Study of foreign churches was advisable; St. Germain l'Auxerrois in Paris, St. Pierre at Chartres, and the Eglise des Augustins in Rouen were particularly recommended as examples of town churches worthy of emulation. Finally, the visual importance of a long unbroken roof line was stressed even at the expense of any symbolic differentiation on the exterior between nave and chancel.

According to Street, "true ancient Christian architecture" had always combined the horizontal and the vertical. The point could not yet be made but the great Perpendicular town churches of England actually met most of his requirements—as Street was eventually to admit when he later dared to be frank about the matter. But it was to be another twenty years and more before the Camdenian ban on the "debased" Third Pointed was finally and flatly revoked. All this new doctrine in Street's article of 1850 is certainly not Ruskinian nor is it exactly Butterfieldian; it seems rather to represent an independent position more balanced and sensible than those of either of the older men.

Other significant books and articles of 1850 and 1851 should be at least mentioned here. *Examples of Architectural Art Chiefly of the 13th to 16th Centuries in Italy and Spain* (1850) by J. B. Waring (1823–1875) and T. R. Maquoid included much trecento as well as quattrocento work and even some examples of Italian Romanesque; in fact, the authors were open proponents of the free, nonacademic use of the round arch. Waring also published at this time *Thirty Designs for Civil Architecture* (1850), which the *Builder* said the "straitlaced" would call "mixed" because there was so much use of molded brick. M. D. Wyatt presented his "Observations on Polychromatic Decoration in Italy from the XIIth to the XVIth Century" before the R.I.B.A. in 1850 also, following up his earlier books on the same subject; and a few preacademic Italian fragments began to be presented individually in illustrations in the *Builder*.

But the great journalistic subject of discussion in the columns of the *Builder* at this time was "copyism." A lively controversy was set off by Pugin's restatement of his own unchanged position which required the most humble emulation of the past; this was answered almost at once by the architectural historian James Fergusson. The latter vigorously condemned the "servile doctrines of copying" and clearly stated the position so familiar today that "truth in [architectural] art consists of representing faithfully the wants and feelings of the people who use [buildings] and of the age which gave birth to [them]." Fergusson also cleverly attacked the symbolical interpretation of Gothic; certainly his remark that Pugin's roof at St. George's, Southwark, was only "symbolical of bad carpentry" can be considered a successful hit at Pugin, if not perhaps at Durandus. Gilbert Scott took up a middle position, as he usually did when controversies got hot, urging that the 19th-century revival of Gothic need not be copyistic but should rather allow for a gradual development of original expression. The educational period of the revival, which had provided a necessary starting point, was nearly completed, he considered, and the time was ripe for some sort of movement forward. This mild but not unplausible proposition quieted Fergusson, at least temporarily; Pugin shortly went mad and died (though not as a result of this controversy).

The youthful Robert Kerr, speaking before the Architectural Association, soon renewed the battle. He asserted that the 19th century already *had* its own style; this could be seen in ordinary houses and simple chapels as well as in the Crystal Palace—"herein is evinced the tendency of the *natural* style of our period," he said. But Kerr had spent some part of his youth in America; there, as was well known to Victorians, radicalism was contagious in all fields of thought—it is even possible that Kerr may have known the sculptor Horatio Greenough's functionalist ideas or their inspiration in the writings of Emerson. The tedious Samuel Huggins of Liverpool, on the other hand, saw the then present as "evidently a crisis in the career of British architecture," which was in fact true enough although not very helpful. Curiously enough neither the new direction Butterfield was taking in actual building at All Saints' nor the new ideas of the *Seven Lamps* played much part in this discussion.

Yet Seddon, with reference both to Fergusson and to Ruskin, had said before the Architectural Association early in the controversy: "We want neither a new nor a universal style, we should know nothing about styles; the very name is a bane and a hindrance to architects, however useful to the antiquary." That is, of course, a recurrent attitude, which many architects—and particularly Walter Gropius—have echoed in attacking 20th-century critics like me. Paradoxically enough it seems usually to indicate a period of stylistic crystallization, often at the hands of those who are firmest in its support. Seddon, indeed, was shortly to be a leading protagonist of the High Victorian Gothic style-phase, whether he recognized it or not. A friend of the Pre-Raphaelites in the Hogarth Club, of which he was one of the few architect-members, he provided a significant link between the advanced painters and the advanced architects of the day. He goes on to explain his position further and perhaps better: "Let us leave to posterity our productions and be sure that if we work simply, neither copying nor striving for singularity, we cannot so far emancipate ourselves from the feelings of our own age and country but that they will give an impress to our work, though we may not discern it for ourselves." Gropius could not make this point more happily.

Insofar as the real outcome of any intellectual or artistic quarrel can ever really be determined by posterity once the emotional connotations originally so stirring to contemporaries have faded, the "copyist" controversy of 1850–51 seems to have resulted in a draw. So also must the parallel but quite separate historical controversy as to whether Ruskin or Butterfield had primary responsibility for the new direction revived Gothic was taking in these years. To the later Victorians a modified copyism seemed within a few years to have won out; after the early 60's little more was to be heard of wholly new styles or of style-less architecture for a generation. Many 20th-century historians, recalling from these years almost nothing but the Crystal Palace and King's Cross Station, forget that for a long time these represented an end point rather than the beginning of a new development; by such writers copyism and the very concept of style, in anything resembling a historic sense, are therefore considered to have received their deathblow in the climactic achievements of ferrovitreous construction. They merely ignore the critical controversy of 1850–51 as it was understood by those involved in it and altogether forget both Butterfield and Ruskin, who then represented rising, not sinking, forces.

In 1852 a whole group of architects, both young and old, began designing buildings, all Gothic but by no means all churches, that clearly indicated a new phase of Victorian architecture was actually under way. Articles full of new ideas were also appearing right and left from the pens of various architects and critics. With the appearance of the *Stones of Venice, 1*, in 1851 Ruskinism became available as a system, while from All Saints' and St. Matthias's something like a Butterfieldian system could also be deduced. Both systems were accessible to all who were interested; it was therefore quite natural that the two should be merged in general practice. Increasing numbers of architects who traveled on the Continent were also bringing back their own sketches of medieval work many of which were published in books or as illustrations in the *Builder*. Papers on related topics were becoming regular features of the meetings of architectural and archaeological societies. Among the younger architects Street was perhaps the most assiduous traveler and easily the most cogent writer.

The large collection of building stones displayed at the Great Exhibition in 1851 called attention to British resources in natural mineral products. Native marbles, alabasters, serpentines, and granites could, when polished, provide as rich and brilliant a repertory of colors as Italian architects had ever had at their disposal. Mechanized methods of polishing the Scottish blue and red granites from Aberdeen and Peterhead were reducing the cost of such luxuries; while the railways made available stones of various colors far from the regions in which they were quarried and worked. Enthusiasm for brick and terra-cotta products continued to rise as well; this was stimulated by the various improved techniques of manufacture developed immediately after the removal of the brick tax in 1851. (Robert's hollow-brick vaults and walls and Edmeston's glazed tile panels for use in cast-iron chassis provide good examples of this.) Finally, the enormous success of the Crystal Palace advertised the potentialities of iron construction as also of the prefabricated or partially prefabricated production of building elements. When Carpenter, of all people, was called upon in 1853 by the Ecclesiological Society to design an iron church that project provided the perfect counterfoil to Paxton's ecclesiologically correct restoration of the medieval church at Baslow near Chatsworth.

The exposition of Ruskin's doctrines in their most consistent form was completed only after the appearance of the two later volumes of the *Stones of Venice* in 1853 and the *Edinburgh Lectures* which were delivered that year and published the following one. Yet the first volume of the *Stones of Venice* (1851) was to some extent an independent treatise. "The Foundations" with which it dealt were primarily the foundations of the sort of architectural criticism which Ruskin intended to apply to the architecture of Venice in his two later volumes; but those critical foundations were, of course, intended also to be much wider in their application. If the examples of positive architectural virtues were most frequently drawn by Ruskin from Venetian (or at least from medieval Italian) monuments, there was also a wealth of reference, favorable and unfavorable, to the architecture of all times and places from ancient Egypt to contemporary Britain.

The *Builder's* leader-review of Volume 1 of the *Stones* was considerably less diffident than that devoted to the *Lamps* two years earlier. George Godwin, the editor (who probably wrote the piece), found the new book more "practical," as doubtless it is, and remarked that it "will assist to pave the way to the rationalism and advancement of architecture." If Godwin stressed the fact that it should serve to educate laymen, he was merely echoing Ruskin's own preface. Ruskin had explained there that he desired to "gain the ear of all kinds of persons," since "in architecture all must commit themselves . . . therefore all of us must have knowledge and act upon it, not be left to the caprice of architects or the mercy of contractors." But it later became evident in the text that Ruskin was writing for the capricious architects also, if not perhaps for the merciless contractors.

Ruskin disclaimed that he had included anything "bearing on the special forms and needs of modern buildings." As the educed "principles were universal" and medieval Venice had been a commercial metropolis like modern London, however, he felt that the treatise as a whole—that is, including the detailed descriptions of Venetian edifices that would fill the later volumes —should be of relevant interest "as illustrating what a mercantile community built for civil uses and domestic magnificence" might be. A separate folio volume of large plates, *Examples of the Architecture of Venice* (1851), offered detailed views of the buildings he most admired, something notably lacking in the *Seven Lamps*.

The eclectic and progressive Godwin could not accept the universality of Ruskin's pretensions any more than those of Pugin. But he welcomed what Ruskin offered as support for that eclectic modulation of neo-Gothic design which was already under way. Neither Godwin nor many professional men outside Camdenian circles could accept the frenzied denunciations of the "pestilent Renaissance," however, which were what most endeared Ruskin to the *Ecclesiologist*.

As with the *Seven Lamps*, the *Ecclesiologist* had to apologize for tardiness in reviewing Volume 1 of the *Stones* but fortunately made up for its delay by providing two long notices in successive numbers. Although protesting Ruskin's anti-Romanist "monomania" and his tasteless attack on Pugin, the reviewer cordially recommended the book without endorsing by any means "all that he [Ruskin] advances that is strictly architectural and artistic." Ruskin's poetic tendency to derive ideal curved forms from the profile of the Matterhorn or of a salvia leaf seemed somewhat farfetched, but the work as a whole was "of extreme value in suggesting and directing thought" (which of course it still is) because it forced readers to accept a "constructional" system of criticism. In the second notice Ruskin's remarks on the use of "constructional colour" in patterns of simple geometric form were quoted with warm approval. "We are delighted to find Mr. Ruskin a champion for the beauty, as well as the strict architectural propriety, of the Italian method of decoration by horizontal bands of colour, in opposition to the dictum of Professor Willis" (who had been attacking the stripings of All Saints' as soon as the walls were high enough to reveal the revolutionary character of their treatment).

The tedious oversystematization of Volume 1 of the *Stones*, with its innumerable short chapters and inevitable repetitions—good pedagogy, perhaps, but prosy reading—received little comment from the reviewers; and Ruskin's extraordinary omissions went largely unnoted, I suppose because such omissions—as of planning in toto and of all vaulting theory—seemed natural to contemporaries, even in a system of architectural analysis called "constructional" by its author. The anonymous critic "Z" 's cogent complaint, made in the *Builder* in 1853, that Ruskin "the reformer of taste and architecture appeared utterly insensible . . . to the value of artistic composition, general character, and effect of ensemble," and the even more precise complaint that he made of detail the "all-in-all of architecture" were, however, echoed by many reviewers of Volumes 2 and 3. Comment on Ruskin's negative attitude to iron construction, including his violent strictures on the Crystal Palace, has appeared in the previous chapter; but it is of interest to note again that this bigoted attitude was not shared by the *Ecclesiologist*.

It would be tedious to conclude this book with a summary of the Ruskinian system of architectural criticism as adumbrated in the *Stones of Venice, 1.* And it is unnecessary. No architect of the 50's seriously attempted to mold his methods of design step by step upon its precepts. Even the designs of Benjamin Woodward (1815–1861), that most Ruskinian of architects, represent but one of many possible ways of interpreting the written doctrine. Despite—or, more truly, because of—Woodward's close personal association with Ruskin, and even the existence of a sort of collaboration on several important projects of the mid-50's, there is much in Ruskinism that neither of Woodward's two Oxford buildings nor yet his important Foreign Office project illustrate at all. The iron and glass roof of his Oxford Museum is at open odds with one of Ruskin's strongest convictions, or so it would appear. That, however, and a fortiori the Union Debating Hall of 1856–57 and the Foreign Office design of the same date lie beyond the boundary set for this book.

The character of Ruskin's influence was extraordinarily complex and cannot even be summarized in this terminal chapter which must come to an end just at the point that influence began to be significant. Ruskin's influence could and did operate on various levels in the 50's and through succeeding decades down into our own time. The most obvious and superficial level, just after 1850, is represented by the acceptance of the study of Italian medieval monuments as a necessary part of a Victorian architect's preparation for practice and, more broadly, the study of all sorts of continental Gothic precedent previously disapproved as unworthy of English emulation. On the deepest level of understanding only a few men of a younger generation whose artistic production did not begin until around 1860 deserve in the end to be considered true Ruskinians. There were no Ruskinians of this order, except for one or two architects' assistants and Oxford undergraduates, in the early 50's.

Still later the original Ruskinian doctrines were so modified by the glosses the author added to successive editions of his early books and by the less systematic but recurrent discussions of architecture in his writing after 1860 that finally almost *all* attitudes toward architecture current between the 50's and the present, except the more strictly academic ones, can claim a relationship to Ruskin. The Ruskinian critical tradition, more remarkable for its subtlety than for its consistency, has never died out. But even Ruskin, for all his changeableness, would be surprised by the actual production of many famous modern architects such as Henri Van de Velde and Frank Lloyd Wright, to name but the eldest, who acknowledge the influence of his thought.

What more and more Victorian architects were to be currently doing in the 50's and after can very often be related to one or another specific recommendation in the *Lamps* or the *Stones,* but Ruskin himself increasingly disapproved the results. After 1860 he even exaggerated rather perversely the extent of his own earlier influence when he came to reject almost all modern Gothic building because of its cheap exploitation of various High Victorian motifs. He was not really the legitimate parent of many of those motifs even if he came to find a breast-beating satisfaction in accepting blame for having introduced them.

Avid readers though Victorian architects were, fascinated by theoretic doctrine and even more eclectic with their minds perhaps than with their eyes, Ruskin's books were on the whole more stimulating than formative in their effect on professional readers. The first volume of the *Stones* particularly, organized so much like a textbook, can repel a mature mind by its specious completeness at the same time that it fascinates by the sensitivity of various critical discriminations. Formally used as the backbone of a program of instruction—in a way it certainly never was in any of the English schools where architecture was taught in the mid-century—the *Stones* might ultimately have created a Ruskinian academicism more rigid than the Puginian academicism of the 40's. But when it is read by independent minds, young or old, the book recurrently shifts the reader away from the doctrine and back to the monuments themselves—or at least to the bits and pieces of monuments which are so subtly and inconsistently discussed.

The truest Ruskinian architecture was ultimately to be designed by men—some of them foreigners as yet unborn—who started from his ethical rather than from his aesthetic premises; these were the men who would at least try to see *everything*—and not just his limited repertory of approved monuments—with a vision and a moral passion comparable in subtlety to his own. The Ruskinian character of Le Corbusier's earliest water-color sketches is almost more striking than are Van de Velde's avowed discipleship or the Ruskinism of much of Wright's theoretical writing.

Of the rising interest in Italian medieval architecture in the years during which the *Stones of Venice* was coming out there can be no question. For this new and significant interest Ruskin usually received specific credit from those who reported on their Italian pilgrimages. Even the travelers who still had eyes for Palladio were more and more ready to look at earlier things also. A hard core of Classicism hardly existed even at the Royal Academy although Cockerell was Professor of Architecture there in the early 50's.

There were still some prominent architects who professed to remain faithful to "Italian," that is, to academic Renaissance, traditions. But they were soon almost as open, in their growing eclecticism, to the allurements of structural polychrome and other supposedly Ruskinian ideas as were the Gothic men. The round-arched early medieval styles of Italy, for instance, and even the quattrocento mode provided wide areas for stylistic compromise and

611

amalgamation. With the increasing pursuit of "character" and of outright innovation in design the boundary between what was considered respectable by men of Gothic upbringing and what was acceptable to those of Renaissance training almost disappeared after the mid-50's.

The main threads in the story of the earliest beginnings of the High Victorian Gothic in the years 1849–51 have been indicated in this chapter; the braiding of them together in the next few years is a fascinating episode which lies outside the defined framework of this book. The years around 1850 were an extraordinarily eventful moment in architectural history. Never before nor again were the threads of Victorian aesthetic life so tautly stretched; nor are there clearer trumpet notes in all of Victorian architecture than the ferrovitreous masterworks of Paxton and Lewis Cubitt and Brunel or deeper organ tones than Butterfield sounded at All Saints', Margaret Street, and St. Matthias's, Stoke Newington.

As the major critical problems of the Renaissance center in the theories and the works which Alberti produced in a short period of years in the mid-15th century, so most of the critical problems of the Victorian Age converge on Butterfield and Ruskin in the years 1849–51. The results of their ideological revolution (or should one say "counter-revolution?") in architecture, which so closely paralleled the Pre-Raphaelites' insurgence in painting, were to mature over a decade and more; but the essential drama, as always with artistic developments, was concentrated in the first years. As previous chapters have shown, the Early Victorian tide was still flowing strong through these years. Yet, since the most exciting moment of the succeeding Victorian architectural phase coincided in date with these later —one can properly say terminal—years of the Early Victorian, the account of that moment has permitted a rising instead of a falling cadence to this book's conclusion.

In other chapters the story has generally been carried down into and even beyond the mid-50's. But enough has been set down concerning the buildings, the books, and the controversies of the very early 50's to make plain that the beginnings of the High Victorian coincide in date with the greatest of Early Victorian achievements. So it has been before and will be again. Only long-continued wars or major population movements set architectural periods absolutely apart from one another. And if the great styles usually overlap (as the Late Gothic, for example, overlaps and even blends with the Early Renaissance) rather than come to neat conclusions, how much more the subordinate style-phases must be expected to do so. Yet to have described here the events which initiated the High Victorian Gothic—one facet only of the High Victorian style-phase as a whole, but the first to crystallize—will help to round out the frame of the Early Victorian at one end, just as the description at the beginning of the book of the latest Georgian architecture of the 30's should have helped to define it at the other.

Only now will it be fully evident how out of date (at least in advanced circles) was the House of Commons, originally designed in the 30's and built through the 40's, even when it was first opened in 1852. Thus it is that the largest edifices, whose building campaigns outlast one and even two successive style-phases, distort architectural history if they are allowed to be its chief representatives with posterity. While Barry and Pugin's Palace was building the complicated music of the first movement of Victorian architecture worked itself to an end. The plain song of Pugin's churches and the ferrovitreous cadenza of Paxton's Crystal Palace, the 16th-century counterpoint of Barry's palaces and the merry "Old English" tunes of the Jacobethan provide the characteristic architectural melodies of the Early Victorian period; the solid and generally tedious drone of the urban housing of the 40's and 50's, varied by the bolder brass passages of the civic and commercial architecture, provides the binding material.

Complex as it is when examined episode by episode, the Early Victorian style-phase as a whole has some sort of inner unity. But no analogy, either with an elaborately orchestrated musical composition or with one of the three-decker novels of the period, can do more than suggest the character of that unity. To attempt to define even a brief style-phase too closely is inevitably to distort it. The pictures which follow must say what the author, even at the end of his book, cannot. Almost all he knows about Early Victorian architecture is in them. If the character of the British building production of the years between the mid-30's and the mid-50's cannot be read in the graphic documents, it can hardly be read anywhere. They epitomize the production of the period as only pictures and not written words can ever successfully do.

INDEX

All buildings are listed under cities and towns, except country houses whose names are considered to represent their location. Roman numerals refer to illustrations (Volume 2).

Dorchester Abbey, 581, 596, 599
Doré, Gustave, 457
Dorking, church, 209
Douai, France, Collège de St. Edmond, 72
Dover: castellated crescent project, 439; Lord Warden Hotel, 554, XVI 27
—— and Croydon Railway, 509
Downes, Charles, *The Building erected . . . for the Great Exhibition,* 530, 540
Downing and Davis, 451
Downside, St. Gregory's Abbey project, 85
Drapers' Company, 420
Duban, Félix, 210, 219
Dublin: Crystal Palace, 549, 550–1, XVI 22, 23; stations, 521
Duc, L. J., 219
Ducie, Earl of, 235
Duncannon, Lord, 260
Duncombe Park, 190
Dunrobin Castle, 195, 208, 244, VII 5
Duquesney, François, 492
Durand, J. N. L., *Précis de leçons d'architecture,* 307, 311
Durandus, 129–30, 132, 136
Dusillon, Pierre Charles, 209–10
Dwyer, John, 484
Dyce, William, 148, 592
Dyer, Charles, 303
Dyers' Almshouses, competition, 235

Eales, Christopher, 326
Eastbourne, 452
Eastern Counties Railway, stations, 510
Eastern Steam Navigation Co., 209
Eastlake, Charles Lock, *History of the Gothic Revival,* 44, 46, 92, 97, 99, 104
—— Sir Charles, 35
Eastnor Castle, 29
ecclesiology, 57, 73
Ecclesiological Society, 57, 77, 132, 151, 152, 153, 579, 580, 593, 603; iron church project, 151, 528, 545, 546, 608. *See also* Cambridge Camden Society; Camdenians
Eckington, station, 505
Edensor, 449
Edinburgh, 416: Ashley Buildings, 470; British Linen Bank, 306, 366; Commercial Bank of Scotland, 360–1, XI 7; Corn Exchange, 327–8, X 29; Donaldson's Hospital, 340; Fettes College, 248, 340; Free Church College, 340, X 40; High School, 341; Improved Dwellings for Working Classes, 470; National Gallery of Scotland, 339–40, X 40; New Town, houses and shops, 396, 420, 479; Physicians' Hall, 175–6, VI 11; Royal Bank of Scotland, New Town

Branch, 366; Royal College of Surgeons, 361; Royal Scottish Institution, 339, X 40; Scott Monument, 123, IV 29; Scottish National Monument, 339; Scottish Provident Institution, 366; Stewart's Hospital, 340; Union Bank of Scotland, 366; Victoria Hall (Tolbooth St. John's) 133, 340; villa districts, 479; Western Bank (Scottish Widows' Fund) 366
Edmeston, James, I, 112
—— —— II, 527, 528
Edward VII, 253
—— VIII, 253
—— the Confessor, 43n
Egerton, Lord Francis, *see* Ellesmere, Earl of
Egypt, Temple of the Sphinx, 520
Eiffel, 242
Elger, 482
Elgin, Lord, 252
Ellesmere, Earl of, 42, 195, 196, 205, 229, 533
Elliott, L., 479
Ellis, 536
Elmes, Harvey Lonsdale, 301, 305, 309, 310, 312, 334, 337, 338, 481, 507
—— James, 301, *Metropolitan Improvements,* 373
Elmslie, E. W., 146
Ely, Cathedral, 287
Emerson, 606
Emmett, J. T., 136, 138–9
Enbrook, 237, VIII 16, 17
Engels, Friedrich, 457
Enshanger, 130
Epping, church, 581
Epsom, station, 511, XV 28
Esdaile, Katherine, 306
Everard, Edward, 38, 41
Evill, William, 524
Exeter: Lower Market, 299, 326; St. Mary Ottery's, 594
Eyambo, King, 515–16

Fair, 395
Fairbairn, Sir William, 386, 460, 499, 519
Famin, A., 36. *See also* Grandjean de Montigny and Famin
Faraday, Michael, 270
Farmer, 227
Fergusson, James, 546, 605, 606
Ferrey, Benjamin, 111, 114, 116, 118, 119, 126, 128, 130, 142, 151, 152, *Recollections of A. N. Welby Pugin and His Father,* 44, 272
Ferrières, France, 243
Fiesole, Italy, 398

INDEX

631

The text pages of both volumes were printed by the Vail-Ballou Press, and the illustration pages by the Meriden Gravure Company.

The ornament on the binding is reproduced from A. N. W. Pugin's book, *Floriated Ornament* (London, 1849).

The view of the Britannia Bridge on the title pages is reproduced from an etching in J. C. Jeaffreson's *Life of Robert Stephenson* (London, 1866).

Insofar as possible, the illustrations have been reproduced directly from contemporary sources, using the offset process. A special 300-line screen was used for the halftone copy in most cases.

The book was designed by Alvin Eisenman.